COLONIAL RECORDS

OF THE

NEW YORK CHAMBER OF COMMERCE,

1768—1784

WITH HISTORICAL AND BIOGRAPHICAL SKETCHES

BY

JOHN AUSTIN STEVENS JR.

NEW YORK:
JOHN F. TROW & CO., 50 GREENE STREET.
1867

JOHN F. TROW & CO.,
PRINTERS, STEREOTYPERS, AND ELECTROTYPERS,
60 Greene Street, New York.

REGISTER OF PROCEEDINGS OF NEW YORK CHAMBER OF COMMERCE.

HEREAS, mercantile societies have been found very usefull in tradeing cities for promoting and encouraging commerce, supporting industry, adjusting disputes relative to trade and navigation, and procuring such laws and regulations as may be found necessary for the benefit of trade in general;

For which purpose, and to establish such a society in the city of New York, the following persons convened on the first Tuesday in, and being the 5th day of, April, 1768:

John Cruger,
Elias Desbrosses,
James Jauncey,
Jacob Walton,
Robert Murray,
Hugh Wallace,
George Folliot,
William Walton,
Samuel Verplanck,
Theophylact Bache,
Thomas White,
Miles Sherbrooke,
Walter Franklin,
Robert Ross Waddle,
Acheson Thompson,
Lawrence Kortright,
Thomas Randal,
William McAdam,
Isaac Low,
Anthony Van Dam,

Who agreed that the said Society of Merchants should consist of

A President,
Vice-President,
Treasurer,
Secretary,

And such a number of merchants as already, or hereafter may become members thereof, to be called and known by the name of

THE NEW YORK CHAMBER OF COMMERCE.

The Members present unanimously chose the following Gentlemen their officers for this year, to commence the first Tuesday in May next:

John Cruger, President.
Hugh Wallace, Vice-President,
Elias Desbrosses, Treasurer,
Anthony Van Dam, Secretary.

Then the following resolutions, being read, were agreed to.

That the members of the Chamber of Commerce shall meet the first Tuesday in every month, to transact such business as may come before them; and establish such rules for the order and good government of the Society as they may *think proper and* find necessary.

That the first Tuesday in May, August, November, and February in every year are declared to be the Grand Quarterly Meetings, at which times the accounts of the Chamber are to be settled, and any new members who desire it and are chosen by ballot are to be admitted.

The officers of said Chamber of Commerce to be chosen yearly by ballot on the first Tuesday in May, and to continue for one year.

Every member of the Society who now is or hereafter may be admitted into the same, shall pay unto the Treasurer for the use of the said Chamber of Commerce five Spanish dollars on his admission, and shall also pay unto the said Treasurer for the aforesaid use the further sum of one Spanish dollar on each of the four quarterly days before mentioned, and such members shall faithfully and truly keep, obey, and conform to all rules and regulations made and entered into by said Chamber of Commerce, which are to be entered into the Books of the said Society to be kept for that purpose, on pain of being dismissed the said Chamber of Commerce, and having his or their names struck off the list.

Any merchant chooseing to become a member of this Chamber of Commerce must give in his name to the President for the time being on the first Tuesday in the month preceeding the Quarterly meeting, and the person proposed is to be balloted for, and if three nays appear he cannot be admitted during the government of the President in whose year he was so refused, but may be proposed the succeeding or any year after, and if not again opposed by three nays then to be admitted, but if any person is three times refused, he is never to be admitted.

A proper room for the meeting of the members of the Chamber of Commerce is to be provided at the expence of the members so that it doth not exceed one shilling per man, which each person is to pay to the Treasurer at their respective meetings.

The members of the Chamber of Commerce doth agree that the Treasurer shall provide for their use a strong chest wherein shall be deposited their cash, books and papers which is to have three different good locks and keys—one key to be kept by the President, one by the Treasurer, and the third by the Secretary; the chest for the present to be kept at the Treasurer's.

No business to be done by the said Chamber of Commerce unless there be twenty-one members present, of which the President or Vice-President to be always one (unless by committees to be appointed for particular purposes), the meeting on the first Tuesday in May next only excepted, when thirteen or more members may do business, and every thing proposed or transacted to be by vote of the members present, and the opinion of the majority of votes to be conclusive and binding on the members, except in admitting new members, which is to be done as is herein before directed.

The President, with the advice of the members of the Chamber is to appoint the place of meeting, nothing to be done but by application to him, who is to examine and sign the Treasurer's accounts, and in general to superintend all the Society's affairs.

The Vice-President in the absence of the President to have the same power and authority as if the President was personally present, who is to keep the President's key when absent.

The Treasurer to provide a proper book at the expence of the said Chamber for keeping the receipt of all money paid to him, and all money laid out by him for the use of the said Society, which are to be fairly entered at the meetings held from time to time, and which are to be audited on the first Tuesday in May in every year, and signed by the auditors to be appointed for that purpose, when he is to deliver over the cash remaining in hand, books and his key to the Treasurer elected, or in the absence of the Treasurer so elected, then to the President, or in his absence to the Vice-President.

The Secretary is to keep a fair register of all proceedings, orders, rules, and regulations of the said Chamber of Commerce, which are to be entered in a proper book to be provided for that purpose at the expence of the said Society. In the absence of the Secretary, the President to appoint one of the members to officiate in his place for the time being, to whom, by a written order from the President, the Secretary is to deliver his key.

Every member not attending the monthly meeting, to forfeit and pay to the Treasurer two shillings, and such who do not attend the quarterly meeting, to pay four shillings for non-attendance, unless some cause, judged reasonable by the Society, is admitted by them as sufficient. Sickness, and being absent at least six miles from the city, to be always allowed sufficient reason for non-attendance.

The President is to appoint a proper person, to be approved of by the Society, as their Doorkeeper and Messenger, who is tc be paid by the Treasurer such sums as may be hereafter directed by the President, for his services.

It is agreed that no new rules, regulations, or orders for the government of this Socieiy shall be made, unless proposed at a preceeding meeting, that there may be time for the general sense of the Society to be known.

The President, or, in his absence, the Vice-President, hath power on any emergency to call a meeting of the said Chamber, and all meetings to be at six o'clock in the evening of every day that their attendance may be required.

The following gentlemen, who are of the Society, not being present, assented to the same:

John Alsop,	Philip Livingston,
Henry White,	James McEvers.

CHAMBER OF COMMERCE.—New York, 3d May, 1768.

Present.

Hugh Wallace, Vice-President.

John Alsop,	Thomas Randal,
Acheson Thompson,	James Jauncey,
Lawrence Kortright,	Robert R. Waddle,
Walter Franklin,	Jacob Walton,
Robert Murray,	Theophylact Bache,
Isaac Low,	Samuel Ver Plank,
Henry White,	George Folliot,
Miles Sherbrooke,	Thomas White.

Elias Desbrosses, Treasurer.
Anth. Van Dam, Secretary.

Several gentlemen, being desirous to be admitted members of the Society, were ballotted for and were elected, as follows:

Robert Watts,	Thomas Marston,
John Harris Cruger,	Peter Hasencliver,
Gerrard Walton,	Alexander Wallace,
Isaac Sears,	Gabriel H. Ludlow,
Jacobus Van Zandt,	Thomas Buchanan,
Charles McEvers,	William Nielson,
John Moore,	Sampson Simson,
Lewis Pintard,	Peter Ketletas,
Levinus Clarkson,	Gerrard W. Beekman,
Nicholas Gouverneur,	Jacob Watson,

Richard Yates.

Ordered—That the Secretary send notice to the several gentlemen elected, in writing, as soon as possible, that they are unanimously chosen.

Resolved and Ordered—That the following gentlemen are appointed a Comittee, untill the first Tuesday in June next, for adjusting any difference between parties agreeing to leave such disputes to this Chamber, and that they do attend on every Tuesday, or oftener, if business

FRAUNCES TAVERN.

1867

require, at such places as they may agree upon, giving notice thereof to the President:

James Jauncey,
Jacob Walton,
Robert Murray,
Samuel Ver Plank,
Theophy. Bache,
Miles Sherbrooke,
George Folliot.

ABSENT MEMBERS.

John Cruger, President,	not well.
William Walton, Jr.,	in Connecticut.
William McAdam,	in the gout.
James McEvers,	not well.
Philip Livingston.	

Ordered and Resolved—That the members of the Chamber do meet at BOLTON & SIGELS'[1]; precisely at the usual hour.

AT A MEETING OF THE CHAMBER OF COMMERCE, IN THE CITY OF NEW YORK, ON THE 7TH DAY OF JUNE, 1768, BEING THE FIRST TUESDAY IN THE MONTH,

PRESENT.

John Cruger, Esq., President.
Hugh Wallace, Vice-President.
Elias Desbrosses, Treasurer.
Antho. Van Dam, Secretary.

James Jauncey,
Jacob Walton,
Robert Murray,
William Walton,
Samuel Ver Plank,
Theophy. Bache,
Thomas White,
Walter Franklin,
Robert Ross Waddle,
Acheson Thompson,
Thomas Randal,
William McAdam,
Isaac Low,
Lawrence Kortright,
Robert Watts,
John Harris Cruger,
Gerrard Walton,
Isaac Sears,
Jacobus Van Zandt,
Charles McEvers,
John Moore,
Lewis Pintard,
Levinus Clarkson,
Nicholas Gouverneur,
Richard Yates,
Thomas Marston,
Peter Hasencliver,
Alexan. Wallace,

George Folliot,
Miles Sherbrooke,
Philip Livingston,
John Alsop,
Henry White,
William Neilson,
Gabr. H. Ludlow,
Thomas Buchanan,
Sampson Simpson,
Gerrard W. Beekman,
Peter Keteltas,
Jacob Watson.

It is proposed that, in future meetings, any member that shall be absent at six o'clock, shall forfeit one shilling, to be paid to the Treasurer.

Resolved and Ordered—That the following gentlemen are appointed a Comittee, until the first Tuesday in July next, for adjusting any differences between parties agreeing to leave such disputes to this Chamber, and that they do attend on every Tuesday, or oftener, if business require it, at such places as they may agree upon, giving notice thereof to the President:

John Alsop,
Acheson Thompson,
Lawrence Kortright,
Isaac Low,
Henry White,
Thomas Randal,
Walter Franklin.

It is proposed that, at the next meeting, or some future one, it shall be declared whether this Society is determined to discourage the paper currency of Pennsylvania[2] from passing in this Colony.

It is proposed that, at the next meeting, or some future one, it shall be declared whether this Society will or not receive the paper currency of New Jersey[3] thereafter in the same advanced proportion as it now in general passes, or a Thirty Shilling Bill Proc. for thirty-two shillings only, and so in proportion.

It is proposed that every gentleman who hath anything to propose to this Society, shall do it in writing.

At a Meeting of the Chamber of Commerce, in the City of New York, on the 5th day of July, being the first Tuesday in this month.

Present.

John Cruger, President.
Vice-President absent.
Elias Desbrosses, Treasurer.
Anth. Van Dam, Secretary.

James Jauncey,
Jacob Walton,
Robert Murray,
William Walton,
Samuel Verplank, (absent)
Theoph. Bache,
Thomas White,
Walter Franklin,
Robert R. Waddle,
Acheson Thompson,
Thomas Randal,
William McAdam,
Isaac Low,
Lawrence Kortright,
George Folliot,
Miles Sherbrooke,
Philip Livingston, (absent)
James McEvers, do.
John Alsop, do.
Henry White,
Robert Watts,
John Harris Cruger,
Gerrard Walton,
Isaac Sears,
Jacobus Van Zandt,
Charles McEvers, (absent)
John Moore,
Lewis Pintard,
Levinus Clarkson, (absent)
Nicholas Gouverneur,
Richard Yates,
Thomas Marston,
Peter Hasencliver,
Alexan Wallace,
Gabriel H. Ludlow,
William Neilson, (absent)
Sampson Simpson,
Peter Keteltas,
Gerr'd W. Beekman,
Jacob Watson.

This Chamber having taken into consideration the proposal of last meeting, whether the paper currency of Philadelphia shall be hereafter discouraged from passing in this Colony, and in consequence thereof there appeared: For passing 14, For not passing 17.

This Chamber having taken into consideration the proposal of last meeting, whether the paper currency of New Jersey shall hereafter be received in the same advanced proportion as it now passes. When it was unanimously determined to take a further time to consider of the same.

It is proposed that it be considered whether the price of flour and bread casks should not be reduced from the present prices, and at what.

It is proposed that there be some method fallen upon to establish a paper currency[4] in this city, and that it be considered of in a future meeting or meetings.

Resolved and Ordered—That the following gentlemen be, and hereby are appointed a Comittee until the first Tuesday in August next, for adjusting any differences between parties agreeing to leave such disputes to this Chamber, and that they do attend on every Tuesday, or oftener, if business require it, at such places as they may agree upon, giving notice thereof to the President:

William Walton,
Thomas White,
Robert R. Waddle,
Robert Watts,
John Harris Cruger,
Gerrard Walton,
William McAdam.

Absent members, viz.:

Samuel Ver Plank,
Philip Livingston,
James McEvers,
William Neilson,
John Alsop,
Hugh Wallace,
Charles McEvers,
Levinus Clarkson.

Members fined for appearing after six o'clock:

Theophy Bache,
Robert Watts,
George Folliot,
Acheson Thompson,
Anthony Van Dam,
Peter Keteltas,
Miles Sherbrooke,
Lawrence Kortright,
John Harris Cruger,
Robert R. Waddle,
Gerrard W. Beekman,
Thomas White,
Peter Hasencliver,
Isaac Sears,
Richard Yates,
James Jauncey,
Gab. H. Ludlow,
Isaac Low,
Thomas Marston,
Alexan Wallace,
Jacob Walton,
Gerrard Walton.

CHAMBER OF COMMERCE.—TUESDAY, 2d August, 1768.

MEMBERS PRESENT.

John Cruger, President.
Hugh Wallace, Vice-President.
Elias Desbrosses, Treasurer.

Jacob Walton,
James Jauncey,
Thomas Randal,
Thomas Buchanan,
William Neilson,
Jacobus Van Zandt,
Richard Yates,
Peter Hasencliver,
Nicholas Gouverneur,
Robert Watts,
Gerrard Walton,
William Walton,
Isaac Sears,
Robert R. Waddle,
Sampson Simpson,
Henry White,
Lawrence Kortright,
Miles Sherbrooke,
Gabriel Ludlow,
Gerrard W. Beekman.

Resolved and Ordered—That the following gentlemen be, and are hereby appointed a Committee until the first Tuesday in September next, for adjusting any differences between parties agreeing to leave such disputes to this Chamber, and that they do attend on every Tuesday, or oftener if business require it, at such places as they may agree upon, giving notice thereof to the President:

Jacobus Van Zandt,
Charles McEvers,
John Moore,
Nicholas Gouverneur,
Richard Yates,
Thomas Marston,
Levinus Clarkson.

The consideration of the Jersey paper currency be referred to some other meeting.

Several gentlemen being desirous to be admitted members of the Society, were balloted for, and were elected as follows:

Richard Sharpe,
Peter Remsen,
William Seton,
Edward Laight,
Henry Remsen, jr.

Ordered—That the Secretary send notice to the several

gentlemen elected, in writing, as soon as possible, that they are unanimously chosen.

This Chamber having taken into consideration the proposal of last meeting, whether the price of flour and bread cask should not be reduced, and to what price,

It was unanimously agreed that, from and after the 15th day of present month of August, no member of this Society will give more than twenty-five shillings and six-pence per ton for flour and bread cask, including nailing.

It is proposed to admit such members who offer monthly, as the quarterly admissions are found too tedious, and that it be considered next meeting.

CHAMBER OF COMMERCE.—TUESDAY, 6th September, 1768.

MEMBERS PRESENT.

John Cruger, President.
Hugh Wallace, Vice-President.
Elias Desbrosses, Treasurer.
Anth. Van Dam, Secretary.

Samuel Ver Plank,
Thomas White,
Walter Franklin,
Robert R. Waddle,
Acheson Thompson,
William McAdam,
Isaac Low,
Philip Livingston,
Henry White,
Peter Remsen,
Henry Remsen,
Robert Watts,
John H. Cruger,
Gerrard Walton,
Isaac Sears,
Jacobus Van Zandt,
John Moore,
Nicholas Gouverneur,
Richard Yates,
Alexander Wallace,
Gabriel H. Ludlow,
William Neilson,
Sampson Simpson,
Gerrard W. Beekman,
Jacob Watson,
William Seton,
Edward Laight.

MEMBERS ABSENT.

James Jauncey,
Jacob Walton,
Robert Murray,
Richard Sharpe,
Chas. McEvers,
Lewis Pintard,

William Walton,	Levinus Clarkson,
Theophy. Bache,	Thomas Marston,
Thomas Randal,	Peter Hasencliver,
Lawrence Kortright,	Thomas Buchanan,
George Folliot,	Peter Keteltas,
Miles Sherbrooke,	James McEvers,

John Alsop.

A proposal of establishing a paper currency in this city, proposed the first Tuesday in July last, being considered of, it is thought proper to defer it to some future meeting.

The proposal of altering the currency of Jersey having been considered of fully, and finding that there would be a manifest injury done to the merchants, traders and inhabitants of this Colony, do resolve, and it is hereby resolved, that no further notice will be taken untill it may become a matter of more concern to this city and province.

Having taken into consideration the proposal of admitting members monthly, instead of quarter days. Resolved unanimously, that any persons offering to become members of this Chamber, that they be balloted for the meeting after that their names be proposed.

It is proposed to this Chamber, whether it is not necessary that there should be some regulations respecting Inland and West India Bills of Exchange,[5] as to damages when returned under protest.

It is proposed that where any person of this Chamber purchases any flour, that they order some of the casks to be started, to try if they are justly tared; if found fraudulent, to have an allowance, and use all means to have the transgressor fined, agreeable to a law[6] of this Colony for that purpose. And it is further proposed to have all flour inspected and weighed when purchased.

It is proposed that Pennsilvania money be taken by

this Chamber at $6\frac{2}{3}$ per cent., as many great inconveniences arise to the trade of this city by refusing it, as hath been determined by this Chamber.

Resolved and Ordered—That the following gentlemen be a Committee, untill the first Tuesday in October next, for adjusting any differences between parties agreeing to leave such disputes to this Chamber, and that they do attend on every Tuesday, or oftener if business require it, at such places as they may agree upon, giving notice thereof to the President:

Philip Livingston,
Isaac Sears,
Lewis Pintard,
Alex. Wallace,
Gabl. H. Ludlow,
Thomas Buchanan,
Peter Hasencliver.

CHAMBER OF COMMERCE.—TUESDAY, 4th October, 1768.

PRESENT.

John Cruger, President.
Hugh Wallace, Vice-President.
Elias Desbrosses, Treasurer.
Anth. Van Dam, Secretary.

Jacob Walton,
Samuel Ver Plank,
Robert R. Waddle,
Miles Sherbrooke,
Henry Remsen,
Robert Watts,
Gerrard Walton,
Lewis Pintard,
Levinus Clarkson,
Thomas Marston,
Alexan. Wallace,
Gab. H. Ludlow,
Thomas Buchanan,
Peter Keteltas,
John Moore.

Fined for appearing after six o'clock:

Hugh Wallace,
James Jauncey,
Thomas Randal,
Isaac Low,
Lawrence Kortright,
Sampson Simpson,
Edward Laight,
Isaac Sears.

ABSENT.

Robert Murray,
William Walton,
Walter Franklin,
Acheson Thompson,

Theoph. Bache,
Thomas White,
Philip Livingston,
John Alsop,
Henry White,
Richard Sharpe,
Peter Remsen,
John H. Cruger,
Jacobus Van Zandt,
William McAdam,
George Folliot,
Chas. McEvers,
Nicholas Gouverneur,
Richard Yates,
Peter Hasencliver,
William Neilson,
Gerrard W. Beekman,
Jacob Watson,
William Seton.

The proposal of last meeting to consider whether it is not necessary that there should be some regulation respecting Inland and West India Bills of Exchange, as to damages when returned under protest.

Resolved—That Messrs. Hugh Wallace, Samuel Ver Plank, Isaac Low, Jacob Walton, and John Moore, be a Committee to adjust or ascertain the damages that ought to be paid on Inland and West India Bills of Exchange, and that they do make report thereon in writing to this Chamber on the next meeting, as fully and clearly as they can.

The proposal of last meeting for starting of flour, in order to see that the casks be duly tared, was considered, and it is Resolved by this Chamber unanimously, that one barrel of every brand-mark, at least, be started to see that it be fairly tared, and if found fraudulent, that they use all means in their power to bring the offenders to justice, agreeable to an Act of the General Assembly.

Resolved—That every member of this Chamber do, in their future purchase of flour, cause the same to be weighed and inspected after purchase, and that the Secretary do cause these resolutions[7] relative to Flour to be advertized in the public newspapers, the cost of which to be paid by the Treasurer.

The proposal for taking Pennsilvania money at $6\frac{2}{3}$ per cent. advance having been reconsidered, it was Resolved by a great majority of this Chamber, that it be hereafter received by any member that inclines to take it at $6\frac{2}{3}$ per cent. advance, being the same proportion that Dollars pass at.

Resolved and Ordered—That the following gentlemen be a Committee, untill the first Tuesday in November next, for adjusting any differences between parties agreeing to leave such disputes to this Chamber, and that they do attend on every Tuesday, or oftner if business require it, at such places as they may agree upon, giving notice thereof to the President:

William Neilson,
Peter Keteltas,
Gerrard W. Beekman,
William Seton,
Edward Laight,
Sampson Simpson,
Jacob Watson.

The following gentlemen, having been proposed at the last meeting, were balloted for, and elected as follows:

John Reade,
Robert Alexander,
Thomas W. Moore.

Ordered—That the Secretary send notice to the several gentlemen elected, in writing, as soon as possible, that they are unanimously chosen.

CHAMBER OF COMMERCE.—TUESDAY, 1st November, 1768.

PRESENT.

John Cruger, President.
Hugh Wallace, Vice-President.
Elias Desbrosses, Treasurer.
Anthony Van Dam, Secretary.
Samuel Ver Plank,
Robert Watts,

Thomas Randal,
John Alsop,
Richd. Sharpe,
Peter Remsen,
John H. Cruger,
Lewis Pintard,
Richard Yates,
Sampson Simpson,
Henry Remsen.

Fined for appearing after six o'clock:

William Walton,
Theophy Bache,
Robert R. Waddle,
Isaac Low,
Miles Sherbrooke,
Henry White,
Charles McEvers,
Alex. Wallace,
Gabriel H. Ludlow,
Thomas Buchanan,
William Neilson,
Gerrard W. Beekman,
Robert Alexander,
Thomas W. Moore,
John Moore.

ABSENT.

James Jauncey,
Jacob Walton,
Robert Murray,
Thomas White,
Walter Franklin,
Acheson Thompson,
William McAdam,
Lawrence Kortright,
George Folliot,
Philip Livingston,
Gerrard Walton,
Isaac Sears,
Jacobus Van Zandt,
Levinus Clarkson,
Nicholas Gouverneur,
Thomas Marston,
Peter Hasencliver,
Peter Keteltas,
Jacob Watson,
William Seton,
Edward Laight,
John Reade.

Messrs. Hugh Wallace, Samuel Ver Plank, Isaac Low, Jacob Walton and John Moore, the Committee appointed at the last meeting to ascertain the damages that ought to be paid and received on Inland and West India Bills of Exchange, Reported that they had considered of the same, and delivered their opinion in writing.

Ordered—That the same be read, which was in the words following:

Agreeable to the desire of the Chamber of Commerce, we, the Committee appointed to consider the necessity there is for some regulation relating to

Inland and West India Bills of Exchange that are returned with protest, for which at present no damages or re-exchange is ascertained.

It is our opinion that the sum of five per cent. damages ought to be paid and received on all Bills from any one Province in North America on another, recoverable here in full of all damages, re-exchange, cost of protest, postage, &c., and that the full amount of the Bill, with damages of five per cent., is due and payable immediately on return of said Bill with protest.

And it is our opinion that the sum of ten per cent. damages ought to be paid and received on all Bills drawn from North America on the West Indias, or from the West Indias on North America, which may be recoverable here in full of all damages, re-exchange, cost of protest, postage, &c.; and that the full amount of the Bill, with the damages of ten per cent., is due and payable immediately on return of the Bill with protest.

All which, however, is submitted to the President and members of said Chamber of Commerce.

Resolved—That the members of this Chamber will in future pay and receive damages on West India and Inland Bills of Exchange, agreeable to the report of the above Committee.

Ordered—That the same Committee do, by the next meeting of this Chamber, consider of, and deliver their opinion in writing respecting Bills on Europe, whether the 20 per cent., as is now generally paid, be in full compensation for damages, cost of protest, postage, &c., and if it shall be received in money by the holder of the Bill so protested at y[e] exchange current when it shall be returned, or in a Bill of Exchange with the addition of the damages.

Ordered—That Messrs. Hugh Wallace, Henry White, Robert Watts, Robert Alexander, Robert Murray, Thomas Randal, John Moore, William Walton, Sampson Simpson, John H. Cruger, and Isaac Low, be a Committee to revise, amend, correct and digest the Articles of this Chamber; and that they do draw up an introduction proper to be inserted in the newspapers, in order to inform the publick their use and design.

And it is proposed that as soon as the articles of the Chamber are revised and corrected, that a number of copies be printed, that each member be served therewith.

It is proposed, that as the General Assembly of this Province is now sitting, that a Committee be appointed to apply to the City Members, and request them to consider of such laws as may be necessary for the regulation of the Trade of this Colony, particularly as to the more effectual Inspection of Flour, Pott-ash, &c.

Ordered—That Messrs. Elias Desbrosses, John Alsop, Samuel Ver Plank, Theophylact Bache, and Isaac Low, be a Committee for the purpose aforesaid, and that they do report to this Chamber, at their next meeting, the result of their application.

This Chamber being informed that there is a combination among the Bolters, Millers, Bakers, and sellers of flour, with respect to the prices of flour and bread casks, and finding they are opposed to the resolution of this Chamber at their meeting on the 2d August last, when the Chamber determined on giving 25s 6d per ton for the same, they have Resolved, Ordered, and do agree that Mr. William Neilson do go to Philadelphia, and purchase there from fifteen hundred to two thousand barrels of flour at the lowest price he can obtain them at, and that he cause them to be shipped to this place, advising this Chamber in what vessels they may be put on board. That on their arrival here such members as are in want shall be first supplied at the [*erased in the manuscript.*] any that remains on hand to be disposed of on account of this Chamber; and, if need be, that each member pay to the Treasurer his proportion of the quantity to be purchased, which, on the sale, shall be repaid his full advance, the loss or gain to be paid or received from the common stock. And Mr. Neilson is further ordered, while at Philadelphia, to correspond with the Secretary, in order to have insurance made on the interest shipped, which the Secretary is to get effected by the consent of the President or Vice-President.

Resolved and Ordered—That the following gentlemen be a Committee, untill the first Tuesday in December next, for adjusting any differences between parties agreeing to leave such disputes to this Chamber, and that they do attend on every Tuesday, or oftner if business require it, at such places as they may agree upon, giving notice thereof to the President:

John Reade,	Jacob Walton,
Robert Alexander,	Robert Murray,
Thomas W. Moore,	Samuel Ver Plank,

James Jauncey.

A SPECIAL MEETING, ON MONDAY, ye 14th NOV., 1768.

John Cruger, President.
Hugh Wallace, Vice-President.
Anth. Van Dam, Secretary.

Thomas Buchanan,	William McAdam,
William Walton,	Samuel Ver Plank,
Levinus Clarkson,	Jacob Watson,
Robert R. Waddle,	Nichs. Gouverneur,
Robert Alexander,	Gabriel H. Ludlow,
Gerrard Walton,	Richard Yates,
Theophy. Bache,	Peter Remsen,
Isaac Low,	Lawrence Kortright,
Sampson Simpson,	Miles Sherbrooke,
Thomas W. Moore,	John Moore,
Robert Murray,	Charles McEvers.

Resolved—That each member of this Chamber do, on the morrow, pay unto the Secretary £50 towards reimbursing Mr. Pintard, now at Philadelphia in the place of Mr. Nielson, who is purchasing flour for this Chamber.

Ordered—That the Secretary send by express all the Bills that may come to his hands from the members, and from £600 or £800 in cash, and that he engage some carefull person for that purpose to go to Philadelphia to carry the money, which is to be delivered to Mr. Lewis Pintard or order.

Several of the sellers of Flour, Bakers, and Bolters attended the meeting, upon notice given them that the Chamber was ready to hear anything that could be said in support of their late demand of raising the price of flour and bread cask from 25s. 6d. to 28s., which they demanded lately on account of flour being rather scarce. But their allegations did not amount to sufficient proof for the Chamber to alter their resolution; and both parties debating thereon, they, the Flour sellers, Bakers, and Bolters, acquiesced with charging in future no more than 25s. 6d. per ton, craving, at the same time, that the Chamber would take into their consideration at their next meeting the difficulty they have to make their principals give into the measures adopted by the Chamber.

CHAMBER OF COMMERCE.—TUESDAY, 6th December, 1768.

PRESENT.

John Cruger, President.
Hugh Wallace, Vice-President.
Anthony Van Dam, Secretary.

John H. Cruger,
Robert Watts,
Sampson Simpson,
Robert Murray,
John Alsop,
John Reade,
Isaac Sears,
Edward Laight,
Jacobus Van Zandt,
Levins Clarkson,
Richd. Sharpe,
William McAdam,
Nichs. Gouverneur,
Lewis Pintard,
Alex. Wallace,
Thomas Marston.

Fined for appearing after six o'clock.

Richard Yates,	Isaac Low,
Thomas W. Moore,	Miles Sherbrooke,
Charles McEvers,	Thomas Randal,
John Moore,	Theoph. Bache,

Thomas Buchanan.

ABSENT.

Elias Desbrosses,	James Jauncey,
Samuel Ver Plank,	Jacob Walton,
Peter Remsen,	Thomas White,
Henry Remsen,	Walter Franklin,
William Walton,	Lawr. Kortright,
Robert R. Waddle,	George Folliot,
Henry White,	Philip Livingston,
Gab. H. Ludlow,	Gerr. Walton,
William Nielson,	Peter Hasencliver,
Gerrard W. Beekman,	Peter Keteltas,
Robert Alexander,	Jacob Watson,

William Seton.

Messrs. Hugh Wallace, Samuel Ver Plank, Isaac Low, Jacob Walton and John Moore, the Committee appointed for to consider of and deliver their opinion in writing respecting Bills of Exchange on Europe, whether the 20 per cent., as is now generally paid, be in full compensation for damages, cost of protest and postage, have made their report in writing, which, being read, was in the words following:

NEW YORK, 6th December, 1768.

In obedience to the order of the Chamber of Commerce, we have considered the necessity there is for some fixed rule of payment for European Bills returned with protest.

And it is our opinion that the sum of twenty per cent. ought to be paid on all European Bills returned protested, in full for all damages, re-exchange, cost of protest, postage, &c., and that all European Bills returned protested ought to be paid immediately on return of said Bill with proper protest, together with the twenty per cent. damages, in money at the current exchange in New York, without regard to the exchange at which said Bill was bought or sold.

All which is humbly submitted by

HUGH WALLACE,
ISAAC LOW,
JACOB WALTON,
JOHN MOORE.

Resolved unanimously, that the same report be entered on the minutes of this Chamber, and that the same is agreed to.

Messrs. Hugh Wallace, Robert Watts, Robert Alexander, Robert Murray, Thomas Randal, John Moore, William Walton, Sampson Simpson, John H. Cruger, and Isaac Low, the Committee to revise, amend, correct and digest the articles of this Chamber, and having made their report in writing, which, being read, was in the words following:

WHEREAS, Mercantile Societies have been found very usefull in tradeing cities for promoting and encouraging commerce, supporting industry, adjusting disputes relative to trade and navigation, endeavoring to procure such laws, establishing such regulations, as may be found necessary for the benefit of trade in general.

THEREFORE, to promote and establish so truly laudable an institution in this city, the following persons met the 5th day of April, 1768, in order to consider of such rules and regulations as might be necessary more effectually to carry the design into execution:

John Cruger,
Elias Desbrosses,
John Alsop,
Henry White,
Walter Franklin,
Robert Ross Waddle,
James Jauncey,
Jacob Walton,
Robert Murray,
Hugh Wallace,
George Folliot,
William Walton,
Philip Livingston,
James McEvers,
Samuel Ver Plank,
Theophy. Bache,
Thomas White,
Miles Sherbrooke,
Acheson Thompson,
Lawrence Kortright,
Thomas Randal,
William McAdam,
Isaac Low,
Anthony Van Dam.

who agree that the said Society of Merchants should consist of

A PRESIDENT,
VICE-PRESIDENT,
TREASURER,
SECRETARY,

And such a number of Merchants as already are, or hereafter may become, members thereof, and be called and known by the name of

THE NEW YORK CHAMBER OF COMMERCE.

The members present unanimously chose the following gentlemen their officers for this year, to commence the first Tuesday in May next:

JOHN CRUGER, President.
HUGH WALLACE, Vice-President.
ELIAS DESBROSSES, Treasurer.
ANTH. VAN DAM, Secretary.

Then the following resolutions being read were agreed to.

That the members of the Chamber of Commerce shall meet the first Tuesday in every month, to transact such business as may come before them, and establish such rules for the order and good government of the Society as they may find necessary.

That the first Tuesday in May, August, November and February in every year are declared to be the Grand Quarterly meetings, at which times the accompts of the Chamber are to be settled, and any new members who desire it, and are chosen by ballot, are to be admitted.

The Officers of said Chamber of Commerce to be chosen yearly by ballot, on the first Tuesday in May, and to continue for one year.

Every member of the Society who now is, or hereafter may be admitted into the same, shall pay unto the Treasurer, for the use of the said Chamber of Commerce, Five Spanish Dollars on his admission, and shall also pay unto the said Treasurer, for the aforesaid use, the further sum of One Spanish Dollar, on each of the four Quarterly days before mentioned. And such members shall faithfully observe and conform to all rules and regulations made and entered into the Books of the said Society (kept by the said Chamber of Commerce for that purpose) on pain of being dismissed the said Chamber of Commerce, and having his or their name struck off the list.

Any person choosing to become a member of this Chamber of Commerce, must give in his name to the President for the time being, on the first Tuesday in the month preceeding the Quarterly Meetings; and the person proposed is to be balloted for, and if three nays appear he cannot be admitted during the government of the President in whose year he was so refused, but may be proposed the succeeding or any year after, and, if not again opposed by three nays, then to be admitted.

A proper room for the meeting of the members of the Chamber of Commerce is to be provided, and the Treasurer is to have Bread and Cheese, Beer, Punch, Pipes and Tobacco, provided at the expence of the members present, so that it doth not exceed one shilling each man, which each person is to pay to the Treasurer at their respective meetings.

The members of the Chamber of Commerce do agree that the Treasurer shall provide for their use a strong chest, wherein shall be deposited their Cash, Books and Papers, which is to have three different good locks and keys—one key to be kept by the President, one by the Treasurer, and the third by the Secretary. The chest, for the present, to be kept at the Treasurer's.

No business to be done by the said Chamber of Commerce unless there be twenty-one members present, of which the President or Vice-President to be always one (unless by Committees to be appointed for particular purposes), the meeting on the first Tuesday in May next only excepted, when thirteen or more members may do business, and everything proposed or transacted to be by vote of the members present, and the opinion of the majority of votes to be conclusive and binding on the members, except in admitting new members, which is to be done as is herein before directed.

The President, with the advice of the members of the Chamber, is to appoint the place of meeting ; nothing to be done but by application to him, who is to examine and sign the Treasurer's accompts, and in general to superintend all the Society's affairs.

The Vice-President, in the absence of the President, to have the same powers and authority as if the President was personally present, and is to keep the President's key when absent.

The Treasurer to provide a proper book for keeping the receipt of all money paid to him, and all money laid out by him for the use of the said Society, which are to be fairly entered at the meetings held from time to time, and which are to be Audited on the first Tuesday in May in every year and signed by the Auditors to be appointed for that purpose, when the Treasurer is to deliver over the cash remaining in hands, books, and his key to the Treasurer next chosen ; or, in absence of the Treasurer so elected, to the President, or in his absence, to the Vice-President.

The Secretary is to keep a fair register of all proceedings, orders, rules and regulations of the said Chamber of Commerce, which are to be entered in a proper book to be provided for that purpose. In the absence of the Secretary, the President to appoint one of the members to officiate in his place for the time being, to whom, by a written order from the President, the Secretary's key is to be delivered.

Every member not attending the Monthly meetings to forfeit and pay to the Treasurer Two Shillings, and such who do not attend the Quarterly meetings to pay Four Shillings for non-attendance, unless some cause, judged reasonable by the Society, is admitted by them as a sufficient excuse; sickness, and being absent at least six miles from the City, to be always allowed sufficient reason for non-attendance.

The President is to appoint a proper person, to be approved of by the Society, as their Door-keeper and Messenger, who is to be paid by the Treasurer such sums as may be hereafter directed by the President for his services.

It is agreed that no new rules, regulations, or orders for the government of this Society shall be made unless proposed at a preceeding meeting, that there may be time for the general sense of the Society to be known.

The President, or in his absence, the Vice-President, hath power, on any emergency, to call a meeting of the said Chamber; and all meetings to be at six o'clock in the evening of every day that their attendance may be required.

December 6, 1768.

Examined and revised by order of the Chamber.

HUGH WALLLACE,	THOMAS RANDAL,
ROBERT MURRAY,	ISAAC LOW,
SAMPSON SIMPSON,	JNO. HARRIS CRUGER.

Resolved—That the same be entered in the minutes of this Chamber.

The same gentlemen report, according to order, the draught proper to be inserted in the newspapers—the use and design of this Chamber—which, being read, was in the words following:

NEW YORK CHAMBER OF COMMERCE,
December 6, 1768.

As Mercantile Societies have been found very usefull in trading cities for promoting and encouraging commerce, adjusting disputes relative to trade and navigation, supporting industry, recommending such laws and establishing such regulations as may be found necessary for the benefit of trade in general,

A considerable number of the Merchants of New York formed themselves into a Society in May last, and have since been joined by the greatest part of the other Merchants in the city, in order to advance so truly laudable an Institution.

They are called the New York Chamber of Commerce; who meet the first

Tuesday of every month, and hear all proposals for the better regulating, encouraging and extending trade and navigation.

A Monthly Committee is appointed, who adjust accounts and settle, gratis, all disputes between merchants and traders which the parties may think fit to submit to their decision.

The Chamber, in general, do everything in their power for the interest of the Community.

A plan of the Institution, with the Rules and Regulations relating to the Chamber, and the method of admitting members, may be seen by applying to

ANTHONY VAN DAM, Secretary.

By order of the Chamber.

HUGH WALLACE,	ROBERT WATTS,
ROBERT MURRAY,	THOMAS RANDAL,
SAMPSON SIMPSON,	JNO. H. CRUGER,

ISAAC LOW.

Resolved—That the same be entered on the minutes of this Chamber.

Ordered—That the Secretary deliver a fair copy of the Articles now read to the printer, and request him to print 300 copies thereof, and that each member be furnished with one.

Ordered—That a fair copy be made of the writing proper to be inserted in the newspapers, to acquaint the publick the use and design of this Chamber, and desire the printers to publish it in the next papers, and to continue it in their papers for six weeks.[8]

Messrs. Elias Desbrosses, John Alsop, Samuel Ver Plank, Theophylact Bache, and Isaac Low, the Committee appointed to apply to the City Members,[9] and request them to consider of such laws as may be necessary for the better regulation of the trade of this Colony, particularly as to the more effectual inspection of Flour, Potash, Pearl-ash, &c., do make their report in the words following:

The Committee, to whom was referred by the New York Chamber of Commerce the consideration of some proper regulation with respect to the inspection of Flour exported from this Colony, so as if possible to retrieve its general disrepute in all parts of the world, and thereby render effectual the intention of the Legislature in providing a law for that purpose,

Do report it as their opinion:

That the Flour from this Colony ought to be at least equal to that exported from Philadelphia; because it is obvious that the wheat brought to this market from Jersey and Maryland is as good, and the wheat from the North River, in particular, much better, than any which comes to Philadelphia. Therefore, that Philadelphia Flour should have the preference at all markets of New York Flour, cannot be attributed to the superior quality of the wheat, but to some defect in its manufacture, and the present mode of inspection.

To remedy which the Committee are of opinion that there ought to be only one Inspector of Flour in this City, as is the practice in Philadelphia; that he ought to appoint as many deputies under him as might be necessary; and that he should be responsible for their conduct, since he might then establish some certain Rule of Inspection, from which his Deputies, being under his immediate direction and controul, would not dare to deviate. Whereas, on the footing the law now stands, of admitting several Inspectors of equal authority, each endeavours to establish a reputation with the Flour Sellers and Factors, and to secure a preference of their business; not by vieing with each other who shall inspect best, but who shall suffer the worst Flour to pass inspection; and there have been instances where one Inspector has condemned, and for that reason not been allowed to proceed any further, when another has given the sanction of his brand to all the remaining parcel of the same sort of Flour.

The Committee are also of opinion, that the Inspector of the Flour ought not only to advert to its being of a proper fineness, but carefully to examine (either by mixing up a little of the Flour into a cake and baking it, or by some other effectual experiment) whether it has not been injured by being ground too close, or in some other way, so as to prevent its riseing and making light white bread; and that he ought not to brand it for exportation if deficient in any of those respects.

The Committee are further of opinion that it would tend greatly towards creating a proper emulation in the manufacturers of Flour, if each of them was obliged to brand the initial letter of his Christian name, and the whole of his sirname, on the casks, together with the name of the County in which he resides; and that the Inspector of Flour be obliged to brand on the casks the name of the Province in which the Flour was manufactured.

The consideration of a law more effectually to inspect Pott and Pearl Ashes, being also referred to this Committee,

They are of opinion that there ought to be only one Inspector of these articles also; that he should distinguish them under the denomination of 1st, 2d and 3d quality; and that the names of the manufacturers, and their places of abode, be also branded on the casks, and that the Inspector also brand on the casks the quality of the Ashes, together with the name of the Province in which they were manufactured.

ELIAS DESBROSSES, ISAAC LOW,
JOHN ALSOP, THEOPHY. BACHE,
SAML. VER PLANK.

Ordered—That the same gentlemen be a Committee to wait on the City members, and inform them of their report, and that it hath been read in this Chamber and approved of.

Ordered—That Messrs. Thomas Randal, Richard Sharpe, Peter Remsen, Henry Remsen, Theophy Bache, Miles Sherbrooke, and George Folliot, be a Committee, untill the first Tuesday in January next, for adjusting any differences between parties agreeing to leave such disputes to this Chamber, and that they do attend on every Tuesday, or oftener if business require it, at such places as they may agree upon, giving notice thereof to the President.

On motion of Mr. Isaac Low, who proposed that, as it may be necessary sometimes for the good of this Chamber, that a Special Meeting of it be called, as lately happened respecting the regulations the Chamber had resolved on about the price of Flour casks,

And, whereas, it is one of the fundamental Rules of this Chamber that no new Rule, Order, or Regulation can be binding on any of the members, except it be proposed for their consideration at least one month previous to its being resolved on,

It is proposed that in cases of sudden emergency only, when it may be thought necessary (agreeable to the established Rule of this Chamber) that a Special Meeting of the members should be called, each of them shall be notified, in writing, by the President or Vice-President, of such meeting; and that in such case any regulation which may be agreed to by a majority of the members then present, shall be binding on all the other members, under the same Penalties and Forfeitures as are provided for the observance of the other Rules and Orders of this Chamber.

ISAAC LOW.

Proposed—That the Thanks of this Chamber be given to Mr. Pintard, for purchasing a cargo of Flour at Philadelphia for them, and that the Treasurer to satisfy Mr. Pintard for his expence and trouble in procuring it. Proposed also, that Mr. Anthony Van Dam do sell, and keep the Accompts of Sales of said Flour, and that he be paid a commission of 2½ per cent. for transacting that business.

CHAMBER OF COMMERCE.—TUESDAY, January 3, 1769.

PRESENT.

John Cruger, President.
Hugh Wallace, Vice-President.
Elias Desbrosses, Treasurer.
Antho. Van Dam, Secretary.

Isaac Low,
Lawrence Kortright,
Sampson Simpson,
Edward Laight,
Robert Murray,
George Folliot,
Henry Remsen,
Walter Franklin,
Theophy Bache,
William Walton,
Samuel Ver Plank,
Thomas Marston,
Thomas W. Moore,
Robert R. Waddle,
Richard Yates.

Fined for appearing after six o'clock :

Richard Sharpe,
John H. Cruger,
Miles Sherbrooke,
Gerrard Walton.

ABSENT.

James Jauncey,
Jacob Walton,
Thomas White,
Thomas Randal,
William McAdam,
John Alsop,
Henry White,
Philip Livingston,
Peter Remsen,
William Seaton,
John Reade,
Robert Alexander,
Robert Watts,
Isaac Sears,
Charles McEvers,
John Moore,
Lewis Pintard,
Levinus Clarkson,
Nicholas Gouverneur,
Peter Hasencliver,
Alexan. Wallace,
Gabriel H. Ludlow,
Thomas Buchanan,
William Neilson,
Peter Keteltas,
Gerrard W. Beekman,
Jacob Watson,
Jacobus Van Zandt.

The consideration of Mr. Low's proposal, That in case of sudden emergency only, when it may be thought necessary (agreeable to the established Rule of this Chamber) that a Special Meeting of the members shall be called, each of them shall be notified in writing of such meeting.

Resolved unanimously—That in case any regulation which may be agreed to by a majority of the members then present at such meeting shall be binding on all the other members, under the same penalties and forfeitures as are provided for the observance of the other Rules and Orders of this Chamber.

The proposal for the Thanks of this Chamber to be given to Mr. Pintard, for the trouble he was at in purchasing a cargo of Flour at Philadelphia on account of this Chamber, having been considered of, it is

Resolved and Ordered—That the Secretary do take an extract from the minutes of this Chamber, and serve Mr. Pintard with the same, thanking him for the pains and trouble he so generously afforded this Chamber in the purchase and shipping at Philadelphia a cargo of

Flour, when they were opposed by the sellers of Flour in this City in the price they had fixed for Flour and Bread Casks, and the Treasurer is hereby directed to pay Mr. Pintard's expences.

Resolved unanimously—That the Secretary be paid by the Treasurer a commission of 2½ per cent. for his trouble of collecting money from the different members, sending it to Philadelphia for the purchase of Flour, selling the same here, collecting the proceeds, and repaying it to the members.

Ordered—That Messrs. William Walton, Thomas White, Walter Franklin, Robert R. Waddle, Lawrence Kortright, William McAdam, and Isaac Low, be a Committee, untill the first Tuesday in February next, for adjusting any differences between parties agreeing to leave such disputes to this Chamber, and that they do attend on every Tuesday, or oftener, if business require it, at such places as they may agree upon, giving notice thereof to the President.

The following gentlemen, having been proposed at the last meeting, were balloted for, and elected, as follows:

Abraham Lynsen,
Isaac Roosevelt,
Nicholas Hoffman.

Ordered—That the Secretary send notice to the several gentlemen so elected, in writing, that they were unanimously chosen.

CHAMBER OF COMMERCE.—TUESDAY, February 7, 1769.

PRESENT.

John Cruger, President.
Hugh Wallace, Vice-President.
Treasurer.
Anth. Van Dam, Secretary.

Robert Murray,
William Walton,
Samuel Ver Plank,
Lawrence Kortright,
Jacob Watson,
Henry Remsen,
John Reade,
Robert Watts,
John H. Cruger,
Abrah. Lynsen,
Gerrard Walton,
Isaac Sears,
William Neilson,
Sampson Simpson.

Fined for appearing after six o'clock:

Miles Sherbrooke,
Walter Franklin,
William McAdam,
Isaac Low,
Peter Remsen,
Thos. W. Moore,
John Moore,
Levinus Clarkson,
Richd. Yates,
Alex. Wallace,
Isaac Roosevelt.

Fined for non-appearance, being Quarter Day:

James Jauncey,
Jacob Walton,
George Folliot,
Theophy. Bache,
Thomas White,
Robt. R. Waddle,
Thomas Randal,
Peter Keteltas,
John Alsop,
Henry White,
Philip Livingston,
Richd. Sharpe,
William Seaton,
Edward Laight, sick,
Robert Alexander,
Gerrard W. Beekman,
Jacobus Van Zandt,
Charles McEvers,
Lewis Pintard,
Nichs. Gouverneur,
Thos. Marston,
Peter Hasencliver,
Gabriel H. Ludlow,
Thos. Buchanan,
Nichs. Hoffman.

Mr. Lewis Pintard, who purchased a quantity of Flour at Philadelphia, and Anthony Van Dam, who was appointed to sell it here, having exhibited their accounts, relating thereto,

Ordered—That Messrs. Robert Watts and Thomas W. Moore be a Committee to audit the same, and make report thereof at the sitting of this Chamber, on the first Tuesday in March next.

Resolved and Ordered—That the following gentlemen be, and hereby are, appointed a Committee, untill the first Tuesday in March next, for adjusting any differences between parties agreeing to leave such disputes to this Chamber, and that they do attend on every Tuesday, or oftner if business require it, at such places as they may agree upon.

Robert Watts,
John H. Cruger,
Gerrard Walton,
Abraham Lynsen,
Isaac Roosevelt,
Nichs. Hoffman,
Jacobus Van Zandt.

As it appears highly necessary for this Chamber to have a decent, large and commodious room to meet in, and that the Room over the Exchange will be proper for that use—

Ordered—That Messrs. Isaac Low, Isaac Roosevelt, Wm. Walton, Lawrence Kortright, and Thomas Randal, be a Committee to wait upon the Mayor and Corporation, and apply to them for the use of the Room[10] over the Exchange, and agree on such terms as they judge reasonable.

Mr. Hugh Wallace acquaints this Chamber that Mr. Nichs. Gouverneur, William McAdam and himself are appointed Arbitrators, to settle a long and intricate account between Col. John Schuyler[a] and Capt. Archibald Kennedy,[b] and desiring that they may be excused from serving on any Committee during the time they may be so employed, which was granted.

Several gentlemen who were proposed at the last meeting, and are desirous of becoming members of this Chamber, were balloted for, and were elected, viz.:

Hamilton Young,
Thomas Walton,
John Thurman.

Ordered—That the Secretary send notice to the several

gentlemen so elected, in writing, that they were unanimously chosen.

CHAMBER OF COMMERCE.—TUESDAY, March 7, 1769.

PRESENT.

John Cruger, President.
Hugh Wallace, Vice-President.
Elias Desbrosses, Treasurer.
Anth'y Van Dam, Secretary.

William Walton,
Peter Remsen,
Henry Remsen,
John Reade,
Isaac Sears,
Jacobus Van Zandt,
Levinus Clarkson,
Richard Yates,
Thomas Buchanan,
Abrah. Lynsen,
Isaac Roosevelt.

Fined for appearing after six o'clock, viz.:

John Cruger, P.
Hugh Wallace, V. P.
Elias Desbrosses, T.
James Jauncey,
Robert Murray,
Theoph Bache,
Walter Franklin,
Isaac Low,
John Alsop,
Richd. Sharpe,
Edward Laight,
Robert Alexander,
John Thurman,
Jacob Walton,
Lawrence Kortright,
Miles Sherbrooke,
Robert Watts,
John H. Cruger,
Gerrard Walton,
John Moore,
Gabriel H. Ludlow,
William Neilson,
Sampson Simpson,
Peter Keteltas,
Jacob Watson,
Nicholas Hoffman.
Thomas Walton,
William Seton,
Thomas W. Moore,
Gerrard W. Beekman.

ABSENT, VIZ.:

George Folliot,
Samuel Ver Plank,
Thomas White, Gout,
Robert R. Waddle,
Thomas Randal,
William McAdam, Gout,
Henry White,
Philip Livingston,
Charles McEvers,
Lewis Pintard,
Nicholas Gouverneur,
Thomas Marston,
Peter Hasencliver,
Alexander Wallace,
Hamilton Young.

Mr. Holt's[c] account appeared for printing 300 copies

of the Articles of this Chamber and two advertisements, amounting to five pounds ten shillings.

Ordered—That the Treasurer do pay that account, and charge this Chamber for the same.

Several gentlemen, having been proposed at the last meeting, were balloted for and elected, as follows:

John Wetherhead,	William Stepple,
Garret Rapelje,	Gerardus Duyckinck.

Ordered—That the Secretary send notice to the several gentlemen so elected, in writing, that they were unanimously chosen.

Messrs. Isaac Low, Isaac Roosevelt, William Walton, Lawrence Kortright, and Thomas Randal, reported that they had waited on the Mayor [d] and Corporation, to ask their assent for the Room over the Exchange, and that they were pleased to say that the Chamber should have the use thereof for one year from the first of May next, if they would put it in such repair as they required, and after that to pay £20 per annum.

Ordered—That Mr. President, Mr. Isaac Low, Thomas Randal, and Sampson Simpson, be a Committee to employ and agree with some fit persons to make tables, &c., and put the said Room in order for the Chamber.

Ordered—That Messrs. John Alsop, Henry White, Philip Livingston, Charles McEvers, Hamilton Young, Thomas Walton, and John Thurman, be a Committee, untill first Tuesday in April next, for adjusting any differences between parties, &c.

CHAMBER OF COMMERCE.—TUESDAY, April 4, 1769.

PRESENT.

John Cruger, President.
Hugh Wallace, Vice-President.
Elias Desbrosses, Treasurer.
Antho. Van Dam, Secretary.

James Jauncey,	Sampson Simpson,
Robert Murray,	John Reade,
Gab. H. Ludlow,	Henry Remsen,
Thomas Buchanan,	Nicholas Hoffman,

William Stepple.

Fined for appearing after six o'clock:

Jacob Walton,	Robert R. Waddle,
Thomas Randal,	Peter Remsen,
Isaac Low,	Abram Lynsen,
William Walton,	Hamilton Young,
Gerrard Walton,	Robert Watts,
John Moore,	Garret Rapelje,
Edward Laight,	Robert Alexander,
Gerrard W. Beekman,	Gerrard Duyckinck,

John Wetherhead.

ABSENT.

Hugh Wallace,	Richard Yates,
George Folliot,	Thomas Marston,
Samuel Ver Plank,	Philip Livingston,
Theophy. Bache,	Isaac Sears,
Miles Sherbrooke,	Lewis Pintard,
Walter Franklin,	Peter Hasencliver,
Lawren. Kortright,	Alexander Wallace,
Henry White,	William Seton,
John Alsop,	William Neilson,
Thomas White,	Peter Keteltas,
William McAdam,	Jacob Watson,
John H. Cruger,	Thomas W. Moore,
Jacobus Van Zandt,	Richard Sharpe,
Charles McEvers,	Isaac Roosevelt,
Levinus Clarkson,	Thomas Walton,
Nicholas Gouverneur,	John Thurman.

As the usual Tare allowed on Firkin'd Butter and Hog's Lard often proves very erroneous and much to the prejudice of the purchasers, It is proposed by Mr. Edward Laight, that the just weight of each Firkin be mark'd on the head of all Butter or Hog's Lard that shall be hereafter bought or sold by the members of this Chamber.

Mr. Anthony Van Dam proposes that when any differences shall be settled by Committees of this Chamber, That the names of the persons who had the dispute, with the sums awarded, shall be entered on the Minutes of this Chamber, and that such gentlemen who have already decided any disputes, who can conveniently give in their award, that they be also entered.

As it is highly necessary that the Quantity of the different species of Goods usually shipped from this Port be ascertained [*and it be fixed what* "] shall be a ton. It is proposed that there be a Committee appointed to enumerate the different quality of Goods usually exported from hence, and fix what shall be a Ton of Flour, Bread, Pork, Beef, Rice, Grain, and all kinds of Lumber, &c., &c., &c.

Mr. William Imlay and Augustus Van Horne, who were proposed at the last meeting, were balloted for and elected.

Ordered—That the Secretary send notice to the gentlemen so elected, in writing, that they were unanimously chosen.

Ordered—That Messrs. Levinus Clarkson, John Moore, Richard Yates, John Wetherhead, Garret Rapalje, Gerrardus Duyckinck, and William Stepple, be a Committee, untill the first Tuesday in May next, for adjusting any differences between parties agreeing to leave such disputes to this Chamber, and that they do attend on every Tuesday, or oftener if business require it, at such places as they may agree upon, giving notice thereof to the President.

CHAMBER OF COMMERCE.—TUESDAY, May 2, 1769.

PRESENT.

John Cruger, President.
Hugh Wallace, Vice-President.
Elias Desbrosses, Treasurer.
Anth. Van Dam, Secretary.

James Jauncey,
Jacob Walton,
William Walton,
Walter Franklin,
Levinus Clarkson,
Sampson Simpson
Jacob Watson,
Peter Remsen,
Henry Remsen,
John Reade,
Nicholas Hoffman,
Thomas Walton,
Garret Rapelje.

Fined for appearing after six o'clock:

Elias Desbrosses,
Robert Murray,
Hugh Wallace,
Samuel Ver Plank,
Theophy. Bache,
Miles Sherbrooke,
Lawrence Kortright,
Thomas Randall,
Edward Laight,
William McAdam,
Isaac Low,
John Alsop,
John H. Cruger,
Gerrard Walton,
Isaac Sears,
Jacobus Van Zandt,
John Moore,
Thomas W. Moore,
Lewis Pintard,
Nichol. Gouverneur,
Richard Yates,
Thomas Marston,
Gabriel H. Ludlow,
Thomas Buchanan,
William Neilson,
Richard Sharpe,
Abram Lynsen,
John Wetherhead,
William Stepple,
William Imlay,
Augustus Van Horne.

ABSENT.

George Folliot,
Thomas White, Gout,
Robert R. Waddel,
Robert Watts, Jersey,
John Thurman, do.
Charles McEvers,
Alexander Wallace,
Peter Keteltas,
Gerrard W. Beekman,
Gerrard Duyckinck,
William Seton,
Robert Alexander,
Isaac Roosevelt,
Hamilton Young.

Mr. President reported that the Honorable House of Assembly had directed him[12] to signify their Thanks to the Merchants of this City and Colony for their Patriotic conduct in declining the Importation of Goods from Great Britain at this juncture,[13] which being read, was in the words following:

GENTLEMEN :—

I have it in charge from the General Assembly to give the Merchants of this City and Colony the Thanks of the House for their repeated disinterested, publick spirited and patriotic conduct in declining the importation or receiving of goods from Great Britain, untill such Acts of Parliament as the General Assembly had declared unconstitutional and subversive of the Rights and Liberties of the People of this Colony, should be repealed.

Ordered—That Mess. Desbrosses, Alsop, Low, Kortright, W. Franklin, and McAdam be a Committee to prepare and deliver in to this Board, a draught of the Thanks to the Honorable House for the particular notice they have taken of the Merchants that compose this Chamber, and that they do, when perfected, wait on the Honorable House therewith as soon as conveniently may be.

Mr. Treasurer reported that the Committee had accordingly drawn up the thanks of this Chamber; after some amendments it was read in the words following:

NEW YORK CHAMBER OF COMMERCE,
May 2, 1769.

The Merchants of the City of New York, at their Monthly Meeting this day, having received by the Speaker the Thanks of the Honorable House of Assembly for their disinterested and steady regard for the Publick Good, are highly sensible of the honour done them, and flatter themselves that their endeavours to promote the Trade of the Colony will always merit and receive the protection and approbation of the Legislature in general, and this Honorable House in particular.

This being the day appointed by the original institution to elect officers for the ensuing year, the following gentlemen were balloted for, when the four former were rechosen, viz.:

JOHN CRUGER, President.
HUGH WALLACE, Vice-President.
ELIAS DESBROSSES, Treasurer.
ANTHONY VAN DAM, Secretary.

The consideration of Mr. Laight's motion to regulate the tare to be allowed on Firkin'd Butter and Hog's Lard is referred to some future meeting.

Mr. Van Dam's proposal respecting the propriety of entering on the Minutes of this Chamber the business that may come before the several Monthly Committees was considered of, and

Ordered—That all future Committees do report unto the next sitting of this Chamber what differences between parties they have adjusted, with their names and sums they have awarded, unless both parties object to the same being inserted, and that such gentlemen who have decided any controversies are desired to deliver in the subject of their awards as soon as may be, and that the same be entered.

Mr. McAdam proposes that the Chamber shall agree what are the usual Commissions for doing business at this place, as well foreign as inland, and prays that a Committee be appointed to make enquiry and report to the Chamber at their next meeting.

Ordered—That the Treasurer, Mr. Simpson, Mr. Pintard, Mr. Kortright, and Mr. Bache be a Committee for that purpose, and that they do make their report at the next meeting of the Chamber.

Mr. Simpson proposes that as an inconvenience attends the Chamber when any of the members depart before the Business before them is done, Moves, that if any member departs without leave first obtained from the President, that they be fined four Shillings.

Ordered—That Mr. Franklin, Mr. Buchanan, Mr. Van Zandt, Mr. Yates, and Mr. H. Remsen be a Committee to audit the Treasurer's Accounts, and sign the same agreeable to the Rules of the Chamber.

Mr. Van Dam's Proposal for fixing the Tonnage of Goods being considered of and being thought very necessary and useful to prevent disputes,

Ordered—That Mr. R. Murray, Mr. Young, Mr. Sherbrooke, Mr. Yates, and Mr. P. Remsen be a Committee to ascertain the Tonnage[14] of this Port, and that they make report in writing on the next meeting of the Chamber.

Ordered—That Mr. Imlay, Mr. Van Horne, Mr. Sears, Mr. Pintard, Mr. Alex. Wallace, Mr. G. H. Ludlow, be a Committee for the month of May, for adjusting any differences between parties agreeing to leave such disputes to this Chamber, and that they do attend on every Tuesday, or oftner if business require it, at such places as they may agree upon, giving notice thereof to the President.

Messrs. Franklin, Buchanan, Yates, Sharpe, and Van Zandt, propose that the Members have a Publick Dinner in the Chamber, and that it be on the second Tuesday in June for this year, at the expence of each member; that absent members pay Five Shillings, and that Two Stewards be appointed on the first Tuesday in June next for this year.

Mr. Henry C. Bogart and Mr. George Ludlow, who were proposed at the last meeting, were balloted for and elected.

Ordered—That the Secretary send notice to the Gentlemen so elected, in writing, that they were unanimously chosen.

CHAMBER OF COMMERCE.—TUESDAY, 6th June, 1769.

PRESENT.

John Cruger, President.
Hugh Wallace, Vice-President.
Elias Desbrosses, Treasurer.
Anthony Van Dam, Secretary.

James Jauncey,
Jacob Walton,
Thomas Randal,
Richard Yates,
Gabriel H. Ludlow,
Thomas Buchanan,
Sampson Simpson,
John Reade,
Henry Remsen,
Abrah. Lynsen,
Isaac Roosevelt,
Nicholas Hoffman,
Lewis Pintard.

Fined for appearing after six o'clock:

Robert Murray,
Isaac Sears,
Alexan. Wallace,
Hamilt. Young,
William McAdam,
Theoph. Bache,
Hugh Wallace,
Henry C. Bogart,
August. Van Horne,
George W. Ludlow,
William Neilson,
William Walton,
William Seton,
Peter Remsen,
Miles Sherbrooke,
Isaac Low,
Robert Watts,
Thomas Walton,
John Thurman.

Fined for non-appearance:

George Folliot,
Samuel Ver Plank, (Bloomandale)[15]
Henry White,
John Alsop,
Thomas White,
Robert R. Waddle,
Charles McEvers, (Bloomandale)
John Moore,
Levinus Clarkson, (Bloomandale)
Nicholas Gouverneur,
Thomas Marston, (flat Bush)[16]
Philip Livingston,
Peter Keteltas,
Gerrard W. Beekman,
Jacob Watson,
Robert Alexander,
Thomas W. Moore,
Richard Sharpe,
John H. Cruger,
Gerrard Walton,
Jacobus Van Zandt, F[17]
Gerrard Duykink,
Peter Hasencliver,
Edward Laight,
William Stepple,
John Wetherhead,
Garret Rapelje,
William Imlay.

The Committee appointed to audit the Treasurer's Accounts having made their report, which, being read, was in the words following,

PURSUANT to an order of this Chamber, of 2d May, We, the Committee appointed to Audit the Accounts of Elias Desbrosses (present Treasurer), have audited the said accounts from the 3d May, 1768, to 29th May, 1769, and do find a Ballance of Sixty-nine Pounds five Shillings and fivepence due from the said Treasurer to the Chamber of Commerce. In Witness whereof, We have signed this Report, the 3d June, 1769.

JACOBUS VAN ZANDT, THOMAS BUCHANAN,
HENRY REMSEN, jun., RICHD. YATES.

The Committee appointed to agree on what are the usual Commissions for doing business at this place, as well Foreign as Inland, report that they had made some progress therein, and desired further time to consider thereof, and to deliver in their report.

Ordered—That leave be given accordingly.

The Committee appointed to ascertain the Tonnage of this Port, having made some progress therein, desired leave to sit again.

Ordered—That leave be given accordingly.

Mr. Low proposed—That, as the Governor, Council and General Assembly of this Province had passed an Act[18] at their last Sessions for the better Inspection of Flour, &c., and therein had provided that all Flour Casks should have Ten Hoops, three of which to be on each head; for the encouragement to the Manufacturers of Flour, the Chamber shou'd agree to pay for all Flour Casks that shall be well and sufficiently made and Hooped with Ten hoops, agreeable to said Law, at and after the rate of Twenty-eight Shillings p Ton for Casks and Nails.

Mr. Low proposed—That for the better order and more effectual doing of business in this Chamber, that every Person who hath any reasons to offer in favour of any proposals made to the Chamber, or any objections to make against them, shall rise and address himself to the

President, on forfeiture of One Shilling for every Offence, and the same to be inflicted on any Person who shall interrupt another while speaking to the President.

The proposal of last meeting for the Chamber to Dine in Publick on Tuesday next being considered of and agreed to,

Ordered—That Cap. Randal and Mr. Low be Stewards to provide a Dinner accordingly, and that notice be given by the Messenger of this Chamber the day before to each Member.

The Committee for March report that they have settled a dispute between

Moses Franks, by John H. Cruger, his Attor'y,
and
Gerrardus Duyckinck;

And having maturely considered the objections made by Mr. Duyckinck, and the allegations of both parties, the Committee, as Arbitrators—to wit, Jacs. V. Zandt, J. Roosevelt, Ab. Lynsen, Nich. Hoffman, and Gerrard Walton—did Award that Gerra's Duyckinck should pay unto the said John Harris Cruger, for the use of the said Moses Franks, the sum of One Hundred and Twenty-eight Pounds Sixteen Shillings and Seven Pence, Sterling Money of Great Britain.

The same Committee having considered of

David Knote, Thomas & Isaac Potter, Joseph & Stephen Fleming, of New Jersey's,
dispute with
Cap. John Anderson,

Wherein the first Party demand of Anderson £106 9s. 2¾d.; but on examining into the Merits of the dispute, awarded Anderson to pay them £65 9s. 10¾d.

The Committee for May report that they settled a dispute between

John Barnes of Bristol,
and
Lambert Garrison;

And having duly considered the Proofs and Allegations of both parties, have awarded the said Garrison to pay the said Barnes the sum of £38 4s. 9d., Sterling money of Great Britain, on or before the first July next ensuing, and that on payment thereof, the said Barnes do execute to said Garrison a discharge in full for that sum and all other expences.

ISAAC SEARS, LEWIS PINTARD,
GAB. H. LUDLOW, ALEXAN. WALLACE,
THOMAS BUCHANAN.

Mr. Joseph Bull having been proposed as a member of this Chamber, and being balloted for, was chosen.

Ordered—That the Secretary send notice thereof, in writing, that he was duly elected.

Ordered—That Messrs. W. Seton, E. Laight, Wm. Neilson, S. Simpson, P. Keteltas, H. C. Bogart, and G. W. Ludlow, be a Committee to hear and determine disputes between parties who shall agree to leave such to this Chamber, and that they do make report thereof, in writing, to this Chamber, what business hath or shall come before them during their appointment.

CHAMBER OF COMMERCE.—TUESDAY, 4th July, 1769.

PRESENT.

John Cruger, President.
Hugh Wallace, Vice-President.
Elias Desbrosses, Treasurer.
Anthony Van Dam, Secretary.

Jacob Watson,
Joseph Bull,
Gab. H. Ludlow,
Lewis Pintard,
William Neilson,
Henry Remsen, Jr.,
Sampson Simpson,
James Jauncey,
Henry C. Bogart,
Augustus Van Horn,
Jacobus Van Zandt,
Thomas Randall,
Nicholas Hoffman,
Robert Watts.

Fined for appearing after six o'clock:

Thomas W. Moore,
William Seton,
Robert R. Waddle,
Isaac Low,
Jno. H. Cruger,
William Stepple,
Theoph Bache,
Levinus Clarkson,
Alexan. Wallace,
Thomas Walton,
Gerrard Beekman,
Gerrard Duyckinck,
Thomas White,
William Walton,
Samuel Ver Plank.

Fined for non-appearance:

Robert Murray,
George Folliot,
Miles Sherbrooke,
Walter Franklin, R. I.
Lawrence Kortright,
Henry White,
John Alsop,
Richard Sharpe,
Isaac Roosevelt,
Gerrard Duyckinck,
William McAdam,
Gerrard Walton,
Charles McEvers,
John Moore,
Nicholas Gouverneur,
Richard Yates,
Thomas Marston,
Peter Remsen,
Hamilton Young,
William Imlay,
Philip Livingston,
Isaac Sears,
Peter Hasencliver,
Thomas Buchanan,
Edward Laight,
Peter Keteltas,
Robert Alexander,
Abram Lynsen, (Setauket)[19]
Garret Rapelje,
George W. Ludlow.

Mr. Low's proposal at last meeting having been considered of, for allowing 28s. p Ton for Flour casks hooped with Ten hoops,

Resolved—That the members of this Chamber, in their future purchase of Flour, are willing to pay Twenty-eight Shillings p Ton for Casks and Nails, provided that they be well and sufficiently made (agreeable to an Act of the Governor, Council, and General Assembly of this Province, passed at their last Sessions,) and hooped with Ten hoops, three of which to be on each Head.

Ordered—That the above resolve be published in the Papers.[70]

The Committee for enquiring what are the usual Commissions as well Foreign as Inland, delivered in their report, which, being read, was in the words following:

PURSUANT to an Order of this Chamber of 2d May, We, the Committee appointed to enquire what are the usual Commissions for doing Business at this Place, have, agreeable to said order, made Inquiry, and do find that the following Commissions are most generally charged, viz.:

Inland,	2½ per cent.	on Sales, exclusive of Storage.	Say from Boston to Philadelphia.
	2½ per cent.	Returns.	
Foreign,	5 "	on Sales, exclusive of Storage.	
	5 "	Returns.	

Bills of Exchange, Indorsing, Selling, or Negotiating,		- -	2½ p ct.
Making Insurance,	½ per cent.	Recovering of Losses, - -	2½ "
Outfit of Vessels,	5 per cent.	Solliciting & Procuring of Freight,	5 "
Collecting in Freight,	2½ per cent.	Receiving or Paying of Money,	2½ "

Which is submitted to the consideration of this Chamber.

LAWRENCE KORTRIGHT, SAMPSON SIMPSON,
LEWIS PINTARD, THEOPH BACHE,
ELIAS DESBROSSES.

The Chamber agree in opinion that the above Commissions are generally charged in this place, and that in case any disputes arise between parties and Referees being chosen out of this Chamber, that they do govern themselves accordingly, except where special agreements have been made to the contrary.

The Proposal of Mr. Low to inflict a fine of One Shilling for any person who hath anything to offer and doth not address himself to the Chair standing, or that interrupts any of the members while speaking to the Chair, being consider'd of,

Resolved—That it is the opinion of the Chamber that the business will be much better attended to if the proposed fine be attended to, and it is unanimously agreed to.

Mr. Leonard Lispenard, Junr., having been proposed at a former meeting, was balloted for and unanimously chosen a member of this Chamber.

Ordered—That the Secretary send notice, in writing, that he was unanimously chosen.

Ordered—That Messrs. G. W. Beekman, J. Watson, J. Reade, R. Alexander, T. W. Moore, R. Sharpe, and Jos. Bull, be a Committee untill the first Tuesday in August next, to hear and determine disputes between parties who shall agree to leave such to this Chamber, and that they do make report thereof, in writing, to this Chamber, what business hath or shall come before them during their appointment.

CHAMBER OF COMMERCE.—TUESDAY, 1st August, 1769.

PRESENT.

John Cruger, President.
Elias Desbrosses, Treasurer.
Anth. Van Dam, Secretary.

John H. Cruger,
Nicholas Hoffman,
Robert Murray,
Sampson Simpson,
Gerrard Walton,
Thomas Walton,
Jacob Watson,
James Jauncey,
Isaac Roosevelt,
Joseph Bull,
Isaac Low,
William Walton,
Abram Lynsen,
Edward Laight,
Richard Yates,
John Moore.

Fined for appearing after six o'clock:

Hamilton Young,
Nicholas Gouverneur,
Samuel Ver Plank,
Thomas W. Moore,
Peter Remsen,
William Stepple,
Isaac Sears,
George Ludlow,
Robert Watts.

Fined for non-appearance:

Hugh Wallace,
Jacob Walton,
George Folliott,
Theophy Bache,
William McAdam,
Jacobus Van Zandt, (Jerseys.)
Charles McEvers,
Levinus Clarkson,
William Neilson,
Peter Keteltas,
Gerrard W. Beekman,
John Reade,
Miles Sherbrooke,
Walter Franklin, (L. I.)
Lawrence Kortright,
Thomas Randall,
Henry White,
John Alsop,
Thomas White,
Robert R. Waddle,
Augustus Van Horne,
Thomas Marston,
Philip Livingston,
Lewis Pintard,
Peter Hasencliver,
Alexander Wallace,
Gabriel H. Ludlow, (N° Castle.)[21]
Thomas Buchanan,
William Seton,
Henry C. Bogart,
Robert Alexander,
Richard Sharpe,
Henry Remsen,
John Thurman,
John Weatherhead,
Garret Rapelje,
Gerrard Duykink,
William Imlay.

Mr. William Walton proposes that the Chamber should take into their consideration the low rates that Gold and Silver Coin passes at, among which are:

English Guineas & half-Guineas,
French " & " "
Moidores & "
English Crowns & "
French Crowns and half-Crowns,
Carolines,
Ducats,
Chequins,
Shillings and Sixpences:

And any other Coins that pass under their value, and prays that a Committee be appointed to ascertain their true value and make report thereof to this Chamber at their next Meeting.

Ordered—That Mr. Wm. Walton, Sam. Ver Plank, Robt. Murray, Ham. Young, and Jno. H. Cruger, be a

Committee for the purpose aforesaid, and that they make report thereof accordingly.

Mr. Moore proposes that as the quality of Lumber is an Article of considerable consequence to this Colony, and that such as is brought to this Market is generally very irregular, that a Committee be appointed to take the matter into consideration and to make a report to the Chamber of such regulations as they may think necessary to be made concerning it.

Ordered—That Mr. Moore, Mr. Yates, Mr. A. Wallace, Mr. Watson, and Mr. Bache be a Committee for the purpose aforesaid, and that they do make report thereof to this Chamber at their next Meeting.

Capt. Thomas Miller having been proposed at a former Meeting, was balloted for and unanimously chosen a member of this Chamber.

Ordered that the Secretary send notice in writing that he was unanimously chosen.

Ordered that Messrs. P. Remsen, H. Remsen, A. Lynsen, I. Roosevelt, N. Hoffman, H. Young, and Thos. Walton be a Committee until the first Tuesday in September next, to hear and determine disputes between parties who shall agree to leave such to this Chamber, and that they do make report thereof, in writing, to this Chamber what business has or shall come before them during their appointment.

The Committee for June, 1769, report

That having been applied to by Mr. H. C. Bogart, on the part and behalf of *Mr. Rhodes*, of Boston, and Mr. Lewis Pintard by procuration of *Peter Pallade* for *Monsr. La Piere* of Port au Prince, wherein *Mr. Rhodes* demands for a * * * * * *

	£	s.	d.
Protested Bill of Exchange of 4325 livres, 15 J currency, - - - - - - - - - -	216	5	-
20 per cent. damages, - - - - - - -	43	4	6
Charges of protest, - - - - - - -		8	
	259	17	6
Interest from 13 Sept., 1765, to 9 June, being 3 years and 8 months & 126 days at 7 per cent.	67	19	6
Cost of Attachment - - - - - - - -	6	11	9
	£334	8	9

The parties being heard by Messrs. Peter Keteltas, William Wilson and Wm. Seton, three of the Committee, who award £266 6s. 6d. to be due to *Mr. Rhodes* from *Vallade* the possessor of *Monsr. La Piere's* effects.

The Committee for July, 1769, report

That, having been applied to by *Capt. William Warnock* of the one part, and *John Franklin* of the other part, who being heard by Messrs. Jacob Watson, Thos. W. Moore, and John Reade, three of the Committee, have awarded that there is due from *John Franklin* to *William Warnock* the sum of £11. 6s. 3d., with this memorandum: Since settling the above account, *Cap. Warnock* says he delivered a keg of rum more than was specified in the bill-lading; and as he delivered a barrel flour short, the matter is left unsettled till *Mr. Franklin's* return from Phil'a.

CHAMBER OF COMMERCE.—TUESDAY, 4th September, 1769.

PRESENT.

John Cruger, Presid't,
John Reade,
Jacob Watson,
Robert Murray,
William Walton,
Lewis Pintard,
G. W. Ludlow,
Samp'n Simpson,
Gerrard Walton,
Joseph Bull,
Jacobus Van Zandt.

Fined for appearing after six o'clock:

Samuel Ver Plank,
Peter Remsen,
Miles Sherbrooke,
Hamilton Young,
James Jauncey,
Thomas Walton,
John Moore,
Gab. H. Ludlow,
Thomas W. Moore.

As a sufficient number of Members were not convened[22] to do business, all the rest were fined for non-attendance.

Hugh Wallace, V. P.,
Elias Desbrosses, T.,
Anthony Van Dam, S.,
Jacob Walton,
George Folliot,
Theophy. Bache,
Walter Franklin,
Lawrence Kortright,
Thomas Randal,
Isaac Low,
Henry White,
John Alsop,
Thomas White,
Robert R. Waddle,
William McAdam,
Robert Watts,
John H. Cruger,
Charles McEvers,
Levinus Clarkson,
Nicholas Gouverneur,
Richard Yates,
Thomas Marston,
Philip Livingston,
Isaac Sears,
Peter Hasencliver,
Alexan. Wallace,
Thomas Buchanan,
William Seton,
Edward Laight,
William Neilson,
Peter Keteltas,
Gerr'd W. Beekman,
Robert Alexander,
Richard Sharpe,
Henry Remsen,
Abram Lynsen,
Isaac Roosevelt,
Nicholas Hoffman,
John Thurman,
John Wetherhead,
Garret Rapelje,
Gerr'd Duykink,
Will. Stepple,
Will. Imlay,
Augus. Van Horn,
Henry C. Bogart.

CHAMBER OF COMMERCE.—TUESDAY, 3d October, 1769.

PRESENT.

John Cruger, P.
V. P.
T.
Anthony Van Dam, S.

Jacob Walton,
Joseph Bull,
Lawrence Kortright,
Isaac Sears,
Theoph. Bache,
Gab. H. Ludlow,
George Ludlow,
Richard Yates,
William Stepple,
Leonard Lispenard,
Henry Remsen,
John Moore,
Hamil. Young,
Thomas Walton,
James Jauncey,
Garret Rapelje,
Thomas Buchanan,
Lewis Pintard,

William Walton,
John H. Cruger,
Miles Sherbrooke,
Augus. Van Horn,
Samuel Ver Plank,
Thomas Marston,
Thomas W. Moore,
Walter Franklin,
Abram Lynsen.

Fined for appearing after six o'clock:

John Thurman.

Fined for non-appearance:

Hugh Wallace,
Elias Desbrosses,
Robert Murray,
George Folliot,
Thomas Randal,
Isaac Low,
Henry White,
John Alsop,
Thomas White,
Robert R. Waddle,
William McAdam,
Robert Watts,
Gerrard Walton,
Jacobus Van Zandt, (Phil'a)
Levinus Clarkson,
Nicholas Gouverneur,
Philip Livingston,
Peter Hasencliver,
Alexand. Wallace,
William Seton,
Edward Laight,
William Neilson,
Sampson Simpson,
Peter Keteltas,
Gerrar. W. Beekman,
Jacob Watson,
John Reade,
Robert Alexander,
Richard Sharpe,
Peter Remsen,
Isaac Roosevelt,
Nichos. Hoffman,
John Weatherhead,
Gerrars. Duykink,
William Imlay,
Henry C. Bogert,
Thomas Miller,
James Beekman,
Samuel Kemble,
Charles McEvers.

The Committee appointed to ascertain the Value of Gold and Silver Coin[23] having made their report, which, being read, was in the words following:

We, the subscribers, being appointed a Committee by the Chamber of Commerce to consider what the undermentioned Coins should pass current for, do report, viz.:

A Johannes, weighing eighteen pennyweight, shall for - - - £6 8
and every smaller coin of the same denomination in like proportion.

	£	s.	d.
A Moidore, weighing six pennyweight eighteen grains, for - and the smaller coins of same denomination in like proportion.	£2	8	
A Caroline, weighing six pennyweight eight grains, for - - -	1	18	
A Spanish Doubleloon, or Four-Pistole piece, weighing seventeen pennyweight eight grains, - - - - - - - - - - and the smaller coins in the same proportion.	5	16	
An English Guinea, weighing five pennyweight six grains, - - Half and Quarter do. in same proportion.	1	17	
A French Guinea, weighing five pennyweight four grains, - - Half do. in same proportion.	1	16	
A Chequeen, weighing two pennyweight four grains - - - -		14	6
An English Crown for - - - - - - - - - - - - - - - Half Crowns in same proportion.		8	9
A French Crown for - - - - - - - - - - - - - - - Half Crowns in same proportion.		8	6
A French Pistole, weighing four pennyweight five grains, - -	1	8	
An English Shilling for - - - - - - - - - - - - - - Sixpence in same proportion.		1	9
A Pistareen for - - - - - - - - - - - - - - - - - -		1	7

And for every grain any of the above specified pieces of Gold shall weigh less than the weight above directed, there shall be deducted four pence, which is humbly submitted by

William Walton, Hamilton Young,
Samuel Ver Plank, Robert Murray,
John H. Cruger.

Resolved—That this Chamber will pay and receive all Gold and Silver in future at the above rates, and Ordered that the substance of the above report be published in Newspapers.[24]

The Committee appointed to report their opinion respecting Lumber, having made their report, which, being read, was in the words following:

We, the subscribers, being appointed by the New York Chamber of Commerce to be a committee for considering the present state of Lumber shipp'd from this Port, and to make report to them of what may appear to us necessary for the further improvement of this article of our Exports, do give as our opinion ;

That our Lumber is at present in disrepute at Foreign Markets, and sells considerably under what is Exported from Philadelphia, which we believe to be in a great measure owing to a want of proper care in the Dimensions and Dressing.

That, in order to give it Reputation, and thereby increase the demand for it, We are of opinion that the following regulations will be of service, viz.:

That every Butt Stave shall be Five feet four inches long, Five inches broad in the narrowest part, clear of Sap, One inch and a quarter thick in the thinnest place, not more than One inch and three quarters thick in any part, and shall not have more than eight worm holes.

That every Pipe Stave shall be Four feet eight inches long, Four inches broad in the narrowest part, clear of Sap, One inch thick in the thinnest place, not more than One inch and a half thick in any part, and shall not have more than seven worm holes.

That every Hogshead Stave shall be Three feet eight inches long, Four inches broad in the narrowest part, clear of Sap, Three quarters of an inch thick in the thinnest place, not more than one inch and one quarter thick in any part, and shall not have more than six worm holes.

That every Barrel Stave shall be Two feet eight inches long, Four inches broad in the narrowest part, clear of Sap, Three quarters of an inch thick in the thinnest place, not more than one inch and one quarter thick in any part, and shall not have more than five worm holes.

That every piece of Hogshead Heading shall be Two feet six inches long, Seven inches broad in the narrowest part, clear of Sap, and the Cantle pieces of the same breadth in the widest part, clear of Sap; both sorts One inch thick, and shall not have more than seven worm holes in each piece, the Cutter having a due regard that there be always a proper proportion of middle pieces in such heading.

That all the aforesaid Staves and Headings shall be regularly split with the grain of the wood, clear of sap, not to exceed the lengths and breadths already mentioned, and be otherwise good and fit for making light casks.

That all Hoops brought to Market in order to be shipped off shall be from fourteen to sixteen feet long, and otherwise good and sufficient.

That Oak Plank of all dimensions shall be clear of Sap and Shakes, edged, and the ends square, and be otherwise good and sufficient.

That Pine Boards of all sorts and dimensions shall be edged clear of Shakes, as long and as broad as possible, and otherwise good and sufficient.

That all Oak Timber brought to Market, in order to be shipped off, shall be square both sides, and ends free of [———] and be otherwise good and sufficient.

That Long Shingles shall be Three feet long, five to eight inches and upwards broad, and three-quarters of an inch thick at the Butts.

That Short Shingles shall be One foot six inches to one foot eight inches long, four inches and upwards broad, and half an inch to five-eights of an inch thick.

That it is further our opinion that, in order to have the above regulations duly complied with, one capable and sufficient person be appointed to inspect and cull all such Staves, Heading, and Hoops as shall be brought to Market for Exportation, with power of substituting others, if necessary, for whose conduct however he is to be accountable.

That one capable and sufficient person be also appointed to inspect and measure all such Oak Plank, Pine Boards excepting such Pine Boards as are sold by the Piece, and square Timber, and inspect all such Shingles as shall be brought to Market for Exportation, with power of substituting others, if necessary, for whose conduct he is to be accountable.

All which matters are humbly submitted to the consideration of the Chamber.

JOHN MOORE,
THEOPY. BACHE,
RICH'D. YATES.

Ordered—That Mr. John Moore, Mr. Yates and Mr. Bache be a Committee to wait on the Mayor[25] and ask the favour of him to recommend it to the Corporation, that it may be passed into a Bye Law[26] of this place.

Mr. James Beekman and Capt. Samuel Kemble, having been proposed at a former Meeting, were balloted for and unanimously chosen Members.

Ordered—That the Secretary send notice in writing that they were unanimously chosen.

Mr. Verplank moves that no Persons be admitted Members of this Chamber, in future, but Merchants.

Mr. H. Remsen proposes that the Rules and Regulations agreed to by this Chamber, and that are now binding, be Printed for the use of the Members, and that whatever Regulations are hereafter agreed upon be Printed every half year.

Ordered—That Mr. Thurman, Mr. Wetherhead, Mr. G. Rapelje, Mr. G. Duyckinck, Mr. Stepple, Mr. Imlay, and Mr. Van Horne, be a Committee until the first Tuesday in November next, to hear and determine disputes between parties who shall agree to leave such to this Chamber, and that they do make report thereof, in writing, what business hath or shall come before them during their appointment.

CHAMBER OF COMMERCE.—TUESDAY, 7th November, 1769.

PRESENT.

John Cruger, P.
Hugh Wallace, V. P.
Elias Desbrosses, T.
Anth. Van Dam, S.

James Jauncey,
Samuel Ver Plank,
Theoph. Bache,
Miles Sherbrooke,
Lawrence Kortright,
Isaac Low,
Henry White,
William Walton,
Robert R. Waddle,
Hamilton Young,
John H. Cruger,
Gerrard Walton,
Jacobus Van Zandt,
Richard Yates,
Thomas Marston,
Lewis Pintard,
Alexan. Wallace,
Gabriel H. Ludlow,
Thomas Buchanan,
John Thurman,
William Neilson,
Sampson Simpson,
Robert Alexander,
Thomas W. Moore,
Peter Remsen,
Henry Remsen,
Abraham Lynsen,
Isaac Roosevelt,
Nicholas Hoffman,
Garret Rapelje,
William Stepple,
Joseph Bull,
William Imlay,
Leonard Lispenard,
Augustus Van Horne.

Fined for appearing after six o'clock:

Samuel Ver Plank,
Charles McEvers,
John Moore,
George W. Ludlow.

Fined for non-appearance:

Robert Murray,
George Folliot,
Walter Franklin,
Thomas Randal,
John Alsop,
Thomas White,
William McAdam,
Peter Hasencliver,
William Seton,
Edward Laight,
Peter Keteltas,
Samuel Kemble, (Jerseys)
Gerrard W. Beekman,
Jacob Watson.

Robert Watts,	John Reade,
James Beekman,	Richard Sharpe,
Levinus Clarkson,	John Wetherhead,
Nicholas Gouverneur,	Gerrard Duyckinck,
Philip Livingston,	Henry C. Bogart,
Isaac Sears,	Thomas Miller, (Sea).

At the desire of several members of the Chamber, since last Meeting, they had requested of the President to apply to Messrs. David Rittenhouse[e] and John Montresor,[f] to take the Latitude of the Flag Bastion in Fort George,[27] in the City of New York. The observations of Mr. David Rittenhouse were as follows:

NEW YORK, October 12, 1769.

SIR,

At your request, in behalf of the Chamber of Commerce of the City New York, I have made the following Observations with the Pennsylvania Sector, of six feet Radius, on the South West Bastion of Fort George, in this city.

ZENITH DISTANCE ON THE MERIDIAN OF CAPELLA:

	°	′	″
Octr. 9 Morn, - - - - - - - -	5	2	0½
10 ditto, - - - - - - - -	5	1	59
OF CASTOR:			
10 Morn, - - - - - - - -	8	19	51
12 ditto, - - - - - - - -	8	19	51

Having carefully computed the Declinations of the above Stars, from their Latitudes and Longitudes, as settled by Dr. Bradley,[g] reduced to the present time and corrected by the aberration of Light and variable motion of the Earth's Axis, I find the Latitude of the place from the observations of

	°	′	″
Capella to be - - - - - - - - -	40	42	9
And from those of Castor, - - - - - -	40	42	7
A mean whereof is the Latitude of the Fort,[28] -	40	42	8

I am, Sir, your very humb. Serv't,

DAVID RITTENHOUSE.

To JOHN CRUGER, Esq., Presid't of the Chamber of Commerce.

Observations were made at the Flag Bastion in Fort George, in the City of New York, principally with the Sector belonging to the Province of Pennsylvania, of six feet Radius, by Messrs. David Rittenhouse and John Montresor, Engineers, October, 1769.

ZENITH DISTANCE OF CAPELLA:

		°	′	″
	h			
October 9th—	3 50, Morn'g, - - - - - -	5	2	0½
10—	3 46, morn'g, - - - - - -	5	1	59

ZENITH DISTANCE OF CASTOR:

		°	′	″
	h			
October 10th—	6 6, Morn'g, - - - - - -	8	19	51
12—	5 58, morn'g, - - - - - -	8	19	51

	°	′	″
Declination of Capella, - - -	45	44	14
Zenith distance of Capella, Refraction,	5	2	5
Latitude, - -	40	42	9
Declination of Castor, - - -	32	22	7
Zenith Distance of Castor, - -	8	19	51
Refraction - - - - - -	0	0	9
Latitude, - - - - - - -	40	42	7

	°	′	″
The mean of the above observations ascertains the Latitude of Fort George in - - - - -	40	42	8

I am, with respect, Sir, your most obedient and most h'ble serv't,

JOHN MONTRESOR.

To John Cruger, Esq., President of the Chamber of Commerce at New York.

Ordered—That the Treasurer do repay unto the Gentlemen that are in advance to Mr. Rittenhouse the sum of Twenty pounds for his services.

Mr. President having also taken an abstract from the

minutes of the above Gentlemen, who were employed by the Commissioners for ascertaining the Line[29] between New York and Jersey—being read, was as follows:

LATITUDES taken by Mr. Rittenhouse and McLean,[h] of Philadelphia, and Capt. John Montresor, Engineer, in September and October, 1769.

	°	′	″
Mahackomach,[30] on Delaware, - - - - - -	41	21	37
On Hudson's River, 79 chains and 27 Links south of the House late Mrs. Corbet's,[31] a marked Rock,	41	0	0
Light House on Sandy Hook,[32] - - - - -	40	27	40
South West Bastion on Fort George, New York, -	40	42	8

Mr. Moore, one of the Committee appointed to wait on the Mayor to desire his influence with the Corporation to procure a Law for the better Cutting of Lumber, reported

That they had waited on the Mayor, and that he was pleased to say that he wou'd urge the matter, and be of all the use in his power; and, furthermore, that he had been waited upon by the Public Repackers of Beef and Pork in this (city), representing that complaints had been frequently made of Beef and Pork shipped from this place, and to that end recommended that the Chamber would consider of a Petition delivered, which, being read, was in the words following:

WE, THE PUBLICK PACKERS[33] of this City, whose names are hereunto subscribed, hearing frequent complaints of Beef and Pork being Rusty, pray the Mayor and Corporation to make the following amendments:

That all Beef and Pork for Sale in this City shall be well Trim'd and filled with pickle before the month of April expires in every year, under the penalty of —— p. barrel.

That all Beef and Pork which shall be brought to this City for sale after the first day of May in every year, shall be pickled within Ten Days after it's landed, under the like penalty.

That all Barrels containing Beef and Pork shall be hooped with —— Hoops, at least.

DANIEL DUNSCOMB,	PETER STOUTENBERG,
RICHARD KIP,	JAMES DUNSCOMB,
THEOPH. ELSWORTH,	JOSEP. GODWIN,
EDWARD LOWNE,	JOHN SILVESTER,
ABRA'M COCK,	JOHN POST.

Ordered—That Messrs. C. McEvers, T. Bache, R. Yates, J. Moore, T. Buchanan, H. White, J. Thurman, and L. Pintard, be a Committee to consider of the nature of the Petition, and wait upon the Mayor and Corporation with their Report, as well as to Report to this Chamber what good purpose it will answer.

Mr. Ver Plank's motion for not admitting any persons Members of this Chamber in future but Merchants,[34] which being considered of, a Majority of the members appeared in favour of the motion.

Resolved—That no persons who are hereafter proposed to be Members of this Chamber be admitted but Merchants.

Mr. Henry Remsen, who proposed that the Rules and Regulations agreed to by this Chamber, and that are now binding, be printed for the use of the members, and that whatever Regulations are hereafter agreed to be Printed every half year.

Resolved—That it is the unanimous opinion that all the Rules and Regulations already entered, and engaged for by the Members, and what other rules may be made, be printed accordingly.

Mr. Alexander McDonald, who was proposed at a former Meeting, was balloted for and unanimously chosen a Member.

Ordered—That the Secretary send notice in writing that he was unanimously chosen.

Ordered—That Mr. H. C. Bogart, Mr. G. W. Ludlow, Mr. Jos. Bull, Mr. L. Lispenard, Mr. Jas. Beekman, Mr. S. Kemble, and Mr. James Jauncey, be a Committee until the first Tuesday in December next, to hear and determine disputes between Parties who shall agree to leave such to this Chamber, and that they do make report thereof in writing what business hath or shall come before them during their appointment.

The Committee for January, 1769, having been applied to by *Watson and Murray, Owners*, and *Isaac Sears, Freighter* of the Ship America, on her Voyage from New York to Lisbon, on prosecuting which she went ashore on Nutten Island,[35] and received some damage, do report:

We, the Subscribers, having been appointed as a Monthly Committee of the New York Chamber of Commerce, have, at the request of the Parties, arbitrated and finally determined who ought to bear the Expenses of Unlading and getting off the Ship America, Cap. Hervey, when said Ship was ashore some time ago, on Nutten Island, on her Voyage from this port (to) Lisbon, and do report it as our opinion that the Freighters ought not to be chargeable with any Expenses which attended the unlading and getting off the said Ship. Witness our hands, this first day of November, 1769, in the City of New York.

LAWRENCE KORTRIGHT,	ROBT. R. WADDELL,
WILLIAM WALTON,	THOMAS WHITE,
ISAAC LOW,	WILLIAM MCADAM.

CHAMBER OF COMMERCE.—TUESDAY, 5 December, 1769.

PRESENT.

Hugh Wallace, V. P.
Elias Desbrosses, T.
Anthony Van Dam, S.

James Jauncey,	Edward Laight,
Isaac Low,	William Neilson,
William Walton,	Sampson Simpson,
Robert R. Waddell,	John Reade,
Robert Watts,	Alexander McDonald,
John H. Cruger,	Lawrence Kortright,
Gerrard Walton,	Thomas W. Moore,
John Moore,	Henry Remsen,
Levinus Clarkson,	Nichols. Hoffman,
Samuel Kemble,	Hamil. Young,
Theophy Bache,	Thomas Watson,
Thomas Marston,	John Thurman,

Isaac Sears,
Lewis Pintard,
Gabr. H. Ludlow,
Thomas Buchanan,
Willliam Stepple,
George W. Ludlow,
James Beekman,
Samuel Ver Plank.

Fined for non-appearance:

John Cruger, P.
Jacob Walton,
Robert Murray,
George Folliot,
Charles McEvers,
Nicholas Gouverneur,
Richard Yates,
Jacob Watson,
Peter Remsen,
Garret Rapelje,
William Imlay,
Joseph Bull,
Miles Sherbrooke,
Walter Franklin,
Thomas Randal,
Henry White,
Philip Livingston,
Peter Hasencliver,
Alexand. Wallace,
Robert Alexander,
Abraham Lynsen,
Gerrard Duykink,
Augustus Van Horne,
Leonard Lispenard,
John Alsop,
Thomas White,
William McAdam,
Jacobus Van Zandt, F.
William Seton,
Peter Keteltas,
Gerrard Beekman,
Richard Sharpe,
Isaac Roosevelt,
John Weatherhead,
Henry C. Bogert,
Thomas Miller, (Sea.)

The Committee appointed to consider the better inspection and Cutting of Lumber exported from this, report

That they had waited on the Mayor, who was pleased to deliver them a draft of a Law for the better inspection and regulation of Lumber, &c., which they exhibited, and being carefully read was [*erased*] and thought would be of great use if made into a Law.

Mr. Simpson proposed that it be considered by the Chamber whether Guineas shou'd not pass for 37s. each that weigh 5 dwt. 3 gr., instead of 5 dwt. 6 gr., as established by this Chamber.

Mr. Simpson also proposed that this Chamber do consider of some method to prevent the clipping or filing[36] Gold Coin, and that every half Johannes weighing 9 dwt. 4 grains and upwards do pass at 65 shillings.

Mr. Van Dam proposed that a Committee be appointed to Inspect and transcribe what Rules and regulations are proper to be printed, in addition to those already done, agreeable to Mr. Henry Remsen, jun'r.'s motion on the 7th November past.

Mr. Low proposed that as it would tend greatly to promote the Benevolent intentions of this Chamber to have it incorporated under proper regulations; and as there is the greatest reason to expect from His Honor the Lieut. Governor and his Council all the Countenance and protection which so usefull an infant Institution justly merits,

Moves that a Committee be appointed from this Chamber to wait on his Honor the Lieut. Governor, praying the favour of him to invest it with a Charter granting such privileges as may be conceived most advancive of the important Ends intended by it; And that the said Committee prepare a Draught of the said proposed Charter for the approbation of the Chamber at their next meeting. I also propose that the rule relative to the Election of Members into this Chamber be reconsidered, and that instead of three black Balls there shall be at least Six, or such greater number as to the Wisdom of the Chamber shall seem meet, to prevent any Person hereafter proposed from becoming a Member thereof.

ISAAC LOW.

Ordered—That Mr. Folliot, Mr. Ver Plank, Mr. Bache, Mr. Sherbrooke, Mr. W. Franklin, Mr. Kortright, and Mr. T. Randall, be a Committee, until the first Tuesday in January next, to hear and determine disputes between parties who shall agree to leave such to this Chamber, and that they do make report thereof in writing what business hath or shall come before them during their appointment.

CHAMBER OF COMMERCE.—TUESDAY, January 2, 1770.

PRESENT.

John Cruger, P.
Hugh Wallace, V. P.
Elias Desbrosses, T.
Antho. Van Dam, S.

James Jauncey,
Walter Franklin,
Lawrence Kortright,
William Walton,
William McAdam,
Gerrard Walton,
Richard Yates,
Lewis Pintard,
Alexan. Wallace,
Gabr. H. Ludlow,
Edward Laight,
William Neilson,
Samp. Simpson,
Robert Alexander,
Henry Remsen,
Isaac Roosevelt,
Thomas Walton,
John Thurman,
Garret Rapelje,
William Stepple,
James Beekman.

Fined for appearing after six o'clock :

Hugh Wallace,
Elias Desbrosses,
Theoph. Bache,
John Moore,
Alexan. McDonald.

Fined for non-appearance:

Jacob Walton,
Robert Murray,
George Folliot,
Samuel Ver Plank,
Miles Sherbrooke,
Thomas Randal,
Isaac Low,
Henry White,
John Alsop,
Thomas White,
Gerr'd W. Beekman,
Jacob Watson,
John Reade,
Thom's W. Moore,
Richard Sharpe,
Peter Remsen,
Abram Lynsen,
Nicholas Hoffman,
Hamilt. Young,
Robert R. Waddle,

John H. Cruger,	Robert Watts,
Jacobus Van Zandt, F.	William Imlay,
Charles McEvers,	Henry C. Bogart,
Levinus Clarkson,	Thomas Miller, (Sea)
Nicholas Gouverneur,	William Seton,
Thomas Marston,	Augus. Van Horne,
Philip Livingston,	George W. Ludlow,
Isaac Sears,	Samuel Kemble, (Sea)
Peter Hasencliver,	John Weatherhead.
Thomas Buchanan,	Gerrard Duykink,
Peter Keteltas,	Joseph Bull,

Leonard Lispenard.

Mr. Simpson's Proposal, whether Guineas should not pass at thirty-seven shillings that weigh 5 dwt. 3 grains, being considered, and it appearing that 5 dwt. 3 grs. is on a medium the general weight of the Guineas amongst us,

Agreed that Guineas of that weight shall pass at thirty-seven shillings, provided they are not apparently defaced.

Whereas, a resolution of this Chamber fixed the lowest weight of half Joha's at Nine pennyweight, induced thereto by the custom of the Merchants in a neighbouring Colony,[37] but finding the scandalous practice of filing and diminishing foreign Gold Coin too much countenanced, to encourage which was by no means the intention of this Chamber, In order to prevent such base practices here,

We declare that we will discourage it by all means in our power, and hold any person guilty of it in contempt, and not proper to be a Member of this Chamber.

Ordered—That Messrs. Charles McEvers, Jacobus Van Zandt, and John Moore, be a Committee to transcribe such Rules and Regulations entered into by this Chamber as are not printed, and that they do prepare the same for the inspection of this Chamber at their next Meeting.

Mr. Low's Proposal for appointing a Committee to

wait on his Honor the Lieut. Governor,[i] praying him to Incorporate this Chamber, was considered of and agreed to defer its consideration till a future Meeting.

The Committee appointed the 7th November last, to consider the nature of the Petition of the Repackers in this City to the Mayor and Corporation respecting the better Inspection of Beef and Pork, report in writing as follows:

We, the Subscribers being appointed by the New York Chamber of Commerce to be a Committee for taking into consideration the present mode of Packing Beef and Pork in this City, and for reporting any regulations that may appear to us necessary for the further improvement thereof, do give as our opinion from the best Information we could procure and from our own experience—

That the size of the Barrels in which Beef and Pork are now packed is generally too large, from whence an inconvenience arises, not only with respect to Stowage, but also with respect to the due preservation of these Articles, as we are of opinion that they cannot be so well preserved in Casks in which the pieces lie loose as in those in which they are compact and close, besides the Sale of these Articles is hurt at foreign Markets by being packed in too large Casks, as upon opening a Barrel it does not appear to be full and therefore it is hastily concluded that it does not contain a sufficient quantity; in order to remedy these inconveniences, we are of opinion that the Barrels should contain not less than thirty nor more than thirty-one gallons.

That the Barrels in which Beef and Pork are packed be made of good seasoned and sufficient Stuff, that the Staves be half an inch thick at the Chine, and $\frac{3}{8}$ of an inch thick at the Bilge, at least, and that the Barrels be hooped with 12 hoops.

That the Packers have power to condemn all Casks that are not made agreeable to the above regulations, and be subjected to a Penalty for branding any Provisions that are not well and sufficiently Cured and Merchantable, and that are not packed in Barrels conformable to said Regulations, and further, that the said Packers be obliged to give Security for their good Behaviour.

That all Beef and Pork sold in this City shall be Inspected, Repacked, and Branded at the time of Sale, and if sold more than once shall be inspected and repacked as often as sold, if Required by the Purchaser.

That every Barrel of Beef shall contain Two hundred and twenty Suttle pounds, and every Barrel of Pork Two hundred and ten Suttle[38] pounds Neat.

That with respect to the Prayer of the Packers Petition, that a Law be passed enacting that all Beef and Pork be pickled before the first Day of May. We are of opinion that the foregoing Regulations, if duly attended to, will of themselves remedy the Evil complained of.

That if a Law [39] be passed for enforcing the above Regulations, we are of opinion it should not take place till the first Day of October next.

All which matters are humbly submitted to the Chamber.

THEOPHY BACHE, JOHN MOORE,
LEWIS PINTARD, RICH'D. YATES.

Mr. Samuel Bayard junr. having been proposed at a former Meeting, was Balloted for and chosen a Member of this Chamber.

Ordered—That the Secretary send him notice in writing that he was duly elected.

Ordered—That Messrs. Isaac Low, H. White, J. Alsop, W. Walton, T. White, R. R. Waddell, and Rob. Watts be a Committee until the first Tuesday in February next, to hear and determine disputes between Parties who shall agree to leave such to this Chamber, and that they do make report thereof in writing to this Chamber what business hath or shall come before them during their appointment.

CHAMBER OF COMMERCE.—TUESDAY, February 6, 1770.

PRESENT.

John Cruger, P.
Hugh Wallace, V. P.
Elias Desbrosses, T.
Anth'y Van Dam, S.

James Jauncey,
Jacob Walton,
Samuel Verplank,
Theophy. Bache,
Lawrence Kortright,
Isaac Low,
Henry White,
John Alsop,
Sampson Simpson,
John Reade,
Thomas W. Moore,
Richard Sharpe,
Peter Remsen,
Henry Remsen,
Abraham Lynsen,
Isaac Roosevelt,

William Walton,
William McAdam,
John H. Cruger,
Gerrard Walton,
Levinus Clarkson,
Richard Yates,
Thomas Marston,
Alexand'r Wallace,
Gabriel H. Ludlow,
Thomas Buchanan,
William Seton,
Edward Laight,
William Neilson,
Nicholas Hoffman,
Thomas Walton,
John Thurman,
Garret Rapelje,
William Stepple,
August's Van Horne,
Henry C. Bogart,
George W. Ludlow,
Joseph Bull,
Leonard Lispenard,
James Beekman,
Alexander McDonald,
Samuel Bayard, jr.

Fined for appearing after six o'clock :

James Beekman,
Anthony Van Dam,
Samuel Bayard,
Isaac Low,
Henry C. Bogart,
Edward Laight,
Robert Watts,
Alexan'r McDonald,
John Moore.

Fined for non-appearance :

Robert Murray,
George Folliot,
Miles Sherbrooke,
Walter Franklin,
Thomas Randal,
Thomas White,
Robert R. Waddell,
Robert Watts,
Thomas Miller, (Sea)
Charles McEvers,
Jacobus Van Zandt,
John Moore,
Nicho's Gouverneur,
Philip Livingston,
Isaac Sears,
Lewis Pintard,
Peter Hasencliver,
Samuel Kemble, (Sea)
Peter Keteltas,
Gerra'd W. Beekman,
Jacob Watson,
Robert Alexander,
Hamilton Young,
John Wetherhead,
Gerrard Duykink,
William Imlay.

Mr. C. McEvers, J. Van Zandt, and J. Moore, the Committee appointed to Transcribe the Rules and Regulations of this Chamber, beg'd leave to sit again.

Mr. Low's proposal for appointing a Committee to

wait on the Governor, praying to incorporate this Chamber, being considered of,

Ordered—That Messrs. I. Low, Wm. McAdam, J. H. Cruger, C. McEvers, R. Sharpe, H. Remsen, Thos. Buchanan, S. Simpson, W. Walton, J. Alsop, and Jno. Thurman, be a Committee, or any six of them, to prepare a draft of a Petition to the Governor and Council, and draft of a Charter to incorporate this Chamber, and that they do prepare and deliver them in at their next meeting.

The Report of the Committee appointed to consider the present mode of Packing Beef and Pork in this City, delivered in at this Board last meeting, being again read, and the whole Chamber taking it into consideration, are of opinion that the mode proposed therein will answer every good purpose for the reestablishing of the credit of these Articles; therefore,

Ordered—That Mr. John Moore, R. Yates, T. Bache, Lewis Pintard, J. Thurman, be a Committee to wait on the Mayor with their report to this Chamber, and pray him to use his influence with the Corporation to take this matter into consideration, and enforce the same by a Law of the Corporation.

Mr. Low proposed that, amongst the judicious Regulations already made for the good Government of this Chamber, there is one wanting which appears to me more essential to preserve the spirit of the Institution than any which has yet been adopted; because, I presume, one of the principal Objects in pursuit is not only amicably to settle and accommodate Accounts and Disputes between Merchants and others who may think fit to submit them to the Arbitrament of this Chamber, but more especially all such Disputes as may arise between its own Members. As, therefore, it is absolutely necessary that the Members should set the Example which they would have others to follow, in order to prevent unnecessary Litigation, I propose, as a standing and invariable Rule of this Chamber for the Future, that the members shall on their Parts never refuse to submit all disputed Matters of Accounts they may be concerned in with each other, or any other Persons whomsoever, to the final Arbitrament and determination of the Chamber collectively, or to such of the Members as may be chosen by the Parties, on pain of being expelled the Chamber, and disqualified from being ever again admitted a Member of it.

Mr. Low proposed that whenever this Chamber shall consist of Eighty members, every Person on being Elected a member hereof, he shall pay the sum of four Pounds on admission, until this Chamber shall consist of Ninety members, after which every member that is admitted shall pay a sum not under Five pounds, until the Chamber consists of One hundred members, and so on *ad infinitum* for the use of this Chamber.

Mr. McAdam proposes to the consideration of this Chamber, whether it is not necessary to have One or more Buoys [40] fixed on the most dangerous Sands in the entrance to this Harbour, and that a Committee be appointed to consult with the Wardens [41] of the Port, and ask them to cause Two or more Buoys to be placed at such places as they shall think proper for the Better preservation of the Navigation in and out of this Port.

Mr. Henry Remsen moves that a Committee be appointed to consider of some plan, the most eligible, for carrying into execution the Whale-Fishery [42] out of this Port, which has proved very beneficial to our neighboring Colonies, it being very evident that we are as well situated for that branch of business as they.

Ordered—That Mr. H. Remsen, H. C. Bogart, W. Franklin, T. Bache, S. Verplank, J. Thurman, R. Yates, and S. Simpson, be a Committee to consult on the subject of the Própsal, and deliver into this Chamber their thoughts in writing at their next Meeting.

Mr. Low proposes that no less than thirty Members shall hereafter be sufficient to transact business in this Chamber, and that instead of three black Balls to disqualify a person from being hereafter Elected a Member of this Chamber there shall be four black Balls whenever there be upwards of thirty Members, when more than forty, five black Balls, and so on, one black Ball for every ten Members that may be present at the election.

Ordered—That Messrs. Jno. H. Cruger, Ger. Walton, J. Van Zandt, C. McEvers, J. Moore, L. Clarkson, and R. Yates, be a Committee until the first Tuesday in March next, to hear and determine disputes between Parties who shall agree to leave such to this Chamber, and that they do make report thereof, in writing, to this Chamber, what business hath or shall come before them during their appointment.

CHAMBER OF COMMERCE.—THURSDAY, 15th Feb., 1770.

SPECIAL MEETING.

PRESENT.

John Cruger, P.
Anthony Van Dam, S.

Theophy Bache,	Peter Keteltas,
Miles Sherbrooke,	Sampson Simpson,
Walter Franklin,	Leonard Lispenard,
Jacobus Van Zandt,	Thomas W. Moore,
Levinus Clarkson,	Henry Remsen, junr.,
Joseph Bull,	Hamilton Young,
Richd. Yates,	John Thurman,
Thomas Marston,	William Stepple,
Lewis Pintard,	James Beekman.

Fined for appearing after six o'clock:

James Jauncey,
Jacob Walton,
Isaac Low,
John Alsop,
Thomas White,
William McAdam,
Robert Watts,
Nicholas Gouverneur,
Thomas Buchanan,
Gerrard W. Beekman,
Robert Alexander,
Nicholas Hoffman,
John Wetherhead,
Augustus Van Horn,
Alexander McDonald,
Samuel Bayard jr.,

Fined for non-appearance:

Hugh Wallace,
Elias Desbrosses,
Robert Murray,
George Folliot,
Samuel Ver Plank,
Charles McEvers,
John Moore,
Philip Livingston,
Isaac Sears,
Peter Hasencliver,
Richard Sharpe,
Peter Remsen,
Abraham Lynsen,
Isaac Roosevelt,
Thomas Walton,
Lawrence Kortright,
Thomas Randal,
Henry White,
William Walton,
Robert R. Waddle,
John H. Cruger,
Gerrard Walton,
Alexan. Wallace,
Gabriel H. Ludlow,
William Seton,
Edward Laight,
William Neilson,
Jacob Watson,
John Reade,
Garret Rapelje,
Gerrard Duyckinck,
William Imlay,
Henry C. Bogart,
George W. Ludlow.
Thomas Miller, } (Sea).
Samuel Kemble, }

The Committee appointed to draw up a draft of a Petition to His Honor the Lieut. Governor praying him to Incorporate this Society, and to draw up a draft of the Charter, Report that they had drawn a draft of the Petition, which being read was in the words following:

To the Honourable CADWALLADER COLDEN, Esquire, Lieutenant Governor and Commander-in-Chief of the Colony of New York, and the Territories depending thereon in America,

IN COUNCIL.[43]

THE PETITION OF JOHN CRUGER, Esquire, President of a Society of Merchants of the City of New York, associated for promoting Trade and Commerce in behalf of the said Society,

MOST HUMBLY SHOWETH

That the said Society, sensible that Numberless inestimable benefits have accrued to Mankind from Commerce, that they are in proportion to their greater or lesser application to it, more or less opulent and potent in all Countries ; and that the Enlargement of Trade will vastly increase the value of real Estates as well as the general opulence of this Country ; have associated together for some time past in order to carry into execution, amongst themselves, and by their Example, to promote in others such measures as were beneficial to these Salutary Purposes. And the said Society having, with great pleasure and Satisfaction, experienced the good Effects which the few Regulations already adopted have produced, are very desirous of rendering them more extensively useful and permanent, and more adequate to the purposes of so benevolent an Institution.

Your Petitioner, therefore, in behalf of the said Society, most humbly prays your Honor to Incorporate them as a Body Politic, and to invest them with such Powers and Authorities as may be thought most conducive to answer and promote the Commercial, and consequently the Landed Interests of this growing Colony.

And your Petitioner, as in duty bound, shall ever pray.

Resolved—That the Petition be engrossed and signed by the President, and that he does wait on His Honor the Lieut. Governor with the same when perfected, and that the Committee before mentioned do attend the President, and such other Gentlemen of the Chamber as please to go.

CHAMBER OF COMMERCE.—TUESDAY, 6th March, 1770.

PRESENT.

John Cruger, P.
Hugh Wallace, V. P.
Elias Desbrosses, T.
Anthon. Van Dam, S.

James Jauncey,	Lewis Pintard,
Samuel Ver Plank,	Alexander Wallace,
Theophy Bache,	William Seton,
Robert R. Waddell,	Edward Laight,

Gerrard Walton,
Jacobus Van Zandt,
John Moore,
Richard Yates,
Thomas Marston,
Isaac Sears,
Sampson Simpson,
Robert Alexander,
Henry Remsen,
Thomas Walton,
Leonard Lispenard,
James Beekman.

Fined for appearing after six o'clock:

Hugh Wallace,
Walter Franklin,
Isaac Low,
Henry White,
William Walton,
John H. Cruger,
Charles McEvers,
Levinus Clarkson,
Nicholas Gouverneur,
Thomas W. Moore,
John Thurman,
Augus. Van Horne,
Henry C. Bogert,
Joseph Bull,
Samuel Bayard,
Robert Watts.

Fined for non-appearance:

Jacob Walton,
Robert Murray,
George Folliot,
Miles Sherbrooke,
Lawren. Kortright,
Thomas Randal,
John Alsop,
Thomas White,
William McAdam,
Philip Livingston,
George W. Ludlow,
Peter Hasencliver,
Gabriel H. Ludlow,
Thomas Buchanan,
William Neilson,
Peter Keteltas,
Gerrard W. Beekman,
Jacob Watson,
John Reade,
Richard Sharpe,
Peter Remsen,
Thomas Miller, (Sea)
Abraham Lynsen,
Isaac Roosevelt,
Nicholas Hoffman,
Hamilton Young,
John Wetherhead,
Garret Rapelje,
Gerr'd Duyckinck,
William Stepple,
William Imlay,
Samuel Kemble, (Sea)
Alexander McDonald.

The President reported to the Chamber that he had with the Committee waited on His Honor the Lieut. Governor, and had presented the Petition praying him to Incorporate this Society, who was pleased to say:

I think it a good Institution, and will always be glad to promote the Commercial Interests of this City, and shall deem it a peculiar happiness that a Society so beneficial to the General good of the Province is incorporated during my administration.

It is proposed, that for the good Offices the Attorney-General[i] has shewn in his readiness to forward the Charter to Incorporate this Chamber, that he be paid Twenty Guineas for his trouble, by the Treasurer.

Mr. John Moore, one of the Committee appointed to wait on the Mayor with their opinion respecting the better curing Beef and Pork Exported from this Colony, Report

That they had waited on the Mayor, who was pleased to say, that He would lay it before the Corporation at their next Common Council, and recommend that a Law[44] should be passed for the more effectual cure and preserving those Articles of Commerce.

Mr. Low's Proposal that the Members of this Chamber shall in future leave to Arbitration matters of Account disputed to a Reference,

Ordered—That the consideration thereof be referred a future meeting.

Mr. Low's Proposal for admitting Members by paying a greater entrance having been very maturely considered of by the whole Chamber,

Resolved—That from and after there be Eighty Members belonging to this Chamber, Each Person admitted afterwards shall pay to the Treasurer for the time being the sum of TEN Spanish DOLLARS, until there be NINETY Members; that from and after there be Ninety Members belonging to this Chamber, Each Person admitted afterwards shall pay to the Treasurer for the time being the sum of TWELVE and a half Spanish DOLLARS, until there be ONE HUNDRED Members; and so on, *ad infinitum*, Two and a HALF DOLLARS for every Ten Members, for the use of the Chamber.

Mr. Low's Proposal, that no less than THIRTY Members be sufficient hereafter to compose a Chamber, having been considered of,

It is thought right there should be no alteration from the first mode. But that part of the motion which respects the admitting of New Members by a greater number of NAYS, it is

Resolved unanimously, that instead of THREE NAYS to disqualify a Person from being hereafter elected, there shall be THREE NAYS when only THIRTY Members are Present at an Election; whenever more than Thirty Members present, FOUR NAYS; when more than FORTY Members present, FIVE NAYS; and so on, ONE NAY for every TEN Members after the Number present exceeds thirty Persons.

Mr. Henry Remsen, one of the Committee appointed to take into consideration the Whale Fishery to be carried on out of this Port, Report that they had made some progress therein, but that they were not sufficiently informed; therefore prayed for leave to sit again.

Ordered—That leave be given accordingly.

Ordered—That Messrs. P. Livingston, T. Marston, I. Sears, L. Pintard, A. Wallace, G. W. Ludlow, and T. Buchanan, be a Committee, until the first Tuesday in April next, to hear and determine disputes between Parties who shall agree to leave such to this Chamber, and that they do make report thereof in writing to this Chamber what business hath or shall come before them during their appointment.

CHAMBER OF COMMERCE.—TUESDAY, 3d April, 1770.

PRESENT.

John Cruger, Pres't.
Hugh Wallace, V. P.

Antho. Van Dam, Sect'y.

Jacob Walton,
Jacob's Van Zandt,
Lewis Pintard,
Gabriel H. Ludlow,
Samson Simpson,
John Reade,
Henry Remsen, jun'r.
Abram Lynsen,
Nicholas Hoffman,
Hamilton Young,
Thomas Walton,
Gerrard Duykink,
William Stepple,
George W. Ludlow,
James Beekman.

Fined for appearing after six o'clock:

Hugh Wallace,
Theophy. Bache,
Miles Sherbrooke,
Lawrence Kortright,
Isaac Low,
William Walton,
Robert R. Waddle,
William McAdam,
Robert Watts,
John H. Cruger,
Levinus Clarkson,
Richard Yates,
Thomas Marston,
Thomas Buchanan,
Edward Laight,
William Neilson,
Thomas W. Moore,
John Thurman,
Henry C. Bogart,
Joseph Bull,
Alexan'r McDonald.

Fined for non-appearance:

Elias Desbrosses,
James Jauncey,
Robert Murray,
George Folliot,
Samuel Ver Plank,
Walter Franklin,
Thomas Randal,
Henry White,
John Alsop,
Thomas White,
Gerrard Walton,
Peter Hasencliver,
Alexand. Wallace,
William Seton,
Peter Keteltas,
Gerrard W. Beekman,
Samuel Kemble, (Sea)
Jacob Watson,
Robert Alexander,
Richard Sharpe,
Peter Remsen,
Isaac Roosevelt,

Thomas Miller, (Sea)
Charles McEvers,
John Moore,
Nicholas Gouverneur,
Philip Livingston,
Isaac Sears,
John Weatherhead,
Garret Rapelje,
William Imlay,
August's Van Horne,
Leonard Lispenard,
Samuel Bayard.

His Honor, Lieutenant Governor Colden, having been pleased to grant a Charter to this Chamber, under the Great Seal[45] of the Province, agreeable to the Petition presented to him by the President in behalf of the Chamber, the said Charter was ordered to be read, together with the address of Thanks presented to His Honor, and his honor's answer.

Ordered—That the same be fairly copied into the minutes of this Corporation, and that the said Charter be deposited with the Treasurer.

Ordered—That as Mr. Banyar,[k] Deputy-Secretary, has been so polite as to make this Chamber a compliment of his Fees for recording the Charter, that the President do return him the thanks of this Corporation for the favour conferred on them.

Ordered—That the Treasurer do pay Mr. Attorney-General Twenty Guineas for his Services in perfecting the Charter incorporating this Chamber, agreeable to the proposal of last meeting.

It is proposed that the Treasurer shall pay the Clerk who engrossed the Charter Eight Dollars for his Services.

Mr. Thurman moves that, as it is the desire of a number of the Inhabitants of this City to have their Estates Insured[46] from Loss by Fire, and that Losses of this sort may not fall upon Individuals, Proposed that the Chamber take into consideration some plan that may serve so good a purpose under the direction of this Corporation.

Mr. Yates moves that a Committee of this Chamber be appointed to wait on the Mayor praying him to use his Influence with the Corporation to make a Law[47] appointing Inspectors for the Inspection of Cornell,[48] Rye Meal, and Indian Meal.

Mr. Yates also proposes that as the Office of Secretary to this Corporation is attended with much trouble and loss of time, moves that the present and future Secretarys may be allowed a Salary, whatever may be judged adequate to their Services.

Mr. William Walton—That this Corporation dine together on the Second Tuesday in May next, and that at the next Meeting three Stewards be appointed to provide a suitable Dinner at the Expence of the Members, and that absent Members pay five Shillings each.

The Committee appointed to Transcribe the Regulations, Rules, and Orders of the Chamber Report :

Agreeable to an Order from the Chamber of Commerce, dated 2d January, 1770,

We, Charles McEvers, Jacobus Van Zandt, and John Moore, being a Committee appointed to Collect and Transcribe from the Minutes of this Board such Rules and Regulations entered into, as are not yet Printed, have duly attended the said Order, and accordingly Selected from the said Minutes the following Resolutions and Orders which we conceive to be the most necessary for Publication :

SEPTEMBER 6th, 1768.

RESOLVED, unanimously, that any Persons offering to become Members of this Chamber be Balloted for the next Meeting after their Names are Proposed.

OCTOBER 4th.

RESOLVED, unanimously, that One Barrel of Flour at least, of every Brand Mark, be Started to see that it be Fairly Tared, and if found Fraudulent, that all possible means be used to bring the Offenders to Justice, agreeable to an Act of the General Assembly.

RESOLVED, also, that every Member of this Chamber do, in their future purchase of Flour, cause the same to be Weighed and Inspected after Purchase, and that the Secretary do cause these Resolutions to be Advertised in the Public News Papers, the Cost of which to be paid by the Treasurer.

RESOLVED, also, by a great Majority of this Chamber, that Pennsylvania Paper Money be hereafter received by any Member that inclines to take it at 6$\frac{2}{3}$ per ct. advance being equal to Spanish Mill'd Dollars at 8s.

RESOLVED, that the Members of this Chamber will, in future, Pay and Receive damages on West India and Inland Bills of Exchange, agreeable to the following Regulations, viz.:

That 5 per ct. damages be paid and received on all Bills drawn from any one Province of North America upon another, Recoverable here in full of all damages, Re-Exchange, Cost of Protest, Postage, &c., and that the full amount of the Bill with damages of 5 per cent. is due and payable immediately on return of said Bill with Protest. That 10 per cent. damages be paid and Received on all Bills drawn from North America on the West Indies, or from thence on North America, which may be recoverable here, in full of all damages, Re-exchange, Cost of Protest, Postage, &c., and that the full Amount of the Bill with damages of 10 per cent. is due and payable immediately on return of the Bill with Protest.

DECEMBER 6th.

RESOLVED unanimously, that 20 p. cent. be paid on all European Bills Returned Protested, in full for all damages, Re-exchange, Cost of Protest, Postage, &c.,

And that all European Bills returned protested be paid immediately on return of said Bill with proper Protest, together with the 20 p. cent. damages in money at the then current Exchange in New York, without regard to the Exchange at which said Bill was bought or sold.

JANUARY 3d, 1769.

RESOLVED unanimously, that in case of sudden Emergency only, when it may be thought necessary (agreeable to the established Rules of this Chamber) that a Special Meeting of the Members shou'd be called, each of them shall be Notified in Writing of such Meeting: And that in case any regulation which may be agreed to by a Majority of the Members then Present shall be Binding on all the other Members, under the same Penalties and Forfeitures as are provided for the observance of the other Rules of this Chamber.

MAY 2d.

ORDERED—That all future Committees do report unto the next Meeting of this Chamber what differences they have adjusted between Parties, with the names of the Parties and the Sums they have awarded, unless the Parties object to it; and that such Gentlemen who have decided any Controversies are desired to deliver in the subject of their Award as soon as may be, that the same be Entered.

JULY 4th.

RESOLVED—That the Members of this Chamber, in their Future purchase of Flour, do agree to pay Twenty-eight Shillings per Ton for the Casks and nails, provided that they be well and sufficiently made (Agreeable to an Act of the Governor, Council and General Assembly of this Province, Passed at their last Sessions) and hooped with Ten hoops, three of which hoops to be on each head.

COMMISSIONS.

The Chamber of Commerce agree in opinion that the following Commissions are generally Charged in this Place, and that in case any disputes between parties should arise, and Referees be chosen out of this Chamber, that they govern themselves accordingly (except where Special Agreement has been made to the contrary), viz. :

Inland Commissions, 2½ p. ct. on Sales, exclusive of Storage ; and 2½ per cent. on Returns, say from Boston to Philadelphia.

Quere, if we should not have one Stated Commission for the Business of the whole Continent.

Foreign Commissions.

5 p. Cent. on Sales, Exclusive of Storage. 5 pr. Cent. on Returns.

Indorsing or Negotiating Bills of Exchange, - -	2½ per cent.
Making Insurance, - - - - - - - -	½ per cent.
Recovering Losses, - - - - - -	2½ per cent.
Outfit of Vessel, - - - - - - -	5 per cent.
Soliciting and Procuring Freight, - - - -	5 per cent.
Collecting Freight, - - - - - - -	2½ per cent.

RESOLVED—That any member Addressing the Chair shall Rise, under the Penalty of One shilling.

RESOLVED—That every Member of this Chamber will pay and receive Gold and Silver in future at the following Rates :

	dt. grs.		£ s.
A Johannes, weighing	10 0	- - - - -	6 8
A Moydore,	6 18	- - - -	2 8
and the small Coins of the same Denomination in like proportion.			
A Caroline, weighing	6 8	- - - - -	1 18
A Spanish Doubleloon, or 4 Pistole piece,	17 8	- - - - -	5 16
and the smaller Coins in proportion.			
An English Guinea,	5 3	- - - - -	1 17
and Half and quarter ditto in proportion.			

	dt.	grs.		£	s.	
A French Guinea,	5	4	- - - -	1	16	
Half ditto in same proportion.						
A Chequin, weighing	2	4	- - - -		14	6
An English Crown, and half Crown in same proportion					8	9
A French ditto, and half ditto in same proportion					8	6
A French Pistole	4	5	- - - -	1	8	
An English Shilling			- - - -		1	9
A Pistereen			- - - -		1	7

And for every Grain any of the above specified pieces of Gold shall weigh less than the Weight above directed, there shall be a Deduction of Four Pence.

RESOLVED—That this Chamber will pay and receive all Gold and Silver in Future at the above Rates, and Ordered that the substance of the above Report be Published in the News Papers.

NOVEMBER 7, 1769.

RESOLVED—That no Persons hereafter be proposed to be Members of this Chamber can be admitted unless they are Merchants Residents of this City.

RESOLVED unanimously—That all the Rules and Regulations already entered into be Printed for the use of the Members, and also that every future Regulation that may be agreed to shall be Printed every half year, for the same purpose.

WHEREAS, a Resolution of this Chamber has fixed the lowest Weight of half Johannes at Nine pennyweight, induced thereto by the Custom of Merchants in a Neighbouring Colony ; but finding the true intent and meaning of the said Regulation perverted by the Base practice of filing and diminishing the Weight of Foreign Gold Coin : to encourage which was by no means the intention of this Chamber,

We declare that we will discourages it by all means in our power, and will hold any guilty of it in contempt and not proper to be a Member of this Chamber.

WHEREAS, a Resolution was entered into by this Chamber on the 3d of October last for Regulating the Weight of sundry Gold Coins, wherein the Weight of Guineas were fixed at Five pennyweight Six Grains, the Chamber, on a further and more mature deliberation, did, on the 2d January, 1770, agree that Guineas Weighing Five pennywht, three Grains, and not apparently defaced, Shou'd be paid and received by the Members of this Chamber at 37s. each.

The Committee, in attention to this Regulation, have in the General List of Coins in October last, fixed the Weight and Value accordingly.

The Committee beg leave to observe to the President and Members of this Chamber, that in the foregoing Regulations they have in some few instances deviated from the Strict Letter of the Book of Minutes, which are humbly Offered to their Consideration.

CHARLES McEVERS,
JACOBUS VAN ZANDT,
JOHN MOORE.

Several Gentlemen having been proposed to be admitted Members of this Corporation, were balloted for and elected, as follows:

Robert C. Livingston,	Isaac Corsa,
Harman Gouverneur,	Jeremiah Platt.

Ordered—That the Secretary send notice to the several Gentlemen Elected, in writing, as soon as possible, that they were duly elected.

Ordered—That Messrs. W. Seton, E. Laight, W. Neilson, Sam'n Simpson, P. Keteltas, G. W. Beekman, and John Reade, be a Committee until the first Tuesday in May next, to hear and determine disputes between parties who shall agree to leave such to this Chamber, and that they do make report thereof in writing to this Corporation.

On SATURDAY, THE 24TH MARCH, A COMMITTEE OF THIS CHAMBER waited on His Honor the Lieutenant Governor with the following Address:

TO THE HONOURABLE CADWALLADER COLDEN, ESQ., &c., Lieutenant Governor and Commander-in-chief of the Colony of New York and the Territories[49] depending thereon in America.

THE ADDRESS of the President and Members of the Corporation of the Chamber of Commerce of the City of New York.

MAY IT PLEASE YOUR HONOUR,

We, the President and Members of the Chamber of Commerce of the City of New York, sensible of Your Honour's desire to encourage every Measure that may tend to promote the Interest of the Colony; take the earliest opportunity of returning you our sincere thanks for the Royal Charter with which you have been pleased to invest us. And we entertain the most greatful sense of the confidence thereby reposed in us by Government.

The important Light in which Your Honour views this Institution has been abundantly evinced by that Readiness so conspicuously manifest in every part of your conduct, from our first Application to its last happy Conclusion.

The Merchants are now, by Your Honour's favour, enabled to execute many Plans of Trade, which, as Individuals, they could not before accomplish, and we flatter ourselves many and great advantages will result to this Colony from their Incorporation—

We beg leave to assure your Honour that our utmost Ambition is to approve ourselves useful Members of the Community, submissive to the Laws, zealous for the Support of Government, and our happy Constitution, and firmly attached to our most Gracious Sovereign ; and that we will exert ourselves on all occasions to promote the General Interest of the Colony, and the Commerce of this City in particular ; that the Utility of the Institution and the Wisdom of its Founder may be equally applauded by the latest Posterity.

Signed by Order of the Chamber,
JOHN CRUGER, President.

To which his HONOUR was pleased to return the following ANSWER :

I return you sincere thanks for this very obliging Address :

The extensive Property of so considerable a Body of the Merchants of this City, united with Principles of Loyalty, afford the strongest assurance of your Zeal in the Support of the Government and our happy Constitution ; while your good Example will, at all times, have the most favorable Influence by promoting that due Obedience to the Laws which is essential to the Security of the Subject. I ardently wish success to this Institution so well adopted to increase the Trade and Opulence, and advance the Prosperity of the Colony.

FORT GEORGE, NEW YORK,
March 24th, 1770.

Mathew Pratt, Pinxt. P. Purdon Graham, Sc.

LIEUT. GOV. CADWALLADER COLDEN.

From the Portrait in possession of the Chamber of Commerce, N.Y.

CHARTER.[50]

GEORGE THE THIRD,[1] by the Grace of God, of Great Britain and Ireland, King, Defender of the Faith, and so forth—To all to whom these presents shall come, Greeting:

WHEREAS, a great Number of Merchants in our City of New York, in America, have, by voluntary Agreement, associated themselves for the laudable Purposes of promoting the Trade and Commerce of our said Province; and Whereas, John Cruger, Esq., the present President of the said Society, by his humble Petition presented in Behalf of the said Society, to our Trusty and well-beloved CADWALLADER COLDEN, Esq., our Lieutenant Governor and Commander-in-Chief of our said Province of New York, and the Territories depending thereon in America, and read in our Council for our said Province, on the Twenty-eighth Day of February, last past, hath represented to our said Lieutenant Governor, That the said Society (sensible that numberless inestimable Benefits have accrued to Mankind from Commerce; that they are, in proportion to their greater or lesser Application to it, more or less Opulent and Potent in all Countries; and that the Enlargement of Trade will vastly increase the Value of Real Estates, as well as the general Opulence of our said Colony) have associated together for some time past, in order to carry into Execution among themselves, and by their Example to promote in others, such Measures as were beneficial to those salutary Purposes; AND that the said Society having, with great Pleasure and Satisfaction, Experienced the good Effects which the few Regulations already adopted, had produced, were very desirous of rendering them more extensively useful and permanent, and more adequate to the Purposes of so benevolent an Institution; AND therefore the Petitioner, in behalf of the said Society, most humbly prayed our said Lieutenant Governor to Incorporate them a Body Politick, and to Invest them with such Powers and Authorities as might be thought most conducive to answer and promote the Commercial and consequently the Landed Interest of our said growing Colony; WHICH PETITION being read as aforesaid, was then and there referred to a Committee of our said Council, and afterwards on the same Day, our said Council, in pursuance of the Report of the said Committee, did humbly advise and consent, that our said Lieutenant Governor, by our Letters Patent, should constitute and appoint the Petitioner, and the Present Members of the said Society, a Body Corporate and Politick, by the Name of "THE CORPORATION OF THE CHAMBER OF COMMERCE IN THE CITY OF NEW YORK, IN AMERICA," agreeable to the Prayer of the said Petition: Therefore, We being willing to further the said laudable Designs of our said loving Subjects, and to give Stability to an Institution from whence great advantages may arise, as well to our Kingdom of Great Britain as to our said Province,

KNOW YE, That of our Especial Grace, certain Knowledge and mere Motion, We have Willed, Ordained, Given, Granted, Constituted, and Appointed, And by these Presents for Us, our Heirs and Successors, DO Will, Ordain, Give, Grant, Constitute, and Appoint, that the present Members of the said Society, Associated for the Purposes aforesaid, That is to say, John Cruger, Elias Desbrosses, James Jauncey, Jacob Walton, Robert Murray, Hugh Wallace, George Folliot, Wm. Walton, John Alsop, Henry White, Philip Livingston, Samuel Verplank, Theophylact Bache, Thomas White, Miles Sherbrooke, Walter Franklin, Robert Ross Waddell, Acheson Thompson, Lawrence Kortwright, Thomas Randal, William McAdam, Isaac Low, Anthony Van Dam, Robert Watts, John Harris Cruger, Gerard Walton, Isaac Sears, Jacobus Van Zandt, Charles M'Evers, John Moore, Lewis Pintard, Levinus Clarkson, Nicholas Gouverneur, Richard Yates, Thomas Marston, Peter Hassencliver, Alexander Wallace, Gabriel H. Ludlow, Thomas Buchannan, Wm. Neilson, Sampson Simson, Peter Ketletas, Gerard W. Beekman, Jacob Watson, Richard Sharpe, Peter Remsen, Henry Remsen, junior, William Seton, Edw. Laight, John Reade, Robert Alexander, Thomas W. Moore, Abraham Lynsen, Isaac Roosevelt, Nicholas Hoffman, Hamilton Young, Thomas Walton, John Thurman, John Weatherhead, Garret Rapelje, Gerrard Duyckink, William Stepple, William Imlay, Augustus Van Horne, Henry C. Bogart, George W. Ludlow, Joseph Bull, Leonard Lispenard, Thomas Miller, James Beekman, Samuel Kemble, Alexander McDonald, and Samuel Bayard, junior, all of our City of New York, in our said Province of New York, Merchants, and their Successors to be Elected by Virtue of this our present Charter, shall for ever hereafter be one Body Corporate and Politick in Deed, Fact, and Name, by the Name, Style, and Title of "THE CORPORATION OF THE CHAMBER OF COMMERCE IN THE CITY OF NEW YORK, IN AMERICA," and them and their Successors by the same Name, WE do by these Presents really and fully Make, Erect, Create, Constitute and Declare One Body Politick and Corporate in Deed, Fact, and Name for ever; And Will, Give, Grant, and Ordain, that they and their Successors, The Corporation of the Chamber of Commerce in the City of New York, in America, by the same Name, shall and may have perpetual Succession, and shall and may by the same Name, be Persons capable in the Law to Sue and be Sued, Implead and be Impleaded, Answer and be Answered, Defend and be Defended, in all Courts and elsewhere, in all Manner of Actions, Suits, Complaints, Pleas, Causes, Matters, and Demands whatsoever, as fully and amply as any other our Liege Subjects of our said Province of New York may or can sue or be sued, implead or be impleaded, defend or be defended, by any lawful Ways or Means whatsoever; And that they and their Successors by the same Name, shall be for ever hereafter Persons Capable and Able in the Law to purchase, take, receive, hold, and enjoy, to them and their Successors, any Messuages, Tenements, Houses, and Real Estates whatsoever, and all other Hereditaments of whatsoever Nature, Kind and Quality they be, in Fee simple, for Term of Life or Lives, or in any other manner howsoever, and also any Goods, Chattels, or Personal Estate whatsoever, as well for enabling them the better to carry into Execution, encourage and promote by just and lawful Ways and Means, such Measures as will tend to promote and extend just and lawful Commerce, as to provide for, aid, and Assist, at their Discretion, such Members of our said Corporation as may be hereafter reduced to Poverty, and their Widows and Children: PROVIDED ALWAYS, the clear Yearly Value of the said Real Estate doth not at any Time exceed the Sum of Three Thousand Pounds Sterling, lawful Money of our Kingdom of Great Britain. And that our said Corporation of the Chamber of Commerce in the City of New York, in America, and their Successors for ever, by the same Name, shall and may have full Power and Authority to Give, Grant, Sell, Lease, Demise and Dispose of the same Real Estate and Hereditaments whatsoever, for Life or Lives, or Years, or for ever; and all Goods, Chattels, and personal Estates whatsoever, at their Will and Pleasure, according as they shall judge to be most beneficial and advantageous to the Good Ends and Purposes abovementioned. And that it shall and may be Lawful for them and their Successors forever hereafter, to have a Common Seal, to serve for the Causes and Business of them and their Successors, and the Same Seal to Change, Alter, Break, and Make new from time to time at their Pleasure. And also that they and their Successors by the same Name, shall and may have full Power and Authority to Erect and Build out of their Common Funds or by any other Ways or Means, for the use of the said Corporation hereby Erected, any House, Houses, or other Buildings, as they shall think necessary and Convenient. And for the better carrying into Execution the Purposes aforesaid, our Royal Will and Pleasure is, and We do hereby Give and Grant to the Corporation of the Chamber of Commerce in the City of New York, in America, and their Successors for ever, that there shall be for ever hereafter belonging to the said Corporation, one President, One or more Vice President or Vice Presidents, One or more Treasurer or Treasurers, And One Secretary ; And for the more immediate carrying into Execution our Royal Will and Pleasure herein, We do hereby Assign, Constitute, and Appoint the above named John Cruger, Esq., to be the present President ; the above named Hugh Wallace to be the present Vice President ; the above named Elias Desbrosses to be the present Treasurer, and the above named Anthony Van Dam to be the present Secretary of our said Corporation hereby Erected, who shall hold, possess, and enjoy their said respective Offices until the first Tuesday in May now next ensuing :—And for the keeping up the Succession in the said Offices, Our Royal Will and Pleasure is, and we do hereby for us, our Heirs and Successors, establish, direct, and require, and give and Grant to the said Corporation of the Chamber of Commerce in the City of New York, in America, and their Successors for ever, that on the said first Tuesday in May now next ensuing, and Yearly, and every Year forever thereafter, on the first Tuesday in May in every Year, they and their Successors shall meet at some convenient place in our said City of New York, to be fixed and ascertained by some of the Bye-Laws or Regulations of our said Corporation, and there, by the Majority of such of them as shall so meet, shall by Ballot, or in such other manner and Form as shall be regulated by the Bye-Laws or Regulations of our said Corporation, Elect or chuse One President, One or more Vice President or Vice Presidents, One or more Treasurer or Treasurers, and One Secretary, to serve in the said Offices for the ensuing Year, who shall immediately enter upon their respective Offices, and hold, exercise, and enjoy the same respectively from the time of such Elections, for and during the Space of one Year, and until other fit Persons shall be Elected and chosen in their respective Places, according to the Laws and Regulations aforesaid. And in case any of the said Persons by these Presents Nominated and Appointed to the respective Offices aforesaid, or who shall hereafter be Elected and Chosen thereto respectively, shall die, or on any Account be removed from such Offices respectively before the time of their respective appointed Services shall be expired, or refuse or neglect to Act in and execute the Office for which he or they shall be so elected and chosen, or is or are herein nominated or appointed, that then, and in any and every such Case, it shall and may be Lawful for the Members of our said Body Corporate hereby erected, to meet at such Time and Times, and at such Place and Places within our said City of New York, and upon such Notices or Summons as shall for that Purpose be established and directed by the Bye-Laws or Regulations of our said Body Corporate, and there, by the Majority of such of them as shall so meet, Elect and choose other or others to the said Offices respectively, in the Place of him or them so dying, removing, neglecting or refusing to Act in manner and Form, and after the same method to be observed in the Annual Elections of the like Officers respectively, by Virtue of these our Letters Patent, and the said Bye-Laws or Regulations of our said Corporation, Hereby giving and granting, that such Person or Persons as shall be so Elected and Chosen by the majority of such of the said Members as shall meet in manner aforesaid, shall have, hold, exercise and enjoy such the Office or Offices to which he or they shall be so Elected and Chosen, from the time of such Election until the first Tuesday in May then next ensuing, and until other or others be legally Chosen in his or their Place and Stead, as fully and amply to all Intents and Purposes whatsoever, as the Person or Persons in whose place he or they shall be chosen might or could have done by Virtue of these Presents. And our Will and Pleasure is, and We do hereby for us, our Heirs and Successors, ordain, direct and require, that every President, Vice President, Treasurer and Secretary to be Elected by Virtue of these Presents, shall, before they Act in their respective Offices, take an Oath or Affirmation to be to them administered by the President, or in his Absence by One of the Vice Presidents of the preceding year, (who are hereby Authorized to Administer the same,) for the faithful and due Execution of their Respective Offices during their Continuance in the same respectively.—And We do further, for Us, our Heirs and Successors, Give and Grant to the Corporation of the Chamber of Commerce in the City of New York, in America, and their Successors forever, that besides the Annual Meeting of our said Corporation herein before Directed and Appointed to be held on the first Tuesday in May in every Year, it shall and may be Lawful for them, their Heirs and Successors, forever hereafter, for promoting and carrying into Execution the laudable Intents and Designs aforesaid, and for the Transacting the Business and Concerns of our said Corporation, to meet together on the first Tuesday in every Month, for ever, at such Place or Places in our said City of New York as shall for that Purpose be established, fixed, ascertained and Appointed by the Bye-Laws and Regulations of our said Corporation:—And that the Members of our said Corporation being so met, or so many of them in Number at the least as shall by the Bye-Laws or Ordinances of our said Corporation be for that Purpose from time to time established, directed, Ordained or Appointed, shall, together with the President, or any one of the Vice Presidents of our said Corporation for the Time being, be a legal Meeting of our said Corporation; and they, or the Major part of them so met, shall have full Power and Authority to adjourn from Day to Day, or for any other Time, as the business of our said Corporation may require, and to do, Execute, and perform all and every Act and Acts, Thing and Things whatsoever which the said Corporation of the Chamber of Commerce in the City of New York, in America, are or shall by these our Letters Patent be Authorized to do, Act or Transact, in as full and ample manner as if all and every of the Members of the said Corporation were present:—And that at any such legal Meeting of the said Corporation, they shall and may in Writing, under the common Seal, make, frame, constitute, establish, and ordain from Time to Time, and at all Times hereafter, such Laws, Constitutions, Ordinances, Regulations, and Statutes, for the better Government of the Officers and Members of the said Corporation, for fixing and ascertaining the Places of Meeting of our said Corporation as aforesaid, and for regulating all other their Affairs and Business as they, or the Major Part of them so legally met, shall Judge best for the general Good of the said Corporation, and profitable for the more effectually promoting the beneficial Designs of their Institution;—

All which Laws, Constitutions, Regulations, Ordinances, and Statutes so to be made, framed, constituted, established, and Ordained as aforesaid, We Will, Command, and Ordain by these Presents for Us, our Heirs and Successors, to be from Time to Time and at all Times hereafter, kept, obeyed, and performed in all things as the same ought to be, on the Penalties and Amercements in the same to be imposed and limited, so as the same Laws, Constitutions, Regulations, and Statutes be reasonable in themselves, and not repugnant or contrary to the Laws and Statutes of that Part of our Kingdom of Great Britain called England, nor of our said Province of New York.—And, for the keeping up and preserving for ever hereafter a Succession of Members for the said Corporation, our Will and Pleasure is, and We do hereby for us, our Heirs and Successors, Ordain, and Give and Grant to the said Corporation of the Chamber of Commerce in the City of New York, in America, and their Successors for ever, that at any of the Stated legal Meetings of the said Corporation, to be held on the first Tuesday in every Month for ever hereafter, but at no other Meeting of our said Corporation, it shall and may be Lawful for them and their Successors for ever, to Elect and choose in such manner and Form, and upon such Terms and Conditions, as shall be directed, ordained, and established for that Purpose by any of the said Bye-Laws, Statutes, Constitutions, or Ordinances of the said Corporation, such and so many Persons to be Members of the said Corporation as they shall think beneficial to the laudable Designs of the said Corporation; Which Persons, and every of them so from Time to Time Elected and Chosen, shall by Virtue of these Presents and of such Election, be Vested with all the Powers, Authorities, and Privileges which any Member of the said Corporation is hereby Invested with. And in case any other extraordinary Meeting or Meetings of the said Corporation shall at any Time or Times be judged necessary for the promoting the Interest and Business of the said Corporation, We do hereby for us, our Heirs and Successors, Will, Declare, and Ordain, that it shall and may be Lawful for our said Corporation to meet from Time to Time, at such Days and Times, and at such Places in our said City of New York, and upon such Notices or Summons as shall for that Purpose from Time to Time be Settled, Established, and Ordained by the Laws, Ordinances, or Statutes of the said Corporation; And that the Members of our said Corporation being so met, or so many of them in Number at the least as by the said

Laws, Ordinances, and Statutes aforesaid shall from Time to Time be Established, Directed, Ordained, and Appointed for that Purpose, shall together with the President, or One of the Vice Presidents of the said Corporation for the Time being, be a legal Meeting of the said Corporation; And they, or the Major part of them so met, shall have full Power and Authority to Act, Transact, do, and Perform all and Singular whatsoever may be Transacted, done, and Performed at any the hereby Stated Meetings aforesaid of the said Corporation, saving and Except the Electing Members, Making laws, Ordinances and Statutes, and Disposing of the real Estate of the said Corporation. And our Will and Pleasure is, that until the same shall be otherwise Regulated as aforesaid, that the Meetings of the said Corporation shall be held in the great Room of the Building commonly called the Exchange, situate at the lower End of the Street called broad Street,[51] in the said City of New York: and that until the same shall be also otherwise regulated as aforesaid, that no Act done in any Meeting of the said Corporation shall be Legal, Good, or Valid, unless the President, or one of the Vice Presidents, and Twenty others of the Members of the said Corporation at the least, be Present, and the Major Part of them consenting thereto. And We do further Give and Grant to the said Corporation of the Chamber of Commerce in the City of New York, in America, that it shall and may be lawful for the President of the said Corporation, at all times hereafter for ever, to Appoint a Door-Keeper, One or more Messenger or Messengers, And all such other Inferior Officers as shall by him be thought necessary for the said Corporation, and to displace them and any or every of them at his Will and Pleasure. PROVIDED NEVERTHELESS, That no such Door-Keeper, Messenger, or other Officer shall hold his or their Office or Offices by Virtue of any such appointment, longer than until the then next lawful Meeting of our said Corporation, unless such Person or Persons so appointed shall be then approved of by the Majority of such of the Members of the said Corporation as shall then be met.—And We do further, of our especial Grace, certain Knowledge, and mere Motion, for us, our Heirs and Successors, Grant and Ordain, that when and as often as the President, or any Vice President, Treasurer or Secretary of the said Corporation, shall misdemean himself in his or their said Offices respectively, and thereupon a Complaint or Charge in Writing shall be exhibited against him or them, by any Member of the said Corporation, at any legal Meeting or Meetings of the said Corporation, that it shall and may be lawful for the Members of the said Corporation then Met, or the Major Part of them, from Time to Time, upon Examination and due Proof, to suspend or discharge such President, Vice President, Treasurer or Secretary, from their Offices respectively, although the Yearly or other Time for their respective Services shall not be expired, any thing before in these Presents contained to the Contrary thereof in any wise notwithstanding.—And further, We do by these Presents, for us, our Heirs and Successors, Give and Grant unto the said Corporation of the Chamber of Commerce in the City of New York, in America, and their Successors forever, that this our present CHARTER shall be deemed, adjudged, and construed in all Cases most favorably, and for the best benefit and advantage of our said Corporation, and for promoting the good Intentions and Designs herein before expressed, inducing us graciously to grant the same; And that this our present Grant, being entered on Record as herein after is expressed, or the Enrollment thereof, shall be for ever hereafter good and effectual in the Law, according to our true Intent and meaning hereinbefore declared, without any other License, Grant, or Confirmation from us, our Heirs and Successors, hereafter by the said Corporation to be had or obtained, notwithstanding the not reciting or misrecital, or not naming or misnaming of the aforesaid Offices, Franchises, Privileges, Immunities, or other the Premises, or any of them, And although no Writ of *ad quo damnum*, or other Writs, Inquisitions, or Precepts hath been upon this Occasion had, made, issued, or Prosecuted, Any Statute, Act, Ordinance, or Provision, or other Matter or thing to the contrary thereof in any wise notwithstanding. IN TESTIMONY whereof, We have caused these our Letters to be made Patent, And the Great Seal of our said Province to be hereunto Affixed, And the same to be Entered on Record in our Secretary's Office, for our said Province, in one of the Books of Patents there remaining.

WITNESS our trusty and well-beloved CADWALLADER COLDEN, Esquire, our Lieutenant Governor and Commander-in-Chief of our said Province of New York, and the Territories depending thereon in America, by and with the Advice and Consent of our Council for our said Province, at FORT GEORGE, in our City of New York, this thirteenth Day of March, in the Year of our Lord One thousand seven hundred and Seventy, and of our Reign the Tenth.

CHAMBER OF COMMERCE.—TUESDAY, 2d May, 1770.

John Cruger, President.
Hugh Wallace, V. P.
Elias Desbrosses, Treasurer.
Anthony Van Dam, Secretary.

James Jauncey,
Jacob Walton,
Isaac Low,
John Alsop,
William Walton,
William McAdam,
Gerrard Walton,
John Moore,
Nicholas Gouverneur,
Lewis Pintard,
Richard Yates,
Gabriel H. Ludlow,
Sampson Simson,
Peter Keteltas,
Gerrard W. Beekman,
John Reade,
Robert Alexander,
Thomas W. Moore,
Richard Sharpe,
Abram Lynsen,
Isaac Roosevelt,
Nicholas Hoffman,
Hamilton Young,
Thomas Walton,
John Thurman,
Gerrard Duyckinck,
William Stepple,
Henry C. Bogert,
George W. Ludlow,
Joseph Bull,
James Beekman,
Alexander McDonald,
Samuel Bayard,
Robert C. Livingston.

Fined for appearing after six o'clock, viz.:

Samuel Verplank,
Henry White,
Thomas White,
Robert R. Waddle,
Isaac Sears,
Alexan. Wallace,
Thomas Buchanan,
August. Van Horne.

Fined for non-appearance:

Robert Murray,
George Folliot,
Theoph Bache,
Miles Sherbrooks,
Walter Franklin,
Acheson Thompson,
John H. Cruger,
Jacobus Van Zandt, gout,
Charles McEvers,
John Weatherhead,
Garret Rapelje,
William Imlay,
Lawrence Kortright,
Thomas Randal,
Philip Livingston,
Robert Watts,
Isaac Corsa,
William Seton,

Levinus Clarkson,
Thomas Marston,
Peter Hasencliver,
Jacob Watson,
Peter Remsen,
Henry Remsen,
Edward Laight,
William Neilson,
Jeremiah Platt,
Leonard Lispenard,
Thomas Miller,
Samuel Kemble,
Harman Gouverneur.

The proposal of Mr. Thurman to take into consideration some plan to be pursued in Insuring Houses from Loss by Fire is referred to a future Meeting.

Mr. Yates's proposal for a Committee to be appointed to wait on the Mayor, praying him to use his influence with the Corporation, to make a Law for the Inspection of Cornel, Rye Meal, and Indian Meal, is also referred to a future Meeting.

Mr. Yates's proposal for allowing the Secretary of this Corporation a Salary [52] for defraying the Expences he is put to having been considered,

Resolved, unanimously, that the present and future Secretary of this Chamber be paid annually, on the first Tuesday in May in every year, by the Treasurer of this Corporation, the sum of Twenty Pounds Currency.

In consequence of the Motion made by Mr. William Walton for this Corporation to Dine together, Messrs. William Walton, Richard Sharpe, William McAdam, and Gerrard W. Beekman were appointed Stewards to order a Dinner [53] in this Chamber on the Second Tuesday of this Month.

Ordered—That the Secretary do forthwith send Notices to and Invite the Lieut. Governor, Council, and Members of the General Assembly,[54] who may be in Town, the Secretaries,[55] the General [56] and his Suit, the Captains of His Majesty's Ships,[57] the Principal Officers of the Customs,[58] and the Mayor of the City.

Ordered—That Messrs. Samuel Verplank, Peter Keteltas, John Reade, John Alsop, and Jacob Walton, be a Committee to audit the Treasurers accounts, and that they do report to this Corporation what Sum is in his hands.

The Charter of Incorporation as well as the Rules of the Chamber, appoint this Day for the Election of Officers for the Current Year, when the following Gentlemen were Elected, viz.:

The Hon.[59] Hugh Wallace, Esq.,	President.
The Hon. Henry White, Esq., Elias Desbrosses, Esq.,	Vice-Presidents.
Theop. Bache,	Treasurer.
Antho Van Dam,	Secretary.

Ordered—That Messrs. R. Alexander, T. W. Moore, R. Sharpe, P. Remsen, H. Remsen, Isaac Roosevelt, and Nicholas Hoffman, be a Committee, until the first Tuesday in June next, to hear and determine disputes between Parties who shall agree to leave such to this Chamber, and that they do make report thereof in writing to this Corporation.

CHAMBER OF COMMERCE.—Tuesday, 5th June, 1770.

Present.

The Hono'ble Henry White, Esqr., Elias Desbrosses, Esqr., } Vice-Presidents.
Anthony Van Dam, Secretary.

John Cruger,	Gerrard W. Beekman,
Jacob Walton,	Jacob Watson,
William Walton,	Robert Alexander,
Gerrard Walton,	Nicholas Hoffman,
Jacobus Van Zandt,	Alexan. Wallace,
John Moore,	Gabriel H. Ludlow,

Charles McEvers,
Richard Yates,
William Seton,
Edward Laight,
Sampson Simson,
Thomas Walton,
William Stepple,
Alexand. McDonald,
Samuel Bayard,
Robert C. Livingston.

Fined for appearing after six o'clock:

Samuel Ver Plank,
Robert R. Waddell,
Robert Watts,
John Harris Cruger,
Thomas Buchanan,
Henry Remsen,
Thomas Miller.

Fined for non-appearance:

Hugh Wallace,
James Jauncey,
Robert Murray,
George Folliot,
Theophy. Bache,
Miles Sherbrooke,
Walter Franklin,
Lawrence Kortright,
Acheson Thompson,
Thomas Randal,
Isaac Low,
John Alsop,
Thomas W. Moore,
Richard Sharpe,
Peter Remsen,
Abram Lynsen,
Hamilton Young,
John Thurman,
Isaac Corsa,
John Weatherhead,
Garret Rapelje,
Gerrard Duyckink,
Thomas White,
Philip Livingston,
William McAdam,
Levinus Clarkson,
Nicholas Gouverneur,
Thomas Marston,
Isaac Sears,
Lewis Pintard,
Peter Hasencliver,
William Neilson,
Peter Keteltas,
John Reade,
William Imlay,
August's Van Horne,
Henry C. Bogart,
Jeremiah Platt,
George W. Ludlow,
Joseph Bull,
Leonard Lispenard,
James Beekman,
Samuel Kemble,
Harman Gouverneur.

The consideration of Mr. Thurman's Proposal for Insuring Houses from Fire is postponed to a future Meeting.

Mr. Pettit[m] having exhibited an account of Expences

for Fire-wood, Candles, &c., amounting to Two pounds fifteen shillings and two pence, and a year's Salary, due the first May last, Proposed that he be paid the same.

John Cruger, Esqr., Moves—That as the Resolution of this Chamber for Regulating Johannes has caused the Evil and Scandalous Practice of clipping every Johannes before it passes in this Colony, and will encourage Foreigners and others to reduce them before they are sent hither; therefore moves that it may be taken into consideration whether it will not be for the Interest of Commerce to Resolve not to take a half Johannes for sixty-four Shillings that does not weigh 9 dwt. 3 grains; if under that weight a deduction to be made.

That as the Committee appointed to ascertain the Tonnage of this Port have not Reported,

Ordered—That Messrs. John Moore and Jacobus Van Zandt be added thereto, and that they do report to this Corporation the quantity of the different species of Goods usually Shipped from this Port, to ascertain the Tonnage thereon.

Ordered—That Messrs. A. Lynsen, H. Young, Thos. Walton, J. Thurman, Jno. Weatherhead, G. Rapelje, and G. Duykinck, be a Committee, until the first Tuesday in June next, to hear and determine disputes between Parties who shall agree to leave such to this Chamber, and that they do make report thereof in writing to this Chamber.

CHAMBER OF COMMERCE.—Tuesday, July 3d, 1770.

Present.

Hon'ble Hugh Wallace, Esqr., President.
Elias Desbrosses, Esqr.,
Hon'ble Henry White, Esqr., } V Presidents.
Theoph. Bache, Treasurer.
Anth. Van Dam, Secretary.

James Jauncey,
Jacob Walton,
Lawrence Kortright,
Isaac Low,
William Walton,
John H. Cruger,
Gerrard Walton,
Jacobus Van Zandt,
John Moore,
Gabriel H. Ludlow,
Peter Keteltas,
Henry Remsen,
Nicholas Hoffman,
Hamilton Young,
William Stepple,
George W. Ludlow,
Alexander McDonald,
Samuel Bayard,
Robert C. Livingston.

Fined for appearing after six o'clock:

Edward Laight,
William Nielson,
Jacob Watson,
Thomas W. Moore,
Abraham Lynsen,
Isaac Corsa,
Jeremiah Platt.

Fined for non-appearance:

Robert Murray,
George Folliot,
Samuel Ver Plank,
Miles Sherbrooke,
Walter Franklin,
Thomas Randal,
John Alsop,
Thomas White,
Robert R. Waddell,
Philip Livingston,
William McAdam,
Robert Watts,
Charles McEvers,
Levinus Clarkson,
Samuel Kemble,
Nicolas Gouverneur,
Richard Yates,
Thomas Marston,
Isaac Sears,
Lewis Pintard,
Peter Hasencliver,
Alexander Wallace,
Thomas Buchanan,
William Seton,
Samson Simson,
Gerrard W. Beekman,
John Reade,
Robert Alexander,
Richard Sharpe,
Peter Remsen,
Isaac Roosevelt,
Thomas Walton,
John Thurman,
John Weatherhead,
Garret Rapelje,
Gerrard Duyckink,
William Imlay,
August. Van Horne,
Henry C. Bogart,
Joseph Bull,
Leonard Lispenard,
Thomas Miller,
James Beekman.

Ordered—That the Treasurer of this Corporation do

pay Mr. Pettit his [*account*[60]] of Money expended for Firewood and Candles, amounting to £2 15s. 2d., and also his Salary of Fifteen Pounds, as Door keeper and Messenger for one year ending the first of May last.

Mr. Cruger's motion for half Joes. to weigh 9dwt. 3g. to pass for 64s., being considered of and greatly debated, on a division, it passed in the Negative.

Mr. Low moves that Jersey money[61] shall not be received or paid by any Member of this Corporation for more than $6\frac{2}{3}$ per cent. advance, from and after the first day of January next ensuing.

Mr. Low also moves that, to prevent that Scandalous practice of clipping half Johannes, that three pence be allowed for every grain which a half Joe. weighs more than nine pennyweight, and that four pence be deducted for every grain it weighs less.

Order'd—That Messrs. W. Stepple, W. Imlay, A. Van Horne, H. C. Bogart, G. W. Ludlow, J. Bull, and L. Lispenard be a Committee until the first Tuesday in August next to hear and determine disputes between Parties who shall agree to leave such to this Chamber, and that they do make report thereof in writing, to this Chamber.

CHAMBER OF COMMERCE.—TUESDAY, August 17, 1770.

PRESENT.

Honble. Hugh Wallace, P.
Elias Desbrosses, } V. P.
Honble. Henry White, } V. P.
Theop. Bache, Treas.
Anthon. Van Dam, Secty.

John Cruger,	Peter Remsen,
James Jauncey,	Isaac Roosevelt,
Samuel Ver Plank,	Thomas Walton,
Isaac Low,	John Thurman,

William Walton,
Thomas White,
Robert R. Waddell,
Robert Watts,
Gabriel H. Ludlow,
Edward Laight,
Sampson Simson,
Peter Keteltas,
Gerrard W. Beekman,
John Reade,
Thomas W. Moore,
Garret Rapelje,
Gerrard Duyckinck,
George W. Ludlow,
James Beekman,
Alexander McDonald,
John H. Cruger,
Gerrard Walton,
Jeremiah Platt,
Henry Remsen,
Abram Lynsen,
Samuel Bayard, Junr.,
Isaac Corsa.

Fined for non-appearance:

Jacob Walton,
George Folliot,
Theoph. Bache,
Miles Sherbrooke,
Walter Franklin,
Lawrence Kortright,
Thomas Randal,
Henry White,
John Alsop,
Philip Livingston,
William McAdam,
Jacobus Van Zandt,
Charles McEvers,
John Moore,
Levinus Clarkson,
Nicholas Gouverneur,
Richard Yates,
Thomas Marston,
Isaac Sears,
Lewis Pintard,
Peter Hasencliver,
Alexander Wallace,
Thomas Buchanan,
William Nielson,
William Seton,
Jacob Watson,
Robert Alexander,
Richard Sharpe,
Nicholas Hoffman,
Hamilton Young, L. I.[62]
John Weatherhead,
William Stepple, L. I.
William Imlay,
Augusts. Van Horn,
Henry C. Bogart,
Joseph Bull,
Leonard Lispenard,
Thomas Miller,
Samuel Kemble,
Robert C. Livingston,
Harman Gouverneur.

On Mr. Low's motion of last Meeting, whether there should not be allowed three pence per Grain on all half Johanneses that weigh more than nine Penny weight being debated in the Chamber, and on a division, passed in the Affirmative.

Resolved, therefore—That the Members of the Corporation will in future pay and receive half Johanneses weighing Nine penny weight at three pounds four shillings, and for every Grain they weigh more to allow three pence, and to deduct four pence for every Grain they weigh less.

Ordered—That Notice be given in the News Papers.[63]

John Cruger, Esq., begs leave to dissent from the above resolution as it tends towards diminishing the value of our Currency, and that it be entered on the Minutes of this Corporation.

Ordered—That this dissent be entered accordingly.

Mr. Low's proposal for receiving and paying Jersey Money, from and after the first January next, at 6⅔ per cent. advance, is postponed till a future Meeting.

Ordered—That Messrs. James Beekman, A. McDonald, S. Bayard, R. C. Livingston, H. Gouverneur, I. Corsa, Jerem. Platt, be a Committee until the first Tuesday September next to hear and determine disputes between Parties who shall agree to leave such to this Chamber, and that they do make report thereof in writing to this Chamber.

CHAMBER OF COMMERCE.—Tuesday, 4th September, 1770.

Present.

Honble. Hugh Wallace, P.
Elias Desbrosses, } V. P.
Honble. Henry White, } V. P.
Theophy Bache, T.
Antho. Van Dam, S.

Samuel Ver Plank,
William Walton,
Robert R. Waddell,
Gerrard Walton,
Jacobus Van Zandt,
Hamil. Young,
Thomas Walton,
John Thurman,
Garret Rapelje,
Gerrard Duyckinck,

Edward Laight,
Sampson Simson,
Jacob Watson,
Thomas W. Moore,
Isaac Roosevelt,
Willliam Stepple,
Augus. Van Horne,
Leonard Lispenard,
James Beekman,
Samuel Bayard.

Fined for appearing after six o'clock :

Hugh Wallace,
Miles Sherbrooke,
Robert Watts,
Alexan. Wallace,
Gabriel H. Ludlow,
Robert Alexander,
Abraham Lynsen,
Harman Gouverneur.

Fined for non-appearance :

James Jauncey,
Jacob Walton,
Robert Murray,
George Folliot,
Theoph. Bache,
Walter Franklin,
Lawrence Kortright,
Thomas Randal,
Isaac Low,
John H. Cruger,
Charles McEvers,
John Moore,
Levinus Clarkson,
Nicholas Gouverneur,
Richard Yates,
Thomas Marston,
Isaac Sears,
Lewis Pintard,
Gerrard W. Beekman,
John Reade,
Richard Sharpe,
Peter Remsen,
Henry Remsen,
Nichols. Hoffman,
John Weatherhead,
William Imlay,
Henry C. Bogert,
Henry White,
John Alsop,
Thomas White,
Philip Livingston,
William McAdam,
Isaac Corsa,
Peter Hasencliver,
Thomas Buchanan,
William Seton,
William Nielson,
Peter Keteltas,
Robert Livingston,
George W. Ludlow,
Joseph Bull,
Thomas Miller,
Samuel Kemble,
Alexander McDonald,
Jeremiah Platt.

The proposal for receiving and paying Jersey Money at $6\frac{2}{3}$ per ct. was further postponed.

Mr. Hugh Gaine [n] Printer's account for Work performed, and Books, &c., furnished this Corporation amounting to £12.15, appeared.

Proposed—That the same be paid.

Ordered—That Messrs. John Cruger, James Jauncey, Jacob Walton, George Folliot, Samuel Verplank, Theophylact Bache, and Miles Sherbrooke, be a Committee until the first Tuesday in October next to hear and determine disputes between parties who shall agree to leave such to this Chamber.

To the Gentlemen Committee of the Chamber of Commerce:

Messrs. *Conyngham & Nesbitt*, of *Philadelphia*, chartered a vessel for Lisbon; the merchant at Lisbon, to whom the Cargo was consigned, sent them by the Master of said Vessel, one hundred half Joes. The Vessel foundered at sea, the Crew were taken up by *Capt. Warden*, of *Glasgow*, who saved part of the materials and brought them to New York where he received a Salvage for them.

Capt. Warden [o] demands a Salvage on the above one hundred half Joes which were in the Captain's chest. Please to give your opinion on this matter whether *Capt. Warden* is entitled to any Salvage, and what?

HUGH & A. WALLACE.

We, the Subscribers, are of opinion that Ten per Cent. on Cash saved in this case is an adequate Salvage.

JOHN CRUGER,
JAMES JAUNCEY,
SAMUEL VERPLANK,
MILES SHERBROOKE,
THEOPH. BACHE.

October 1, 1770.

CHAMBER OF COMMERCE.—TUESDAY, 2d October, 1770.

PRESENT.

Hon'ble Henry White, P. V. P. T.

Antho. Van Dam, S.

John Cruger,
James Jauncey,
Walter Franklin,
Isaac Low,
William Walton,
Robert Watts,
Gerrard Walton,
John Moore,
Lewis Pintard,
Gabriel Ludlow,
Edward Laight,
Sampson Simson,
Gerrard W. Beekman,
Nicholas Hoffman,
Thomas Walton,
George W. Ludlow,
Joseph Bull,
James Beekman,
Samuel Bayard,
Henry White, F.
John Thurman, F.

Fined for non-appearance:

Hugh Wallace,
Elias Desbrosses,
Jacob Walton,
Robert Murray,
George Folliot,
Samuel Ver Plank,
Theophy. Bache,
Miles Sherbrooke,
Lawren. Kortright,
Thomas Randal,
John Alsop,
Thomas White,
Robert R. Waddell,
Philip Livingston,
William McAdam,
John H. Cruger,
Samuel Kemble,
Harman Gouverneur,
Jacobus Van Zandt,
Charles McEvers,
Levinus Clarkson,
Nichol's Gouverneur,
Richard Yates,
Thomas Marston,
Isaac Sears,
Peter Hasencliver,
Alexan. Wallace,
Thomas Buchanan,
William Seton,
William Neilson,
Peter Keteltas,
Jacob Watson,
John Reade,
Robert Alexander,
Alexand. McDonald,
Isaac Corsa,
Thomas W. Moore,
Richard Sharpe,
Peter Remsen,
Henry Remsen,
Abram Lynsen,
Isaac Roosevelt,
Hamilton Young,
John Weatherhead,
Garret Rapelje,
Gerrard Duyckink,
William Stepple,
William Imlay,
August's Van Horne,
Henry C. Bogert,
Leonard Lispenard,
Thomas Miller,
Robert C. Livingston,
Jeremiah Platt.

Mr. John Moore Proposed that the Charter of this Corporation be read at every Quarterly Meeting.

Mr. Moore also Proposed that a Proper Stove[64] be erected at the lower end of this Room, for the comfort of the members the approaching Winter.

Order'd—That the Treasurer do pay Mr. Hugh Gaine's Account, amounting to Twelve pounds fifteen shillings.

Mr. Isaac Low beg'd leave to propose to the Chamber some reasons that may avail to bring into repute the lost character of Flour[65] Exported from this market, in the words following:

MR. PRESIDENT:

The Disrepute which the Flour, the grand Staple of this Colony, suffers at all markets, calls aloud on the Legislature and every Member of the Community to contribute their sincere endeavours to effect a thorough reform, and, if possible, to retrieve its lost Reputation; and as nothing can be more worthily the object of the serious attention of this Corporation than to promote so desireable an end, I beg leave to propose to their consideration some of the means which appear to me most conducive to remedy the Defects so much complained of, and so severely felt by every principal Exporter of Flour in this City.

First, then, I conceive, and it is demonstrably evident, that the grand Reason why Philadelphia has so much the preference of New York Flour is because the former chiefly use French Burr Stones[66] for Grinding their Wheat, while there is scarce a single pair of them employed by any of the Millers in this Colony. For remedy whereof, I propose that the Fund of this Chamber, and as much more, to be collected by Subscription from each Member of it, as shall be sufficient to purchase Ten or Twenty Pair of French Burr Stones, shall be appropriated for that purpose. That application be made to the Owners of Ships in the London Trade, either to bring over the said Stones as Ballast, or at a very moderate Freight, instead of Coals or Grind Stones; and that when the said Stones arrive here, they shall be disposed of at Prime Cost to any Miller in this Colony only who shall apply for them.

The prevalence of habit is such, that it is extremely difficult to induce People to abandon old Customs, especially where doing so is likely to be attended with considerable Expence, although, as in the present instance, there is a moral certainty of Success. I conceive, therefore, it is absolutely necessary to introduce, on the most easy Terms to the Purchasers, such a number of French Burr Stones as may appear to this Chamber adequate to the Design; not only to Evince their great utility, but to excite an Emulation in our Millers, as is already the case in Pennsylvania, to use none else; which may be easily effected by this Chamber, after a few of them are introduced, by giving a due preference to the Flour which shall be ground by them.

But the quality of the Stones is not the only, tho' the principal reason to which is to be attributed the defects in our Flour.

In Philadelphia, I am informed that no Flour may be brought to market but in cover'd Waggons and under the Decks of Boats, and that the Transgressors in either case are subject to very severe Penalties, which are invariably inflicted without respect to Persons.

Some means ought, therefore, to be devised and recommended to the Legislature to enforce like Regulations in this Colony, as also with regard to the Weight and Size of the Barrels, to prevent the Flour from being packed too hard, which is a very great fault in our Flour in general, and to have the wheat Skreened on Delivery.

An Amendment to the Inspection Act of Flour was, if I remember right, recommended by this Chamber and adopted by the Legislature last year: That the Inspectors should not only have a particular regard to the fineness of the Flour but also to Grinding—That it should be lively and rise well in the Baking, which I am told is, with proper Judges, very easy to determine. But experience has evinced that a due regard has not been paid to these particulars, especially the latter of them—whence I infer that our present Inspectors are either from their great Age become too dim sighted, and want the sense of feeling to distinguish properly, or that they do not sufficiently understand their Duty. I therefore propose, that if Younger Men and better Judges can be found, they be recommended to the Legislature as Inspectors of Flour; which, as we confessedly have better Wheat ought to have the preference, rather than be in disgrace, as is notoriously the present case at all Markets. And if the Regulations I have thought it my duty to recommend to this Chamber together with such others as their better Judgements may suggest be properly attended to, I flatter myself that in a very short time the lost Reputation of our Flour will not only be retrieved, but that it will in fact be equal, if not superior to any made on this Continent.

The advantages which will result from so desireable an Event are too obvious to require any Arguments with the Members of this Corporation, cheerfully to embrace the means which shall appear to them most likely to promote the great object of their steady pursuit, THE GOOD OF THEIR COUNTRY—with same view, and for no other reason, I also beg leave to propose to the consideration of this Chamber, whether the Fees for Inspecting Pot Ashes,[67] which is so rapidly become a considerable Staple of this Colony, ought not to be recommended to the Legislature to be reduced. Since, from the vast unexpected increase of that Commodity, the Fees of Inspection are, in the opinion of many, become greatly more than adequate to the Services;

which operates against its being brought to this Market; and the contrary ought to be encouraged by every means in our power, whether therefore some further Regulations ought not to be made relative to Cooperage, and another Inspector appointed at the West end of the City to save Proprietors the Expence of double Cartage, and whether all Pott Ash should not be brought in Covered Waggons, and under the Decks of Boats, under severe Penalties to the Transgressors. All which is humbly submitted to the consideration of this Chamber.

ISAAC LOW.

CHAMBER OF COMMERCE.—TUESDAY, 7th Nov., 1770.

PRESENT.

Honble. Hugh Wallace, P.
Elias Desbrosses, } V. P.
Honble. Henry White, }
Theop. Bache, Treas.
Antho. Van Dam, Secty.

James Jauncey,
Jacob Walton,
Walter Franklin,
Thomas White,
William McAdam,
John H. Cruger,
William Seton,
Sampson Simpson,
Peter Keteltas,
Peter Remsen,
Abram Lynsen,
Isaac Roosevelt,
Joseph Bull,
Leonard Lispenard,
James Beekman,
Alexan. McDonald,
Samuel Bayard, jr.,
Robert C. Livingston,
Jacobus Van Zandt,
Gabriel Ludlow,
Nicholas Hoffman,
Hamilton Young,
Isaac Corsa.

Fined for appearing after six o'clock:

Isaac Low,
Lewis Pintard,
John Thurman.

Fined for non-appearance:

Robert Murray,
Theoph. Bache,
Miles Sherbrooke,
Lawrence Kortright,
Gerrard Walton,
Gerrard W. Beekman,
Jacob Watson,
John Reade,
Robert Alexander,
Thomas Moore,

Charles McEvers,
John Moore,
Levinus Clarkson,
Nicholas Gouverneur,
Richard Yates,
Thomas Marston,
Isaac Sears,
Peter Hassencliver,
Alexan. Wallace,
Jeremia Platt,
George Folliott,
Thomas Randal,
John Alsop,
William Walton,
Thomas Buchanan,
Edward Laight,
William Nielson,
Richard Sharpe,
Thomas Walton,
Samuel Ver Plank,
Robert R. Waddel,
Philip Livingston,
Robert Watts,
John Weatherhead,
Garret Rapalje,
Gerrard Duykinck,
William Steppel,
William Imlay,
August. Van Horne,
Henry C. Bogert,
George W. Ludlow,
Thomas Miller,
Samuel Kemble,
Harman Gouverneur.

Mr. Low's proposal of last meeting was read and considered of, respecting of Flour, when Mr. Marschalk,[p] who was attending produced several Samples of Flour, as well as Bread baked from it, which the Chamber approved of, as being greatly improved in its quality, especially such as was ground with Burr Stones; and it is recommended by this Corporation that the Members hereof do give a preference in their purchase of such Marks as have been exhibited, as well as to those Millers who shall use Burr Stones in future. To Skreen the Wheat is also recommended, with German Mill Skreens;[68] and it appears also to the Chamber that having two Inspectors is of bad consequence, and

It is proposed that this Chamber apply to the Assembly, at their next Meeting, to appoint only One Inspector.[69]

And it appears that there are several Burr Stones already sent for, and that therefore it does not seem necessary for this Chamber to send for any at this time.

That this Chamber apply to the Assembly to oblige the Millers to Brand the first Letter of their Christian,[70] and their whole Sirname at length on each barrel.

Upon considering Mr. Low's Proposal relating to Pot-ash, it is thought proper to postpone that matter till another Meeting, when this Corporation may be better informed what quantity is shipp'd off, and what expence attends the Inspection.

Order'd—That Messrs. R. White, McAdam and J. Thurman do prepare an Advertisement for Mr. Gaine's next Paper,[71] to be signed by the Secretary, signifying the approbation of this Chamber to the quality of several Samples of Flour exhibited by Mr. Marschalk, one of the Inspectors, who is required to attend Monthly with an account of such Millers as improve in ye manufacture of Flour.

Ordered—That Messrs. Robert R. Waddell, P. Livingston, W. McAdam, R. Watts, J. H. Cruger, G. Walton, and J. Van Zandt, be a Committee, until the first Tuesday in December next, to hear and determine disputes between Parties who shall agree to leave such to this Corporation.

We, the underwritten Arbitrators, indifferently chosen by *John Dunlap* and *Lewis Pintard* to inspect Mr. L. Jouet's charges at Hispaniola for the Snow Peggy and Polly, do award the said *John Dunlap* to allow the said *Lewis Pintard*, out of the Hire of the said Snow, the Sum of Seventy-one pounds Eight shillings and one penny New York Currency, subject to the Sum of Seven pounds Eighteen Shillings and two pence N. York Curr'y, to be repaid *Capt. Dunlap* by *Lewis Pintard*, if Peter Saunders, a Sailor who was put in Prison at the Cape, should come to New York and Recover the same from *Capt. Dunlap*, or the owner.

Witness our hands in New York, this 11th [———] 1770

JOHN ALSOP,
ISAAC LOW,
WILLI WALTON.

CHAMBER OF COMMERCE.—TUESDAY, December 4, 1770.

PRESENT.

Hon'ble Hugh Wallace, P.
Elias Desbrosses, } V. P.
Theop. Bache, T.
Antho. Van Dam, S.

John Cruger,
James Jauncey,
Isaac Low,
John Alsop,
William Walton,
Robert R. Waddell,
John H. Cruger,
Gerrard Walton,
John Moore,
Sampson Simson,
Jacob Watson,
Robert Alexander,
Peter Remsen,
Thomas Walton,
August's Van Horne,
Joseph Bull,
Robert C. Livingston,
Isaac Corsa.

Fined for appearing after six o'clock:

Hugh Wallace,
Nicho's Hoffman,
Theophy Bache,
George W. Ludlow,
Lewis Pintard,
Alexa. McDonald,
Samuel Bayard.

Fined for non-appearance:

Jacob Walton,
Samuel Ver Plank,
Lawrence Kortright,
Thomas White,
Robert Watts,
Levinus Clarkson,
Thomas Marston,
Gabriel H. Ludlow,
Edward Laight,
Gerrard W. Beekman,
Richard Sharpe,
Isaac Roosevelt,
John Weatherhead,
William Stepple,
Leonard Lispenard,
Harman Gouverneur,
Thomas Buchanan,
William Neilson,
John Reade,
Henry Remsen,
Hamilton Young,
Garret Rapelje,
William Imlay,
James Beekman,
Jeremi Platt,
George Folliot,
Walter Franklin,
Henry White,
William McAdam,
Charles McEvers,
Richard Yates,
Alexander Wallace,

Robert Murray,
Miles Sherbrooke,
Thomas Randall,
Philip Livingston,
Jacobus Van Zandt,
Nicholas Gouverneur,
Isaac Sears,
William Seton,
Peter Keteltas,
Thomas W. Moore,
Abram Lynsen,
John Thurman,
Gerrard Duyckinck,
Henry C. Bogert,
Samuel Kemble.

The following Gentlemen having been proposed at the last Meeting were balloted for and elected; Daniel Phenix, Walter Buchanan, Benjamin Booth, and John Amiel.

Ordered—That the Secretary send notice to the several Gentlemen, so Elected, in writing that they were unanimously chosen.

Ordered—That Messrs. Charles McEvers, L. Clarkson, N. Gouverneur, R. Yates, Thos. Marston, I. Sears, and Louis Pintard, be a Committee till the first Tuesday in January next, to hear and determine disputes between parties who shall agree to leave such to this Corporation.

The Members of this Corporation having met shortly after the arrival of His Excellency, the Earl of Dunmore, when it was unanimously thought proper to address him on his appointment to this Government: the same was prepared and approved of, and a majority of the Members presented his Lordship with the following address:

To his Excellency, the Right Honourable John,[q] Earl of Dunmore, Captain General, and Governor in Chief, in and over the Province of New York, and the Territories depending thereon in America, Chancellor and Vice-Admiral of the same:

May it Please Your Lordship,

The Corporation of the Chamber of Commerce, of the City of New York, beg leave to present to Your Lordship their sincere and most respectful Congratulations on Your safe Arrival to your Government, and to assure your Lordship of their zealous and steady attachment to his most Gracious Majesty, King George the Third; whose affectionate Regard for his People of this Colony is so conspicuously manifested in the appointment of Your Lordship to preside over us.

It will be the constant Endeavour of this Corporation to answer the Expectations which induced the Worthy Lieutenant Governor to invest us with a Royal Charter; as also to evince to Your Lordship the Utility of the Institution, by promoting Trade and Commerce, so essential to the Prosperity of the Colony, adjusting controverted and intricate Accounts, and by preventing, as much as possible, a spirit of Litigation, ever highly injurious to a Mercantile City.

We hope for Your Lordship's Favour and Approbation, and shall esteem it a peculiar happiness if we can be instrumental in rendering the Residence of a Governor of Your Lordship's high and distinguished Rank agreeable, your administration easy to your Lordship, happy and advantageous to the Colony.

By order of the Corporation,
HUGH WALLACE, President.

To which his Lordship was pleased to return the following Answer:

GENTLEMEN: Your address is highly pleasing to me; you may depend on my approving every Measure of yours which may tend to promote the true Commercial Interest of this Colony.

CHAMBER OF COMMERCE.—TUESDAY, 1st January, 1771.

PRESENT.
Hon. Hugh Wallace, P.

Antho. Van Dam, Sect'y.

John Cruger,	Edward Laight,
James Jauncey,	Samson Simpson,
William Walton,	William Stepple,
John H. Cruger,	Joseph Bull,
Lewis Pintard,	Samuel Kemble,
Thomas Buchanan,	Isaac Corsa,
William Seton,	Lawrence Kortright,
Henry Remsen,	John Alsop,
Nicholas Hoffman,	William McAdam,
John Thurman,	Isaac Sears,

Harman Gouverneur,
Jacob Walton,
Walter Franklin,
Robert R. Waddle,
Gerrard Walton,
Alexand. Wallace,
Gabriel H. Ludlow,
William Neilson,
John Reade,
Daniel Phenix,
Benja. Booth,
John Amiel.

Fined for appearing after six o'clock:

John Moore,
George Ludlow,
Jacob Watson,
Benj. Booth,
William Imlay.

Fined for non-appearance:

Elias Desbrosses,
Miles Sherbrooke,
Thomas White,
Jacob's Van Zandt,
Nicholas Gouverneur,
Peter Hasencliver,
Robert Alexander,
Peter Remsen,
Hamilton Young,
Thomas Walton,
Henry C. Bogart,
James Beekman,
Robert C. Livingston,
George Folliot,
Thomas Randal,
Philip Livingston,
Charles McEvers,
Richard Yates,
Peter Keteltas,
Thomas W. Moore,
Abram Lynsen,
John Weatherhead,
Garret Rapelje,
Leonard Lispenard,
Alexan'r McDonald,
Jeremiah Platt,
Samuel Ver Plank,
Henry White,
Robert Watts,
Levinus Clarkson,
Thomas Marston,
Gerrard W. Beekman,
Richard Sharpe,
Isaac Roosevelt,
Gerrard Duykink,
August Van Horn,
Thomas Miller,
Samuel Kemble,
Walter Buchanan.

It is proposed by Mr. John Cruger that the President, or one of the Vice-Presidents, with seven or five Members have power to adjourn their Meeting provided any Number of Members less than Twenty-one appear at their future stated Meetings, but not to do Business.

Ordered—That Messrs. A. Wallace, G. H. Ludlow,

T. Buchanan, W. Seton, E. Laight, W. Neilson and Sampson Simson, be a Committee until the first Tuesday in February next, to hear and determine disputes between Parties who shall agree to leave such to this Corporation.

We, the Subscribers, of the Committee of the Chamber of Commerce for the Month of January, being applied to in a matter of disputed Accounts between *Peter Townsend* and *Thomas Budd*, are of opinion and do Award that the said *Peter Townsend* is to pay unto the said *Thomas Budd* the sum of £44 16s 6d New York Currency, which appears to be the Ballance due him for his Services at Sterling Iron Works,[72] agreeable to articles executed by *Peter Townsend* the 4th. January, 1766. And further we do Award, that as it appears to us the said *Thomas Budd* having been improperly kept out of his Wages, was obliged to commence a Suit against the said *Peter Townsend*, in Hakinsack Court,[73] in New Jersey—the Charges that have occurred in Law by that means till this day must be paid by the said *Peter Townsend* as taxed, if required by the Chief Justice of that Province,[r] which Award we now give indented under our hands and seals this 18th January of our Lord, 1771.

WILLIAM SETON, WM. NEILSON,
ALEX. WALLACE, G. H. LUDLOW,
THOMAS BUCHANAN.

We, the subscribers, are of opinion that *Mr. Dennis McCready* is to deliver *Mr. Patrick Loughan* 34 Hogsheads of uncleaned Merchantable Flax seed here, and that the said *Loughlan* shall pay on delivery of said 34 hhds. of seed, Ten pounds seven shillings in New York Currency to the said *Dennis McCready*. We are further of opinion that the money paid by *Mr. Dennis McCready* to Mr. Daniel Criddon remains the property of *Mr. Dennis McCready* only.

ALEX. WALLACE, E. LAIGHT,
THOS. BUCHANAN, WM. NEILSON,
SAMS. SIMSON, G. H. LUDLOW.

We, the Subscribers, are of opinion and do award that *Walter and Thomas Buchanan & Co.* are, in ten days, to pay to *Robert Munro*, £162 10 2½ New York Currency, to deliver him free of all incumbrances the Schooner Dolphin, now in this Port, with all her Sails, Rigging, and other appurtenances, also the Sails now in their possession, that did belong to the said *Munro's* Vessels, excepting those of the Ship Dispatch and Schooner Providence. Also they, the said *Walter and Thomas Buchanan & Co.*, are to reconvey fully and amply the title of all the Estate, with the Schedulle annexed, which was conveyed by the said *Robert Munro* to *Walter Buchanan*, at Imlaytown[74] in Chaleur Bay, on the 9th of October, 1770, excepting the Schooner Providence, which was sold here and credited on their account. They are also to fully impower the said *Munro* and give him sufficient authority to receive from David Coll, or any other person or persons under him, them, or either of them, all the Effects belonging to the said *Munro* which were taken in possession by *Walter Buchanan*, or by his order. In consideration of which they, the said *Walter and Thomas Buchanan & Co.*, are to hold as their property, the Sloop Dispatch, the Schooner Providence, and also all the Goods they have here on hand, formerly belonging to the said *Munro*, excepting the Schooner Dolphin and all the Sails as above recited.

N. B. Full discharges to be given on both sides, and the *Buchanans* to pay the Expences attending the reference and Award.[75]

ALEX. WALLACE, SAMS. SIMSON,
WM. SETON, G. H. LUDLOW,
EDWARD LAIGHT.

January —, 1771.

CHAMBER OF COMMERCE.—TUESDAY, February 5, 1771.

PRESENT.

Honble. Hugh Wallace, P.
Honble. Henry White, V. P.
Antho. Van Dam, S.

Miles Sherbrooke,
Robert Watts,
John Moore,
Alexan. Wallace,
Sampson Simpson,
Henry Remsen,
Hamil't Young,
Garret Rapelje,
Lawrence Kortright,
Gerrard Walton,
Thomas Marston,
Gabriel H. Ludlow,
Gerra'd W. Beekman,
Abram. Lynsen,
Thomas Walton,
William Stepple,
Isaac Low,
Jacobus Van Zandt,
Lewis Pintard,
William Seton,
Jacob Watson,
Isaac Roosevelt,
John Thurman,
George W. Ludlow,
Joseph Bull,
Harman Gouverneur,
James Beekman,
Isaac Corsa,
Samuel Bayard,
Daniel Phenix,
John Amiel.

Fined for non-appearance:

Elias Desbrosses,
James Jauncey,
George Folliot,
Thomas Randal,
John Alsop,
William Walton,
Thomas White,
Robert R. Waddell,
Philip Livingston,
William McAdam,
John H. Cruger,
Charles McEvers,
Levinus Clarkson,
Nicho's Gouverneur,
Richard Yates,
Theoph. Bache,
Jacob Walton,
Samuel Verplank,
Isaac Sears,
Peter Hasencliver,
Edward Laight,
William Neilson,
Peter Keteltas,
John Reade,
Robert Alexander,
Thomas W. Moore,
Richard Sharpe,
Peter Remsen, S.[76]
Nicholas Hoffman,
John Weatherhead,
John Cruger,
Robert Murray,
Walter Franklin,
Gerrard Duyckink,
William Imlay,
August. Van Horne,
Henry C. Bogart,
Leonard Lispenard,
Thomas Miller,
Samuel Kemble,
Alexan. McDonald,
Robert C. Livingston,
Jeremiah Platt,
Walter Buchanan,
Benj. Booth.

The Proposal of John Cruger, Esq. having been considered of, that the President or one of the Vice-Presidents, with seven or five Members, have power to adjourn, provided any number of the Members, less than twenty-one, appear at their future stated Meetings, but not to do business.

Resolved—That it is the opinion of this Corporation, and they do determine that the President or one of the Vice-Presidents, for the time being, with five other Members shall have power to adjourn, provided any number of the Members less than twenty-one appear at the future stated Meetings.

Mr. Jacob Watson proposes that this Corporation

procure a set of Weights and Scales for weighing Gold, which shall be allowed to be a Standard[77] by the Members of this Corporation.

Mr. Watson also proposes to this Corporation, that instead of Seamens Months advance pay[78] in Cash, that they give Notes of hand payable in three days after their departure from Sandyhook.

Ordered—That Messrs. H. Remsen junr., A. Lynsen, I. Roosevelt, N. Hoffman, H. Young, Thos. Walton, and J. Thurman, be a Committee until the first Tuesday in March next, to hear and determine disputes between Parties who shall agree to leave such to this Corporation.

We, the Subscribers, as a Committee of the Corporation of the Chamber of Commerce, established by Royal Charter, in the City of New York, in America, being requested by Mr. *Anthony Van Dam*, on the part and behalf of *Mr. William Castel* and Captain *Joseph Smith*, late Commander of the Sloop Bellesarius, to settle our account against the said Sloop and *William Castel*, and having heard the Allegations of both Parties, with the Evidences produced, do hereby award and determine that the said *Anthony Van Dam* as agent and special bail for the said *William Castel*, doth pay unto the said Captain *Joseph Smith*, the sum of Fifty-two pounds, eighteen shillings, and three pence Currency, and no more in full for and in lieu of his Account exhibited to us, as also for the profits and advantages arising in Sugar and Molasses he claims as his due as well as for all loss, cost of Suit and other damages he hath been put to for the recovery hereof. Witness our hands this fourth day of February, 1771.

SAMPSON SIMSON, GABRIEL H. LUDLOW,
WILLIAM NEILSON.

We, the Subscribers, have considered the Dispute subsisting between Messrs. *Grant & Fine*, Freighters of the Brigt ——— to Quebec, and *Henry Law and Totten & Crosfield*, part owners, do determine that the quantity each hh'd. should contain, to fix the Freight, is one hundred and twelve Gallons [79] outside contents of each hogshead.

ANTHONY VAN DAM,
JACOBUS VAN ZANDT,
ROBERT WATTS.

New York, February 24th, 1771.

CHAMBER OF COMMERCE.—TUESDAY, 5th March, 1771.

PRESENT.

Theophy. Bache, T.
Anthony Van Dam, S.

John Cruger,
James Jauncey,
Miles Sherbrooke,
William Walton,
Robert R. Waddell,
William McAdam,
Robert Watts,
Gerrard Walton,
John Moore,
Thomas Marston,
Isaac Sears,
Gabriel H. Ludlow,
Edward Laight,
Sampson Simson,
Peter Ketletas,
Jacob Watson,
Thomas W. Moore,
Henry Remsen,
Abram Lynsen,
Hamil. Young,
Thomas Walton,
John Thurman,
William Stepple,
George W. Ludlow,
Leonard Lispenard,
James Beekman,
Samuel Bayard, jr.,
Robert C. Livingston,
Daniel Phenix,
Walter Buchanan,
Benjamin Booth,
Thomas Buchanan.

Fined for non-appearance:

Hugh Wallace,
Elias Desbrosses,
Henry White,
Jacob Walton,
George Folliot,
Samuel Verplank,
Walter Franklin,
Lawrence Kortright,
Thomas Randal,
Isaac Low,
John Alsop,
Thomas White,
Philip Livingston,
John H. Cruger,
Isaac Corsa,
Jacobus Van Zandt,
Charles McEvers,
Levinus Clarkson,
Nicholas Gouverneur,
Alexan. Wallace,
William Seton,
William Neilson,
Gerrard W. Beekman,
John Reade,
Robert Alexander,
Richard Sharpe,
Jeremiah Platt,
Peter Remsen,
Isaac Roosevelt,
Nicholas Hoffman,
John Weatherhead,
Garret Rapelje,
Gerrard Duyckink,
William Imlay,
August Van Horne,
Henry C. Bogert,
Joseph Bull,
Thomas Miller,

Richard Yates,
Lewis Pintard,
Peter Hassencliver,
Samuel Kemble,
Alexan. McDonald,
Harman Gouverneur,
John Amiel.

Mr. Jacob Watson's Proposal for to procure a set of Weights and Scales for Weighing of Gold having been Considered of,

Ordered—That Jacob Walton, Hamilton Young and Alexander Wallace, be a Committee for that purpose, and that they appoint a proper Goldsmith to receive the Same, and that the person so appointed to regulate any Weights and Scales belonging to the Members of this Corporation, who shall require the same.

Ordered—That Messrs. P. Ketletas, G. W. Beekman, J. Watson, J. Reade, R. Alexander, T. W. Moore, and R. Sharpe be a Committee until the first Tuesday in April next, &c.

Messrs. S. Hake and J. Ramsay being Proposed at a former Meeting, were balloted for and chosen Members.

Ordered—That the Secretary send Notice in Writing that they were duly Elected.

CHAMBER OF COMMERCE.—TUESDAY, 2d April, 1771.

PRESENT.

Honble. Hugh Wallace, P.
Elias Desbrosses, V. P.
Theoph. Bache, T.
Antho. Van Dam, S.

James Jauncey,
William Walton,
William McAdam,
Robert Watts,
John H. Cruger,
Samuel Verplank,
Gerrard Walton,
Thomas Marston,
Sampson Simson,
Isaac Low,
Joseph Bull,
James Beekman,
Isaac Corsa,
Samuel Hake,

Fined for appearing after six o'clock:

Theoph. Bache,
Lawrence Kortright,
Robert. R. Waddell,
William Stepple,
Benjam. Booth,
Miles Sherbrooke,
Nicholas Gouverneur,
Lewis Pintard,
Alexan. McDonald,
Thomas Buchanan,
Walter Franklin,
Alexan. Wallace,
Thomas Walton,
Robert C. Livingston.

Fined for non-appearance:

Henry White,
George Folliot,
Thomas Randal,
John Alsop,
Thomas White,
Philip Livingston,
Jacobus Van Zandt,
Jacob Watson,
Thomas W. Moore,
Abraham Lynsen,
Hamilton Young,
Garret Rapelje,
August Van Horne,
Leonard Lispenard,
Samuel Bayard,
Daniel Phenix,
John Ramsay,
John Cruger,
Charles McEvers,
John Moore,
Levinus Clarkson,
Nicholas Gouverneur,
Richard Yates,
Isaac Sears,
John Reade,
Richard Sharpe,
Isaac Roosevelt,
John Thurman,
Gerrard Duyckinck,
Henry C. Bogert,
Thomas Miller,
Harman Gouverneur,
Walter Buchanan,
Robert C. Livingston,
Jacob Walton,
Gabriel H. Ludlow,
William Seton,
Edward Laight,
William Nielson,
Peter Ketletas,
Gerrard W. Beekman,
Robert Alexander,
Henry Remsen,
Nicholas Hoffman,
John Weatherhead,
William Imlay,
George W. Ludlow,
Samuel Kemble,
Jeremiah Platt,
John Amiel.

Mr. William Walton moves that as the Lieut. Governor was very kind in favoring this Corporation with a Charter and as there is now a good Limner in Town that Mr. President be desired to request the favour of Mr.

Colden to sit for his Picture[80] to be put up in the Chamber as a Memorial of their Gratitude.

It is proposed that this Corporation Dine together in next Month, and that at next Meeting Stewards be appointed to provide a Suitable Dinner at the Expence of each of the Members.

Ordered—That Messrs. J. Weatherhead, G. Rapelje, G. Duyckink, W. Stepple, W. Imlay, A. Van Horne, and H. C. Bogert, be a Committee, until the first Tuesday in May next, to hear and determine disputes between Parties who shall agree to leave such to this Corporation.

CHAMBER OF COMMERCE.—TUESDAY, 7th May, 1771.

PRESENT.

The Hon'ble Hugh Wallace, P.
Elias Desbrosses, } V. P.
Theoph. Bache, T.
Antho. Van Dam, S.

John Cruger,	John Reade,
William Walton,	Garret Rapelje,
Lewis Pintard,	James Beekman,
Sampson Simson,	Daniel Phenix,
Thomas Walton,	Thomas Buchanan,
William Stepple,	John Alsop,
Jeremia Platt,	John H. Cruger,
John Amiel,	William Neilson,
Samuel Ver Plank, (absent)	Hamilton Young,
Robert Watts,	Gerrard Duyckinck,
Gabriel H. Ludlow,	Samuel Bayard,

Walter Buchanan.

Fined for appearing after six o'clock :

Hugh Wallace,	Edward Laight,
Elias Desbrosses,	Gerrard W. Beekman,
Theoph. Bache,	Jacob Watson,
James Jauncey,	Thomas W. Moore,
Jacob Walton,	Henry Remsen,
Miles Sherbrooke, (absent)	Isaac Roosevelt,
Walter Franklin, (absent)	Nicholas Hoffman,

Lawrence Kortright, (absent)
Isaac Low,
Robert R. Waddle,
Gerrard Walton,
Jacobus Van Zandt,
John Moore,
Isaac Sears,
Henry C. Bogert,
George W. Ludlow,
Joseph Bull,
Alexand. McDonald,
Robert C. Livingston,
Isaac Corsa,
Benjam. Booth,
Augus. Van Horne.

Fined for non-appearance:

Henry White,
George Folliot,
Miles Sherbrooke,
Walter Franklin,
Acheson Thompson,
Robert Murray,
Lawrence Kortright,
Thomas Randall,
John Thurman,
John Weatherhead,
William Imlay,
Thomas White,
Philip Livingston,
William McAdam,
Charles McEvers,
Levinus Clarkson,
Nicholas Gouverneur,
Richard Yates,
Thomas Marston,
Leonard Lispenard,
Thomas Miller,
Samuel Kemble,
Peter Hasencliver,
Alex. Wallace,
William Seton,
Peter Keteltas,
Robert Alexander,
Richard Sharpe,
Peter Remsen, (Ill)
Samuel Ver Plank,
Abram Lynsen,
Harman Gouverneur,
Samuel Hake,
John Ramsay.

Mr. Walton's Proposal, that a Portrait of Lieut. Governor Colden be taken, was unanimously agreed to, and

Ordered—That the Hon'ble Hugh Wallace do wait upon the Lieut. Governor, and Request the favour of him to sit for his Picture, which the Treasurer of this Corporation will pay for; and that when finished it be hung up in the Chamber in memory of their Gratitude for granting them a Charter of Incorporation.

In consequence of the Proposal of last Meeting for this Corporation to Dine together, the following Gentlemen were appointed Stewards, viz.: G. Walton, Thomas W. Moore, John H. Cruger, and Robert Watts, who are ordered to provide a Genteel Dinner,[81] and wait upon Lord Dunmore to know when it will be convenient for him to do them the Honor of Dining with them, and that they send notices to and write the Governor and his Secretary,[82] the Lieut. Governor and his Secretary, the Secretary of the Province, the General and his Suit, the Council, the Members of the General Assembly that are in Town, the Field Officers doing duty in this City,[83] the Captains of his Majesty's Ships, the Principal officers of the Customs, and the Mayor of the City.

Order'd—That absent Members pay Eight Shillings towards the Expence of the Dinner.

Robert G. Livingston, jr., having been proposed at a former Meeting, was balloted for, and chosen a Member of this Corporation.

Order'd—That the Secretary send notice in writing that he was duly Elected.

Order'd—That Messrs. G. W. Ludlow, J. Bull, L. Lispenard, James Beekman, Alex. McDonald, Samuel Bayard, and Robert C. Livingston, be a Committee, until the first Tuesday in June next, to hear and determine disputes between Parties who shall agree to leave such to this Corporation.

The Charter of Incorporation, as well as the Rules of this Chamber, appoint this Day for the Election of Officers for the current year, when the following Gentlemen were balloted for, duly Elected, and sworn to perform the Trust reposed in them.

President, ELIAS DESBROSSES, Esqr.

Vice-Presidents, { HENRY WHITE, Esqr.
THEOP. BACHE.

Treasurer, WILLIAM WALTON.

Secretary, ANTHONY VAN DAM.

CHAMBER OF COMMERCE.—TUESDAY, 4th June, 1771.

PRESENT.

Elias Desbrosses, P.
} V. P
William Walton, T.
Anthony Van Dam, S.

James Beekman,
Nicholas Hoffman,
Peter Ketletas,
Edward Laight,
George W. Ludlow,
Alexand'r Wallace,
Thomas Buchanan,
Robert C. Livingston,
Thomas W. Moore,
William Neilson,
Jeremiah Platt,
Hamilton Young,
Isaac Corsa,
John Reade,
Isaac Roosevelt,
John Ramsay,
Sampson Simson.

Fined for appearing after six o'clock :

Samuel Hake,
Robert G. Livingston,
Isaac Sears,
Isaac Low,
Lewis Pintard,
Jacobus Van Zandt,
Leonard Lispenard,
Daniel Phenix.

Fined for non-appearance :

Henry White,
Theophy. Bache,
John Amiel,
Gerrard W. Beekman,
Henry C. Bogert,
Joseph Bull,
Samuel Bayard,
Walter Buchanan,
Benjam. Booth,
John Cruger,
John Alsop,
Peter Hasencliver,
James Jauncey,
William Imlay,
Lawrence Kortright,
William Stepple,
Acheson Thompson,
John Thurman,
John H. Cruger,
Levinus Clarkson,
Gerrard Duyckink,
George Folliot,
Walter Franklin,
Nicholas Gouverneur,
Harman Gouverneur,
Gerrard Walton,
William McAdam,
Charles McEvers,
John Moore,
Thomas Marston,

Samuel Kemble,
Philip Livingston,
Gabr. H. Ludlow, (out of Town)
Abram. Lynsen,
Robert Murray,
Robert Alexander,
Peter Remsen,
Henry Remsen,
Garret Rapelje,
Miles Sherbrooke,
William Seton,
Richard Sharpe,
Thomas Miller,
Alexand. McDonald,
Thomas Randal,
John Weatherhead,
Samuel Verplank,
Augustus Van Horne,
Hugh Wallace,
Jacob Walton,
Thomas White,
Robert R. Waddle,
Robert Watts,
Jacob Watson.

In May, 1770, Messrs. Robert Murray, Hamilton Young, Miles Sherbrooke, Rich. Yates, and Peter Remsen, were appointed a Committee to ascertain the usual Tonage of this Port, and in June, 1770, Messrs. John Moore and Jacobus Van Zandt were added to said Committee, who have hitherto made no report.

Ordered—That the said Committee do, at the next Meeting of this Chamber, deliver in a Report accordingly, and that they do also collect such information as they can, what is usually reckoned a Ton of Goods of as many species as possible, Exported from Britain, because the mode now practiced is too uncertain either for Shippers of Goods or Ship Owners, which will prevent many disputes if adopted by this Corporation.

Ordered—That Messrs. Thomas W. Moore, Hamilton Young, and Henry Remsen, be a Committee to audit the Treasurer's Account for the last year, and that they do make Report thereof at next Meeting.

Thomas Petitt, Door Keeper, exhibited an account for repairing the Windows 16s. 3d., a quire paper 1s. 6d., and his Year's salary of £15, being due the 1st of last Month. Proposed that the same be paid.

Ordered—That Messrs. Harman Gouverneur, Isaac

Corsa, Jerem. Platt, Daniel Phenix, Walter Buchanan, Benjamin Booth, and John Amiel, be a Committee, until the first Tuesday in July, to hear and determine disputes between Parties who shall agree to leave such to this Corporation.

CHAMBER OF COMMERCE.—TUESDAY, 2d July, 1771.

PRESENT.

Elias Desbrosses, P.
William Walton, T.

John Alsop,	Joseph Bull,
Samuel Bayard,	Samp. Simson,
John Cruger,	Richard Sharpe,
John H. Cruger,	Jacobus Van Zandt,
Isaac Corsa,	Jacob Walton,
Peter Keteltas,	Robert Watts,
Henry C. Bogart,	Isaac Low,
Leonard Lispenard,	George W. Ludlow,
Robert C. Livingston,	Hamil. Young,
Robert G. Livingston,	John Reade,
Lewis Pintard,	Isaac Sears,
Daniel Phenix,	Gerrard Walton,

Alexand. Wallace.

Fined for appearing after six o'clock:

Theoph Bache,	Thomas Marston,
Walter Buchanan,	Thomas W. Moore,
Nicholas Hoffman,	John Amiel,
William Stepple,	Jerem. Platt,
Antho. Van Dam,	William Seton.

Fined for non-appearance:

Henry White,	Gabriel H. Ludlow,
James Beekman,	Edward Laight,
Benja. Booth,	Abram Lynsen,
Thomas Buchanan,	William McAdam,
Levinus Clarkson,	Miles Sherbrooke,

Gerrard Duyckinck,
George Folliot,
Walter Franklin,
Nicholas Gouverneur,
Harman Gouverneur,
Peter Hassencliver,
John Ramsay,
Samuel Verplank,
Thomas White,
John Weatherhead,
Robert Alexander,
Samuel Hake,
James Jauncey,
William Imlay,
Lawrence Kortright,
Samuel Kemble,
Philip Livingston,
August. Van Horne,
Robert R. Waddle,
Jacob Watson,
Gerrard W. Beekman,
Charles McEvers,
John Moore,
Thomas Miller,
Alexander McDonald,
William Nielson,
Thomas Randal,
Peter Remsen,
Henry Remsen,
Isaac Roosevelt,
Garret Rapelje,
John Thurman,
Hugh Wallace,
Thomas Walton,
Richard Yates.

Thomas Petitt, Doorkeeper to this Corporation, having exhibited his Account at the last Meeting, amounting to £15 17s 9d for One Year ending the first of May last,

Ordered—That the Treasurer pay the same.

The Committee appointed to audit Mr. Bache the late Treasurer's accounts, Report

That they have examined the same and find a Ballance of £91 13 4 remaining in his hands.

Ordered—That he do pay the same into the hands of Mr. William Walton the present Treasurer and that he doth deliver the Book of Accounts to him at the same time.

This Corporation finding it very inconvenient that the Mail[84] for the Packet to England is made up the first Tuesday in the Month, which is the Day appointed to hold their Monthly Meetings—agreed that a Representation thereof be made and presented to Mr. FOXCROFT,[s]

Deputy Post Master General for North America—and that The Honble. Hugh Wallace, Mr. Theoph Bache, and William Walton be a Committee to draw up and present him with a Representation of the inconvenience attending the Members of the Corporation, and request the favour of him to appoint another Day for that purpose.

Ordered—That Messrs. Thomas Buchanan, S. Hake, J. Ramsay, Robt. G. Livingston, H. Wallace, J. Cruger and James Jauncey be a Committee until the first Tuesday in August next, to hear and determine disputes between Parties, who shall agree to leave such to this Corporation.

SPECIAL MEETING.—Friday, 12th July, 1771.

PRESENT.

Elias Desbrosses, P.
Theoph Bache, V. P.
Anthon. Van Dam, Secty.

John Cruger,	Robert C. Livingston,
Jeremiah Platt,	Daniel Phenix,
Samuel Verplank,	Hamilton Young,
Alexan. Wallace,	Leonard Lispenard, Jun.,
George W. Ludlow,	Richard Yates,
Gerrard Walton,	Edward Laight,
Augus. Van Horne,	Lewis Pintard,
Isaac Roosevelt,	James Jauncey,
Robert Watts,	Gabriel H. Ludlow,
John Ramsay,	Alexan. McDonald.

Proposed—That as his Excellency William Tryon,[t] Esqr., is arrived to this his Government, that a Committee be appointed to draw up an address to be presented to him by this Corporation.

Ordered—That Messrs. J. Moore, S. Verplank, R. C. Livingston, W. McAdam, T. Bache, J. Jauncey, J. H. Cruger, Isaac Low and Peter Ketletas be a Committee to draw up an address to congratulate his Excellency Governor Tryon on his arrival to his Government, and that they do prepare the same ready to be delivered on Monday Evening next, to this Chamber at six o'clock.

SPECIAL MEETING.—MONDAY, 15th July, 1771.

PRESENT.

Elias Desbrosses, P.
Theop. Bache, } V. P.
Henry White, } V. P.
Anthon. Van Dam, S.

William Stepple,	John Thurman,
George W. Ludlow,	Walter Franklin,
Gerrard Duykink,	James Beekman,
John Reade,	Edward Laight,
Samuel Hake,	Isaac Roosevelt,
Samuel Bayard,	Gabriel H. Ludlow,
William Nielson,	Gerrard W. Beekman,
Richard Yates,	John Amiel,
Lewis Pintard,	Daniel Phenix,
John Cruger,	Gerrard Walton,
Peter Keteltas,	Alexan. McDonald,
Samp. Simson,	John H. Cruger,

John Moore.

The Committee appointed to draw up an Address to Congratulate his Excellency, Governor Tryon, on his appointment and arrival to his Government of New York Report

That they have prepared an Address, which was order'd to be read, and is in the words following:

TO HIS EXCELLENCY, WILLIAM TRYON, Esquire, Captain General and Governor in Chief in and over the Province of New York and the Territories depending thereon in America, Chancellor and Vice-Admiral of the same.

MAY IT PLEASE YOUR EXCELLENCY,

The Corporation of the Chamber of Commerce of the City of New York beg leave to present your Excellency their most cordial and sincere Congratulations on your arrival in this Province with your Lady and Family.

His most gracious Majesty having promoted our late Worthy Governor the Right Honourable the Earl of Dunmore, to the Government of the Dominion of Virginia, we esteem ourselves happy in the Appointment of a Gentleman of your Excellency's eminent Abilities and amiable Character to the command of this Province.

The Chamber of Commerce, instituted on Principles of general Utility, flatter themselves with enjoying under your Excellency's Administration that Patronage and Protection which they have experienced from your Worthy Predecessors; and your Excellency may be assured that it will be the constant Endeavour of this Corporation to deserve your Favour, by promoting the Trade and Commerce of this City, so essentially necessary for its Increase and Prosperity.

Attached, from Principle, to our most gracious Sovereign and our happy Constitution, we promise ourselves the utmost Happiness under the Government of your Excellency, distinguished for your Services to both; and we beg leave to assure your Excellency, that it will be our constant Aim to render your Administration easy and agreeable to yourself, as we are confident it will be highly beneficial to the Colony.

By Order of the Corporation,

ELIAS DESBROSSES, President.

New York, July 22d, 1771.

HIS EXCELLENCY'S ANSWER to the Corporation of the Chamber of Commerce of the City of New York:

GENTLEMEN,

This polite and warm Address of the Corporation of the Chamber of Commerce is highly pleasing to me, and claims my very sincere Acknowledgements.

I am most truly sensible of the Honour I derive from his Majesty's gracious Appointment of me to succeed the Earl of Dunmore in the Government of this Province, and no less happy in the Testimonies you give me of being acceptable to its Inhabitants.

As it is my Duty, so it is no less my earnest Intention, to advance by every means in my power the Honour, Prosperity and true Interests of this flourishing Colony: an Institution, therefore, tending to the Extension of Commerce upon just Principles, will always be entitled to my Zealous Protection.

I accept with grateful respect your kind Assurances of contributing to the ease of my Administration, and I promise myself real Advantage in the concurrence of a Body of your Consideration, actuated by Principles so beneficial to Commerce, favourable to Government, and Honourable to your Society. WILLIAM TRYON.

CHAMBER OF COMMERCE.—TUESDAY, August 6, 1771.

PRESENT.

Elias Desbrosses, P.
Theoph. Bache, V. P
William Walton, T.
Antho. Van Dam, S.

Henry C. Bogart,
John Cruger,
Isaac Corsa,
Walter Franklin,
Harman Gouverneur,
Nicholas Hoffman,
Samuel Hake,
Peter Keteltas,
Isaac Low,
James Beekman,
Gabriel H. Ludlow,
Edward Laight,
George W. Ludlow,
Leonard Lispenard,
Robert C. Livingston,
John Moore,
William Nielson,
Daniel Phenix,
Hamil. Young,
Samuel Bayard,
John Reade,
Henry Remsen,
Isaac Roosevelt,
Samp. Simson,
William Stepple,
John Thurman,
Hugh Wallace,
Gerrard Walton.

Fined for appearing after six o'clock:

Elias Desbrosses,
William Seton,
Walter Buchanan,
Robert R. Waddell,
John H. Cruger.

Fined for non-appearance:

Henry White,
John Alsop,
Robert Alexander,
John Amiel,
Gerrard W. Beekman,
Joseph Bull,
Benja. Booth,
Thomas Buchanan,
Levinus Clarkson,
Gerrard Duyckink,
George Folliot,
Nicholas Gouverneur,
William McAdam,
Charles McEvers,
Thomas Marston,
Thomas W. Moore,
Thomas Miller,
Alexand. McDonald,
Jeremiah Platt,
Richard Yates,
Thomas Randal,
Garret Rapelje,
John Ramsay,
Miles Sherbrooke,

Peter Hasencliver,
Jacob Watson,
James Jauncey,
William Imlay,
Samuel Kemble,
Philip Livingston,
Robert G. Livingston,
Robert Murray,
Richard Sharpe,
Samuel Verplank,
Jacobus Vanzandt,
Augus. Vanhorne,
Jacob Walton,
Thomas White,
Robert Watts,
Alexand. Wallace,
John Weatherhead.

Ordered—That Messrs. Jacob Walton, George Folliot, Sam. Verplank, Miles Sherbrooke, Thomas Randal, John Alsop, and Thomas White, be a Committee until the first Tuesday in September next, to hear and determine disputes between Parties who shall agree to leave such to this Corporation.

CHAMBER OF COMMERCE.—TUESDAY, 3d September, 1771.

PRESENT.

Hon'ble Henry White, Esqr., } V. P.
Theoph. Bache, } V. P.
William Walton, Tres'r.
Anth. Van Dam, S.

Samuel Bayard,
Walter Franklin,
Harman Gouverneur,
Nicholas Hoffman,
Samuel Hake,
James Jauncey,
John Cruger,
Edward Laight,
George W. Ludlow,
Leonard Lispenard,
Robert G. Livingston,
Alexand. McDonald,
Isaac Corsa,
Lewis Pintard,
Daniel Phenix,
John Reade,
John Ramsay,
Isaac Sears,
Sampson Simpson.

Fined for appearing after six o'clock :

Henry White,
Miles Sherbrooke,
John Amiel,
John Thurman,
Hamil. Young,
John Moore,
Richard Yates.

Fined for non-appearance:

Elias Desbrosses,
Gerrard Beekman,
Joseph Bull,
Henry C. Bogert,
James Beekman,
Walter Buchanan,
John Alsop,
Lawrence Kortright,
Peter Keteltas,
Samuel Kemble,
Philip Livingston,
Gabriel H. Ludlow,
Robert Alexander,
Jerem. Platt,
Thomas Randal,
Henry Remsen,
Isaac Roosevelt,
Garret Rapelje,
Benjam. Booth,
Thomas Buchanan,
John H. Cruger,
Levinus Clarkson,
Gerrard Duyckink,
George Folliot,
Walter Franklin,
Nicholas Gouverneur,
Harman Gouverneur,
Peter Hasencliver,
William Imlay,
Alexan. Wallace,
Abram. Lynsen,
Robert C. Livingston,
Robt. G. Livingston, (Albany)
Robert Murray,
William McAdam,
Charles McEvers,
Thomas Marston,
Thomas W. Moore,
Thomas Miller,
William Nielson,
John Weatherhead,
William Seton,
Richard Sharpe,
William Stepple,
Samuel Verplank,
Jacobus Vanzandt,
Augus. Van Horne,
Hugh Wallace,
Jacob Walton,
Thomas White,
Gerrard Walton,
Jacob Watson.

The Committee for considering the Tonnage and recommending a general Plan, having presented a Calculation according to Order, which being read was considered of, and agreed to refer it to a future Meeting.

Ordered—That Messrs. Walter Franklin, Robert R. Waddell, P. Livingston, William McAdam, Robert Watts, John H. Cruger, and Gerrard Walton, be a Committee untill the first Tuesday in October next, to hear and determine disputes between parties who shall agree to leave such to this Corporation.

CHAMBER OF COMMERCE.—TUESDAY, 1st October, 1771.

PRESENT.

Elias Desbrosses, P.
Theop. Bache, V. P.
William Walton, T.
Antho. Van Dam, S.

Robert Alexander,
Joseph Bull,
James Beekman,
Samuel Bayard,
Thomas Buchanan,
Thomas W. Moore,
John Reade,
Garret Rapelje,
John Ramsay,
Jacob Watson,
John Cruger,
Nicho. Hoffman,
James Jauncey,
Isaac Low,
Edward Laight,
Lewis Pintard,
William Stepple,
John Thurman,
Jacobus Van Zandt,
Hamilton Young,
Leonard Lispenard,
Robert C. Livingston,
Robert G. Livingston,
John Moore,
Thomas Marston,
Daniel Phenix,
Gerrard Walton,
Alexan. Wallace,
Thomas Walton.

Fined for non-appearance:

Henry White,
John Alsop,
John Amiel,
Gerrard W. Beekman,
Henry C. Bogert,
Walter Buchanan,
Benjam. Booth,
John H. Cruger,
Levinus Clarkson,
Isaac Corsa,
Gerrard Duyckinck,
George Folliot,
Walter Franklin,
Nicholas Gouverneur,
Harman Gouverneur,
Peter Hassencliver,
Samuel Hake,
William Imlay,
George W. Ludlow,
Robert Murray,
William McAdam,
Charles McEvers,
Thomas Miller,
Alexan. McDonald,
William Nielson,
Jeremiah Platt,
Thomas Randal,
Henry Remsen,
Isaac Roosevelt,
Miles Sherbrooke,
Isaac Sears,
William Seton,
Sampson Simson,
Richard Sharpe,
Samuel Verplank,
August. Van Horne,

Lawrence Kortright,	Hugh Wallace,
Peter Kettletas,	Jacob Walton,
Samuel Kemble,	Thomas White,
Philip Livingston,	Robert R. Waddell,
Gabriel H. Ludlow,	Robert Watts,
Abraham Lynsen,	John Weatherhead,

Richard Yates.

The Report of the Committee respecting Tonnage, which was read at last Meeting, was again read and debated upon.

Ordered—That the same Report be recommitted to the same Committee, and that they do report thereon at the next Meeting of this Corporation, and that Mr. Robert C. Livingston be added to the Committee.

Ordered—That Messrs. Lawrence Kortright, Isaac Low, Jacobus Van Zandt, Charles McEvers, John Moore, Richard Yates and Thomas Marston, be a Committee until the first Tuesday in November next, to hear and determine Disputes between Parties, who shall agree to leave such to this Corporation.

CHAMBER OF COMMERCE.—Tuesday, 5th Nov., 1771.

Present.

Elias Desbrosses, P.
Theop. Bache, V. P.
Antho. Van Dam, S.

John Alsop,	Robert C. Livingston,
Robert Alexander,	Robert G. Livingston,
John Amiel,	William McAdam,
Gerrard W. Beekman,	Charles McEvers,
Joseph Bull,	John Moore,
James Beekman,	Thomas Marston,
Samuel Bayard,	Jacob Watson,
Walter Buchanan,	Thomas W. Moore,
Thomas Buchanan,	Lewis Pintard,
John Cruger,	Jeremiah Platt,

John H. Cruger,
Isaac Corsa,
Walter Franklin,
Thomas Walton,
James Jauncey,
William Imlay,
Isaac Low,
Gabriel H. Ludlow,
Edward Laight,
George W. Ludlow,
Leonard Lispenard,
Daniel Phenix,
John Reade,
Henry Remsen, Jun'r,
Garret Rapelje,
John Ramsay,
William Stepple,
Jacobus Van Zandt,
Jacob Walton,
Gerrard Walton,
Alexand. Wallace,

Alexan. McDonald, Augustus Van Horne, } after six o'clock.

Fined for non-appearance:

Henry White,
William Walton,
Henry C. Bogert,
Benjam. Booth,
Levinus Clarkson,
Gerrard Duyckinck,
George Folliot,
Nicholas Gouverneur,
Harman Gouverneur,
Peter Hassencliver,
Nicholas Hoffman,
Samuel Hake,
Lawrence Kortright,
Peter Ketletas,
Samuel Kemble,
Philip Livingston,
Abraham Lynsen,
Robert Murray,
Thomas Miller,
William Neilson,
Thomas Randal,
Isaac Roosevelt,
Miles Sherbrooke,
Isaac Sears,
William Seton,
Sampson Simson,
Richard Sharpe,
Acheson Thompson,
John Thurman,
Samuel Verplank,
Hugh Wallace,
Thomas White,
Robert Watts,
John Wetherhead,
Richard Yates,
Hamilton Young.

The Report of the Committee respecting the Tonnage[85] proposed to be adopted, having been recommitted to the same Committee to report thereon after making some alterations in the words following:

WE, THE SUBSCRIBERS, being a Committee appointed by this Corporation to take into consideration the present uncertain State of the Tonnage of this Port, and to make report of such regulations as we should deem necessary for the better ascertaining the same, are of opinion that those following, if adopted, may be of publick utility, viz.:

1st. That twenty-two hundred gross weight be deemed a Ton of Flour, Tallow, Hams, Butter, Hog's Lard, Beef in Keggs, Pott Ash, dry'd Cod in hogsheads, Candles, Soap, Chocolate, Sugar, Honey, Beeswax, Rice, Coffee, Cocoa, Tobacco, and Starch.

2d. That twelve hundred weight be a Ton of Bread in bulk, and eleven hundred weight if in bags.

3d. That eight Barrels be a Ton of Beef, Pork, wet Fish, Pitch Tar, and Turpentine.

4th. That forty Bushels, Winchester[86] measure, be a Ton of Wheat, Indian Corn, and other Grain, and that thirty-two bushels Water measure be a Ton of Salt, and thirty-six bushels ——— measure be a Ton of Coals in bulk.

5th. That eleven hundred gross weight be a Ton of Bread in Casks of all denominations.

6th. That two hundred and fifty-two gallons, reckoning the full contents of the Casks, be a Ton of Oil, Wine, Rum, Molasses, and Beer.

7th. That twenty hundred weight be a Ton of Bar and Pig Iron, Logwood, Fustick, &c., as also of dry'd Cod Fish in Bulk.

8th. That thirty-two Bushels, Winchester measure, be a Ton of Flaxseed, Pease, Indian Corn, and other Grain in Casks.

9th. That Forty cubick feet be a Ton of Mahogany, square Timber, Oak Plank, Pine Boards; as also of Beaver Furs and Peltry[87] in Bales and hhds., and of Bale Goods of all kinds.

10th. That considering the great irregularity of Staves usually brought to this Market, and of consequence how impracticable it would be to fix upon a standard for ascertaining their Tonnage, we are of opinion that the Freight of all Staves, Headings, and Hoops, should be rated by the thousand, to be regulated according to the quality.

11th. We are also of opinion, for the same reason, that the Freight of Cotton, Sarsparilla, and dry'd Hides, be rated by the pound.

All which is humbly submitted to the Corporation of the Chamber of Commerce, by their most obedient servants,

HAMILTON YOUNG, MILES SHERBROOKE,
RICHARD YATES, JOHN MOORE,
JACOBUS VANZANDT.

New York, 3d September, 1771.

Voted and carried in the affirmative—That this Corporation will determine thereon at this Meeting.

Voted by a great majority—That the proposed plan shall be carried into execution.

Dissented—John Cruger, Esq.

Voted and Ordered—That the Members of this Corporation do, from and after the first day of May, one thousand seven hundred and seventy-two, when they agree to Lett or Hire any Vessel or Vessels, and do it by the Ton, that the Goods of the several denominations, as reported by the Committee, shall be adopted a Ton invariably. This Resolution, however, shall not debar or restrain any or either of the Members from making a bargain for the whole Vessel by the Run, by the Month, or by Barrel, Piece, or Bushel.

Mr. McAdam's Proposal, viz. :—Soon after the establishment of this Society, I proposed to your consideration whether it was for the Interest of the Community that Jersey paper money should pass in this Province higher than it is taken for in the Treasury of the Province of New Jersey.

The Loss and inconvenience arising to the Traders in this City from the present practice of passing Jersey money for more than its acknowledged value by their own Legislature, will, I hope, plead my excuse for renewing my proposal that this Corporation may enter into an agreement to fix a time when they will no longer depreciate their own Currency by accepting that of another above par. I therefore propose, that a time[88] may be fixed that this Corporation do agree to pay and receive Jersey money at the same rate it is received and paid in their own Treasury. WILLIAM MCADAM.

November 5, 1771.

Lewis Johnston[u] against *William Bayard.*[v] } In an action of debt for £450 Currency, being on a supposition that he had paid Mr. Bayard for a Bill of Exchange, value £300 sterling, which Mr. Johnston never received.

What gave rise for this action is this, viz. :—

Mr. Johnston, at sundry times, bought Bills of *Mr. Bayard* to the amount of £6,021, 3s 6d Sterling. Some time in the year 1768 or 69, the said *Mr. Johnston*, in order to frame an Account and transmit it to his Friends in England, sent to *Mr. Bayard* a list of Bills, which he had bought of him, and desired that he would let him know the Exchange he had given for them, as he had not kept any account thereof. *Mr. Bayard*, in order to do that, had recourse to his Bill Book and furnished him with the Account, at the same time, informed him that he had remitted a Bill entered in his Book of £300 Sterling, sold in September, 1757, dated 9th March, 1757. *Mr. Johnston* charges this Bill with the rest, to the Proprietors, but on examining the account find that no such Bill was ever sent them. *Mr. Johnston*, therefore, draws this conclusion, that he must have paid *Mr. Bayard* for this Bill, and therefore demands the money without producing any receipt or proof of his having paid it. *Mr. Bayard* says that he has received payment from some one, and makes no demand of payment. It appears that from the Papers exhibited to us by *Mr. David Johnston* and *Mr. Bayard*, and that the Society of Proprietors,[89] of Jersey, were determined to send Mr. Morris[w] home on their business, and voted the sum of £400 sterling should be awarded him toward defraying his Expences. Mr. Parker called upon *Mr. Bayard* and took up the Bills, viz. : 1 set of £300, dated the 9th of March, 1757, drawn by Apthorp & Son on the Contractors, and another set of £100 sterling drawn by Capt. Gordon, which were entered in the two several Bill Books to *Mr. Johnston* as sold to him, being one of the Proprietors. It also appears, from two Receipts, that *Mr. Bayard* did receive the Sum of £573 17s 7d Currency from Andrew Johnston, Esq., by the hands of James Parker in part of these very Bills. *Mr. Lewis Johnston*, therefore, could not have paid for them, and the presumption is still greater when you consider that the Treasurer of the Society[90] only kept an account of them, for *Mr. Lewis Johnston* had not any knowledge of the matter from the 10th September, 1757, until the year 1768–9; and surely, if he had advanced *Mr. Bayard* £540 currency for Bills which he had not received, he would not have left so considerable a sum in his hands so long. It appears, further, that *Mr. Lewis Johnston* did purchase of *Mr. Bayard*, in the year 1760, Bills to the amount of £500 sterling, and made full payment at several times without making any demand for the sum in contest.

New York, 29th November. We, therefore, the Arbitrators, chosen to give an Award, do say, that *Lewis Johnston* hath no demand upon *Mr. Bayard;* but that he pay all costs of suit.

John Alsop,
Anthy. Van Dam,
Theop. Bache.

CHAMBER OF COMMERCE.—TUESDAY, 3d December, 1771.

PRESENT.

Henry White, V. P.
William Walton, T.
Anthony Van Dam, S.

John Alsop,
Joseph Bull,
James Beekman,
Thomas Buchanan,
John Cruger,
John H. Cruger,
Isaac Corsa,
Walter Franklin,
Nicholas Hoffman,
Samuel Hake,
Jacob Watson,
James Jauncey,
Lawrence Kortright,
Isaac Low,
Robert C. Livingston,
Robert G. Livingston,
William McAdam,
Thomas Marston,
John Moore,
Lewis Pintard,
Daniel Phenix,
Henry Remsen, jr.,
Garret Rapelje,
Isaac Sears,
William Stepple,
Jacobus Van Zandt,
Jacob Walton,
Robert R. Waddell,
Robert Watts,
Gerrard Walton,
Thomas Walton.

Fined for appearing after six o'clock :

Samuel Bayard,
Charles McEvers,
John Thurman.

Fined for non-appearance :

Elias Desbrosses,
Theoph. Bache,
Robert Alexander,
John Amiel,
Gerrard Beekman,
Henry C. Bogert,
Walter Buchanan,
Benj. Booth,
Levinus Clarkson,
Gerrard Duyckink,
Peter Ketletas,
John Ramsay,
Miles Sherbrooke,
William Seton,
Samps. Simson,
Richard Sharpe,
Acheson Thompson,
Samuel Ver Plank,
Augus. Vanhorne,
George Folliot,
Nicholas Gouverneur,
Harman Gouverneur,

Samuel Kemble,	Peter Hasencliver,
Philip Livingston,	William Imlay,
Gabriel H. Ludlow,	Thomas Miller,
Edward Laight,	Alexan. McDonald,
Abram Lynsen,	William Neilson,
George W. Ludlow.	Jeremiah Platt,
Leonard Lispenard,	Thomas Randal,
Robert Murray,	Hugh Wallace,
Thomas W. Moore,	Thomas White,
John Reade,	Alexan. Wallace,
Isaac Roosevelt,	John Weatherhead,

Richard Yates.

This Corporation, at their last Meeting, determined on the mode of Tonnage to be adopted from and after the first Day of May next.

Anthony Van Dam proposed that the Report of the Committee for ascertaining the Tonnage and the order and Resolution of this Corporation, be published[91] in the News Papers once a Month until June next.

Mr. McAdam's Motion for altering the mode of passing Jersey Money by the Members of this Chamber, being debated, is postponed until the first Tuesday in February next.

Ordered—That Messrs. Sampson Simson, Peter Ketletas, G. W. Beekman, Jacob Watson, John Reade, Robert Alexander, and Thomas W. Moore, be a Committee until the first Tuesday in January next, to hear and determine disputes between Parties, who shall agree to leave such, &c.

CHAMBER OF COMMERCE.—Tuesday, 7th January, 1772.

Present.

Theoph. Bache, V. P.
William Walton, T.
Anthony Van Dam, S.

Henry C. Bogert,
Joseph Bull,
James Beekman,
Samuel Bayard,
Benjam. Booth,
John Cruger,
Levinus Clarkson,
Walter Franklin,
Samuel Hake,
James Jauncey,
Edward Laight,
George W. Ludlow,
Leonard Lispenard,
Robert C. Livingston,
Thomas Marston,
Alexand. McDonald,
John Reade,
Henry Remsen,
Miles Sherbrooke,
Isaac Sears,
John Thurman,
Jacobus Van Zandt,
Thomas Walton,
Hamilton Young,

Fined for non-appearance:

Elias Desbrosses,
Henry White,
John Amiel,
Gerrard W. Beekman,
Walter Buchanan,
Thomas Buchanan,
John H. Cruger,
Isaac Corsa,
Gerrard Duyckink,
George Folliot,
Nicholas Gouverneur,
Harman Gouverneur,
Peter Hassencliver,
Nicholas Hoffman,
William Imlay,
Lawrence Kortright,
Peter Ketletas,
Samuel Kemble,
John Alsop,
Isaac Low,
Philip Livingston,
Gabriel H. Ludlow,
Abram Lynsen,
Robert Murray,
William McAdam,
Charles McEvers,
John Moore,
Thomas Miller,
William Neilson,
Lewis Pintard,
Jeremiah Platt,
Daniel Phenix,
Thomas Randal,
Henry Remsen,
Isaac Roosevelt,
Garret Rapelje,
Robert Alexander,
John Ramsay,
William Seton,
Sampson Simson,
Richard Sharpe,
William Stepple,
Acheson Thompson,
Samuel Verplank,
August Van Horne,
Hugh Wallace,
Jacob Walton,
Thomas White,
Robert R. Waddell,
Robert Watts,
Gerrard Walton,
Alexan. Wallace,
John Weatherhead,
Jacob Watson,
Richard Yates.

Anthony Van Dam's Proposal for publishing the Report of the Committee for ascertaining the Tonnage of this Port:

Ordered—That the same be published in the three[92] several News Papers of this City until June next.

Walter Franklin proposes that as Flour is one of our Staple Articles, it is needful it should be brought to Market and Exported with the least Expence possible: therefore moves that the Chamber agree not to pay anything for the weighing of Flour after the first of March next.

Ordered—That Messrs. R. Sharpe, H. Remsen, J. Roosevelt, Nich's Hoffman, H. Young, T. Walton, and J. Thurman, be a Committee until the first Tuesday in February next, to hear and determine disputes between Parties, who shall agree to leave such to this Corporation.

CHAMBER OF COMMERCE.—TUESDAY, 4th February, 1772.

PRESENT.

Henry White, V. P.
William Walton, T.
Anthony Vandam, S.

Robert Alexander,
John Amiel,
Joseph Bull,
Samuel Bayard,
Thomas Buchanan,
Walker Franklin,
Harman Governeur,
Samuel Hake,
James Jauncey,
Alexander Wallace,
Isaac Low,
George W. Ludlow,
Leonard Lispenard,
Robert C. Livingston,
John Moore,
Thomas Marston,
Thomas Miller,
Alexander McDonald,
William Neilson,
Hamilton Young,
Daniel Phenix,
Henry Remsen, jun.,
Isaac Roosevelt,
Garret Rapelje,
Jacobus Van Zandt,
Augusts. Van Horne,
Robert R. Waddell,
Robert Watts,
Gerrard Walton.

Fined for appearing after six o'clock:

Lawrence Kortright,
Lewis Pintard,
Hugh Wallace.

Fined for non-appearance:

Elias Desbrosses,
Theophy. Bache,
John Alsop,
Gerrard W. Beekman,
Henry C. Bogert,
James Beekman,
Walter Buchanan,
Benj. Booth,
John Cruger,
John H. Cruger,
Peter Hasencliver,
Nicholas Hoffman,
William Imlay,
Peter Keteltas,
Samuel Kemble,
Philip Livingston,
Gabriel Ludlow,
Edward Laight,
Abram Lynsen,
Robert G. Livingston,
John Reade,
John Ramsay,
Miles Sherbrooke,
Isaac Sears,
William Seton,
Samson Simpson,
Richard Sharpe,
William Stepple,
John Thurman,
Samuel Verplanck,
Levinus Clarkson,
Isaac Corsa,
Gerrard Duyckinck,
George Folliott,
Nicholas Gouverneur,
Robert Murray,
William McAdam,
Charles McEvers,
Jeremiah Platt,
Thomas Randal,
Richard Yates,
Jacob Walton,
Thomas White,
John Weatherhead,
Jacob Watson.

Mr. McAdam's and Mr. Franklin's Proposals are postponed till next Meeting.

Ordered—That Messrs. J. Wetherhead, G. Rapelje, G. Duyckinck, W. Stepple, W. Imlay, A. Van Horne, and H. C. Bogart, be a Committee, until the first Tuesday in March next, to hear and determine disputes between Parties who shall agree to leave such to this Corporation.

CHAMBER OF COMMERCE.—TUESDAY, 3d March, 1772.

PRESENT.

Elias Desbrosses, P.
Theop. Bache, V. P.
William Walton, T.
Antho. Van Dam, S.

John Alsop,
Robert Alexander,
James Beekman,
Samuel Bayard,
George W. Ludlow,
Leonard Lispenard,
Robert C. Livingston,
William McAdam,
Daniel Phenix,
Isaac Roosevelt,
Miles Sherbrooke,
William Stepple,
Benja. Booth,
Levinus Clarkson,
Nicholas Hoffman,
Samuel Hake,
Lawrence Kortright,
Edward Laight,
John Moore,
Thomas Marston,
Thomas Miller,
Alexan'r McDonald,
William Neilson,
Jeremiah Platt,
John Thurman,
Jacobus Van Zandt,
August Van Horn,
Hugh Wallace,
Alexand. Wallace,
Jacob Watson.

Fined for appearing after six o'clock:

Henry Remsen, junr.,
Robert Watts.

Fined for non-appearance:

Henry White,
John Amiel,
Gerrard W. Beekman,
Henry C. Bogart,
Joseph Bull,
Walter Buchanan,
Thomas Buchanan,
John Cruger,
John H. Cruger,
Isaac Corsa,
Gerrard Duyckink,
George Folliot,
Walter Franklin,
Abram Lynsen,
Robert G. Livingston,
Robert Murray,
Charles McEvers,
Thomas W. Moore,
Lewis Pintard,
Thomas Randal,
Hamilton Young,
John Reade,
Garret Rapelje,
John Ramsay,
Isaac Sears,
William Seton,

Nicholas Gouverneur,	Sampson Simpson,
Harman Gouverneur,	Richard Sharpe,
Peter Hassencliver,	Samuel Ver Plank,
James Jauncey,	Jacob Walton,
William Imlay,	Thomas White,
Peter Keteltas,	Robert R. Waddle,
Samuel Kemble,	Gerrard Walton,
Isaac Low,	Thomas Walton,
Philip Livingston,	John Wetherhead,
Gabriel H. Ludlow,	Richard Yates.

Mr. Walter Franklin's Motion of the 7th January last, having been duly considered at the last and present Meetings of this Corporation, to whom it was referred; and it appearing very evident that the Staple or Export of this Province ought to be shipped with as little charge as that of any Sister Colony. And the Merchants of this City have in most instances paid the Venders of Flour, &c., at the rate of one penny half-penny for half weighing, which is thought to be an unreasonable charge.

Resolved, unanimously—That from and after the first day of May next ensuing, the Members of this Corporation, when they purchase Flour, shall not pay one penny half penny per Barrel for half weighing as is at present charged in some of the Weigh Notes by Sellers of Flour.

Mr. William McAdam's motion of the 5th November last being read in the words following:

Soon after the establishment of this Society, I proposed to your consideration whether it was for the interest of the Community that Jersey paper Money should pass in this Province higher than it is taken for in the Treasury of the Province of New Jersey. The loss and inconvenience arising to the Traders in this City, from the present practice of passing Jersey Money for more than its acknowledged value by their own Legislature, will, I hope, plead my excuse for renewing my proposal; that this Corporation may enter into an agreement to fix a time when they will no longer depreciate their own Currency by accepting that of another above par.

I therefore propose that a time be fixed that this Corporation do agree to pay and receive Jersey money at the same Rate it is received and paid in their own Treasury.

November 5th, 1771. WILLIAM MCADAM.

And the same having been referred to their consideration, at the succeeding stated Meeting in December following, when it was adjourned for further deliberation to the first Tuesday in February, then again deferred to this day, Whereupon it was moved whether this Corporation would go upon the subject, and debates arising thereon it was put to the vote and passed in the affirmative, 19 for—16 against.

The question was then put that when the Members of this Corporation shall pay or receive any Jersey money they shall accept it on the same terms that it passes for in the Jersey Treasury, that is to say—

A Bill of	£6	Proclamation money	for	16	Dollars,	or	£6	8s	New York	Cur'y.	
A Bill of	3	"	"	" 8	"	or	3	4	"	"	"
A Bill of	1 10s	"	"	" 4	"	or	1	12	"	"	"
A Bill of	15s	"	"	" 2	"	or		16 shillings.			

And in like proportion for Bills of a less denomination, which was also carried in the affirmative, 19 for—15 against.

Then a debate arose when it should take place, and it was argued that as many people might be possessed of some of that currency, who live in the remote parts of this Province, who had taken it at its common current Value, and that it would be right to give them an opportunity of parting with it without Loss, who might perhaps very ill afford to suffer by means of this agreement, and on a division whether it should be carried into execution in 6 or 9 months—

Votes appeared for six months 19, and for nine months 15.

Thereupon Ordered—That the Members of this Corporation, from and after the third day of September next ensuing, shall, in all their dealings and Commercial Concerns, when they receive or pay Jersey money, accept and pay the same agreeable to the above Resolution.

Furthermore Ordered—That a copy of the foregoing Resolutions be delivered to the Printers of the GAZETTE and JOURNAL, and that the same be published[93] therein that all the Members may be apprised thereof.

Mr. John Schuyler having been proposed to be admitted a Member of this Corporation was balloted for and elected. Ordered—That Mr. Schuyler be informed in writing, that he was duly elected a Member of this Corporation.

Ordered—That Messrs. G. W. Ludlow, J. Bull, L. Lispenard, James Beekman, A. McDonald, S. Bayard, and R. C. Livingston, be a Committee until the first Tuesday in April next.

CHAMBER OF COMMERCE.—TUESDAY, 7th April, 1772.

PRESENT.

Elias Desbrosses, P.
Theoph. Bache, V. P.
William Walton, T.
Antho. Van Dam, S.

Henry C. Bogert,	Thomas Marston,
Joseph Bull,	Lewis Pintard,
James Beekman,	Daniel Phenix,
John Cruger,	Miles Sherbrooke,
Isaac Corsa,	William Stepple,
James Jauncey,	Jacobus Van Zandt,
Gabriel H. Ludlow,	Jacob Watson,
Edward Laight,	Hamil. Young.

Fined for appearing after six o'clock:

Theophy Bache,
William Walton,
Samuel Bayard,
John H. Cruger,
Walter Franklin,
Isaac Low,
William McAdam,
John Moore,
Thomas McDonald,
William Neilson,
John Reade,
Isaac Sears,
John Thurman,
Jacob Walton,
Gerrard Walton,
Alexan. Wallace.

Fined for non-appearance:

Henry White,
John Alsop,
Robert Alexander,
John Amiel,
Gerrard W. Beekman,
Walter Buchanan,
Benjamin Booth,
Thomas Buchanan,
Levinus Clarkson,
Gerrard Duyckinck,
George Folliot,
Nicholas Gouverneur,
Harman Gouverneur,
William Imlay,
Lawrence Kortright,
Peter Keteltas,
Samuel Kemble,
Philip Livingston,
Abram Lynsen,
George W. Ludlow,
Leonard Lispenard,
Robert C. Livingston,
Robert G. Livingston,
Robert Murray,
Charles McEvers,
Thomas W. Moore,
Thomas Miller,
Jeremiah Platt,
Thomas Randal,
Henry Remsen,
Isaac Roosevelt,
Garret Rapelje,
John Ramsay,
William Seton,
Sampson Simson,
Richard Sharpe,
Acheson Thompson,
Samuel Verplanck,
August's Van Horne,
Hugh Wallace,
Thomas White,
Robert R. Waddell,
Robert Watts,
Thomas Walton,
John Weatherhead,
Richard Yates.

Thomas Pettit, Doorkeeper and Messenger, acquainted this Corporation that he had paid for glazing the Windows, which with his Salary to the first Tuesday in May next, amount to £15 16 6, he prays to be paid for.

Mr. William McAdam proposes that this Corporation dine together on the second Tuesday in May next, and that at the Meeting the first Tuesday in that Month, three Stewards be named to provide a Dinner and that each Member that may be absent at Dinner to pay eight Shillings.

Ordered—That Mr. Petit put the Room in proper Order.

Ordered—That Messrs. H. Gouverneur, I. Corsa, J. Platt, D. Phenix, Walter Buchanan, B. Booth, and John Amiel, be a Committee until the First Tuesday in May next, to hear and determine disputes between Parties.

CHAMBER OF COMMERCE.—TUESDAY, 5th May, 1772.

PRESENT.

Elias Desbrosses, P.
Theop. Bache, } V. P.
William Walton, } V. P.
Antho. Van Dam, S.

John Amiel,
Joseph Bull,
James Beekman,
Samuel Bayard,
John Cruger,
Isaac Corsa,
Walter Franklin,
Samuel Hake,
Peter Ketletas,
Edward Laight,
Leonard Lispenard,
Robert C. Livingston,
John Moore,
Lewis Pintard,
Daniel Phenix,
John Reade,
Henry Remsen, Jun'r,
Isaac Roosevelt,
John Schuyler,
Henry White,
Jacob Walton,
Gerrard Walton,
Alexander Wallace,
Robert R. Waddle,
Hamilton Young.

Fined for appearing after six o'clock:

Theoph. Bache,
Henry C. Bogert,
Isaac Low,
Alexan. McDonald,
William Stepple,
Thomas White,
John Thurman,
Augus. Van Horne,

William Neilson,
Jeremiah Platt,
Thomas Randal,
Thomas Walton,
Hugh Wallace,
Richard Yates.

Fined for non-appearance:

John Alsop,
Robert Alexander,
Gerrard W. Beekman,
Thomas Buchanan,
Walter Buchanan,
Benjamin Booth,
John H. Cruger,
Levinus Clarkson,
Gerardus Duyckinck,
George Folliot,
Nicholas Gouverneur,
Harman Gouverneur,
Nicholas Hoffman,
John Weatherhead,
James Jauncey,
William Imlay,
Lawrence Kortright,
Samuel Kemble,
Philip Livingston,
Gabriel H. Ludlow,
George W. Ludlow,
Abram Lynsen,
Robert G. Livingston,
Robert Murray,
William McAdam,
Charles McEvers,
Thomas Marston,
Jacob Watson,
Thomas W. Moore,
Thomas Miller,
Garret Rapelje,
John Ramsay,
Miles Sherbrooke,
Isaac Sears,
William Seton,
Sampson Simson,
Richard Sharpe,
Acheson Thompson,
Samuel Verplank,
Jacobus Van Zandt,
Robert Watts.

Thomas Petitt's account amounting to £15 16 6 having been laid before this Corporation at last Meeting,

Ordered—That the Treasurer do pay the same.

The Ceiling of the Chamber being much damaged from the leak in the Cupolo,[94] proposed that it be repaired, and that Messrs. Robert C. Livingston, Thomas Randall, and L. Pintard be a Committee to employ proper workmen to put it in order.

Proposed—That seven Guineas be paid to Capt. Isaac L. Winn[x] in addition to the ten Guineas already paid Mr. Bache, late Treasurer, for a Seal[95] of this Corporation.

Ordered—That Messrs. Peter Keteltas, Robert R. Waddell, and Joseph Bull, or any two of them, be a Committee to audit the Treasurer's Accounts till this day.

Mr. William Walton proposed that Mr. Patrick McDavitt be ballotted as a Member of this Corporation at the next Meeting of the Chamber.

In consequence of Mr. McAdam's proposal of last Meeting for this Corporation to dine together, Messrs. William McAdam, John Moore, and John Reade, are appointed Stewards, who are ordered to provide a suitable Dinner for the Corporation,[96] and wait upon his Excellency GOVERNOR TRYON to know when he will do this Corporation the honour to dine with them, that they send written Notices to and invite the Governor and his Secretary, Lieut. Governor Colden and his Sectry., the Sectry. of the Province, General Gage and his Suit, the Members of his Majesty's Council, the Members of the Assembly that are in Town, the Field Officers doing Duty in this City, the Captain of his Majesty's Ship, the Principal Officers of his Majesty's Customs, and the Mayor of this City, and it being debated whether absent Members should pay Eight Shillings or more was put to the Vote and carried, 20 for paying Eight Shillings, 19 against.

Mr. John Moore's proposal, viz.:

As the Quarterage, paid by the Members of this Corporation, is by many thought heavy, I propose that it may be abolished—

And further—I propose that the money now in the hands of Treasurer, or that may hereafter be in his hands, shall be put out at Interest, upon good security, for the benefit of this Corporation:—I also propose—that the

President for the time being have charge of the Seal of this Corporation.

The Charter of this Corporation, as well as the Rules of the Chamber, appoint this day for the Election of Officers for the Current year, when the following Gentlemen were balloted for and duly Elected, and sworn to perform the trust reposed in them, viz.:

Hon. HENRY WHITE, Esq., President.
THEOP. BACHE, WILLIAM WALTON, } Vice-Presidents.
ISAAC LOW, Treasurer.
ANTHONY VAN DAM, Secretary.

Ordered—That Messrs. Samuel Hake, John Schuyler, Robert G. Livingston, John Cruger, Hugh Wallace, James Jauncey, and J. Walton, be a Committee, until the first Tuesday in June next, to hear and determine Disputes between Parties who shall agree to leave such to this Corporation.

CHAMBER OF COMMERCE.—TUESDAY, 2d June, 1772.

PRESENT.

The Hon'ble Henry White, P.
Theop. Bache, V. P.
Isaac Low, T.
Antho. Van Dam, S.

Joseph Bull,
John Cruger,
Isaac Corsa,
Elias Desbrosses,
Nicholas Hoffman,
Gabriel H. Ludlow,
George W. Ludlow,
Edward Laight,
Leonard Lispenard,
Robert C. Livingston,
Lewis Pintard,
John Reade,
Henry Remsen,
Isaac Roosevelt,
Richard Sharpe,
James Jauncey,
Peter Keteltas,
Alexa. Wallace,
Thomas Marston,
William Neilson,
Hamilton Young,
John Thurman,
Jacobus Van Zandt.

Fined for appearing after six o'clock:

Thomas Buchanan,
James Beekman,
Robert G. Livingston,
William McAdam,
Charles McEvers,
Robert R. Waddell.

Fined for non-appearance:

John Alsop,
Robert Alexander,
Gerrard W. Beekman,
Henry C. Bogart,
Samuel Bayard,
Walter Buchanan,
Benjam Booth,
John H. Cruger,
Levinus Clarkson,
Gerardus Duyckink,
George Folliot,
Walter Franklin,
Nicholas Gouverneur,
Harman Gouverneur,
Samuel Hake,
Thomas White,
Jacob Watson,
William Imlay,
Lawrence Kortright,
Samucl Kemble,
Philip Livingston,
Abram Lynsen,
Robert Murray,
John Moore,
Thomas W. Moore,
Thomas Miller,
Alexan. McDonald,
Jeremiah Platt,
Daniel Phenix,
Thomas Randal,
Garret Rapelje,
John Ramsay,
Robert Watts,
Richard Yates,
Miles Sherbrooke,
Isaac Sears,
William Seton,
Sampson Simpson,
Richard Sharpe,
William Stepple,
John Schuyler,
Acheson Thompson,
Samuel Verplank,
August. Van Horne,
William Walton,
Jacob Walton,
Thomas Walton,
Gerrard Walton,
Hugh Wallace,
John Weatherhead.

Ordered—That Messrs. Thomas Randall, Lewis Pintard, and Rob. C. Livingston, be a Committee to employ proper persons to repair the Cupola, &c., of the Chamber, and that the Treasurer advance the sum, not exceeding fifty pounds, towards the same.

Ordered—That seven Guineas be paid to Captain Winn by the Treasurer, being the sum advanced by him for the Seal of this Corporation.

Messrs. P. Keteltas, R. R. Waddell, and Joseph Bull, the Committee, reported that they had audited Mr. Walton's account, and that there remained £215 15s 9d in his hands, and the Arrears for that year is £59 2s.

Mr. Moore's Proposal for abolishing the Quarterage heretofore paid, was carried by a great Majority.

Ordered—That the Money in the hands of the Treasurer be put out at Interest on such Security as the President, Vice-Presidents and Treasurer shall approve of.

Ordered—That the President for the time being Keep the Seal of this Corporation in his possession.

Whereas the Reduction of Jersey Money to its real Value was thought necessary by this Chamber and carried into a Resolution to receive and pay a Jersey £3 Bill for £3 4s and no more. It is conceived this Regulation will be grievous to some Individuals, and as this Chamber [*is*] moved by just principles, I can not but conclude that each Member will readily bear an equal proportion of the Burthen. I therefore move that each Member of this Corporation shall and may Receive Jersey money (for Outstanding Debts that now are or shall become due the 1st September next only) at the rate of £3 5s for a Jersey £3 Bill until the 1st May, 1773, and pay such Jersey £3 Bill at £3 4s, and bring in an Account attested of such difference, and that whatever Loss may arise on the receiving and paying such Money, shall be equally borne by all the Members of this Corporation.

JOHN THURMAN, Jun'r.

MR. PRESIDENT:

Whereas, a number of the Members of this Chamber were not present at the time the Vote was carried for reducing Jersey Money, and as most of the Merchants who do not belong to it are warmly opposed to altering the present mode of receiving it, by which means a number of the Chamber will be evident sufferers, I move the matter may be reconsidered.

June 2d, 1772. JOSEPH BULL.

Mr. Patrick McDavitt was balloted for and refused.

Ordered—That Messrs. Jacob Walton, Hugh Wallace, George Folliot, Thomas White, Miles Sherbrooke, Walter Franklin, and Robert R. Waddell, be a Committee until the first Tuesday in July next, to hear and determine disputes between Parties, who shall agree to leave such to this Corporation.

CHAMBER OF COMMERCE.—TUESDAY, July 8th, 1772.

PRESENT.

Hon'ble Henry White, P.
Theop. Bache, } V. P.
William Walton, }
Isaac Low, T.
Anthony Van Dam, S.

Henry C. Bogert,
Joseph Bull,
James Beekman,
Samuel Bayard,
Benjam. Booth,
John Cruger,
Isaac Corsa,
Elias Desbrosses,
Walter Franklin,
Samuel Hake,
James Jauncey,
Peter Ketletas,
Edward Laight,
Robert C. Livingston,
Robert G. Livingston,
Charles McEvers,
Alexa. McDonald,
William Neilson,
Daniel Phenix,
John Reade,
Henry Remsen,
Isaac Sears,
Sampson Simson,
John Schuyler,
John Thurman,
Jacob Walton,
Thomas White,
Jacob Watson.

Fined for appearing after six o'clock :

John Amiel,
Gerra'd W. Beekman,
John H. Cruger,
Gerardus Duyckink,
Nicholas Hoffman,
Isaac Low,
William McAdam,
John Moore,
Thomas W. Moore,
Jeremiah Platt,
Thomas Randal,
Isaac Roosevelt,
John Ramsay,
William Seton,
Richard Sharpe,
William Stepple,
Henry White,
William Walton,
Gerrard Walton,
Alexan. Wallace,
Robert R. Waddell,
Richard Yates.

Fined for non-appearance :

John Alsop,
Robert Alexander,
Thomas Buchanan,
Walter Buchanan,
Levinus Clarkson,
George Folliot,
Nicholas Gouverneur,
Harman Gouverneur,
Peter Hassencliver,
William Imlay,
John Wetherhead,
Lawrence Kortright,
Samuel Kemble,
Philip Livingston,
Gabriel H. Ludlow,
George W. Ludlow,
Abram. Lynsen,
Leonard Lispenard,
Robert Murray,
Thomas Marston,
Thomas Miller,
Hamilton Young,
Lewis Pintard,
Garret Rapelje,
Miles Sherbrooke,
Acheson Thompson,
Samuel Ver Plank,
Jacobus Van Zandt, (Ill)
Augustus Van Horne,
Thomas Walton,
Hugh Wallace,
Robert Watts.

Mr. Livingston, one of the Committee to employ proper Persons to repair the Cupola, reported that they had applied to Peter Mersillisy to make an Estimate of the repairs, produced the same amounting to £92 11s. 4d. which the Chamber think excessive high.

Ordered—That Mr. G. Walton be added to the Committee, who are to apply to some other Workman, and see whether the Cupola cannot be repaired without new shingling[97] the Roof.

Mr. Thurman's Motion of last meeting being debated, was unanimously carried in the negative.

Mr. Bull's Motion for reconsidering the receiving and paying of Jersey Money, was Debated and Carried; 29 for Standing to their resolution; 22 against.

Ordered—That Messrs. T. Randal, J. Alsop, P. Livingston, W. McAdam, J. H. Cruger, G. Walton, and C. McEvers, be a Committee, until the first Tuesday in August next, to hear and determine disputes between Parties.

CHAMBER OF COMMERCE.—TUESDAY, 4th August, 1772.

PRESENT.

William Walton, V. P.
Antho. Van Dam, S.

Samuel Bayard,
John H. Cruger,
Elias Desbrosses,
Lawrence Kortright,
Edward Laight,
Leonard Lispenard,
Daniel Phenix,
Henry Remsen,
Isaac Roosevelt,
Sampson Simpson,
William Stepple,
Jacobus Van Zandt,
Gerrard Walton,
Jacob Watson.

Fined for appearing after six o'clock:

Theophy. Bache,
John Cruger,
Gabr. H. Ludlow,
John Moore,
Miles Sherbrooke,
Henry White.

Fined for non-appearance:

John Alsop,
Robert Alexander,
Gerrard W. Beekman,
Henry C. Bogert,
Joseph Bull,
William McAdam,
Charles McEvers,
Thomas Marston,
Thomas W. Moore,
Thomas Miller,

Thomas Buchanan,
James Beekman,
Walter Buchanan,
Benjamin Booth,
Levinus Clarkson,
Isaac Corsa,
Gerardus Duyckink,
George Folliott,
Walter Franklin,
Nicholas Governeur,
Harman Governeur,
Nicholas Hoffman,
Samuel Hake,
Peter Hassencliver,
James Jauncey,
William Imlay,
Peter Keteltas,
Samuel Kemble,
Isaac Low, (Out)
Philip Livingston,
George W. Ludlow,
Abram Lynsen,
Robert C. Livingston,
Robert G. Livingston,
Robert Murray,
Alexander McDonald,
William Neilson,
Lewis Pintard,
Jeremiah Platt,
Thomas Randal,
John Reade,
Garret Rapelje,
John Ramsay,
Isaac Sears,
William Seton,
Richard Sharpe,
John Schuyler,
Acheson Thompson,
John Thurman,
Samuel Ver Plank,
Augusts. Van Horne,
Jacob Walton,
Thomas Walton,
Hugh Wallace,
Alexan. Wallace,
Robert R. Waddell,
Robert Watts,
Thomas White,
John Weatherhead,
Richard Yates,
Hamilton Young.

Ordered—That the Committee appointed to employ proper Persons to repair the Cupola get it done in the cheapest and best manner as soon as possible.

SIR,

Whereas, there is a Law pass'd by the Chamber of Commerce, which takes place the third of Sept. next, preventing any of the Members taking Jersey Currency for more than it passes for in that Province, and knowing it will be too much against my Interest to take that Money any other ways than it now passes, it puts me under the disagreeable necessity to request my name to be struck out as member of that honourable Board.

ISAAC SEARS.

To H. White, Esq., President.

Ordered—That his name be struck off accordingly.

Ordered—That Messrs. J. Van Zandt, J. Moore, L.

Clarkson, Richd. Yates, T. Marston, L. Pintard, and A. Wallace, be a Committee, until the first Tuesday in September next, to hear and determine disputes between Parties who shall agree to leave such to this Corporation.

CHAMBER OF COMMERCE.—TUESDAY, 1st September, 1772.

PRESENT.

Hon'ble Henry White, P.
William Walton, V. P.
Anthony Van Dam, S.

John Amiel,
Joseph Bull,
John Cruger,
Isaac Corsa,
Elias Desbrosses,
Nichol. Hoffman,
James Jauncey,
George W. Ludlow,
Thomas White,
Edward Laight,
Leonard Lispenard,
Thomas Moore,
Alexan. McDonald,
Lewis Pintard,
Jeremi. Platt,
Daniel Phenix,
John Reade,
Henry Remsen,
Isaac Roosevelt,
Garret Rapalje,
John Ramsay,
William Seton,
Sampson Simson,
John Schuyler,
Hugh Wallace.

Fined for appearing after six o'clock:

Samuel Bayard,
Benjam. Booth,
Peter Keteltas,
Gab. H. Ludlow,
Augus. Van Horne,
Robert R. Waddell.

Fined for non-appearance, W.[98]

John Alsop,
Robert Alexander, (England)
Theophy. Bache,
Gerard W. Beekman,
Henry C. Bogert,
Thomas Buchanan,
James Beekman,
Walter Buchanan,
Abram Lynsen, (W. I.)
Robert C. Livingston, (Manor)
Robert G. Livingston,
Robert Murray, (London)
William McAdam, (Gout)
Charles McEvers,
John Moore,
Thomas Marston,

John H. Cruger,
Levinus Clarkson, (Boston)
Gerardus Duyckinck,
George Folliot, (L. Island)
Walter Franklin, (Rho. Island)
Nicholas Gouverneur, (Nash)[99]
Harman Gouverneur,
Peter Hassencliver, (England)
Nicho's Hoffman,
Samuel Hake, (Ill)
William Imlay,
Lawrence Kortright,
Samuel Kemble, (London)
Isaac Low,
Philip Livingston,
Thomas Miller, (London)
William Nielson,
Thomas Randal,
Miles Sherbrooke,
Richard Sharpe,
William Stepple,
Acheson Thompson, (Ireland)
John Thurman,
Samuel Ver Plank, (L. Island)
Jacobus Van Zandt, (New Eng)
Jacob Walton,
Gerard Walton,
John Wetherhead,
Richard Yates,
Hamilton Young, (L. I.)

MAY IT PLEASE THE PRESIDENT,

This Chamber having lately entered into a Resolve to alter the Currency of Jersey Bills, which at present I apprehend will be inconvenient for me to comply with, I am therefore under the disagreeable necessity of declining to be any longer a Member of this Corporation, and request the favour my name may be Erased.

I am, with much esteem, thy assured friend,

JACOB WATSON.

Septem. 1st, 1772.

Ordered—That his name be struck off accordingly.

Ordered—That Messrs. G. H. Ludlow, W. Seton, E. Laight, W. Neilson, S. Simpson, P. Ketletas, and G. W. Beekman, be a Committee until the first Tuesday in October to hear and determine disputes between parties who shall agree to leave such to this Corporation.

CHAMBER OF COMMERCE.—TUESDAY, October 6, 1772.

PRESENT.

Honble. Henry White, P.
William Walton, V. P.
Anthony Van Dam, S.

John Alsop,
Henry C. Bogart,
Joseph Bull,
Samuel Bayard, jr.,

Benj. Booth,
John Cruger,
John H. Cruger,
Elias Desbrosses,
James Jauncey,
William Imlay,
Edward Laight,
Leonard Lispenard,
Gabriel H. Ludlow,
George W. Ludlow,
Robert C. Livingston,
William McAdam,
John Moore,
Alexand. McDonald,
John Reade,
William Stepple,
John Schuyler,
John Thurman,
August's Van Horne,
Robert R. Waddell,
Hamilton Young.

Fined for appearing after six o'clock:

Robert Alexander,
Walter Franklin,
William Seton,
Samuel Verplank,
Hugh Wallace,
Richard Yates.

Fined for non-appearance:

John Amiel,
Thomas Buchanan,
Walter Buchanan,
Levinus Clarkson,
Isaac Corsa,
George Folliot,
Nicholas Gouverneur,
Peter Hassencliver,
Samuel Hake,
Abram Lynsen,
Robert G. Livingston,
Peter Keteltas,
Samuel Kemble,
Robert Murray,
Charles McEvers,
Thomas Marston,
Thomas W. Moore,
Thomas Miller,
Lewis Pintard,
Garret Rapelje,
John Ramsay,
Sampson Simson,
Acheson Thompson,
Gerrard Walton,
Alex. Wallace,
Thomas White,
John Weatherhead.

The President exhibited Mr. Pratt's[z] account amounting to thirty-seven pounds for taking Governor Colden's portrait in full length,[100] to be placed in the Chamber.

Ordered—That the same lie till next Meeting.

Proposed—That a Frame be made for the Lieut. Governor's Picture.

Several Gentlemen of the Chamber have, in consequence of the alteration of Jersey Money, sent in their resignations, which were read and accepted, and are as follows:

Isaac Roosevelt,
James Beekman,
Nicholas Hoffman,
Daniel Phenix,
Gerrard W. Beekman,
Henry Remsen,
Gerardus Duyckinck,
Harman Gouverneur,
William Neilson.

Moreover—Messrs.

John Thurman,
William Imlay,
John Schuyler,
Leonard Lispenard,

Declared—That they were, from necessity, obliged to receive Jersey money as formerly, and requested their resignations might also be accepted, which was granted.

Ordered—That Messrs. John Reade, Robert Alexander, Thomas W. Moore, Richard Sharpe, Hamilton Young, John Weatherhead, and William Stepple, be a Committee, until the first Tuesday in November next, to hear and determine Disputes between Parties who shall agree to leave such to this Corporation.

CHAMBER OF COMMERCE.—Tuesday, 3d Nov., 1772.

Present.

Honble. Henry White, President.
Theophy Bache, William Walton, } Vice-P.
Isaac Low, Treasurer.
Anthony Van Dam, Secrty.

John Alsop,
Robert Alexander,
John Amiel,
Samuel Bayard,
Benjam. Booth,
John Cruger,
John H. Cruger,
Isaac Corsa,
Elias Desbrosses,
James Jauncey,

Peter Ketletas,
Gabriel H. Ludlow,
Robert C. Livingston,
William McAdam,
John Moore,
Lewis Pintard,
William Seton,
Richard Sharpe,
William Stepple,
Samuel Ver Plank,
August Van Horne,
Gerrard Walton,
Alexr. Wallace,
Thomas White.

Fined for non-appearance :

Henry C. Bogert,
Joseph Bull,
Levinus Clarkson,
George Folliott,
Walter Franklin,
Nicholas Gouverneur,
Peter Hassencliver,
Samuel Hake,
Samuel Kemble,
George W. Ludlow,
Abram Lynsen,
Robert G. Livingston,
Robert Murray,
Charles McEvers,
Thomas Marston,
Thomas W. Moore,
Thomas Miller,
Alex. McDonald,
Thomas Randal,
Garret Rapelje,
John Ramsay,
Sampson Simpson,
Acheson Thompson,
Jacob Walton,
Hugh Wallace,
Robert R. Waddell,
Robert Watts,
John Wetherhead,
Richard Yates.

Ordered—That the Treasurer do pay Mr. Pratt for taking Governor Colden's portrait, £37.

Ordered—That Messrs. J. Moore, Gerard Walton, and Richard Sharpe, be a Committee to agree for a Frame for Governor Colden's Picture, which is to be placed in the Chamber as soon as it is finished.

Mr. Robert C. Livingston, one of the Committee appointed to employ proper workmen for repairing the Cupola of the Chamber, exhibited Jonathan Blake's[aa] account for work performed thereon, amounting to Twenty Pounds which the said Committee had agreed for.

Ordered—That it lie for the Vote of the Chamber until next Meeting.

Thomas Petit also produced his account for Fire Wood, Candles, and glazing of Windows, £3 15s. 5d.

Ordered—That also remain till next meeting.

Messrs. Edward Laight and Hamilton Young, have sent their resignation to the President, praying that their Names may be erased as they cannot any longer, consistent with their Interest, continue to be Members under the Restriction of Jersey Money passing agreeable to the Laws of this Chamber.

Whose Resignations were accepted of.

Ordered—That Messrs. Augustus Van Horne, Joseph Bull, Thomas Miller, Alexander McDonald, Samuel Bayard, and Robert C. Livingston, be a Committee, until the first Tuesday in December next, to hear and determine Disputes between parties who shall agree to leave such to this Corporation.

CHAMBER OF COMMERCE.—TUESDAY, Dec. 1, 1772.

PRESENT.

Honble. Henry White, P.
William Walton, V. P.
Isaac Low, T.
Antho. Van Dam, S.

John Alsop,
John Cruger,
Isaac Corsa,
Elias Desbrosses,
James Jauncey,
Peter Keteltas,
Robert C. Livingston,
William McAdam,
Thomas Miller,
Lewis Pintard,
Samuel Verplank,
Augustus Van Horne,
Jacob Walton,
Gerrard Walton,
Richard Yates.

Fined for appearing after six o'clock:

John Alsop,
Samuel Bayard,
Samuel Kemble,
Alexander Wallace.

Fined for non-appearance :

Theophy. Bache,
Henry C. Bogert,
Benjam. Booth,
John H. Cruger,
Levinus Clarkson,
George Folliot,
Walter Franklin,
Nicholas Gouverneur,
Peter Hassencliver,
Samuel Hake,
Gabr. H. Ludlow,
George W. Ludlow,
Abram. Lynsen,
Robert Murray,
Charles McEvers,
John Moore,
Alexand. McDonald,
Thomas Randal,
William Seton,
Sampson Simson,
Richard Sharpe,
William Stepple,
Acheson Thompson,
Hugh Wallace,
Thomas White,
Robert R. Waddle,
Robert Watts,
John Weatherhead.

Ordered—That the Treasurer do pay unto Jonathan Blake the sum of Twenty Pounds for work performed and Materials furnished in repairing the Cupola of the Chamber.

Ordered—That the Treasurer do pay Thomas Petit, three Pounds, fifteen Shillings, and five Pence, for Fire Wood, Candles, and Glazing Windows, in full.

Ordered—That Messrs. Hugh Wallace, Elias Desbrosses, Samuel Kemble, Isaac Corsa, Benjamin Booth, Samuel Hake, and Robert G. Livingston, Jun'r, be a Committee untill the first Tuesday in January next, to hear and determine Disputes between Parties, who shall agree to leave such to this Corporation.

Mr. John Amiel hath sent in his Resignation to the President, requesting that his Name may be erased, as he can not, consistent with his Interest, any longer continue to be a Member under the Restriction of Jersey Money passing agreeable to the Laws of this Chamber.

Which was accepted.

CHAMBER OF COMMERCE.—TUESDAY, 5th January, 1773.

PRESENT.

Hon'ble Henry White, President.
William Walton, Theoph. Bache, V. P.
Isaac Low, Treasurer.
Anth. Van Dam, Secretary.

John Alsop,
Benjam. Booth,
John Cruger,
John H. Cruger,
Elias Desbrosses,
Walter Franklin,
James Jauncey,
William McAdam,
William Stepple,
Jacob Walton,
Gerrard Walton,
Hugh Wallace,
Richard Yates.

Fined for appearing after six o'clock:

Robert C. Livingston,
Thomas Miller,
Samuel Verplank,
Alexand. Wallace.

Fined for non-appearance:

Robert Alexander,
Henry C. Bogert,
Joseph Bull,
Samuel Bayard, Jun'r,
Levinus Clarkson,
Isaac Corsa,
George Folliot,
Nicholas Gouverneur,
Peter Hasencliver,
Samuel Hake,
Peter Keteltas,
Samuel Kemble,
Gabriel H. Ludlow,
George W. Ludlow,
Abram. Lynsen,
Robert G. Livingston,
Robert Murray,
Charles McEvers,
John Moore,
Alexand. McDonald,
Thomas Randal,
William Seton,
Sampson Simson,
Richard Sharpe,
Acheson Thompson,
Augus. Van Horne,
Thomas White,
Robert R. Waddle,
Robert Watts,
John Weatherhead.

Ordered—That Messrs. Samuel Verplank, Walter Franklin, Thomas Randal, John Alsop, Thomas White,

Robert R. Waddel, and William McAdam, be a Committee until the first Tuesday in February next, to hear and determine Disputes between Parties, who shall agree to leave such to this Corporation.

CHAMBER OF COMMERCE.—TUESDAY, February 3d, 1773.

PRESENT.

Theophy Bache, } V. P.
William Walton, }
Antho. Van Dam, Secretary.

John Alsop,
Henry C. Bogert,
Isaac Corsa,
Elias Desbrosses,
Walter Franklin,
William McAdam,
William Stepple,
August. Van Horne,
Alexan. Wallace,
Richard Yates.

Fined for appearing after six o'clock:

Theophy Bache,
Hugh Wallace.

Fined for not appearing:

Robert Alexander,
Joseph Bull,
Samuel Bayard,
Benja. Booth,
John Cruger,
Levinus Clarkson,
George Folliot,
Nicholas Gouverneur,
Peter Hassencliver,
Samuel Hake,
James Jauncey,
Peter Ketletas,
Samuel Kemble,
Isaac Low,
Gabriel H. Ludlow,
George W. Ludlow,
Abram Lynsen,
Robert C. Livingston,
Robert G. Livingston,
Robert Murray,
Charles McEvers,
John Moore,
Thomas Miller,
Alexander McDonald,
Thomas Randal,
William Seton,
Sampson Simson,
Richard Sharpe,
Acheson Thompson,
Samuel Verplank,
Gerrard Walton,
Thomas White,
Robert R. Waddle,
Robert Watts,
Henry White,
Jacob Walton,
John Weatherhead.

As a sufficient Number of the Members did not appear, the Corporation adjourned till the first Tuesday in March.

CHAMBER OF COMMERCE.—TUESDAY, 2d March, 1773.

PRESENT.

Honble. Henry White, President.
William Walton, Vice do.
Isaac Low, Treasurer.
Anthon. Van Dam, Secretary.

Samuel Bayard,
Isaac Corsa,
Elias Desbrosses,
Robert C. Livingston,
William McAdam,
William Stepple,
Gerrard Walton,
Alexanr. Wallace.

Fined for appearing after six o'clock:

John H. Cruger,
Benjamin Booth,
Charles McEvers,
Richard Yates,

Fined for not appearing:

John Alsop,
Robert Alexander,
Theophylact Bache,
Henry C. Bogert,
Joseph Bull,
Benjamin Booth,
John Cruger,
Levinus Clarkson,
George Folliott,
Walter Franklin,
Nicholas Gouverneur,
Peter Hassencliver,
Samuel Hake,
James Jauncey,
Peter Keteltas,
Samuel Kemble,
Gabriel H. Ludlow,
George W. Ludlow,
Abram Lynsen,
Robert G. Livingston,
Robert Murray,
John Moore,
Thomas Miller,
Alexan. McDonald,
Thomas Randal,
William Seton,
Sampson Simson,
Richard Sharpe,
Acheson Thompson,
Samuel Verplanck,
Augustus Van Horne,
Jacob Walton,
Hugh Wallace,
Thomas White,
Robert R. Waddell,
Robert Watts,
John Weatherhead.

CHAMBER OF COMMERCE.—TUESDAY, April 6th, 1773.

PRESENT.

Honble. Henry White, President.
Theophy. Bache, William Walton, Vice-Presdts.
Isaac Low, Treasurer.
Anthon. Van Dam, Secretary.

Robert Alexander,
John H. Cruger,
Isaac Corsa,
Elias Desbrosses,
James Jauncey,
Robert C. Livingston,
William Stepple,
Augustus Van Horne,
Jacob Walton,
Gerrard Walton,
Hugh Wallace,
Alexand. Wallace,
Thomas White,
Samuel Bayard.

Fined for appearing after six o'clock:

Benjam. Booth,
John Cruger,
Charles McEvers,
Thomas Miller,
Samuel Verplank.

Fined for non-appearance:

John Alsop,
Henry C. Bogart,
Joseph Bull,
Levinus Clarkson,
George Folliot,
Walter Franklin,
Nicholas Gouverneur,
Peter Hassencliver,
Samuel Hake,
Peter Ketletas,
Samuel Kemble,
Gabriel H. Ludlow,
George W. Ludlow,
Abram Lynsen,
Robert G. Livingston,
Robert Murray,
John Moore,
Alexan'r. McDonald,
Thomas Randal,
William Seton,
Sampson Simson,
Richard Sharpe,
Acheson Thompson,
Robert R. Waddel,
Robert Watts,
John Wetherhead,
Richard Yates.

The President having made this Corporation acquainted that the Honble. House of Assembly, in their last Sessions, did grant [101] the sum of Two Hundred Pounds per

Annum for five years, to be paid to the Treasurer of this Corporation, for the encouragement of a Fishery on this Coast, for the better supplying the Markets of this City with Fish.[102] In pursuance of the laudable Intentions of the Legislature, it was proposed:

That a Premium of Forty Pounds be paid to the Owners and Crew of any one Boat or Vessel who shall supply this Market with the greatest quantity of Fish—Skate and Ray excepted taken with a Trawl[103] net—from the first of May next, to the 1st of May, 1774.

That a Premium of Thirty Pounds be paid to the Owners and Crew of any one Boat or Vessel who shall supply this Market with the next greatest quantity of Fish—Skate and Ray excepted taken with a Trawl net—from the first Day of May next, to the first Day of May, 1774.

That a Premium of Thirty Pounds be paid to the Owners and Crew of any one Boat or Vessel who shall supply this Market with the greatest quantity of Live Cod Fish, from the first Day of November next ensuing, to the first Day of May, 1774.

That a Premium of Twenty Pounds be paid to the Owners and Crew of any one Boat or Vessel who shall supply this Market with the next greatest quantity of Live Cod Fish, from the first Day of November next, to the first Day of May, 1774.

That a Premium of Twenty Pounds be paid to the Owners and Crew of any one Boat or Vessel who shall supply this Market with the greatest quantity of Live Sheeps-Head, from the first Day of May next, to the first Day of May, 1774.

That a Premium of Fifteen Pounds be paid to the Owners and Crew of any one Boat or Vessel who shall supply this Market with the next greatest quantity of Live Sheeps-Head, from the first Day of May next, to the first Day of May, 1774.

THAT A PREMIUM of Ten Pounds be paid to the Owners and Crew of any one Boat or Vessel who shall supply this Market with the greatest quantity of fresh Mackarel, from the first day of May next to the first day of May, 1774.

THAT A PREMIUM of Five Pounds be paid to the Owners and Crew of any one Boat or Vessel who shall supply this Market with the next greatest quantity of fresh Mackarel, from the first day of May next to the first day of May, 1774.

Ordered—That Messrs. Theophy Bache, J. Walton, James Jauncey, and Capt. Thomas Miller, be a Committee to advertise the foregoing Premiums in the newspapers that are proposed to be given for taking Fish and supplying the Market therewith.

Messrs. William Jauncey, Johnston Fairholme, and Daniel Ludlow proposed to become Members.[104]

Ordered—That Messrs. John H. Cruger, Gerrard Walton, Charles McEvers, Richard Yates, Alexander Wallace, and John Weatherhead, be a Committee until the first Tuesday in May next to hear and determine Disputes between Parties who shall agree to leave such to this Corporation.

CHAMBER OF COMMERCE.—TUESDAY, 4th May, 1773.

PRESENT.

Honble.	Henry White,	President.
	Theophy. Bache, William Walton,	Vice-Presidents.
	Isaac Low,	Treasurer.
	Anthony Van Dam,	Secretary.

Isaac Corsa,
John Cruger,
Elias Desbrosses,
James Jauncey,
Robert C. Livingston,
William McAdam,
William Stepple,
August Van Horne,
Samuel Verplank,
Jacob Walton,
Alexr. Wallace.

Fined for appearing after six o'clock:

Benj. Booth,
Walter Franklin,
Hugh Wallace,
Robert R. Waddell,
Richard Yates.

Fined for non-appearance:

John Alsop,
Henry C. Bogart,
Joseph Bull,
Samuel Bayard,
John H. Cruger,
Levinus Clarkson,
Nicholas Gouverneur,
Peter Hasencliver,
Samuel Hake,
Peter Keteltas,
Samuel Kemble,
Gabriel H. Ludlow,
George W. Ludlow,
Abraham Lynsen,
Robert G. Livingston,
Robert Murray,
Charles McEvers,
Thomas Miller,
Alex. McDonald,
Thomas Randal,
Sampson Simson,
Acheson Thompson,
Gerrard Walton,
Thomas White,
Robert Watts,
Jno. Wetherhead.

The Committee appointed to advertise the Premiums for supplying this Market with Fish, report

That they had caused an Advertisement to be inserted in two[105] of the Newspapers of this City.

Ordered—That all Persons who mean to apply for the aforesaid Premiums that they do, every Fare[106] they make, carry an account thereof to the Secretary of this Board for the Time being, who is to keep a regular account thereof, and that the Persons make oath before a Magistrate of the quantity brought to Market, each time, if required.

Ordered—That Mr. Verplank, Mr. Robt. C. Livingston, and Mr. Yates, be a Committee to audit the Treasurer's Accounts, or any two of them, and that they report the same at their next Meeting.

Thomas Petit's Account amounting to £7 6s for glazing Windows and other petty charges, being exhibited with his Salary of £15, proposed to be considered at next Meeting.

Ordered—That Messrs. John Alsop, Joseph Bull, Samuel Bayard, Benjamin Booth, John Cruger, and Elias Desbrosses, be a Committee until the first Tuesday in June next, to hear and determine Disputes between Parties, who shall agree to leave such to this Corporation.

The Charter of this Corporation, as well as the Rules of the Chamber, appoint this Day for the Election of Officers for the Current Year, when the following Gentlemen were balloted for and duly elected, and all but the Treasurer, who was absent, were sworn to perform the trust reposed in them.

THEOPHY BACHE, President.
WILLIAM WALTON, } Vice-Pres.
ISAAC LOW, }
JOHN ALSOP, Treasurer.
ANTHONY VAN DAM, Secretary.

CHAMBER OF COMMERCE.—TUESDAY, June 1st, 1773.

PRESENT.

William Walton, Vice-Pres't.
John Alsop, Treasurer.
Anthony Van Dam, Secretary.

John Cruger,
John H. Cruger,
Elias Desbrosses,
Johnst. Fairholme,
Robert C. Livingston,
William McAdam,
Samuel Verplank,
Henry White,
Gerrard Walton,
Hugh Wallace,
Alexand. Wallace.

Fined for non-appearance:

Theophy Bache,
Henry C. Bogert,
Joseph Bull,
Samuel Bayard,
Benjamin Booth,
Levinus Clarkson,
Isaac Corsa,
Walter Franklin,
Nicholas Gouverneur,
Peter Hasencliver,
Samuel Hake,
James Jauncey,
Peter Ketletas,
Samuel Kemble,
Isaac Low,
Abram Lynsen,
Robert G. Livingston,
Robert Murray,
Charles McEvers,
Thomas Miller,
Alexan. McDonald,
Thomas Randal,
Sampson Simson,
William Stepple,
Acheson Thompson,
Augus. Van Horne,
Jacob Walton,
Thomas White,
Robert R. Waddle,
Robert Watts,
Richard Yates.

CHAMBER OF COMMERCE.—New York, 3d June, 1773.

SPECIAL MEETING.

Present.

Theophy Bache, President.
William Walton, Isaac Low, } Vice-Pres.
John Alsop, Treasurer.
Anthony Van Dam, Secretary.

Hugh Wallace,
Alexander Wallace,
John Cruger,
Jacob Walton,
William Stepple,
Thomas White,
Johnston Fairholme,
Samuel Kemble,
Thomas Miller,
Charles McEvers,
Augustus Van Horne,
Gerrard Walton,

Samuel Bayard,	John H. Cruger,
Robert R. Waddle,	James Jauncey,
Elias Desbrosses.	

Mr. President made this Corporation acquainted that he had been requested by several of the Members to convene a Meeting to address General Gage[bb] on his Departure for England.[107]

Ordered—That Mr. President, Mr. Desbrosses, and Mr. John Harris Cruger, be a Committee to prepare a Draft of an Address to General Gage, and that they do report the same this Afternoon.

Mr. Francis Lewis, and Mr. James Seagrove were proposed to become Members of this Chamber.

CHAMBER OF COMMERCE.—NEW YORK, 3d June, 1773.

SPECIAL MEETING.

PRESENT.

Theophy. Bache, President.
William Walton, Isaac Low, Vice-Presidents.
Anthony Van Dam, Secretary.

John Cruger,	Thomas Miller,
Hugh Wallace,	Charles McEvers,
John H. Cruger,	Augustus Van Horne,
Jacob Walton,	Henry White,
Gerrard Walton,	James Jauncey,
Samuel Bayard,	Thomas Randal,
Johnston Fairholme,	Robert R. Waddel,
Walter Franklin.	

The Committee appointed to draw up an Address to General Gage reported that they had perfected a Draft, and submitted it to the consideration of the Corporation, which, being read, was approved of, and is in the words following:

TO HIS EXCELLENCY THE HONOURABLE THOMAS GAGE, General and Commander-in-Chief of his Majesty's Forces in North America.

THE HUMBLE ADDRESS of the CORPORATION of the Chamber of Commerce of the City of New York.

MAY IT PLEASE YOUR EXCELLENCY,

When we review your conduct as Commander-in-Chief of his Majesty's Forces, and reflect on the Happiness derived to this Colony from your eminent Justice, from the Discipline and good Order of the Army, and your constant Attention to secure to North America the solid Effect of a Series of Victories so glorious to the British arms; [108] when to these we unite your engaging Manners and polite and obliging Deportment, we feel, Sir, in common with the rest of our Fellow-Citizens, the liveliest Sentiments of Esteem and Respect for a character so truly valuable. These Impressions, as they increase the Regret with which we consider the approach of your Departure for England, cannot fail of exciting in us a warm Desire thus publickly to testify the high sense we entertain of your exalted Merit.

We are persuaded, Sir, that as you take with you the deserv'd Applause of the Colonies, and the cordial Affections of the Inhabitants of this City, long honored by your immediate Residence, so your Zeal and Fidelity in the Discharge of a Trust the most important will recommend you to the Favour and approbation of our gracious Sovereign.

Permit us to wish your Excellency, your amiable Lady and Family, an agreeable Passage to your Native Country, and every Degree of Felicity, both in publick and private Life, so justly due to your distinguished Virtues.

By order of the Chamber,

THEO. BACHE, Presd't.

CHAMBER OF COMMERCE,
NEW YORK, 4th June, 1773.

Order'd—That Messrs. Gerrard Walton, Charles McEvers, Johnston Fairholme, be a Committee (and John H. Cruger) to wait on his Excellency Genl. Gage, with a fair Copy of the Address, and know his Pleasure when he will be waited on by this Corporation to receive the same.

The Committee appointed to wait on Genl. Gage reported,

That he was pleased to say it would be agreeable to him to receive the Address of this Corporation on the Morrow, at two o'clock, at which Time all the Members were desired to attend at the Chamber.

HIS EXCELLENCY'S ANSWER to the Gentlemen of the Corporation of the Chamber of Commerce of the City of New York.

GENTLEMEN,

It is a circumstance the most flattering to me, that my Publick and Private conduct should meet the approbation of so respectable a Body, and I return you my best thanks for your polite and affectionate Address.

I have resided long amongst you, and lived happily with you and your Fellow-citizens; so it is Natural that I should leave you with Regret and Concern, and I beg you to believe that I carry with me Sentiments the most friendly to the Colonies in general, and the warmest wishes for the Prosperity and Happiness of the Inhabitants of New York.

CHAMBER OF COMMERCE.—TUESDAY, 6th July, 1773.

PRESENT.

Theophylact Bache, President.
Anthony Van Dam, Secretary.

John Cruger,	Gerrard Walton,
Hugh Wallace,	Henry White,
Alexan'r Wallace,	Richd. Yates,
Elias Desbrosses,	Isaac Corsa.

Fined for appearing after six o'clock:

John Alsop,	Samuel Bayard,

Robt. C. Livingston.

CHAMBER OF COMMERCE.—TUESDAY, 3 August, 1773.

PRESENT.

Theophylact Bache, President.
William Walton, } Vice-Presidents.
Isaac Low, }
Anthony Van Dam, Secretary.

John Cruger,	Robert Waddel,
John Harris Cruger,	William McAdam,
Elias Desbrosses,	William Stepple,
Hugh Wallace,	Samuel Verplank,

Augustus Van Horne.

CHAMBER OF COMMERCE.—TUESDAY, 7 Sept., 1773.

PRESENT.

William Walton, Vice-President.
Anthony Van Dam, Secretary.

John Cruger,
John Harris Cruger,
Elias Desbrosses,
James Jauncey,
Thomas Randal,
Augustus Van Horne,
Gerrard Walton.

CHAMBER OF COMMERCE.—TUESDAY, 5th October, 1773.

PRESENT.

Theophylact Bache, President.
William Walton, Vice-President.
John Alsop, Treasurer.
Anthony Van Dam, Secretary.

John Cruger,
John Harris Cruger,
Elias Desbrosses,
Walter Franklin,
Thomas Randal,
Augustus Van Horne,
Gerrard Walton.

CHAMBER OF COMMERCE.—TUESDAY, 2d Nov., 1773.

PRESENT.

William Walton, Isaac Low, } Vice-Presidents.
John Alsop, Treasurer.
Anthony Van Dam, Secretary.

Joseph Bull,
Isaac Corsa,
Elias Desbrosses,
James Jauncey,
Thomas Randal,
Augustus Van Horne,
Gerrard Walton.

CHAMBER OF COMMERCE.—TUESDAY, 7th December, 1773.

PRESENT.

Theoph. Bache,
William Walton,
Isaac Low,
John Alsop, Treasurer.

Richard Sharpe,
John Cruger,
Elias Desbrosses,
Charles McEvers,
Miles Sherbrooke,
William Seton,
George Ludlow,
John Moore,
Isaac Corsa,
Richard Yates,
Benj. Booth,
Samuel Hake,
Thomas Randal,
Gabriel H. Ludlow,
Joseph Bull,
Augustus Van Horne,
Robert Alexander,
Robert C. Livingston,
Gerrard Walton,
John H. Cruger,
Samuel Bayard,
Alexander Wallace,
Lewis Pintard,
James Jauncey.

Messrs. James Seagrove, Francis Lewis, and William Jauncey, who were proposed at a former Meeting to become Members of this Corporation, were Balloted for and passed in the affirmative.

Ordered—That the Secretary send notice to the Several Gentlemen so elected, in Writing, that they were unanimously chosen.

Mr. Alsop, the Treasurer, was this night Qualifyed. Gilbert Bennit, John Cox, and John Bennit, proposed a petition to this Corporation, which was read and ordered to lay for further consideration.

Mr. Robert C. Livingston's Motion:

This Corporation, having by a Vote passed the 2nd March, 1772, Agreed to receive and pay Jersey Money at the same Value it is estimated by the Treasurer's in that Colony, which was then and is still thought to be a necessary and Just regulation, but as I humbly conceive it would be more expedient for this Corporation to permit the Members to receive and pay it at the rate at which it passed current before this regulation took place.

I therefore beg leave to move that every Member of this Corporation may be at liberty to receive and pay Jersey Money as it formerly passed.

Mr. Charles McEver's Motion:

That, as many of the Members of this Corporation have sent in their resignations, and others have absented themselves from the usual Meetings of this Chamber on Account of the regulation entered into for the receiving and paying of Jersey Money, which they from Necessity could not conform to without prejudice to their Business, and as Mr. Livingston has moved this Chamber, that in future the Members may be at liberty to receive and pay Jersey Money as it formerly passed, should his Motion be agreed to: I beg leave to move that those Gentlemen who have sent in their resignations, and those who have absented themselves from this board may be again received, and that notice may be sent them to attend the Chamber as usual.

Ordered—That the foregoing Motions be entered and taken into consideration.

CHAMBER OF COMMERCE.—TUESDAY, January 4th, 1774.

PRESENT.

Theoph. Bache, President.
William Walton, Isaac Low, V. P.
John Alsop, Treasurer.
Antho. Van Dam, Secretary.

Joseph Bull,
John Cruger,
John H. Cruger,
Isaac Corsa,
Elias Desbrosses,
Samuel Hake,
Peter Keteltas,
George Ludlow,
Leonard Lispenard,
John Moore,
Francis Lewis,
Lewis Pintard,
William Stepple,
Jacob Walton,
Robert R. Waddell,
Robert Watts.

Fined for appearing after six o'clock:

James Jauncey,
William Jauncey,
Charles McEvers,
Thomas Miller,
James Seagrove.

Mr. Robert C. Livingston's Motion that every Member of this Corporation be at liberty to receive and pay Jersey Money as it formerly passed, having been debated, was agreed to.

Mr. Charles McEvers having proposed at the last Meeting that such Gentlemen who have sent in their resignations, and those that have withdrawn themselves from this board, may be again received, having been considered and deliberating therein, it was unanimously

Resolved—That those Gentlemen that have sent or given in their resignations be informed that the Chamber are at liberty to receive and pay Jersey money as formerly, notwithstanding they conceive the evil tendency of receiving it for more than its real value in their Treasury, which does in the event depreciate our own Currency. That if they choose to offer themselves to become members again of this Corporation by being balloted for under the same restrictions as heretofore, except that no fine or expence will attend their admission, and that time is given them untill the first Tuesday in May next for that purpose.

Ordered—That the Secretary deliver to the Doorkeeper and Messenger a fair Copy of this resolution, to be by him shown and served upon each of the following Gentlemen, who appear on the registry of this Corporation to have given in their resignations, viz.:

Gerrard Duykink,
Henry Remsen,
William Imlay,
John Amiel,
Daniel Phenix,
John Schuyler,
Isaac Sears,
Jacob Watson,
James Beekman,
William Neilson,
Leo. Lispenard,
Hamilton Young,
Isaac Roosevelt,
Gerrard W. Beekman,
John Thurman,
Edward Laight,
Nich's Hoffman,
Harman Gouverneur.

[*A true copy.*] ANTHONY VAN DAM, Sec'ry.

Ordered—That Messrs. Robert Alexander, Henry C. Bogert, Joseph Bull, Samuel Bayard, Benjamin Booth, John Cruger, and John H. Cruger, be a Committee, untill the first Tuesday in February next, to hear and determine Disputes between Parties who shall agree to leave such to this Corporation.

CHAMBER OF COMMERCE.—Tuesday, 1st February, 1774.

PRESENT.

Theophylact Bache, President.
William Walton, } Vice Do.
Isaac Low, [6] [109] } Vice Do.
Anthony Van Dam, Secretary.

Joseph Bull,
John Cruger,
Isaac Corsa,
Elias Desbrosses,
Francis Lewis,
William McAdam,
Thomas Miller, [6]
Lewis Pintard,
William Jauncey, [6]
Gerrard Walton,
Alexan. Wallace,
Robert R. Waddell. [6]

CHAMBER OF COMMERCE.—Tuesday, 1st March, 1774.

PRESENT.

Theophylact Bache, President.
William Walton, Vice.
Anthony Van Dam, Secretary.

Joseph Bull,
Samuel Bayard,
Isaac Corsa,
Peter Keteltas,
George Ludlow,
Miles Sherbrooke,
Gerrard Walton,
Hugh Wallace,
Robert R. Waddel,
Robert Watts.

CHAMBER OF COMMERCE.—Thursday, 24th March, 1774.

SPECIAL MEETING.

PRESENT.

Theophylact Bache, President.
Isaac Low, Vice.
John Alsop, Treasurer.
Anthony Van Dam, Secretary.

Peter Keteltas,	Miles Sherbrooke,
Charles McEvers,	Gabriel H. Ludlow,
Johnston Fairholme,	James Jauncey,
Alex'r Wallace,	Samuel Bayard, Jun'r,
Samuel Hake,	Richard Sharpe,
Elias Desbrosses,	Joseph Bull,
Robert R. Waddel,	Richard Yates,
Robert Alexander,	John Moore,

William Jauncey.

The President, at the request of several of the Members of this Corporation who were desireous to address his Excellency GOVERNOR TRYON before his embarkation[110] for England, having convened a Chamber, and one being drawn up, was read, after some alterations and amendments was agreed to.

Ordered—That Messrs. William Walton, Isaac Low, John Alsop, John Moore, Johnston Fairholme, and Elias Desbrosses, be a Committee to wait on his Excellency with a fair Copy, and know his pleasure when he will be pleased to receive the same.

CHAMBER OF COMMERCE.—TUESDAY, 5th April, 1774.

PRESENT.

Theoph. Bache, President.
William Walton, Vice.
Anthony Van Dam, Secretary.

Robert Alexander,	George Ludlow,
Joseph Bull,	Gabriel H. Ludlow,
John Cruger,	John Moore,
John H. Cruger,	William Stepple,

Robert Watts.

Fined for appearing after six o'clock :

Elias Desbrosses, Johnston Fairholme,
Robert R. Waddel.

CHAMBER OF COMMERCE.—TUESDAY, 2d May, 1774.

PRESENT.

Theoph. Bache,	President.
William Walton,	Vice President.
Anthony Van Dam,	Secretary.
Robert Alexander,	Garret Rapelje,
John H. Cruger,	William Stepple,
Isaac Corsa,	Richard Sharpe,
Walter Franklin,	James Seagrove,
Robert C. Livingston,	Gerrard Walton,
George Ludlow,	Robert Watts,
William McAdam,	Richard Yates.

Fined for appearing after six o'clock :

William Jauncey,	John Moore,
Francis Lewis,	Robert R. Waddel,
Jacob Walton,	Miles Sherbrooke,
Thomas Miller,	Augustus Vanhorne.

Mr. Leonard Lispenard, Junr., having desired that he might be readmitted a Member of this Corporation, and Mr. William Laight having been proposed at a former meeting, were balloted for, and unanimously chosen Members of this Corporation.

Ordered—That the Secretary do send them notice in writing that they have been unanimously chosen.

Ordered—That Mr. Richard Yates, Mr. John Moore, Mr. Miles Sherbrooke, and Mr. Gerard Walton, be a Committee to audit the Treasurer's accounts, until this day, and that they report the same to this Corporation.

Ordered—That Messrs. William McAdam, William Stepple, William Jauncey, Robert Watts, and Francis Lewis, be a Committee to examine the Claims of Fishermen that have furnished this Market with such Fish as this Corporation have thought fit to grant a Bounty thereon, and prescribe such mode of Proof as will be necessary to entitle them thereto, such report to (*be*) made at a future meeting; and the same Committee are appointed to report the necessary premium to be given the ensuing season.

Mr. Barnard Romans[cc] having formerly requested the countenance and Protection of this board to his design of publishing by Subscription several Maps of East and West Florida,[III] &c., and his Letters being read and refered to the next meeting of this Corporation :

Proposed—That Eleven sets be subscribed for, in addition to one set the President hath engaged for, and that any member be furnished with them at first cost.

Ordered—That Messrs. Robert Alexander, Theoph. Bache, Joseph Bull, Benj. Booth, Thomas Buchanan, John Cruger, and Elias Desbrosses, be a Committee to hear and determine Disputes that may be left to the Chamber, until the first Tuesday in June next.

The Charter, as well as the Laws of this Corporation, appoints this day for the Election of Officers, when the following Gentlemen were balloted for and duly Elected :

WILLIAM WALTON, President.
ISAAC LOW, } Vice Presidents.
JOHN ALSOP, }
WILLIAM MCADAM, Treasurer.
ANTHO. VAN DAM, Secretary.

Mr. William Walton, William McAdam, and Anthony Van Dam, being present, were duly sworn agreeable to the charter to exercise their respective Offices.

The President, having been desired by several Members of the Corporation to convene a chamber to Address the Governor before his departure for England, the same was agreed to and was waited on to deliver the same, which together with his answer, were in the words following:

To His Excellency, William Tryon, Esqr.:—Captain General and Governor in Chief of the Colony of New York, and Territories depending thereon in America, Chancellor and Vice-Admiral[112] of the same.

The Humble Address of the Corporation of the Chamber of Commerce of the City of New York:—

May it please your Excellency:

When publick spirit unites with private virtue in forming the character of a Chief Magistrate, and the representative of the Sovereign is distinguished no less by his inclination than ability to advance the interests of the Province over which he presides, the people become deeply interested in his welfare, and will omit no opportunity of testifying their gratitude and esteem.

Influenced by these considerations, We, the Members of the Corporation of the Chamber of Commerce, Join with the General voice of the Colony, in deploring your Excellency's departure from a country which owes much to your care, and has flourished under the auspices of a mild, a wise, and an impartial administration.

With pleasure, Sir, we have beheld you, the Governor of a Province, and not of a Party, nor can we forbear doing Justice to that Generosity of temper and liberality of sentiment which has led your Excellency to consider every rank and class of People among us, as equally loyal subjects of the same Sovereign, and equally entitled to his favours and munificence.

It is with real concern we anticipate the time when the Community will cease to reap advantage from your counsels, the poor lament the absence of their benefactor, and the inhabitants of this City regret the loss of a Governor, whose affability, ease of access, and friendly deportment had conciliated their affection and regard.

We, indeed, derive no little consolation from the abilities and probity of the Gentleman[113] on whom the command will devolve, of whose attatchment to our Interest We have had ample proofs, and to whose attention to the advancement of Commerce, We owe our existence as a Corporation.

Permit us, most sincerely, to wish Your Excellency and family a safe and pleasant passage to your native Country; may health and happiness ever attend you, and may you speedily return crowned with the approbation and favour of your Royal Master, to a Country where your name will descend with honour to future generations, and your administration form a bright page in their annals.

By order of the Corporation,

Theophy. Bache, President.

HIS EXCELLENCY'S ANSWER:

GENTLEMEN:

I should be destitute of sensibility if I did not receive this very affectionate address of the respectable Chamber of Commerce with great satisfaction.

Your generous approbation of my publick and private conduct, your concern at my departure, and solicitude for my health and happiness, which furnish a testimonial so honourable to my administration demand the warmest returns of esteem and gratitude. However my Gracious Sovereign may be pleased to dispose of me, I trust you will believe that the prosperity of this loyal colony, the increase of its trade and riches, and its permanent reputation and tranquility, will not cease to be objects very near my heart.

In leaving a country, to which I have so much reason to be attached, it is a pleasing reflection that the Government will devolve on a Gentleman whose long and faithfull services entitle him to the confidence of the Crown, and whose great abilities and experience as well as inclination will lead him, upon all occasions, to consult the interest of his Sovereign, and promote the felicity of the people intrusted to his care.

WILLIAM TRYON.

CHAMBER OF COMMERCE.—TUESDAY, June 7th, 1774.

PRESENT.

William Walton, President.
Isaac Low, Vice President.
William McAdam, Treasurer.
Antho. Van Dam, Secretary.

Joseph Bull,
Isaac Corsa,
Samuel Hake,
Leonard Lispenard,
William Laight,
Garret Rapelje,
Lewis Pintard,
Gerrard Walton.

Fined for appearing after six o'clock:

Francis Lewis,
John Cruger,
James Seagrove,
Jacob Walton,
Anthony Van Dam.

CHAMBER OF COMMERCE.—TUESDAY, July 5th, 1774.

PRESENT.

William Walton, President.
Isaac Low, John Alsop, Vice Presidents.
Antho. Van Dam, Secretary.

John Cruger,
Isaac Corsa,
Gabriel H. Ludlow,
William Laight,
Lewis Pintard,
Alexander Wallace,
Robert Watts.

Fined for appearing after six o'clock:

Theoph. Bache,
Francis Lewis,
Gerrard Walton,
William Stepple,
John Moore,
Miles Sherbrooke,
Robert R. Waddle,
Richard Sharpe,
James Seagrove,
Richard Yates.

The Committee appointed to examine fishermen's Claims, report:

That *Peter Parks* exhibits ample proof that he hath brought to this City and exposed to sale in the Publick Market upwards of Eight hundred live Cod Fish, between the first day of Nov., 1773, and the first day of May, 1774.

Ordered—That the Treasurer do pay unto the said *Peter Parks* the sum of Thirty Pounds, it appearing from the Committee's report and Vouchers, lodged with the Secretary of this Corporation, that he hath brought the greatest quantity of Live Cod Fish to Market, within the period prescribed by a Vote of this Corporation, on the first Tuesday in April, 1773.

That *Robert Heartshorn* exhibits proof that he hath, at Divers times, between the first day of May, 1773, and the first day of May, 1774, sent to this Market four hundred and fifty-six Sheepshead.

Ordered—That the Treasurer do pay unto the said *Robert Heartshorn*, the sum of Twenty Pounds, it appearing from the Committee's report, and Vouchers lodged with the Secretary of this Corporation, that he hath sent by divers persons, employed by the said *Heartshorne*, the greatest quantity of Live Sheeps-head to the publick Market[114] in this city, within the period prescribed by a Vote of this Corporation on the first Tuesday in April, 1773.

Ordered—That in case any other persons claim the Bounty on Fish brought to this Market, between the first day of May, 1773, and the first day of May, 1774, that when full proof is made to the satisfaction of the Committee appointed to examine fishermen's claims, upon the different species on which this Corporation have voted such Bounty : That the Committee aforesaid do draw an order on the Treasurer for the respective sums, and in favour of such persons as shall be justly intitled thereto, which the Treasurer is hereby ordered to pay and charge this Corporation therewith.

In obedience to the order of the Corporation of the Chamber of Commerce, the Committee appointed by them have considered what premiums are proper to be proposed to encourage bringing Fish to the publick Market in this City for the present year, Report as their opinion :

THAT THE SUM of Fifty Pounds be paid to the owners and crews of any one Vessel or Boat who shall supply this Market with the greatest quantity of Fish—Skate and Ray excepted—not less than one thousand pounds weight taken with a Trawl net, from the first day of May, 1774, to the first day of May, 1775.

THAT THE SUM of Twenty Pounds be paid to the owners and crew of any one Boat or Vessel who shall supply this Market with the next greatest quantity of Fish—Skate and Ray excepted—not less than seven hundred and fifty pounds weight, taken with a Trawl net within the same period.

THAT THE SUM of Thirty Pounds be paid to the owners and crew of any one Boat or Vessel who shall supply this Market with the greatest quantity of Live Cod Fish, not less than one thousand fish in number, from the 1st day of November, 1774, to the 1st day of May, 1775.

THAT THE SUM of Twenty Pounds be paid to the owners and crew of any one Boat or Vessel who shall supply this Market with the next greatest quantity of Live Cod Fish, not less than seven hundred and fifty Fish in number, within the same period.

THAT THE SUM of Twenty Pounds be paid to the owners and crew of any one Boat or Vessel who shall supply this Market with the greatest quantity of Live Sheeps-head Fish, not less than one thousand Fish, from the first day of May, 1774, to the 1st day of May, 1775.

THAT THE SUM of Fifteen Pounds be paid to the owners and crew of any one Boat or Vessel who shall supply this Market with the next greatest quantity, not less than seven hundred and fifty Fish, within the same period.

THAT THE SUM of Ten Pounds be paid to the owners and crew of any one Boat or Vessel who shall supply this Market with the next greatest quantity, not less than five hundred Sheeps-head, within the same period.

THAT THE SUM of Ten Pounds be paid to the owners and crew of any one Boat or Vessel which shall supply this Market with the greatest quantity of fresh Mackarel, not less than seven thousand Fish, from the first day of May, 1774, to the first day of May, 1775.

THAT THE SUM of Five Pounds be paid to the owners and crew of any one Boat or Vessel who shall supply this Market with the next greatest quantity, not less than five thousand Mackaral, within the same period.

THAT THE SUM of Twenty Pounds be paid to the owners and Crew of any one Boat or Vessel who shall supply this Market with the greatest quantity of dryed Herring, sufficiently cured, from the first day of March, 1774, to the first day of July, 1775. Which is humbly submitted.

FRAN'S LEWIS.
WILLIAM STEPPLE.
ROBERT WATTS.

Ordered—That the above Report be published in the several newspapers, which may tend to promote a greater supply of Fish to the Inhabitants of this City, and answer the end intended by an Act of the Gouverneur Council and General Assembly of this Province.

The following gentlemen having been proposed at a former meeting to be Elected Members of this Corporation, were balloted for, and duly Elected:—Mr. John Schuyler, Edward Laight, Isaac Sears, Gerrard W. Beekman.

Order'd—That the Secretary send them written certificates of their admission.

Mr. John Alsop and Mr. Isaac Low were qualified to serve as Vice Presidents for the ensuing year, agreeable to their Election on the first Tuesday in May last.

Order'd—That Messrs. Theoph. Bache, Isaac Corsa, Geo. Folliot, Walter Franklin, Samuel Hake, and James Jauncey, be a Committee, untill the first Tuesday in August next, to hear and determine disputes between Parties who chose to leave such to their determination.

CHAMBER OF COMMERCE.—TUESDAY, 3d August, 1774.

PRESENT.

William Walton, President.
Isaac Low, } Vice do.
John Alsop, }
Anthony Van Dam, Secretary.

Joseph Bull, Gabriel H. Ludlow,
John Cruger, William Laight,
Robt. R. Waddle, William Stepple,
Alex'r Wallace.

Fined for appearing after six o'clock:

Isaac Low.

CHAMBER OF COMMERCE.—TUESDAY, 6th September, 1774.

PRESENT.

William Walton, President.
Anthony Van Dam, Secretary.

Samuel Bayard,
John Cruger,
John H. Cruger,
Isaac Corsa,
Elias Desbrosses,
Johnston Fairholme,
William Laight,
William Stepple,
Gerrard Walton,
Hugh Wallace,
Robert Watts.

Fined for appearing after six o'clock:

William Walton,
Johnston Fairholme,
Cerrard Walton,
Hugh Wallace.

The consideration of the motion made for subscribing for Eleven more of Mr. Roman's Drafts that he is now publishing, being debated,

Voted—That Eleven sets be subscribed for on account of this Corporation, and that any Member in want thereof be furnished therewith at first Cost.

Ordered—That the Treasurer do pay unto Mr. Barnard Romans the first subscription money for Eleven sets, taking his Receipt.

Ordered—That Messrs. Samuel Bayard, John H. Cruger, Johnston Fairholme, William Jauncey, Peter Keteltas, Lawrence Kortright, and Philip Livingston, be a Committee to hear and determine disputes that may be left to the Chamber untill the first Tuesday in December next.

CHAMBER OF COMMERCE.—TUESDAY, 4th October, 1774.

PRESENT.

William Walton, President.
William McAdam, Treasurer.
Anthony Van Dam, Secretary.

Joseph Bull,
Benjamin Booth,
John Cruger,
Isaac Corsa,
Leonard Lispenard,
Edward Laight,
John Moore,
Lewis Pintard,

George Ludlow,
Gabriel Ludlow,
William Stepple,
Gerrard Walton,
Robert Watts.

Fined for appearing after six o'clock:

Robert Watts.

CHAMBER OF COMMERCE.—TUESDAY, 1st November, 1774.

PRESENT.

William Walton, President.
John Alsop, } Vice do.
Isaac Low, }
Anthony Van Dam, Secretary.

Theophylact Bache,
John Cruger,
John H. Cruger,
Elias Desbrosses,
Robert C. Livingston,
George Ludlow,
Gabriel H. Ludlow,
Francis Lewis,
William Laight,
John Moore,
Miles Sherbrooke,
Richard Sharpe,
James Seagrove,
Samuel Verplanck,
Augustus Van Horne,
Gerrard Walton,
Robert R. Waddle,
Robert Watts.

Fined for appearing after six o'clock:

Isaac Low,
John Moore,
Miles Sherbrooke,
James Seagrove,
Robert R. Waddle.

CHAMBER OF COMMERCE.—TUESDAY, December 6th, 1774.

PRESENT.

William Walton, President.
Isaac Low, Vice President.
William McAdam, Treasurer.
Anthony Van Dam, Secretary.

Joseph Bull,
John H. Cruger,
Isaac Corsa,
George Ludlow,
Francis Lewis,
William Laight,
William Stepple,
Gerrard Walton.

Fined for appearing after six o'clock:

John Moore, Anthony Van Dam,
Alex'r Wallace.

CHAMBER OF COMMERCE.—TUESDAY, 3d January, 1775.

PRESENT.

William Walton, President.
Anthony Van Dam, Secretary.

Joseph Bull,
John Cruger,
Isaac Corsa,
William Laight,
Robert R. Waddle.

Fined for appearing after six o'clock:

Francis Lewis.

CHAMBER OF COMMERCE.—TUESDAY, February 7th, 1775.

PRESENT.

William Walton, President.
John Alsop, Vice Pres.
Anthony Van Dam, Secretary.

Joseph Bull,
William Laight,
John H. Cruger,
Johnston Fairholme,
John Cruger,
Richard Sharpe,
Gerrard W. Beekman,
Edward Laight,
Isaac Corsa,
John Schuyler.

Fined for appearing after six o'clock:

Samuel Bayard, James Seagrove,
Gerrard Walton.

CHAMBER OF COMMERCE.—TUESDAY, March 7th, 1775.

PRESENT.

William Walton, President.
Anthony Van Dam, Secretary.

Theophy. Bache,
Joseph Bull,
Isaac Corsa,
William Laight,
Robert Murray,
Miles Sherbrooke,
Robert R. Waddle.

CHAMBER OF COMMERCE.—TUESDAY, April 4th, 1775.

PRESENT.

William Walton, President.
William McAdam, Treasurer.
Anthony Van Dam, Secretary.

Elias Desbrosses,
Peter Ketletas,
William Stepple,
Hugh Wallace,
Alexan. Wallace.

Fined for appearing after six o'clock :

Joseph Bull,
William McAdam,
Gerrard W. Beekman,
Jacob Walton,
Edward Laight,
Robert R. Waddell.

CHAMBER OF COMMERCE.—TUESDAY, 2d May, 1775.

PRESENT.

William Walton, President.
Isaac Low, Vice President.
William McAdam, Treasurer.
Anthony Van Dam, Secretary.

Theoph. Bache,
Joseph Bull,
John Cruger,
Isaac Corsa,
Elias Desbrosses,
George Ludlow,
Francis Lewis,
William Laight,
Edward Laight,
Charles McEvers,
William Stepple,
Augustus Van Horne,
Gerrard Walton,
Robert R. Waddle,
Hugh Wallace.

Ordered—That Messrs. William Laight, William Seton, Miles Sherbrooke, James Seagrove, and William Stepple, be a Committee to Audit the Treasurer's accounts until this day, and that they report the same to this Corporation at their next meeting.

Ordered—That the Treasurer pay unto Mr. Bernard Romans, or his Order, One hundred and eight Dollars, being the last payment for Twelve Complete Setts of Charts of the Navigation to and in the new ceded Countries to the Southward of Georgia,"[115] which he hath lately transmitted to the Secretary.

Ordered—That Messrs. Peter Ketletas, Joseph Bull, Gabriel H. Ludlow, and Edward Laight, be a Committee to examine Fishermen's Claims, that have furnished this Market with such Fish as this Corporation have thought fit to grant a Bounty thereon, and prescribe such mode of Proof as will be necessary to entitle thereto, and that they, or any three of them give an order on the Treasurer for the Payment, when it shall appear who are the Objects of such Bounty, and that they make report thereof to this Corporation.

Ordered—That Messrs. Robert C. Livingston, Geo. Ludlow, Gabriel H. Ludlow, Leonard Lispenard, Junr., William Laight, Robert Murray, and John Moore, be a Committee to hear and determine Disputes that may be left to this Chamber, until the first Tuesday in June next.

The Charter as well as the Laws of this Corporation appoints this Day for the Election of Officers when the following Gentlemen were balloted for and duly Elected.

Isaac Low,	President.
John Alsop, Vice	Presidents.
William McAdam, Vice	
Charles McEvers,	Treasurer.
Anthony Van Dam,	Secretary.

Then Messrs. Isaac Low, William McAdam, Charles McEvers, and Anthony Van Dam, the Officers elected that were present, were duly sworn, agreeable to the Charter, to execute their respective offices.[116]

CHAMBER OF COMMERCE.

HE STATE OF PUBLIC AFFAIRS[117] having been such as not to require a meeting of the Chamber of Commerce at an earlier period, no measures were taken for that purpose untill it was conceived that the Increase of Commerce,[118] in consequence of the Latitude it derived from the Commissioners'[119] benevolent proclamation,[120] rendered a revival of so usefull an Institution absolutely necessary.

At the request, therefore, of a number of the Members, the President issued notices for convening as many of them as were now in New York and its vicinity, and the following Members appeared accordingly, in the Upper long room at the Coffy House.[121]

SPECIAL MEETING.—MONDAY, 21st June, 1779.

PRESENT.

Isaac Low, President.
William McAdam, Vice President.
Anthy. Van Dam, Secretary.

William Walton,	Alcxand'r Wallace,
Isaac Corsa,	Robert R. Waddel,
Robert Murray,	William Laight,
John Moore,	Thomas Buchanan,
William Seton,	Gabriel H. Ludlow,
Thomas Miller,	William Stepple,
Edward Laight,	Richard Yates,
Hugh Wallace,	Gerrard Walton,
Henry White,	Augustus Van Horne,
Benj. Booth,	Lawrence Kortright.

A draft of a Letter to the Commandant[122] was then produced in the words following:

NEW YORK, June 21, 1779.

SIR:

We beg leave to inform your Excellency that the Subscribers are Members of a Society known by the Style and Title of a Chamber of Commerce which, before the present unnatural rebellion, met under certain regulations (of which we have the honor of inclosing a copy), and determined the principal matters relative to trade in this City.

The good effects of this Institution having been felt and acknowledged by all persons concerned in Trade, and the increase of Commerce encouraged by the Proclamations of his Majesty's Commissioners, together with the success of Private Ships of War,[123] has induced the Merchants in general (who are ready to join us agreeable to our regulations) to solicit a renewal of our Meetings in order that the many mercantile differences which so frequently happen may be adjusted.

As Commandant of the City, we esteemed it our duty to lay before you the intent of our proposed meetings and at the same time we beg leave to assure you that our assistance, when called upon, will at all times be ready to facilitate the Public good.

We have the honor to be, Sir, your Excellency's Most ob't and most humble servants.

HIS EXCELLENCY DANIEL JONES,[dd] Esq.,
Commandant of New York, &c.

The question being put resolved nem. con. that it be engrossed and signed by the members present and transmitted by the President to the Commandant—it was signed accordingly.

The following Gentlemen were appointed till the first Tuesday in July next, to hear and determine disputes between Parties who shall agree to leave such to the determination of this Corporation:

William Walton,	John Moore,
Isaac Corsa,	William Seton,
Robert Murray,	Thomas Miller,

Edward Laight.

CHAMBER OF COMMERCE.—TUESDAY, 6th July, 1779.

PRESENT.

William McAdam, Vice President.
Anthony Van Dam, Secretary.

August Van Horne, George Ludlow,
William Seton, Robert Murray,
Gerrard Walton, Benj. Booth,
Alex. Wallace, William Walton,
Gabriel H. Ludlow, Rob. R. Waddel,
Isaac Corsa, Thos. Buchanan,
Edward Laight, William Stepple,
Hugh Wallace, William Laight,
Thomas Miller, Henry White,
Law. Kortright.

The Vice President having received a Letter from his Excellency Gen'l Jones in answer to one Subscribed by this Corporation at their last Meeting, (*it*) was ordered to be entered on the Minutes, and is in the words following:

NEW YORK, June 25th, 1779.

GENTLEMEN:

I have laid the Letter you favored me with before the Commander in Chief, and I have the Pleasure to acquaint you that his Excellency approves of the Gentlemen of the Chamber of Commerce renewing their Meetings as formerly. I was happy to hear of this Institution and regret only that I have not had the benefit of your assistance sooner to procure to New York every advantage our present situation would admit of, which I have always had much at Heart. You may therefore Gentlemen be assured every Proposal coming from you, for the good of the City, shall meet with my hearty concurrence and assistance, and when I Quit my present Command I shall recommend to my Successor the usefull assistance that I think may be drawn from your Institution.

I have the honour to be, Gentlemen,
Your most Obedient and Humble Servant,
D. JONES, Lt. Gen'l. Commandant.

The Gentlemen of the
Chamber of Commerce, New York.

Committee to hear and determine disputes until the first Tuesday in August.

Hugh Wallace,
Thomas Buchanan,
Gab'l H. Ludlow,
William Stepple,
Richard Yates,
Gerrard Walton,
Augustus Van Horne.

The following Gentlemen were balloted for, and chosen members of this Chamber:

Fred Rhinelander,
Jacob Watson,
Nich's Hoffman,
John Thurman,
John Miller,
Smith Ramadge,
Neil Jameson.

CHAMBER OF COMMERCE.—MONDAY, 12th July, 1779.

SPECIAL MEETING.

PRESENT.

Wm. McAdam, Vice President.
Anthony Van Dam, Secretary.

Hugh Wallace,
Thomas Buchanan,
Thomas Miller,
Alex'r Wallace,
Gerrard Walton,
Jacob Watson,
William Walton,
Robt. Murray,
Edward Laight,
Isaac Corsa,
William Seton,
William Laight,
Law. Kortright,
Gab. H. Ludlow,
Smith Ramadge,
Robt R. Waddell,
John Miller,
Fred Rhinelander,
Will'm Stepple.

At the request of the Superintendent General, by his Letter, a Special Meeting of the Chamber was called by desire of the Commandant, and Mr. ELLIOT ee laid before the Corporation the following Letter:

MAJOR GENERAL PATTISON ff desires that the Committee of the Chamber of Commerce will meet on Monday next, to consider on the most effectual means to be used for the better Cleansing the City, and for the raising a necessary Fund for defraying the Expence thereof, as likewise to propose such Fines and Penaltys as may be thought sufficient to prevent the Inhabitants from throwing the Filth and Rubbish from their Houses into the Streets, and to oblige them to convey it to certain Places that may be assigned in each Ward for depositing it, and from thence to be regularly taken away at stated times by Scavengers to be employed for that Purpose. Hospitals, Barracks, and all Public Buildings to be comprehended in whatever regulations may be propos'd for carrying into execution this very necessary and salutary Plan. The Commandant likewise wishes to know the opinion of the Chamber of Commerce respecting the expediency of regulating the markets with regard to the Prices to be paid for Butchers'meat;[124] and further, to prevent the danger of Fire, to which the City is now exposed from the Quantities of Naval Stores that are dispers'd through the Town. The General, before he gives any order on this important point, requests to know what Plan the Merchants would wish to propose, that might Combine the safety of the Public together with the Conveniencys of Trade.

NEW YORK, 10th July, 1779.

ANDREW ELLIOT, Superintendent, &c., &c., &c.

Whereupon the following Gentlemen were appointed a Committee to take the said Letter into consideration, and to report to this Chamber thereon against Monday Evening next at six o'clock: William Walton, Jacob Watson, William Laight, Lawrence Kortright, Isaac Corsa, Isaac Low, John Thurman, William Stepple, Benjamin Booth, Nicholas Hoffman, John Miller, Fred'ck Rhinelander, Augustus Van Horne.

CHAMBER OF COMMERCE.—MONDAY, 19th July, 1779.

SPECIAL MEETING.

PRESENT.

Isaac Low, President.
Anthony Van Dam, Secretary.

Jacob Watson, Richard Yates,
Isaac Corsa, Gabriel H. Ludlow,
Alexander Wallace, John Thurman,
Robert Murray, Lawrence Kortright,
John Moore, William Stepple,
Smith Ramadge, John Miller,
Gerrard Walton, Fred'ck Rhinelander,
Edward Laight, Nicholas Hoffman,
Hugh Wallace, William Laight,
Augustus Van Horne.

In pursuance of the order of this Corporation, the Committee laid before them their report in the words following:

THE COMMITTEE of the Chamber of Commerce, to whom is referred MAJOR GENERAL PATTISON'S Recommendations to lay before him a Plan for the better cleansing the Streets in this City, &c., Beg leave to observe,

That as the want of proper regulations for that Purpose has been long complained of by everybody; they are the more happy to find that the Commandant regards it as an object of his earliest attention; and is so ready to give the sanction of his authority effectually to remedy so crying an Evil,—and although this business does not come within the proper Sphere of the Chamber of Commerce, as not appertaining to Trade, they very cheerfully accept the Task, and shall be very happy if they can furnish any Hints that may be honored with the Commandant's approbation.

But we presume it is not so necessary to devise a new Plan, as to revise that which was formerly in Practice. This City was once as remarkable for its cleanliness as it is now for the contrary.

If, therefore, the same Regulations are adopted which experience manifested to be so Salutary and Proper, we conceive they will be more likely to produce the same good Effects, than any other we might be able to suggest for that Purpose.

The old Corporation ordinances,[125] matured after various amendments by Time and Reflection, contain excellent Regulations for Cleaning and Paving the Streets, and also provide amply against Storing Naval Stores within the confines of the City, and as the Police[126] are possessed of these Ordinances, and the inhabitants probably attached to old Customs, we beg leave to recommend an adoption of them, not only with regard to the above Particulars, but in all other respects where they may be found usefull. And if Hospitals,[127] Barracks, and all other Public Buildings are (as the Commandant generously promises) " to be comprehended in the regulations for carrying into execution this Very necessary and Salutary Plan," we conceive every difficulty will be entirely removed. Very different has been the former usage relative to these Public Buildings, for notwithstanding repeated representations, it seemed to be the opinion that nothing further was necessary than to throw the Straw and Dirt into the middle of the Streets and leave it to the Inhabitants and Scavengers to remove in any way they pleased. Experience has abundantly evinced that to have all the Dirt and Rubbish removed by Scavengers at the Public expence, exceeds almost all computation ; and it will be difficult to devise funds adequate to the Purpose, amidst the necessity there is for large expenditures for the use of the Poor, and other indispensable Occasions. Scavengers may nevertheless be found very usefull, and a Plan was once handed to the Superintendent and some Progress made therein, of advertising for and employing Scavengers under the immunity of an exclusive right to take the Dirt and Rubbish out of the Streets for their own use. To this it was objected by some Person in Power,[123] "*that it would interfere with the common right of Mankind, because every Person who pleased had a right to take Dirt out of the Streets.*" An Hypothesis in our Idea founded neither in Reason or Fact ; and we still think the Mode proposed would be the cheapest and best, of employing Scavingers.

With regard to regulating the Price of Butchers meat, Experience justifies our apprehensions that the remedy may prove worse than the Disease. But we are of opinion that limiting the Time of Butchers, Greenwomen,[129] or Hucksters, being in the Market, may be attended with very good effects. We therefore beg leave to recommend that no Butchers, Greenwomen, Poulterers, Sellers of Vegetables, or any Hucksters, to be in the Market (Saturday afternoons excepted) after 10 o'clock in the morning, from the Month of April to October; and not after 11 o'clock the remaining Part of the Year. And that no fresh Provisions (Fish excepted), Vegetables or Poultry, should be suffered to be put into Stores or Cellars, on Penalty of being forfeited for the use of the Alms House.[130]

We beg leave to recommend to your Consideration, whether it is not expedient to lower the Prices of Cartmen,[131] which are certainly much higher than they ought to be, as an industrious Cartman may, as they now Stand, earn from 40s to 100s p. day.[132] These high wages have rendered them so very nice and Choice, about what and for whom they will Cart ; that it is highly expedient the Police should revise the old Laws[133] respecting Cartmen, and confine them more strictly to their Duty.

We are of opinion that if the Wages of Cartmen were reduced one third from their Present prices they would still be amply sufficient.

Ordered—That a fair Copy be made of the above Report, and delivered to the Commandant by the President.

CHAMBER OF COMMERCE.—TUESDAY, 3d August, 1779.

PRESENT.

Isaac Low,	President.
William McAdam,	Vice President.
Anthony Van Dam,	Secretary.

William Stepple,	Alexa. Wallace,
William Seton,	Robert R. Waddel,
Thomas Miller,	Fred. Rhinelander,
Nicholas Hoffman,	John Moore,
Gerrard Walton,	Edward Laight,
Robert Murray,	Hugh Wallace,
John Thurman,	Benj. Booth,
William Laight,	George Ludlow,
William Walton,	Jacob Watson,
John Miller,	Isaac Corsa,
Smith Ramadge,	Gabriel H. Ludlow.

A Letter from Mr. ELLIOT, signifying the Commandant's desire that the Chamber would furnish a Table of Rates for Cartmen's Wages, being read in the words following:

NEW YORK, 3d August, 1779.

GENTLEMEN:

I am directed by the Commandant to request you to lay before him a Table of such Rates as you think ought to be allowed to Cartmen in this City.

Those now established were fixt by the Gentlemen of the Old Insurance Office,[134] at a time when Provision was higher, but Forage lower than at present.

I have the honor to be, Gentlemen,

Your very obedt. hble. servt.,

ANDREW ELLIOT, Supert. Genl.

The Gentlemen of the Chamber of Commerce.

Ordered—That the following Persons be a Committee for that Purpose, and that they report a Table of the said Rates to MR. ELLIOT, with all convenient speed: William McAdam, John Miller, Benjam. Booth, Fred Rhinelander, Edward Laight, Alexander Wallace, Smith Ramadge.

The said Committee are appointed untill the first Tuesday in September, to hear and determine disputes between parties who are willing to submit the same to this Corporation.

Mr. Booth having presented proposals of the Rate of Storing Gun-Powder afloat:[135]

Ordered—That the Monthly Committee do take into consideration Mr. Booth's proposals about Powder, and report to this Corporation the best and cheapest rates of storing Gun Powder, and the most proper places for that Purpose.

Several Gentlemen having been proposed to become Members of this Corporation, the following were ballotted for and duly elected.

Samuel Donaldson,	John Taylor,
William Kenyon,	Thomas C. Williams,
William Backhouse,	Thomas Goodwin,
Patrick McDavitt,	Harding Burnley,
Daniel McCormick,	John L. McAdam,
Walter Spens,	Oliver Templeton,
Henry Thompson,	John Oothout,
John Murray,	John Tench,
Charles Nicoll,	Edward Goold,

William Ustick.

Ordered—That the Secretary send notice to the respective Gentlemen in writing, that they are duly elected Members of this Corporation.

Resolved and Ordered—That the Fines for non-attendance at any Meetings of the Chamber be strictly levied, agreeable to the standing rules thereof.

CHAMBER OF COMMERCE.—TUESDAY, 7th Sept., 1779.

PRESENT.

Isaac Low, President.
William McAdam, Vice President.
Anth. Van Dam, Secretary.

Robert Murray,	John Murray,
Edward Goold,	John Miller,
Edward Laight,	John Tench,
William Kenyon,	William Stepple,
Jacob Watson,	John Oothout,
Isaac Corsa,	Benjm. Booth,
Willm. Backhouse,	William Seton,
Smith Ramadge,	John Moore,
Patrick McDavitt,	Daniel McCormick,
William Ustick,	William Laight,
Thos. C. Williams,	Oliver Templeton,
Samuel Donaldson,	Robert R. Waddell,

Alex. Wallace.

Mr. Booth having made further proposals to the Chamber, respecting the Storage of Gun Powder :

Ordered—That it be referred to the Committee of last month, and that Mr. John Moore be added thereto.

This Corporation having occupied the LONG ROOM of the COFFY-HOUSE :

It is proposed that Mrs. Smith[136] be paid at the Rate of Fifty Pounds per annum, commencing the 1st May last, the Chamber finding Firewood and Candles, and that John Norris,[gg] Doorkeeper and Messenger, do furnish the same.

It is proposed that there be allowed and paid to John Norris, Door Keeper and Messenger, the sum of Forty pounds per annum, commencing the first day of May last.

It is proposed that Thomas Petit, the former Door

Keeper be paid his accustomed salary to the first day of May, 1775.

Ordered—That Messrs. Robert R. Waddel, Lawrence Kortright, Jacob Watson, Richard Sharpe, Nicholas Hoffman, Samuel Kemble, and William Kenyon, be a Committee, untill the first Tuesday in October next, to hear and determine disputes between Parties who shall agree to abide their determination.

CHAMBER OF COMMERCE.—TUESDAY, 5th October, 1779.

PRESENT.

Isaac Low, President.

} Vice Presidents.

Secretary.

Lawrence Kortright,	John Murray,
William Laight,	Jacob Watson,

Gabriel H. Ludlow.

Fined for appearing after six o'clock :

Isaac Low,	Benj. Booth,
Fred. Rhinelander,	Nicholas Hoffman,
John Tench,	Thomas C. Williams,
William Stepple,	Patrick McDavitt,
William Kenyon,	Smith Ramadge,
William Backhouse,	Robert R. Waddell,
John Thurman,	John Moore,
John Oothout,	Danl. McCormick,
Alex. Wallace,	Oliver Templeton.

Resolved—That in consequence of the proposal of last Meeting to pay Mrs. Smith rent for the Long Room of the Coffy-House, that she be paid at the rate of £50 per annum, to commence the 1st May last, by the Treasurer for the time being, in quarterly or half year payments.

Resolved—That the Treasurer, for the time being, do also pay unto John Norris, Door Keeper and Messenger, a salary of Forty pounds per annum, commencing the first day of May last, and

Resolved—That the Treasurer for the time being do pay to Thomas Petit, the former Doorkeeper, his salary for one year ending the first day of May, 1775, the sum of £15.

Ordered—That Messrs. William Backhouse, Charles Nicoll, John Murray, Samuel Donaldson, John L. McAdam, Patrick McDavitt, and Oliver Templeton, be a Committee, untill the first Tuesday in November next, to hear and determine Disputes between parties that shall submit the same to their decision.

A Petition signed John Van Vart, Henry Shier, and John Machet in behalf of themselves and others, the Cartmen of the City of New York, requesting that the Chamber would revise the rates as lately affixed by the office of Police, and (attending to the difference of labor, Provisions, Provender, &c.,) make such an alteration as the Wisdom and Justice of the Chamber shall think meet, which being considered, it was

Resolved—That it be recommended that the following Rates be affixed :

For every common Load, &c., - -	2s	6d.
Load of Hay, - - - - - -	8	
Rum, Wine, Moll's, Sugar, -	4	6

and that the different Articles be taken out and housed, as was formerly accustomed.

Ordered—That the Committee of the month consider and report their opinion, the Price of Labor now demanded by Artificers,[137] &c., at the next meeting.

CHAMBER OF COMMERCE.—FRIDAY, 12th October, 1779.

SPECIAL MEETING.

PRESENT.

Isaac Low, President.
Anthony Van Dam, Secretary.

Edward Laight,
William Laight,
John Tench,
Fred Rhinelander.

Fined for appearing after six o'clock :

William Kenyon,
Robert Murray,
Thos. Buchanan,
Will'm Backhouse,
John Oothout,
Saml. Donaldson,
Walter Spens,
Thomas Goodwin,
John Murray,
Will'm Stepple,
Jacob Watson,
Gerrard Walton,
Robert R. Waddell,
Alex'r Wallace,
John Moore,
Isaac Low,
Dan'l McCormick,
Gabriel H. Ludlow,
Patrick M'Davitt,
Lawrence Kortright,
Thomas C. Williams,
Edward Goold,
Oliver Templeton,
Smith Ramadge,
William Pagan.

THE CORPORATION of the Chamber of Commerce being convened this Even'g for the express purpose of reconsidering a report of the Monthly Committee relative to a disputed account between Messrs. *Ward & Selkrig*, *James Selkrig & Co.*, *& Alexander Selkrig*, with *David Black*, in consequence of a Memorial of the said *David Black* to the Police and to the Commandant complaining of Ill language, Injustice, and great partiality of the Monthly Committee to whom the said controversies were referred. The Chamber report that they have carefully examined and attended to the several allegations of the Complainant. That it appears to the Chamber their Committee were at great pains to investigate the Truth. That the injurious reflections cast on them, and particularly on Mr. Waddle, were without the least foundation ; and that Mr. Black's objections to the determination of the Committee appear from a number of concurring circumstances calculated rather to evade the payment of a just debt by mere Subterfuges than to shew any solid reason for his refusal. The Chamber, therefore, cannot but confirm the opinion of their Committee without the least deviation or exception whatever.

CHAMBER OF COMMERCE.—TUESDAY, 2d November, 1779.

PRESENT.

Isaac Low, President.
Anthony Van Dam, Secretary.

Gerrard Walton,	Oliver Templeton,
William Laight,	William Ustick,
John Tench,	John Moore,
William Kenyon,	Charles Nicoll,
William Backhouse,	Patrick McDavitt,
Frederick Rhinelander,	John Oothout,
Daniel McCormick,	Will'm Stepple,
Jacob Watson,	Saml. Donaldson,
Smith Ramadge,	Alex. Wallace,
John Murray,	Benj'm Booth,
Isaac Corsa,	John L. McAdam,
Robert Murray,	Thomas Goodwin,
Robert R. Waddell,	John Miller.

The Chamber having had the terms laid before them by Mr. Booth for storing Gunpowder at different meetings on board a Vessel fitted for that purpose, received the following

RATES:

Every Quarter Cask of Gun-powder received on board the Powder Vessel to pay—three shillings.

Every such Quarter Cask delivered out of the Vessel, provided it has been on board no longer [*than*] three months—three shillings.

Every such Quarter Cask remaining on board longer than three Months to pay at the rate of three pence p. month afterwards over and above the rates above-mentioned.

By a Quarter Cask is meant the fourth part of one hundred pound weight of Gun-powder. All other packages to pay in proportion.

But since the Chamber of Commerce approved of the foregoing rules, Mr. Booth has made a new calculation, and is happy to find that he shall be able to lessen the last charge of three Shillings, payable on delivery, to Eighteen

Pence, at which rate the Storage of 100 lbs. for the first three months will be only 18s, and the accounts will be made out accordingly.

The above rates for Storing Gunpowder on board a Ship is approved of by this Corporation.

Ordered—That Messrs. John Oothout, John Taylor, Thos. C. Williams, John Tench, Walter Spens, Thos. Goodwin, Edward Goold, be a Committee, untill the first Tuesday in December next, to hear and determine disputes between parties who shall leave such to this Chamber, and that they do make report thereof to this Corporation.

The following Gentlemen having been propos'd at a former meeting to become members of this Corporation, were balloted for, and duly elected:

William Pagan, Andrew Kerr.

Ordered—That the Secretary send notice to them in Writing, that they are duly elected Members of this Corporation.

It is Proposed and Ordered—That as Mr. William McAdam is dead, and Mr. John Alsop is absent,[138] who were Vice Presidents of this Corporation—that two others be balloted for at the next Monthly Meeting agreeable to the Charter.

CHAMBER OF COMMERCE.—TUESDAY, 7th Dec., 1779.

PRESENT.

Isaac Low, President.
Anthony Van Dam, Secretary.

John Murray, William Ustick,
Isaac Corsa, Robert Murray,
William Kenyon, Alex. Wallace,
Richard Yates.

Fined for appearing after six o'clock:

William Stepple,	William Laight,
Oliver Templeton,	Patrick McDavitt,
Daniel McCormick,	Edward Goold,
John Tench,	Hugh Wallace,
Andrew Kerr,	Robert R. Waddell,
John Oothout,	Fred. Rhinelander,
William Pagan,	Thomas Goodwin,
Walter Spens,	John Moore,
John Miller,	Thomas C. Williams,
John L. McAdam,	Smith Ramadge,

Thomas Buchanan.

It having been represented that the Powder-Ship will not be safe during the Winter at her present moorings.

Ordered—That Messrs. John Miller, Will'm Laight, and Will'm Ustick, be a Committee to enquire a proper situation for the security of the Powder-Ship during the Winter, and that the Proprietor be desired to have Her removed at a convenient time to such as they shall Judge most safe.

The Corporation proceeded, in consequence of the resolve of last Meeting, to the election of two Vice Presidents in the place of William McAdam, deceased, and John Alsop, absent, when

The Hon'ble Hugh Wallace,

Mr. Thomas Buchanan,

were duly elected to serve to the first Tuesday in May next, and untill others were chosen, who were sworn accordingly to perform the trust reposed in them agreeable to Charter, and took their Seats accordingly.

Messrs. William Lowther and Henry Brevoort, being proposed at a former Meeting, were balloted for and duly elected Members of this Corporation.

Ordered—That Notice be sent them by the Secretary in writing that they were duly elected.

John Murray moves that the dispute between *Henry White, Esqr.*, and *Donaldson & White*, determined by a Committee of this Chamber, be heard by the Chamber of Commerce at large, for to be approved or disapproved by this Corporation.

John Oothout moves that this Corporation direct any future Committee to keep a Book in which they shall enter every opinion given on any disputed matter referred to them by the Commandant, the Police, or mutual references of Individuals, and that the said Book of proceedings be brought into the Chamber at every monthly meeting for their inspection, and delivered to the succeeding Committee.

Ordered—That Messrs. Robert Murray, William Walton, Daniel McCormick, William Ustick, William Pagan, Andrew Kerr, and Augustus Van Horne, be a Committee untill the first Tuesday in January next, to hear and determine disputes between parties, who shall agree to leave such to this Corporation, and that they do report the same in writing at their next meeting.

CHAMBER OF COMMERCE.—Tuesday, 4th January, 1780.

PRESENT.

Isaac Low, President.
Anthony Van Dam, Secretary.

Richard Yates,	Jacob Watson,
Edward Laight,	Daniel McCormick,
William Laight,	Fred. Rhinelander,
John Miller,	Thos. C. Williams,
Andrew Kerr,	Gerrard Walton,
Oliver Templeton,	William Backhouse,
John Murray,	Robert Murray.

Fined for appearing after six o'clock:

Isaac Low,	Samuel Donaldson,
William Kenyon,	Alexan. Wallace,
William Ustick,	Augustus Van Horne,
Anthony Van Dam,	William Pagan,
John Moore,	William Lowther.

Ordered—That Messrs. John Moore, Robert R. Waddel, Lawrence Kortright, Robert Watts, Gerrard Walton, William Lowther, and Henry Brevoort, be a Committee untill the first Tuesday in February next, to hear and determine disputes between Parties that shall submit the same to this Corporation, and that they report their proceedings to this Chamber.

A MEMORIAL of Messrs. *Shedden & Goodrich* of the said City, Merchants, requesting the Chamber to reconsider a disputed account between them and *Capt. McDonald* being read, the CHAMBER accordingly revised and carefully investigated the proceedings of the Committee; see no reason to differ with them in opinion, and therefore confirm it in all respects.

AN APPLICATION of *Issacher Polock* to have a rehearing on a dispute settled by the last month's Committee between *Barrack Hays* and said *Issacher Polock;* the latter appealing to the Chamber at large, asserting that he had more evidence in support of his claim, and several witnesses, being duly sworn before the Police, to give in their evidence, all which being duly attended to: The CHAMBER at large nevertheless confirm the determination of the Committee, that is to say

That it is the opinion of the Committee of the Chamber of Commerce that *Mr. Issacher Polock* do pay unto *Mr. Barrack Hays* one hundred and fifty pounds Currency in full for his half commissions, the matter of dispute between them.

Ordered—That Mr. John Murray's motion be considered at a future Meeting.

Ordered—That Mr. John Oothout's motion be considered at next Meeting.

CHAMBER OF COMMERCE.—TUESDAY, 1st February, 1780.

PRESENT.

Isaac Low, President.
Thomas Buchanan, Vice-President.
Anthony Van Dam, Secretary.

William Laight,
Edward Laight,
Alexr. Wallace,
Henry Brevoort,
Robert R. Waddell.

Fined for appearing after six o'clock:

Frederick Rhinelander,
William Backhouse,
William Walton,
Walter Spens,
Charles Nicoll,
Jacob Watson,
Thomas Buchanan,
Gerrard Walton,
Augus. Van Horne,
William Seton,
William Kenyon,
Robert Murray,
William Stepple,
William Lowther,
Thomas C. Williams,
Smith Ramadge,
Andrew Kerr,
John Oothout,
Daniel McCormick,
William Ustick,
John Thurman,
Patrick McDavitt,
John Moore,
William Pagan,
John Miller.

Ordered—That Messrs. Robert Watts, Richard Yates, Alexander Wallace, Gabriel H. Ludlow, Thomas Buchanan, Jacob Watson, and William Seton, be a Committee untill the first Tuesday in March next to hear and determine disputes between parties that shall submit the same to this Corporation, and that they report their proceedings to this Chamber.

Mr. John Moore proposed that as the PRIMAGE of Goods brought into this port, where primage is not specified in the Bill of Lading, is at present in a state of uncertainty, some paying 5 per cent. and others refusing to pay anything, that this Corporation, if agreeable to them, will take the same into their Consideration, and allot such primage as to them shall seem meet.

Mr. David Seabury having been proposed at a former meeting, was ballotted for and duly elected a member of this Corporation.

Ordered—That notice be sent to him by the Secretary, in writing, that he was duly elected a Member of this Corporation.

CHAMBER OF COMMERCE.—TUESDAY, 15th February, 1780.

SPECIAL MEETING.

PRESENT.

Isaac Low, President.
Thomas Buchanan, Vice-Presidt.
Anthony Van Dam, Secretary.

Robert Murray,
Will'm Kenyon,
John Miller,
William Stepple,
William Lowther,
Andrew Kerr,
Alex'r Wallace,
Will'm Laight.

Fined for appearing after six o'clock:

Patrick McDavitt,
David Seabury,
Daniel McCormick,
Gabriel H. Ludlow,
Richard Yates,
Augustus Van Horne,
Jacob Watson,
William Seton,
Frederic Rhinelander,
Robert Watts,
Thomas C. Williams,
Thomas Buchanan,
William Backhouse,
William Pagan,
Oliver Templeton,
Charles Nicoll,
Samuel Donaldson,
Robert R. Waddell.

This Special Meeting having been called to take into consideration a Letter from the Police relative to a petition of *Mr. William Tongue*, who had been deprived of His License as a Vendue Master, for refusing to comply with the determination of the Committee of this Corporation in paying for a Vessel sold by him for Mr. Lee, and the Police refusing to restore to the said *William Tongue* his License as a Vendue Master,[139] unless he be recommended for that Purpose by this Chamber—They are of opinion, that there was great propriety in the punishment inflicted on *Mr. Tongue* for not fulfilling his duty as a Vendue Master, yet, having at length complied with what was requested of Him, they have no objection to *Mr. Tongue's* being restored to his former Employment.

A Petition from the Bakers, setting forth that the price of Flour being advanced beyond the assized price of Bread, and that therefore they cannot afford to carry on their Business.

Ordered—That the President inform the Police, that on the most minute enquiry, the Chamber are of opinion that Good Flour cannot now be purchased under Three Pounds p. Hundred Weight.

A Dispute having arisen between *Mr. William Pagan* and *Mr. Robert Dale*, joint owners in a Privateer, what Commissions, or if any, ought to be allowed on the men's shares to the acting owner, for transacting the Business, where no previous agreement is made between the owners themselves, and the Question being put after debate thereon, in the words following, viz.:

Whether the Commission charged by *Mr. Pagan* on the Crew's Shares, shall be divided between the Owners, or wholly retained by *Mr. Pagan*, he having paid the said crew.

Resolved in the affirmative, by a majority of the Chamber—That *Mr. Pagan* retain the whole of the said Commissions of 5 p. ct. on the Crew's share.

CHAMBER OF COMMERCE.—TUESDAY, 7th March, 1780.

PRESENT.

Isaac Low, President.
Thos. Buchanan, Vice-President.
Anthony Van Dam, Secretary.

Fred. Rhinelander,
William Laight,
Robert Murray,
Gab'l H. Ludlow,
William Kenyon,
Oliver Templeton,
Gerard Walton,
William Lowther,
Alex'r Wallace,
William Backhouse,
Edward Laight.

Fined for appearing after six o'clock:

Samuel Donaldson,
John Miller,
Thomas C. Williams,
Smith Ramadge,
Daniel McCormick,
Patrick McDavitt,
John Moore,
Robert R. Waddle,
David Seabury,
Rich'd Yates,
Tho's Buchanan,
Charles Nicoll.

A representation by Mr. Miller and Agent Walter,[hh] of the Insecurity of the Powder-Ship, the following Gentlemen were appointed a Committee to confer with proper Judges the propriety of fixing a Conductor to secure her against lightning,[140] and a practical mode of receiving and delivering Powder; John Moore, Samuel Donaldson, Smith Ramadge, Gerrard Walton, John Miller, who are to report at their next meeting.

Ordered—That the Thanks of this Corporation be given to Lieut. Walter for his great attention and care of the Powder-Ship in the Walloon Bay[141] during the Winter.

SIR :—

I have the Pleasure to inclose you an order of the Chamber of Commerce in Testimony of the high sense they entertain of your Services in preserving the Powder-Ship, and I have the honor to remain, Sir, your most obt. Hbl. Servant, ISAAC LOW, Presidt.

Chamber of Commerce.

Ordered—That Messrs. Fred. Rhinelander, John Miller, Smith Ramadge, Will'm Laight, Will'm Kenyon, Rich'd Sharpe, Nich's Hoffman, be a Committee untill the first Tuesday in April next, to hear and determine disputes between parties, that shall submit the same to this Corporation, and that they report their proceedings to this Chamber.

The Committee of the month are ordered to report the Primage due where no bargain hath been made.

Mr. Richard Smith, having been proposed at a former Meeting, was balloted for and duly elected a Member of this Corporation.

Ordered—That notice be sent to him by the Secretary in writing that he was duly elected.

Ordered—That Mr. President represent to the Commandant & Police regulations respecting bread, which was drawn up as follows :—

The various artifices practiced by the Bakers to take undue advantages of the community, are too palpable and notorious to require illustration, and call loudly for redress.

The Chamber of Commerce, therefore, whom the police have honored constantly to consult on such occasions, having discussed this subject at large at their last monthly meeting, think it incumbent on them to propose for the consideration of the Police the following regulations as most likely to remedy the impositions daily practiced by the Bakers, finding on enquiring that the Best Flour can now be purchased from 50s to 52 p. cwt., and that Flour at Vendue does not exceed 40s p. cwt.

They are of opinion there might also to be two sorts of bread ; and that the former regulations (now totally neglected) of stamping the initial Letters of the Bakers names on all their Bread, should be revised and Strictly enforced under certain penalties, if omitted.

That Bread of the finest and best Flour should be baked into long loaves of two Pounds weight, for Fourteen Coppers.[142]

That all other Flour of inferior quality, or that is in the least degree Musty or Sour should (by way of distinction) be baked up into round loaves of Two and a half Pounds weight, and sold at the same price of the Long Loaves.

That any Baker presuming to bake other than the best Flour into Long instead of Round Loaves, or of less weight than is mentioned, should forfeit all the Bread so manufactured for the use of the Alms House.

And that the Bakers may be strictly watched and kept to their duty, a public Inspector[143] of judgement and reputation should be appointed to vissit their Bake Houses at discretion to see that their Bread is made in the manner above directed, and in case any inhabitants are served with Bread deficient in any of the particulars before mentioned, it shall be expected as a duty they owe to the community that they immediately send such bread to the Inspector who should be authorized and required to levy from the Bakers a fine of ——— for every loaf of such Bread.

CHAMBER OF COMMERCE.—TUESDAY, 4th April, 1780.

PRESENT.

Isaac Low, President.
Anthony Van Dam, Secretary.

Richard Sharpe,	William Lowther,
William Stepple,	William Backhouse,
Gerrard Walton,	Robert R. Waddel,

Fined for appearing after six o'clock:

Daniel McCormick,	Alexander Wallace,
Robert Murray,	David Seabury,
William Ustick,	John Moore,
John Miller,	William Donaldson,
Patrick McDavitt,	John Oothout,
William Pagan,	John Thurman,
Gabriel H. Ludlow,	Frederick Rhinelander,
Oliver Templeton,	William Laight.

Disputes daily arise with respect to Freights and other contracts made abroad for Sterling money.

Resolved—That all contracts for Sterling money

payable in New York, are to be paid in Dollars at Four Shillings and Six Pence, Guineas at Twenty-one Shillings and Half Johannes at Thirty-six Shillings Sterling, unless otherwise expressed.[144]

THE MAGISTRATES OF POLICE have thought proper to mention several abuses in the sale of Butter, Tallow, Candles, Soap and other articles.

It is the opinion of the Corporation that all such articles shall be weighed at the Time of sale and sold by the pound, and not by invoice as hath been scandalously practised by some.

They have also represented that many daring cheats and abuses, respecting the sale of Beef and Pork have been practised of late.

Ordered—That Messrs. John Moore, William Pagan, Samuel Donaldson, Robert R. Waddel, John Miller, and Daniel McCormick, be a Committee and report to the President, the most probable means to prevent the like practices as early as possible that he may communicate the same to the Magistrates of Police.

Ordered—That Messrs. Hugh Wallace, William Stepple, William Backhouse, Charles Nicoll, John Murray, Samuel Donaldson, John L. McAdam, be a Committee untill the first Tuesday in May next, to hear and determine disputes between parties submitting such to their determination, and that they report their proceedings to the Corporation.

CHAMBER OF COMMERCE.—TUESDAY, 2d May, 1780.

PRESENT.

Isaac Low, President.
Hugh Wallace, } Vice-Presidents.
Thomas Buchanan, }
Anthony Van Dam, Secretary.

William Stepple,
Robert Murray,
William Lowther,
Augustus Van Horne,
John Murray,
Richard Sharpe,
William Laight,
David Seabury.

Fined for appearing after six o'clock:

Robert R. Waddel,
William Ustick,
Gerrard Walton,
Jacob Watson,
William Pagan,
Thomas Buchanan,
Alexander Wallace,
Daniel McCormick,
Gabriel H. Ludlow,
Edward Laight,
William Seton,
John Miller,
Patrick McDavitt,
Samuel Donaldson,
Smith Ramadge,
Richard Smith,
Isaac Low,
Henry Brevoort,
Richard Yates,
Hugh Wallace,
Oliver Templeton,
Will'm Kenyon,
Thomas C. Williams,
John Thurman.

THE ROYAL CHARTER, as well as the LAWS of this Corporation, appoints this Day for the Election of officers for the ensuing Year, when the following Gentlemen were balloted for, and duly elected:

ISAAC LOW,	President.
HUGH WALLACE, THOMAS BUCHANAN,	Vice-Presidents.
ROBERT R. WADDLE,	Treasurer.
ANTHONY VAN DAM,	Secretary.

And they being all present, were duly sworn agreeable to the Charter to execute their respective offices.

Ordered—That Messrs. Smith Ramadge, John Thurman, Oliver Templeton, Alexander Wallace, and John Miller, be a Committee to Audit Mr. Charles McEvers, late Treasurer's accounts, from the last Audit to this day, and report in writing; and that the late Treasurer do pay any balance to Mr. Robert R. Waddel, the Treasurer elect.

John Norris, the former Doorkeeper, dyed lately, and Richard Harris[ii] was chosen to succeed him, who is to be paid the like Salary in quarterly payments of forty Pounds p. annum.

A Letter from the Superintendent,[145] enclosing one[146] from his EXCELL'Y GENERAL ROBERTSON,[jj] relative to the encouragement thought necessary to be given to Privateers[147] and other mercantile concerns, was laid before the Chamber.

Ordered—That Messrs. Hugh Wallace, Henry White, Thomas Buchanan, Samuel Donaldson, Gerrard Walton, and William Seton, be a Committee to draw up answers to the above Letters, expressive of the approbation and Thanks of this Chamber for the regard manifested by the said Letter to the mercantile Interest of this City, and that the Chamber meet at six o'clock on Tuesday next that the said Letters may be laid before them for their approbation.

Ordered—That Messrs. John Oothout, Thomas C. Williams, Walter Spens, Patrick McDavitt, Oliver Templeton, Richard Smith, and David Seabury, be a Committee, untill the first Tuesday in June next, to hear and Determine disputes between parties submitting such to their determination, and that they report their proceedings to the Corporation.

CHAMBER OF COMMERCE.—TUESDAY, 9th May, 1780.

SPECIAL MEETING.

PRESENT.

Hugh Wallace, Thomas Buchanan,	Vice-Presidents.
Robert R. Waddell,	Treasurer.
Anthony Van Dam,	Secretary.

Will'm Laight, Edward Laight,
Will'm Backhouse.

Fined for appearing after six o'clock:

John Murray,
Daniel McCormick,
William Seton,
William Lowther,
David Seabury,
John Oothout,
Charles Nicoll,
Oliver Templeton,
John McAdam,
William Pagan,
Jacob Watson,
Richard Yates,
Thos. C. Williams,
Patrick McDavitt,
Gerrard Walton,
John Miller,
Smith Ramage,
Richard Smith,
Fred. Rhinelander,
Andrew Kerr,
Hugh Wallace,
Thomas Buchanan.

The Committee appointed at last Meeting to draw up answers to his Excellency GENERAL ROBERTSON and the Superintendant Generals Letters laid before them, report the following Drafts.[148]

TO HIS EXCELLENCY JAMES ROBERTSON, Esq., Captain General and Governor in Chief of the Province of New York and Territories thereon depending in America, Vice-Admiral of the same, and Major-General of his Majesty's Forces.

NEW YORK, 2d May, 1780.

SIR,

It is with great Pleasure we avail ourselves of this first General Meeting of the Chamber of Commerce since your Excellency's Arrival to congratulate you on this Event, and with unfeigned Sincerity to assure you that it gives us the highest Satisfaction to find our gracious Sovereign has been pleased to intrust the Re-establishing and securing the Happiness of this Province to your Excellency, who we know to be not only perfectly well acquainted with its real Interests, but capable and desirous of promoting them.

The recent Instance your Excellency has given of your Attention to our mercantile Interest, not only calls for our immediate Acknowlegements, but convinces us how firmly we may rely on your Support.

Both Duty and Inclination will therefore strongly excite our Endeavours to promote your Excellency's Happiness; nor shall we esteem any Means so effectual as by cheerfully contributing our Assistance to every Measure that may be adopted for the public good.

We have the Honour to be Your Excellency's
Most obedient humble Servants.
ISAAC LOW, President.

By order of the Chamber of Commerce.

HIS EXCELLENCY'S ANSWER :

GENTLEMEN :

I am much obliged by a Mark of Esteem from the Chamber of Commerce, whose Opinions have ever been received with Respect, and followed with Advantage. Duty and Inclination make me wish Trade to flourish : a Return of this will bring with it a Return of Happiness to the Province. Commerce, which enlarges the Mind and destroys Prejudices, is ever favourable to Freedom, and will not only shew, but make the People feel, the Blessings of his Majesty's Government, so that a Truth well known in Britain will be acknowledged all over America, that the importance and prosperity of both countries depend upon their Union.

Respect for the Body of Merchants will not only make me attentive to their Advice, but receive it with Gratitude, as their Lights will prevent me from mistaking the true Interests of Trade.

CHAMBER OF COMMERCE.—TUESDAY, 6 June, 1780.

PRESENT.

Isaac Low, President.
Thomas Buchanan, Hugh Wallace, } Vice-Presidents.
Robert R. Waddel, Treasurer.
Anthony Van Dam, Secretary.

William Stepple,
Edward Laight,
David Seabury,
William Laight,
William Lowther,
Andrew Kerr,
Alex. Wallace,
Patrick McDavitt,
Gabriel H. Ludlow.

Fined for appearing after six o'clock :

John Oathout,
John Moore,
Will'm Ustick,
Thomas Buchanan,
Oliver Templeton,
Gerrard Walton,

Augustus Van Horne,
Richard Sharpe,
William Pagan,
Lawrence Kortright,
Jacob Watson,
Fred. Rhinelander,
Samuel Donaldson,
Smith Ramadge,
Hugh Wallace,
John Murray,
Richard Smith,
Isaac Low,
Daniel McCormick,
John Miller,
Charles Nicoll.

Mr. Thomas Buchanan moves that the Thanks of this Corporation be given to CAPT. NEWMAN[kk] of the late CARTERET PACKET,[149] and that he be presented with a Piece of Plate, value about 20 Gui's, and that the Seal of the Corporation be engraved thereon, as a token of their regard for preserving the Mails by that Ship when attacked by Four Privateers,[150] the back of Long Island.

Ordered—That Messrs. Edward Goold, Thomas Goodwin, John Taylor, Robert Murray, William Pagan, John Tench, and William Walton, be a Committee untill the first Tuesday in July next to hear and determine Disputes between Parties submitting such to their determination, and that they report their proceedings to the Corporation.

CHAMBER OF COMMERCE.—TUESDAY, 4th July, 1780.

PRESENT.

Thomas Buchanan, Vice-President.
Robert R. Waddle, Treasurer.
Anthony Van Dam, Secretary.

John Moore,
Alex. Wallace,
Edward Laight,
William Laight,
William Lowther,
Aug's Van Horne,
Patrick McDavitt.

Fined for appearing after six o'clock:

William Pagan,
William Kenyon,
Gabriel H. Ludlow,
Richard Smith,

John Miller,
Samuel Donaldson,
Jacob Watson,
Oliver Templeton,
John Oothout,
William Stepple,
John Tench,
Rich'd Sharpe,
Edward Goold,
Daniel McCormick,
Thomas Buchanan,
Lawrence Kortright.

Resolved—That in pursuance of the motion made at the last Meeting of the Chamber—That the Thanks be given, and the Thanks of this Corporation is accordingly given, to CHARLES NEWMAN, Esq., Commander of his Majesty's late CARTERET PACKET BOAT, for preserving, when attacked by four Rebel Privateers, to the Southward of Long Island, and bringing, at a great risque, in his boat[151] to the Post Office[152] in this City, the Public and private dispatches: and in Testimony of his merit, it is ordered that a piece of Plate be presented to him of the value of Twenty Guineas, or thereabouts, whereon shall be engraved the representation of the Seal of this Corporation—underneath thereof:

PRESENTED *by the Corporation of the Chamber of Commerce of New York, to* CHARLES NEWMAN, *Commander of his Majesty's late Packet, the* CARTERET, *for his great attention and Prudence, in saving and bringing, at all hazards, his Mail to New York.*

Ordered—That Mr. Thomas Buchanan, and Mr. Richard Smith, be a Committee to order the above piece of Plate to be made, and presented to Captain NEWMAN, and that the Treasurer do pay for the same.

Capt. NEWMAN having been presented with the Thanks in writing, and attending replied, also in writing, in the following words:

NEW YORK, July 4, 1780.

SIR,

I beg the favor of you to return my most respectful thanks to the Chamber of Commerce for so honorable a testimony which they have been pleased to shew of their approbation of my conduct, in preserving the Mails and Public Despatches in my late unfortunate situation. This mark of Distinction from so respectable a body of Merchants will ever be remembered with gratitude, and they may be assured it shall always be my Study, whilst I have the honor to command one of his Majesty's Packets, to accelerate and promote the Correspondence of this City as much as it lies in the power of, Sir, your most obedient and most humble servant, CHARLES NEWMAN.

ISAAC LOW, Esqr., President of the Chamber of Commerce.

Ordered—That Copys of the Vote of Thanks, and Capt. NEWMAN's answer, be delivered to the Printers for their Insertion.[153]

Messrs. Abraham Walton and Vincent Pearce Ashfield, having been proposed at former Meetings, were unanimously chosen members of this Corporation.

Ordered—That the Secretary send them notice in writing that they were duly elected.

Ordered—That Messrs. Daniel McCormick, William Ustick, Andrew Kerr, Augustus Van Horne, William Lowther, Henry Brevoort, William Laight, be a Committee, untill the first Tuesday in August next, to hear and determine disputes between parties submitting such to their determination, and that they report their proceedings to the Corporation.

CHAMBER OF COMMERCE.—TUESDAY, 1st August, 1780.

PRESENT.

Isaac Low, President.
Robert R. Waddel, Treasurer.
Anthony Van Dam, Secretary.

William Stepple, John Tench,
William Backhouse, Abram Walton,
Gerrard Walton, Gabriel H. Ludlow,
Jacob Watson, Augustus Van Horne,
William Laight, John Moore,
William Lowther.

Fined for appearing after six o'clock:

Patrick McDavitt,
David Seabury,
Harding Burnley,
Oliver Templeton,
Charles Nicoll,
Robert R. Waddel,
Smith Ramadge,
William Pagan,
Frederic Rhinelander,
Vincent P. Ashfield,
John Miller,
Thomas C. Williams,
Daniel McCormick.

Ordered—That Messrs. Thomas Buchanan, Jonn Moore, Abra'm Walton, William Seton, Gabriel H. Ludlow, Vincent P. Ashfield, and Edward Laight, be a Committee untill the first Tuesday in September next, to hear and determine disputes between parties, submitting such to their determination, and that they report their proceedings to this Corporation.

CHAMBER OF COMMERCE.—FRIDAY, 11th August, 1780.

SPECIAL MEETING.

PRESENT.

Isaac Low,	President.
Thomas Buchanan,	Vice-President.
Robert R. Waddel,	Treasurer.
Anthony Van Dam,	Secretary.

John Tench,
Andrew Kerr,
Charles Nicoll,
William Pagan,
Augustus Van Horne,
William Backhouse,
Gabriel H. Ludlow,
John Miller,
John Oothout,
John Moore,
William Laight.

Fined for appearing after six o'clock:

Anthon. Van Dam,
John Murray,
Samuel Donaldson,
Richard Sharpe,
Abram Walton,
Thomas Buchanan,
Walter Spens,
Richard Smith,

Robert R. Waddel,	Oliver Templeton,
William Kenyon,	Gerrard Walton,
Thomas C. Williams,	William Stepple.

An Embargo[154] having been laid by the Admiral on Shipping to answer the purpose of Manning his Majesty's Fleet, the Merchants become desirous of applying to be relieved from the heavy expence daily accumulating on Ships and Goods, wish to express their application to the Commander in Chief to be relieved if it shall be thought expedient for the Public Service, and

A draft of a Memorial[155] to the Commander in Chief being read, was ordered to be fairly Copied and signed by the President, and that he deliver it to the Superintendant General with a desire of him to wait upon the Commander in Chief therewith.

[*There is no copy of this Memorial on the Minutes.*]

CHAMBER OF COMMERCE.—Monday, 14th August, 1780.

SPECIAL MEETING.

Present.

Isaac Low,	President.
Thomas Buchanan, Hugh Wallace,	Vice-Presidents.
Robert R. Waddle,	Treasurer.
Anthony Van Dam,	Secretary.

William Laight,	Oliver Templeton,
Edward Laight,	Thomas C. Williams,
Jacob Watson,	Harding Burnley,
Vincent P. Ashfield,	John Miller,
Richard Smith,	John Moore,
Alexand. Wallace,	August's Van Horne,
Smith Ramadge,	John Murray,
Daniel McCormick,	William Seton,
William Kenyon,	Samuel Donaldson,
Abraham Walton,	Gabriel H. Ludlow,
John Tench,	William Pagan.

A LETTER[156] from the Superintendant General premised that he had waited on the Commander in Chief, who was pleased to say that it was his intention to take off the Embargo as early as possible, and that he had written to ADMIRAL ARBUTHNOT[11] to that purpose, and also expressed his great Satisfaction of the Merchants' readiness in furnishing their Seamen for the Navy.[157]

A LETTER[158] from the Commandant was read in the words following:

[*There is no copy of these Letters on the Minutes.*]

CHAMBER OF COMMERCE.—TUESDAY, 5 September, 1780.

PRESENT.

Isaac Low, President.
Robert R. Waddel, Treasurer.
Anthony Van Dam, Secretary.

William Walton, William Lowther,
William Stepple, William Backhouse,
John Moore, Richard Smith,
Henry Brevoort.

Fined for appearing after six o'clock:

Gabriel H. Ludlow, Smith Ramadge,
Thomas C. Williams, John Murray,
Daniel McCormick, Samuel Donaldson,
Charles Nicoll, Andrew Kerr,
John Tench, Vincent P. Ashfield,
Richard Sharpe.

Ordered—That Messrs. Gerrard Walton, Lawrence Kortright, Richard Yates, Alexand. Wallace, Jacob Watson, John Miller, Fredk. Rhinelander be a Committee untill the first Tuesday in Oct. next, to hear and determine Disputes between Parties submitting such to their determination, and that they report their proceedings to this Corporation.

CHAMBER OF COMMERCE.—TUESDAY, 3d October, 1780.

PRESENT.

Isaac Low, President.

William Walton,	Thomas C. Williams,
Edward Laight,	Oliver Templeton,
David Seabury,	John Murray,
William Stepple,	Jacob Watson,
Samuel Donaldson,	Alexan. Wallace,
William Laight,	Abraham Walton,
William Lowther,	John Moore,

Andrew Kerr.

Fined for appearing after six o'clock :

John Miller,	Will'm Backhouse,
Smith Ramadge,	Gerrard Walton,
Richard Smith,	Daniel McCormick,
Isaac Low,	Charles Nicoll,
Will'm Pagan,	Richard Yates,

Fred. Rhinelander.

Ordered—That Mr. John Oothout, President of the Committee of August, Mr. Gerrard Walton, President of the Committee of September, Mr. Thomas C. Williams of the August Committee, Mr. Alexander Wallace of the September Committee, Mr. John Moore, Mr. Edward Laight, and Mr. William Pagan be a joint Committee to hear and determine a Controversy between Mr. Samuel Rogers, Capt. of the Privateer Auctioneer[159] of the one part, and the agents and owners of the Privateer on the other part.

Resolved—That it be a Standing instruction to the Presidents of each monthly Committee in future that if any matter shall be referred by the POLICE, which does not immediately relate to Trade, it shall be return'd back to the POLICE,[160] as this Chamber cannot consistently with their INSTITUTION interfere in any other matters.

Ordered—That Messrs. Richard Sharpe, Smith Ramadge, Harding Burnley, Nicholas Hoffman, William Kenyon, William Backhouse, and Charles Nicoll, be a Committee untill the first Tuesday in November next, to hear and determine Disputes between Parties submitting such to their determination, and that they report their proceedings to this Corporation.

CHAMBER OF COMMERCE.—TUESDAY, 7th November, 1780.

PRESENT.

Isaac Low, President.
Thomas Buchanan, Vice-Presd.
Robert R. Waddle, Treasurer.
Anthony Van Dam, Secretary.

William Lowther,
Harding Burnley,
Oliver Templeton,
William Laight,
Charles Nicoll,
Richard Sharpe,
William Walton,
Andrew Kerr,
Daniel McCormick,
David Seabury,
Patrick McDavitt,
William Stepple,
Edward Laight,
Abraham Walton,
Alexander Wallace,
John Oothout,
Vincent P. Ashfield,
Robert Alexander,
Samuel Donaldson,
Jacob Watson,
Gerrard Walton,
Gabriel H. Ludlow,
William Backhouse,
Smith Ramadge,
John Moore,
Richard Yates,
John Miller.

Fined for appearing after six o'clock :

Frederick Rhinelander,
John McAdam,
Thomas Buchanan,
Thomas C. Williams,
John Murray,
Lawrence Kortright.

The Committee appointed to Audit the late Treasurer's accounts having reported that the said accounts had not yet been rendered for that purpose,

Ordered—That the Secretary write a Letter to the Treasurer requesting him to furnish the said Accounts so that they may be audited and reported at the next monthly meeting of the Chamber.

Ordered—That Messrs. Samuel Donaldson, John Murray, Patrick McDavitt, John Oothout, Edward Goold, John McAdam, Thomas C. Williams, be a Committee untill the first Tuesday in December next, to hear and determine disputes between parties, submitting such to their determination, and that they report their proceedings to this Corporation.

CHAMBER OF COMMERCE.—TUESDAY, 5th December, 1780.

PRESENT.

Isaac Low,	President.
Thomas Buchanan,	Vice do.
Robert R. Waddle,	Treasurer.
Anthony Van Dam,	Secretary.

Richard Sharpe,	William Kenyon,
Gerrard Walton,	William Lowther,
Alexander Wallace,	John Murray,
Patrick McDavitt,	William Laight,
Samuel Donaldson,	Abraham Walton,
Frederick Rhinelander,	Jacob Watson,
William Walton,	John Tench.

Fined for appearing after six o'clock :

John Moore,	Richard Smith,
Richard Yates,	Smith Ramadge,
John Miller,	John McAdam.

The MAGISTRATES OF POLICE having recommended the consideration of a dispute between *Abraham Cuyler, Esqr.*,[mm] and *Sheffield Howard, Esqr.*,[nn] security for *Will'm Tongue*,[oo]

Auctioneer, with respect to a ballance due *Mr. Cuyler*, *Mr. Howard* not attending. It was the opinion of the Chamber that the President acquaint the Magistrates of Police of that circumstance, and that they will meet purposely on Friday next, to hear *Mr. Howard's* reasons that they may form their opinion.

The Season of the Year requires that the Powder-Ship should be removed.

Ordered—That Mr. Miller direct that the Powder-Ship be transported to Walloon Bay for the Winter.

Ordered—That Messrs. William Pagan, Oliver Templeton, John Tench, William Ustick, Robert Alexander, Andrew Kerr, and William Lowther, be a Committee untill the first Tuesday in January next, to hear and determine disputes between parties submitting such to their determination, and that they report their proceedings to this Corporation.

Messrs. Joseph Allicocke, Joshua Watson, having been proposed at a former meeting, were balloted for and duly elected Members of this Corporation.

Ordered—That the Secretary send them notices in writing that they were duly elected.

CHAMBER OF COMMERCE.—Friday, 8th December, 1780.

SPECIAL MEETING.

Present.

Isaac Low, President.
Thomas Buchanan, Vice do.
Robert R. Waddle, Treasurer.
Anthony Van Dam, Secretary.

Gerrard Walton,
Edward Laight,
William Walton,
Frederick Rhinelander,
David Seabury,
Vincent P. Ashfield,
William Lowther,
William Stepple,

William Backhouse,
John Miller,
Abraham Walton,
William Laight,
Henry Brevoort,
Jacob Watson,
Richard Yates,
Augustus Van Horne,
Gabriel H. Ludlow,
John Murray.

Fined for appearing after six o'clock:

Smith Ramage,
John Moore,
Lawrence Kortright,
Alex'r Wallace,
John Tench,
Andrew Kerr,
Samuel Donaldson,
Thomas C. Williams,
Patrick McDavitt,
William Kenyon,
Daniel McCormick.

In pursuance of the resolution of this Corporation at last Meeting to attend to the complaint of *Abraham Cuyler, Esq.*, against *Sheffield Howard, Esq.*, as security of *William Tongue*, Auctioneer, recommended by the Police.

The Corporation having heard the parties and debates arising thereon, it did appear,

That *Cuyler* put into the hands of *Tongue* (when some other person was his security) a quantity of Merchandise to be sold for his account on or about the —— day of November last, between which time and the 25th January last, *Tongue* had disposed of part thereof to the amount of £86 6 1½, when for some irregularity in his conduct the Magistrates of Police deprived him of his Lycence and gave notice to this Corporation that if they or any of their Friends had any demands on him to make it known that justice might be done. Afterwards he was reinstated in his business having still *Cuyler's* goods in hand except to the amount of £86 6 1½ as aforesaid, when *Mr. Sheffield Howard* became his security for his faithfull conduct. Afterwards *Tongue* compleated the Sale of the Goods and furnished an account thereof and made payments thereon on which there now remains a ballance of £217 13 2½ curr'y.

In discussing this business, some urged that the first payment in the time of *Mr. Howard's* security should go in discharge of the first part of the Goods sold under the former security, others that no part of the Money paid after *Howard* became Security should go in discharge of a Debt before he became surety.

Wherefore a motion was made* by the Secretary, and Seconded

That it appears to this Corporation there is a ballance due from *William Tongue* to *Abraham Cuyler*, *Esq.*, the sum of £217 13 2½ Currency on the whole produce of Acc't of Sales being £644 1 2½. That £81 11 the net proceeds of £86 6 1½ was a Transaction under the Security of *Hosmer* as related. That the Securitys of each must bear a proportion of the deficiency, and therefore the last Security entered into the first of March is accountable to Mr. Cuyler in the sum of £190 0 2½ on a division,

For the Motion - - -	25
Against it - - - -	7
	18

CHAMBER OF COMMERCE.—TUESDAY, 2d January, 1781.

PRESENT.

Isaac Low, President.
Thomas Buchanan, Vice-President.
Robert R. Waddle, Treasurer.
Anthony Van Dam, Secretary.

William Laight,
Jacob Watson,
Edward Laight,
William Backhouse,
Vincent P. Ashfield,
Frederick Rhinelander,

William Lowther,
William Walton,
Gerrard Walton,
Abraham Walton,
Smith Ramadge,
David Seabury.

Fined for appearing after six o'clock:

John Moore,
Alex'r Wallace,
Samuel Donaldson,
Andrew Kerr,
Joshua Watson,
Augustus Van Horne,
Oliver Templeton.

Ordered—That Messrs. William Walton, William Stepple, John Taylor, Daniel McCormick, David Seabury, Henry Brevoort, and William Laight, be a Committee untill the first Tuesday in February next, to hear and determine disputes between parties submitting such to their determination, and that they report their proceedings to this Corporation.

Mr. Walton moves that any Gentleman of the Monthly Committee do pay 8 Dollars, if they do not attend the whole committee, and 4s. each night, without satisfactory excuse.

CHAMBER OF COMMERCE.—TUESDAY, 6th February, 1781.

PRESENT.

Thomas Buchanan, Vice-Pres't.
Robert R. Waddel, Treasurer.
Anthony Van Dam, Secretary.

William Laight,
Gerrard Walton,
William Ustick,
Andrew Kerr,
William Walton,
Vincent P. Ashfield,
Frederick Rhinelander,
Richard Sharpe,
Henry Brevoort,
Jacob Watson,
Alexan'r Wallace,
William Backhouse,
John Moore,
Edward Laight,
Joseph Allicocke,
William Lowther,
Patrick McDavitt,
Daniel McCormick.

Fined for appearing after six o'clock :

Thomas Buchanan,	Augustus Van Horne,
Joshua Watson,	Robert Alexander,
John Miller,	David Seabury,

Edward Goold.

The CHAMBER having taken up the Motion of Mr. Abraham Walton, at last meeting, and debating thereon :

Ordered—That every Member of this Corporation who shall be hereafter appointed of the Monthly Committee, do pay a Fine of Four Shillings for not attending each night that there shall be business, and that they are duly notified, provided that the whole Fines do not exceed Eight Dollars to a member for the Month : and if they fail attending at all for the Month, to pay said Eight Dollars to the Chairman of the Committee, to defray their expences. The attending Members to be judge of the excuse offered for being absent.

Ordered—That Messrs. John Moore, William Seton, Augustus Van Horne, Abraham Walton, Vincent P. Ashfield, Joshua Watson, and Joseph Allicocke, be a Committee, untill the first Tuesday in March next, to hear and determine Disputes between parties submitting such to their determination, and that they report their proceedings to this Corporation.

Messrs. James Douglas, John Ponsonby, William Hodgzard, and Alexn'r Forteath, having been proposed at a former meeting, were balloted for, and duly elected Members of this Corporation.

Ordered—That the Secretary send them notices in writing that they were duly elected.

CHAMBER OF COMMERCE.—TUESDAY, 6th March, 1781.

PRESENT.

Isaac Low, President.
Thomas Buchanan, Vice-Pres't.
Robert R. Waddell, Treasurer.
Anthony Van Dam, Secretary.

Smith Ramadge,
Alex'r Wallace,
William Backhouse,
William Kenyon,
Gerrard Walton,
Abram Walton,
Oliver Templeton,
Frederick Rhinelander,
Augustus Van Horne,
William Laight,
John Moore,
William Lowther,
John Tench,
Alexnr. Forteath,
Henry Brevoort,
Edward Laight,
Andrew Kerr,
William Walton,
Joseph Allicocke,
John Miller,
Joshua Watson.

Fined for appearing after six o'clock :

Daniel McCormick,
John Oathout,
William Seton,
David Seabury,
Richard Yates,
Patrick McDavitt,
John Ponsonby,
Richard Sharpe,
James Douglas,
William Pagan,
Thomas Buchanan,
Vincent P. Ashfield,
Jacob Watson,
William Hodgzard,
John Murray,
Samuel Donaldson.

Ordered—That Messrs. Hugh Wallace, Edward Laight, Gab'l H. Ludlow, Richard Yates, Gerrard Walton, James Douglas, and John Ponsonby, be a Committee untill the first Tuesday in April next, to hear and determine disputes between parties submitting such to their determination, and that they report their proceedings to this Corporation.

A REPRESENTATION from Messrs. Taylor & Rogers, by some of the Members to this Corporation. It appears that the dutys on a cargo of Wine, arrived from Madeira in the Snow[161] Friendship, has been demanded from them by the Hon. Andrew Elliott, Esqr., as Collector of the Customs of this Port.[162] And it also appears by an Act of Parliament,[163] passed in the —— Year of His Majesty's Reign, that the Commander-in-Chief for the time being is to make the necessary regulations respecting the Trade of this Port, and the Collection of such Dutys appearing to this Corporation as contrary to Act of Parliament, and a very particular hardship on the Importer and Consumer.

Mr. Donaldson begs leave to move that an address be presented to the Commander in chief representing the sentiments of this Chamber on that subject, praying relief from the operation of the Collection of such dutys.

Ordered—That the following Gentlemen be a Committee to draw up and address, viz.: Isaac Low, Thomas Buchanan, Gerrard Walton, John Moore, William Lowther, Will'm Laight, and John Miller, and report it to this Corporation now sitting.

The Committee having reported a draft of the address, was in the words following:—

To His Excellency, Sir Henry Clinton,[pp] Knight of the most honorable order of the Bath, General, Commander in Chief of all his Majesty's Forces within the Colonies laying in the Atlantic Ocean from Nova Scotia to West Florida inclusive.

The Memorial of the President and Corporation of the New York Chamber of Commerce, incorporated by Royal Authority,

Humbly Sheweth,

That your Memorialists encouraged by your Excellency's experienced attention to Protection of Person, Property, and Mercantile Interest within the British Lines, as also the Confidence the Military Government has reposed in them, in respect to disputes in which Trade is concerned, presume to lay before your Excellency the state of Trade since the passing of the prohibitory Act, from which Period no regular Plan of Trade for this Port (Except such as was carried by Licences) was established, till the arrival of his Majesty's Commissioners in the Summer of 1778, by which means the Merchants' Int'rest was not only left in a most precarious situation but in some instances suffered severely.

At the expiration [164] of the Commissioners' Proclamation, they would have experienced the same bad effects, had not your Excellency so timely exerted your Authority in their favor, by ordering [165] the Officers Superintending the Exports and Imports (from whom we have ever experienced attention and despatch) to continue in the same Line of Duty.

The Act of Parliament that now regulates the Trade of New York, and which took place here the 24th of October last. leaves to your Excellency the entire regulation of Exports and Imports, (a power that we are sensible is essentially necessary during the operation of the Prohibitory Act to be in the Commander in Chief, in order to secure the necessary supplies both to the Garrison and the Inhabitants under Protection,) and your Excellency agreeable to the Powers vested in you by that Act, having continued the former appointments in the Superintendant's office, confining them as before to their Salaries without burdening Trade with any Tax for Fees. We are greatly alarmed by a recent Advertisement [166] from Andrew Elliott, Esqr., Superintendant of the Port, demanding all duties that were formerly payable when the Merchants enjoyed the Benefits of the Acts of Parliament that imposed the Same, and which all the American Ports not mentioned in the Prohibitory Act, have ever enjoyed, and to which Benefits Georgia [167] is again restored.

The said Act of Parliament regulating the Trade of New York admits of no Exportation to Foreign Ports, the Merchant's Profit on importing Wines from Mad'a and the Azores arose formerly from the Exportation of the Produce of this Country; Adventurers to those Ports are now obliged to send their vessels in Ballast with Bills or Specie to purchase their Cargoes, which from the expence of Navigation and high Insurance makes the Trade not an object for the Merchant, and the Wines come high to the Consumer; and was it not for the supplies of Wine that come from Portugal by Licences, this Garrison [168] would suffer greatly for the want of so necessary an Article.

Exportation thus stopped makes the demanding the duties on Wines from Madeira and the Azores, not only operate to the prejudice of the Garrison, but appears to us inconsistent with the Spirit of the Act that makes them payable.

The duties laid on foreign Sugars, Indigo, and all Coffee, are conditional, either to be paid here, or, if exported to Great Britain within twelve months, to be paid there. The Duties [169] are so high on all those articles, that it would always be the interest of the Merchant to export them agreeable to the Act of Parliament; but the supplies, particularly of Sugar, depending almost solely on captures,[170] the consumption of the Garrison has made it necessary to prevent the exportation of that article. Therefore, as the Exporting condition of the act is not allowed of, we cannot think it reasonable that the Duty should be exacted.

Being cut off from Foreign Trade, and our circumscribed situation [171] not affording country Produce to be exported to the British West India Islands, the Merchant imports Melasses [172] under the same disadvantage that he does Wines from Madeira and the Azores.

From the above state of our situation, we rest assured that your Excellency's just discernment will view in a proper light the objections we make to the demand of Duties now made by ye Superintendent.

AND MOST HUMBLY PRAY your Excellency will be favourably pleased to suspend the Superintendent's demand of duties, which, if enforced, will be attended with the most fatal effects to the supply of this Garrison and the Mercantile Interest.

Ordered—That the President and Vice-President do wait upon the Commander in Chief and present the same.

Jacob Watson moves—That this Corporation take into consideration the utility of appointing a Committee to draw up a form of a CHARTER [173] such as would be most advantageous to this City, consistent with the Constitution offered us by Great Britain, to be laid before a future Meeting of this Corporation for their approbation, and when approved, to be presented to the GOVERNOR, [174] who has signified his willingness to confirm it.

CHAMBER OF COMMERCE.—THURSDAY, 8th March, 1781.

SPECIAL MEETING.

THE PRESIDENT having directed the Doorkeeper to convene the Members to receive the Commander in Chief's reply to their Memorial, presented by the President and Vice-President, which was in these words:

NEW YORK, March 7th, 1781.

SIR,

I have the honor to acquaint you, in answer to the Memorial presented to me this Day, in behalf of the Corporation of the New York Chamber of Commerce, that I shall take the earliest opportunity to transmit a Copy thereof to His Majesty's Secretary of State for the

American Department, in order that the same may be laid before the King for his Royal consideration: And, as I shall be happy at all times to pay every attention in my power to the Representations of so respectable a Body as the Merchants of the City of New York, I shall with great pleasure comply with the Prayer of their Petition, and will not fail to communicate to them, through you, Sir, the Royal Pleasure thereupon, as soon as I am honored with the King's commands upon a subject so interesting.

I have the honor to be, Sir,

Your Most Obedient and Most Humble Servant,

H. CLINTON.

ISAAC LOW, Esqr.,

President of the Chamber of Commerce, New York.

Ordered—That they do express the Thanks and Grateful Acknowledgements of this Corporation to His Excellency the Commander in Chief for his readiness and great dispatch given to their representation which is here inserted—

SIR,

The Chamber of Commerce consider it as their indispensable duty, and have therefore directed me to return your Excellency their best Thanks most respectful and grateful Acknowledgements not only for the readiness with which Your Excellency complied with the Prayer of their Petition, but also for the very great Dispatch given to that Business.

They regard it, Sir, as a striking proof [*of your*] Excellency's attention and regard for the Mercantile Interest of this City which the United Wisdom of the Nation has thought expedient to place under Your Excellency's immediate Patronage and Protection, together with that of other places on this Continent, under a similar Predicament, and while they hope for a favourable ultimate Decision to their, and such other Representations as Your Excellency shall think expedient to transmit for his Majesty's Royal Consideration; they beg leave to assure Your Excellency that nothing will contribute more to their Happiness than to have it in their Power, upon all occasions, to merit as they most anxiously wish, the Honour of Your Excellency's approbation.

By Order of the CHAMBER OF COMMERCE.

NEW YORK, March 8th, 1781.

CHAMBER OF COMMERCE.—TUESDAY, 3d April, 1781.

PRESENT.

Isaac Low, President.
Robert R. Waddle, Treasurer.
Anthony Van Dam, Secretary.

Jacob Watson,
William Backhouse,
John Moore,
David Seabury,
Andrew Kerr,
Oliver Templeton,
Vincent P. Ashfield,
Patrick McDavitt,
William Laight,
Abram Walton,
Gerrard Walton,
Joseph Allicocke,
William Lowther,
Frederick Rhinelander,
Daniel McCormick.

Fined for appearing after six o'clock :

Alexa'r Forteath,
Joshua Watson,
William Pagan,
John Miller,
James Douglass,
Edward Laight,
William Kenyon,
Smith Ramadge,
Alex'r Wallace.

Ordered—That Messrs. Alexander Wallace, Chairman, Frederick Rhinelander, Robert R. Waddel, John Miller, Smith Ramage, Alexander Forteath, and William Hodgzard be a Committee, untill the first Tuesday in May next, to hear and determine disputes between Parties submitting such to their Determination, and they report their proceedings to this Corporation.

Mr. Strachan[175] having hyred the COFFEE HOUSE where this Corporation meet for the Dispatch of Business.

Ordered—That William Pagan and Anthony Van Dam be a Committee to agree with said Mr. Strachan for the use of the large Room in the Year as often as the Corporation shall require it, and a Room for the Monthly Committees, provided that the Yearly Rent does not exceed Eighty Pounds Currency, he finding Firewood and Candles as often as they meet.

Mr. Watson's motion at last meeting for a Committee to be appointed for drawing up a Draft of a Charter for the City and County of New York, having been debated,

Ordered—That Mr. President, William Walton, Jacob Watson, Thomas Buchanan, Anthony Van Dam, William Laight, Wm. Lowther, Law. Kortright, Robert Murray, William Seton, John Moore, Frederick Rhinelander, William Backhouse, Samuel Donaldson, and Gerrard Walton, do prepare the same as soon as possible, and lay it before this Corporation at a future meeting thereof.

The President having been desired to Write to Charles McEvers, Esqr., late Treasurer, to furnish his accounts that they might be audited by the Committee appointed in May last, was in the Words following:

SIR,

The Chamber of Commerce, at their last Meeting, having on Enquiry found that you had not yet been kind enough to furnish Mr. Waddel, their present Treasurer, with a State of your accounts, nor delivered over to him the Money remaining in your Hands as late Treasurer according to their Annual Custom.

I am directed to request that favour of you; and that you will be so obliging as to comply with it, so that your accounts may be audited at their next meeting, being the First Tuesday in May.

I am, Sir, your most obedient Humble Serv't,

ISAAC LOW, Presid't
Chamber of Commerce.

NEW YORK, 15th March, 1781.

CHAMBER OF COMMERCE.—TUESDAY, 1st May, 1781.

PRESENT.

Isaac Low,	President.
Hugh Wallace,	Vice-President.
Thomas Buchanan,	Do.
Robert R. Waddel,	Treasurer.

Augustus Van Horne,	Vincent P. Ashfield,
Andrew Kerr,	John Moore,
Joseph Allicocke,	Richard Sharpe,
Fred'ck Rhinelander,	David Seabury,
William Lowther,	John Ponsonby,

William Backhouse.

Fined for appearing after six o'clock :

Hugh Wallace,	James Douglass,
Gerrard Walton,	Thomas Buchanan,
Isaac Low,	Samuel Donaldson,
Jacob Watson,	John Murray,
Smith Ramadge,	Robert Alexander,
Daniel McCormick,	Anthony Van Dam,
William Laight,	Alexander Wallace,
William Walton,	Richard Yates,
Alexander Forteath,	William Pagan,

John Miller.

The Committee for revising the old and preparing a New Charter for the City of New York, reported that they had made some progress therein, and prayed leave to sit again.

Ordered—That leave be given accordingly.

Ordered—That Messrs. Jacob Watson, Nicholas Hoffman, John Murray, William Backhouse, Lawrence Kortright, Richard Sharpe, and William Kenyon, be a Committee, untill the first Tuesday in June next, to hear and determine disputes between parties submitting such to their determination, and they report their proceedings to this Corporation.

The Royal Charter as well as the Laws of this Corporation appoint this Day for the Election of officers for the ensuing year, when the following Gentlemen were baloted for and duly elected :

Isaac Low, President.
Thomas Buchanan, }
Jacob Walton, } Vice-Presidents.
Robert R. Waddell, Treasurer.
Anthony Van Dam, Secretary.

And all except Mr. Jacob Walton, who was not present, were duly sworn, agreeable to the Charter, to execute their respective offices.

Ordered—That the President and Vice-Presidents do write to the Admiral or the Commander of his Majesty's Navy for the time being, representing the Distress[176] of the Commerce of this Coast, and praying that one or more Cruisers may protect the Vessells coming to and departing from this Port, and such other Convoys as they may think expedient.

Ordered—That Mr. Samuel Donaldson, Mr. Andrew Van Horne, and Mr. Andrew Kerr, be a Committee to Audit Mr. Treasurer's accounts from the time of his appointment untill this Day.

Mr. Pagan and Mr. Van Dam reported that they had been with Mr. Strachan, present proprietor of the Coffy House, who accepted of the proposed sum of £80, finding the Chamber with Fire Wood, and Candles, and the Grand Chamber once a Month, and Committees a room whenever they require it, and also upon Extra occasions.

CHAMBER OF COMMERCE.—Monday, 8th May, 1781.

SPECIAL MEETING.

Present.

Isaac Low, President.
Thomas Buchanan, Vice-President.
Robert R. Waddell, Treasurer.
Anthony Van Dam, Secretary.

Augustus Van Horne,
Gerrard Walton,
Robert Murray,
Alexan'r Forteath,
John Miller,
Frederick Rhinelander,
Joseph Allicocke,
Oliver Templeton,
John Murray,
Samuel Donaldson,
David Seabury,
John Moore,
Patrick McDavitt,
Richard Yates,
John McAdam,
Abram Walton,
Richard Sharpe,
Alexander Wallace,
William Walton,
William Backhouse,
John Oothout,
William Pagan,
William Kenyon,
Daniel McCormick,
Lawrence Kortright,
William Laight,
Edward Goold,
James Douglass,
John Ponsonby.

The Committee to draw up a representation and write to Admiral Arbuthnot the situation of the Trade and Commerce of this City, reported that they had done so and laid a Copy thereof before the Chamber, which was in the words following :—

Sir :—

I am directed by the Chamber of Commerce to represent to your Excellency,

That the Port of New York is from the Nature of its situation become the principal deposit and Magazine of all military as well as Mercantile Stores and Provisions from Great Britain and Ireland.

That its intercourse also with the West Indies and his Majesty's American Colonies is very considerable.

That, consequently, the best Cruizing Ground for the Enemy, perhaps in the World, is within a small distance of Sandy Hook.

That more Property has constantly been captured by their Privateers within Fifty Leagues of that Place, than perhaps upon all the rest of the Atlantic Ocean.

That the Success Rebel Privateers have met with in a few Days Cruize, (when they can be out and home again, and many of them in so short a Time having actually made large Fortunes,) will greatly encourage others to engage in the same enterprises.

That from every information many stout Privateers are fitting out in the different Rebel Ports to infest this Coast, and that unless effectual measures be taken to defeat and blast their designs, very few except Vessels of great Force, will either get safe in or out of this Port.

That from the many captures which have already been made, the Premiums of Insurance[177] are so much enhanced in London, as greatly to discourage the Importer.

That from former Experience (notwithstanding the different Convoys of Provisions for the Navy and Army, have generally arrived more fortunately than could well have been expected) they, as well as the Inhabitants of the Garrison, have at different times experienced great Inconveniences, and must have been reduced to the most complicated distress had it not been from the large supplies derived from private Importers.

That by late advices, the Garrison of Gibraltar[178] exhibits to public View a striking instance of the salutary and invaluable advantages which flow from private importations ; and that from this exuberant Source even the Navy in this Port are at this Day enabled to purchase a supply of Bread.

Thus from the preceding, and many other considerations which might be adduced, the Chamber of Commerce humbly conceive that no other object so easily attainable can be of so great importance as the effectual Protection of the Trade of this Port.

That with all due deference to your Excellency's better judgment, they conceive that a couple of fast sailing Frigates, constantly to cruize between Delaware and Block Island,[179] and making the Light House at Sandy Hook once or Twice a Week, as the Winds might permit, would effectually protect the Trade of this Port from all Invaders.

That the doing so, considered only as a mere act of Prevention, would distress the Rebels more than any Captures made from them could effect: it being notorious that their principal Resource and dependence is, and has been, from the success of their Privateers, and that they have derived more supplies by these means than from all their importations, together with those of their Allies, during the Rebellion.

That, therefore, the Chamber of Commerce are fully convinced that if the nature of the public service will permit, your Excellency will pay every attention that so important an object may seem to require.

That so deeply are they impressed with the magnitude of its importance, that they not only conceive it to be their indispensable Duty to impart their Ideas of it to your Excellency ; but in case it should not be in your Excellency's power to afford the desired relief, to pray it may be granted from Home as soon as possible : convinced that the Rebellion can NEVER be happily terminated untill so great a source of supply to feed and nurture it can be effectually prevented.

I am directed also to represent the Fishery upon the Banks[180] of Shrewsbury as an object of great importance to this Garrison : and that unless a proper armed vessell can be appointed daily to protect the Fishermen from the Gun and Whale Boats[181] that are preparing upon the adjacent Shores to attack them, they will find it totally impracticable to pursue that Business.

Amongst the Variety of important services which must constantly engage your Excellency's attention, the Chamber of Commerce can easily conceive the embarrassment they must occasion, to which you should give a preference, but they presume the objects they have mentioned are of too much consequence not to attract your Excellency's mature consideration; and they are convinced your Excellency will be happy to afford every assistance in your power.

By order of the Corporation of the Chamber of Commerce.

I have the honor to be, Sir, &c.,

ISAAC LOW, Presid't.

To His Excellency MARRIOTT ARBUTHNOT, Esqr.,
Admiral, &c., &c.

Also, Admiral ARBUTHNOT'S Answer, as follows:

ROYAL OAK,[182] OFF NEW YORK, 3d May, 1781.

SIR,

I have just received the Letter you have honored me with, pointing out the necessity of Frigates being constantly employed in cruizing off Sandy Hook, for the protection of the Trade bound to this place, as well as for protecting the Fishery upon the Banks of Shrewsbury, and to prevent the Rebel Privateers from making such near advances to this Port as they have lately done, in which they are reported to have met with too much success.

It gives me no small concern that you should suppose I have been in the smallest respect inattentive to this service in the Arrangement of the King's Ships[183] under my command, because, since my return from Charlestown, the greater part of my Force hath been upon this Coast, and during my stay at Gardner's Bay[184] Frigates have not only been cruizing almost constantly off the Barr, but between Montock Point[185] and the Delaware.

As far as circumstances could permit since my leaving Gardner's Bay I have detached Cruizers off this part of the Coast. I am sorry to say it has not been in my power to Station a single Frigate for the protection of the Trade bound to Halifax,[186] a Post not inferior to any in America.

With respect to the protection of the Fishermen employed on the Banks of Shrewsbury for supplying your Market, I cannot help mentioning to you that early after I took the Command on this Station I purchased a Vessel mounting Twelve Carriage Guns; she was fitted out at a considerable expence; I requested that the City would Man her, that I would pay the Men, and that her Services should never be diverted to any other purpose than giving such protection; my offer was received with a strong degree of coolness and till now I have never had any further solicitations on the subject.

I am, Sir, Your most obedient
Humble Servant,
M'T. ARBUTHNOT.

ISAAC LOW, Esq., &c., &c.

WHEN a Report was ordered to be written and signed by the President.

SIR,

I had the Honor of receiving, on the 5th Instant, Your Excellency's answer to the representations of the Chamber of Commerce relative to the requested Protection of the Trade of this Port which I took the first opportunity of laying before them.

It is with concern they find you have supposed any part of their Letter to imply a particular inattention in Your Excellency to this Service, as they flatter themselves no part of it will bear *such* Construction, nor was anything more distant from their Intention than to give cause of the least Offence.

They meant only to impart to Your Excellency their ideas of the Mode (never hitherto altogether adopted) of affording *effectual* Protection to this Port, submitting the result, as in duty bound, to Your Excellency's discretion and better judgement.

That it is not in Your Excellency's Power to afford all the Protection you wish to the Trade bound to Halifax as well as to this Port, we equally lament and although we would not draw a comparison between the two Ports in Point of Harbor for *Large*[187] Ships, so neither can we suppose Your Excellency means to be understood that the one can bear the least competition with the other as to the Importance arising from the Value of Imports and Exports which renders the Port of New York so immediately and eminently the *superior* Object of Protection.

With regard to Your Excellency's Request to the City to Man a Vessel for the Protection of the Fishery on the Banks of Shrewsbury, the Chamber of Commerce beg leave to assure Your Excellency that no application was ever made to this Corporation upon that subject or in all probability they had taken it up with the same Zeal which they doubt not Your Excellency will admit they manifested to procure Volunteers for Manning His Majesty's Ships under your Command.

And if your Excellency will be so good as to furnish a proper Vessel with Provisions and Ammunition to protect the Fishermen on the Banks of

Shrewsbury for the benefit of this Market, the Chamber of Commerce will cheerfully exert their endeavours and they doubt not they will be able in a short time not only to procure as many Men as Your Excellency may think sufficient for that purpose but also to raise Funds for paying them, provided protection from injuries can be granted by Your Excellency to the Men, and that they shall be discharged[188] as soon as the Fishing season is over.

NEW YORK, May 8th.

His Excell'y MARRIOTT ARBUTHNOT, Esq., Admiral, &c., &c.

CHAMBER OF COMMERCE.—TUESDAY, 5th June, 1781.

PRESENT.

Isaac Low, President.
Robert R. Waddel, Treasurer.
Anthony Van Dam, Secretary.

William Walton,
Oliver Templeton,
William Backhouse,
Andrew Kerr,
Gerrard Walton,
John Moore,
Patrick McDavitt,
William Kenyon,
Fred. Rhinelander,
Augustus Vanhorne,
Alexander Wallace,
William Laight.

Fined for appearing after six o'clock:

John Miller,
Edward Laight,
James Douglass,
John Taylor,
Vincent P. Ashfield,
Samuel Donaldson,
Joshua Watson,
Joseph Allicocke,
William Lowther,
William Pagan,
Isaac Low,
Robert Alexander,
David Seabury,
Jacob Watson,
Edward Goold,
John Ponsonby,
Hugh Wallace,
John Tench.

Ordered—That Messrs. John McAdam, Edward Goold, William Pagan, Samuel Donaldson, John Oothout, Oliver Templeton, and William Ustick, be a Committee untill the first Tuesday in July next, to hear and determine disputes between Parties submitting such to their determination, and that they report their proceedings to this Corporation.

The COMMITTEE appointed to Audit the Treasurer's Account, reported:

WE, THE SUBSCRIBERS, being appointed to examine the Account of Robert Ross Waddel, Esqr., as Treasurer to the Corporation of the New York Chamber of Commerce, do report, that from the 8th June, 1780 to the 2nd May, 1781 the Treasurer has received on account of the Corporation, the Sum of Two Hundred Pounds, and paid away the Sum of One Hundred and Ninety-six Pounds, Four Shillings, and Four Pence, N. York currency, and that the Sum of Three Pounds, 15s. 8d, now remains in his hands, being the exact Ballance of the Cash Account, which on examining and comparing with the Vouchers for Payment therein charged, we do find to be just and True in every particular.

SAMUEL DONALDSON.
ANDREW KERR.
AUGUST'S VAN HORNE.

NEW YORK, 5th June, 1781.

The President communicated ADMIRAL ARBUTHNOT'S reply to his last LETTER, written by order of the Chamber, as follows:

ROYAL OAK, OFF SANDY HOOK,
27th May, 1781.

SIR,

I have received your Letter of the 8th Instant, in the name of the Corporation of the Chamber of Commerce.

I have taken such measures for the Protection of the Port of New York as are proportioned to the General and extensive scale of service by which I am to regulate my Conduct. It is to be understood that offence to his Majesty's enemies, as well as protection to the Loyal part of the Community, necessarily engages a degree of our consideration.

I shall always with pleasure bear testimony to the ready and cheerfull assistance which the City gave to the raising Volunteers, after the arrival of REAR ADMIRAL GRAVES,[qq] and I doubt not but the Zeal which operated so powerfully in that instance will be equally exerted on every other important occasion.

I have the honor to be, Sir, Your mo. obed't Hum'l Serv't,

M'T. ARBUTHNOT.

ISAAC LOW, Esqr.,
President of the Chamber of Commerce, N. York.

CHAMBER OF COMMERCE.—TUESDAY, 3d July, 1781.

PRESENT.

Isaac Low,	President.
Thomas Buchanan,	Vice do.
Robert R. Waddel,	Treasurer.
Anthony Van Dam,	Secretary.

William Walton,	James Douglass,
William Lowther,	William Laight,
John Miller,	John Moore,
Jacob Watson,	Abraham Walton,
Gerrard Walton,	John McAdam.

Fined for appearing after six o'clock:

Vincent P. Ashfield,	Frederick Rhinelander,
Thomas Buchanan,	Oliver Templeton,
Isaac Low,	John Oothout,
Joshua Watson,	Robert R. Waddel,
Samuel Donaldson,	Richard Sharpe,
William Pagan,	John Murray,
Alexander Wallace,	Edward Goold.

A LETTER was communicated by the President from the Magistrates of Police with some Papers therein inclosed, respecting the ill practices of many of the Licenced Auctioneers,[189] whereupon the following Persons were appointed a Committee to report to this Corporation at an early day,—Oliver Templeton, Frederick Rhinelander, John Murray, Joshua Watson, John Oothout.

Ordered—That Messrs. John Taylor, John Tench, Henry Brevoort, Daniel McCormick, William Laight, William Lowther, and Andrew Kerr, be a Committee untill the First Tuesday in August next, to hear and determine disputes between parties submitting such to their determination, and that they report their proceedings to this Corporation.

CHAMBER OF COMMERCE.—THURSDAY, 19th July, 1781.

SPECIAL MEETING.

PRESENT.

Isaac Low, President.
Thomas Buchanan, Vice do.
Anthony Van Dam, Secretary.

William Laight,	Joseph Allicocke,
Vincent P. Ashfield,	Hugh Wallace,
Daniel McCormick,	David Seabury,
John Murray,	Thomas Buchanan,
William Lowther,	William Hodgzard,
William Backhouse,	Andrew Kerr,
Alexander Wallace,	John Oothout,
Alexander Forteath,	John Miller,
Patrick McDavitt,	Richard Yates,
John Moore,	John Tench,
Augustus Van Horne,	Richard Sharpe,
Samuel Donaldson,	Isaac Low,
Frederick Rhinelander,	William Pagan,

Oliver Templeton.

The COMMITTEE appointed to report on the ill practices of some of the Licenced Auctioneers, made the same, which being Read, was in the Words following :—

IN ORDER to remedy the Inconveniences and injuries to Trade, arising from the improper disposal of Goods at Public Vendue, and exposing Merchandise for sale on Stands in different parts of this City. It is the opinion of your Committee,

THAT ALL LICENCES heretofore issued to Vendue Masters be called in and new ones granted to them only who shall be recommended by the Chamber of Commerce.

THAT NO PEDLAR or Petty Chapman[190] be permitted to Hawk goods for sale or sell them at any Stands erected or to be erected for that purpose near the Market Places or in any of the Public Streets of this City.

THAT THE PROCLAMATION of the 12th January, 1779,[191] be chiefly adhered to, and for every offence against the Same or the above further regulation, such offender shall incur a Penalty of One Hundred Pounds, one half of which to be appropriated for the use of the Poor of this City, and the other half for the benefit of the Informer.

OLIVER TEMPLETON.
JOHN MURRAY.
FRED'K RHINELANDER.
JOHN OOTHOUT.

CHAMBER OF COMMERCE, 18th July, 1781.

And it being debated, when

THE CORPORATION of the Chamber of Commerce beg leave to recommend to the Magistrates of Police to enforce the Proclamation of the 12th January, 1779, and to call in the Lycences of all those Auctioneers who have transgressed the same which will effectually remedy the evils complained of in the MEMORIAL.

Messrs. *Winthrop*[II] *& Kemble*,[192] owners of the Ship Vigilant from Jamaica, demand freight from *Mr. Augustus Van Horne* for 20 hhds. sugar and 40 Puncheons of Rum, which being surveyed by the WARDENS[193] OF THE PORT, most of the Former were found washed out and Sea damaged, and some Rum Puncheons injured by distress of weather, having met with a Gale of Wind in which she sprung a dangerous Leak, no fault being attributed to the Stowage, yet *Mr. Van Horne* alledges that it is a hardship to pay freight for empty hhds.

The Bill of Lading being exhibited to the Corporation does express that £6 10s sterling p. hh'd shall be paid for freight of the Sugars and £5 per hh'd for the Rum. Some part of the Latter was recd. by *Mr. Van Horne* before it was discovered that any of his Sugars were washed out, and debates arising on the propriety of the demand it was the opinion of the Chamber (except Mr. Lowther and Mr. Moore)—

That—The full freight of six Pounds ten Shillings Sterling for the Sugar hh'ds, and Five Pounds Sterling for the Rum is due notwithstanding that almost all the Sugar was washed out and some of the Rum-Puncheons injured or stove.[194]

CHAMBER OF COMMERCE.—TUESDAY, 7th August, 1781.

PRESENT.

Isaac Low, President.
Thomas Buchanan, Vice-President.
Anthony Van Dam, Secretary.

William Lowther,
Gerard Walton,
Joshua Watson,
Alexander Forteath,
John Tench,
John Moore,
Daniel McCormick,
William Backhouse,
James Douglass,
William Ustick,
David Seabury,
Oliver Templeton,
Isaac Low,
Joseph Allicocke,
Vincent P. Ashfield,
William Laight,
Patrick McDavitt,
Thomas C. Williams,
Thomas Buchanan.

Ordered—That Messrs. Vincent P. Ashfield, Joshua Watson, Abraham Walton, Joseph Allicocke, John Ponsonby, David Seabury, and Harding Burnley, be a Committee untill the first Tuesday in September next, to hear and determine disputes between parties submitting such to their determination, and that they report their proceedings to this Corporation.

The COMMITTEE of last month complain to the Chamber at large that having been desired by the POLICE to adjust a dispute between *Messrs. Banan & Burke* complainants against *Capt. Stone*, that they had returned their opinion to the Police upon which the said Bannon very grossly insulted them, that they had Represented the same to the Magistrates of Police, eight days past, who had taken no notice thereof.

Ordered—That the President do write to the Magistrates of Police, representing their surprise that no notice was taken of their Committee's complaint, and that unless the Committees can be protected from injurious treatment they will be under the necessity to decline the trouble of any future decisions.

CHAMBER OF COMMERCE.—TUESDAY, 4th September, 1781.

PRESENT.

Isaac Low,	President.
Thomas Buchanan,	Vice do.
Robert R. Waddel,	Treasurer.
Anthony Van Dam,	Secretary.

John Moore,	William Laight,
Vincent P. Ashfield,	William Backhouse,
William Kenyon,	Jacob Watson,
James Douglass,	David Seabury,
William Lowther,	Fred'k Rhinelander,

Andrew Kerr.

Fined for appearing after six o'clock:

August. Van Horne,	Samuel Donaldson,
Alexan'r Forteath,	Daniel McCormick,
Alexan'r Wallace,	John Murray,
Patrick McDavitt,	Abraham Walton,
Richard Yates,	John Tench,
Thomas C. Williams,	John Oathout,

Thomas Buchanan.

Mr. President reported that, in pursuance of the order of the Chamber, he had wrote to the Magistrates of Police, had received their Answer and a Letter from Mr. Bannon, which were ordered to be entered.

GENTLEMEN.

The Committee for the last Month have complained to the Chamber of Commerce that in consequence of having given their decision in a dispute between Messrs. Banan & Burke, complainants against Capt. Stone, the said Banan treated them with very gross insulting Language; that they had represented the same to the Magistrates of Police more than a Week ago, and that no notice had been taken of it.

I am therefore directed by the Chamber of Commerce to express their surprise that no notice had been taken of their Committee's complaint by the Magistrates of Police, and at the same time to represent, that however the Monthly Committee may possibly have erred in their Judgement, no Individual can be justified in loading them with abusive or indecent Language. Unless therefore they can be protected from Licentious and injurious Treatment, and Delinquents punished for their offences against the Rules of propriety and Decorum, the Chamber must be under the necessity of declining the trouble of any further decisions.

SIR,

We are favored with yours of Wednesday last relative to the complaint of the Committee for the last Month against Mr. Bannon, and in answer must beg leave to inform you—That immediately on receiv'g the inclosed Letter we summoned Mr. Banan to appear before us to answer for his conduct; he immediately came and confessed great concern for what had happened, and declared his willingness to wait on all the Gentlemen (Mr. Lowther excepted) and make a proper submission. The reason he alledged against making any apology to Mr. Lowther was, that Mr. Lowther had struck him without his ever having spoken to him. As this was confirmed to us we really thought there was good ground for his objection, as Mr. Lowther had taken his own satisfaction. Mr. Mathews informed Mr. Tench of what Mr. Banan had said, and expected to have had an Answer from that Gentleman whether anything more was required. Mr. Banan has called on MR. MATHEWS several times to know what he is to do, and is ready to make any concessions to the Committee (Mr. Lowther excepted). The great assistance the Police have received from the Chamber, which will be always acknowledged with the highest sense of gratitude, will induce them at all times to pay every attention to any representation from the Chamber, and to take every step in their power to have such persons as the Chamber may complain of brought to a proper sense of their Duty, and the great obligations they are under to the Chamber for their trouble and attendance. We are, with great respect, Sir,

Your most obed't and Hum'le Serv'ts,

D. MATHEWS, Mayor.[88]

WM. WALTON,[195] Magistr. of Police.

OFFICE OF POLICE, 14th August, 1781.

ISAAC LOW, Esqr.

SIR,

Mr. Burke, my partner, having bo't a parcell of Staves from a *Mr. Stone*, upon which contract he gave him as earnest £3. 4s., which he kept 24 Hours, and then came and offered 3 Guineas to be off of the bargain, which *Mr. Burke* refused, alledging very justly he was acting for other people as well as for himself, whereupon *Mr. Stone* returned the earnest; in consequence we were obliged to Police him, and at my request the Gentlemen of the Police submitted the decision to the Chamber of Commerce, who accordingly met and decided the matter in favor of *Mr. Stone*, wherein I am satisfied they have impartially given their opinion, from the evidence that came before them. I made it my business to see Mr. Tench, the Chairman of that Committee the Day following, to request he would direct me to have a rehearing of this matter, whereupon some conversation passed that I am sorry was construed into an insult to the Chamber of Commerce, which I assure you was never intended, as no man can hold that Body in greater esteem than I do; and if I said anything on that Evening through Hate or Passion, I am sorry for it, and do now beg their Pardon: had they known me well they would not deem me capable of saying anything that would give offence to any man—particularly to a Body of respectable Men who meet at their own expense for the good of Trade and their fellow-Citizens. Therefore I hope they will suspend any resentment to me on that head, as they may be assured I am, with great respect, their and your most obedient hle. servant,

OWEN BANAN.

NEW YORK, 17th August, 1781.

Mr. ISAAC LOW, President of the Chamber of Commerce.

Ordered—That Messrs. John Moore, William Hodgzard, Gab'l H. Ludlow, James Douglass, Richard Yates, William Seton, and Alexander Forteath, be a Committee untill the first Tuesday in October next, to hear and determine Disputes between Parties submitting such to their determination, and that they report their proceedings to this Corporation.

Messrs. Thomas Charles Williams and *Thomas Roy* having submitted matters of disputed accounts to the Committee of last Month, who have decided thereon :

It was debated whether the Chamber should or not take up the dispute, there being the following clause at the Foot of the Bond of submission:

"N. B.—This Penalty is understood that it does not exclude either party from appealing to the Chamber at large."

Resolved almost unanimously—That they will rehear the dispute.

The Parties being required to attend, and having exhibited their Accounts and Vouchers, which being read, and neither of them having any new matter to offer, It was

Resolved unanimously by this Corporation—That their Committee's opinion be confirmed in every part of it.

CHAMBER OF COMMERCE.—TUESDAY, 2d October, 1781.

PRESENT.

Isaac Low, President.
Thomas Buchanan, Vice-Presid't.
Robert R. Waddel, Treasurer.
Anthony Van Dam, Secretary.

John Moore,	James Douglass,
Vincent P. Ashfield,	Gerrard Walton,
Andrew Kerr,	Daniel McCormick,
Alexa'r Wallace,	John Murray,
John Miller,	Fred'k Rhinelander,
Thomas C. Williams,	Oliver Templeton,
Richard Sharpe,	David Seabury,
Joseph Allicocke,	Patrick McDavitt,
Jacob Watson,	William Lowther,

William Pagan.

MR. PRESIDENT communicated to the Chamber Copy of a Letter that he had written to the Superintendant-General on the indecent behaviour of Mr. Bannon, a Letter from the Superintendant, and one from Mr. Banon, which were read and ordered to be entered on the minutes as follows:

SIR,

Inclosed you will be pleased to find, agreeable to your request the Letter from the Magistrates of Police, and another from Mr. (Banan) relative to the indecent and abusive Language from the latter to the Monthly Committee—The Offence having been given to the Committee, to those Members alone can concessions with propriety be made: and untill that was done, the Chamber of Commerce at large thought it incumbent on them, in justice to their Committee, to direct that no future decisions should be given.

This Resolution it was the duty of my Station to communicate to the Police, and that is the only Agency I have had in the matter.

I have the honor to be, Sir, &c., &c.,

ISAAC LOW.

The Hon'ble ANDREW ELLIOT, Esq.
21st Sept., 1781.

NEW YORK, 2d October, 1781.

SIR,

I beg to inclose the two Letters you was so good as to favour me with, together with a Letter from Mr. Owen Banan to Mr. John Tench. Your delivering it will oblige me, it appearing calculated to answer the purpose for which it is intended.

As I was and still am of opinion that Mercantile disputes cannot be adjusted in a more proper or more equitable way than by a reference to respectable Merchants, it gave me great satisfaction when the method was so generally agreed to, and I flattered myself that, notwithstanding the trouble it gave individuals, that it would at least continue as long as I had any concern in the Superintendency. I shall be much concerned if these my Expectations should be disappointed. The present Juncture of Affairs [196] does not seem favorable for any new plans to be adopted. It has long been proposed (I hope Events are not distant that may admit of a Trial) to revive at least such part of the civil Authority [197] by which Justice may be administered to the Community. Individuals will then be freed from the Burthen of adjusting Mercantile disputes, and I shall be relieved from a most fatiguing anxious situation. But I beg you will assure the Chamber of Commerce that in all situations I shall ever retain the highest sense of the Assistance and Support they have afforded me.

I am, with regard, Sir,
Your most obed't, and most humble Serv't,
ANDREW ELLIOT, Super't General.

ISAAC LOW, Esq., Pres't Ch. of Commerce.

SIR,

The satisfaction I have on enquiry that you have impartially decided on the matter in dispute between Mr. Stone and Mr. Burke (my partner) induces me to take this opportunity to assure you that the Conversation that passed, on the Evening following, twixt you and I was never intended as an insult to your decision on that head, and, if you think so, that I am sorry for it, and do now assure you (though a Stranger) no man can respect the Chamber of Commerce more than I do, from the Laudable purposes, I am informed, they meet on for the good order of Trade and the Convenience of their fellow Citizens; therefore hope you will be kind enough to assure the Committee of your meeting of those my sentiments and that I am, with great respect, Theirs and your most obe't servant,

OWEN BANNON.

NEW YORK, October, 1781.

Mr. JOHN TENCH, President of a former Committee of the Chamber of Commerce.

And debates arising thereon whether the concession made by Mr. Banan is satisfactory or not,

Agreed—That it is satisfactory.

The Committee for last month, not having done any business, they are hereby appointed for the Present month and untill the first Tuesday in November next.

MR. PRESIDENT having communicated a Letter from the Hon'ble GEORGE K. ELPHINSTON,[tt] Commander of his MAJESTY'S Ship WARWICK,[198] Convoy to Troop Ships and private Merchantmen to Halifax and Quebec, representing the Ill conduct of two of the Convoy belonging to this Port.

Ordered—That the President give the Thanks of this Corporation to CAPT. ELPHINSTON for the information therein: that CAPT. ELPHINSTON be requested to order the Copy of the Log Books for the further information of this Corporation, And that they may have his leave to publish his Letter.

WARWICK, OFF NEW YORK, 28th Sept., 1781.

GENTLEMEN :

Some time ago His Majesty's Ship under my Command was ordered to protect a Fleet of Troop Ships to Quebec. About the time of sailing [199] many private traders applyed for Instructions which were very readily granted, and every possible attention for their Security given. Yet, notwithstanding, two Brigs [200] belonging to this Port found means to quit the Convoy and are said to have been taken by the Rebels. I therefore think it incumbent on me to inform any gentlemen who may have insured any part of these Brigs that I have reason to suspect their Conduct and that any information that the Log Books of the WARWICK or GARLAND [201] can furnish is at the Insurer's [202] service.

I am, with much esteem, Gentlemen,

Your most ob'dt and hon'ble servant,

G. K. ELPHINSTON.

CHAMBER of COMMERCE, New York.

SIR,

I am happy in taking the earliest opportunity of conveying the gratefull sense the Chamber of Commerce entertain for the Favor conferred on them by your Letter of 28th Ult., relative to the two Vessells belonging to this Port who quitted your Convoy bound to Quebec and are since said to be taken by the Rebels. As a Mercantile Body, the Chamber hold themselves bound to the Community to avail themselves of every means in their Power to detect the Frauds which there is so much reason to apprehend have been practised on both sides of the water since the commencement of this most unnatural Rebellion. [203] I am, therefore, directed by the Chamber of Commerce to return you the Thanks of that Corporation, which I am proud to have the honor of doing, for your kind communication, and also to accept your further obliging offer of the Extracts relative to those Vessells from the Log Books of the WARWICK and GARLAND; which, together with your Letter on that subject, they beg to have your permission to Publish.

I have the Honor to be, with great respect, by order of the Corporation of the Chamber of Commerce, Sir,

Your most obedient and most H'ble Servant,

ISAAC LOW, President.

The Hon'ble Cap. ELPHINSTON.

NEW YORK, October 3d, 1781.

CHAMBER OF COMMERCE.—TUESDAY, 4th October, 1781.

SPECIAL MEETING.

PRESENT.

Isaac Low,	President.
Thomas Buchanan,	Vice do.
Robert R. Waddle,	Treasurer.
Anthony Van Dam,	Secretary.

James Douglass,	William Hodgzard,
John Murray,	William Seton,
John McAdam,	Frederick Rhinelander,
William Backhouse,	Joseph Allicocke,
Richard Sharpe,	Daniel McCormick,
Thomas C. Williams,	Alexan'r Forteach,
Gerrard Walton,	Henry Brevoort,
John Ponsonby,	Joshua Watson,
Augustus Van Horne,	Oliver Templeton,
John Miller,	William Walton,
William Laight,	Abram Walton,
William Lowther,	Samuel Donaldson,
William Ustick,	Patrick McDavitt,
John Moore,	John Tench,

David Seabury.

The President communicated a Letter from Governor Robertson, signifying that the Admiral was in want of a number of Seamen to man the Fleet [204] in this particular Season of events ; wherefore, this Corporation, taking the Governor's requisition into consideration, think it of the utmost importance to his Majesty's service that every aid be given thereto; they unanimously agree that this Corporation will raise among themselves the Sum of Four Hundred Guineas, to be paid in Bountys [205] to the Seamen that shall enter as Volunteers.

CHAMBER OF COMMERCE.—TUESDAY, 6th November, 1781.

PRESENT.

Isaac Low,	President.
Robert R. Waddel,	Treasurer.
Anthony Van Dam,	Secretary.

Jacob Watson,
William Lowther,
William Laight,
Gerrard Walton,
William Backhouse,
Henry Brevoort,
Augustus Van Horne,
William Walton.

Fined for appearing after six o'clock:

Alexanr. Forteath,
Andrew Kerr,
William Pagan,
Fred'k Rhinelander,
William Ustick,
James Douglas,
Samuel Donaldson,
John Moore,
John Miller,
Patrick McDavitt,
Daniel McCormick.

Ordered—That Messrs. Gerrard Walton, Frederick Rhinelander, Lawrence Kortright, Augustus Van Horne, Alexander Wallace, and John Miller, be a Committee untill the first Tuesday in December next, to hear and determine disputes between parties submitting the same to their determination, and that they do report their proceedings to this Corporation.

DISPUTES having arisen between the owners of Vessells and Freighters on Voyages intended to be made to Virginia, which have not been performed, and it appears that *William Lowther*, owner of one Vessell, and *Mr. Hodgzard*, owner of another; *Mr. Douglas*, a Freighter for himself and others, desire to have the opinion of the Chamber at large.

And debates having arisen, it was determined—

THAT a moiety of the Freight paid shall be detained by the owner of the Vessell, or if any have not paid they then do pay half the agreed freight, the Voyage having been set aside by the mutual consent.

CHAMBER OF COMMERCE.—TUESDAY, 4th December, 1781.

PRESENT.

Isaac Low, President.
Thomas Buchanan, Vice-Pres't.
Robert R. Waddle, Treasurer.
Anthony Van Dam, Secretary.

William Laight,
Patrick McDavitt,
John Oothout,
Alexan'r Wallace,
John Moore,
Abram Walton,
William Lowther,
Edward Laight,
Jacob Watson,
Thomas C. Williams,
Gerrard Walton,
William Backhouse,
Vincent P. Ashfield,
Oliver Templeton.

Fined for appearing after six o'clock:

John Murray,
John Miller,
John Tench.

Ordered—That Messrs. Samuel Donaldson, William Backhouse, Richard Sharpe, John Murray, Jacob Watson, William Kenyon, and John McAdam, be a Committee untill the first Tuesday in January next, to hear and determine disputes between parties submitting such to their determination and that they do report their proceedings to this Corporation.

CHAMBER OF COMMERCE.—TUESDAY, 2d January, 1782.

PRESENT.

Isaac Low, President.
Anthony Van Dam, Secretary.

Edward Laight,
Jacob Watson,
William Lowther.

After six o'clock:

William Backhouse,
James Douglas,
David Seabury.

Committee for January: William Pagan, Edward Goold, John Oothout, Oliver Templeton, John Tench, William Ustick.

CHAMBER OF COMMERCE.—TUESDAY, 5th February, 1782.

PRESENT.

Isaac Low, President.
Thomas Buchanan, Vice-Prt.
Robert R. Waddel, Treasurer.
Anthony Van Dam, Secretary.

Oliver Templeton,
William Kenyon,
William Backhouse,
Samuel Hake,
Patrick McDavitt,
William Laight,
William Pagan,
John Tench,
David Seabury,
Augustus Van Horne,
Edward Laight,
Abram Walton,
Jacob Watson,
Gerrard Walton,
John Miller.

Fined for appearing after six o'clock:

Isaac Low,
Daniel McCormick,
Frederick Rhinelander,
Robert R. Waddel,
John Oothout.

Ordered—That Messrs. William Lowther, Henry Brevoort, John Taylor, William Laight, Patrick McDavitt, Richard Smith, and David Seabury, be a Committee untill the first Tuesday in March next, to hear and determine disputes between parties submitting such to their determination, and that they do report their proceedings to this Corporation.

MR. PRESIDENT having convened many of the Members on the 9th Ultimo in consequence of a Letter rec'd from the Magistrates of Police, intimating that the arrival of the Provision Fleets[206] had reduced the price of Flour, he was directed to reply thereto, and both

Letters are now ordered to be transcribed in the minutes as follows :—

POLICE, 8th January, 1782.

SIR,

We are informed from the arrival of the Provision Fleet, and a number of Prizes,[207] that the price of Flour is at present reduced, and in all probability will continue so for some time. The Chamber of Commerce favoring us with the average price of Flour, and their opinion of the necessary alteration in the price of Bread, we shall immediately lay it before the Commandant for his orders to regulate Bread accordingly. If the Chamber of Commerce would be so good as to favor us Monthly with their opinion in regard to the price of Flour and Bread, we should esteem it a favor.

We are, with much esteem,

Sir, Your most obedt. hble servts.,

ANDREW ELLIOT, Supert. Genl.
D. MATHEWS, Mayor.

ISAAC LOW, Esqr.,
President of the Chamber of Commerce.

GENTLEMEN,

I convened the Chamber of Commerce yesterday, on purpose to take into consideration the Letter you honored me with relative to the Price of Flour. It is their opinion that the present price of the best fresh Flour may be estimated at 56s. p. ct., and, as it is a common practice with the Bakers to give Eight Pounds of Bread for Seven Pounds of Flour, and as they also gave a Loaf weighing Two Pounds for sixteen Coppers[208] when the Price of Flour was estimated at 70s. per ct., the Chamber of Commerce think they can at the present price, equally, if not better, afford to give a Quarter of a Pound more in each Loaf for Fourteen Coppers.

Upon this principle, then, the Long Loaf of the best flour ought to weigh Two Pounds and a Quarter, and the Round Loaf Two Pounds and Three Quarters for one shilling. The Chamber are, however, sorry to be under the necessity of reminding the Police that the last regulation of the heavy round Loaves has never, that they can learn, been regarded. And it is too evident to require illustration, that unless it be vigilantly and strictly enforced [*it*] must entirely defeat the whole intention of regulating the Price of Bread, and throw all the difference between the price of good and bad Flour altogether into the Bakers' Pockets.

If, therefore, the Bakers *can* be compelled to make no long Loaves of any but the best Flour, and to make up all other that is in the least degree deficient in fineness or any other respect into the round heavy Loaves, and that both the long and round Loaves be properly baked and dryed, and not delivered, as is too often the case, in so moist a state as to defeat the intention of Weighing, the Chamber will be both proud and happy to contribute their aid to a Measure in which the Good of the Public is so deeply interested. But untill then all other Efforts must prove nugatory and vain.

I have the honor to be,

By order of the Chamber of Commerce,

Gentlemen, &c.,

ISAAC LOW, President.

CHAMBER OF COMMERCE.—TUESDAY, 4th March, 1782.

PRESENT.

Thomas Buchanan, Vice-President.
Robert R. Waddel, Treasurer.
Anthony Van Dam, Secretary.

Edward Laight,
William Laight,
William Backhouse,
Gerrard Walton,
William Lowther,
William Kenyon,
Frederick Rhinelander.

Fined for appearing after six o'clock:

William Pagan,
Vincent P. Ashfield,
Joshua Watson,
John Murray,
Thomas C. Williams,
David Seabury,
Patrick McDavitt,
Thomas Buchanan,
James Douglass,
Richard Smith,
Oliver Templeton,
John Miller,
Andrew Kerr,
Samuel Hake,
John Ponsonby.

GOVERNOR ROBERTSON enclosed a MEMORIAL of the Proprietors of Wharfs[209] in this City, praying for an increase of the pay of Vessels Wharfage,[210] which being debated, the consideration thereof was postponed untill the next meeting, that they may inform themselves on the Merits of the Petition.

Ordered—That Messrs. Vincent P. Ashfield, Joshua Watson, Abram Walton, James Douglass, Samuel Hake, Joseph Allicocke, and John Ponsonby, be a Committee untill the first Tuesday in April next, to hear and determine disputes between parties submitting the same to their determination, and that they do report their proceedings to this Corporation.

CHAMBER OF COMMERCE.—TUESDAY, 2d April, 1782.

PRESENT.

Isaac Low, President.
Anthony Van Dam, Secretary.
David Seabury, Alexander Wallace,
William Kenyon.

Fined for appearing after six o'clock:

William Backhouse,	Samuel Donaldson,
James Douglass,	John Taylor,
John McAdam,	Daniel McCormick,
Richard Smith,	John Tench,
Richard Sharpe,	Joshua Watson,
William Lowther,	William Ustick,
Patrick McDavitt,	Joseph Allicocke,
John Murray,	Samuel Hake.

Ordered—That Messrs. William Seton, Gabriel H. Ludlow, Edward Laight, Richard Yates, Daniel McCormick, Hugh Wallace, and Gerr'd Walton, be a Committee, untill the first Tuesday in May next, to hear and determine disputes between parties submitting such to their determination, and that they do report their proceedings to this Corporation.

THE PETITION of Owners of Wharfs to Governor ROBERTSON having been duly considered by the Chamber, they are of opinion:

THAT ALL OWNERS OF WHARFS who shall produce a Certificate from the Wardens of the Port that their Wharves are in perfect repair and good condition, shall hereafter be intitled to receive from all Masters and Owners of Vessells that shall lay fast'ned thereto, for every Vessell not exceeding 100 Tons Carpenter's measurement, at the rate of three shillings p. Day; for all Vessells above 100 Tons and not exceeding 300 Tons, 4s 6d p. Day; and all Vessels above 300 Tons 6s p. Day.

That all Vessells laying in the outside Berths of the above description to pay one half of the above rated Wharfage.

WHEREUPON the President wrote the following Letter to his Excellency the GOVERNOR:

SIR,

I have the honor to inclose the opinion of the Chamber of Commerce on the Petition your Excellency was pleased to refer to their consideration, relative to the increase of wharfage and putting and keeping the Wharf in repair, so necessary for the accomodation of Trade.

Those Regulations they conceive will be perfectly agreeable, as well to those who pay as to those who receive Wharfage; and should they be honored with your Excelly's approbation, may be put into immediate execution.

The PRESIDENT laid before the Chamber Copies of Letters from Capt. ST. CLAIR[uu] to the President, and one from him to Capt. St. Clair, [*which*] were in the words following:

COMMANDANT'S OFFICE, 2d March, 1782.

SIR,

In consequence of an application from *Mr. William Lyon* and *Mr. John McCole* (recommended by the Magistrates of Police) to have a matter of theirs, which has been before a Committee of the Chamber of Commerce, laid before the Chamber at large, the Commandant requests you will please to direct the Gentlemen who compose that body to meet, when it may be convenient to you and them, to hear the parties and report to him your opinion. I have the honor to be, Sir, your most obed't H'ble Serv't,

JNO. ST. CLAIR, Secr'y.[211]

CAPT. ST. CLAIR:

As I was lame, and could not attend the Chamber of Commerce, I sent the Letter you honored me with to Mr. Buchanan, the Vice-President, who Informs me that they investigated very minutely the proceedings of their Committee from the papers which they were possessed of relative to Claims of *Mr. William Lyon* and *Mr. John McCole*, which were not (as they supposed) passed over unnoticed, but, on the contrary, fully considered; and the Chamber do intirely concur with the Monthly Committee that the Claimants are not intitled to any damages from the Vessel, Master, or Mariners, for any deficiency or supposed embezzlement alledged against them. I have, &c.,

ISAAC LOW.

CHAMBER OF COMMERCE.—TUESDAY, 7th May, 1782.

PRESENT.

Isaac Low, President.
Thomas Buchanan, Vice-Pres't.
Robert R. Waddell, Treasurer.
Anthony Van Dam, Secretary.

Patrick McDavitt,
Alex'r Wallace,
William Backhouse,
Will'm Kenyon,
John Miller.

Fined for appearing after six o'clock:

Joshua Watson,
Robert R. Waddel,
Thomas Buchanan,
Thomas C. Williams,
William Pagan,
Samuel Donaldson,
Samuel Hake,
Oliver Templeton,
John Oothout,
Vincent P. Ashfield,
William Laight,
John Ponsonby,
Richard Sharpe,
Daniel McCormick,
David Seabury,
Frederick Rhinelander,
Richard Yates.

The PRESIDENT laid before the Chamber a Letter from ADMIRAL DIGBY[vv] to GOVERNOR ROBERTSON, dated the 3d April, when a *Special Meeting* took the same into consideration, and thereupon ordered the President to reply thereto. Both Letters are here transcribed, and Mr. President's Letter approved of:

NEW YORK, April 3d, 1782.

SIR,

There are already above one Thousand Men out in Privateers, and four more ready, to man which will take above 200 men. I must therefore beg your Excellency will withhold granting any more Commissions till the return of some of the large Privateers whose cruizes are expired, as there are two frigates[212] now in the port that cannot be sent to sea for want of men.

At the same time, I beg it may be understood that I mean to give all the encouragement to Privateers in my power, whenever the King's service will permit.

But I must beg leave to take this opportunity of informing your Excellency that unless they are kept within bounds, it will be impossible to carry on the King's service; and that the Perseverance, belonging to Messrs. King[213] & Kemble, and commanded by Mr. Ross,[214] has sailed without my pass, and returned to the Hook and sailed again after bidding defiance to the Guard Ship and King's Boats, which, if suffered to pass unnoticed, must in the end prove a great detriment to my Intentions. I have the honor to be

Your Excellency's very ob't servant,

(Signed,) ROBT. DIGBY.

HIS EXCELLENCY LIEUT. GEN. ROBERTSON.

SIR,

I took the earliest opportunity of laying before the Chamber of Commerce the Letter relative to privateers which Your Excellency received from the Admiral and did me the honor to inclose for that purpose.

The Chamber of Commerce are exceeding sorry to find his Excellency the Admiral intimates that encouraging privateers is incompatible with and prejudicial to the King's Service.

They flattered themselves the reasons urged in a Memorial (a copy of which we now beg leave to inclose) presented to his Excellency on that subject should, after his arrival to this Command, had convinced him of the contrary position

That there may be Individuals (from which perhaps no Community is exempt) who may be disposed to transgress or have actually violated the Stipulations set forth in that Memorial in which privateers were permitted to fit out, the Chamber of Commerce cannot but sincerely regret and would wish they might on due conviction be punished according to the nature of their offence, but to take out a great part of the best men and put them on board Men of War and thereby in a manner breaking up the Cruise without regularly trying the offenders are terms too hard for any owners, however opulent, to attempt to combat.

The best human Laws and Institutions are liable to abuse, but to abolish them altogether for that reason were to render the remedy far worse than the disease and therefore cannot be the *bounds*, within which unless privateering be kept, his Excellency the Admiral means to be understood it will be impossible to carry on the King's Service.

Past uniform experience abundantly justifies us in observing to your Excellency that however difficult it may be to carry on the King's Service, unless Privateers are kept within bounds, it will be found much more so if these bounds be reduced to too narrow a compass.

Due encouragement to Privateers is in other words only to tempt both Landsmen as well as Seamen by the most powerful inducements, that of making it their Interest, to resort from all parts of the Continent to this port. Nor has any Maxim obtained more universal assent than that all wise Governments should assiduously consult and attend to the Temper and Genius of the people, and it is notorious that the Genius of no people was ever more peculiar or conspicuous than that of the Americans for Privateering.[215] If therefore, that Genius be counteracted it must necessarily produce the evils inseparable from such conduct in all other Cases.

Within bounds or due encouragement being however indefinite Terms, we beg leave to explain to Your Excellency what we mean by the latter, as we wish upon an important an occasion to be well understood.

Due encouragement then in our idea to privateers, or in other words to increase the number of Seamen in this Port, and thereby upon any grand emergency more effectually to man his Majesty's Ships consists in a few simple obvious Principles, not merely to be published to the world, but strictly and invariably adhered to, viz:

To impress no man returning from Captivity by Cartel or Escape untill their return to this Port after performing one Voyage.

To impress no man on shore or from any outward bound Vessels, but that this Port should really and truly be an asylum to all of the above description, except as is before mentioned, on some grand emergency, for, rather than be liable to an impress on board Men of War on their arrival here before they have made a Voyage, experience has fully evinced they will enter on Board Merchant Vessels and Privateers amongst the Rebels.

If, therefore, there were Ten Thousand men instead of only One Thousand in Privateers from this Port, it were far less an Evil considered in the most unfavorable light, even supposing not one of them could ever be got to enter on Board the King's Ships, than to have them in Privateers acting against us, which would certainly be the alternative.

Having thus presumed to give your Excellency our Candid sentiments about Privateers; We beg leave to add that although it may not be thought expedient to give encouragement to them in the full extent we have mentioned: unless his Excellency, the Admiral, can permit Privateers to fit out and Man in this Port upon more liberal and permanent Principles than are now granted, particularly as to the number of Men on board each Privateer, what is called encouragement is only specious and does not merit that appelation. For at present, Privateers, instead of running to Men of War for protection, and giving as they might often do, important intelligence, they avoid and run from them as they would from an enemy for fear of losing many of their Men; and therefore rather than have Privateering admitted upon the present loose footing, the Chamber of Commerce evidently wish, and here they are confident they express the general sentiments of the Citizens of New York, that if his Excellency, the Admiral, can reconcile it with his Ideas of promoting the King's Service, Privateering out of this Port may be not only restrained within bounds, but altogether suppressed, for, although some may thereby be deprived the pleasure of being enriched by the Spoils of their Enemies, all will at least be relieved from the stinging reproach of obstructing his Majesty's Service.

On the footing of favor they wish not to be gratified in Privatereing, nor on any other than that of its being considered and encouraged as one of the best means of annoying and humbling his Majesty's Enemies.

The late unfortunate disasters, the few arrivals, and the peculiar dulness of Trade, all conspire to render the want of Seamen greater than usual: but when it is considered how many Vessels have been purchased and manned for the Public Service,[216] besides the King's Ships of various denominations, and the great number of Seamen which this Port has constantly furnished, We rather wonder whence they could be collected than that no more have offered, and in this important point of View we are confident this Port can be exceeded by none upon this Continent, and perhaps is not far below the second in Great Britain.

Ordered—That Messrs. William Backhouse, Augustus Van Horne, Frederick Rhinelander, John Miller, Jacob Watson, Will'm Kenyon, and Alexander Wallace, be a Committee untill the first Tuesday in June next, to hear and determine disputes between parties submitting such to their determination, and that they do report their proceedings to this Corporation.

The Royal Charter, as well as the Laws of this Corporation, appoint this Day for the Election of Officers for the ensuing Year, when the following Gentlemen were balloted for, and duly elected:

Isaac Low,	President.
Thomas Buchanan, Jacob Walton,	Vice-Presidents.
Robert R. Waddle,	Treasurer.
Anthony Van Dam,	Secretary.

And all except Mr. Jacob Walton, who was not present, were duly sworn agreeable to the Charter to execute their respective offices.

Ordered—That the Committee of the Month Audit the Treasurer's Accounts.

Ordered—That Mr. Treasurer demand from each Member 40s. in advance towards the expence of the Chamber, and that it be repaid, or a proportion thereof, out of the Fines to be collected.

CHAMBER OF COMMERCE.—Tuesday, 4th June, 1782.

Present.

Anthony Van Dam, Secretary.

Vincent P. Ashfield, Joseph Allicocke,
Richard Sharpe, William Backhouse.

Committee in Rotation to hear and determine disputes until the first Tuesday in July next: John Murray, Samuel Donaldson, John L. McAdam, Patrick McDavitt, John Oothout, Edward Goold, Thomas Goodwin.

CHAMBER OF COMMERCE.—Tuesday, 2d July, 1782.

Present.

Isaac Low, President.
Anthony Van Dam, Secretary.

Gerrard Walton, William Laight,
William Backhouse.

Fined for appearing after six o'clock:

David Seabury,
John Murray,
William Kenyon,
Samuel Donaldson,
Robert R. Waddell,
Oliver Templeton,
Isaac Low,
Andrew Kerr,
Daniel McCormick,
Samuel Hake,
Edward Goold,
Vincent P. Ashfield,
Patrick McDavitt,
Alexan. Wallace,
Richard Sharpe,
Fred. Rhinelander,
Thomas Buchanan,
John Oothout,
Thomas Goodwin.

THE REGISTER of the Monthly Committee's decisions being mislaid:

Ordered—That the Committee for the present month, or any member, make enquiry for the same; when found, deliver it to the SECRETARY, that their reports may be entered.

Ordered—That Messrs. Oliver Templeton, John Taylor, Andrew Kerr, John Tench, Henry Brevoort, William Pagan, and William Ustick, be a Committee, untill the first Tuesday in August next, to hear and determine disputes between parties submitting the same to their determination, and that they do report their proceedings to this Corporation.

Ordered—That the President do write to GENERAL ROBERTSON, requesting to know whether the Letter written to him on the subject of Privateering had been laid before the ADMIRAL, and whether any or what Answer had been given thereto; and also that he write to the Admiral, representing that the Trade and Fishery was unprotected, and requesting that some means may be pursued so as to encourage the Fishermen to take Fish for a supply to this Garrison, and that its Commerce may not be annoyed by the Privateers and Whaleboats that infest even the Narrows.[217]

CHAMBER OF COMMERCE.—TUESDAY, 6th August, 1782.

PRESENT.

Isaac Low, President.
Thomas Buchanan, Vice do.
Anthony Van Dam, Secretary.

William Backhouse,
Patrick McDavitt,
William Lowther,
Oliver Templeton,
Alexander Wallace.

Fined for appearing after six o'clock:

John Murray,
David Seabury,
Andrew Kerr,
Thomas Buchanan,
Vincent P. Ashfield,
Frederick Rhinelander,
Richard Yates,
Jacob Watson,
Samuel Hake.

COMMITTEE IN ROTATION to hear and determine Disputes between parties until the first Tuesday in September next: Richard Smith, William Lowther, David Seabury, William Laight, Abraham Walton, Vincent P. Ashfield, and Daniel McCormick.

CHAMBER OF COMMERCE.—TUESDAY, 3d September, 1782.

PRESENT.

Isaac Low, President.
Robert R. Waddell, Treasurer.
Anthony Van Dam, Secretary.

William Lowther,
William Backhouse,
William Laight,
Vincent P. Ashfield.

Fined for appearing after six o'clock:

John Murray,
Henry Brevoort,
Richard Yates,
Joseph Allicocke,
Samuel Hake,
John Oothout,
David Seabury,
John Tench,
William Pagan,
Jacob Watson,
Richard Smith,
Richard Sharpe,

Patrick McDavitt,	Joshua Watson,
Alexan'r Wallace,	Fred. Rhinelander,
Robert R. Waddell,	Samuel Donaldson,

Abraham Walton.

Ordered—That Messrs. John Ponsonby, Joseph Allicocke, Samuel Hake, Richard Yates, William Seton, Hugh Wallace, and Gabriel H. Ludlow, be a Committee untill the first Tuesday in Oct. next, to hear and determine Disputes between Parties submitting such to their judgment, and that they do report their proceedings to this Corporation.

DISPUTES having subsisted between *Robert Wilkins, assured*, and *John Porteous*[218] *& Patrick Reed, assurers*, on the Kitty and Polly from St. Augustine to New York, which was referred by the Magistrates of Police to the Monthly Committee, who thought that as their decision might be brought into precedent, prayed the opinion of the Chamber at large, who having heard the Evidences, it did appear:

That the Kitty and Polly departed from New York to St. Augustine, where the Factor was to load her back to New York; before the Owners heard of her Arrival there they caused Insurance to be made from St. Augustine to New York on Vessell and Goods.

Her fate was not known when a dispatch Vessell arrived from St. Augustine, the master informed that the Kitty and Polly[219] was to sail from St. John's River, a member of St. Augustine, the same day, or about that time that the dispatch Vessell departed; on which the Broker, at the desire of *Mr. John Tench*, was directed to inform the Assurers of that circumstance, and to learn their opinion whether the risque was still good. The Broker related that he had waited upon *Mr. John Porteous*, one of the underwriters, who replied that he considered the Vessell out of time, and therefore declared off the risque, but did not see *Mr. Patrick Reed*, the other underwriter. The assured was advis'd presently that after that it would be best to avoid difficulties to offer the *Assurers* an advance premium, rather than leave the matter in an uncertain state; if that could not be effected to promote a new Insurance, which could not be procured, when the *Assured* desired the Broker to propose to the underwriters to leave it to reference whether the *Assurers* were on or not: His evidence was that they, or one of them, totally declined a submission to an award of Arbitrators. These overtures were before the fate of the Kitty and Polly was known. All the parties attended who had an Agency in this business, and it was generally agreed that the risque from St. John's River was rather less hazardous than from the Harbor of St. Augustine, and the Assurers themselves acknowledged that they would as readily have wrote from St. John's River, as from the Town of St. Augustine, when the application was first made.

It may be remarked that *Mr. John Tench* as well as *Mr. Robert Wilkins* were interested in this Vessell and Cargo. That all the Insurance for the concerned was directed to be done by *Mr. Tench.* That *Mr. Tench* having doubts, when the dispatch Boat arrived, about the Vessell's sailing from St. John's instead of St. Augustine Harbor, he applied to the underwriters on his Policy, who agreed that a note should be made thereon, taking the risque from St. John's. This led him to make the same application to the Assurers on *Mr. Wilkins'* policy, through the Broker, which was done without the privity of *Mr. Wilkins*, and he (*Mr. Wilkins*) knew of nothing being done therein untill the underwriters, or one of them, refused to continue the risque. From all the Facts being collected, and that it appears by the Protest of the Master that he sailed in and with the said Kitty and Polly, at the time the Master of the Dispatch Vessel did; that she was taken the third day after her departure, and sent into Georgetown.[220] Two points arise that are disputable.

1st. WHETHER St. John's River can be considered at and from Augustine, and

2d. WHETHER, if so, that the underwriters are held to pay the loss, as they declined being on the Risque after they had declared off, before it was known she was taken.

TO THE FIRST it was debated and generally acknowledged that St. John's is the principal port of Newfoundland, as Kingston is the principal port of Jamaica, yet that if a Vessell is insured from Newfoundland or Jamaica, tho' she sails from an outport, so [*although*] the Kitty and Polly sail'd from St. John's River in St. Augustine it is held to be valid.

TO THE SECOND, when it was asked, and the underwriters declared off the Risque, it did not appear to the Chamber that they were discharged because it was requiring their sentiments to avoid Disputes, and the assured never gave up his Claim.

This Corporation divided thereon, and a great Majority were of opinion that the Underwriters were bound to pay a total loss agreeable to the Policy.

Mr. John Strachan having been proposed at a former

Meeting, was balloted for and unanimously elected a Member of this Corporation.

Ordered—That notice be sent to him by the Secretary, in writing, that he was unanimously elected.

CHAMBER OF COMMERCE.—TUESDAY, 1st October, 1782.

PRESENT.

Isaac Low, President.
Thomas Buchanan, Vice-President.
Anthony Van Dam, Secretary.

William Laight,
Samuel Hake,
Joshua Watson,
John Strachan,
William Backhouse,
Jacob Watson,
Frederick Rhinelander.

Fined for appearing after six o'clock:

Oliver Templeton,
John Oothout,
Thomas Buchanan,
Joseph Allicocke,
John Murray,
William Pagan,
John Miller.

COMMITTEE IN ROTATION to hear and determine disputes between parties untill the first Tuesday in November next: Augustus Van Horne, Gerrard Walton, Joshua Watson, John Strachan, John Miller.

CHAMBER OF COMMERCE.—TUESDAY, 5th November, 1782.

PRESENT.

Isaac Low, President.
Anthony Van Dam, Secretary.

Alexander Wallace,
Gerrard Walton,
William Laight,
William Pagan.

Fined for appearing after six o'clock:

Joseph Allicocke,
John Oothout,
John Strachan,
William Backhouse,

Frederick Rhinelander, Augustus Van Horne,
John Miller, Patrick McDavitt,
Jacob Watson.

COMMITTEE IN ROTATION to hear and determine disputes between parties untill the first Tuesday in December next: William Kenyon, Jacob Watson, Richard Sharpe, Alexan'r Wallace, Frederick Rhinelander.

CHAMBER OF COMMERCE.—TUESDAY, 3d December, 1782.

PRESENT.

Isaac Low, President.
Thomas Buchanan, Vice-Pres't.
Robert R. Waddle, Treasurer.
Anthony Van Dam, Secretary.

Jacob Watson, John Murray,
Richard Sharpe, Oliver Templeton,
William Backhouse, John Taylor,
William Laight, Edward Laight,
Richard Yates, David Seabury,
Alex. Wallace.

Fined for appearing after six o'clock:

John Strachan, Samuel Hake,
John Miller, Joseph Allicocke,
Daniel McCormick.

Ordered—That Messrs. Patrick McDavitt, William Backhouse, John L. McAdam, John Murray, and Samuel Donaldson, be a Committee untill the first Tuesday in January next, to hear and determine disputes between parties submitting such to their determination, and that they do report their proceedings to this Corporation.

The COMMANDANT having recommended a rehearing of a dispute between the owners of the Kidnapper and

Ranger, and having heard the parties, the CHAMBER at large confirm their Committee's Opinion.

CHAMBER OF COMMERCE.—TUESDAY, 7th January, 1783.

PRESENT.

Isaac Low, President.
Thomas Buchanan, Vice-President.
Robert R. Waddel, Treasurer.
Anthony Van Dam, Secretary.

Edward Laight,
William Lowther,
William Backhouse,
Gerrard Walton,
Alexan. Wallace,
John Strachan,
John Murray,
William Walton.

Fined for appearing after six o'clock:

John Oothout,
John Miller,
Jacob Watson,
Andrew Kerr,
John Ponsonby,
Patrick McDavitt,
Oliver Templeton,
William Ustick,
John Tench,
Samuel Donaldson.

Ordered—That Messrs. Oliver Templeton, John Tench, John Oothout, Edward Goold, and Thomas Goodwin, be a Committee untill the first Tuesday in February next, to hear and determine disputes between parties submitting such to their determination, and that they do report their proceedings to this Corporation.

Mr. Strachan, partner to *Lee & Strachan*, having made an application to the Commandant and the Police, and they requesting the Chamber at large to take up a dispute between them and *Robert Hoakesley*, and debates thereon arising the Corporation decided, thereupon it appeared that there were for rehearing - - 5
against it - - 17

Mr. John McKenzie having been proposed at a former meeting, was balloted for and unanimously elected.

Ordered—That the Secretary send him notice in writing that he was unanimously elected a Member of this Corporation.

CHAMBER OF COMMERCE.—TUESDAY, 4th February, 1783.

PRESENT.

Isaac Low, President.

William Lowther,	John Murray,
David Seabury,	Andrew Kerr,
Samuel Donaldson,	Samuel Hake,
Thomas Goodwin,	William Backhouse,
John McKenzie,	John Ponsonby.

Fined for appearing after six o'clock:

Vincent P. Ashfield,	William Laight.

COMMITTEE IN ROTATION to hear and determine disputes untill the first Tuesday in March next: Andrew Kerr, John Taylor, William Ustick, John McKenzie, and William Pagan.

CHAMBER OF COMMERCE.—TUESDAY, 4th March, 1783.

PRESENT.

Isaac Low, President.
Robert R. Waddell, Treasurer.
Anthony Van Dam, Secretary.

Jacob Watson,	Thomas Goodwin,
Joshua Watson,	John Ponsonby,
Frederick Rhinelander,	Edward Laight,
John Murray,	John Tench,
William Laight,	Samuel Hake,

William Lowther,	Andrew Kerr,
John McKenzie,	John Oothout,
William Backhouse,	Patrick McDavitt,
Oliver Templeton,	William Pagan,
David Seabury,	John Strachan.

Messrs. Alexander Leckie, William Trenholm, Samuel Elam, and John Glover, having been proposed at a former Meeting were balloted for and unanimously elected.

Ordered—That the Secretary send them notice in writing that they were unanimously elected Members of this Corporation.

Ordered—That Messrs. Abram Walton, William Lowther, Daniel McCormick, William Laight, and David Seabury, be a Committee, untill the first Tuesday in April next, to hear and determine disputes between Parties submitting such to their determination, and that they do report their proceedings to this Corporation.

Mr. Treasurer reported that he had rec'd from Mr. McEvers, former Treasurer, the Books belonging to this Corporation, and

The President laid before the Chamber a Letter rec'd from Mr. McEvers, which was read, and ordered to be entered on the Minutes.

Sir,

My Friend Colonel Cruger[221] this Morning communicated to me that the Chamber of Commerce have (in consequence of my silence on a Letter rec'd from you as their representative, and from Mr. Van Dam) conceived an opinion of an intentional contempt to a Body corporate for whom I would wish to testify every mark of respect and esteem. As I ever have thought myself much honored in my appointment as an Officer to that Board, I of course do and shall continue to feel with greater concern the information received through my Friend.

In the first place, I beg leave to say that the Idea of Contempt is removed from me beyond any descriptive distance; and in the next place, that the cause of my silence was founded in the hope of long before this to have separated from my present small dependence as much as would have enabled me to have answered the purport and requisition of your Letter. This, with concern, I may say that I am not yet able to do, and that my wishes in this respect have long been thwarted by many in this City, who can and ought to give me my own. The Book and other matters in my charge belonging to the Board shall be sent to your present Treasurer on my return to my country Quarters; and I have only to add that you will, I hope, at your next Meeting, do me the justice to represent the anxiety I have expressed to you on this occasion.

I am, with regard, Sir,

Your most obd't serv't,

CHARLES MCEVERS.

CHAMBER OF COMMERCE.—TUESDAY, 1st April, 1783.

PRESENT.

Isaac Low, President.
Robert R. Waddel, Treasurer.
Anthony Van Dam, Secretary.
William Lowther, John Strachan,
John McKenzie.

Fined for appearing after six o'clock:

William Backhouse,
William Trenholm,
William Kenyon,
Isaac Low,
Robert R. Waddel,
Thomas Buchanan,
David Seabury,
Samuel Elam,
Daniel McCormick,
John Murray,
Oliver Templeton,
Patrick McDavitt,
Jacob Watson,
Alexand'r Leckie,
Gerrard Walton,
John Ponsonby,
John Glover,
William Laight.

Ordered—That Messrs. Vincent P. Ashfield, John Ponsonby, Alexander Leckie, Joshua Watson, and William Trenholme, be a Committee, untill the first Tuesday in May next, to hear and determine disputes between parties submitting such to their determination, and that they do report their proceedings to this Corporation.

CHAMBER OF COMMERCE.—TUESDAY, 6th May, 1783.

PRESENT.

Isaac Low, President.
Robert R. Waddell, Treasurer.
Anthony Van Dam, Secretary.

William Backhouse, Samuel Elam,
William Pagan, Gerrard Walton,
Alexand'r Leckie, William Lowther,
John McKenzie.

Fined for appearing after six o'clock:

William Kenyon, Patrick McDavitt,
John Glover, Samuel Hake,
William Walton, Daniel McCormick,
John Miller, Oliver Templeton,
John Oothout, Robert Waddel,
John Strachan, William Laight,
Isaac Low, Frederick Rhinelander,
Thomas Buchanan.

Ordered—That Messrs. John Strachan, Samuel Elam, William Seton, John Glover, and Edward Laight, be a Committee untill the first Tuesday in June next, to hear and determine disputes between parties submitting such to their determination, and that they do report their proceedings to this Corporation.

The CHARTER as well as the laws of this Corporation appoint this day for the choice of Officers, when the following Gentlemen were duly elected to serve the current year, and untill others be elected:

THOMAS BUCHANAN, President.
GERRARD WALTON, } Vice-Presidents.
WILLIAM WALTON, }
ROBERT R. WADDELL, Treasurer.
ANTHONY VAN DAM, Secrctary.

And the Vice-Presidents, Treasurer and Secretary being sworn to execute their several offices, Mr. Buchanan having declined qualifying, when the Charter directs in such an event that another be chosen at the next meeting.

Ordered—That Mr. Strachan, Mr. Glover, and Mr. Elam, be a Committee to audit the Treasurer's accounts and report thereon.

CHAMBER OF COMMERCE.—TUESDAY, 20th January, 1784.

PRESENT.

	President.
Gerard Walton, William Walton,	Vice do.
Robert R. Waddel,	Treasurer.
	Secty.

Andrew Kerr,	Thomas Randall,
Will'm Laight,	Edward Goold,
John Miller,	Jacob Watson,
John Alsop,	Saml. Donaldson,
William Backhouse,	William Lowther,
George Ludlow,	August. Van Horne,
Oliver Templeton,	John Murray,
Robert Murray,	Jacobus Van Zandt,
Theoph. Bache,	Dan'l Ludlow,
Walter Buchanan,	Sam'l Elam.

Mr. Bache's Motion seconded by R. R. Waddell—Whereas, a number of Gentlemen formerly Members of this Corporation, and who Resigned their seats on Account of a difference of sentiment Respecting the passing of Jersey money,[222] and are now desirous of Becoming Members of the said Corporation. Mr. Bache proposes to the Chamber that the following Persons are admitted to be Members[223] and Restored to their seats without being Balloted for:—Henry Remsen, Daniel Phenix, Isaac Sears, James Beekman, William Neilson, and Isaac Roosevelt.

Ordered—That Notice be sent to those Gentlemen to attend the Chamber at the next meeting.

William Backhouse's Motion seconded by Wm. Laight. The Admittance to be a Member of the Chamber of Commerce is thought too high for the Propriety of Increase of the Chamber. William Backhouse Proposes that the fee of Admittance should be reduced to the sum of Eight Dollars.[224]

The following Gentlemen wish to become Members of this Corporation: [225]

Eleazer Miller, Cornelius Ray,[ww] and Archibald Gamble, Proposed by Henry Remsen and Rob't R. Waddell; Viner Vanzandt, Proposed by Jacobus Vanzandt; Sam'l Broome, Jacob Morris, James Stewart, John Woodward, Comfort Sands,[xx] Robert Bowne,[yy] Moses Rogers, Sam'l Franklin, William Denning, John Shaw, Joseph Hallett, William Malcom, and Joshua Sands,[zz] Proposed by John Murray.

Ordered—That the Treasurer pay the Bill of this night.

NOTE.

The Colonial Records properly close with the Meeting of 6 May, 1783.

The Colonial period may be considered to have ended with the evacuation of the City by the British and its occupation by the American forces on the 25th November, 1783.

In the spring of 1784 "a Number of the Members of the Chamber and other Citizens, on their return to this City, taking into Consideration the state of the Chamber, and being advised by Counsel that the Charter of the said Chamber had been forfeited and lost by reason of the Misuser and Nonuser of the same, they thought it most adviseable to petition the Legislature for a confirmation of the said Charter * * * * the Legislature taking the same into Consideration granted the Prayer of their Petition, and did, on the Thirteenth day of April, pass a Law Intitled 'An Act to remove doubts concerning the Chamber of Commerce, and to confirm the Rights and Priviledges thereof.'"

A Meeting was held on the 20th April, 1784, and the Chamber was reorganized. The Act of the Legislature altered the name of the Institution to THE CHAMBER OF COMMERCE OF THE STATE OF NEW YORK.

OFFICERS

OF THE

NEW YORK CHAMBER OF COMMERCE,

1768–1784.

PRESIDENTS.

PAGE	ELECTED		RETIRED	PAGE
4	1768 April 5	JOHN CRUGER...........	2 May 1770	100
100	1770 May 2	HUGH WALLACE........	7 May 1771	128
128	1771 May 7	ELIAS DESBROSSES.......	5 May 1772	158
158	1772 May 5	HENRY WHITE.........	4 May 1773	179
179	1773 May 4	THEOPHYLACT BACHE....	2 May 1774	191
191	1774 May 3	WILLIAM WALTON.......	3 May 1775	202
202	1775 May 2	ISAAC LOW.............	6 May 1783	295
295	1783 May 6	———————*...........	13 April 1784	—

VICE-PRESIDENTS.

PAGE	ELECTED		RETIRED	PAGE
4	1768 April 5	Hugh Wallace..........	2 May 1770	100
100	1770 May 2	Henry White...........	5 May 1772	158
100	1770 May 2	Elias Desbrosses.......	7 May 1771	128
128	1771 May 7	Theophylact Bache......	4 May 1773	179
158	1772 May 5	William Walton.........	2 May 1774	191
179	1773 May 4	Isaac Low.............	3 May 1775	202
191	1774 May 2	John Alsop†............	7 Dec. 1779	218
202	1775 May 3	William McAdam‡......	1 Oct. 1779	—
218	1779 Dec. 7	Hugh Wallace.........	1 May 1781	254
218	1779 Dec. 7	Thomas Buchanan.......	1 May 1781	295
254	1781 May 1	Jacob Walton..........	6 May 1783	295
295	1783 May 6	Gerard Walton.........	13 April 1784	—
295	1783 May 6	William Walton........	13 April 1784	—

* *Thomas Buchanan*, elected May 6, 1783, but declining to qualify, the office was vacant until 13th April, 1784. † *John Alsop* retired from the city, 1776.

‡ *William McAdam* died, 1st Oct. 1779.

TREASURERS.

PAGE	ELECTED		RETIRED	PAGE
4	1768 April 5	Elias Desbrosses........	2 May 1770	100
100	1770 May 2	Theophylact Bache......	7 May 1771	128
128	1771 May 7	William Walton.........	5 May 1772	158
158	1772 May 5	Isaac Low.............	4 May 1773	179
179	1773 May 4	John Alsop............	2 May 1774	191
191	1774 May 2	William McAdam.......	3 May 1775	202
202	1775 May 3	Charles McEvers.......	2 May 1780	228
228	1780 May 2	Robert Ross Waddell....	13 April 1784	—

SECRETARY.

4	1768 April 5	Anthony Van Dam......	13 April 1784	—

MEMBERS OF THE NEW YORK CHAMBER OF COMMERCE. 1768–1784.

PAGE	ELECTED		LAST PRESENT	PAGE
18	1768 Oct. 4	Alexander, Robert......	5 June 1781	259
241	1780 Dec. 5	Allicocke, Joseph.......	3 Dec. 1782	290
7	1768 April 5	Alsop, John............	20 Jan. 1784	296
116	1770 Dec. 4	Amiel, John............	3 Nov. 1772	168
234	1780 July 4	Ashfield, Vincent Pearce..	4 Feb. 1783	292
3	1768 April 5	Bache, Theophylact.....	20 Jan. 1784	296
211	1779 Aug. 3	Backhouse, William......	20 Jan. 1784	296
71	1770 Jan. 2	Bayard, Samuel jr.......	7 Feb. 1775	200
8	1768 May 3	Beekman, Gerard William.	4 April 1775	201
59	1769 Oct. 3	Beekman, James........	8 July 1772	161
44	1769 May 2	Bogart, Henry C........	3 Feb. 1773	173
116	1770 Dec. 4	Booth, Benjamin........	2 Nov. 1779	216
218	1779 Dec. 7	Brevoort, Henry........	3 Sep. 1782	286
8	1768 May 3	Buchanan, Thomas......	6 May 1783	295
116	1770 Dec. 4	Buchanan, Walter.......	20 Jan. 1784	296
48	1769 June 6	Bull, Joseph...........	2 May 1775	201
211	1779 Aug. 3	Burnley, Harding.......	7 Nov. 1780	239
8	1768 May 3	Clarkson, Levinus.......	3 Mar. 1772	150
87	1770 April 3	Corsa, Isaac...........	7 Dec. 1779	217
3	1768 April 5	Cruger, John..........	2 May 1775	201
8	1768 May 3	Cruger, John Harris.....	7 Feb. 1775	200
3	1768 April 5	Desbrosses, Elias	2 May 1775	201
211	1779 Aug. 3	Donaldson, Samuel	20 Jan. 1784	296
245	1781 Feb. 6	Douglass, James........	2 April 1782	278

PAGE	ELECTED		LAST PRESENT	PAGE
38	1769 Mar. 7	Duyckinck, Gerardus.....	8 July 1772	162
293	1783 Mar. 4	Elam, Samuel..........	20 Jan. 1784	296
177	1773 April 6	Fairholme, Johnston*....	7 Feb. 1775	200
3	1768 April 5	Folliott, George.........	3 Jan. 1769	32
245	1781 Feb. 6	Forteath, Alexander.....	6 Nov. 1781	273
3	1768 April 5	Franklin, Walter........	2 May 1774	190
293	1783 Mar. 4	Glover, John J.........	6 May 1783	295
211	1779 Aug. 3	Goodwin, Thomas.......	4 Mar. 1783	292
211	1779 Aug. 3	Goold, Edward..........	20 Jan. 1784	296
87	1770 April 3	Gouverneur, Harman....	4 Feb. 1772	148
8	1768 May 3	Gouverneur, Nicholas....	2 April 1771	125
124	1771 Mar. 5	Hake, Samuel...........	6 May 1783	295
8	1768 May 3	Hasencliver, Peter.......	2 Aug. 1768	13
245	1781 Feb. 6	Hodgzard, William......	4 Oct. 1781	272
34	1769 Jan. 3	Hoffman, Nicholas.......	5 Oct. 1779	213
40	1769 April 4	Imlay, William..........	6 Oct. 1772	167
206	1779 July 6	Jameson, Niel†.........	————	——
3	1768 April 5	Jauncey, James..........	24 Mar. 1774	189
185	1773 Dec. 7	Jauncey, William........	2 May 1774	190
59	1769 Oct. 3	Kemble, Samuel........	3 June 1773	180
211	1779 Aug. 3	Kenyon, William........	6 May 1783	295
217	1779 Nov. 2	Kerr, Andrew...........	20 Jan. 1784	296
8	1768 May 3	Keteltas, Peter..........	4 April 1775	201
3	1768 April 5	Kortright, Lawrence.....	8 May 1781	255
13	1768 Aug. 2	Laight, Edward.........	4 Mar. 1783	292
190	1774 May 2	Laight, William.........	20 Jan. 1784	296
293	1783 Mar. 4	Leckie, Alexander.......	6 May 1783	295
185	1773 Dec. 7	Lewis, Francis..........	2 May 1775	201
51	1769 July 4	Lispenard, Leonard, jr....	4 Oct. 1774	198
7	1768 April 5	Livingston, Philip.......	6 Sep. 1768	14
87	1770 April 3	Livingston, Robert C....	1 Nov. 1774	199
128	1771 May 7	Livingston, Robert G., jr..	8 July 1772	161
3	1768 April 5	Low, Isaac.............	6 May 1783	295
218	1779 Dec. 7	Lowther, William........	20 Jan. 1784	296
177	1773 April 6	Ludlow, Daniel‡........	20 Jan. 1784	296

* *Fairholme, Johnston,* proposed at meeting of April 6, 1773. His election not noticed on minutes—appears in his seat, June 1, 1773, p. 180.

† *Jameson, Niel,* does not appear ever to have taken his seat.

‡ *Ludlow, Daniel,* proposed at meeting of April 6, 1773. His election not noticed on minutes—appears in his seat, January 20, 1784, p. 296.

PAGE	ELECTED		NAME	LAST PRESENT	PAGE
8	1768	May 3	Ludlow, Gabriel H......	8 Dec. 1780	242
44	1769	May 2	Ludlow, George W......	20 Jan. 1784	296
34	1769	Jan. 3	Lynsen, Abraham.......	5 Mar. 1771	123
211	1779	Aug. 3	McAdam, John Loudon..	2 April 1782	278
3	1768	April 5	McAdam, William.......	7 Sep. 1779	212
211	1779	Aug. 3	McCormick, Daniel.....	6 May 1783	295
211	1779	Aug. 3	McDavitt, Patrick.......	6 May 1783	295
64	1769	Nov. 7	McDonald, Alexander...	6 Oct. 1772	167
8	1768	May 3	McEvers, Charles.......	2 May 1775	201
7	1768	May 3	McEvers, James*.......	———	
292	1783	Jan. 7	McKenzie, John........	6 May 1783	295
8	1768	May 3	Marston, Thomas.......	2 June 1772	158
206	1779	July 6	Miller, John............	20 Jan. 1784	296
53	1769	Aug. 1	Miller, Thomas.........	3 Aug. 1779	210
8	1768	May 3	Moore, John...........	4 Dec. 1781	274
18	1768	Oct. 4	Moore, Thomas William..	8 July 1772	162
211	1779	Aug. 3	Murray, John...........	20 Jan. 1784	296
3	1768	April 5	Murray, Robert.........	20 Jan. 1784	296
8	1768	May 3	Neilson, William.........	8 July 1772	161
211	1779	Aug. 3	Nicoll, Charles..........	7 Nov. 1780	239
211	1779	Aug. 3	Oothout, John	6 May 1783	295
217	1779	Nov. 2	Pagan, William.........	6 May 1783	295
116	1770	Dec. 4	Phenix, Daniel..........	1 Sep. 1772	165
8	1768	May 3	Pintard, Lewis..........	4 Oct. 1774	198
87	1770	April 3	Platt, Jeremiah.........	1 Sep. 1772	165
245	1781	Feb. 6	Ponsonby, John.........	1 April 1783	294
206	1779	July 6	Ramadge, Smith........	1 May 1781	253
124	1771	Mar. 5	Ramsay, John...........	1 Sep. 1772	165
3	1768	April 5	Randall, Thomas........	20 Jan. 1784	296
38	1769	Mar. 7	Rapalje, Garret.........	7 June 1774	193
18	1768	Oct. 4	Reade, John............	6 Oct. 1772	167
13	1768	Aug. 2	Remsen, Henry, jr......	1 Sep. 1772	165
13	1768	Aug. 2	Remsen, Peter..........	4 Dec. 1770	115
206	1779	July 6	Rhinelander, Frederick..	6 May 1783	295
34	1769	Jan. 3	Roosevelt, Isaac........	1 Sep. 1772	165
153	1772	Mar. 3	Schuyler, John..........	7 Feb. 1775	200
222	1780	Feb. 1	Seabury, David..........	1 April 1783	294
185	1773	Dec. 7	Seagrove, James........	7 Feb. 1775	200

* *McEvers, James,* never took his seat. He died 8th September, 1768.

PAGE	ELECTED		LAST PRESENT	PAGE
8	1768 May 3	Sears, Isaac............	8 July 1772	161
13	1768 Aug. 2	Seton, William...........	4 Oct. 1781	272
13	1768 Aug. 2	Sharpe, Richard.........	3 Dec. 1782	290
3	1768 April 5	Sherbrooke, Miles.......	7 Mar. 1775	200
8	1768 May 3	Simson, Sampson.........	1 Sep. 1772	165
225	1780 Mar. 7	Smith, Richard...........	3 Sep. 1782	286
211	1779 Aug. 3	Spens, Walter...........	11 Aug. 1780	235
38	1769 Mar. 7	Stepple, William.........	8 Dec. 1780	241
288	1782 Sep. 3	Strachan, John...........	6 May 1783	295
211	1779 Aug. 3	Taylor, John............	3 Dec. 1782	290
211	1779 Aug. 3	Templeton, Oliver.......	20 Jan. 1784	296
211	1779 Aug. 3	Tench, John............	4 Mar. 1783	292
3	1768 April 5	Thompson, Acheson.....	5 July 1768	11
211	1779 Aug. 3	Thompson, Henry*......	———	
36	1769 Feb. 7	Thurman, John..........	2 May 1780	228
293	1783 Mar. 4	Trenholm, William......	1 April 1783	294
211	1779 Aug. 3	Ustick, William.........	7 Jan. 1783	291
3	1768 April 5	Van Dam, Anthony.....	6 May 1783	295
40	1769 April 4	Van Horne, Augustus...	20 Jan. 1784	296
8	1768 May 3	Van Zandt, Jacobus.....	20 Jan. 1784	296
3	1768 April 5	Verplanck, Samuel......	1 Nov. 1774	199
3	1768 April 5	Waddell, Robert Ross...	20 Jan. 1784	296
8	1768 May 3	Wallace, Alexander......	7 Jan. 1783	291
3	1768 April 5	Wallace, Hugh.........	19 July 1781	262
234	1780 July 4	Walton, Abraham.......	3 Sep. 1782	287
8	1768 May 3	Walton, Gerard.........	20 Jan. 1784	296
3	1768 April 5	Walton, Jacob..........	4 April 1775	201
36	1769 Feb. 7	Walton, Thomas........	5 May 1772	156
3	1768 April 5	Walton, William........	20 Jan. 1784	296
8	1768 May 3	Watson, Jacob..........	20 Jan. 1784	296
241	1780 Dec. 5	Watson, Joshua.........	4 Mar. 1783	292
8	1768 May 3	Watts, Robert..........	15 Feb. 1780	222
38	1769 Mar. 7	Wetherhead, John.......	15 Feb. 1770	76
7	1768 May 3	White, Henry...........	6 July 1779	205
3	1768 April 5	White, Thomas.........	3 June 1773	180
211	1779 Aug. 3	Williams, Thomas Charles	7 May 1782	280
8	1768 May 3	Yates, Richard.........	3 Dec. 1782	290
36	1769 Feb. 7	Young, Hamilton.......	6 Oct. 1772	167

135 Members.

* *Thompson, Henry*, does not appear ever to have taken his seat.

TABULAR VIEW OF ELECTIONS TO THE CHAMBER.

1768–1784.

MONTHS.	1768	1769	1770	1771	1772	1773	1774	1775	1776	1777	1778	1779	1780	1781	1782	1783	1784	TOTALS.
January	....	3	1	....	....	....	....	....	....	....	....	....	....	....	....	2	1	7
February	....	3	....	....	....	....	....	....	....	....	....	....	1	4	....	....	....	8
March	....	4	....	2	1	....	....	....	....	....	....	....	1	....	....	3	....	11
April	24	2	4	....	....	....	....	....	....	....	....	....	....	....	....	....	....	30
May	21	2	....	1	....	1	1	....	....	....	....	....	....	....	....	....	....	26
June	....	1	....	....	....	....	....	....	....	....	....	....	....	....	....	....	....	1
July	....	1	....	....	....	....	....	....	....	....	....	4	2	....	....	....	....	7
August	5	1	....	....	....	....	....	....	....	....	....	19	....	....	....	....	....	25
September	....	....	....	....	....	....	....	....	....	....	....	....	....	....	1	....	....	1
October	3	2	....	....	....	....	....	....	....	....	....	....	....	....	....	....	....	5
November	....	1	....	....	....	....	....	....	....	....	....	2	....	....	....	....	....	3
December	....	..	4	....	....	3	....	....	....	....	....	2	2	....	....	....	....	11
	53	20	9	3	1	4	1	....	....	....	....	27	6	4	1	5	1	135

TABULAR VIEW OF ATTENDANCE AT THE CHAMBER.

1768 – 1784.

MONTHS.	1768	1769	1770	1771	1772	1773	1774	1775	1776	1777	1778	1779	1780	1781	1782	1783	1784	AVERAGE.
January	....	23	28	39	27	22	26	8	....	....	....	....	24	23	8	22	23	23
February ..	....	28	54	34	35	14	16	16	....	....	....	....	32	27	23	13	....	26
March.....	....	42	39	34	36	16	13	9	....	....	....	....	26	40	24	23	....	28
April	20	30	38	31	34	24	15	13	....	....	....	....	24	27	21	22	....	25
May	19	46	46	49	42	21	25	19	....	....	....	....	34	33	25	23	....	32
June......	44	35	32	28	33	14	16	....	....	....	....	23	35	32	5	....	....	26
July.......	40	33	31	37	54	10	21	....	....	....	....	21	25	25	23	....	....	27
August....	23	28	36	36	22	13	11	....	....	....	....	25	27	22	16	....	....	23
September.	31	20	32	29	34	9	14	....	....	....	....	28	21	27	26	....	....	25
October ...	26	30	23	33	34	11	16	....	....	....	....	23	26	23	17	....	....	24
November .	30	42	31	46	29	11	22	....	....	....	....	28	36	22	15	....	....	27
December..	28	35	27	37	23	28	14	....	....	....	....	30	24	21	20	....	....	26
Average..	29	33	35	36	33	16	17	13	....	....	....	25	28	27	19	21	23	26

This Table includes only the attendance at Regular Meetings.—A Quorum was of 21 members.

NOTE.

The following Memoranda include the names of all the Old Members who continued or renewed their connection with the Chamber after its reorganization.

Names of Old Members subscribed to Petition to Legislature of the State of New York for confirmation of Charter.

1784, ———	John Alsop,	James Beekman,	Gerad. Duyckinck,
	Daniel Phœnix,	Jeremiah Platt,	Thomas Randall,
	Isaac Roosevelt,	Isaac Sears,	Jacob's Van Zandt.

Names of Old Members present at Reorganization of the Chamber according to Act of Legislature.

1784, Apr. 20.—	John Alsop,	James Beekman,	Gerad. Duyckinck,
	Daniel Phœnix,	Isaac Roosevelt,	Jacob's Van Zandt,
		Isaac Sears.	

Names of Old Members proposed at meeting for Reorganization and readmitted by ballot.

1784, May 4.—		Henry Remsen.	
1784, June 1.—	John J. Glover,	Peter Keteltas,	William Neilson,
		John Ramsay.	
1784, Aug. 3.—		Francis Lewis.	
1785, Mar. 1.—		Walter Buchanan.	

Names of Old Members readmitted by resolution of 13 *February*, 1787, *upon appearance at a Stated Meeting.*

1787, Mar. 6.—	Wm. Backhouse,	Patrick McDavitt,	Oliver Templeton.
1787, April 3.—	Edward Goold,	William Laight,	Daniel Ludlow,
	Gerard Walton,	John Miller,	John Oothout,
	George W. Ludlow,	Robert R. Waddell.	
1787, May 1.—		Theophylact Bache.	
1787, June 5.—	John Thurman,	Daniel McCormick,	William Lowther.
1787, July 3.—		John Murray.	
1787, Aug. 7.—		William Walton.	

NOTES TO REGISTER OF PROCEEDINGS

OF

NEW YORK CHAMBER OF COMMERCE.

HISTORICAL.

NOTE 1, PAGE 9. BOLTON & SIGELL'S.—This Public House, which, under various names and keepers, was a celebrated resort throughout the latter half of the last century, stood, and still stands, on the south-east corner of Broad and Dock, now Broad and Pearl Streets. It was built in the early part of the century by the Delancey family, on land originally conveyed by Colonel STEPHANUS VAN CORTLANDT to ETIENNE (STEPHEN) DE LANCEY, his son-in-law, on the 11th April, 1700. About the middle of the century it was occupied by Col. JOSEPH ROBINSON, as appears by the following advertisement in Hugh Gaine's Mercury, May 28, 1757:—"DELANCY, ROBINSON & Co. have removed their Store to the House wherein the late Col. JOSEPH ROBINSON lived, being the Corner House next the Royal Exchange, where they continue to sell all sorts of European and East India Goods, Shoes, Stockings, and Shirts, white and checked, fit for the Army, with a variety of other goods." The firm continued their business here until 1761.

On the 15th January, 1762, this property passed by deed into the ownership of SAMUEL FRANCIS, the most noted publican of the day, who here opened a tavern, called the "Queen's Head," under the sign of "Queen Charlotte."

In 1765 FRANCIS retired from this enterprise, and was succeeded by one JOHN JONES; but in the year 1766 he also withdrew.

BOLTON & SIGELL put forward their first advertisement in Holt's New York Journal of January 15, 1767, in the following style:—"BOLTON & SIGELL Take this method to acquaint the Public that they propose to open, on Monday next, a Tavern and Coffee House at the House of MR. SAMUEL FRANCIS, near the EXCHANGE, lately kept by MR. JOHN JONES, and known by the name of the 'Queen's Head Tavern,' where Gentlemen may depend upon receiving the best of Usage. As Strangers, they are sensible they can have no Pretentions to the Favour of the Public but what results from their readiness upon all occasions to oblige. Dinners and Public Entertainments provided at the shortest notice. Breakfasts in readiness from 9 to 11 o'clock. Jellies in the greatest Perfection, also Rich and plain Cakes sold by the weight."

The house seems to have enjoyed a fair share of patronage.

The Societies met here as they had done in the time of the favorite host FRANCIS, and the Chamber of Commerce continued to hold its monthly meetings here until it secured a Room of its own.

But it is doubtful whether the business was a prosperous one, at least the connection of the hosts was not of long duration. In Holt's New York Journal of February 8, 1770, appeared this notice:—"The partnership of BOLTON & SIGELL being this day dissolved, all those to whom they are indebted are desired to send in a state of their demands, and it is hereby humbly requested of those gentlemen who are indebted to them that they will be pleased to discharge their accounts, to enable MR. SIGELL to settle his affairs as soon as possible. The business, for the future, will be carried on solely by RICHARD BOLTON, who begs leave to solicit the continuance of the Public's favour. The most respectful attention shall be employed to secure the approbation of every gentleman who pleases to frequent the house.—February 5, 1770."

MR. BOLTON retired in May of the same year, and FRANCIS again returned. It was under the last occupancy of FRANCIS, or, as he signed himself at a later period, SAMUEL FRAUNCES, that his house, under the title of "Fraunces' Tavern," acquired its celebrity. Here Washington bade farewell to his officers on the 4th December, 1783, an affecting and historic scene. To this event is owing the present name of the house, "Washington's Head Quarters." It is now a hotel of the most ordinary description, and has been kept by one E. BEUERMEYER for a period of about twenty years.

NOTE 2, PAGE 10. PAPER CURRENCY OF PENNSYLVANIA.—The financial position of this colony was at this period in a better condition than that of New York, and their trade was in a more flourishing state. While exchange on Great Britain was selling at 175 and 170 in New York in exchange for currency, it only commanded in Pennsylvania 165 to 160, and so settled was this difference, that in the Almanacs of the Day "Arbitrations of the most common Courses of Exchange on London between New York and Philadelphia" were regularly published. Hugh Gaine's Pocket Almanac for 1771 gives a short table showing the equivalents from £160 to £190. As an instance, exchange in New York at £160 = exchange in Philadelphia at £150; at £175 = £164 1*s.* 3*d.*; £190 = £178 2*s.* 6*d.*

In the same year is published a curious Arbitration of a Remittance in Dollars.—"1000 dollars, upon an average, weigh 866 ounces; then suppose 866 ounces of silver at 5*s.* 6*d.* = £238 3*s.* 0*d.*, Freight and Insurance and Brokerage, three per cent., £7 3*s.* 0*d.*, leaves £231 0*s.* 0*d.*, which with Exchange at 75 is equal to £404 5*s.* 0*d.*, while 1000 Dollars are equal to £400 0*s.* 0*d.*; so that when Dollars are worth 5*s.* 6*d.* sterling per ounce in London, it is a Trifle better to remit them than Bills at 75, provided there is no other Commission than Brokerage 1-2 per cent. charged on sale of said Dollars."

From this it is clear that the Pennsylvania money, which the Chamber voted (October 4, 1760) to take at 6⅔ per cent. advance, was the legal tender currency of that province, and the advance a premium over the legal tender currency of New York.

NOTE 3, PAGE 10. PAPER CURRENCY OF NEW JERSEY.—At what rate this currency of the neighboring colony should be received was a question which greatly disturbed the harmony of the Chamber for several years.

Originally introduced in the June meeting in 1768, its discussion was postponed from time to time, but was again brought forward by Mr. William McAdam, 5th November, 1771 (page 143), and a vote was taken 3d March, 1772, when it was resolved that it should not be received for more than it passed for in the Jersey Treasury (pages 152 and 153). The inconvenience which this decision occasioned in the early transaction of business was so great that numbers of the members felt obliged to resign their seats. The Chamber finally rescinded their vote on the 4th January, 1774, and invited the return of the retired members (page 187).

New Jersey also labored throughout her colonial history under great money difficulties. In 1723, Governor Burnet advised Lord Carteret that the Assembly had provided "for ten years to come for the supporting of Government, in order to obtain paper money which their necessities made inevitable."—*Col. Doc.* v. 705.

NOTE 4, PAGE 12. PAPER CURRENCY IN NEW YORK.—The following account of the rise of Paper Money in the Colony of New York is given by Governor Clinton, in a letter to the Board of Trade, dated Fort George in New York, 26th November, 1749. "When Mr. Hunter came Governor into this Province, early in the year 1710, a strong Faction was then formed in the Assembly, as now, on Republican and levelling Principles, with a noted Republican (William Nicoll of Suffolk County) at the head of the Faction and speaker of the Assembly, who obstinately refused to grant any Revenue for support of Government in any manner conformable to the King's standing Instructions. Though Mr. Hunter dissolved the Assembly several times, it was to no purpose, the Faction still prevailed." The bills drawn by Mr. Hunter, by order of Queen Anne, for the Canada expedition, were all returned protested. Mr. Hunter and all the officers being so far distressed, he was under a necessity of making compliances to the Assembly, in order to obtain a support for himself and the other officers of Government. Mr. Hunter was likewise obliged to consent to a very large emission of Paper Money, and from this a Paper Currency had its first rise in this Government."—*Colonial Documents*, vi. 535.

The great colonial historian concurs in this statement: in an account of the expedition of 1709 to Canada, he says, "It was at this juncture our first act for issuing bills of credit was passed; an expedient without which we could not have contributed to the expedition, the treasury being then totally exhausted."—*Smith's New York*, 1,198.

Governor Robert Hunter, in a letter dated at New York, August 7, 1718, to the Lords of Trade, says, "Our money bills are equal to silver over the greatest part of the English continent, and 30 per cent. better than the country bills upon the change at Boston itself—our credit better than any of our neighbors."

Lieutenant-Governor Clarke, in a letter also to the Board of Trade, New York, February 17th, 173 7/8, relates the manner in which the payment of these bills was secured. "About 20 years ago the excise on strong liquors, which before that time had all along been appropriated to the Revenue, was given towards the sinking a large sum of Paper Money then struck to pay the debts of the Government; this fund will expire in 1739, when I am informed there will be nigh twenty thousand pounds unsunk."—*Col. Doc.* vi. 111.

Meanwhile, as the sinking fund absorbed the legal tender notes, other Paper Currency was issued. The large expenditures attendant upon the French War had increased its volume, and greatly depreciated its value in all the colonies. In 1767 the rates for sterling exchange had risen in New York to 175, in Pennsylvania to 165. Meanwhile Parliament endeavored to correct the evil, but its measures were too stringent to suit the colonists, and on the 19th September, 1764, the Assembly "reported a resolution to petition the Commons upon the many inconveniences that will attend the Act of Parliament entitled An Act to prevent Paper Bills of Credit hereafter to be issued in any of his Majesty's Colonies and Plantations in *America* from being declared a legal Tender in Payments of Money, and to prevent the legal Tender of such Bills as are now subsisting from being prolonged beyond the Periods limited for calling in and sinking the same."—*Journal of Assembly*, 11, 754.

Parliament disregarded this petition, and a crisis in the money affairs of the Colony was soon precipitated. The situation was certainly a difficult, indeed, considering the high rates of sterling and of coin, an anomalous one. Governor Moore, in a letter to the Earl of Hillsborough, dated Fort George, May 14, 1768, thus explains the position of affairs :—"After the first day of November next there will be none of the Bills formerly issued current, the Lyon Dollars (a species of money brought here by the first Dutch settlers) are rarely now seen. These and Bills of Credit issued before the Statute passed 16th December, 1737, are the only kinds of money that were ever made a Tender in this Colony. After the first day of November, therefore, we shall have nothing to make a legal tender with." In the same letter he says, "The Colony had always kept up the Credit of their Paper Currency, and taken particular care it should not be depreciated." This was not difficult under the sinking fund system. The necessities became so urgent, however, that on the 5th January, 1770, Governor Colden assented to a Bill for emitting £120,000 in Bills of Credit, but he writes to Hillsborough that "the making of them a tender is carefully avoided, except at the loan offices and Treasury."—*Col. Doc.* viii. pp. 198-206.

This Bill was sanctioned by Parliament the same year.

The desires of the merchants, therefore, beset with the currency of neighboring colonies at the period when the subject was brought to the notice of the Chamber, are easily comprehended even at this distance of time. So late as 1780, the almanacs of the time continued to give tables of rates of Pennsylvania and Jersey money reduced to New York currency. They must have formed a large part of the circulating medium of the city. See *Hugh Gaine's New York Almanacs*, 1770–1780.

NOTE 5, PAGE 15. WEST INDIA BILLS OF EXCHANGE.—The trade of New York with the West Indies was chiefly with the English islands of Jamaica, Nevis, Antigua, St. Christopher, and the Barbadoes. The rate of damages on protested bills between New York and the islands has remained unchanged until the present day, ten per cent. being added on the return.

NOTE 6, PAGE 15. LAW OF THE COLONY OF NEW YORK AS TO TARE.—On the 24th November, 1750, 24, George II, the General Assembly passed "An ACT to prevent the Exportation of unmerchantable Flour, and the false taring of Bread and Flour Casks," *providing*, I. That all Bolters and Bakers should have Trade marks and enter them with their names with the Clerk of the Sessions. II. That all Wheat Flour be made merchantable, fine, and be well packed. III. A penalty of Five Shillings for every false tare on Casks. IV. That no Flour be exported before it is inspected; and that the Inspectors brand each cask with the Province Arms and the initial letters of their own name and Sir-name. V. That all disputes between owners and Inspectors be determined by three indifferent judicious persons on warrant from a Magistrate. VI. Empowers Inspectors to search vessels for Flour not branded; such Flour to be forfeited. VII. Appoints FRANCOIS MARSCHALK, JOHN LIVINGSTON, and HENDRICK BOGERT, Inspectors; their successors to be named by the Mayor and Aldermen of the City; all Inspectors to be sworn. VIII. Inspectors forbidden, under penalty of £50, from purchasing any Flour they condemn. IX. For a penalty of 20 shillings for any neglect or delay of Inspectors to inspect when required. X. For a penalty of £100 for counterfeiting brand marks. XI. And a penalty of £100 for emptying branded Casks to export therein Flour not branded. XII. For the manner of recovering the fines. XIII. That the ACT take effect 21st March, 1751, and continue till 1st day of June, 1752.—*Journal of the Assembly of New York*, I, 294.

This Act was continued 11 November, 1752, with an addition thereto, *and again* continued 24 December, 1757, till January 1, 1765, with amendments.

NOTE 7, PAGE 17. ADVERTISEMENT OF RESOLUTIONS AS TO PURCHASE OF FLOUR.—This Advertisement, under the signature of Anthony Van Dam, Secretary, appears in *Holt's New York Journal or General Advertiser*, Thursday, 6 Oct., 1768.

NOTE 8, PAGE 29. ADVERTISEMENT OF USE AND DESIGN OF THE CHAMBER OF COMMERCE.—This advertisement may be seen in *Holt's New York Journal or General Advertiser* for Thursday, 8th December, 1768.

NOTE 9, PAGE 28. CITY MEMBERS OF THE ASSEMBLY.—New York was at this time (December, 1768) represented in the General House of Assembly by PHILIP LIVINGSTON, JAMES DE LANCEY, JACOB WALTON, and JAMES JAUNCEY; all, with the exception of the second named, Merchants and Members of the Chamber of Commerce.

They had been elected in the preceding March. "Never," says the *New York Journal* of the 10th March, "was an Election in this place carried on with so great an Ardour on all sides." To the usual exciting elements in the Canvass was added a sharp struggle between the Merchants and the Lawyers for supremacy in the Colony, which ended in the total defeat of the latter. The result of the poll is stated in *Gaine's New York Gazette and Weekly Mercury* of March 14th: PHILIP LIVINGSTON 1320; JAMES DE LANCEY 1204; JACOB WALTON 1175; JAMES JAUNCEY 1052; JOHN MORIN SCOTT 870; AMOS DODGE 257, [Total, 5878 votes.]

The Chamber could therefore apply with confidence to their fellows the City Members to consider of Laws for the better regulation of the Trade of the Colony.

The firm opposition of this Assembly to the encroachments of the Crown rendered its members obnoxious to the Government, but endeared them to the people. This Assembly having been dissolved by the Governor, SIR HENRY MOORE, a new Election was ordered. This extract from *Gaine's N. Y. Mercury* of January 9, 1769, shows the feeling with which the old representatives were regarded: "At a meeting of a great number of the Freeholders and Freemen of this City on Wednesday evening last, at the Change, in order to consult as to the propriety of re-electing the late Members for the City for their spirited Conduct in asserting and supporting the Rights of their Constituents; MR. PHILIP LIVINGSTON having publicly declined serving again, MR. JOHN CRUGER [the late Mayor] was nominated, and has accordingly joined the other Members: At this Meeting it was mentioned that Thanks should be returned the late Members for their spirited Conduct in the late Assembly, which motion was agreed to and the public Approbation signified by three huzzas."

The Election was held on the GREEN on the 23d January, 1769, when these Gentlemen were returned by a great majority.

NOTE 10, PAGE 36. ROOM OVER THE EXCHANGE.—The Merchant's Exchange was a building raised upon arches at the lower end of Broad Street. Originally projected by the Merchants of the City, who voluntarily subscribed for its erection, the Corporation in the spring of 1752 voted a sum of money towards its completion, and appointed an Assistant to the Board of Managers chosen by the Subscribers.

The control of the building, both as to the mode of construction, and the rental, seems to have been almost immediately assumed by the City Government.

On the 13th day of July, 1753, the Corporation "Ordered that the second story of the Exchange now a building at the lower end of Broad Street, be not exceeding fifteen feet in height, and not less than fourteen; and that the Room be arched from the height of the said fourteen feet, and that a Cupola be erected on said Exchange, under the direction of the Committee appointed for completing the said Exchange."

The ROOM was completed in the fall of the year, and on the 15th January, 1754, was rented to Mr. OLIVER DELANCEY, a merchant of the City, for the sum of £50. On the 10th January, 1755, it passed, with the rest of the building, for the sum of £30, into the hands of Messrs. KEENE and LIGHTFOOT, who at once applied it to public uses. A Coffee Room was opened below stairs, and the Upper Room was leased for balls, concerts, and the temporary occupation of Societies. In 1756 ALEXANDER LIGHTFOOT obtained a renewal of the lease in his own name at the rate of £40. In 1757 Mrs. SARAH LIGHTFOOT, probably the widow of the afore-named, again took the building at the same terms. The LIGHTFOOTS do not appear to have met with success in their enterprise, and in 1758 Mr. ROPER DAWSON, a merchant, secured a lease for three years, of the upper Room and the Room below stairs, for the annual rent of £50. On the 26th Feb., 1759, it was advertised in the *New York Mercury*, "ROPER DAWSON, in the Room over the Exchange, now sells at a low Rate for short payment: a large and General assortment of European and India Goods, amongst which are Broad Cloths, Gilt Leather for Hangings and Screens, Green Tea." In 1763 Mr. DAWSON was still the occupant of the building. In 1764 one TURNER hired the same premises at £80, but the next year a new tenant appears of the name of THOMAS JACKSON, at a rate of £60.

No further entries appear on the minutes of the Corporation until the 15th February, 1769, when "Messrs. ISAAC LOW, THOMAS RANDALL, WILLIAM WALTON, ISAAC ROOSEVELT, and LAURENCE KORTRIGHT, personally made application to this Board for the use of the EXCHANGE HOUSE for one year, from the first day of May next, for the CHAMBER of COMMERCE, on such terms as they shall think fit and reasonable; this Board taking the same into consideration, thereupon *resolved and ordered*, that the said EXCHANGE HOUSE be let to them accordingly for one year, on their putting the same in good repair, and permitting this Corporation to make use of it as often as they shall judge necessary."

The terms of the agreement were reported to the Chamber by their Committee, at the Meeting of the 7th March, 1769—to be a free occupation from the 1st of May following, on condition of proper repairs, and "after that £20 per annum." The Royal Charter, granted to the Chamber of Commerce on the 13th March of the year 1770, required "that the Meetings of the said Corporation shall be held in the GREAT ROOM of the Building commonly called the Exchange, situate at the lower End of the Street called broad Street." Here the Chamber remained until the meetings were suspended in May, 1775, on the breaking out of hostilities.

NOTE 11, PAGE 40. "AND IT BE FIXED WHAT."—There is here an omission in the Record, the probable sense of which these words are introduced to supply.

NOTE 12, PAGE 41. THANKS OF THE ASSEMBLY TO THE MERCHANTS.—"Monday, April 10, 1769. Journal of the General Assembly, Session begun 4 April, 1769. MR. LIVINGSTON moved 'That the Thanks of this House be given to the Merchants of this City and Colony for their repeated disinterested public-spirited and patriotic conduct in declining the importation or receiving of goods from Great Britain, until such Acts of Parliament as the General Assembly had declared unconstitutional and subversive of the rights and liberties of the people of this colony should be repealed; and that MR. SPEAKER signify the same to the Merchants at their next monthly meeting. Ordered: That Mr. Speaker signify the thanks of this house to the Merchants of this City at their next monthly meeting accordingly.'"

The mover of this resolution, MR. PHILIP LIVINGSTON, who sat in this Assembly as a representative of the Manor of Livingston, was a member of the Chamber. The Speaker of the House was JOHN CRUGER, unanimously chosen on the 4th of April to preside over the Assembly. Being at the same time President of the Chamber, he was directed to convey the Thanks of the House to its members.

REPLY OF THE CHAMBER to the Thanks of the House:

"A Committee from the Merchants of the City of New York, attending at the door, were called in, and MR. JOHN ALSOP, in behalf of the said merchants, addressed himself to the Speaker in the words following:—

"SIR,—The Merchants of the City of New York, at their monthly meeting this day, having received by the SPEAKER the thanks of the Honorable House of the Assembly for their disinterested and steady regard for the public good, are highly sensible of the honor done them; and flatter themselves that their endeavors to promote the trade of the Colony will always merit and receive the protection and approbation of the Legislature in general, and this Honorable House in particular."—*Journal of the Assembly*, Session begun 4th April, 1769.

NOTE 13, PAGE 42. NON-IMPORTATION AGREEMENT.—"City of New York, October 31, 1765. At a general meeting of the Merchants of the City of New York trading to Great Britain, at the House of Mr. George Burns, of the said City, Inn-holder to consider what was necessary to be done in the present Situation of Affairs with respect to the STAMP ACT, and the melancholy state of the N. American Commerce, so greatly restricted by the Impositions and Duties established by the late Acts of Trade: They came to the following Resolutions, viz.:—

"FIRST, That in all orders they send out to Great Britain for Goods or Merchandize of any nature, kind, or Quality whatsoever, usually imported from Great Britain, they will direct their Correspondents not to ship them unless the STAMP ACT be repealed: It is nevertheless agreed, that all such Merchants as are Owners of, and have Vessels already gone and now cleared out from Great Britain, shall be at Liberty to bring back in them on their own Accounts, Crates and Casks of Earthenware, Grindstones, Pipes, and such other bulky articles as Owners usually fill up their Vessels with.

"SECONDLY. It is further unanimously agreed that all Orders already sent Home shall be countermanded by the very first conveyance; and the Goods and Merchandize thereby ordered, not to be sent unless upon the Condition mentioned in the foregoing Resolution.

"THIRDLY. It is further unanimously agreed that no Merchant will Vend any Goods or Merchandize sent upon Commission from Great Britain that shall be shipped from thence after the first Day of January next, unless upon the Condition mentioned in the first Resolution.

"FOURTHLY. It is further unanimously agreed that the foregoing Resolutions shall be binding until the same are abrogated at a general Meeting hereafter to be held for that Purpose.

"In witness whereof we have hereunto respectively subscribed our Names."

[*This was subscribed by upwards of Two Hundred principal Merchants.*]

In consequence of the foregoing Resolutions, the Retailers of Goods of the City of New York subscribed a Paper in the Words following:—

"We, the under-written, Retailers of Goods, do hereby promise and oblige ourselves not to buy any Goods, Wares, or Merchandizes, of any Person or Persons whatsoever, that shall be shipped from Great Britain after the first Day of January next; unless the STAMP ACT shall be repealed. As witness our Hands. Oct. 31, 1765."—*John Holt's New York Gazette or Weekly Post Boy*, Thursday, 7th November, 1765.

NOTE 14, PAGE 44. TONNAGE OF THE PORT OF NEW YORK. —The word Tonnage is here used in a special sense. It refers not to the number of tons of Shipping, but to the weight and measurement of goods. See the Report of the Committee made 5th November, 1771, page 141–2.

NOTE 15, PAGE 45. BLOOMANDALE (corruption for Bloomendale). Bloomingdale was part of the Out Ward. Its once wide extended limits are now restricted to that part of the 22d Ward lying between the 8th Avenue, the Western boundary of the Central Park, and the North River, extending from 42d to 125th Street. This beautiful piece of country, situated on the picturesque bank of the Hudson, was a favorite country residence of the wealthy citizens. The Five-Mile Stone (from the City Hall) stands near the corner of 74th Street and the Bloomingdale Road, opposite the grounds lately owned by Mr. Pelatiah Perit. The Six-Mile Stone is near 96th Street, in front of the property of Dr. Williams. The distance from the New York limits being about six miles, in the Colonial times, the note on the minutes refers to a residence there as a sufficient excuse for absence from the regular meeting of the Chamber under its By-Laws. (See Revised Rules and Regulations, page 28.)

NOTE 16, PAGE 45. FLATBUSH, Kings County, Long Island.—This ancient settlement of the Dutch was begun by them in 1651, upon which they conferred the name of Midwout, or Middlewood. It is bounded north by Brooklyn, south by Jamaica and the Bay, Flatlands and Gravesend, and west by Gravesend; containing an area of about 700 acres. In 1652, Governor Stuyvesant gave the inhabitants a patent for a portion of the present town, including the village.—*Thompson's Long Island*, vol. 2, 200.

NOTE 17, PAGE 45. F.—This letter, which occasionally appears after the names of members fined for absence or late appearance, is supposed to be a private memorandum of Mr. VAN DAM, Secretary, regarding the Fine imposed; probably a note of its payment on the spot.

NOTE 18, PAGE 46. ACT OF THE GENERAL ASSEMBLY AS TO INSPECTION OF FLOUR.—On the 20th May, 1769, 9th George III., the General Assembly of the Colony of New York passed an act to amend an act entitled an "act to prevent the exportation of unmerchantable Flour, and the false taring of Bread and Flour Casks," its preamble reciting "that notwithstanding the act of 24 George, such great abuses have been committed in the manufacture of Flour, that this great staple of the Colony has, in a very considerable degree, lost its reputation in all places to which it has usually been exported, which renders some new regulation necessary." The act provides: I. That Flour be inspected before exportation. II. That none but such as is merchantable be branded. III. The Inspection to be *at or after* the sale. IV. Two Inspectors, and no more, appointed, who are to share the profits equally; viz., FRANCIS MAERSCHALK and HENRY BOGART—the Inspectors to be sworn. V. Ten Hoops to be put on every Cask. VI. That the act remain in force till Jan. 1, 1775.—*Journal of General Assembly*, vol. 2, 536.

NOTE 19, PAGE 49. SETAUKET, or Seatalcott, anciently called Ashford, and sometimes Cromwell Bay, is the oldest English settlement in the Town of Brookhaven, County of Suffolk, Long Island. Its name is derived from the once powerful tribe that possessed it, and was applied to the whole territory of the town previous to its being called Brookhaven, the latter name becoming more general after the conquest of New Netherlands in 1664.—*Thompson's Long Island*, vol. 1, 433.

A post-village of Brookhaven Township, Suffolk County, New York, on the north side of Long Island, 58 miles E. by N. from New York. It has a good harbor, and contains many churches and stores.—*French's New York Gazetteer*, page 633.

NOTE 20, PAGE 50. ADVERTISEMENT OF RESOLUTION AS TO FLOUR CASKS.—New York Chamber of Commerce, July 4, 1769. *Resolved*—That the Members of this Chamber in their future Purchases of Flour, are willing to pay Twenty-Eight Shillings per Ton for Casks and Nails, provided they be well and sufficiently made, agreeable to an Act of the Governor, Council, and General Assembly of the Province, passed at their last Sessions, and hooped with ten Hoops each, three of which are to be on each Head. ANTHONY VAN DAM, Secretary.

The Act of Assembly for the better Inspection of Flour takes Place the 1st of September next, when all Flour Casks are to be hooped as above; but as many of the Manufacturers of Flour may chuse to send theirs to market before that time, the Merchants who compose the Chamber think it will be of use to advertise the Country of their willingness to come into a Measure that must in some measure pay for the two extra Hoops on each Cask of Flour; and as the Flour of this Province has got into a general Disrepute abroad, from its bad Quality, it is hoped that the manufacturers will take more Pains in future to regain the Credit that it was in for a number of Years; the Inspectors will do their Duty therein, it may be depended upon, according to the new Regulations that will then take place.—*Hugh Gaine's New York Gazette and Weekly Mercury*, Monday, 10th July, 1769.

NOTE 21. PAGE 52. NORTH CASTLE, Westchester County, N. Y. —The Township of North Castle is situated 6 miles North of White Plains, 36 miles from New York, and 129 miles from Albany; bounded North by New Castle and Bedford, East by Poundridge, South Easterly by the State of Connecticut and the Town of Harrison, and West by Mount Pleasant." North Castle was at first styled *The White Fields*, and subsequently (upon its division into several patents), the *Liberty of North Castle*. The present Township was organized on the 7th March, 1788.—*Bolton's Westchester*, vol. 1, p. 466.

NOTE 22, PAGE 55. SUFFICIENT NUMBER OF MEMBERS WERE NOT CONVENED.—This was the first Meeting of the Chamber adjourned for want of a Quorum. 20 members appear to have been in their seats. The By-Laws required the presence of 21 to transact business.—(See Rules, page 27.)

NOTE 23, PAGE 56. GOLD AND SILVER COIN.—Governor Moore, in a Letter to the Earl of Hillsborough, dated at Fort George, May 14, 1768, writes: "After the first day of November next, there will be none of the Bills formerly issued current, the LYON DOLLARS (a Species of money brought here by the first Dutch Settlers) are rarely now seen. These, and Bills of Credit issued before the Statute (passed 16 Dec., 1737) are the only two kinds of money that were ever made a Tender in this Colony." *Colonial Documents*, vol. viii. p. 72.

Hence arose the need of some agreement among Merchants to determine the Value at which the various coins in use should pass current among themselves. The Coins named in the Report are the

JOHANNES, a Portuguese gold coin of the value of eight dollars; contracted often into *Joe*, a *Joe*, or *Half Joe*. It is named from the figure of King John, which it bears (Noah Webster's Dict., N. Y., 1828). Defoe in his Fictions alludes constantly to "Pieces of Eight."

MOIDORE, a Portugal gold coin, in value 27s Sterling.—Bailey's Etymological Dictionary, London, 1760.

CAROLINE, a German coin. Hugh Gaine in his Almanac for 1772 styles it the "*German Caroline;*" a coin weighing 6 dwt. 8 grs., valued at £1 18s.

DOUBLOON, Doublon, a Spanish coin containing the value of two Pistoles. —Sam. Johnson, Dict., Lond. 1790.

——— a Spanish and Portuguese coin, being double the value of the Pistole.—Webster's Dict.

GUINEA [English], a known Sort of Gold Coin current at £1 1s., value at Standard Rate £1, weighing 5 Pennyweight 9⅗ Grains.—The new World of Words, by Edward Phillips, London, 1720.

——— [of Guinea in Africk], a Gold coin, in value 21s.—Bailey's Dict.

GUINEA [French]. What this coin was is uncertain; whether a French coinage of African gold, or a name in use for some piece of French money approximating in value to the English coin of the same name.

CHEQUEEN, *Zechin*, or *Zachin*, a Gold coin worth about seven shillings and six Pence Sterling; so called from *La Zecha*, a Place in the City of Venice where the Mint is settled. There is also a Turkish Zechin, valued at nine shillings.—Edward Phillips' Dict.

——— *Zechin*, or *Zachin*, a Gold coin worth about 7s and 6d Sterling. —Bailey's Etymo. Dict., 1760.

——— *Sequin*; sometimes written CHAQUIN and *Zechin*.—Webster's Dict.

CROWN [English], a coin or Piece of Money of five Shillings value.—Edw. Phillips' new World of Words, 1720.

——— [French], 4 Shillings 6 Pence.—Edw. Phillips' new World of Words, 1720.

PISTOLE, a Spanish Piece of Gold worth seventeen Shillings Sterling. The *French Pistole*, or *Louis d'Or*, is also settled at same value.—Phillips' Dict.

——— a French or Spanish Piece of Gold worth 17s.—Bailey's Dict.

SHILLING, an English silver coin worth Twelve Pence, and of which Twenty make a Pound Sterling; alltho' among our Saxon Ancestors it consisted but of Five Pence.—Phillips' Dict.

PISTAREEN, a Silver Coin of the value of 17@18 cents, or 9d Sterling.—Webster's Dict.

The rates given in the report of the Committee are evidently in exchange for the depreciated currency of the day, and not in the legal tender of the Province.

NOTE 24, PAGE 56. PUBLICATION IN NEWSPAPERS AS TO RATES FOR GOLD AND SILVER COIN.—New York Chamber of Commerce, October 3, 1769. At a meeting of the Chamber of Commerce this Day, it was unanimously agreed—That all the Members will receive and pay the undermention'd Gold and Silver Coins at the following Rates, and their lesser Denominations in the same proportion, viz.:—(Here follow the rates.)

That for every Grain any of the above specified Gold Coins shall weigh less than the above respective Weights, Four Pence must be deducted therefrom. ANTHONY VAN DAM, Secr'y.—*Hugh Gaine's New York Gazette and Weekly Mercury*, Monday, October 6, 1769.

NOTE 25, PAGE 69. THE MAYOR AND CORPORATION.—During the Colonial period under the English rule, the Mayors of the City were appointed by the Governors of the Province. The Aldermen and Assistants were elected by Freeholders of the several Wards, and were always men of substance, character, and public spirit. The Corporation was in 1768-9:—*The Worshipful* WHITEHEAD HICKS, ESQR., *Mayor;* Simon Johnson, Esqr., *Recorder.* For the SOUTH WARD:—Francis Filkin, Esqr., *Alderman;* Mr. John Abeel, *Assistant.* For the WEST WARD:—Abraham P. Lott, Esqr., *Ald.;* Mr. Peter T. Curtenius, *Ass't.* For the NORTH WARD:—George Brewerton, Esqr., *Ald.;* Mr. Benjamin Huggitt, *Ass't.* For the EAST WARD:—Elias Desbrosses, Esqr., *Ald.;* Mr. Jacob Brewerton, *Ass't.* For the DOCK WARD:—Andrew Gautier, Esqr., *Ald.;* Mr. James Van Varick, *Ass't.* For MONTGOMERIE WARD:—Benjamin Blagge, Esqr., *Ald.;* Mr. Huybert Van Wagner, *Ass't.* For the OUT WARD:—Cornelius Roosevelt, Esqr., *Ald.;* Mr. Mathew Buys, *Ass't.*

1769-70: *The Worshipful* WHITEHEAD HICKS, ESQR., *Mayor;* Thomas Jones, Esqr., *Recorder.* The Aldermen and Assistants were the same as the previous year, except that John Dyckman, Esqr., succeeded Cornelius Roosevelt as Ald. of the OUT Ward.

NOTE 26, PAGE 59. BY-LAW OF THE CORPORATION AS TO THE INSPECTION OF LUMBER.—On the 7th June, 1770, the Common Council repealed the Old Law, and passed a Law entitled "a Law to ascertain the Size, Dimensions, and Quality of Stave Heading Hoops, Board, Timber, Shingles, and Plank, which shall be brought to this City for sale," and ordered its publication in the Gazette. This Law was to take effect Sept. 1770, and the Inspectors and Measurers ordered by it were Isaac Shardavine, Francis Many, Theophilus Hardenbroock, John Blanch.—*Minutes of Common Council*, vol. vii.. p 49.

NOTE 27, PAGE 61. FORT GEORGE.—This defensive work, the first beginnings of which date back to the earliest Dutch settlement of the City, stood at the lower end of Broadway, opposite the present Bowling Green, and faced on the North and East the streets now known as Battery Place and Whitehall Street. During the Dutch occupation, and throughout the period of English Colonial rule, this was the chief point of interest in the Province of New York. Within its walls were located the Governor's House, and for many years here stood the only place of worship for the inhabitants of the City. In the varied phases of the struggle between England and Holland for Colonial power as well as naval supremacy, its fortunes were those of the Province whose fate its possession decided: with each new master its name was changed.

Fort Manhattes and *Fort Amsterdam* under the Dutch flag, it became *Fort James* when Gov'r Stuyvesant surrendered its control, and with it the hopes of Holland in the New Netherlands, to the English forces. Recaptured by the Dutch, it received the name of *Fort William Hendrick*, but its old title was restored when, on the treaty of peace, it returned to its English masters. Seized by the train-bands of the City on the news of the revolution which put the Prince of Orange on the English throne, it was called *Fort William* in his honor, and thenceforth, as became a ROYAL FORT, its name changed with each new coronation. *Fort Anne* from 1702 to 1714, on the accession of the first George in the latter year its title was altered for the last time, and during the remainder of its existence, covering nearly a century, it was known as FORT GEORGE.

During this period it assumed the form of a square earthwork, with bastions on the four corners faced with stone set in mortar. Covering a surface nearly two acres in extent, it enclosed an interior plain about 150 feet square, on which were erected the Governor's house and other buildings.

Built for the defence of the city, it seems never to have answered any efficient purpose, and its history is one of bloodless surrenders. Its Dutch and English masters were equally unfortunate. Governors and Captains alike struck their flags at the first summons. Perhaps this was the misfortune, and not the fault, of its commanders; the control of the river passages no doubt rendered the Fort of no value for the defence of the city which clustered behind its ramparts.

If not famous in War, it was brilliant in Peace. After the fire which in 1741, during the rule of Governor Clarke, wholly destroyed the old buildings, a new mansion was erected on a more imposing scale. Here stately Governors held their court, and the intellect and wealth and beauty of the Province paid homage to the representative of kingly power.

During the Stamp Act excitement in the fall of 1765, on the 1st November, the Lt. Governor, Colden, was hung in effigy before the Fort. The gates were closed and the guns were turned on the people; but General Gage, the British commander, peremptorily forbade the soldiers to fire. The next day the citizens again resolving to march to the Fort, Gov. Colden did not await the carrying out of the threat, but yielded to the popular will, and delivered up the obnoxious papers to the safekeeping of the City authorities.

On the night of the 29th December, 1773, the Government House, then occupied by Governor Tryon, took fire, and was wholly destroyed; and here ceases the interest attached to the Fort as the Headquarters of the chiefs of the State.

Its history during the revolutionary struggle presents nothing of interest. It remained a British military post until the evacuation of the city in 1783, on the 25th November of which year General Knox entered it with the American forces, and ran up the flag of the new Confederation.

A few years later, about 1788, the whole structure was removed, and a mansion erected on its site for the occupation of the President of the United States; but the seat of Government being changed to Philadelphia before its completion in 1791, it was applied to the occupancy of the Governor of New York, and later served for the United States Custom House.

Note.—The above facts are chiefly taken from the admirable sketch of the history of the Fort in New York published by *D. T. Valentine, Esq.*, in the *Manual of the Corporation for* 1864, pp. 624 to 647.

NOTE 28, PAGE 61. LATITUDE OF FLAG BASTION, FORT GEORGE.—In a description of the Fort in 1671, it is stated that "within it, and in the outermost bastion towards the river, stands a windmill and a very high staff, on which a flag is hoisted whenever any vessels are seen in Godyn's Bay" (now known as the Lower Bay). This outermost bastion was the South-west Bastion, where the flag-mount seems to have been located from the earliest period.

The Latitude of New York was established by one of the first scientific men of the day, David Rittenhouse, as 40° 42′ 8″.

The Report of the United States Coast Survey Office for 1858 (page 54), referring to the Observations of the Year, states, that "the Latitude of the Station (Rutherford Observatory, No. 175 Second Avenue) was ascertained from 89 observations, which were made upon 24 pairs of stairs, by Sub-Assistant Goodfellow, with the Coast Survey Zenith Telescope, No. 5. The Latitude was determined at 40° 43′ 48″."

NOTE 29, PAGE 63. LINE BETWEEN NEW YORK AND JERSEY.—It was in this year, 1769, that, at the request of a Board of Commissioners authorized by the Legislature of New York and New Jersey, the celebrated David Rittenhouse fixed the point where the parallel which divides New York from Pennsylvania was to be traced westward. The northern limit of New Jersey upon Hudson River is the 41st degree of latitude. The point where this parallel intersects the shore was fixed by the surveyors at this time. The northern limit of both Pennsylvania and New Jersey, upon the Delaware, is the 42d degree of latitude; and this parallel, continued westward, divides Pennsylvania from New York. Rittenhouse was appointed by Pennsylvania as commissioner to meet a commission from New York, and determine the place where this parallel intersects the Delaware."—*Dunlap's New York*, vol. ii.

On the 12th April, 1769, the New York Commissioners, John Cruger, William Bayard, John Morin Scott, Benj. Kissam, Henry Holland, and Fred. Philipse, informed Governor Moore, who in turn, on the 15th, advised Governor Penn that they had prevailed on Captain Bernard Ratzers to make some preliminary surveys on the Delaware River."—*Pennsylvania Archives*, 1760–76, pp. 338, 339.

The King's Commissioners, Charles Stewart, President; Andrew Elliot, Samuel Holland, Andrew Oliver, Charles Morris, and Jared Ingersoll, met at the Long Room called the Chamber of Commerce, in the City of New York, the 7th day of October, 1769.—*Whitehead's New Jersey Boundary.*

NOTE 30, PAGE 63.—MAHACOMAC on Delaware: corruption for Mahackamach, a stream of water which flows into the Delaware. The Commissioners who met in 1769 reported that the Fork or Branch formed by the junction of the stream of water called the Mahackamach, with the River called Delaware or Fishkill, is the Branch (as laid down on Vischer's Map) intended and referred to in the deed from the Duke of York, which Fork or Branch was found by an observation taken by the surveyors appointed by the Court, to be in the Latitude 41° 21′ 37″.—*Whitehead's Northern Boundary, Proc. N. J. Hist. Soc.* viii. p. 181.

NOTE 31, PAGE 63.—HOUSE LATE MRS. CORBET'S. The House

of CORBET was afterward called Sneydon's Landing. It was on the west shore of the Hudson River, opposite Dobb's Ferry.

The Commissioners to establish the Boundary Line in 1769, report in reference to this point: "We are further of opinion that the Northern Boundary on Hudson's River, being by the words of the said Deed from the Duke of York, expressly limited to the Latitude of 41° should be fixed in that Latitude, which Latitude we have caused to be taken in the best manner by the surveyors appointed by the Court, and which falls at a rock on the west side of Hudson's River marked by the said surveyors, being 79 chains and 27 links to the southward on a meridian from Sneydon's House formerly Corbets'."—*Whitehead's Northern Boundary*, *Proc. N. J. Hist. Soc.* viii. p. 181.

NOTE 32, PAGE 63. LIGHT HOUSE ON SANDY HOOK.—The origin of the Sandy Hook Light House was a memorial of the Merchants of the City to the Lt. Governor of the Province. The reference to this paper may be found in the Message of the Governor to the General Assembly, 3d April, 1761.

GENTLEMEN: The erecting a convenient Building for a Light House near *Sandy Hook* is an object so worthy your consideration and a provision for it so essential to the welfare of our commercial Interests and the Preservation of a very useful Part of the Community, that I cannot avoid recommending the MEMORIAL I received on this subject to your closest attention. The Example of other Trading Places is a proof how necessary these Land Marks have been tho't for the safety of Navigation, and the late severe losses by Shipwreck on our own Coasts, will, I persuade myself, lead you to a measure so well calculated to guard against the like Accidents for the future.

The spot best adapted and the only one proper for its Situation for this end lying within the Province of *New Jersey*, it may prevent any delay or obstruction to the Design, in case you determine to carry it into Execution, that I have it in my power to communicate your Resolves to that Government while the Branches of the Legislature are convened.

CADWALLADER COLDEN.

The Message and Memorial were referred to the Members of the City of New York, Richmond, and Westchester County.

On the 4th April, Alderman [Philip] Livingston from the Committee reported, That it appeared to them that a Light House on Sandy Hook is necessary for the security of the Trade of this Colony.

That His Honour, the President, be humbly requested to make Application to the Governor of New Jersey to desire him to apply to the General Assembly of that Colony for their assistance in this useful Design which will be of great service to the Trade of that Colony though not to so great a degree as to that of this.

That as they have been credibly informed that the Proprietor of Sandy Hook is very unreasonable in his Demand for a small quantity of Land necessary for the Purpose of building a Light House, they also conceive it necessary that his Honour be desired to apply to the said Governor of New Jersey, to desire that he will be pleased to recommend it to the other Branches of the Legislature there, to interfere in such a Manner as that the Proprietor of the said Land do convey or dispose of the same at a reasonable Price.

That they conceive it would be proper for the House to make Provision for the purchasing of the said Land, and building the Light House in such Proportion as shall be agreed on with the Colony of New Jersey.

And that the Expence of maintaining and supporting of the said Light House be supported by a small duty of Tonnage on Vessels.

Which report he read in his Place and afterwards delivered it at the Table: where the same were again read and agreed to by the House.

[Whereupon it was] Resolved that an humble Address be presented to his Honor the President, that he will be pleased to acquaint the Governor of New Jersey that this House, from the Representation of several Merchants of this Province, is convinced of the necessity and utility of a Light House being built on Sandy Hook; that the House hath been credibly informed that the Proprietor of the Land which would be proper for the Building the said Light House on is so very extravagant in his Demand that it is out of the Power of private Persons to come to any agreement with him; that as the Land lays within the Colony of New Jersey, and is of but little value to the Proprietor, yet as the Erecting of the said Light House is of the utmost Importance to this and the Colony of New Jersey, this House is willing to give the said Proprietor a very valuable consideration for the same; and that therefore his Honor would be pleased to desire his Excellency Governor Boone to recommend it to the Assembly of his Government to prevail with the Proprietor of the said Land in such a Manner as to oblige him to convey or dispose of the same at a reasonable rate, that the Trade of these Colonies may not be any longer subject to the Inconveniences they have so long laboured under for want of the said Light House.

Ordered—That Alderman Livingston and Mr. Bayard wait on his Honor the President with the same Address.

Alderman Livingston moved for leave to bring in a Bill for enabling certain Persons to raise by Way of Lottery a certain sum of Money towards erecting and building a Light House.

Ordered that leave be given accordingly.

Alderman Livingston then (according to leave) presented to the House a Bill entitled, "An Act to enable the Persons therein named to raise a sum not exceeding ——— Pounds by way of Lottery, for building a Light House," which was read the first Time and ordered a second Reading.—*Journal of the Votes and Proceedings of the General Assembly*, vol. ii., p. 655.

May 8, 1761. The Engrossed Bill entitled, "An Act for raising a Sum not exceeding *Three Thousand Pounds* by way of Lottery for building a Light House," was read the third time. Resolved that the Bill do pass.—*Journal of the Assembly*, vol. ii., p. 659.

By this Act, John Cruger, Philip Livingston, Leonard Lispenard, and William Bayard, Esquires (the City Members), were authorized to establish the Lottery; and raised the sum of £2,664 15s. 6d., May 2, 1762. The Assembly vested the Title to the land purchased in the aforenamed gentlemen as Trustees, and, 22d May, 1762, passed an "Act to make Trespasses committed on Sandy Hook, in the colony of New Jersey, actionable in the colony of New York." In December they authorized the raising of a further sum of *Three Thousand Pounds*. The scheme was as follows: "The Lottery is to consist of 10,000 Tickets, at Forty Shillings each, whereof 1,684 are to be fortunate, subject to *Fifteen* per cent. Deductions."—*Weyman's New York Gazette*, Jan. 17, 1763. This Lottery was drawn at Mr. Burns' Long Room at the Province Arms, Monday, the 13th June, 1763.

26th Feb. 1772. An Act was passed "to lay a Duty of Tonnage on Vessels for defraying the expense of the Light House at Sandy Hook." The Tonnage duty so levied, was of one Penny half Penny for every Ton of measurement, exempting all vessels engaged in whaling while so engaged, and all coasting vessels not over 50 Tons' burthen, wholly owned by persons residing between Cape Henry and New Hampshire.

The New York Magazine for August, 1790, gives an engraving of the Light House at that time, and adds these particulars: "The land was purchased for the purpose from Robert and Easick Hartshorn, containing about four acres of barren land for the *moderate price* of £750. The Light House is built of stone, and measures, from the surface of the earth to the top of the lanthorn, 106 feet. The base is 32 feet in diameter, and tapers off at the foot of the lanthorn to 16 feet. The light may be seen at the distance of 10 leagues. It stands in 40° 25′ N. Lat., and 73° 30′ W. Long. from London."

This Light House was refitted by the United States Government in 1857. Its reflector gave place to a Fresnel lens of the third order. It is officially described as "a fixed white light," and as standing in 40° 27′ 39″ North Latitude, and 73° 59′ 49″ West Longitude.

NOTE 33, PAGE 63. PUBLIC PACKERS OF THE CITY.—From the earliest period of English Government these were public officers. On the 3d November, 1740, the General Assembly passed "an Act to prevent Abuses in the Repacking of Beef and Pork," which, in its preamble, recites the abuses committed and the complaints of "putting the Brand mark of the City of New York on Barrels containing Beef and Pork imported from other places, particularly North Carolina, Virginia and Maryland, to the Disreputation and Undervaluing of the Beef and Pork of this Colony exported from hence," and provides an oath to be taken by the "*Repackers of Meat*," and other stringent measures.

NOTE 34, PAGE 64. MERCHANTS ONLY TO BE ADMITTED. --The immediate cause of this resolution cannot now be ascertained. It was probably an expression of the strong feeling of rivalry which had long existed between these classes, and had shown itself in the Assembly elections of the previous year, when the lawyers were defeated by the merchants at the city polls.

NOTE 35, PAGE 65. NUTTEN ISLAND.—Governor's Island, originally called *Nutting Island*, because of the quantity of hazel and other nuts growing there, and furnishing the winter's supply to the citizens. In later times, says Knickerbocker, it was cultivated in gardens for the use of the Colonial Governors—"once a smiling garden of the Sovereigns of the Province."—*Watson's Annals*, p. 189.

This island was known to the Indians by the name of Pugganck, and by the Dutch was called *Nutten* or *Nut Island*. Governor Wouter Van Twiller bought this island in his own name from the Indian owners. It does not seem to have been sold to any individual proprietor after the sale to Van Twiller. It was ceded to the United States by an Act of the Legislature, Feb. 15, 1800, and is now occupied solely as a military station of the United States army.—*Valentine's Manual for* 1855, p. 497.

NOTE 36, PAGE 67. CLIPPING OF COINS.—With the depreciation of the currency in the Colony, caused by the new issues at the period of the French war and the general stagnation of commerce, the debasement of coin by *clipping* and *washing* had become a general and annoying evil. As the coins were foreign (the Lyon dollar introduced by the Dutch being the only *legal tender* of coin in the Colony), the Assembly was powerless to remedy the evil. The Chamber, therefore, established a rate which soon became the custom in trade. The value of the Lyon dollar was fixed as early as 1720; "seventeen pennyweight for fifteen pennyweight of Sevil Pillar or Mexican Plate." It soon after became a scarce coin.

NOTE 37, PAGE 69. CUSTOM OF MERCHANTS IN A NEIGHBOURING COLONY.—This reference is probably to New Jersey. The prints of the day make no allusion to the subject.

NOTE 38, PAGE 70. SUTTLE POUNDS.—This word, which does not appear in any of the modern dictionaries, in Johnson of 1790, or Bailey's Etymological Dictionary of 1760, is given in "*The New World of Words or Universal English Dictionary*" of *Edward Phillips*, London, of 1720, thus—"SUTTLE WEIGHT" (among merchants), the pure Weight of commodities after the Allowance for Tare is deducted."

NOTE 39, PAGE 71. REGULATIONS AS TO INSPECTION OF BEEF AND PORK.—The Report of the Committee of the Chamber was laid before the Common Council by the Mayor, 21st March, 1770.—*Common Council Minutes*, vol. vii. p. 35. (For the action taken by the Board, see Note 44.)

NOTE 40, PAGE 74. BUOYS IN THE HARBOR.—"For the Safety of Vessels coming into and going to Sea from the Port of New York, the Masters and Wardens of the said Port did last week place a large Can Buoy on the South West Spit of the East Bank, in eighteen feet Water at low water, bearing from the Light House on Sandy Hook N. W. and by W. half W., and from the Bluff at Staten Island making the Narrows, S. half East. Vessels going down must keep in five Fathom Water till they open the Buoy with the Point of Sandy Hook, which will clear them of the Spit. They find that the first of the Flood sets about S. W. and by W. for two Hours, and is apt to draw vessels over upon the West Bank.

"The day after placing the Buoy, a Boat going down was seen to run directly upon it, supposed intentionally to destroy it. If any Person will discover the Boatman to the Master and Wardens that was so wickedly bent on injuring the mark set to prevent Vessels running into Danger, so that he may be punished, he will receive the Thanks of the said Master and Wardens."—*Gaine's New York Gazette and Weekly Mercury*, June 17, 1771.

NOTE 41, PAGE 74. WARDENS OF THE PORT.—Among the Colonial MSS at Albany there is a warrant dated June 10, 1758, appointing a *Master* and eight *Wardens* for the Port of New York. A definition of their duties appears at a later period. The General Assembly, on the 13th December, 1763, passed an Act empowering the Governor or Commander-in-Chief of the Colony for the time being, "to appoint one fit and proper Person to be *Master*, and three or more fit and proper Persons to be *Wardens of the said Port of New York.* Their duty—To examine and commission all Branch Pilots; to survey all damaged Goods or Vessels brought into Port (*Gaine's Laws of New York*, p. 433); to maintain the Light House and collect the Tonnage dues; to place and keep in Repair such Buoys as they shall think necessary (26th February, 1772)."—*Ibid.* 636.

A notice issued from the *Wardens' office*, Feb. 18, 1772, offering a reward for the recovery of a lost Buoy, gives the names of John Griffiths, Daniel Stiles, and Anthony Van Dam, as acting *Wardens.*—*Holt's New York Journal*, Feb. 20, 1772.

NOTE 42, PAGE 74. WHALE FISHERY OF NEW YORK.—"An

Act for the Encouragement of Whaling," passed by the General Assembly, 18 September, 1708, enacted "That hereafter any Indian that is bound to go to Sea a Whale-fishing, shall not at any Time or Times, between the first day of November and the fifteenth day of April following, Yearly, be sued, arrested, molested, detained, or kept out of that Employment."—*Gaine's Laws of New York*, p. 71.

A notice of this enterprise appears in 1768: "A very beneficial Branch of Trade has been long neglected in this Province—that is *Whaling*, but we now have some Hopes of seeing it revived, as *Mr. Robert Murray* and *Messrs. Franklins* have, at their own Expence, fitted out a Sloop for that Purpose, which sailed Last Sunday. In Holland a merchant that is not concerned in the Whale Fishery is dispised by all the trading Part of the Country; and we are told that the Island of Nantucket alone, last season, got oil, &c., to the amount of £70,000."—*Holt's New York Journal*, April 21, 1768.

The Law of 1772, levying Tonnage dues, exempted "all vessels engaged in Whaling."

No action seems to have been taken by the Chamber on the proposal of Mr. Remsen; but a few years later a Society was formed. Their first notice appears in *Rivington's New York Gazetteer*, June 2, 1774: "WHALE FISHERY.—Notice is hereby given that the subscription roll of the *United Whaling Company*, established in this City, will be kept open until the sailing of the first vessel. Application to be made to J. Allicocke, Secretary." On the 30th June of same year, the public are advertised that "it is expected the first whaling vessel will sail next week."

"On Tuesday last, May 30, being the first Anniversary of the *New York United Whaling Company*, the following members were elected by Ballot for the ensuing year: PHILIP LIVINGSTON, Esq., President: CHARLES MCEVERS, Esq., Treasurer: Captains, William Heyer, Patrick Dennis, John Barton; and Messrs. Isaac Stoutenburgh, Anthony Van Dam, and Joseph Allicocke (Secretary), Committee for purchase of Vessels and Sale of Oils."—*Gaine's N. Y. Gazette*, June 5, 1775.

On the 24th July, 1776, in *Gaine's New York Gazette or Weekly Mercury*: "The members of the *United Whaling Company* in the City of New York are desired to meet at the Merchants' Coffee House, the 6th of August next. This is published at the earnest request of all the members now in Town. Those who cannot give their attendance personally are desired to appoint some Persons to act for them, otherwise they must abide by the Transactions of that Evening. All Persons having any accounts against the Company are requested to get them ready at that time." This was evidently the closing notice of the Company.

NOTE 43, PAGE 76. HIS MAJESTY'S COUNCIL FOR THE PROVINCE OF NEW YORK.—A Body of twelve who received their appointments directly from the Home Government. The Council was in 1770 composed of Hon. Cadwallader Colden (Lieut. Gov.), appointed in 1722; Hon. Daniel Horsmanden, Esq., 1733; Hon. Sir William Johnson Bart, 1751; Hon. John Watts, Esq., 1757; Hon. Oliver De Lancey, Esq., 1760; Hon. Joseph Reade, Esq., 1764; Hon. Roger Morris, Esq., 1764; Hon. Charles Ward Apthorp, Esq., 1765; Hon. Henry Cruger, 1767; Hon. Hugh Wallace, 1769; Hon. Henry White, 1769.

The following changes occurred in the composition of the Council during the remainder of the Provincial rule:

Hon. William Axtell, Esq., appointed 1771, in place of Hon. Joseph Reade, Esq.; Hon John Harris Cruger, Esq., 1773, in place of Henry Cruger, Esq.; Hon. James Jauncey, Esq., 1775.

NOTE 44, PAGE 79. LAW AS TO CURING BEEF AND PORK.—The subject was laid before the Common Council 21st March, 1770. "Mr. Mayor produced to the Board a paper proposing Regulations for the package of Beef and Pork within this city as drawn up by a Committee of the Chamber of Commerce appointed for that purpose, which, being read it was thereupon ordered by this Board that *Daniel Dunscomb*, one of the *Public Packers* of this city, be served with a copy of said Regulations in order that he may communicate the same to those in the like Office that their sentiments may be had at the next Common Council."—*Common Council Minutes*, vol. vii. p. 35.

As no further action appears, it is to be inferred that the Regulations proposed were adopted by the Packers without the formality of a law.

NOTE 45, PAGE 82. THE GREAT SEAL OF THE PROVINCE, granted by King George III.—Engraved on the one side with the Effigy of the King in his royal robes, and two Indians kneeling and offering presents—with the following inscription around the circumference: "*Sijillum Provinciae Nostrae Novi Eboraci In America.*" The reverse contained the Royal Arms and Titles.

The first notice of a new seal is found in a letter of Lieut. Gov. Colden to the Lords Commissioners for Trade and Plantations, dated Jan. 10, 1761: "What gives me most concern is that the General Assembly of this Province dissolves by the King's death, as there is no provision made in this case, either by Act of Parliament, or by Act of this Province. The Council is of opinion that I cannot make use of the old seals without the King's warrant for that purpose. If so I cannot call a New Assembly, and if I should take upon me to do it from the necessity of affairs, the legality of the suits may be called in question."—*N. Y. Col. Doc.*, vol. vii. p. 453.

In the great fire of the 29th December, 1773, which totally consumed the Government House in Fort George, this seal was one of the few things saved. Gov. Tryon, in a letter of the 31st December, 1773, to Earl Dartmouth, relating the disaster, says: "The Great Seal, which was found this evening, notwithstanding the intenseness of the heat, has suffered no injury."—*N. Y. Colonial Documents*, vol. viii. p. 407.

Richard Jackson, the King's Attorney, in a letter to the Lords of Trade, 20th April, 1779, on the power of the King to appoint a seal to be used for the Great Seal of the Province, speaks of being informed "that it was surmised that said seal is at this time in the power of the rebels."—*N. Y. Colonial Documents*, vol. viii. p. 762.

NOTE 46, PAGE 82. FIRE-INSURANCE.—This motion of Mr. John Thurman (3d April, 1770), seems to have been the first proposal for insurance against fire in New York. Its consideration was postponed by the Chamber, 2d May, 1770 (page 99), and again, 25th June, 1770 (page 101), and never taken up in the Colonial period.

The first Fire-Insurance Company in New York was organized by John Pintard. The first notice appeared in 1787.

"*Mutual Assurance Company* for insuring houses from loss by Fire in New York.—Whereas the insuring of houses and buildings from loss by fire has been found of great and public utility wherever it has been practiced; and although societies have been instituted in different places, yet none have hitherto been formed in this city for that laudable and beneficent purpose.

"A number of respectable citizens, as well for their own mutual security as for the common security and advantage of their neighbors and fellow-citizens, with the view of promoting the insurance of houses and other buildings from loss by fire upon the most equal terms, and without any views of private or separate gain or interest, have established a company by the name of *The Mutual Assurance Company*, for insuring houses from loss by Fire in New York.

"The utility of an institution in its purpose so laudable cannot fail to attract the notice of every citizen, being of so great importance to the security of property and the happiness of families, that it is presumed that no person of prudence will be found to neglect it.

"The office is now opened at No. 57 King Street, where such persons as incline to insure their houses and other buildings, may, on application, receive every necessary information. JOHN PINTARD, Secretary, June 15, 1787."—*New York Packet*, July 24, 1787.

This Company was incorporated under the name of the "*Mutual Insurance Company of the City of New York*," March 28, 1809.—*Private Laws of New York*, 32d Session, p. 154.

NOTE 47, PAGE 83. INSPECTOR OF MEAL.—The consideration of this proposal to apply to the Common Council for the appointment of an Inspector of Meal, was postponed in May, but was not again brought up. No such application appears in the Common Council Minutes.

NOTE 48, PAGE 83. CORNEL.—In grinding the seed of either Wheat or Rye, before Flour-bolting was so perfect as now, much of the grain which was crushed or coarsely ground could not be bolted. This part, after the bran was taken from it, was known as Wheat Cornel or Rye Cornel.—*MSS. Note of Thomas F. Devoe.*

NOTE 49, PAGE 87.—COLONY OF NEW YORK AND TERRITORIES DEPENDING THEREON.—"In the Duke of York's commission to his several Lieutenant Governors, Major Edmund Andross, on the first day of July, 1664, and Col. Thomas Dongan, on the 3d day of September 1682, among other descriptions of the boundaries of this province are expressly comprehended all the land from the West side of Connecticut River to the East side of Delaware Bay.

"King William and Queen Mary, by their Commission dated the 4th day of January in the first year of their reign, appointed Henry Slaughter to be Governor of the province of New York *and the territories depending thereon;* the boundaries whereof to Connecticut river on the east, by the above and many other grants, commissions, and public acts, were notorious.

"In all subsequent acts and commissions this colony is described by the same general words *the province of New York and the territories depending thereon;* and its boundaries have never been altered by the government here or at home."—*A Statement of the Right of New York to its eastern boundary on Connecticut River. Journal of the Assembly*, 8th March, 1773.

NOTE 50, PAGE 89. CHARTER OF THE CHAMBER.—This instrument is on record in the office of the Secretary of State, Albany, as well as in the minutes of the Chamber, and may be found printed in Jones & Varick's edition of the *Laws of New York*, vol. i. p. 113, and in 1st *Greenleaf*, 78, and in *King's Sketch of the History of the Chamber.* The original has been many years lost. *Mr. Prosper M. Wetmore*, when Secretary of the Chamber, made some interesting statements concerning the old document:

"In my search for objects of interest connected with the past history of the Chamber, my attention was naturally directed to the original charter, granted by Lieut. Gov. Colden, in the name of His Majesty George III., and which I knew had been in existence some few years previously. Every effort in my power was made at the time, and has been continued since, but as yet without success, for the recovery of this interesting link in our historical chain.

"There is a bit of history, also, connected with this old charter. Some five-and-twenty years ago, Admiral Walton, of the British Navy, succeeded by inheritance to the property of his family in this city; and on taking possession, among a vast accumulation of miscellaneous lumber, boxes, baskets, and chests, articles of domestic economy, dragoon saddles and Hessian muskets, in the spacious attic of 'Walton House,' in Pearl street, was found the original charter of the Chamber of Commerce. It was very large, about three feet in width, with the massive waxen seal of the crown, six inches in diameter, attached, and the whole carefully encased in tin and enclosed in mahogany. The Admiral immediately made known the discovery to Mr. Pintard, who took possession of the document.

"Secretary Van Dam was known to have been an intimate friend, probably a relative, of the Walton family. William Walton had once been President of the Chamber. These facts may account for the situation in which the charter had been found, and we must therefore believe that this instrument had lain undisturbed in the recesses of Walton House for the period of nearly half a century.

"On the night of the great fire, the mahogany case containing the charter, was seen in the room occupied by the Chamber at the Exchange. As everything portable was supposed to have been removed from the building before its destruction, I indulged for some time a confident hope of being able to recover the old charter. In this, I regret to say, I have been disappointed. If it was saved from the fire, it has ever since been so carefully guarded that the most diligent research has not been successful in tracing its whereabout. Like the old seal, it may yet turn up in some unexpected manner, and then our memorials of an existence of fourscore years will be complete."—*Letter to Hon. Charles King, N. Y.*, Nov. 20, 1848. (See * p. 371.)

NOTE 51, PAGE 96. THE STREET CALLED BROAD.—Originally the line of a brook or inlet. Its early name was the "*Heeren-gracht*," or *Gentlemen's Canal.* It was called the *Moat* in the time of Governor Kieft, and the *Great Dyke* at the close of the English Governor Lovelace's administration (1672), when it was ordered to be cleaned, and when also the streets of the city were paved. The Dutch called it *Breede-gracht* (Broad-Canal), as well as *Heeren-gracht.* Three years after this view (viz., 1676), the gracht (canal) was ordered to be filled up and the street levelled and paved.—*Moulton's New Orange*, p. 31.

NOTE 52, PAGE 99. SALARY OF THE SECRETARY.—This seems to have been a nominal sum to cover the expenses incurred for clerk-hire.

NOTE 53, PAGE 99. ANNUAL DINNER OF THE CHAMBER (Tuesday, 9th May, 1770).—No notice of this entertainment appears in the public prints of the day.

NOTE 54, PAGE 99. MEMBERS OF THE GENERAL ASSEMBLY, 1769-1775.—The last Assembly which sat in the colony of New York under Colonial authority. Summoned by writ of Sir Henry Moore, Governor of the

Province, in 1769, this Assembly organized with the election of John Cruger as Speaker. During the excited period which preceded the Revolution, it held a middle course. Although it lost the popular favor by its compliance with many of the obnoxious requirements of the "Mutiny Act," it was by no means pliant or submissive to the exactions of the Crown, and owed its long duration to the fears which the Governors entertained of the result of a new election. It was never prorogued, but adjourned, *sine die*, on the 3d of April, 1775.

LIST OF THE ASSEMBLY:—John Cruger, James De Lancey, Jacob Walton, and James Jauncey, Esquires, city and county of New York; Jacob H. Ten Eyck and Philip Schuyler, Esquires, city and county of Albany; Jacobus Mynderse, Esquire, town of Schenectady; Abraham Ten Broeck, Esquire, manor of Rensalaer; Robert R. Livingston, Esquire, manor of Livingston; Charles De Witt and George Clinton, Esquires, Ulster County; Leonard Van Kleeck and Dirch Brinckerhoff, Esquires, Dutchess County; Jo. De Noyells and Sam. Gale, Esquires, Orange County; John Thomas and Frederick Philipse, Esquires, Westchester County; John De Lancey, Esquire, Borough of Westchester; Piere Van Cortlandt, Esquire, manor of Cortlandt; Jo. Rapalje and Simon Boerum, Esquires, King's County; Dan. Kissam and Zea Seaman, Esquires, Queen's County; William Nicoll and Jesse Woodhull, Esquires, Suffolk County; Benjamin Seaman and Christopher Billop, Esquires, Richmond County.

In 1772, Isaac Wilkins replaced Piere Van Cortlandt, Esquire, as representative for the manor of Cortlandt; Samuel Wells and Crean Brush, Esquires, were chosen as representatives of Cumberland County. In 1774, Guy Johnson and Hendrick Fry, Esquires, were chosen as representatives for Tryon County.

NOTE 55, PAGE 99. SECRETARIES OF THE COUNCIL.—In the year 1770 these gentlemen were—Secretary and Clerk of the Council, George Clarke, Esq., continued in office until the close of the war; Deputy Clerk of the Council, Goldsborow Banyar, Esq., succeeded by Samuel Bayard, Jun., Esq., in 1774, who retained the post till the close of the war.

NOTE 56, PAGE 99. THE GENERAL AND HIS SUIT.—General and Commander-in-Chief, his Excellency the Honourable THOMAS GAGE, Esq. In 1770 his Aids-de-Camp were Capts. Stephen Kemble and Henry Dobson; Secretary, Gabriel Maturin, Esq. In 1773 Major Kemble was promoted to the post of Deputy-Adjutant-General. In 1774 the Aids of General Gage were Major Robert Donkin and Lieut. Harry Rooke. In the spring of 1774 General Gage was appointed Military Governor of Massachusetts, and transferred his head-quarters to Boston.

NOTE 57, PAGE 99. CAPTAINS OF HIS MAJESTY'S SHIPS.—A list of Ships in commission, with their commanders, at Stations in the North America, in the year 1770: *Romney* (50 guns), Samuel Hood, Commodore, Captain John Cosner; *Rippon* (60), Samuel Thompson; *Berlin* (32), Sir Tho. Adams; *Garland* * (20), ——— ; *Launceston* * (44), John Gill; *Deal Castle* (20), M. Jacobs; *Glascow* * (20), William Allen; *Squirrel* (20), J. Botterell; *Viper* (10), Robt. Linzee; *Beaver* (14), H. Bellew.—*Schomberg's Naval Chronology.*

The vessels [*] thus marked are those which appear in New York history.

NOTE 58, PAGE 99. PRINCIPAL OFFICERS OF THE CUSTOMS. —*Collector of Customs and Receiver-General of the Quit Rents*, Andrew Elliott, Esq., appointed 1764, continued in office until 1783. *Deputy Collector*, John Moore, Esq., continued in office till 1783. *Comptroller*, Lambert Moore, Esq., continued in office till 1783. *Naval Officer*, Charles Williams, Esq., succeeded in 1773 by Peter De Lancey, Esq., and in 1774 by Samuel Kemble, Esq. *Surveyor and Searcher*, Alexander Colden, Esq., succeeded in 1773 by Richard Colden, Esq., and in 1777 by Samuel V. Bayard.

NOTE 59, PAGE 100. THE TITLE OF HONORABLE.—This title was in the Colony only accorded to the members of the Council. At this time *Hugh Wallace* and *Henry White* were both members of the Council.

NOTE 60, PAGE 104. [ACCOUNT.]—An omission here occurs in the minutes, which this word, from the context, properly supplies.

NOTE 61, PAGE 104. JERSEY MONEY.—The rate at which the paper money of New Jersey should be taken was before the Chamber as early as June, 1768 (page 10), and its consideration postponed to July of the same year (page 11). Here introduced, July, 1770, in a definite form, its consideration was again postponed to August (page 106), and September (page 107). For the action of the Chamber, see *Note* 88 *to page* 143.

NOTE 62, PAGE 105. L (ONG) I (SLAND).—These letters set against the name of absent members indicate that they were at the time of meeting in Long Island, six miles distant from the city, which exempted from fine under the rule. (See page 7).

NOTE 63, PAGE 106. NOTICE OF RESOLUTION AS TO HALF JOES.—This advertisement, signed by *Anthony Van Dam*, *Secretary*, may be seen in the issue of Thursday, August 16, 1770, of *Holt's New York Journal, or the General Advertiser* (No. 1441).

NOTE 64, PAGE 110. STOVE FOR THE CHAMBER.—This now common convenience of modern times was a comparatively recent invention at this time (1770). *Benjamin Franklin*, in "an account of the new-invented Pennsylvania Fire-places, Philadelphia," 1744, describes the fire-places before in use as follows: "1. The large open fire-places used in the days of our fathers and still generally in the country and in kitchens. 2. The newer-fashioned fire-places, with low breasts and narrow hearths. 3. Fire-places with hollow backs, hearths and jambs of iron (described by M. Guager in his tract entitled *La Mécanique de Feu*), for warming the air as it comes into the room. 4. The Holland stoves, with iron doors opening into the room. 5. The German Stoves, which have no opening in the room where they are used, but the fire is put in from some other room, or from without. 6. Iron pots, with open charcoal fires, placed in the middle of a room." In his autobiography, *Franklin* gives the year 1742 as that of his invention. The *Franklin Stove*, as it is now called, was soon in general use through all the Colonies. Those for public buildings he describes as "in the form of temples cast in iron, with columns, cornices, and every member of elegant architecture."—*Sparks's Life of Franklin*, vi. pp. 34, 38, 398.

NOTE 65, PAGE 110. FLOUR EXPORTS.—From the earliest period of the English settlement, *Flour* was one of the chief products of New

York. "The petition of the merchants" to Lord Cornbury, in 1702, com mences with the statement: "That the principall staple of the Trade of this Province is the manufactory of wheat, expended chiefly in the West Indies by the English," &c.—*Col. Doc.* iv. 1133.

"Flour is also a main article (of our Exports), of which there is shipped about 80,000 barrels per annum."—*Description of the Colony*, 1756, *in Smith's New York*, 2, 331.

"The natural produce and Staple Commodities of this Province are Wheat, Indian Corn, Oats, Rye, &c., &c."—*The Report of Governor Tryon to the Earl of Dartmouth on the Province of New York, Col. Doc.* viii. 449.

NOTE 66, PAGE 110. FRENCH BURR STONES.—The Burr Stone, or "*Buhr Stone*," a hard silicious stone, remarkable for its cellular structure and rough surface, however worn and levelled.—*Bigelow.*

A sub-species of silex or quartz, occurring in amorphous masses. Compact like horn-stone, but containing a greater or less number of irregular cavities. It is used for mill-stones.—*Cleaveland.*

The French stone has preserved its superiority, and is at this time one of the regular imports to the United States from Havre.

NOTE 67, PAGE 111. INSPECTION OF POT-ASHES.—The General Assembly, on the 19th December, 1766, passed "an Act to prevent Frauds by the Adulteration of Pot-Ash and Pearl-Ash," which, in its preamble, recites "that the Manufacture of Pot-Ash and Pearl-Ash hath been lately introduced into this Colony, and is likely to become a considerable Article of Remittance to Great Britain," and provides measures to punish offenders. On the 12th March, 1772, a further Act appointed an Inspector, and allowed a charge of "*Four pence* for every Hundredweight; one half to be paid by the Purchaser, and the other half by the Vender."—*Gaine's Laws of New York,* 486 & 655.

NOTE 68, PAGE 113. GERMAN MILL SCREENS.—The use of this improvement for the cleaning of flour is another evidence of the effort made by the New York Colony to keep up the character of this important staple.

NOTE 69, PAGE 113. APPLICATION TO ASSEMBLY FOR ONE INSPECTOR.—This application does not appear upon the Minutes of the Assembly. Other regulations, adopted at the Twenty-ninth Session, 1770–1771, provided for greater strictness on the part of the Inspectors.—*Gaine's Laws of New York*, p. 610.

NOTE 70, PAGE 114. LAW AS TO BRANDING OF FLOUR.—The General Assembly, on the 10th of February, 1771, passed "an Act further to regulate the Inspection and Branding of Flour."

The third section enacted "That from and after the first day of June next, no Inspector of Flour, appointed for the City of New York, shall brand or mark, as inspected, any Cask of Flour whatever, manufactured, unless the initial Letter of the Christian Name, and the Sirname at Length of the manufacturer are first branded thereon,—this Act to remain in force until the first day of January one thousand seven hundred and seventy-five."—*Gaine's Laws of New York*, p. 608.

NOTE 71, PAGE 114. ADVERTISEMENT AS TO FLOUR.—*Chamber of Commerce,* Tuesday the 16th of November, 1770—Mr. Francis Marschalk, Inspector of Flour, produced to the Chamber several samples of flour, and bread made of it. He informed the Chamber that of late, several millers had much improved in the manufacture of flour, particularly those who used French burr stones for grinding, and German skreens for cleaning the wheat. AGREED, that the members of this Corporation will give all the encouragement in their power to the makers of good flour, by giving their marks a due preference, and will carefully avoid buying any flour of an inferior quality. AND, Mr. Marschalk was desired to attend the Chamber at their monthly meetings to inform the Corporation what improvements have been made, and to leave in writing the names and brand marks of the makers of good and bad flour.—ANTHONY VAN DAM, Secry.—*Hugh Gaine's New York Gazette*, November 19, 1770.

NOTE 72, PAGE 119. STERLING IRON WORKS.—"The Stirling Iron Works are still in operation. They are situated on the outlet of Stirling Pond, about five miles southwest of the Sloatsburgh Station on the Erie Railway. They are owned by descendants of Peter Townsend, and have now been in operation about one hundred years." These works were run during the Revolution for the Continental Army. On the 2d of February, 1778, a contract was entered into with Noble Townsend, the proprietor, by order of Genl. Putnam, for the celebrated chain stretched across the Hudson River from West Point to Constitution Island.—*Boynton's West Point*, p. 56.

NOTE 73, PAGE 119. HACKENSACK.—The port and county-town of Bergen County, on the right bank of the Hackensack river, fifteen miles from its mouth, twelve from New York, and sixty-three from Trenton.—*Gordon's Gazetteer of New Jersey*.

NOTE 74, PAGE 120. IMLAY-TOWN, ON CHALEUR BAY.—Chaleur Bay, in Lower Canada, projects west and northwest from the Gulf of St. Lawrence. It has the British Province of New Brunswick on the south, and the district and county of Gaspee on the north. On its north there are the townships of Hopetown, Cox, Hamilton, North Richmond, Maria and Carlton. The river Ristigouche empties into this fine bay.—*Morse's American Gazetteer*, 1804.

Imlay-Town must have been an unimportant place, as it neither appears here nor on the celebrated chart, *The Atlantic Neptune* of 1778.

NOTE 75, PAGE 120. EXPENSES OF REFERENCE AND AWARD.—From this it appears that the arbitrators received a fee for their services. The same policy has been renewed by the Chamber, and the amounts received are set aside to increase its Library of Mercantile Law.

NOTE 76, PAGE 121. S(ick).—This letter set against the name of an absent member, indicated absence on account of sickness and an exemption from fine.

NOTE 77, PAGE 122. STANDARD GOLD SCALES.—As no public notice appears of this standard, it is probable, if adopted at all, that its use was confined to the members of the Chamber.

NOTE 78, PAGE 122. ADVANCE PAY OF SEAMEN.—An early effort to check the desertion of Seamen before sailing. The ships of war, always in want of seamen, would never return a sailor to a merchant-vessel.

NOTE 79, PAGE 122. FREIGHT ON MOLASSES CASKS.—The custom of the present day is to pay freight on the gross gauge of the casks, at a price for each 110 gallons of such gross gauge.

NOTE 80, PAGE 126. PICTURE OF COLDEN.—This portrait, a full length, may be fairly claimed as a fine specimen of early American Art. The artist, *Matthew Pratt*, was a native of Philadelphia, who painted portraits occasionally in New York.—*Dunlap's Arts of Design in the United States*, p. 101; see also page 167 of *Register of Proceedings.*

It originally hung in the Long Room over the Exchange which was occupied by the Chamber from 1770 till 1775. Whether on the renewal of meetings at the Merchants' Coffee House, in 1779, it followed its owners, is not now known. If so, it was removed at the close of the war, and appears to have fallen into the keeping of the family of the Lieutenant Governor. On the first day of February, 1791, it is recorded on the minutes of the Chamber: "Mr. Vice-President Murray gave information that a picture of Cadwallader Colden, Esq., Lieut. Governor of the late Province of New York, who originally incorporated this Chamber, and which had been drawn by order and at the desire of its members, was now in good preservation and in hands which were willing to restore it to the former owners." Whereupon the Chamber resolved that the President be requested to write to the person in whose possession the Painting is, and ask its restoration to this Corporation. On the 7th May, 1793, the Records show that the picture was returned by Mr. Cadwallader Colden (son of the Lt. Governor). The picture was then placed upon the walls of the room used by the Chamber in the Merchants' Coffee House, and afterwards, on their changing their place of meetings to the Tontine Building, in 1795, it was removed to that place.

On the 15th April, 1817, the American Association of Fine Arts requested the loan of this, and the fine full-length of Hamilton, by Trumbull, also the property of the Chamber, as the Representative of the Merchants of New York for whom it was painted, and the two portraits were placed in their hands under certain agreements. They continued for many years to make a part of the exhibition of the Academy.

On the 1st of May, 1827, the Chamber having taken rooms in the Merchants' Exchange, it was ordered that the pictures should be repaired, their frames re-gilded, and that they be hung in their hall, which was on the lower floor of the building, on the right of the main entrance.

On the morning of December 16th, 1835, the second day of the Great Fire, they were saved from the flames which consumed the building, and, covered with canvas, were deposited in the garret of a store in Wall Street (the memory of the precise number of which is now lost; it was between Water Street and the River), where they lay for many years. When *Mr. Prosper M. Wetmore* was appointed *Secretary of the Chamber*, in 1843, he instituted a search for the old properties of the Corporation, and accidentally fell upon a clue which led to their recovery. So quickly, in the stir and movement of this busy city, things of yesterday pass from memory and sight. It was only known then of the package, that it contained pictures which were supposed to belong to the Chamber. The canvas had never been opened.

The pictures were again repaired and hung in the Room occupied by the Chamber in the Merchants' Bank.

On the 6th February, 1844, they were again transferred, in accordance with the following order: *Resolved*—"That the Secretary be authorized to deposit for safe keeping and due preservation, in the Library of the New York Historical Society, the full-length portraits of Lt. Gov. Colden and General Alexander Hamilton, belonging to this Chamber, the same to be returned to the possession of the Chamber whenever it shall desire to reclaim them.

On the removal of the Historical Society to its fire-proof building in the Second Avenue, corner of Eleventh Street, these portraits were transferred, and now form part of its fine and growing gallery of American portraits, awaiting the time when the merchants of New York shall erect a building for the Chamber, worthy of its ancient honor and present usefulness.

NOTE 81, PAGE 128. ANNUAL DINNER of the Chamber, May, 1771.—No notice of this entertainment appears in the public prints of the day.

NOTE 82, PAGE 128. THE GOVERNOR AND HIS SECRETARY.—"On Thursday morning last, October 17, 1770, his Excellency, the Right Honorable, the *Earl of Dunmore*, the Governor, arrived at Sandy Hook, in his Majesty's ship, the Tweed, . . . and about three in the afternoon landed at the White-Hall, accompanied by Sir William Draper, Lord Drummond, the Commander of the Tweed, and *Capt. Foy*, his Lordship's Secretary."—*Holt's New York Journal, for* Thursday, October 25, 1770.

NOTE 83, PAGE 128. FIELD OFFICERS ON DUTY IN NEW YORK.—The 6th Regiment was at this time stationed in New York. The Field Officers were *Colonel John Scott*, with the rank of Major General, *Lieut. Colonel D. Templer*, and *Major Charles Preston.—Gaine's New York Almanac for* 1771.

NOTE 84, PAGE 132. MAIL FOR THE PACKET FOR ENGLAND.—"*The names of his Majesty's Packet-Boats with their Commanders, that are stationed between Falmouth and New York:* The Earl of Halifax, Balderson; the Harriott, Oake; the Duke of Cumberland, Goodridge; the Lord Hyde, Goddard. (And a fifth one building in our yards.)

"The mail for North America is made up at the General Post Office in London, the first Wednesday in every month, and the mail for England is made up at the Post Office in New York the first Tuesday in every month, and dispatched from each office without delay."—*Gaine's Almanac for* 1772.

The mail had been previously made up on the first Saturday in every month.—*Gaine's Almanac for* 1771.

A notice of a change to Wednesday first appears in 1774.—*Gaine's Almanac for* 1774.

NOTE 85, PAGE 141. TONNAGE OF THE PORT.—This word is here used in a restricted sense, different from its present meaning. It refers to the tonnage of goods by weight or measurement, and not to the capacity of vessels.

NOTE 86, PAGE 142. WINCHESTER MEASURE.—"A standard English Dry Measure originally kept at Winchester, in England, and used till 1826, when the imperial bushel was introduced."—*Worcester.*

"The *Winchester* bushel is 18½ inches wide and 8 inches deep, and contains 2150.22 cubic inches; while the imperial Standard Bushel contains 2208.1907 cubic inches."—*Simmons.*

NOTE 87, PAGE 142. PELTRY.—Edward Phillips, in his New World of Words (1720), defines *Pelt* as the "Skin of a Beast,"—*Peltry*, a word so often met with in Colonial history does not appear in *Phillips*, *Bailey*, or *Johnson*. *Webster* quotes *Smollett* as authority, and defines it as "the skin of animals producing fur."

"The fur trade, though very much impaired by the French wiles and encroachments, ought not to be passed over in silence. The building of Oswego has conduced, more than anything else, to the preservation of this trade. *Peltry* of all kinds is purchased with rum, ammunition, blankets, strouds, and wampum, or conque-shell bugles. (It is computed that formerly we exported 150 hogsheads of beaver and other fine furs per annum, and 200 hogsheads of Indian-dressed deer skins, besides those carried from Albany into New England. Skins undressed are usually shipped to Holland."—*Description of the Colony in* 1756; *Smith's New York*, II, 332.

NOTE 88, PAGE 143. RESTRICTION UPON TAKING OF JERSEY MONEY.—This subject had been several times brought before the Chamber, and as often postponed (see pages 10, 11, 104, 106, 107). It was, November 5, 1771, again introduced. Again postponed, a vote was at last taken, 3d March, 1772, when, by a majority of 19 to 16, the restriction was imposed. So many of the members resigned in consequence, that on the 4th January, 1774 (page 187), the vote was rescinded.

The *General Assembly of New York* took up the subject on the 9th March, 1774, and passed "an Act to prevent the depreciating the Paper Currency of this Colony."

"WHEREAS the Paper Currency or Bills of Credit issued in the neighboring Colonies are not made a legal Tender by any Act of this Colony and yet for Convenience do pass therein as money, and are often received in this Colony at a higher Value than they were emitted for by the Colony issuing the same, to the great Discredit and Depreciation of the Bills of Credit of this Colony, the Prejudice of Individuals, the draining the Colony of their Gold and Silver imported therein, and to the obstruction and detriment of Commerce.

"Be it therefore Enacted, &c., That after the first day of May next no person shall either pass, exchange, pay or receive any Bill of Credit of any of the neighboring Colonies for any sum or at any Rates more than the sum payable therefor at the Treasury of that Colony in which the same was issued, upon Pain of forfeiting a sum equal to the value of the Bills so passed, &c." The following are the Rates at which they are to pass: Jersey Bill for £6, in N. Y. currency £6. 8; for £3 in N. Y. currency, £3. 4, &c., &c.—*Gaine's New York Gazette*, May 2, 1774.

NOTE 89, PAGE 144. SOCIETY OF PROPRIETORS OF NEW JERSEY.—The original Lords Proprietors of East Jersey were Lord Berkeley and Sir George Carteret, to whom the Duke of York on the 24th June, 1664, granted the portion of his tract since known by this name. In 1680, shortly after the death of Sir George Carteret, the property was offered at public sale—"William Penn, with eleven associates of the Quaker persuasion becoming the purchasers for £3,400. . . . Their deeds of lease and release were dated 1st and 2d February, 1681–2, and subsequently each of them sold one half their respective rights to a new associate, making in all twenty-four proprietaries."—*Whitehead's East Jersey under the Proprietary Governments*, vol 1. p. 83.

For many years the Province was under the rule of the Proprietors, who chose their own Governor, but so much dissension occurred that, in 1702, the "pretended right of Government," as it is designated in the act of surrender, was yielded to the Crown. The Jerseys were united with New

York under one Governor, during the administration of Lord Cornbury. Upon the surrender the proprietors secured valuable concessions.—*Douglass' British Settlement* (1755), p. 281.

NOTE 90, PAGE 144. TREASURER OF SOCIETY OF PROPRIETORS.—*James Parker* was elected President of the Board of Proprietors of the Eastern Division of the State of New Jersey, April 10, 1771, and the following year was re-elected. He also was Treasurer for the same time.—*Note from J. Lawrence Boggs, Register.*

NOTE 91, PAGE 146. ADVERTISEMENT AS TO TONNAGE.—The *Report* of the Committee of 3d September, 1771, signed by Hamilton Young, Miles Sherbrooke, Richard Yates, John Moore, and Jacobus Van Zandt, and the *Resolution* of 5th November, 1771, may be seen in *Gaine's New York Gazette and Weekly Mercury for* 27th January, 1772.

NOTE 92, PAGE 148. THREE NEWSPAPERS IN THE CITY (January, 1772).—" *The New York Gazette and the Weekly Mercury*, printed by *Hugh Gaine*, Printer and Bookseller and Stationer, at the Bible and Crown, in Hanover Square (established 3d August, 1752, discontinued 13th October, 1783).

" *The New York Journal, or the General Advertiser*, containing the freshest articles both Foreign and Domestick, Printed and Published by *John Holt*, on Hunter's Quay, Rotton Row (established May 29, 1766, discontinued in 1785).

" *The New York Gazette, or the Weekly Post Boy*, containing the freshest Advices, Foreign and Domestick. Established by *James Parker* in January 1742–3. August 27, 1770, *Samuel Inslee* and *Anthony Carr* published this paper, and continued it two years."—*Isaiah Thomas' History of Printing in America*, vol. ii. p. 293–298.

NOTE 93, PAGE 153. ADVERTISEMENT OF RESOLUTION AS TO JERSEY MONEY.—A long advertisement of the action taken by the Chamber, March 3, 1772, with regard to the charge for weighing of flour; and a full statement of the motion and resolution as to the rates at which "*Jersey money*" should be taken, appeared in *Holt's New York Journal, or General Advertiser for* Thursday, March 12, 1772.

NOTE 94, PAGE 156. CUPOLA ON THE EXCHANGE.—This was built in accordance with the instructions of the Common Council, who on the 13th July, 1753, " *Ordered* that the second story of the Exchange, now a building at the Lower End of Broad street be not exceeding fifteen feet in height and not less than fourteen, and the Room be arched from the height of the said fourteen feet, and that a CUPOLA be erected in said Exchange, under the direction of the Committee appointed for completing the said Exchange."—*Common Council Minutes*, vol. v. p. 340.

NOTE 95, PAGE 156. SEAL OF THE CHAMBER.—This Seal was made in London, and brought out by Captain Winn, who commanded one of the vessels in the trade at the time. It is of solid silver, about three inches in diameter, and one inch in thickness. Mr. *Prosper M. Wetmore*, who was Secretary of the Chamber from 1843 to 1849, relates a singular incident of its loss and recovery : " A somewhat curious story attaches to this Seal. Some years after the Revolution, a gentleman interested in the affairs of this country, in looking through a sort of curiosity shop in London where a miscellaneous collection of personal effects was displayed to catch the eye of a purchaser, fortunately discovered this signet of the Chamber of Commerce of New York. He immediately secured the valuable estray, and with commendable patriotism restored it to the proper custody."—*Note of Mr. Wetmore to Mr. Charles King; History of Chamber of Commerce.*

The President was the designated custodian of the Seal by resolution of 2d June, 1772 (p. 160). It seems probable that the last Colonial President, Mr. Isaac Low, took it with him on his retirement with the British troops in 1783, and that it afterwards found its way into the shop from whence it was rescued.

The device was engraved on the piece of plate presented June 3, 1780, to Captain Newman for saving the Mails of the Carteret Packet (page 233). The Seal is still in fine preservation, in the custody of the Secretary, and is constantly used in authentication of documents.

NOTE 96, PAGE 157. ANNUAL DINNER OF THE CHAMBER, (1772).—No notice of this entertainment appears in the public prints of the day.

NOTE 97, PAGE 163. ROOF OVER THE EXCHANGE.—This shingled roof is another evidence of the poor and temporary character of the public buildings of the last century.

NOTE 98, PAGE 165. W.—A private memorandum of the Secretary, the meaning of which is now lost.

NOTE 99, PAGE 166. NASH.—The meaning of this abbreviation is obscure. From the context, it is doubtless intended as a designation of some locality.

NOTE 100, PAGE 167. COST OF PORTRAIT.—A comparison of the encouragement to art a century since, and now, may be drawn from the price paid for the full-length portrait of Governor Colden, £37, and the cost of the full-length of Mr. President Perit in 1863, $1,000.

NOTE 101, PAGE 175. ACT OF THE ASSEMBLY AS TO FISH BOUNTIES.—This Act, passed by the Twenty-ninth General Assembly, 8th March, 1773, "for the encouraging a Fishery on the Sea Coast for the better supply of the Markets in the City of New York," is recorded in *Gaine's Laws of New York*, page 742.

NOTE 102, PAGE 176. FISH OF NEW YORK.—The fish here mentioned are deep sea-fish. The object of the bounty was to foster a fishery on the coast. The RAY is still abundant in the waters about New York. *Mr. Devoe* in his *Market Assistant* describes several varieties under the names of Clear-nosed Ray, Spotted Ray, Whip-sting Ray, Cow-nosed Ray, Broad-sting Ray. The SKATE is called, by him, a variety of the Ray, and is described under the name of Smooth Skate.

NOTE 103, PAGE 176. TRAWL NET.—"Trawler-men.—A sort of Fishermen that us'd unlawful Arts and Engines to destroy the Fish upon the River Thames."—*Edward Phillips' Dict.* (1720.)

Troll.—To fish for a pike with a rod which has a pulley towards the bottom.—*Samuel Johnson.*

The net so called was probably the ordinary Fisherman's net. The Skate and Ray were excepted because of their great number and poor quality.

NOTE 104, PAGE 177. PROPOSED MEMBERS.—The only entry on the minutes about which there is some uncertainty. Of the three members proposed at the April meeting, one, *Johnston Fairholme*, appears at the June meeting, without any notice being given of his election. *William Jauncey* was admitted 7th December, 1773. *Daniel Ludlow* takes his seat Jan. 20, 1784, without any notice appearing of his election.

NOTE 105, PAGE 178. ADVERTISEMENT OF FISH PREMIUMS. —"Chamber of Commerce, New York, 6th April, 1773. Whereas the Legislature of the Province of New York have, by an Act passed the 8th March last, directed that the Overplus of the Duty of Excise, collected in the said City and County, be annually paid, for the first five years next after the passing of said Act, to the Treasurer of the Corporation of the Chamber of Commerce, to be, by the said Corporation of the Chamber of Commerce, disposed of in such Manner as they shall think most proper for encouraging a Fishery on the Sea Coast, for the better supplying the Markets in the City of New York. In order therefore that the Intention of the Legislature may be fully answered, and the Inhabitants of this City receive the Benefit of so laudable a Donation; It is resolved and agreed that the following Premiums hereafter mentioned be paid by the Treasurer of the Chamber of Commerce to such Persons who, upon application and due Proof made, to the satisfaction of the Chamber, shall be entitled to the same, viz., &c."—*Rivington's New York Gazetteer*, April 29, 1773 (No. 2).

The notices of the Committee appointed by the Chamber to award the premiums for the year ending May 1, 1774, calling on all claimants to meet at the house of Thomas Doran, on the New Dock, may be seen in *Gaine's N. Y. Gazette for* May 9, 1774.

The Committee for 1774-1775 met at Mrs. Brock's (a tea-house opposite the Battery) three days at the close of June.—*Rivington's N. Y. Gazetteer*, June 22, 1775.

NOTE 106, PAGE 178. FARE.—This is a very unusual use of this word, which is generally applied to the money received for a passage, not to the trip of the carrier; yet it can hardly be termed incorrect, since both Spenser and Milton use the word in the sense of "to go." Here it means the fisherman's voyage.

NOTE 107, PAGE 181. DEPARTURE FOR ENGLAND OF GENERAL GAGE.—"On Tuesday, about eleven o'clock, his Excellency the Hon. General Gage, with his Lady, their son and two daughters, Miss Morris, Major Sheriffe, and the Captains Kemble and Dobson, embarked on board the Ship Earl of Dunmore, Capt. Lawrence, for London. The Royal Artillery were under arms, and saluted his Excellency with 17 guns, a great company of gentlemen attended his Excellency to the ship, expressing in very fervent terms their wishes of safety and felicity to this most valuable and sincerely beloved personage, his truly amiable lady and family." —*Rivington's New York Gazetteer for* Thursday, June 10, 1773 (No. 8).

NOTE 108, PAGE 182. SERIES OF GLORIOUS VICTORIES.—The allusion is here to the successes of British arms in the French war. The expeditions, from the commencement of hostilities, in 1755, to the Treaty of Peace with France and Spain, 1763, which resulted favorably, were: "1755, against the French in Nova Scotia, General Winslow with an army of Provincials chiefly; 1758, against Louisburg and the Islands of Cape Breton and St. John, Admiral Boscawen and General Amherst;

against Frontenac, Col. Bradstreet with Regulars and Provincials detached from General Abercrombie's army; against Fort du Quesne with Regulars and Provincials, General Forbes; 1759, against Niagara, Gen. Prideaux and Sir Wm. Johnston with Regulars and Provincials; against Ticonderoga and Crown Point with Regulars and Provincials, Gen. Amherst; against Quebec, Gen. Wolfe; 1760, against Montreal, General Amherst with Regulars and Provincials; against Havana, Earl of Albemarle and Admiral Pocock with an army of Regulars and Provincials; 1762, against Newfoundland, Lord Colville and Col. Amherst with Regulars and Provincials."—*Extract from Hugh Gaine's Almanac for* 1771.

NOTE 109, PAGE 188. [6].—A memorandum of the Secretary, probably a note of payment of fines.

NOTE 110, PAGE 189. EMBARKATION OF GOVERNOR TRYON FOR ENGLAND.—"On Thursday morning, about ten o'clock, Mrs. and Miss Tryon, accompanied by several Ladies of this City, embarked at Murray's Wharf, on board the Mercury pacquet (Dillon), and presently after his Excellency the GOVERNOR proceeded on foot from his house in Broad Street, attended by several of the Honourable gentlemen of his Majesty's Council and of the Assembly, the Clergy of the different Churches, the Mayor and Corporation, and a vast concourse of the inhabitants, to the water side, where he was received by his Honour the Lieutenant Governor, and after taking a most affectionate leave of them, went on board, under a salute of three vollies of Captain Lasher's company of Grenadiers, which were taken up by Captain Samuel Tudor's company of Artillery, who fired a round of nineteen guns; these were succeeded by salutes from a battery of Philip Livingston, Esq.; at St. George's Ferry, Long Island, his Majesty's ship the Swan, several other vessels, and from Fort George; which were returned by artillery on board the Mercury; the pilot-boat, with a number of Gentlemen and a fine band of music, waited on his Excellency to Sandy Hook, where they took their leave; and on Sunday morning, at six o'clock, the pacquet proceeded to sea, with a steady north-west wind.—Thursday, April 14, 1774, *Rivington's New York Gazetteer.*

NOTE 111, PAGE 191. MAPS OF EAST AND WEST FLORIDA. —This is hardly a proper designation of the work of *Captain Bernard Romans*, which is entitled "*a concise Natural History of East and West Florida*, containing an account of the Natural Produce of all the Southern Part of British America, in the three Kingdoms of Nature, particularly the Animal and Vegetable, &c., &c., &c., to which is added by way of appendix, Plain and Easy Directions to Navigation over the Bank of Bahama, the Coast of the *Two Floridas*, the North of Cuba, and the Dangerous Gulph Passage, &c., &c., illustrated with Twelve Copper Plates, and Two whole Sheet Maps. New York, 2 vols., 12mo, 1775. In the list of subscribers which precedes the book may be seen the name of the Chamber of Commerce for the twelve copies ordered by it.

NOTE 112, PAGE 192. CHANCELLOR AND VICE ADMIRAL.—The Governor of the Colony held both these offices. *Smith*, in his History of New York, gives a full account of the Court of Chancery, and the discontent on the part of the people and the Assembly at the exercise of the functions of Chancellor by the Governor. The practice of the Court, he says, was copied after Chancery in England. The title of Vice Admiral was of course nominal.

NOTE 113, PAGE 192. GENTLEMAN ON WHOM THE COMMAND WILL DEVOLVE.—On the departure of Governor Tryon for England, the Government fell upon Lieutenant Governor Colden, who often held this post in the temporary absences of the Chiefs of State. This was the last time he held the command. Governor Tryon returned in 1775.

NOTE 114, PAGE 195. THE PUBLIC MARKET.—There were eight Markets in New York at this time (1774). The Old Slip Market, established 1691, removed 1779; Coenties Slip Market, 1691–1776; the Fly Market at the foot of Maiden Lane, 1699–1822; the Exchange Market, foot of Broad Street, 1738–1799; the Peck Slip Market, 1763–1792; the Bear Market, 1771 (Washington Market was built near its site in 1812); the Crown or Mesiers' Market, at Thurman's Slip, on the North River, 1771–1776; the Oswego Market, junction of Broadway and Maiden Lane, 1772–1811.

Of these the Old Fly Market was the most celebrated. "It could claim the merit of being the best and most liberally supplied with all the various articles used for human food."—*Devoe's Market Book.*

NOTE 115, PAGE 202. NEW CEDED COUNTRIES.—The new ceded countries to the southward of Georgia.—East and West Florida were ceded to England by Spain, on the Ratification of Peace by England, with France and Spain, on the 10th February, 1763.

NOTE 116, PAGE 202. SWORN TO EXECUTE THEIR RESPECTIVE OFFICES.—The Chamber did not meet again until June, 1779, when the sessions were resumed. The officers chosen in May, 1775 (except John Alsop, who left the city on the British occupation), served in 1779.

NOTE 117, PAGE 203. STATE OF PUBLIC AFFAIRS (1775–1776).—For four years the City of New York had been in a state of unquiet which rendered commerce uncertain and irregular, and was by no means favorable to the meetings of an organized body whose functions were those of Peace. Upon the news of the Lexington fight the citizens rose in mass, and on the 5th of May, 1775, appointed a Committee of Safety to take charge of the Government, and business was at once suspended. In June of the same year, at the request of the "Provincial Congress," General Wooster, who was encamped at Harlem, took command of the city. After the disastrous battle of Long Island, in September, 1776, the British under Lord Howe resumed their authority, which was maintained until the close of the war. Many of the citizens left the city with the American troops, and in their turn many of the refugees from Boston and other places within the American lines, came to New York for protection, and established themselves here.

The fatal fire of 1776, which consumed a large part of the City, caused also a derangement of trade from which it did not recover for many years. A second calamity of the same nature visited the city in 1778.

NOTE 118, PAGE 203. INCREASE OF COMMERCE, 1779.—The City of New York was, during the Revolutionary war, the head-quarters of the British army in America, and its great dépôt of supplies. During the succeeding year the captures of American vessels had been very numerous. Governor Tryon alludes to this in his Proclamation of the 8th March, 1779: "The City of New York is become an immense magazine of all Kinds of Supplies for a very extensive Commerce."—*Gaine's New York Gazette*, March 15, 1779.

NOTE 119, PAGE 203. HIS MAJESTY'S COMMISSIONERS.—In the year 1778 (Eighteenth George III.), Parliament passed an "Act to enable his Majesty to appoint Commissioners with sufficient powers to treat, counsel and agree upon the means of quieting the disorders now existing in certain of the Colonies, Plantations, and Provinces in North America." The Commissioners were the EARL OF CARLISLE, GEORGE JOHNSTONE, and WILLIAM EDEN. To these were joined LORD HOWE and Sir WILLIAM HOWE, but they did not act, the former being chiefly with the fleet and the latter having returned to England. General (Sir HENRY) CLINTON took the place of General Howe on the Commission. Dr. ADAM FERGUSON, Professor of Moral Philosophy in the University of Edinburgh, was the Secretary.—*Sparks's Writings of Washington*, v. 397.

NOTE 120, PAGE 203. PROCLAMATION OF THE COMMISSIONERS.—Failing in their purpose to treat with the Congress which declined to negotiate except on the basis of American Independence, the Commissioners proceeded to use such of their powers as seemed most fit to strengthen the cause of the King. On the 26th of September, 1778, the EARL OF CARLISLE, Sir HENRY CLINTON, and WILLIAM EDEN issued a PROCLAMATION in which they announce their desire "to give all immediate relief and security to the trade carried on by his Majesty's loyal subjects at the Port of New York—they therefore suspend so much of the Acts of Parliament of 1776 as prevents the exportation of goods formerly allowed to be shipped from this port to Great Britain, Ireland, Newfoundland, Halifax, Rhode Island, East and West Florida, and the British West Indies; the articles of stores and provisions, naval and military stores, excepted." They also gave license and warrant to the captains of vessels making prizes to "send all such captures to the ports of New York and Newport in Rhode Island," and authorize that the captures "may be exported into and landed in Great Britain or any other part of his Majesty's Dominions," upon payment of the usual duties.—*Gaine's New York Gazette*, October 5, 1778. (For renewals of this Proclamation see Note 164.)

NOTE 121, PAGE 203. THE MERCHANTS' COFFEE HOUSE.—The place where this building stood is now known as the South East corner of Wall and Water Streets, and is the site now occupied by the Journal of Commerce. A *Coffee House* was kept here at a very early period, which gave the name of *Coffee House Slip* to the slip at the foot of Wall street.

A notice of letters left there by the captain of a vessel in August, 1744, for the printer of the chief newspaper of the day, shows that it was a general resort. "*Whereas*, about a Fortnight ago, three or four Letters, directed to the Printer of this Paper, were left at the *Merchants' Coffee House* in this city, among many other Letters by Captain Romar from South Carolina; which Letters have been by ill-minded Persons either destroyed or conveyed away unknown." Signed by JAMES PARKER; who offers a reward for their recovery, and adds in a Postscript, "the keeper of the said *Coffee House's* late Usage to me, obliges me to have no more favourable Sentiments of him than the Case will allow."—*Parker's Post Boy*, (No. 84), Aug. 27, 1744.

A second notice, the same year, shows the date at which the dock was put out at Wall Street: "*To be Sold*, by Isaac Abrahams, newly come from England, on the *New Dock*, near the *Merchants' Coffee House*, all manner of Dantzick cordial Liquors, Rum and Brandy and Raspberry Brandy, Dr. Forbeno's Bitters with Directions and Hungary Water at reasonable

Rates. Also, all sorts of New Market caps and other sorts for Gentlemen and Ladies."—*Parker's Post Boy* (No. 95), November 12, 1744.

The location of the building is established by an advertisement which appears a few years later in the newspaper of the same printer, which had then changed its name: "To be sold by Publick Vendue, on Wednesday, the 5th instant, at Two of the Clock in the Afternoon, at the *Meal Market*, near the *Merchants' Coffee House* in New York, the Sails, Rigging, Anchors, Cables, &c., belonging to the Snow Noble Jane, lately lost near the East Bank."—*The New York Gazette revived in the Weekly Post Boy* (No. 298), October 3, 1748.

The next year a quaint advertisement defines the exact locality with more precision: To be sold by Henry Clopper, at the *corner* of the Meal Market, near the *Merchants' Coffee House*, "All sorts of men's and women's Saddles, Saddlers' Ware, Breed, Fringe, Plush, Brass Furniture, Brass Nails and Tacks, and a large assortment of Horse Whips. He also has several riding Chairs and Kittereens ready made for Sale, after the newest Fashion. He also mends Coaches, Chaises, Chairs, and Kittereens, after the cheapest and best manner."—*Parker's New York Gazette, revived in the Weekly Post Boy* (No. 323), March 27, 1749.

Its position in relation to the Meal Market is fully settled by a notice which appeared a few years later of James Murray, Druggist, "at the sign of the Bell, near the *Merchants' Coffee House*, opposite the *Meal Market*, New York."—*Gaine's New York Mercury* (No. 150), June 23, 1755.

For a few years, from 1751 to 1754, this was the great resort for the merchants of the city. The journals abound in evidences of the favor it enjoyed. Vendues of ships and prizes, of cargoes of goods, of houses, land, and negroes, follow each other in rapid succession. The captains engage for freight or passage here, and lost articles are to be returned to this general place of meeting.

At this time the house was on the river, which came up to Water Street. A proof of this is found in a mercantile notice: "To be sold, on board the Snow *Jamaica Planter*, Samuel Whyting, Master, now lying opposite the *Merchants' Coffee House*, a few barrels of the best Red Herrings."—*Gaine's New York Mercury* (No. 207), Monday, July 6, 1756.

The house now begins to lose its old reputation. The *Meal Market*, ill cared for, had been for many years a great nuisance to the neighbors. The *New Exchange*, with its rival *Coffee House*, began to draw away the throng which had made the *Merchants' Coffee House* the business centre.

Who kept the *Merchants' Coffee House* during this long period is uncertain. A notice some years later is one of the first to be met with of a keeper of the House. "*The Merchants' Coffee House*, late in the occupation of *Mrs. Ferrari*, and now of *Elizabeth Wragg*, on the opposite cross corner to the New House, is now fitted up in a most neat and commodious manner for the reception of Merchants and other Gentlemen who will please to favour her with their Company; where may be had Breakfast every morning, and Relishes at all Hours. Coffee as usual, &c."—*Holt's New York Journal and General Advertiser* (No. 1531), May 7, 1772.

As no further mention appears on the minutes of any change of place of meeting, it is presumed that the Chamber of Commerce continued to hold its sessions here until May 6, 1804, when a long break occurred in its history.

When it was revived on the 4th of March, 1817, by the active instrumentality of Mr. John Pintard, for many years after its honored Secretary, it met at the *Tontine Coffee House*, on the north-west corner of Wall and Water Streets, a few paces distant from the site of the OLD MERCHANTS' COFFEE HOUSE.—*MSS. Minutes of the Chamber*, vol. i. p. 576.

NOTE 122, PAGE 204. COMMANDANT OF NEW YORK.—Major-General DANIEL JONES succeeded Major-General JAMES ROBERTSON in this Post. His first Proclamation, dated May 4, 1778, appointing ANDREW ELLIOT Superintendent-General of the Police, appeared in *Gaine's New York Gazette and Weekly Mercury*, May 4, 1778.

Major-General JONES served until the next year. On the 7th July, 1779, the following notice was published: "His Excellency, the Commander-in-Chief, has been pleased to appoint Major General PATTISON Commandant of the Garrison of New York, in the room of Lieut. General JONES.—*Rivington's Royal Gazette*, July 7, 1779.

NOTE 123, PAGE 204. SUCCESS OF PRIVATE SHIPS OF WAR.—Governor Tryon, in a PROCLAMATION issued March 8, 1779, giving notice "that ample provision is made by the laudable Ardor of his Majesty's loyal Subjects for the employment of all Seamen, Ship-carpenters, and other Landsmen, resorting to this Port, in short and successful Cruises against his Majesty's Enemies," says, "I have already issued one hundred and twenty-one Commissions to as many private Vessels of War,—that in the short space of Time elapsed since the eighteenth of September last the Prize Vessels arrived here amount to above six hundred thousand Pounds Lawful money of New York, at the ancient currency of eight Shillings a milled Dollar."—*Gaine's New York Gazette*, March 15, 1779.

This statement was verified by the publication, a few days later, of "A List of Vessels commissioned as Letters of Marque from the Port of New York, since the 8th of September, 1778 (121 in number), and of their prizes" (165 in number), published in *Gaine's New York Gazette and Weekly Mercury*, March 22, 1779.

NOTE 124, PAGE 207. PRICE OF BUTCHERS' MEAT.—During the whole war there was a great scarcity of fresh meats in the City, and the Chamber naturally advised the Commandant to place no restrictions upon its sale, "*as the remedy may* prove worse than the disease."—(*See Page* 209.)

NOTE 125, PAGE 208. OLD CORPORATION ORDINANCES.—By an old law of the City it was ordained that "all and every Citizen, Free-holders, House-keepers and Inhabitants living within the Six Wards on the South side of the *Fresh Water*, shall, on every *Friday*, Weekly, either by themselves or Servants, rake and sweep together all the Dirt, Filth and Soil lying in the Streets before their respective Dwelling Houses or Lots of Ground, upon Heaps; and on the same Day, or on the *Saturday* following, shall cause the same to be carried away and thrown into the River or some other Convenient Place, under the Penalty of Six Shillings for each Neglect, Refusal, or Default." The Inhabitants were also required "to well and sufficiently pave, or cause to be well and sufficiently paved with Good and sufficient Pebble Stones suitable for Paving, all or so much of the Streets, Lanes, and Alleys within the (said) City as shall front the respective Buildings and Lots of Ground that belong to them respectively."

The Chamber seems to have recommended a mixed plan. On the 27th July, eight days after the recommendation made by them, a notice was issued from the OFFICE OF POLICE inviting "any person or persons that may be inclined to contract for the cleaning the Streets of the City *under the immunity of an exclusive right* to take all the manure and rubbish for their own use, to give their proposals."—*Gaine's New York Gazette*, August 2, 1779.

The next year General JAMES PATTISON, then Commandant, issued a Proclamation (6th April, 1780) essentially renewing the OLD CORPORATION ORDINANCES.—*Gaine's New York Gazette and Weekly Mercury*, April 10th, 1781.

NOTE 126, PAGE 208. POLICE OF THE CITY.—"*Proclamation* by Major-General JONES Commanding his Majesty's Forces on the Island of New York, Long Island, Staten Island, and the Posts depending—WHEREAS it is thought expedient, in order to give necessary assistance to the Commandant of the City, that a Superintendent-General of the Police should be appointed: I do hereby appoint ANDREW ELLIOT, Esq., Superintendent-General of the Police of the City of New York, and its Dependencies, with Powers and Authorities to issue such orders and Regulations from Time to Time as may most effectually tend to the Suppression of Vice and Licentiousness—the Support of the Poor—the Direction of the Nightly Watch—the Regulation of Markets and Ferries and all other matters in which the Œconomy, Peace, and Good Order of the City of New York and its Environs are concerned. The Superintendent-General will be assisted in the Administration of the Police by DAVID MATTHEWS, Esq., Mayor of this City: and I do hereby enjoin and require all Persons whatever, to pay due Obedience to the Superintendent-General, the Mayor and all others acting in Authority under them in the Execution of their Duty; and all Military Officers Commanding Guard, to assist them when it shall be found necessary. *Given under my Hand at* Head Quarters in New York, this 4th day of May, 1778—DANIEL JONES. By order of the General, Nathaniel Philips, Sec'y.—*Gaine's New York Gazette,* May 4, 1778.

NOTE 127, PAGE 208. HOSPITALS.—The principal Hospital of the City was, at the close of the last century, and has since been, "the New York Hospital," situated on the west side of Broadway, opposite the upper end of Pearl Street. During the Revolutionary War some of the churches were used for this purpose by the military authorities, who had little regard for other than the Established Church.

The first of the New York Hospitals which has for near a hundred years been distinguished for the care and purity of its free management, has been thus described:

"In the year 1770, some of the most respected and public-spirited inhabitants of the City of New York subscribed considerable sums of money for the purpose of erecting and establishing a public Hospital; and a petition was presented by Peter Middleton, John Jones and Samuel Bard, three eminent physicians, to Lieutenant Governor Colden, then administering the government of the Colony of New York, for a charter of incorporation, which was, in consequence, granted the following year by the Earl of Dunmore, Governor and Commander-in-chief of the Province. By this charter, dated the 13th of June, 1771, the Mayor, Recorder, Aldermen and Assistants, of the City of New York, the Rector of Trinity Church, one Minister from each of the other churches of different denominations then in the city, the President of King's (now Columbia) College, and a number of the principal and most respectable inhabitants of the city, were named as members, and incorporated under the name of the 'Society of the Hospital of the City of New York in America.' Twenty-six governors were also named for the management of the affairs and business of the Institution, who held their first meeting on the 25th July, 1771. Through the influence of Dr. John Fothergill and Sir William Duncan considerable contributions were made to the Society by many inhabitants of London and other places in Great Britain, and in 1772, the Legislature of the Province of New York granted an annual allowance of 800 pounds (2000 dollars) in aid of the institution for twenty years. In 1773 the governor of the Hospital purchased of Mr. Barclay and Mr. Rutgers, five acres of ground for the erection of a suitable edifice. A plan of a building having been procured by Dr. Jones, the foundation was laid the 27th of July, 1773; but on the 28th of February, 1775, when it was almost completed, the building accidentally took fire and was nearly consumed. By this misfortune the Society suffered the loss of seven thousand pounds ($17,500), and the execution of their benevolent plan would have been wholly frustrated had not the Legislature, in March, 1775, granted them the sum of 4,000 pounds towards rebuilding the house and repairing the loss they had sustained. But the War of Independence, which took place in the same year, prevented the completion of the edifice. During the war the building was occupied by British and Hessian soldiers as barracks, and occasionally as a hospital."—*An Account of the New York Hospital.*

NOTE 128, PAGE 209. PERSON IN POWER.—Efforts to discover the author of the sage remark quoted in the text have proved unavailing.

NOTE 129, PAGE 209. GREENWOMEN.—This word does not appear in any of the early Dictionaries of the language. It was applied to the women who sold greens and vegetables.

NOTE 130, PAGE 209. THE ALMS HOUSE.—"Certain persons of humanity and opulence, in 1774, presented a well-written petition to Robert Lurting, Esq., the Mayor, and to the Corporation, on the utility of erecting a good and substantial building for the reception of various classes of poor, and as a house of correction. Whereupon Messrs. Roome, Bayard, Pell, and Burger, who were Aldermen, with three other gentlemen, were appointed a Committee to fix upon a suitable piece of ground, and to purchase materials for the purpose. They eventually chose a spot then called the *Vineyard;* the very place on which now stands the City Hall. The house was erected; was sixty-five feet by twenty-four, two stories high, with good cellar apartments. . . . When the war commenced between England and America, in the year 1776, it became necessary to remove the poor, first to Westchester and afterwards to Poughkeepsie, under the charge of Mr. John Forbes. During the war, however, the poor and refractory were received into the Alms House, then under the care of Mr. William Littlewood; who was permitted to draw King's rations for nine months to support the poor. . . . . In consequence of the destructive fire which took place in the city on the 21st September, 1776, three hundred destitute persons were received into this institution."—*John Stanford's Sketch, in Valentine's Manual,* 1862, p. 658.

NOTE 131, PAGE 209. PRICES OF CARTMEN.—"*Cartmen's Rates.* By order of the Commandant. The following Rates for Cartmen being recommended by the *Chamber of Commerce,* are to take place from and after Monday, the 20th inst., viz.:

"For Loading, Carting, and unloading Fire-wood and every other common Load, to any place within this city, *Two Shillings.* For a Load of Hay, *Six Shillings.* For every Hogshead of Rum, Sugar, Melasses, and for every Pipe of Wine or other Strong Liquors, *Four Shillings.* For a Hogshead of Tobacco, *Three Shillings.* For a Load of Coal, containing one-third of a Chaldron, *Three Shillings.* For a Whole-Shot Cable, 12 inches circumference, or upwards, *Fifteen Shillings;* under 12 and above 7 inches,

Ten Shillings; seven inches and under, *Seven Shillings and Sixpence;* Half-Shot one third of the Whole-Shot. The above Rates are to be paid for Carting to any Place within this City, not exceeding One Mile, and in the same Proportion for a greater Distance. Any Cartman demanding or receiving, on and after the 20th day of this Month, a greater Price for Carting a load than the Prices settled by the above rates, or refusing to take up the first Load that is offered him on the Stand, shall, upon Proof being made before the Police, forfeit FORTY SHILLINGS for every such offence, one Half to the Informer, the other Half to the City Alms House. Any Person after that Day who shall be discovered acting as a City Cartman, without having obtained a License agreeable to former Orders, and the Number of his License marked in a conspicuous manner, with red Paint, upon each side of his Cart, will be confined and punished for a Breach of Orders. Office of Police, Sept. 16, 1779. ANDREW ELLIOT, Superintendant General. DAVID MATHEWS, Mayor. PETER DUBOIS, Magistrate of Police."—*Gaine's New York Gazette or Weekly Mercury*, September 20, 1779.

NOTE 132, PAGE 209. FORTY TO ONE HUNDRED SHILLINGS.—This amount in New York currency was the equivalent of twenty-four to sixty shillings sterling, *i. e.*, from five to twelve dollars gold in modern computation. This is on the basis of the Tables of Reduction published in *Gaine's Universal Register* for 1779, p. 106.

NOTE 133, PAGE 209. OLD LAWS CONCERNING CARTMEN.—The first regulation on this subject was the PROCLAMATION of Major-General JAMES ROBERTSON, Commandant in New York, issued 29th December, 1777, the Preamble of which reads: "*Whereas*, it has been represented to me that the Inhabitants of this City are daily suffering great Inconveniences, as well from the Irregularity of the public Cartmen thereof in declining, under various Pretences, carting for the Inhabitants, when required, as by the exorbitant and increasing demands which they insist on receiving for their services: For correcting all such Abuses for the future, I do hereby establish the following REGULATIONS: *First*—That no Cartman be allowed to cart without first obtaining a Licence from me for that Purpose, (which will be given out to him gratis), and having the number put upon his cart. *Secondly*—That no Cartman, upon the Request of any Person or Persons, shall refuse, decline, or neglect, upon any improper or false Pretence or Excuses whatsoever, to carry from or to any part of the City of New York, any Load or Loads of any kind whatever. *Thirdly*—That the Fare of the said Cartmen shall be as follows." (Here follow the regulations.)—*Gaine's New York Gazette and Weekly Mercury*, Jan. 5, 1778.

The Rates of which the Chamber complained were established later in the year by military authority.

"*By order of the Commandant*, the following rates are established for Carting, to take place from and after the Tenth day of this instant, December, viz.: For loading, carting and unloading Firewood, and every other common load, to any place within this city, not exceeding one mile, *Three Shillings*. For carting Firewood, or any other common load to any further distance, after the same rate. For every load of Hay, *Eight Shillings*. For every Hogshead of Rum or Molasses, *Six Shillings*; and in the same proportion for Tierces or Barrels. For every Hogshead of Sugar, *Six Shillings;* for Tierces or Barrels in the same proportion. For every Hogshead of Tobacco, *Four Shillings*. For every Load of Coals, consisting of one-third of a chaldron, *Three Shillings*. For every Cable, whole shot, of five inches circumference to seven inches, *Ten Shillings*. For every cable, half shot, of like dimensions, *Six Shillings*. For every cable, whole shot, upwards of seven inches circumference to ten inches, *Twelve Shillings*. For every cable, half shot, of like dimensions, *Eight Shillings*. For every cable, whole shot, upwards of ten inches circumference, *Twenty Shillings*. For every cable, half shot, of like dimensions, *Twelve Shillings*. Any Cartman demanding, or receiving, on or after the Tenth day of this Month, a greater price for carting a load than the price settled by the above rates, shall, upon proof being made before the Police, forfeit FORTY SHILLINGS for every such offence, one-half to the informer, the other half to the City Alms House. All persons that in future intend acting as City Cartmen, are desired, before the Twentieth day of this month, to give in their names at the Police Office, where they will receive Licences gratis. Any person after that day, who shall be discovered acting as City Cartman, without having obtained such a License, and the number of his Licence marked with red paint upon each side of his cart, will be taken into custody. Superintendant General's Office, New York, December 7, 1778. ANDREW ELLIOT, Superintendant General. DAVID MATHEWS, Mayor. PETER DUBOIS, Magistrate of Police."—*Gaine's New York Gazette*, Dec. 14, 1778.

NOTE 134, PAGE 210. THE OLD INSURANCE OFFICE.—The names of the Gentlemen of the Old Insurance Office who advised the Superintendent in 1778 as to the proper rate for Cartmen's Wages are not recorded. This was of course a Marine Office. There was no Fire Office in New York until after the Revolutionary War.

As early as 1759 there was an Office of Insurance known by this name. An advertisement in that year, the first in the New York Journals, reads: "The OLD INSURANCE OFFICE is kept at the Coffee House as usual; where all Risques whatsoever are underwrote at very moderate Premiums, and due attendance given from Twelve to one and from six to eight by KETELTAS & SHARPE, Clerks of the Office."—*Gaine's New York Mercury*, November 5th, 1759.

They had been directed to the advertising of their office perhaps by the appearance, a few months previous, of a new and rival office—" *The New York Insurance Office* is opened at the house of the Widow Smith, adjoining the Merchants' Coffee House, where all risks are underwrote at moderate premiums. Constant attendance will be given from the hours of eleven to one, and from six to eight in the evening, by ANTHONY VAN DAM, Clerk of the Office."—*Gaine's New York Mercury*, August 27th, 1759.

A third was announced during the war. " *The New Insurance Office* is opened at the Merchants' Coffee House, where attendance is given from twelve to two o'clock in the day, and from seven to nine o'clock in the evening, by WILLIAM BRANTHWAITE, Broker."—*Gaine's New York Gazette*, July 6th, 1778.

The *New York Insurance Office*, which appears to have been closed, again opened its doors.

" The *New York Insurance Office* is again opened at the Coffee House, where the Underwriters will attend from twelve to two o'clock at noon and from six to eight in the evening. It is requested that those who want insurance will apply at office hours."—*Gaine's New York Gazette*, Sept. 8, 1777.

A further advertisement shows that these offices were the resort of underwriters only, and not established companies, where all interested participated in the risks, losses, and profits, as under the modern systems. Indeed, the application of the mutual or company systems in the city dates from a period subsequent to the War.

"CUNNINGHAM & WARDROP, Having annexed to their Business that of *Insurance Brokers*, beg leave to inform their friends they have opened a PUBLIC INSURANCE OFFICE.

"Where *Policies* are received and offered to the merchants and underwriters of the City in general.

"The benefits which will in all probability result to the Commercial Interests of the place from such an Institution are obvious, and they flatter themselves with meeting with favour and encouragement from the Public in general. December 17, 1779."—*Rivington's Royal Gazette*, December 29, 1779.

NOTE 135, PAGE 211. STORING GUN-POWDER AFLOAT.—In the preamble to an ordinance passed "for the better securing of the City of New York from the Dangers of Gun-powder," it is recited that "the Corporation of this City of New York, in order to secure the said City and the inhabitants thereof from the Danger they were exposed to by large Quantities of Gun-Powder being kept in Houses, Shops and Stores, did erect and build a suitable and convenient Magazine, or Powder House, on an Island in the Fresh Water of this City, for the Receipt of all the Gun-Powder which was or should be imported into the said City."—*Holt's Corporation Ordinances*, 1763, p. 39.

This island was in the Little Collect, a part of the Collect Pond about where Duane and Centre Streets now cross each other. On the breaking out of war and the large increase of Powder at this central point, a change became necessary, and it was removed to a Powder ship. For many years afterwards this plan was continued. The site of the Powder House was too near the line of city fortification for safety.

NOTE 136, PAGE 212. MRS. SMITH AT THE COFFEE HOUSE.—No notice of Mrs. Smith as keeper of the Merchants' Coffee House appears in the newspapers. That this was the Coffee House in question is evident from a reference to the resolution with regard to the new engagement of the Chamber with Mr. Strachan, who hired the *Merchants' Coffee House*, May 1, 1781 (*see Page* 251 *and Note* 175). There was in 1759 a Widow Smith who kept a house "adjoining the Coffee House where the NEW YORK INSURANCE OFFICE was opened in August of that year" (*see Note* 134), as may be seen by the Advertisement of Anthony Van Dam, Secretary, in *Gaine's N. Y. Mercury*, Aug. 27, 1759.

NOTE 137, PAGE 214. PRICES OF ARTIFICERS.—In a letter from the journeymen to the master-printers of New York, asking for an increase of three dollars to their weekly wages, a statement is made as to the prices of the day. "There is scarcely a common laborer but gets a dollar per day and provisions, and the lowest mechanicks from 12 to 16*s*. per day."—*Rivington's Royal Gazette*, Nov. 14th, 1778.

NOTE 138, PAGE 217. ABSENCE OF MR. JOHN ALSOP.—Mr. Alsop, who was chosen First Vice-President of the Chamber, 2 May, 1775, (p. 202) was a member of the First and Second Continental Congress. On the passage of the Declaration of Independence he resigned his seat, and withdrew to Middletown, Connecticut. He did not return to New York until after the evacuation by the British in 1783.

NOTE 139, PAGE 223. VENDUE MASTER.—These officers were licensed in conformity with an order issued in 1779.

"*By order of the Commandant.* From and after the 20th of this month, no person or persons will be allowed to act as Vendue-Masters for the sale of any kind of goods at Public Auction, but such as shall receive a licence from the Officers of the Police for that purpose, before whom the person applying for a licence must take an oath not to be concerned in any collusive sales, in order to raise the price of any article of trade or provisions ; and, at the same time, must give approved security in the sum of FIVE THOUSAND POUNDS, New York currency, for the faithful execution of their duty, as well as for the security of their employers. In all cases where it may be necessary to have proof by whose orders any parcel or piece of goods were sold at Vendue, the proof to lay with the Vendue-Master who sold such goods ; if he fails in this, to forfeit his licence. All damaged goods to be sold as such, otherwise the purchaser will not be obliged to take them. Shipping and other materials, naval stores, prize goods, provisions and liquors of all sorts, cabinet ware, and the effects of strangers deceased, may be sold on the wharf, or near the Coffee-House Bridge by the licensed Vendue-Masters. Dry-goods, and all other goods that do not come under the above denominations, when intended for public Vendue, are only to be sold in Auction Rooms provided by the licensed Vendue-Masters for that purpose. Permission will be granted to any of the licensed Vendue-Masters when required for the disposing of household furniture at private houses. For the more ready discovery of any person or persons that may attempt acting contrary to this rule, all licenced Vendue-Masters are desired to fix over the door of their Auction Rooms, ——'s LICENCED AUCTION ROOM, and to advertise in the newspapers their street and number of the house. New York, January 12, 1779. ANDREW ELLIOT, Superintendant General. DAVID MATHEWS, Mayor. PETER DUBOIS, Magistrate of Police."—*Gaine's New York Gazette*, Jan. 18, 1779.

NOTE 140, PAGE 224. LIGHTNING CONDUCTOR on the Powder Ship.—The cause of the alarm felt by the Chamber may be traced to the fearful explosion of a Powder-Ship two years previous. This explosion took place a few days after the Great Fire of 1778.

The following accounts were published in the papers of the day : "Yesterday about one o'clock a flash of lightning struck a magazine of damaged powder on board the Ordnance Sloop *Morning Star*, lying in the East River, which occasioned the most awful explosion ever perceived in New York, where most of the houses received very great damage. It had an effect similar to that of an earthquake, and occasioned a tremendous alarm to every resident in the city."—*Rivington's Royal Gazette*, Wednesday, August 5, 1778.

"Last Tuesday afternoon, about one o'Clock, during a heavy Rain, accompanied with Thunder, the Lightning struck the Ordnance Sloop *Morning Star*, lying off the Coffee House in the East River, with 248 Barrels of Gun-Powder on board ; it produced a most tremendous Explosion. A Number of Houses were unroofed, many Windows broke, and some Furniture demolished by the Blast ; the Effects of which were similar to an Earthquake. Happily there was only one Man in the Vessel when the Accident happened. —*Gaine's N. Y. Gazette and Weekly Mercury*, Monday, August 10, 1778.

The invention of Lightning Rods was at this time comparatively recent. "It was in the Spring of 1752 that Franklin thought of trying the experiment with a kite ; and it was during one of the severe thunder-storms of that year that the immortal kite was flown. In Poor Richard's Almanac for 1753, appeared a notice of 'How to secure Houses, &c., from Lightning.'" —*Parton's Franklin*, 1, 289–297.

NOTE 141, PAGE 224. WALLOON BAY.—This is the well-known Wallabout, where the United States Navy Yard is now situated (Brooklyn, N. Y.). The name of Walloon is said to be derived from the early settlement of the *Walloons* at this point.

NOTE 142, PAGE 226. PRICE OF BREAD.—The first Regulation of the Military Authorities as to the price of Bread was made January 10th, 1777, shortly after the capture of the City: "*Whereas* many complaints are made by the Inhabitants that BREAD is become extravagantly high, either from the Exactions of Bakers or Forestallers, it is become necessary to renew a mode that was formerly followed in this place, of fixing an Assize. The Price of the best Flour being now Thirty shillings the Hundred, and that of Fuel and Labour considerably increased, I find that it is the Opinion of the most respectable Inhabitants that a Loaf of Bread of the finest Flour, weighing *Three Pounds Four Ounces*, should be sold for *Fourteen Coppers*, and in the same Proportion for Loaves of a lesser Weight. Any Person who exacts more will be taken into Custody and the Bread in their Possession will be given to the Poor." JAMES ROBERTSON.—*Gaine's New York Gazette*, January 13, 1777.

During the war there were occasional Variations, and necessity arose for changes in the Regulations. On the 22d of January, 1779, a second rule was issued, on this occasion from the "Office of Police":—"Assize of Bread. *Two Pounds for Twenty-one Coppers.* Public Notice is hereby given, that from and after the first day of February next, all the Bakers in this City are to make their Loaves of *Two Pounds Weight*, and that no Baker or Retailer of Bread shall, from and after that date ask, demand, or receive any more or greater sum than *Twenty-one Coppers* for each such Loaf weighing *Two Pounds;* and that from and after the first day of February next, every Baker within this City shall put a mark with the initial letters of his Christian name and surname upon the Loaf-Bread he shall expose to sale, and shall make his Bread Good, and according to the aforesaid Assize, under penalty of forfeiting all such Bread as shall be defective in Quality or deficient in Weight, to the Alms-house in this city; and any person who shall ask, demand or receive any more or greater sum for a Loaf of Bread weighing Two Pounds, shall, for every such offence, forfeit the sum of Five Pounds to be applied to the use of the Poor of this City. The Weight of all Loaves being fixed at Two Pounds, it is intended for the convenience of the Poor, and to avoid fractions in the Weight, which rendered detections of fraud in the assize more difficult.—ANDREW ELLIOT, Superintendent-General. D. MATHEWS, Mayor. PETER DUBOIS, Magistrate of Police."—*Gaine's New York Gazette*, January 25, 1779.

On the 7th July, 1779, an order was issued by the same Magistrate: "All loaf Bread to weigh Two Pound each loaf for *fourteen* coppers each."—*Gaine's New York Gazette*, July 12, 1779.

On the 18th February, 1780, they announce "the Assize of Bread is to continue at *Two Pounds* each Loaf, but the Price of each Loaf is to be *Fifteen Coppers*."—*Gaine's New York Gazette*, February 21, 1780.

On the 15th of March, 1780, they directed that "all Bread made of Flour of the first Quality must be baked into *Long Loaves* of Two Pounds each, stamped with the Initials of the Baker's name, and sold for Fourteen Coppers each Loaf. And all Bread made of merchantable Flour of an inferior Quality must be baked into Sound Loaves weighing Two Pounds and one-half each, stamped with the Initials of the Baker's name, and sold for *Fourteen Coppers* each Loaf."—*Rivington's Royal Gazette*, March 18, 1780.

On the 20th November, 1780, they order "that all Bread made of wheat flour of the first Quality must be baked into *Long Loaves* of Two Pounds' weight each, and stamped with the Initials of the Baker's name, and sold for *Sixteen Coppers* each Loaf." (Bread of the second quality in proportion as before.)—*Gaine's New York Gazette*, November 27, 1780.

On the 11th January, 1782, the Loaves are ordered to be of Two Pounds and one quarter Weight each, and sold at *Fourteen Coppers.—Rivington's Royal Gazette*, January 12, 1782.

On the 6th May, 1783, appeared the last order, that the Loaves be of *Three Pounds'* Weight, and sold for *Fourteen Coppers.—Rivington's Royal Gazette*, May 7, 1783.

NOTE 143, PAGE 226. INSPECTOR OF BREAD.—The recommendation of the Chamber, that a Public Inspector of Bread be appointed, was immediately adopted.

On the 15th March an order was issued with certain regulations, and announcing that "In order that the above Regulations may be duly enforced, JERONIMUS ALSTYNE is appointed *Inspector of Bread*, with directions and powers constantly to visit the several Bake-Houses in the City, and to make Seizure of all such Bread as he may find deficient either in the above-mentioned Qualities, Weight or Stamp."—*Gaine's N. Y. Gazette*, March 27, 1780.

On the 11th January, 1782, BALTHAZAR CREAMER was appointed *Inspector of Bread.*

NOTE 144, PAGE 227. VALUE OF COINS.—On the 30th April, 1777, Sir WILLIAM HOWE, Commander-in-Chief, issued the following PROCLAMATION: "*Whereas* many Inconveniences arise from Merchants and others in this City, charging their Goods and Wares, in sterling Money instead of Currency of the Province, I have therefore thought fit to issue this Proclamation, hereby strictly charging and commanding that the Prices asked for all Goods, Wares, Merchandises and Provisions, hereafter to be sold in this City shall be in Currency agreeable, to the following rates: *A Guinea* weighing 5 Pennyweight 7 Grains, one Pound, Seventeen Shillings and Four Pence; *A Half Johannes*, 9 Pennyweight 3 Grains, Three Pounds 4 Shillings: *a Moidore*, 6 Pennyweight 22 Grains, two Pounds Eight Shillings; *a Spanish milled Dollar*, Eight Shillings; *an English Shilling*, One Shilling and Nine Pence; of which all persons are to take notice and govern themselves under pain of Military Execution."—*Gaine's N. Y. Gazette*, May 12, 1777.

The contracts for Sterling alluded to in the text were, in the opinion of the Chamber, to be settled for in Coin. The advance over the value of the Coin in Great Britain was the ordinary premium on Specie; the Exchange does not enter into the question. Such is essentially the practice at the present day: the seller requires the Sterling money or its equivalent.

NOTE 145, PAGE 229. LETTER FROM THE SUPERINTENDENT.—ANDREW ELLIOT, afterwards Lieut. Governor, held the office of Superintendent of Police at this time. No mention is to be found of the letter here alluded to.

NOTE 146, PAGE 229. LETTER FROM GENERAL ROBERTSON.—General Robertson arrived in New York from England by way of Savannah on the 23d March, 1780—"And was inducted into the office of the Governor of the Province of New York on the 27th." He at once set about his duties. The Letter here referred to does not appear in any of the newspapers. It seems to have been addressed to the Superintendent of Police.

If addressed to the Chamber, it would have been formally acknowledged in their Letter of 2d May, 1780.

NOTE 147, PAGE 229. ENCOURAGEMENT TO PRIVATEERS.—In the early days of the war the British authorities had shown great unwillingness to encourage private ships of war. Their hope was then to restore good feeling between the Home Government and the Colonies. This was made a strong charge against Lord Viscount Howe on his return to England. One of the private pamphlets printed to show the (supposed) weakness of his rule has these striking passages :

"You suffered the rebel merchants to carry on a constant and extensive trade with all their ports, and even from Egg Harbor, within twenty leagues of your head-quarters. And when the Loyalists at New York, enraged at your inactivity, and the losses they daily sustained, offered to destroy the Rebel Ships in that port, provided you would give them permission with a small share of your assistance, they were not obtained. In short, my Lord, you suffered the Rebels to import whatever was necessary to relieve their distress, and to support that Rebellion you were sent to suppress. . . . The Rebels were continually fitting out privateers in almost all their ports. These were constantly intercepting the British merchandise in the European as well as the American seas. In consequence of these in the month of April, 1777, authority from the Admiralty was sent over to his Majesty's loyal subjects for the like commission against the people in rebellion. . . . . . . Many (of the Loyalists) applied to the Governors for their commissions, and many privateers would have been immediately fitted up could they have been obtained. But through your *influence and interference these commissions were refused.* . . . . . . The reason and the only reason assigned is an apprehension in your Lordship that the *privateers* would take from the fleet under your command the seamen necessary to fight and navigate. . . . . . . Nothing, therefore, was necessary to remove this objection but a Proclamation prohibiting the Captains of privateers from taking British seamen. . . . . . . Since his Lordship's resignation the Rebel Navy has been in a great measure destroyed by the small British force remaining in America, and the privateers sent out from New York. Their navy, which consisted at the time of his Lordship's departure of thirty vessels, is now reduced to eight. And the number of privateers fitted out in New England amounting to one hundred and upwards, is now less than forty ; the prices of all foreign necessaries and articles of commerce are raised more than 200 per cent., exclusive of the depreciation of their money. And so great is the risk of their trade that no insurance can be procured in America."—*Letter to Lord Viscount H——e on his naval conduct in America*, signed by "*The Friend of your Country*." London, 1779.

These and similar representations had their effect in England.

Governor Tryon's views were plainly set forth in a letter to Vice-Admiral Arbuthnot, dated 29th June, 1779, in which he expresses his "wish for some early and explicit declaration in support of the public faith pledged by Admiral Gambier (and himself)." He states the crews commissioned from this port to amount to upwards of six thousand men ; and he complained that the "Proclamation of Sir George Collier, of the 13th instant, however well intended or proper for the prevention of Desertion from the King's Ships, cannot fail of damping the ardour of the Merchants and Adventurers."—*N. Y. Col. Doc.* viii. 772.

In what mode General Robertson proposed to aid this already flourishing business does not appear. He probably relieved the ships from the effect of the Proclamation of Admiral Arbuthnot, issued Sept. 14, 1779, giving notice of impressment on board privateers and merchant vessels of an equivalent for all deserters from the British fleet. The last appearance of this advertisement was on the 22d April, 1780, in *Rivington's Royal Gazette.* Governor Robertson's first Proclamation was issued on the 15th of the same month.

NOTE 148, PAGE 230. DRAFTS OF LETTERS TO AND FROM GENERAL ROBERTSON.—These letters, the entry of which on the minutes had been previously omitted, were recorded thereon in February, 1867, by the Editor (the Secretary of the Chamber). They were found in *Rivington's Royal Gazette* for Saturday, 13th May, 1780, and in *Hugh Gaine's New York Gazette and Weekly Mercury* for Monday, 15th May, 1780.

NOTE 149, PAGE 232. THE CARTERET PACKET.—On Wednesday (May 24) arrived the CARTERET PACQUET, Capt. Newman, in about forty days from Falmouth.—*Rivington's Royal Gazette* for Saturday, May 27, 1780.

"PUBLICK AUCTION.—This Day, will be sold at the Coffee House, the Ship CARTERET, packet, Burthen about 230 tons, copper bottomed. As she now lies Stranded near Jones's Inlet, on the South side of Long Island, with all her materials on board, and those brought on shore, consisting of anchors, cables, sails, standing and running rigging, guns, provisions, &c., &c., &c. Inventory to be seen with DANIEL MCCORMICK."—*Gaine's New York Gazette,* June 5, 1780.

"TO BE SOLD AT PRIVATE SALE, All the Stores and Materials lately belonging to the Ship CARTERET PACKET, consisting of cables, anchors, sails, standing and running rigging, masts, spars, pumps, a complete six-oar'd cutter, 24 feet long, and a new yawl; also, six pair double fortified six-pounders, and two pair of four-pounders, with carriages, breechings, tacklings, rammers and spunges, and a quantity of shot. Enquire of No. 1, Mill Street."—*Rivington's Royal Gazette,* July 5, 1780.

"ON MONDAY NEXT, X o'clock, on the Dock below the Coffee House, will be Sold by Templeton and Stewart, all the Stores and Materials lately belonging to the Ship CARTERET Packet, &c., &c." (the notice similar in other respects to the preceding).—*Rivington's Royal Gazette* for Saturday, July 8, 1780.

No account appeared in New York of the attack upon the CARTERET except in the resolution of the Chamber.

The following account appeared in the American papers: "Providence, May 27, 1780.—We learn that four privateers, three of them belonging to New London, on Wednesday last (May 24), drove a copper-bottomed ship ashore on Long Island Beach, 6 miles from Sandy Hook; she mounted 22 nine-pounders, and by some papers found on board proved to be the London Packet from Falmouth, which place she left the 15th of April. Her crew, 55 in number, escaped with the mail. . . . Some valuable effects were taken from on board the packet, but a fleet from New York heaving in sight and some frigates standing for the privateers, they were obliged to leave her."—*Pennsylvania Packet,* June 13, 1780.

The next year Captain Newman again appears as the Commander of a *Carteret Packet;* whether the old stranded ship saved and repaired, or a new one, does not appear. She is noticed as having arrived from Falmouth, and as being at Staten Island June 26, 1781.—*Rivington's Royal Gazette,* June 30, 1781.

NOTE 150, PAGE 232. PRIVATEERS OFF LONG ISLAND.—At this time the American privateers were extremely bold and successful. The

French occupation of Newport had called away many British cruisers from the station. A short time after the running ashore of the Carteret, the Mercury Packet, Captain Dillon, was captured and taken into Philadelphia, and the cutter of the Hon. Major Cochrane was attacked a small distance from the Hook.—*Gaine's New York Gazette and Weekly Mercury*, August 21st, 1780.

Another instance will serve to show the audacity of these adventurous men. "*Extract from the Log-Book of the Sloop Comet, Captain Kemp.*— The 7th of June last, being in company with the sloop Hawk, Capt. Humpstead, was chased by the Iris and escaped. On the 9th, making the east end of Long Island, saw a wreck ashore; out boat with an armed party; went ashore. Took possession of a battery of 10 guns, from which the men had fled on seeing the boat going ashore; found the wreck to be the Hawk, which the Iris had drove ashore, her materials being partly carried off by the inhabitants of Long Island, who had erected the battery; took off two of her guns, spiked the rest; took an anchor and cable, with several other articles. On the 12th, at half-past four A.M., about two miles off Sandy Hook, got in shore of 15 sail, out of which number we captured and manned eight, viz.: schooners Free Mason, Lilly, and Sally; sloops Polly, Driver, Dove, Elizabeth, and Elizabeth, all of which Captain Kemp brought safe to port on the 16th, with twenty-eight prisoners." —*Pennsylvania Packet, Philadelphia*, June 24th, 1780.

NOTE 151, PAGE 233. CAPTAIN NEWMAN'S ESCAPE IN HIS BOAT.—The following account of the escape of Captain Newman was published in a London paper of August 12th, 1780. "By a brig which is put into Lisbon from New York, we are informed that His Majesty's packet-boat the Cartwright, Capt. Newman, with the mail on board from Falmouth, was on the 16th of June chased by three American privateers, and run on shore at Sandy Hook; but Captain Newman, ordering his men to hoist out his boat immediately, which they did, got the mail on board the boat, after which they rowed away, and the privateers kept chasing them for several leagues, firing all the time, but Capt. Newman had the good luck to escape to New York."—*Upcott Collection of Newspaper Cuttings, N. Y. Hist. Soc.*, vol. vi. p. 27.

NOTE 152, PAGE 233. POST OFFICE (1780).—The Post Office was at this time in Broad Street, as appears from the following advertisements, and there it remained till the close of the war.

"RUN AWAY, a Negro Wench named HAGER, about 18 years of age, born in this town; she is about five feet high, had on a white drilling short gown and green petticoat. Whoever brings her to the *General Post Office in Broad Street*, or gives intelligence where she may be found, shall be handsomely rewarded. She is supposed to have gone on board the fleet." —*Rivington's Royal Gazette* (No. 270), May 1st, 1779.

"PAPER HANGINGS.—A very elegant assortment of plain and printed, from 4 to 16*s.* per piece, may be had at the Paper Hanging Manufactory, *No.* 23 *Broad Street, nearly opposite the Post Office*," &c. &c.—*Gaine's New York Gazette and Weekly Mercury* (No. 1542), May 7th, 1781.

"TO BE SOLD, and possession given the first of May next, a two-story brick house, No. 17 *Broad Street* opposite the *General Post Office*, &c.—*Gaine's New York Gazette and Weekly Mercury* (No. 1643), April 14th, 1783.

NOTE 153, PAGE 234. PUBLICATION OF VOTE OF THANKS. —The Vote of Thanks to Captain Newman, together with his reply, was published in *Rivington's Royal Gazette*, July 5th, 1780, and *Gaine's New York Gazette and Weekly Mercury*, July 10th, 1780.

NOTE 154, PAGE 236. EMBARGO ON SHIPPING.—This Embargo does not appear in the newspapers. It was no doubt a practical embargo enforced by the fleet of Admiral ARBUTHNOT. The British officers had great difficulty in keeping their men. Desertions were constant, and recapture rare. On assuming command of the ships on the station, Admiral ARBUTHNOT issued a Proclamation from on board the *Russel* off New York, September 14th, 1779, declaring, "that in future, for every seaman or seafaring man that may desert from the King's ships or transports here, I will press, man for man, out of the privateers and merchant vessels." This continued as a standing Proclamation, and appears in all the newspapers.—*Supplement to Gaine's New York Gazette*, March 6th, 1780.

NOTE 155, PAGE 236. MEMORIAL TO THE COMMANDER IN CHIEF.—No copy of this paper is to be found in any of the journals of the time. Sir HENRY CLINTON held the title of "General and Commander in Chief of all His Majesty's Forces within the Colonies lying on the Atlantic Ocean from Nova Scotia to West Florida, inclusive." He and MARRIOTT ARBUTHNOT, Vice Admiral of the Blue, Commander in Chief of His Majesty's Ships in North America, were "His Majesty's Commissioners to restore Peace and Good Government in the several Colonies in Rebellion in North America."

Sir Henry Clinton returned to New York on the 17th June from the expedition to the Carolinas, which resulted in the reduction of Charleston. —*Gaine's New York Gazette*, June 19th, 1780.

The Admiral was with the squadron off Rhode Island which had recently been taken possession of by the French fleet under Admiral Tiernay. —*Rivington's Royal Gazette*, August 2d, 1780.

The Commander in Chief addressed the Admiral at this port in the letter alluded to (*page* 237).

NOTE 156, PAGE 237. LETTER FROM SUPERINTENDENT-GENERAL.—No copy of this letter anywhere appears. The post of Superintendent General of Police was held by ANDREW ELLIOT. The trade of the City was all carried on under permits from this office, in accordance with the Proclamation of Sir William Howe of July 7th, 1777.

NOTE 157, PAGE 237. MERCHANTS' READINESS TO SUPPLY SEAMEN.—On the two occasions which were critical in the affairs of the British fleet, the presence of the French squadron at Newport in the fall of 1780 and the dangerous position of Cornwallis in 1781, those merchants, who were still loyal to the Crown, came forward to the aid of the British Commanders.

NOTE 158, PAGE 237. LETTER FROM THE COMMANDANT. —There is nothing to show what was the purport of this communication. It nowhere appears. The Commandant at this time was Major General DANIEL JONES.

NOTE 159, PAGE 238. THE PRIVATEER AUCTIONEER.—A well-known cruiser. "The schooner *Auctioneer*, Captain Joseph Nash, intends sailing on a Cruise on Wednesday next. The Owners and Officers would wish such Commanders as have men missing from His Majesty's service to send on board and examine the Crew.

"N.B.—Those who have any demands on the outfit of said Schooner are desired to send their Accounts, to be paid before she sails, to Barrach Hays and Tertulos Dickenson."—*Gaine's New York Gazette*, February 22d, 1779.

In the list of vessels commissioned as letters of marque, published in 1779, SAMUEL ROGERS appears as the captain of the privateer *Mars* of 16 guns.—*Gaine's New York Gazette*, March 22d, 1779.

NOTE 160, PAGE 239. THE POLICE.—The Police here referred to had the entire government of the city in civil affairs. By a notice issued April 28th, 1779, "the business of the Commandant in civil matters" was transacted at the OFFICE OF POLICE.—*Gaine's New York Gazette*, May 3d, 1779.

NOTE 161, PAGE 247. THE SNOW FRIENDSHIP.—This name for a vessel, which sounds strangely to modern ears, was quite common in the last century.

"A vessel equipped with two masts resembling the main and foremasts of a ship, and a third small mast just abaft the mainmast carrying a trysail."—*Marine Dictionary*.

NOTE 162, PAGE 247. COLLECTOR OF CUSTOMS.—On the death of ARCHIBALD KENNEDY, Collector of the Port of New York, ANDREW ELLIOT was appointed to that office. His Commission was dated January 19th, 1764. He held the post till the close of the War.—*N. Y. Col. Doc.* viii. 96.

NOTE 163, PAGE 247. ACT OF PARLIAMENT.—This Act was put in force by General CLINTON. "PROCLAMATION.—In pursuance of an Act made and passed in the twentieth year of His Majesty's reign entitled, 'An Act to allow the exportation of provisions, goods, wares and merchandize from Great Britain, to certain towns, ports, or places in North America which are or may be under the protection of His Majesty's arms; and from such towns, ports or places to Great Britain and other parts of His Majesty's dominions,' I DO HEREBY appoint and authorize the officers who were appointed to superintend the imports and exports at New York, by his Excellency Sir WILLIAM HOWE, in his Proclamation issued 17th July, 1777, and who were afterwards continued in that duty by a Proclamation issued by his Majesty's Commissioners on the 26th of September, 1778; and who since the expiration of the Proclamation last mentioned, have acted under my authority to perform the duties required by the above-mentioned Act, agreeable to the limitations, restrictions, and regulations therein mentioned.

"And I do further appoint and authorize the officers who have under my authority superintended the imports and exports at Charleston, South Carolina, since its reduction, to perform at that place the duties required by the afore-mentioned Act, agreeable to the limitations, restrictions and regulations therein mentioned.

"All masters of trading vessels, merchants, traders and others, are hereby strictly commanded to pay due obedience to the Superintendents, and their officers at the above-mentioned ports in the execution of their duty, as they shall answer the contrary at their peril: And all officers, civil and military, are required to aid and assist them in every case, where the same shall be found necessary.

"The Superintendents, their Deputies, and all Persons acting under them at the above-mentioned ports, having their salaries appointed as a full compensation for the services required of them, no fees are to be offered on any account whatever.

"Given under my Hand, at Head-Quarters in New York, the 24th day of October, 1780. H. CLINTON."—*Gaine's New York Gazette*, October 30th, 1780.

NOTE 164, PAGE 248. EXPIRATION OF COMMISSIONERS' PROCLAMATION (OF 1778).—The PROCLAMATION issued by the EARL of CARLISLE, Sir HENRY CLINTON and Mr. WILLIAM EDEN, His Majesty's Commissioners at New York, 26th September, 1778 (see Notes 119, 120) suspending the Act of Parliament of 1776, "prohibiting all trade and intercourse with certain Colonies," declared that the new orders "should continue in force for three calendar months."—*Gaine's New York Gazette*, October 5th, 1778.

A few days before the departure for England of the Earl of Carlisle and Mr. Eden, upon the Petition of the merchants and Traders of the City (signed by William Walton, President), 14th November, 1778, the three Commissioners, under date 18th November, extended by a new Proclamation the privileges granted by the old, until the 1st of June, 1779.—*Gaine's New York Gazette*, November 23d, 1778.

A further renewal, under the signature of Sir Henry Clinton and Mr. Eden, on the 22d April, 1779, declared the regulations to be in force from the first day of June, 1779, to the first of December next ensuing (1779).—*Rivington's Royal Gazette*, September 29th, 1779.

NOTE 165, PAGE 248. ORDERS OF SIR HENRY CLINTON.—On the expiration of the last renewal of the Proclamation of the Commissioners authorizing trade, General CLINTON assumed the responsibility of continuing the privileges extended by it to the commerce of New York. In his Proclamation of Oct. 24, 1780, he says that "the officers appointed to superintend the imports and exports at New York, since the expiration of the Proclamation of the Commissioners have acted under *my authority*."—(*See Note* 163.)

After the departure of Carlisle and Eden, Sir HENRY CLINTON, Commander-in-Chief of the Army, and MARRIOTT ARBUTHNOT, Vice Admiral, were appointed the *King's Commissioners*, "to restore Peace and Liberty" to the revolted Colonies.

NOTE 166, PAGE 248. ADVERTISEMENT OF SUPERINTENDENT AS TO DUTIES.—"*Public Notice is hereby given*, That I am ordered to demand and receive Duties on Prize Goods and on all other Goods liable to Duties, imported under License, as also on all Goods liable to Duties imported into New York by Virtue of the Act passed in the last Session of Parliament. Of which all agents for prizes, merchants, and traders, are hereby required to take due notice, and govern themselves accordingly. The Duties will be received at the Superintendent's Office, No. 215 Water-Street, where attendance will be daily given for that purpose by ANDREW ELLIOT. New York, February 24, 1781."—*Rivington's Royal Gazette*, February 28, 1781.

A similar notice, dated 10th Sept., calling for all "Duties on Prizes condemned at the Port of New York since October, 1776," appeared in *Rivington's Royal Gazette*, September 18, 1778.

NOTE 167, PAGE 248. RESTORATION OF GEORGIA TO TRADE.—In the winter of 1775-6, the British Parliament passed an Act to prohibit all Trade and Intercourse with certain of the Colonies "during the continuance of the present Rebellion within the said Colonies respectively," of which Georgia was one.—*N. Y. Col. Doc.*, viii. 668.

After the fall of Charleston Sir HENRY CLINTON and Admiral ARBUTHNOT, "His Majesty's Commissioners to restore the Blessings of Peace and Liberty to the several Colonies in America," issued a Proclamation dated Charleston, 1st June, 1780, in which they declare "that as soon as the situation of the Province will admit the Inhabitants will be reinstated in the Possession of all those Rights and Immunities which they heretofore enjoyed under a free Government, exempt from Taxation, except by their own Legislature."—*Gaine's New York Gazette*, June 27, 1780.

"The Province of Georgia having been mostly reduced by the King's troops, civil government was re-established on the 4th March, 1779; and on the 13th of July following, Governor Wright and the other Crown Officers, who had taken refuge in England, returned to Georgia and entered anew upon the administration of their several offices."—*Stevens's History of Georgia*, ii. 185.

NOTE 168, PAGE 248. NEW YORK GARRISON.—The garrison at New York was at this time very large. It was determined by Washington "twelve months beforehand at all hazards to give out and cause it to be believed by the highest military as well as civil officers, that New York was the destined place of attack."—*Sparks's Washington*, ix. 403.

Washington's estimate of the force in New York at this time appears in a Letter of Instructions addressed from New Windsor to General Knox, 10th February, 1781: "In the conference between Count de Rochambeau and myself [held at Hartford, Sept. 21, 1780], it was agreed that if, with the aid of our allies, we can have a naval superiority through the next campaign, and an army of *thirty thousand men, or double the force of the enemy at New York and its dependencies*," &c., &c. This estimates the garrison at this period at *fifteen thousand* men.—*Sparks's Washington*, vii. p. 407.

NOTE 169, PAGE 248. DUTIES ON IMPORTS.—"Articles subject to Duty on Importation into any British American Plantation from Foreign Plantations:

"Wines from Madeira and the Western Islands, the Ton of 252 Gallons, £7 0*s.* 0*d.*; White or Clayed Sugars the 112 lb., £1 7*s.* 0*d.*; other Sugars the 112 lb., £0 5*s.* 0*d.*; Molasses the Gallon, £0 0*s.* 1*d.*; Coffee the 112 lb., £2 19*s.* 0*d.*; Indigo the Pound, £0 0*s.* 6*d.*'—*Gaine's Universal Register for* 1780.

NOTE 170, PAGE 248.—SUPPLY OF SUGAR DEPENDENT ON CAPTURES.—The West India Trade had been nearly broken up by Privateers, who were freed in a great measure from the molestation of the British cruisers engaged in watching the movements of the French Fleet.

NOTE 171, PAGE 249. CIRCUMSCRIBED SITUATION OF NEW YORK, Feb. 1781.—Outside of the British lines the country about New York was firmly held by the patriots. The American army had gone into quarters at the close of November, "The Pennsylvania line near Morristown, the New Jersey regiments at Pompton, and the eastern troops in the Highlands. The head-quarters of the Commander-in-Chief (Washington), were at New Windsor. The French army remained at Newport, except the

Duke de Lauzun's legion, which was cantoned at Lebanon, in Connecticut."—*Sparks's Washington*, i. 345.

Major General Heath commanded at West Point, and the militia of Ulster, Orange, and Dutchess were on the alert to cut off all supplies from the inland to the city. Skirmishes were constant between opposing forces in Westchester, and as near the British lines as Morrisania.—*Sparks's Washington*, vii. 427. *Heath's Memoirs*, 268–273.

NOTE 172, PAGE 249. MELASSES.—This spelling is of early date: though adopted by *Webster*, (who calls "*Molasses* an incorrect orthography of *Melasses*,") and certainly true to the derivation of the word, it has fallen into disuse. *Bailey's* Dictionary, edition of 1763, gives both varieties, while *Johnson* discards "*Melasses*," and quotes a variation of "*Molosses*," which is still more strange to modern ears.

NOTE 173, PAGE 249. CHARTER FOR NEW YORK CITY.—The action of the Chamber on this subject does not appear to have reached any conclusion.

The condition of affairs was not such in the fall of 1781, after the capture of Cornwallis, as to warrant any political changes. Concessions were too late at that period.

The present Charter was granted to the City on the 15th January, 1730, by Lieut. Governor John Montgomerie, in the reign of George the Second. It was amended in 1830, 1849, and 1857.—*Kent's Charter of New York*.

NOTE 174, PAGE 249. GOVERNOR OF THE COLONY.—"Tuesday night (22d March, 1780) arrived from England by way of Savannah, in Georgia, his Excellency *Major-General* (James) ROBERTSON, Governor of the Province of New York."

"On Thursday the Commission of General ROBERTSON was opened in the Presence of General Tryon and the Gentlemen of his Majesty's Council, when his Excellency took the oaths of Qualification, and was inducted into the office of Governor of the Province of New York; the General's Commission was afterwards read at the City Hall, and his Excellency there publicly proclaimed our Governor."—*Gaine's N. Y. Gazette and Weekly Mercury*, March 27, 1780.

He was succeeded by ANDREW ELLIOT in the spring of 1783.

NOTE 175, PAGE 251. MR. STRACHAN AT THE COFFEE HOUSE.—"JAMES STRACHAN, now at the *Queen's Head Tavern* on the Dock—Thanks the Gentlemen of the *Navy* and *Army*, also the Public in general for the great Regard shewn by them to his Interest since his Residence there; and informs them that on May Day next he intends to open business at the place well known by the name of the MERCHANTS' COFFEE HOUSE, where he intends to pay attention not only as a *Coffee House*, but as a *Tavern* in the truest sense; and to distinguish the same as the CITY TAVERN and COFFEE HOUSE. With constant and the best attendance. Breakfasts from seven to eleven. Soups and Relishes from eleven to half-past one. Public or private Dinners will be provided on the shortest Notice. Tea, Coffee, &c., in the afternoons as in England. The Viands and Liquors of every Quality will be as good as Town and Country can afford, and every Exertion made use of to give universal satisfaction. New York, April 27, 1781."—*Gaine's New York Gazette* for Monday, April 30, 1781.

A few days later he issues the same notice, except that he informs them "that, on Thursday last, being May Day, he opened Business at the place known as 'The MERCHANTS' COFFEE HOUSE.'"—*Rivington's Royal Gazette* for Wednesday, May 2, 1781.

NOTE 176, PAGE 254. DISTRESS OF BRITISH COMMERCE, (May, 1781.)—The American privateers, quiet during the winter, had again renewed their cruises, and with little interference, the English squadrons hesitating to separate, while the French fleets hung together awaiting an opportunity to strike a great blow in concert with the land-forces of the allies.

"The first Rebel Privateer that has appeared on our coast this Spring was the Schooner Eagle, Captain Hindman, belonging to the Province of North Carolina, but last from New London, of 8 guns and 20 men."—*Gaine's New York Gazette*, April 9, 1781.

"We learn that there are several stout Privateers now fitting out in the Eastern Ports, which we hear are intended to intercept the fleet from England, bound to Quebec, &c., &c., as they did some Time ago; but we hope that they will be disappointed, as we make no doubt whatever vessels may come out will have a proper Convoy." (The same paper gives the account of eight captures by New London privateers since 8th inst.)—*Gaine's New York Gazette*, April 30, 1781.

Governor Robertson, then in command at New York, writing on the 6th May, 1781, to Lord George Germaine, says that he hopes "soon to be able to revive the spirit of Privateering; the obstructions to this have given the Rebels but too many opportunities lately of carrying into their Ports many of our Ships, and great numbers of their own."—*N. Y. Col. Doc.* viii. 811.

NOTE 177, PAGE 256. PREMIUMS OF INSURANCE AT LONDON.—From the beginning of the war the rates of insurance had been very high. On the 17th February, 1778, the Duke of Richmond stated in Parliament "that the price of insurance, to the West Indies and North America, is increased from 'two, to two and one half to five per cent.' *with convoy*; but, without convoy and unarmed, the said insurance has been made at *fifteen per cent.* But generally ships under such circumstances cannot be insured at all."—*Annual Register for* 1778, page 127.

NOTE 178, PAGE 256. GARRISON AT GIBRALTAR.—Gibraltar was at this time besieged by land and sea by the French and Spanish forces. The advices of the abundant supplies of the Garrison referred to were the following: *London dispatches of December* 26, 1780, *received at New York by His Majesty's Sloop of War the Cormorant.* "This morning some dispatches were received from Gibraltar, which were brought over in the Neptune Frigate, arrived at Plymouth, by which we are informed that every Thing remained quiet; and that they had plenty of provisions."—*Gaine's New York Gazette*, April 23, 1781.

"The privates in Gibraltar receive fresh meat three times a week. Beef is at two pence a pound. An officer writes that the whole army and navy of the enemy can never put their Sovereign in possession of that fortress while there is provision for the garrison."—*Rivington's Royal Gazette*, April 25, 1781.

NOTE 179, PAGE 256. BLOCK ISLAND.—"This island lies in the open sea about 14 miles S.S.W. from Judith Point and 13 N.E. from Montauk Point, on Long Island, N. Y. It is about 8 miles in length and varies from 2 to 4 miles in width."—*Hayward's New England Gazetteer.*

NOTE 180, PAGE 256. SHREWSBURY BANKS.—"Shrewsbury River is a continuation of Sandy Hook Bay. This arm of the bay from the mouth of the Nevisink River is about 5 miles long with an average breadth of a mile and a half. It is separated from the Nevisink by a neck of land 2 miles wide."—*Gordon's Gazetteer of New Jersey.*

The Fisheries on the *Shrewsbury Banks* were a main source of supply to the New York market. During the war they were greatly interfered with by the patriot privateers.

NOTE 181, PAGE 256. GUN AND WHALE BOATS NEAR SHREWSBURY.—The Shrewsbury River was a favorite resort of the bold Captain Hyler and his Whaleboatmen. It was hardly to be expected that he would allow the Fishermen engaged in the supply of the New York market to go toll-free while he was attacking armed vessels. The following is one of many instances of his treatment. He seems neither to have allowed commutation nor to have granted passes, as was the habit of the Admiral on the station. "Last Tuesday night Mr. Hyler took two Fishing Boats near the Narrows and ransomed them for 100 dollars each: one of these Boats he has since captured."—*Gaine's New York Gazette,* July 15, 1782.

NOTE 182, PAGE 257. THE ROYAL OAK.—This vessel, well known in the history of the Revolutionary War, was a Frigate of 74 guns (1603 tons), built at Plymouth in 1769. At the close of the war (1784), she was sent to Portsmouth to repair. In 1797 she was fitted for a prison-ship, and stationed at Portsmouth.—*Exshaw's Register.*

The ROYAL OAK was the flag-ship of Admiral ARBUTHNOT. He was on board at Gardner's Bay, Feb. 1781, watching the French fleet (*Remembrancer* for 1782, p. 315), and also in the action off Cape Henry, with the French squadron under M. de Ternay on the 16th of March, 1781.—*Schomberg's Naval Chronology,* iv. 376.

NOTE 183, PAGE 257. THE KING'S SHIPS UNDER ADMIRAL ARBUTHNOT.—"The squadron that sailed from Spithead for North America under the command of Rear Admiral Arbuthnot, on the 1st of May, 1779.

"Ship *Europe,* 64 guns, Commander MARRIOT ARBUTHNOT, Rear Admiral of the *Blue,* Captain Ardesoife; *Robust* [74], Philips Cosby; *Russell,* F. S. Drake; *Defiance,* Max Jacobs."—*Schomberg's Naval Chronology,* iv. 342.

"A list of the squadron under the command of Vice Admiral ARBUTHNOT in the action off Cape Henry, with that of the French under M. de Ternay, on the 16th March, 1781.

"Ship *Royal Oak* [74 guns], Commander MARRIOTT ARBUTHNOT, Esq., Vice Admiral of the *White,* Captain Swiney; *London* [98], Thomas Graves, Esq., Rear Admiral of the *Red,* Captain D. Graves; *Robust* [74], Ph. Cosby; *Bedford* [74], Edmund Affleck; *America* [64], Samuel Thompson; *Prudent* [64], Thomas Berwick; *Europe,* [64] Smith Child; *Adamant* [50], Gideon Johnstone; *Iris* [32], —— ; *Pearl* [32], George Montagu; *Guadaloupe* [28], Hugh Robinson.—*Schomberg's Naval Chronology,* iv. 376.

NOTE 184, PAGE 257. GARDNER'S BAY.—"The East extremity of Long Island is divided by Great and Little Peconic, and *Gardner's Bays* into two narrow unequal branches, between which are Gardner's, Shelter and Robin's Islands."—*French's New York Gazetteer,* page 631.

The British Squadron anchored here in the summer of 1780. "From the

Oyfter
Constable Point
Dutch Church
ISLAND
Richmond
Old Town
New Town
Ferry
The Narrows
Gravesend Bay
Coney Id
ITON BAY
Sandy Hook

secure position of *Gardner's Island* the British Fleet (of sixteen ships of war) continued to watch the movements (of the Americans and French in Newport Harbor) and virtually to blockade the ships and army of the French. —*Arnold's History of Rhode Island*, ii. 462.

NOTE 185, PAGE 257. MONTOCK POINT.—"The eastern extremity of Long Island. The eastern part of East Hampton consists of a narrow peninsula, to which the name *Montauk* is applied."—*French's Gazetteer of the State of New York*, p. 634. "The *Peninsula of Montock* contains about 9000 acres."—*Thompson's Long Island*, I. 307.

NOTE 186, PAGE 257. TRADE WITH HALIFAX.—"The exports from Great Britain to this country (Nova Scotia) consist chiefly of linen and woollen cloths and other necessaries for wear, of fishing tackle and rigging for ships. The amount of exports at an average of three years before the new settlement was about twenty-six thousand five hundred pounds. The only articles obtained in exchange are timber and the produce of the fishery, which, at a like average, amounted to thirty-eight thousand pounds. The whole population of Nova Scotia and the islands adjoining is estimated at fifty thousand. This estimate, it is supposed, is considerably too large. . . . Halifax is the capital of the Province. It has a good harbour. . . . It is said to contain fifteen or sixteen thousand inhabitants."—*Winterbotham's View of America*, iv. 42.

NOTE 187, PAGE 258. NEW YORK HARBOR FOR LARGE SHIPS.—"Though most of the charts are marked with only 3½ fathoms of water on the bar, the outside of Sandy Hook, yet the most experienced pilots declare they always found the depth 4 fathoms. After getting over the bar the water is deeper all the way to New York. Ships of war can go up the east river through Hell Gate and the Sound, between Long Island and the Continent into the ocean. Sir James Wallace in the *Experiment* of 50 guns when chaced by the French fleet off the East end of Long Island in 1777, came through the Sound, Hellgate and the East River to New York. The tide flows up Hudson's or the North River 180 miles. Before the rebellion ships went from London Bridge to Albany, which is 170 miles up the river; only 6 miles below it, it was necessary to lighten them by taking out part of the cargo."—*Political Magazine*, 1781, vol. 2.

NOTE 188, PAGE 259. DISCHARGE OF SEAMEN.—One of the great troubles under which the British labored arose from the cruel treatment of men on board their vessels. From this cause, while there were always enough sailors to man the privateers commanded by their own townsmen, they could not be brought to enlist in the King's service. Occasional notices of what is called a "*Hot-Press*," appeared in the journals.

On the 6th May, 1781, Governor Robertson informed Lord George Germaine that "the French Men of War and Transports with Troops on board lay ready to sail at Rhode Island, while that under Admiral ARBUTHNOT, having landed 1400 sick and scorbutic men is here unable to go to sea for want of hands. On the Admiral's requisition, with the Commander-in-Chief's consent, other applications having proved ineffectual, all the sailors here have been pressed for the Fleet. This at present puts a stop to privateering; but on my representation to the Admiral that by encouraging privateers and giving all men an easy access to them, We not only hurt the enemy's Trade, but lessen their army; whereas by pressing we force the sailors to fly and man the Rebel Ships of War, he has promised that as soon as the important blow, he now meditates, is struck, or as soon as a sufficient number of his Sick recover, he will *discharge all the men* now impressed and will not renew a measure, which nothing but his and the present state of his and the Enemy's Fleet could justify."—*N. Y. Col. Doc.* viii. 811.

NOTE 189, PAGE 261. LICENSED AUCTIONEERS.—For the regulations for the government of *Licensed Auctioneers* or Vendue Masters, see the orders of the Magistrates of Police, under date 12th January, 1779 (*Note* 139).—*Gaine's New York Gazette*, Jan. 18, 1779.

NOTE 190, PAGE 262. CHAPMAN.—Edward Phillips, in *The New World of Words* (1720), defines this word as "a Buyer or Customer;" Bailey, in his Dictionary, gives the same definition (1763); Johnson essentially follows his predecessors, "a Cheapner; one that offers as a purchaser," and gives Shakespeare, Ben Jonson, and Dryden as authorities; Webster, while giving the old meaning, adds a second definition, "a seller, or market-man."

In the present day the word is held in usage to signify a Peddler. In the text the word seems to apply to a small seller in market places as distinct from a traveling peddler.

NOTE 191, PAGE 262. PROCLAMATION AS TO VENDUE MASTERS.—For a copy of this Proclamation see *Note* 139. It was dated 12th January, 1779, and published in *Gaine's New York Gazette*, Jan. 18, 1779.

NOTE 192, PAGE 263. WINTHROP & KEMBLE.—Advertisements of this firm are occasionally met with in the newspapers at this time. "*Winthrop & Kemble*, have for sale at their store, No. 11 Water Street, Port Wine in pipes, quarter casks and bottles; Madeira in ditto, ditto; Muscovado Sugar in hogsheads, tierces, and barrels; Loaf Sugar; Claret in cases of six dozen; Nails, and a few boxes of Spermaceti Candles; Green and Sushong Teas."—*Gaine's N. Y. Gazette*, Feb. 8, 1779.

NOTE 193, PAGE 263. WARDENS OF THE PORT.—A Proclamation of JAMES PATTISON, Commandant of New York, 1st September, 1779, gives the names of the Wardens and the Districts assigned to their superintendence.

"From the Ship Yards to the Crane, *Capt. Thomas Crowell;* from the Crane to the Fly Market, *Capt. Thomas Vardill;* from the Fly Market to the Old Slip, *Mr. Anthony Van Dam;* from the Old Slip to Whitehall, *Capt. John Griffith.*"—*Gaine's New York Gazette*, September 6, 1779.

A Proclamation of SAMUEL BIRCH, Commandant, dated 11th February, 1782, gives the names of the same Wardens, and assigns to them the care of the same districts.—*Rivington's Royal Gazette*, March 13, 1782.

NOTE 194, PAGE 264. FREIGHT ON BROKEN HOGSHEADS.—The decision of the arbitration committee of the Chamber, that freight is due on empty and broken hogsheads, no matter what the contents, if the examination of the Port Wardens shows the cargo to have been well and properly stowed, has been borne out by the practice of New York Merchants and by the decisions of the courts.

NOTE 195, PAGE 266. WILLIAM WALTON, MAGISTRATE OF POLICE.—This was, no doubt, the WILLIAM WALTON who had been the President of the Chamber. The office of Magistrate of Police was one of the most important in the city. He succeeded Peter Dubois in that office. The last proclamation of Peter Dubois as Magistrate was dated 26th February, 1780; the first of WILLIAM WALTON, 11th Jan., 1782.—*Rivington's Royal Gazette*, Jan. 12, 1782.

NOTE 196, PAGE 269. JUNCTURE OF AFFAIRS.—The state of affairs at the beginning of October, 1781, was by no means favorable for the adoption of new plans. The shadows of defeat were falling fast upon the British cause. New York was in great anxiety to hear of the fate of the fleet which had sailed under Admiral Graves for the relief of Cornwallis, who was closely besieged in Yorktown by Washington and Rochambeau.

"Lord Cornwallis had been completely roused from his dream of security by the appearance, on the 28th of March, 1781, of the fleet of Count de Grasse within the Capes of the Delaware. Awakened to his danger, Cornwallis meditated a retreat to the Carolinas. It was too late. York River was blocked up by French ships; James River was filled with armed vessels covering the transportation of the troops. His lordship reconnoitred Williamsburg; it was too strong to be forced, and Wayne had crossed James River to join his troops to those under the Marquis. Seeing his retreat cut off in every direction, Cornwallis proceeded to strengthen his ranks, sending off repeated expresses to apprise Sir Henry Clinton of his perilous situation." —*Irving's Washington*, vol. iv. 340.

On the 26th September Sir Henry Clinton informs Lord George Germaine that he had "received a Letter from the Admiral, dated the 9th inst., to inform him that the enemy being absolute masters of the navigation of the Chesapeake, there was little probability of anything getting into York River but by night, and an infinite risk to supplies sent by water, at the same time acquainting me that he had on the 5th a partial action with the French fleet of 24 sail of the line, and that the fleets had been in sight of each other ever since."—*Political Magazine*, 1781, ii. 668.

The fleet under Admiral Graves had been too tardy in its movements, and De Barras, who sailed with the grain and stores for the besieging enemy on the Peninsula, had arrived in safety. On the arrival of the English squadron at the mouth of the Chesapeake, De Grasse sailed out with the French ships, and in an action, which lasted several hours, the English were hardly handled—"they were so mutilated, that they had not speed enough to attack the French."—*Gordon's History*, iv. 183; *Operations of De Grasse; Bradford Club.*

"Sir Henry Clinton determined, therefore, to hazard everything for the preservation of Virginia, and having embarked seven thousand of his best troops, sailed for the Chesapeake under convoy of a fleet augmented to twenty-five sail of the line. This armament did not leave the Hook till the day in which the capitulation was refused at Yorktown."—*Marshall's Washington*, iv. 476.

The fears entertained by the British officials in New York were soon justified by the result. Lord Cornwallis surrendered on the 19th October to the allied armies. "The land forces became prisoners to Congress, but the seamen and ships were assigned to the French admiral."—*Gordon's Hist.* iv. 196.

NOTE 197, PAGE 269. REVIVAL OF CIVIL AUTHORITY.—From the time of the entrance of the British troops into the city, New York was under martial law. The interests of the military service may have required this course; but it is certain that it was one unexpected in Great Britain, and distasteful in the last degree, even to those who adhered to the Crown, in America.

When Lord Howe took command, in the fall of 1776, an address was delivered to him, signed by Daniel Horsmanden, Oliver DeLancey, and 946 others of the inhabitants who remained in the city; and a short time after an equally loyal address was presented to him from the loyalists of Queens' County. It was observed of these Petitions, in the Debates of Parliament, in 1777, "That the Constitutional supremacy in one and the Constitutional authority of Great Britain in the other, were very guardedly expressed, all mention of Parliament being omitted, and the great question of unconditional submission, left totally at large. . . . These petitions were not attended to nor were they restored to the rights which they expected in consequence of the declarations as well as of the late law for the appointment of the Commissioners."—*Annual Register* for 1777, pub. in 1778, page 13.

After the restoration of Georgia by the return of its Governor, the inhabitants of New York became restive and anxious for a renewal of civil rule. After a long and bitter experience, the great mass of the people hailed with delight the final triumph of the American cause and of the cause of liberty.

NOTE 198, PAGE 270. HIS MAJESTY'S SHIP WARWICK.—This ship, under the command of Captain Elphinstone, arrived in New York on the 26th June, 1781, "a part of the Convoy to the Cork Fleet," which had touched at Charleston, South Carolina, with reinforcements for Lord Rawdon.—*Gaine's New York Gazette*, July 2d, 1781.

The Warwick, of 50 guns, was built in 1767. She remained on the American station until the close of the war, and appears in the Register of 1784 as a Receiving Ship at Chatham.—*Exshaw's Registers.*

NOTE 199, PAGE 271. SAILING OF TROOP SHIPS.—The coast was so covered with privateers, that no public notice was given of the date at which this expedition sailed. It appears that it was in July, from the following notice.

"The Quebec and Halifax fleets, which left this port in July last, under command of his Majesty's ships *Warwick*, Hon. K. Elphinstone, Commander, and the *Garland*, Captain Chamberlain, arrived at Halifax on the 6th day after they left Sandy Hook. — *Gaine's New York Gazette and Weekly Mercury*, September 24th, 1781.

NOTE 200, PAGE 271. TWO BRIGS ESCAPE THE CONVOY.—These were probably the two vessels referred to in a Boston letter of the 16th August as having been sent in. "Also two brigs from New York bound to Quebec were captured by a privateer from Portsmouth."—*The New Jersey Gazette*, September 5th, 1781.

Their companions were more fortunate, if the British account can be relied upon. "We are informed that a great number of rebel privateers having concocted a design of intercepting the fleet of British merchantmen bound for Quebec, and taken their stations in and about the Gulf of St. Lawrence, they were presently made prizes of by the British cruisers. It is said Admiral Edwards had taken the trade under his protection, apprised of the formidable number of rebel privateers in the Gulf, twenty-six sail of which have been secured; their names we have in vain endeavoured to procure for insertion in this paper; besides the Congress of 26 guns, the following ships are named, the Alexander, the Marquis, and the Neptune. The whole, large and small, carry from twelve to twenty-six guns each."—*Rivington's Royal Gazette*, September 22d, 1781.

NOTE 201, PAGE 271. HIS MAJESTY'S SHIP GARLAND.—This ship, built in 1748, according to *Beatson*, carried 24 guns, and was under the command of Captain Chamberlain. She was on the American station until 1783. In the next year her name disappears from the Registers.—*Exshaw's Registers.*

This ship had been long known on the American station. On the voyage from Cork, as part of the convoy of the Provision Fleet for America, she had the fortune to take a celebrated privateer, which was the cause of much rejoicing and boasting among her officers.

"Extract of a letter from an officer on board the *Garland:* 'On Wednesday last (June 2), we took the *Fair American*, privateer, so remarkable for depredations she has committed on the British trade for the two years past, and always escaping our cruisers by her swiftness of sailing. This, I think, will incontrovertibly, ascertain a fact which some people affect not to value, but which is nevertheless true, '*that the Garland sails superior to all the cruisers on the coast.*' "—*Rivington's Royal Gazette*, January 9, 1782.

NOTE 202, PAGE 271. THE INSURER.—Underwriting was not, as now, the business of companies. One or more individuals would take the risks on such terms as could be agreed upon. The insurance offices were only places of meeting for those whose habit it was to do this business.

NOTE 203, PAGE 271. "THIS MOST UNNATURAL REBELLION."—This phrase, so much used during the late Rebellion (1861–65), and in the text appearing in a letter of ISAAC LOW, President of the Chamber (October 3, 1781), is to be found in a Proclamation of Sir William Howe of the 21st April, 1777, commencing, "*Whereas* for the more speedy and effectual suppression of *the unnatural* Rebellion *subsisting in North America*," *etc.*—*Gaine's New York Gazette*, April 28th, 1777.

NOTE 204, PAGE 272. THE BRITISH FLEET.—Sir Henry Clinton, in a letter to Lord George Germaine, dated on board the London, off Chesapeake, 29th October, 1781, says, "Rear Admiral Graves sailed from Sandy Hook on the 19th inst., and arrived off Cape Charles on the 24th, when we had the mortification to hear that Lord Cornwallis had prepared terms of capitulation to the enemy on the 17th. . . . We are, unfortunately, too late to relieve him, which, being the only object of the expedition, the Admiral has determined upon returning with his fleet to Sandy Hook."—*Political Magazine*, 1781, page 670.

NOTE 205, PAGE 272. BOUNTY OF CHAMBER TO SEAMEN.—A curious Proclamation of Mr. Isaac Low, as President, has been preserved in the Pennsylvania Packet. It was probably issued as a handbill in New York, and for that reason did not find its way into the newspapers:

"TO ALL HONEST HEARTS AND SOUND BOTTOMS.

"Not to step forth when all's at stake were a reflection too indignant and insupportable for the breast of an English seaman.

"It is on such grand occasions that those useful men have always shone in their true light, and astonished the world by their intrepidity and feats of valour.

"Perhaps there never was a period when an exertion of all their powers was more seriously called for.

"Without their most strenuous assistance, not only the great exertions of the noble peer and the gallant army he commands, who have already performed wonders, may be rendered of no effect, but also the endeavours of their brave sympathetic fellow soldiers, who would so eagerly fly to their assistance, be defeated.

"All seamen and able-bodied landsmen are therefore called upon by the Admiral to offer their services and fight under his banners. Nor will they be called upon in vain, or it would be the first invitation of the kind that honest British tars ever refused, or were backward in accepting.

"Yard arm and yard arm never yet failed evincing their prowess over their old implacable foe.

"Greater encouragement was never held out in any country; not from the degrading supposition that their zeal and ardour require any other stimulation than what flows from a love of their country; but only by way of vieing with them, who, in their different stations, should be foremost on this truly grand and important occasion.

"With this view the Admiral and Governor authorize the publication of what cannot but be called great allurements, and the Chamber of Commerce and the other loyal inhabitants will add a bounty of Three Guineas to each volunteer who goes upon this important service, besides plenty of honest grog to cheer their hearts and drink the king's health and success to his arms.

"'Hearts of oak are our ships;
Hearts of oak are our men.
We always are ready, steady, boys, steady.
We'll fight and we'll conquer again and again.'

"This noble chorus again echoed with propriety, will make the heart of the young Prince * leap for joy and glory in the profession of a sailor.

"By order of the Chamber of Commerce and a number of respectable inhabitants there assembled. ISAAC LOW, President."—*News from Chatham, published in the Pennsylvania Packet*, Tuesday, October 30, 1781.

NOTE 206, PAGE 275. ARRIVAL OF PROVISION FLEETS.—"Last Saturday (January 5) arrived here from Cork a fleet of twenty-five victuallers, convoyed by his Majesty's Ship Quebec, of 38 guns, commanded by Christopher Mason, Esq., and the Grana, of 28, by Captain Fortescue. They left Cork the 29th of October. On the 27th of December that part of the convoy destined for Carolina, was sent up to Charlestown. On the 28th they sailed from the bar of that port, and eight days after, viz. on the 5th of January, with the remaining convoy for this garrison, anchored in New York Harbour."—*Rivington's Royal Gazette*, January 9, 1782.

NOTE 207, PAGE 276. ARRIVAL OF PRIZES.—In the twenty days preceding the date of the Letter of the Superintendent, the British privateers had met with more than usual success. On the 19th December the privateer sloop Prince William Henry brought in the Brig *Experiment*, bound from Philadelphia to North Carolina. On the 2d January the Orpheus brought in two vessels laden with flour. On the 23d January his Majesty's Ship Adamant sent in the schooner *Delaware*, laden with three hundred and fifty barrels of flour. The same day the King's Ship Garland sent in the "*Fair*

* Prince William Henry, afterwards William the Fourth, third son of George the Third, arrived at Sandy Hook September 25, 1781.—*Rivington's Royal Gazette*, September 26, 1781.

American, rebel privateer, so remarkable for the depredations she has so long committed on the British trade. The *Fair American* had on board upward of 550 barrels of flour, which she was to unload at the Havana." On the 3d his Majesty's Ship the Chatham sent in the *Sally*, bound from Philadelphia to St. Croix, with a cargo of flour, bread, etc.

These arrivals, together with that of the Cork fleet on the 9th, were a great relief to the city.

NOTE 208, PAGE 276. PRICE OF BREAD, JANUARY, 1782.—On the 11th January, 1782, on the advice of the Chamber given in their letter of the 8th idem (page 276), the Magistrates of Police ordered that *Loaves of Two Pounds and a Quarter* weight each should be sold for *Fourteen Coppers* each.—*Rivington's Royal Gazette*, January 12, 1782. For Bread Regulations during the British occupation, *see Note* 142.

NOTE 209, PAGE 277. WHARVES.—The recommendation of the Chamber (page 279) was followed by the authorities. On the 12th April, 1782, SAMUEL BIRCH, Commandant of New York, issued a Proclamation: "*Whereas* the proprietors of wharves on the East River, by their petition, have prayed an encrease of Wharfage, on condition of putting and keeping the said wharfs in repair, and the prayer of the said petitioners appearing to be just and equitable, I have thought fit hereby to declare and order that such owners of wharfs on the East River as shall produce certificates from the Wardens of the Port, that their wharfs are in proper repair and good condition, shall hereafter be entitled to receive from all masters of vessels that shall lay fastened thereto as follows, viz." (here follow the rates proposed by the Chamber of Commerce; *see page* 279.)—*Gaine's New York Gazette*, April 22, 1782.

"The wharfs, till the first January, 1779, had been occupied by his Majesty's Ships and transports in government service, without paying any wharfage; but as many of them belonged to Loyalists, it was determined, that on the proprietors making oath as to the property, and that no persons without the British lines (with an exception in regard to any copartner in such wharf), were interested or concerned therein, the Commandant gave his permission to such proprietor to occupy his wharf or part of a wharf, and receive the usual and customary wharfage on condition that such proprietor kept the said wharf in good and sufficient repair. Captain Kennedy and Mr. Lefferts owned one of the wharfs in the Commissary General's department; Captain Kennedy was allowed and paid by the Commissary General one dollar per day for his half; but as Mr. Lefferts was without the British lines, nothing was allowed him. This wharf, as well as all others in the Commissary General's department and the stores, were kept in constant repair at the expense of government. Wages and material being very high, had the Owners been in full possession of their property and rented the same for any moderate sum, many of them would have been losers, had they been obliged to have kept the premises in repair."—*Butler's Case; New York City in the American Revolution; N. Y. Mercantile Library*, p. 156.

NOTE 210, PAGE 277. RATES OF WHARFAGE (1782).—"WHEREAS the Proprietors of Wharves on the East River, by their petition, have prayed an encrease of Wharfage on condition of putting and keeping the said Wharves in repair, and the prayer of the said petitioners appearing to be just and equitable, I have thought fit hereby to declare and order that such owners of wharfs on the East River as shall produce certificates from the Wardens of the Port that their wharfs are in proper repair and good condition, shall hereafter be entitled to receive from all masters of vessels that shall lay fastened thereto, as follows, viz.:

"For every vessel not exceeding one hundred tons carpenter's measurement, at the rate of Three Shillings per day. For all vessels above one hundred tons, and not exceeding three hundred tons, at the rate of Four Shillings and Six Pence per day. For all vessels above three hundred tons, at the rate of Six Shillings per day. That all vessels laying on the out-side berths be subject to one-half wharfage, according to their measurement.

"*Given under my Hand, this* 12th day of April, 1782.—SAMUEL BIRCH. By order of the Commandant: John St. Clair, Secretary."

NOTE 211, PAGE 279. SECRETARY OF THE COMMANDANT.—"New York, September 23d. The Commandant of New York has appointed Mr. JOHN ST. CLAIR to be his Secretary."—*Gaine's New York Gazette*, September 25th, 1780.

NOTE 212, PAGE 281. TWO FRIGATES DETAINED.—Another instance of the difficulty which the British Commanders had in manning their vessels in America, and of the aversion with which the service was regarded (*see Note* 188).

NOTE 213, PAGE 281. KING AND KEMBLE.—The name of King and Kemble is not met with as a firm; their connection was probably only that of joint ownership in the privateer brig Perseverance.

NOTE 214, PAGE 281. CAPTAIN ROSS OF THE PERSEVERANCE.—Two captains of this name appear on the "List of Vessels commissioned as Letters of Marque from the Port of New York, since the 8th September, 1778," published 1779—James Ross of the Privateer Roebuck, 20 guns, and Stewart Ross of the Pollux, 18 guns. The Captain who treated the Admiral with so little respect was probably one of those old hands who were not respecters of persons.

NOTE 215, PAGE 282. GENIUS OF AMERICANS FOR PRIVATEERING.—The journals of the last century bear ample witness to the truth of this remark. One is struck with surprise at the unending roll of captured ships on both sides. During the Spanish and French Wars the American rovers reaped rich harvests of plunder from the unfortunate merchantmen who fell in their way. The same success followed in the War of 1812 with Great Britain. The colonists were a hardy, adventurous race, ready for every enterprise of individual hazard.

Many of the British statesmen were fully alive to the results which would follow to their commerce from the adventurous spirit of the hardy seamen of the American coast. In 1776 they had warned the Ministry that "the prohibition of commerce with the Colonies would compel them of necessity to convert their merchant ships into privateers, whereby our West India islands would be totally ruined, and our foreign commerce in general suffer greater injury than in any war in which we have ever been involved."—*Annual Register* for 1776, page 109.

The fears of these observers were fully justified when no English vessel could safely sail without a convoy, and *John Paul Jones* had struck terror into the residents of the English coast. In the debate of 1777 it was stated that the *home* trade had been destroyed by the "swarms of American privateers which had during the war infested and insulted our coasts," and allusion was made "to the terror into which the metropolis of Ireland had been thrown, and the need of fortifying for the first time in all our wars of its harbour," &c.—*Annual Register* for 1778.

NOTE 216, PAGE 283. VESSELS MANNED FOR PUBLIC SERVICE.—The proclamation of Governor Tryon (*see Note* 123), issued in 1779, gives a statement of the number of private ships of war which were sent out from New York. Their number was constantly increasing; to this must be added the transports fitted out for the numerous expeditions along the coast.

NOTE 217, PAGE 285. PRIVATEERS AND WHALE-BOATS INFEST THE NARROWS.—Every day the Privateers became more bold. Towards the close of the War the fishing, on which the inhabitants greatly depended for food, was almost suspended. Captain HYLER with his boats was active and vigilant in his efforts to annoy the British.

"Friday last a number of Fishing Boats were just on the eve of being captured on the Banks by Hyler's Boats; but luckily the Lark Privateer, inward bound, saved them from being convoyed to Middletown, &c."—*Gaine's New York Gazette*, June 17th, 1782.

On the very day of the meeting of the Chamber a daring feat of this nature was performed, which was probably the immediate cause of the motion on the subject.

"On the 2d instant, in New York Bay, Captains Hyler and Story, with two whale-boats, boarded and took the schooner Skip Jack mounting 6 carriage guns besides swivels, but soon after burnt her, finding they could not get her off, it being at noon, in sight of the Guard Ship, and several other ships of War lying at Sandy Hook. This schooner was tender to the Admiral's ship. Hyler brought off the captain and 9 or 10 hands, the others having escaped in their boats on the approach of the whale-boats. Captain Hyler, about the same time, took three other small vessels which were on the trading scheme, one of them being loaded with calves, sheep, &c., bound from New Jersey to New York."—*The Pennsylvania Packet*, July 16th, 1782.

"About 12 o'clock (Tuesday 2d July), five boats under the command of Mr. Hyler, took a Tender of 8 guns near Sandy Hook; the Guard Ship got under way immediately, but there being little Wind she could not recover the Prize, which was carried off, and afterwards burnt in the Shrewsbury River."—*Gaine's New York Gazette and Weekly Mercury*, July 8th, 1782.

Captain Adam Hyler, of New Brunswick, the hero of these exploits, was famous for his daring adventures. A notice of his death on the 6th September, 1782, pays a tribute to his courage: "his many heroick and enterprising acts in annoying and distressing the enemy endeared him to the patriotick part of all his acquaintance."—*The New Jersey Gazette*, September 25th, 1782.

NOTE 218, PAGE 287. JOHN PORTEOUS.—A curious advertisement of this person appears in 1780. "*Best Hats.* In the military and most fashionable cock, with gold and silver buttons and loops; and a variety of feathers, &c., and a few, well-sorted small packages just imported in the last ships from London, and to be sold cheap for cash by JOHN PORTEOUS, next door to the Admiral's in Hanover Square.

"Also carriage-guns, three and four pounders, compleat; swivels and a variety of shot. An elegant pair of looking-glasses, some bales of coarse woollens, cloths and other articles in the dry good way, and a very fine night glass."—*Gaine's New York Gazette*, September 11th, 1780.

There is in the St. Memin Collection (No. 662) a portrait of *John Porteous* (1809), who is described as a planter of Beaufort, S. C.

NOTE 219, PAGE 287. THE KITTY AND POLLY.—This vessel was probably one of the schooners, the capture of which was reported in the newspapers. "Yesterday arrived a small sloop from St. Augustine, after being chased by two rebel gallies of four nine-pounders each, which have taken three schooners bound to this port; their station is off the Light-house, and it is said they cruise in concert, the better to check arrivals and injure our commerce. The sloop was charged with dispatches, but in the chase they were thrown overboard."—*Letter from New York*, 3d July, published in the *Pennsylvania Packet*, July 21, 1782.

The fate of this vessel is an example of the hazard which attended all trade during the war. The *Kitty and Polly* had been formerly the *Shark* Privateer.—*Rivington's Royal Gazette*, February 16, 1782.

NOTE 220, PAGE 288. GEORGETOWN.—The reference in the arbitration is to Georgetown, South Carolina, situated at the mouth of the Santee River. At this time it was in possession of the patriot forces under General Marion, who was a native of the Georgetown District. Its fine harbor made it a valuable refuge for the American cruisers.

The *New Jersey Gazette* of the 4th September gives a notice of "a ship said to have been brought into George-Town, South Carolina, by a privateer of that place, with 250 slaves on board, taken on their way to Jamaica from Savanna."

NOTE 221, PAGE 293. COLONEL CRUGER.—*John Harris Cruger* was one of the earliest members of the Chamber, elected at its first meeting for business, 3d May, 1768 (page 8). He was last in his seat Feb., 1775 (page 201). On the breaking out of the war he was appointed Lieutenant Colonel Commandant of the First Battalion of Oliver De Lancey's Loyal Brigade. He greatly distinguished himself by his services to the Crown in the Southern campaign, especially by his gallant defence of Post Ninety-six, besieged by General Greene in 1780.

NOTE 222, PAGE 296. JERSEY MONEY.—This would indicate that the old trouble concerning the rate at which *Jersey Money* should pass in New York was at last settled, but the subject was again to come before the Chamber. On the 3d April, 1787, a committee was raised to consider whether "countenance should be given to this circulation," who reported, May of same year, "that the Chamber ought not for the present to interfere."—*MSS. Minutes of the Chamber*, i. pp. 344, 345.

NOTE 223, PAGE 296. RESTORATION OF MEMBERS WITHOUT BALLOT.—Of these persons, ISAAC SEARS resigned 4th August, 1772 (p. 64), the rest named on the 6th Oct., 1772 (p. 168).

None of them had availed of the privilege of re-admission without entrance-fee granted by resolution of the Chamber, 4th Jan. 1774 (p. 187).

NOTE 224, PAGE 297. ADMITTANCE FEE TO CHAMBER.—On the organization of the Chamber, April 5, 1768, the entrance-fee was fixed at FIVE SPANISH DOLLARS (page 4). On the 6th March, 1770, a sliding scale of increase was adopted, from Ten Spanish Dollars upwards, to take effect when the Chamber should reach Eighty members (page 79). The proposition to reduce this fee to Eight Dollars, made 20th January, 1784 (page 297), was never voted upon. On the re-organization of the Chamber, 20th April, 1784 (*see Note, page* 298), the old fee of Five Spanish Dollars was restored. On the 15th April, 1817, shortly after the second revival of the Institution, the sum was raised to Ten Dollars, at which it has remained until the present day, except that the Chamber has waived the payment of dues of new members for the calendar year of admission.

NOTE 225, PAGE 297. NEW MEMBERS PROPOSED.—Of the members proposed at this, the only meeting of the Old Corporation between the close of the war and the re-organization of the Chamber under the Act of the Legislature, Cornelius Ray, Viner Van Zandt, Samuel Broome, Jacob Morris, Comfort Sands, Robert Bowne, William Malcom, and Joshua Sands, were petitioners to the Legislature for the confirmation of the Charter, and are named in the Act of Re-Incorporation.

There were elected 4th May, 1784, James Stewart; June 8, 1784, Samuel Franklin, William Denning, Archibald Gamble, and John Shaw; May 1, 1787, Moses Rogers.

The others, named Eleazer Miller, John Woodward, and Joseph Hallet, do not appear on the books of the Chamber.—*MSS. Minutes of the Chamber of Commerce*, vol. i.

---

* *NOTE ON THE OLD CHARTER.*

About the year 1821 or 1822, Mr. Andrew Warner, now of the Bank for the Savings of Merchants' Clerks, then a clerk in the Mutual Insurance Company, of which Mr. John Pintard, the Secretary of the Chamber, was at the time also the Secretary, at his instance called on Admiral Walton, at the Walton House. Mr. Daniel Crommelin Verplanck, the husband of Ann, sister of the Admiral, had been charged by him to inform the officers of the Chamber that, on taking possession of the old house, on his return to America, he had found there the original Charter of the Chamber. Mr. Warner was received at the old mansion, then in fine order and condition, by the Admiral and his wife, and there took possession of the valuable estray. It was then in a mahogany box, oblong, with a circle at one end to allow of the entry of the old Colonial Seal.

NOTES TO REGISTER OF PROCEEDINGS

OF

NEW YORK CHAMBER OF COMMERCE.

BIOGRAPHICAL.

NOTE a, PAGE 36. JOHN SCHUYLER, Colonel.—A grandson of Philip Pietersen Schuyler, of Amsterdam, the first of the name in America, and son of Arent Schuyler, who settled in New Jersey. Col. John Schuyler lived at Bellville, New Jersey, where the family owned valuable copper-mines. A curious account of his house and family is to be met with in the Journal of Isaac Bangs, a private in a Massachusetts regiment stationed near Bellville in 1775, communicated to the New Jersey Historical Society: "Mr. Schuyler's Mansion House is a large, grand and magnificent building, built partly of stone and the rest brick, most beautifully situated upon an eminence on the East Bank of what is called the Hackensack." His farm was several miles in extent, and included fine deer-parks. The copper-mines had greatly enriched the family.—*Letter from S. Alofsen, Esq., of Jersey City; Proceedings N. J. Hist. Soc.* xii. 120.

NOTE b, PAGE 36. ARCHIBALD KENNEDY.—This name was first borne in America by a Scotch gentleman who came to New York in 1714, and soon after was appointed to the office of Receiver General and Collector of the Port. In 1727 he was, on the recommendation of Governor Burnet, appointed one of the King's Council. He married Catharine Schuyler, who was of one of the old colonial families. He died in New York.

CAPTAIN ARCHIBALD KENNEDY received his commission as Captain in the Royal Navy, 4th April, 1757. In December, 1763, he was in command of the *Blonde*, 32 guns. He is best known as, for many years, the Captain of the *Coventry*, a 28 gun ship. During the Stamp Act excitement Governor Colden proposed to put the instruments on board this ship, but Captain Kennedy declined to receive them.

He married as his second wife Anne, eldest daughter of Hon. John Watts, of New York. His property consisted of several houses situated at the lower end of Broadway and near the Battery. The old Kennedy House, No. 1 Broadway, is still standing. It was for a time occupied by Washington as his headquarters, and is now called the Washington Hotel. On the death, in 1792, of the great-grandfather of Captain Kennedy, the 2d Earl of Carlisle (a Scotch earldom), he succeeded to the title. He died 29th December, 1794.—*Col. Doc.* vii. 822; *Valentine's Manual*, 1864, 590.

NOTE c, PAGE 37. JOHN HOLT.—This New York printer was born in Virginia. He commenced life as a merchant, and was at one time the Mayor of Williamsburg, Virginia. Failing in business, he came to New York, and formed a connection with James Parker, then about to open a press in New Haven. Returning to New York in 1760, he managed the *New York Gazette and Post Boy*, first for Parker, and later on his own account. In

1766 he established the *New York Journal*, the well-known liberal paper of the Stamp Act period. When the British entered New York in 1776 he removed to Kingston, where his press was destroyed in Vaughan's expedition. He re-established himself at Poughkeepsie. In 1783 he resumed the publication of his paper in New York. A memorial card, issued shortly after his death by his wife, says he "patiently obeyed Death's awful summons on the 30th of January, 1784, in the 64th year of his Age."—*Thomas's History of Printing*, ii. 105.

NOTE d, PAGE 38. WHITEHEAD HICKS, Mayor of New York.—The eldest son of Thomas and Margaret Hicks was born at Flushing, L. I., August 24th, 1728. Destined for the legal profession, he was placed in the office of the Hon. William Smith, and was the fellow-student of William Smith, junior, the historian, and William Livingston, afterwards Governor of New Jersey. Mr. Hicks was admitted to the Bar of New York October 22d, 1750, and soon received a share of the best practice of the city.

In October, 1766, he was chosen by Sir Henry Moore to succeed Mr. John Cruger as Mayor of the City of New York, and held the office until 14th February, 1776, when he was appointed one of the Judges of the Supreme Court of the Colony. He immediately retired to Bay-Side, Flushing, where he remained until his death, on the 4th October, 1780. Quiet from timidity, he was unmolested during the War. He married Charlotte, the only child of John Brevoort, October 5, 1757.—*Col. Doc.* viii. 594.

NOTE e, PAGE 61. DAVID RITTENHOUSE.—An American mathematician and astronomer, born in Germantown, Penn., April 8, 1732. His knowledge and abilities having attracted public attention, he was commissioned by the Proprietary Government, in 1763, to determine the initial and most difficult portion of the boundary line since known as Mason and Dixon's. He was subsequently employed in determining the boundaries between New York, New Jersey, and Pennsylvania, and several other States, both before and after the Revolution. In 1777 he was made Treasurer of Pennsylvania, and held that office till 1789. In 1791 he was chosen to succeed Dr. Franklin as President of the American Philosophical Society, and in 1792 was made Director of the United States Mint, which position he resigned in 1795, and in that year was elected a Fellow of the Royal Society of London. He died in Philadelphia, June 26, 1796.—*New American Cyclopædia*, xiv. 98.

NOTE f, PAGE 61. JOHN MONTRESOR.—An ensign in the 48th Regiment in the Braddock expedition, where he was wounded, and was appointed to a lieutenantcy in the same corps on the 4th July, 1755. He obtained a grant of land in Willsboro, Essex Co., N, Y., in 1764, and in 1766 quitted the army. He seems later to have occasionally practised the profession of a civil engineer. In the year 1772 he purchased the island then known as *Little Barne's* or *Talbot's*, now called *Randall's Island*, and resided there with his family until the close of the War, when he returned to England with the British troops.—*Col. Doc.* vii. 533; *Valentine's Manual*, 1855, 499.

NOTE g, PAGE 61. JAMES BRADLEY, DR.—An English Astronomer, born at Sherbourne, Gloucestershire, March, 1692. In 1721 he was appointed Savilian professor of Astronomy, and in 1727 published his brilliant discovery of the *aberration of light*. Ten years afterwards he published the equally valuable discovery of the *nutation of the earth's axis*. In 1742 he succeeded Dr. Halley as Astronomer Royal, and in 1752 he received a pension in consideration of the "advantage of his astronomical labors to the commerce and navigation of Great Britain." He died at Chatford, 13th July, 1762.—*New American Cyclopædia*, iii. 612.

NOTE h, PAGE 63. ARCHIBALD McLEAN.—A Civil Engineer of distinction in Pennsylvania. In 1777 he was appointed Prothonotary or Register and Recorder of Deeds for York County. In 1779 he was one of the persons appointed to receive subscriptions in Pennsylvania, agreeably to the resolve of Congress, for procuring Twenty Millions of Dollars on Interest. In Feb., 1781, he was appointed with John Lukins to extend the line commonly called Mason and Dixon's line five degrees of longitude from Delaware river, and to run a meridian line north to the Ohio river from the western termination of the same for a perpetual boundary between Virginia and Pennsylvania.—*Pennsylvania Archives.*

NOTE i, PAGE 70. CADWALLADER COLDEN, Lieutenant Governor of the Colony of New York.—He was the son of the Rev. Alexander Colden, of Dunse, in Scotland, where he was born Feb. 17, 1688; graduated in Edinburgh in 1705, and engaged in the study of medicine and mathematics till 1708. He then emigrated to America, and practised physic in Philadelphia till 1715. On his return to Scotland that year, he married Alice Christie, daughter of a clergyman at Kelso. In 1716 he returned to his practice in Philadelphia, and in 1718 removed to New York, and, abandoning his profession, turned his attention to public affairs. He was successively appointed Surveyor General of the Colony, Master in Chancery, Member of the Council, and Lieutenant Governor. His name is connected with the Stamp Act period, one of the most instructive in New York history. He was a skilful politician. He died at his residence at Flushing, called Spring Hill, on the 20th September, 1776, at the age of eighty-eight years.—*Thompson's History of Long Island*, ii. 87.

NOTE j, PAGE 79. JOHN TABOR KEMPE, Attorney General of the Province of New York.—This gentleman was the son of William Kempe, an English Barrister who was appointed His Majesty's Advocate and Attorney General for New York in 1751, and whose arrival with his family is announced in the *New York Gazette* for Nov. 6, 1752. The father did not live long to enjoy his honors, and upon his death, in 1759, his son John Tabor Kempe, who had been admitted to practice at the New York Bar the preceding year, succeeded him in the office. John Tabor Kempe married Grace, daughter of Hon. Daniel Coxe, of New Jersey, through whom he became possessed of a large landed estate in that Colony. Mr. Kempe remained in New York during the War and took the King's side. His estate was confiscated. He returned to England at the Peace.—*Col. Doc.* vii. 926.

NOTE k, PAGE 82. GOLDSBROW BANYAR, Deputy Clerk of his Majesty's Council.—He was born in London, in the year 1724, and is said to have come to this country about 1737. He was appointed Auditor General in 1746, and sworn in as Deputy Secretary of the Province, Deputy Clerk of the Council, etc., which office he retained until the year 1747, when he was succeeded by Samuel Bayard, Jr. In 1752 he was appointed Register of the Court of Chancery, and the next year Judge of the Probate. At the breaking out of the War he retired to Rhinebeck. In 1767 he married Elizabeth Mortier, daughter of the Paymaster General and widow of John Appy, Judge Advocate of the British Army. After the Peace he removed to Albany, where he died on the 4th November, 1815, at the age of 91, leaving to his descendants a large estate.—*Col. Doc.* viii. 189.

NOTE l, PAGE 89. GEORGE THE THIRD.—Son of Frederick, Prince of Wales, and of Augusta, Princess of Saxe-Gotha, was born 24th May, 1738. On the death of his grandfather, October 25, 1780, he was proclaimed King of Great Britain and Ireland, under the name of George III. On the 8th September, 1761, he married Princess Charlotte, of Mecklenburgh Strelitz (born May 19, 1744, crowned Sept. 22, 1761). From 1787 to 1789 there was an interregnum in the affairs of England, the King's reason being obscured. He died at Windsor Castle, Jan. 29, 1820, in the 82d year of his age and 60th of his reign. His reign was marked by the loss of the Colonies, the acquisition of India, and the Continental War which followed the French Revolution.—*Blake's Biographical Dictionary*, p. 379.

NOTE m, PAGE 101. THOMAS PETTIT.—Appointed Messenger and Doorkeeper of the Chamber as early as 1770; was a favorite person in this class of employment. On the 30th May, 1774, he was chosen Messenger of the Committee of Correspondence of Fifty-one, and his name is to be found on the Journals of the Council of Safety, 14th May, 1777, as their Doorkeeper. In 1780 he lived next door to the *Theatre Royal*, and sold tickets of admission. He died October 13th, 1780.—*Gaine's New York Gazette*, Oct. 16, 1780.

NOTE n, PAGE 108. HUGH GAINE.—This well known Printer and Bookseller was an Irishman by birth. He served his apprenticeship in Belfast. In 1752 he established the *New York Mercury*, and located himself in Hanover Square, where his sign of the "Bible and Crown" was one of the well-known landmarks of old New York. Here he remained for fifty years. When the British came into the city he crossed to Newark with his press, but soon returned. The *New York Mercury* was discontinued after the Peace in 1783. He died in New York April 25, 1807, aged eighty-one years, and was buried in Trinity Church Yard.—*Thomas's History of Printing*, ii. 103.

NOTE o, PAGE 108. CAPTAIN WARDEN, of the *Rose*, arrived in New York in 42 days from *Madeira*, on the 2d August, 1770, and sailed for *Leith* on the 11th October following.—*Holt's New York Journal*, Nos. 1439 and 1449.

It was, no doubt, upon his arrival trip, that he saved the crew of the vessel bound from Lisbon to Philadelphia, alluded to in the text.

NOTE p, PAGE 113. FRANCIS MAERSCHALK.—By an Act of the General Assembly, passed May 20, 1769, FRANCIS MAERSCHALK and Henry Bryant were named Inspectors of all Flour to be shipped for exportation. Their names are recorded in *Gaine's Register* for 1775.—*Gaine's Laws of New York*, 537.

The family of MAERSCHALK were interested in the flour-trade in different ways. In 1740 the Council authorized JOHN MAERSCHALK to store meal in the *Meal Market*.—*Devoe's Market Book*, 250.

NOTE q, PAGE 116. JOHN MURRAY, IVTH EARL OF DUNMORE.—The grandson of Lord Charles Murray, Master of the Horse to Queen Mary, who was raised to the peerage of Scotland 16th August, 1686, as Earl of Dunmore. His two sons, John and William, succeeded him in turn. John, IVth Earl of Dunmore, was the son of William, IIId Earl, and Catharine, daughter of Lord William Murray. He was one of the Representative Peers of Scotland from 1761 to 1784. He married, 21st February, 1759, Lady Charlotte Stewart, daughter of Alexander, Vth Earl of Galloway. Commissioned Governor of New York on the 2d January, 1770, he commenced his rule October 19th, 1770, and continued in power until July 9th, 1771. Lord Botetourt, Governor of Virginia, having died, he was promoted to the Government of that Province. He did not assume his new government until 1772.

On the 22d April, 1776, he went on board the Foway Man of War, and carried on predatory excursions against the neighboring country. Forced to retire to St. Augustine, he fired Norfolk. At the request of the Assembly of Virginia, he had named one of his daughters *Virginia*. He was in 1786 appointed Governor of the Bahama Islands: he died in England in March 1809. One of his daughters, *Augusta*, married Prince Augustus Frederick, Duke of Sussex.—*Burke's Peerage; N. Y. Col. Doc.* viii. 209.

NOTE r, PAGE 119. FREDERICK SMYTH, Chief Justice of the Colony of New Jersey.—On the death of Robert Hunter Morris, February 20th, 1764, Charles Read was appointed to succeed him as Chief Justice. He officiated, however, but a few months. Whether the appointment gave dissatisfaction, or was designed only as a temporary one, the fact is he was soon displaced and consented again to take the place of Second Judge which he had held for some time before Mr. Morris's death. The last Chief Justice of the Colony of New Jersey was FREDERICK SMYTH. He was appointed on the 17th October, 1764, and continued in office until the adoption of the Constitution of 1776. In 1772 he was one of the Commissioners to examine into the burning of the Gaspee by the Whigs of Rhode Island. When the War broke out he removed to Philadelphia. His reputation as a judge was considerable, and he maintained the character of a firm and consistent loyalist.—*New Jersey Hist. Soc. Coll.* iii. 159.

NOTE s, PAGE 132.—WILLIAM FOXCROFT.—The Deputy Postmasters General for the Northern District were in 1771 Benjamin Franklin and William Foxcroft. They were succeeded in 1775 by John Foxcroft and Hugh Finley.—*Gaine's New York Almanacs*, 1771–1775.

NOTE t, PAGE 133. WILLIAM TRYON.—Governor of the Colony of New York. He entered the British army as Lieutenant and Captain of the 1st Regiment of Foot Guards 12th October, 1751; in 1757 married Miss Wake, a lady of fortune, and on 30th Sept. 1758, became Captain and Lieutenant Colonel in the Guards. He was appointed Lieut. Governor of North Carolina in 1764, and Governor in July, 1765. In July, 1771, he was promoted to the administration of the New York Colony. He resigned the government on the 21st July, and was appointed Lieutenant General 20th November, 1782. Before the War he seems to have been generally esteemed, but his subsequent career in America is "as notorious as it was odious." He died in London, 27th January, 1788.—*Col. Doc.* viii. 798.

NOTE u, PAGE 144. LEWIS JOHNSTON.—The sixth son of the well-known Dr. John Johnstone, a druggist of Edinburgh, who emigrated to America, and, settling first at New York in 1685, removed about 1707 to Amboy, New Jersey. Through his wife, Eupham Scot, he became possessed of a grant from the proprietors of Jersey of five hundred acres, on condition of residence upon it. He died 7th September, 1732. LEWIS was born in

October, 1704, and adopting the profession of his father, was much respected, both as a man and a physician. His education was received in Holland. He married Martha, daughter of Caleb Heathcote, of New York. He died November 22, 1773, and it was said of him that "he was a physician of the highest reputation and very greatly beloved by all who knew him."—*Whitehead's Contributions to East Jersey History*, 71.

NOTE v, PAGE 144. WILLIAM BAYARD.—An eminent merchant and head of the house of William Bayard and Company. He was one of the Committee of Correspondence appointed in 1774, upon the news of the passage of the Boston Port Bill; but it does not appear that he had any strong sympathy with the Whig movement. He remained in the city during the British occupation, and signed the loyal address to Lord Howe in the fall of 1776. At the close of the War he went to England. His property in New York was confiscated. Governor Franklin, of New Jersey, recommended him to Lord George Germaine for relief. He died very aged, in 1804, at his seat, Greenwich House, Southampton, England.—*Sabine's Loyalists*, i. 217.

NOTE w, PAGE 144. ROBERT HUNTER MORRIS.—One of the proprietors of New Jersey. He was the second son of Lewis Morris (proprietor of Morrisania, and first Governor of the Province of New Jersey), and Isabella, daughter of James Graham, Attorney General of New York. He was for nearly twenty-six years one of the Council of the Colony, and was also Lieutenant Governor of Pennsylvania from October, 1754, to August, 1756. He was also Chief Justice of New Jersey, which office he resigned in the fall of 1757. He died February 20th, 1764.—*Smith's New Jersey*, 438, 439.

NOTE x, PAGE 156. ISAAC L. WINN.—A captain in one of the London merchant vessels. His arrival in the Downs with his ship, the Duchess of Gordon, is noticed in *Holt's New York Journal*, February 27th, 1772. An announcement of her arrival on Saturday evening, 11th April, 1772, in eight weeks from London, with the newest advices, appeared in the same journal, 16th of same month. It was, no doubt, upon this ship that Captain Winn brought out the SEAL for the Chamber. The Duchess of Gordon has an interesting record. It was on board this ship, in New York Harbor, under protection of the Asia Man of War, that Governor Tryon took refuge on the 30th October, 1775, and in her cabin the Council meetings were for a time held. Captain Winn also appears in the Revolutionary period. In September, 1775, having sailed in a sloop bound to the eastward, and suspected of a design for furnishing the army and navy of the enemy, he was overtaken by Isaac Sears, who pursued him, by order of the General Committee, above Hellgate, and brought before the Committee of Safety. He cleared himself so entirely of suspicion, that he received a certificate of good conduct.—*N. Y. Col. Doc.* viii. 643; *Journal of Prov. Congress*, i. 141.

NOTE y, PAGE 162. PETER MERSILLIS, a Master Carpenter.—The family continued in this branch of mechanics for a long period. Their names may be found, as carpenters, in the New York Directories until quite recently.

NOTE z, PAGE 167. MATTHEW PRATT.—This early American painter was born in Philadelphia on the 23d September, 1734. His taste for portrait painting showed itself when he was still quite young, but he did not adopt it as a profession until he became a member of the family of Mr. Benjamin West, then living in London, with whom there was a distant matrimonial connection. In 1768 he returned to Philadelphia, and, under the patronage of the leading families of the city, soon rose to a considerable local eminence. Art was so little encouraged that he was compelled to add sign painting to portrait painting. He occasionally painted in New York.—*Dunlap's Arts of Design*, i. 98.

NOTE aa, PAGE 169. JONATHAN BLAKE.—A leading and patriotic mechanic. His name appears on the Journals of the New York Committee of Correspondence as Chairman of the Body of Mechanics, signifying "their concurrence with the other inhabitants of the City in the nomination of the Committee."—*Force's American Archives*, i. 295.

NOTE bb, PAGE 181. THOMAS GAGE, General and Commander in Chief of His Majesty's Forces in North America.—An active officer during the French War, he was appointed Governor of Montreal in 1760, and succeeded General Amherst, in 1763, in the chief command of the British forces in America. He resided for many years in New York, and greatly endeared himself to the people by his peremptory orders to the troops not to fire on the citizens who threatened the Fort in New York, in the Stamp Act excitement of the fall of 1765. He sailed from New York for England on 8th June, 1773. On the news of the destruction of the tea reaching England, he was sent for by the King (George III.), and engaged with four regiments to reduce the Colonies to submission. Appointed Military Governor of the Massachusetts Bay, he arrived in Boston on the 17th May, 1774. The expedition to Concord to seize the stores there, which resulted in the Battle of Lexington, was made by his command. After the disastrous Battle of Bunker Hill, June 17th, 1775, he was superseded by General Howe, and sailed for England 10th October of same year. He died at his home, in Portland Place, London, April 2d, 1787.

NOTE cc, PAGE 191. BERNARD ROMANS.—Born in Holland. Removing to England, when quite young, he there received his education as an engineer. He was employed on various occasions by the British Government. While engaged in the map and history of Florida (1773), he made some investigations on the Compass, which were printed in the Transactions of the American Philosophical Society. He was aided in the construction of the map by Abel Buell, of Killingworth, Conn., an ingenious mechanician. On the breaking out of the War, he was appointed, by the New York Committee of Safety, to fortify the Hudson River, and on the 29th August, 1775, commenced the erection of the first of the "Fortifications in the Highlands." On the 18th September of the same year he submitted his plans to Congress. On the 8th February, 1776, he was appointed, by the Committee of Safety of Pennsylvania, Captain of the Company of Matrosses (Artillery), raised by order of Congress. He remained in service until near the close of the War, when he was captured at sea by the British on his way from Connecticut to the Carolinas. He is said to have died about 1783.—*Boynton's West Point*, 21 ; *Journals of N. Y. Prov. Congress ; Minutes of Prov. Council Penn.* x. 479.

NOTE dd, PAGE 204. DANIEL JONES, of the Second Foot.—He received the appointment of Lieutenant General in the Army in 1779.—*Annual Register*, xxii. 243.

NOTE ee, PAGE 206. ANDREW ELLIOT, Superintendent General.—He was the third son of Sir Gilbert Elliot, Baronet, Lord Justice Clerk of Scotland. On the death of Archibald Kennedy, Collector of the Port of New York, he was appointed to the vacant post by a Commission dated 19th January, 1764, and held the office till the evacuation of the city. He also held the office of Superintendent General during the War, and, together with the Mayor and a Magistrate of Police, administered the civil government of the City. He was appointed Lieutenant Governor in 1780, and held the chief power from 17th April to 25th November, 1783. He married a Philadelphia lady. His daughter Elizabeth married Lord, afterwards Earl, Cathcart in 1779.—*N. Y. Col. Doc.* viii. 96.

NOTE ff, PAGE 206. JAMES PATTISON, Major General.—He was appointed Captain of the Artillery, 1st August, 1747; Lieutenant Colonel in the army in 1761; Colonel Commandant of Artillery, 25th April, 1777; Major General 19th February, 1779. He accompanied the expedition against Charleston in 1780; was raised to the rank of Lieutenant General, 28th September, 1787, and of General in the army, 26th January, 1797. He died in London, March 1st, 1805, aged 81 years.—*Gentleman's Magazine*, lxxv. 291.

NOTE gg, PAGE 212. JOHN NORRIS.—This name appears as early as 1735, in the following curious advertisement. "To be sold, Wrought or Unwrought, Curious fine flat purple Stones brought from Hide Park for Tombs-Stones, Head-Stones, Hearth-stones, Step-stones, Paving-stones, &c. Whoever has occasion for any of the afore said Stones may apply to *John Norris*, at the house of Mr. *Edward Hicks*, merchant in New York.—*Bradford's N. Y. Gazette*, No. 492, March 24th to 31st, 1735.

The doorkeeper of the Chamber was a maker of Wigs, as appears by a notice of his death. "Last week died at his House in this City, Mr. JOHN NORRIS, Peruke Maker."—*Gaine's N. Y. Gazette*, April 24th, 1780.

His death is incidentally mentioned in connection with the appointment of his successor by the Chamber, May 2d, 1780 (*see page* 229).

NOTE hh, PAGE 224. LIEUTENANT WALTER.—This gentleman, who received the thanks of the Chamber for his care of the Powder Ship, was probably connected with the British Navy, and detailed for this service. Whose agent he was does not appear.

NOTE ii, PAGE 229. RICHARD HARRIS.—The doorkeepers of the Chamber were unfortunate this year. The death of Richard Harris is recorded on the same day with that of his predecessor, Thomas Pettit. He died Friday, 13th October, 1780.—*Gaine's New York Gazette*, October 16th, 1780.

NOTE jj, PAGE 229. JAMES ROBERTSON, Lieutenant General and Governor in Chief.—He was appointed Major of the 1st Battalion of the 60th or Royal American Regiment, December, 1755; was at Louisbourg in 1758; promoted to be Lieutenant Colonel 8th July, 1758; with Amherst on Lakes George and Champlain in 1759. In 1772 he became Colonel in the army. In July, 1775, he was stationed at Boston; appointed Major General in America, 1st January, 1776. He was with Lord Howe at Staten Island. He returned to England in 1777, and became Major General in the army, 29th August of that year. On the 4th May, 1779, he was commissioned Governor of New York, and was sworn in 23d March, 1780. He became

Lieutenant General 20th November, 1782; embarked at New York for England, 15th April, 1783; and died in 1788.—*N. Y. Col. Doc.* viii. 706.

NOTE kk, PAGE 232. CHARLES NEWMAN.—For a full account of the loss of the Carteret Packet, see *Historical Notes* 149, 150, 153, pp. 352, 354.

NOTE ll, PAGE 237. MARRIOT ARBUTHNOT, Vice Admiral of the Blue, the son of Robert Arbuthnot.—He was a native of Weymouth, in Dorsetshire, and entered the naval service at an early age. He was appointed Lieutenant in 1739. He successively commanded the *Jamaica* Sloop, the *Triton* [24 guns], the *Garland* [20], the *Portland* [50], and the *Terrible* [74]. On the breaking out of the American War he was appointed Commissioner at the Navy Yard at Halifax. After the trial of Admiral Keppel, in which he participated, he was raised to the rank of Vice Admiral of the Blue, and appointed Commander in Chief in North America. He commanded the squadron which sailed from New York for the Carolinas, on the 26th December, 1779, on the expedition which resulted in the reduction of Charleston. Having returned to New York, and being reinforced by Admiral Graves, he sailed for Rhode Island, where the French squadron was laying in Newport harbor. The English fleet lay at Gardner's Bay. The French fleet, under M. de Ternay, put to sea on the 8th of March, 1781, and were pursued by Admiral Arbuthnot. A long but indecisive action took place off Cape Henry.

Admiral Arbuthnot, having received his orders of recall in July, 1781, shifted his flag from the *Royal Oak*, where it had been for some time flying, to his old ship the *Roebuck*, and resigning the command to Admiral Graves, sailed for Spithead. This closed his active command. On the 24th September, 1787, he was made Vice Admiral of the Red, and on the 1st February, 1793, Admiral of the Blue squadron. He died at his house in Great Suffolk Street, Charing Cross, on the 31st January, 1794, aged 83.—*Ralfe's Naval Biography*, i. 129; *The Naval Chronicle*, xxiii. 265.

NOTE mm, PAGE 240. ABRAHAM CUYLER.—Of Albany. Confined at Hartford, he applied to the New York State Convention in August, 1776, for leave to visit his family. Released, after some delay, he was authorized to raise a battalion for the King's service. He was at Jamaica, recruiting, in 1779. He was attainted and his property confiscated. In 1781 he went to England. He returned to Albany, but soon withdrew to Canada, where he died in 1810, aged sixty-eight.—*Sabine's Loyalists*, i. 356.

NOTE nn, PAGE 240. SHEFFIELD HOWARD.—Little is known of this gentleman. He lost a large amount of property during the War. His daughter, Anna, married Major Bingham, and, a widow, became the wife of Sir Thomas Hay, Baronet.—*Sabine's Loyalists*, i. 548.

NOTE oo, PAGE 240. WILLIAM TONGUE.—A Broker and Auctioneer, Hanover Square, two doors from Wall Street, opposite Hugh Gaine's printing office. He was an addresser of Lord Howe in 1776. Like most of the Vendue Masters, his sales were chiefly made on the Coffee-house Bridge. His advertisements are frequently met with about the period 1780–81. In his announcement "that he has opened a Merchant Broker's Office," at the corner house near the Exchange, he says he has had experience in London and America for upward of twenty-five years.—*Rivington's New York Gazetteer*, Sept. 22, 1774.

NOTE pp, PAGE 247. SIR HENRY CLINTON, Commander in Chief.—He was the grandson of Francis, sixth Earl of Lincoln; and after service in the Hanoverian War was sent to America as Major General in 1775. He took part in the battle of Bunker Hill, and commanded at the battle of Long Island, September, 1776, which resulted in the evacuation of New York by the American troops. In 1777 he made an ineffectual effort to open the Hudson and relieve Burgoyne. Forced to withdraw from Philadelphia by General Washington, he led in person the expedition which captured Charleston in the spring of 1780. He sailed from New York to relieve Cornwallis with seven thousand men, on the very day of the surrender of Yorktown. He was superseded by General Carleton in 1781; returned to England in 1782, and was appointed Governor of Gibraltar. He died soon after.—*New American Cyclopædia*, v. 352.

NOTE qq, PAGE 260. THOMAS GRAVES, Rear Admiral of the Red.—He was the second son of Admiral Thomas Graves, and was born at Thankes in Cornwall. He went to sea at an early age. He was raised to the rank of Lieutenant on the 25th June, 1743. His first command was the *Hazard* Sloop, in 1754, and successively the *Unicorn* of 28 guns; the *Antelope* [60]; the *Temeraire* [74]; and the *Raisonable* [60]. In 1776 he was chosen a Representative in Parliament for the borough of East Looe. In 1777 he was appointed to the Nonsuch, and afterwards transferred to the Conqueror. While on the West India station he received information of his elevation to a flag as Rear Admiral of the Blue on the 19th March, 1779. On his return to England he was commissioned to the *London* of 98 guns. In 1780 he sailed for America with a reinforcement of six sail of the line for the squadron under Admiral Arbuthnot, and arrived at New York on the 13th July. On the 26th September he was raised to the rank of Rear Admiral of the Red.

On the recall of Admiral Arbuthnot in July, 1781, the command devolved on Rear Admiral Graves. Intelligence reaching him soon after of the sailing of De Barras from Rhode Island, he put to sea on the 31st August, and pushed for the Chesapeake, where they were engaged by the French fleet under De Grasse. A long but indecisive action took place, in which the English were severely handled, and Admiral Graves was forced to abandon the effort to dislodge the French from their position. "The result of this encounter decided the fate of the war." On his return to New York he was reinforced by Rear Admiral Digby, who had been appointed Commander in Chief on the American station, but who waived his rank till the close of the expedition undertaken to relieve Lord Cornwallis. Owing to delay in the outfit the fleet only sailed from New York on the 19th October, the day of the surrender at Yorktown. On hearing of the surrender Admiral Graves returned to New York, and resigned his command to Admiral Digby.

On the 24th Sept., 1787, he was made Vice Admiral; and on the 12th April, 1794, Admiral of the Blue. He was wounded at the battle of the Nile 1st June, 1794, and was rewarded with an Irish peerage. On the 1st June, 1795, he was made Admiral of the White.

He married, in 1771, Elizabeth, daughter of William Piere Williams, and died in February, 1802.—*Ralfe's Naval Biography*, i. 174.

NOTE rr, PAGE 263. FRANCIS BAYARD WINTHROP.—The Winthrop, of Winthrop & Kemble, was probably the F. B. Winthrop who signed the Boston address to General Gage in 1775 and a loyalist. He married

Miss Marston, eldest daughter of Mr. Thomas Marston, of New York, in April, 1779.—*Gaine's New York Gazette*, April 26, 1779.

He was residing at 29 Wall Street in 1798.—*Longworth's City Directory*, 1798.

Note ss, Page 266. DAVID MATHEWS, Mayor of New York.—Upon the resignation of Whitehead Hicks, in February, 1776, he was appointed Mayor of the City, and, by permission of the Provincial Congress, was qualified by Governor Tryon, on board the ship *Duchess of Gordon* in the harbor. "He was among those who were implicated in the intricacies of the Hickey Plot. There is nothing in the evidence, however, which justifies the suspicion that he was really concerned in it, beyond acting as a messenger in delivering money to Forbes from Tryon. He was removed into Connecticut and held in close custody there for some time. He was Registrar of the Court of Admiralty in 1782. After the War he was President of the Council and Commander in Chief of the Island of Cape Breton. While at Flatbush, in the summer of 1778, he narrowly escaped being captured by Marriner, his expedition being undertaken for that purpose.—*New York City during the Revolution, Mercantile Library*, 67; *Sabine's Loyalists*, ii. 50.

Note tt, Page 270. GEORGE KEITH ELPHINSTONE, the Honorable.—He was the fifth son of Lord Elphinstone, and born in 1746. He went to sea in February, 1762, on board the *Gosport*. In 1772 he was made commander of the *Scorpion*, 14 guns. In 1778 he was appointed to the *Warwick*, of 50 guns, and in January, 1781, he captured, after a smart contest, a Dutch ship of war of 50 guns and 300 men. During the remainder of the War Captain Elphinstone was on the American station under Admiral Digby. In the election of 1785 he was returned for the County of Stirling. In March, 1797, he was raised to the dignity of a baron of the Kingdom of Ireland by the title of Baron Keith; and on the 5th December, 1801, of the United Kingdom. He was promoted for various distinguished services, and on the 9th November, 1805, was made Admiral of the White. In May, 1814, he was created Viscount Keith. He died at Tullian House on the 16th March, 1823, aged 77 years.—*Mackenzie's Naval Biography*, page 144.

Note uu, Page 279. JOHN ST. CLAIR.—Captain St. Clair was appointed Secretary to James Robertson, Commandant, on the 23d September, 1780.—*Gaine's New York Gazette*, Sept. 25th, 1780.

Note vv, Page 280. ROBERT DIGBY, Rear Admiral of the Blue.—He was the third son of Hon. Edward Digby and Charlotte, only surviving daughter of Sir Stephen Fox and sister of Henry Lord Holland. He was appointed Post-Captain August 5, 1755, and his first ship was the *Solebay*, of 24 guns. He commanded in turn the *Biddeford*, the *Rochefort*, of 60 guns. On the breaking out of war with France, Captain Digby was commissioned to the *Ramillies*, of 74 guns. He was made Rear Admiral of the Blue 19th March, 1779. In May he hoisted his flag on board the *Prince George*, and Prince William Henry (afterwards William IV.) was placed under his charge. He twice relieved the Garrison of Gibraltar with supplies. In 1781 he was appointed to the chief command on the American station, but finding on his arrival that Admiral Graves was engaged in an effort to relieve Cornwallis, he waived his rank. On the 24th September, 1787, he was made Vice Admiral, and on the 12th April, 1794, Admiral of the Blue.

He married, in August, 1784, Eleanor, daughter of Andrew Elliot, Esq. (who had been Lieutenant Governor of New York), and widow of Mr. Jauncey.—*Balfe's Naval Biography*, i. 192.

NOTE WW, PAGE 297. CORNELIUS RAY.—The son of Richard Ray and Sarah Bogert, born in New York, 25th April, 1755. He married in Albany, July, 1784, Elizabeth, daughter of Peter Edward Elmendorff, of Kingston, Ulster county. Mr. Ray was an active merchant in New York, but during the Revolutionary War retired to Albany. At the Peace he returned to the city. On the establishment of the United States Bank he was chosen President of the Branch in this city, and so continued until the expiration of its charter in 1810. He was elected President of the Chamber of Commerce in May, 1806, and so continued until 1819, when he declined further service. He died in 1829.—*King's History of the Chamber of Commerce*, page 91.

NOTE XX, PAGE 297. COMFORT SANDS.—The son of John Sands and Elizabeth Cornwall, born at Sands' Point, Long Island, 26th Feb., 1748. In 1762 he went to New York and lived with Joseph Duke, a merchant in Peck Slip. In 1769 he commenced business on his own account, and on the 3d June of the same year he married Sarah, daughter of Wilkie Dodge, of Cow Neck. He had acquired a considerable property before the War broke out. He was one of the Committee of Observation in 1774, and a member of the Provincial Congress from Nov., 1775, to July, 1776. He was chosen Auditor General of the Public Accounts by the New York Convention in 1776, and held the post till October, 1781, when he resigned. In 1783 he formed a partnership with his brother Joshua, and conducted a large mercantile business in New York. The firm continued till 1794. He was several times chosen to represent New York City in the Assembly. He was one of the first directors of the Bank of New York in 1784, and in 1794 was elected President of the Chamber of Commerce. Few persons were more active and useful during the trying period of the Revolution, or enjoyed to a greater degree the public confidence.—*Thompson's Long Island*, ii. 465.

NOTE YY, PAGE 297. ROBERT BOWNE.—The son of John Bowne and Dinah Underhill, born at Flushing, in the year 1744. He married Elizabeth Hartshorne. His name does not appear in New York during the War.—*Thompson's Long Island*, ii. 389–90.

NOTE ZZ, PAGE 297. JOSHUA SANDS.—The son of John Sands and Elizabeth Cornwall. He was connected with his brothers, Comfort and Richardson, in a contract with Robert Morris, to supply the northern army with provisions for 1782. In 1783 he formed a partnership with his brother Comfort, and they transacted a mercantile business, under the name of *Comfort & Joshua Sands*, till 1794. (Their place of business was at 137 Water Street.)—*Thompson's Long Island*, ii. 466.

TABLE OF NEW JERSEY BILLS REDUCED TO NEW YORK CURRENCY.

Agreeable to a Law of the Colony of New York.

GAINE'S NEW YORK ALMANAC, 1775.

No. of Bills.	Bill of 1*s*.			Bill of 1*s*. 6*d*.			Bill of 3*s*.			Bill of 6*s*.			Bill of 12*s*.			Bill of 15*s*.			Bill of 30*s*.			Bill of £3.		
	£	*s*.	*d*.	£	*s*.	*d*.	£	*s*.	*d*.	£	*s*.	*d*.	£	*s*.	*d*.	£	*s*.	*d*.	£	*s*.	*d*.	£	*s*.	*d*.
1	0	1	0¾	0	1	7⅛	0	3	2⅜	0	6	4¾	0	12	9½	0	16	0	1	12	0	3	4	0
3	0	3	2⅜	0	4	9½	0	9	7⅛	0	19	2⅜	1	18	4¾	2	8	0	4	16	0	9	12	0
5	0	5	3⅞	0	8	0	0	16	0	1	12	0	3	4	0	4	0	0	8	0	0	16	0	0
7	0	7	5½	0	11	2¼	1	2	4¾	2	4	9½	4	9	7⅛	5	12	0	11	4	0	22	8	0
10	0	10	7⅞	0	16	0	1	12	0	3	4	0	6	8	0	8	0	0	16	0	0	32	0	0
11	0	11	8⅝	0	17	7⅛	1	15	2⅜	3	10	4¾	7	0	9½	8	16	0	17	12	0	35	4	0
14	0	14	11	1	2	4¾	2	4	9½	4	9	7⅛	8	19	2⅜	11	4	0	22	8	0	44	16	0
16	0	17	0¾	1	5	7⅛	2	11	2⅜	5	2	4¾	10	4	9½	12	16	0	25	12	0	51	4	0
18	0	19	$2\frac{3}{3}$	1	8	9½	2	17	7⅛	5	15	2⅜	11	10	4¾	14	8	0	28	16	0	57	12	0
20	1	1	3⅞	1	12	0	3	4	0	6	8	0	12	16	0	16	0	0	32	0	0	64	0	0

TABLE OF NEW JERSEY BILLS REDUCED TO NEW YORK CURRENCY.

GAINE'S POCKET ALMANAC,

1774.

No. of Bills.	Bill of 1*s.*			Bill of 1*s.* 6*d.*			Bill of 3*s.*			Bill of 6*s.*			Bill of 12*s.*			Bill of 15*s.*			Bill of 30*s.*			Bill of £3.		
	£	*s.*	*d.*	£	*s.*	*d.*	£	*s.*	*d.*	£	*s.*	*d.*	£	*s.*	*d.*	£	*s.*	*d.*	£	*s.*	*d.*	£	*s.*	*d.*
1	0	1	1	0	1	7½	0	3	3	0	6	6	0	13	0	0	16	3	1	12	6	3	5	0
3	0	3	3	0	4	10½	0	9	9	0	19	6	1	19	0	2	8	9	4	17	6	9	15	0
5	0	5	5	0	8	1½	0	16	3	1	12	6	3	5	0	4	1	3	8	2	6	16	5	0
7	0	7	7	0	11	4½	1	2	9	2	5	6	4	11	0	5	13	9	11	7	6	22	15	0
10	0	10	10	0	16	3	1	12	6	3	5	0	6	10	0	8	2	6	16	5	0	32	10	0
11	0	11	11	0	17	10½	1	15	9	3	11	6	7	3	0	8	18	9	17	17	6	35	15	0
14	0	15	2	1	2	9	2	5	6	4	11	0	9	2	0	11	7	6	22	15	0	45	10	0
16	0	17	4	1	6	0	2	12	0	5	4	0	10	8	0	13	0	0	26	0	0	52	0	0
18	0	19	6	1	9	3	2	18	6	5	17	0	11	14	0	14	12	6	29	5	0	58	10	0
20	1	1	8	1	12	6	3	5	0	6	10	0	13	0	0	16	5	0	32	10	0	65	0	0

A TABLE OF THE VALUE AND WEIGHT OF COINS

AS THEY NOW PASS IN

England, Pennsylvania, New Jersey, New York, Massachusetts Bay, South Carolina and Georgia.

GAINE'S NEW YORK POCKET ALMANACK, 1780.

SPECIES.	Standard Weight.		Sterling Money.			Pennsylvania and New Jersey.			New York.			Lawful Money.			South Carolina.			Georgia.		
	dwts.	*grs.*	£	*s.*	*d.*	£	*s.*	*d.*	£	*s.*	*d.*	£	*s.*	*d.*	£	*s.*	*d.*	£	*s.*	*d.*
English Guineas	5	7	1	1	0	1	14	0	1	17	4	1	8	0	7	7	0	1	3	0
French ditto	5	5	1	1	1	1	13	6	1	16	0		ditto						ditto	
English Crown	17	1	0	5	0	9	7	6	0	8	9	0	6	8	1	15	9	0	5	0
English Shilling	0	0	0	1	0	0	1	6	0	1	9	0	1	4	0	7	0	0	1	0
Six-pence	6	0	0	0	6	0	0	9	0	0	9				0	3	6	0	0	6
Spanish Dollar	0	0	0	4	6	6	7	6	0	8	0	0	6	0	1	12	6	0	5	0
Johannes	18	6	3	12	0	6	0	0	6	8	0	4	16	0	26	0	0	4	0	0
Half Johannes	9	3	1	16	0	3	0	0	3	4	0	2	8	0	13	0	0	2	0	0
French Milled Pistole	4	4	0	16	0	1	6	6	1	8	0	1	2	0	6	0	0	0	18	0
Spanish ditto	4	6	0	16	6	1	7	0	1	9	0		ditto		6	0	0	0	18	0
Doubloon	17	8	3	6	0	5	8	0	5	16	0	4	8	0	24	0	0	3	12	0
French Crown	17	6	0	5	0	0	7	6	0	8	6	0	6	8	1	15	0	0	5	0
Pistole Piece	4	8	0	16	0	1	7	0	1	8	0	1	2	0	6	0	0	0	18	0

VALUE OF COINS.

LONDON.

Abstract of the Proclamation relative to the Gold Coin.

GAINE'S POCKET ALMANAC.

1775.

"*YESTERDAY, the* 24*th of June*, 1774, *his Majesty's Proclamation was published respecting the Gold Coin. The following is the substance of the most material Passages in it, viz.:*

"'*Whereas the Commissioners of the Treasury, by their Order of the* 23*d July last, did direct all Officers of the Revenues to cut, break, and deface all Pieces of Gold Coin of this Realm that should be tendered to them in Payment more deficient in Weight than the Rates settled in the Table following, viz.: Guineas coined since the* 31*st of December*, 1771, 5 *dwt.* 8 *gr. Half Guineas during the same Period*, 2 *dwt.* 16 *gr. Guineas coined during the present Reign and prior to the* 1*st January*, 1772, 5 *dwt.* 6 *gr. Half Guineas during the same Period*, 2 *dwt.* 14 *gr. Quarter Guineas during the same Period*, 1 *dwt.* 7 *gr. Guineas coined prior to the Commencement of the present Reign*, 5 *dwt.* 3 *gr. Half Guineas during the same period*, 2 *dwt.* 13 *gr. His Majesty declares and commands that all Guineas, Half Guineas, or Quarter Guineas more deficient in weight than the Rates before mentioned, be not allowed from henceforth to be current, or to pass in any Payment in Great Britain.*

"'*His Majesty further commands that from and after the* 15*th of July next ensuing, all Guineas, Half Guineas, and Quarter Guineas, more deficient in Weight than the Rates specified in the following Table, viz.: Guineas coined since the* 31*st December*, 1771, 5 *dwt.* 8 *gr. Half Guineas during the same period*, 2 *dwt.* 16 *gr. Guineas coined prior to the* 1*st of January*, 1772, 5 *dwt.* 6 *gr. Half Guineas during the same Period*, 2 *dwt.* 14 *gr. Quarter Guineas during the same Period*, 1 *dwt.* 7 *gr. be not allowed to be current, except in Payments to be made at the Exchequer, or to the Collectors of the Revenues, or to the Bank of England, or to the several Persons in different Country Towns mentioned in this Proclamation.*'"

TABLE SHOWING THE VALUE IN NEW YORK OR PENNSYLVANIA CURRENCY

For sums from One Penny to £100, computing the Exchange in New York Currency at 171 3-7 for £100 sterling, and in Pennsylvania Currency at 160 5-7, the Par of Exchange at 4*s.* 8*d.* per Dollar.

GAINE'S POCKET ALMANAC, 1775.

	£	*s.*	*d.*	£	*s.*	*d.*	£	*s.*	*d.*	£	*s.*	*d.*	£	*s.*	*d.*	£	*s.*	*d.*	£	*s.*	*d.*
Sterling			1		1	0		5	0		10	0		15	0	1	0	0	2	0	0
New York			$1\frac{5}{7}$		1	$8\frac{4}{7}$		8	$6\frac{6}{7}$		17	$1\frac{5}{7}$	1	5	$8\frac{4}{7}$	1	14	$3\frac{3}{7}$	3	8	$6\frac{6}{7}$
Pennsylvania			$1\frac{17}{28}$		1	$7\frac{4}{14}$		8	$\frac{3}{7}$		16	$\frac{6}{7}$	1	4	$1\frac{2}{7}$	1	12	$1\frac{5}{7}$	3	4	$3\frac{3}{7}$
Dollars		$\frac{1}{56}$			$\frac{3}{14}$			$1\frac{1}{14}$			$2\frac{1}{7}$			$3\frac{3}{14}$			$4\frac{2}{7}$			$8\frac{4}{7}$	

	£	*s.*	*d.*	£	*s.*	*d.*	£	*s.*	*d.*	£	*s.*	*d.*	£	*s.*	*d.*	£	*s.*	*d.*	£	*s.*	*d.*
Sterling	5	0	0	10	0	0	20	0	0	30	0	0	40	0	0	50	0	0	100	0	0
New York	8	11	$5\frac{1}{7}$	17	2	$10\frac{2}{7}$	34	5	$8\frac{4}{7}$	51	8	$6\frac{6}{7}$	68	11	$5\frac{1}{7}$	85	14	$3\frac{3}{7}$	171	8	$6\frac{6}{7}$
Pennsylvania	8	0	$8\frac{4}{7}$	16	1	$5\frac{1}{7}$	32	2	$10\frac{2}{7}$	48	4	$3\frac{3}{7}$	64	5	$8\frac{4}{7}$	80	17	$1\frac{1}{7}$	160	14	$3\frac{3}{7}$
Dollars		$21\frac{3}{7}$			$42\frac{6}{7}$			$85\frac{5}{7}$			$128\frac{4}{7}$			$171\frac{3}{7}$			$214\frac{2}{7}$			$428\frac{4}{7}$	

PRICES CURRENT IN NEW YORK,

1765–1775.

From John Holt's *New York Gazette or Weekly Post Boy*, 1765–1766; *New York Journal or General Advertiser*, 1767–1775.

STAPLE ARTICLES.	1765 May 2.	1766 May 8.	1767 May 7.	1768 May 5.	1769 May 4.	1770 May 3.	1771 May 16.	1772 May 7.	1773 May 6.	1774 May 5.	1775 May 4.
	£ s. d.	£ s. d.	£ s. d.	£ s. d.	£ s. d.	£ s. d.	£ s. d.	£ s. d.	£ s. d.	£ s. d.	£ s. d.
Wheat per Bushel..	5 9	5 9	6 0	6 9	5 6	5 6	7 6	8 0	8 0	7 4	6 4
Flour..............	15 0	16 0	18 0	19 0	16 0	15 6	20 0	21 0	21 6	19 6	16 0
Brown Bread	13 0	16 0	17 0	19 0	16 8	14 0	20 0	21 0	22 0	16 0	14 0
West India Rum...	3 3	3 2	3 4	3 6	4 1	3 6	3 6	3 6	3 6	3 8	3 5
New England Rum.	2 4	2 9	2 7	2 4	2 6	2 6	2 6	2 6	2 6	2 6	2 6
Muscovado Sugar..	56 0	70 0	50 0	50 0	56 0	55 0	53 0	56 0	52 0	62 0	65 0
Single Refined do..	1 2	1 4	1 2	1 0	2 0	2 0	1 0	1 0	1 1	1 1	1 2
Molasses..........	1 8	2 0	2 0	2 0	1 10	2 0	1 11	1 10	1 11	1 10	2 0
Beef per Barrel....	55 0	50 0	48 0	45 0	45 0	46 0	48 0	50 0	55 0	60 0	48 0
Pork	70 0	75 0	72 0	75 0	90 0	80 0	80 0	4 15 0	4 17 6	75 0	65 0
Salt	2 0	2 6	3 0	2 3	2 0	2 6	2 0	2 0	2 6	2 6	3 0
Bohea Tea.........	7 0	6 2	5 3	4 6	4 0	4 6	5 3	4 2	4 0	4 6	{ Liberty and Property.
Bees-wax..........	1 8	1 6	1 6	2 7	1 8	1 9	1 10	1 9	2 5	2 3	2 3
Chocolate per doz..	1 1 0	1 3 0	1 1 0	1 0 0	1 1 0	19 0	20 0	18 0	17 0	21 0	19 0
Nut Wood.........	30 0	28 0	35 0	32 0	30 0	28 0	32 0	35 0	30 3	30 0	35 0
Oak Wood	20 0	18 0	24 0	23 0	18 0	18 0	20 0	22 0	18 0	18 0	20 0

TABLE OF INSURANCE.

Extract from William Walton's Book of Insurance, 1773–1776.

1773.		Vessels.	Masters.	Voyages.	Sums.		Prem.
Jan.	1	S. Albany	Bunyan	New York to London	£100	A	2½
"	4	B. Mary	Anderson	New York to Newry	125	A	2½
"	5	On ditto	Ditto	Ditto to Newry, Liverpool, and New York . .	140	A	5
"	"	Sl. Sally	Albertson	New York to Philadelphia	50	A	2
"	6	Sh. Robert	Russel	New York to Newry	75	A	2½
"	"	On ditto	Ditto	Ditto and ditto till goods are landed . . .	75	A	3
"	"	On ditto	Ditto	Ditto and ditto	65	A	2½
"	7	On ditto	Ditto	Ditto and ditto till landed	50	A	3
"	8	B. New Diana	Wilson	New York to Dublin and Liverpool . . .	400	A	3
"	"	Sl. Mississippi	Goodridge	New York to New Orleans, with leave to touch .	250	A	4
"	"	Sn. Peggy	Cummings	New York to Belfast	55	L	2½
"	"	Sl. Sally	Hunt	New York to So. Carolina	60	A	2
"	12	Sl. Betsy	McCrahan	N. Carolina to Antigua, 2 Islands, and N. Carolina	45	a	6
"	13	Sc. Friends	Riddle	St. Martin's, Bermuda	50	A	1½
"	14	B. Elizabeth	Ashfield	New York to Curacoa	85	A	2½
"	"	B. Betsy	Schermerhorn	New York to So. Carolina and New York . .	50	A	3½
"	"	Sl. James	Humphreys	So. Carolina to St. Croix, leave to try market .	50	A	2½

Part of the entries of this year are in the writing of Anthony Van Dam, Secretary of the New York Insurance Office.—Ed.

TABLE OF INSURANCE.

Extract from Jacob Walton's Book of Insurance, 1777–1781.

1779.	Vessels.	Masters.	Voyages.	Sums.	Prem.	Ret'rn.
June 15	B. Lord Camden	Morgan	Bermuda to St. Kitts	£135	15	2
" 21	Sl. Nancy	Montaine	New York to Bermuda	60	12	—
" 22	Sc. Polly	McNiel	Grenada to New York	90	25	10
July 2	Sc. Rachel		St. John's River to St. Augustine and New York	60	50	—
" 5	Brig Diligence	McCreight	New York to Glasgow	50	25	10
" 6	Brig Speedwell	Lansfield	New York to London	55	25	10
" 7	Brig Chancery	Johnson	Georgia to Jamaica	130	25	5
	Sl. Sally	Hunt	Providence to New York	55	25	10
" 9	Brig Fannie	McKinley	New York to Oporto	125	25	—
" 12	Brig Kitty	Wilson	St. Kitts to Halifax	70	30	5
	Brig Speedwell	Sarsfield	New York to London	60	25	10
" 14	Sc. Ferret	Finley	St. Eustatia to New York	60	30	5
" 16	Brig Adventurer	Huntington	To Rhode Island	200	15	7

From a Memorandum Book in possession of the Walton Family.

IMPORTS AND EXPORTS

OF THE

AMERICAN COLONIES FROM AND TO GREAT BRITAIN—1700 TO 1780.

From Lord Sheffield's Observations.

Average.	Imports.			Exports.			Average.
	£	s.	d.	£	s.	d.	
1700—1710	267,205	3	4	265,783	0	10	1700—1710
1710—1720	365,645	7	11¾	392,653	17	1½	1710—1720
1720—1730	471,342	12	10½	518,830	16	6	1720—1730
1730—1740	660,136	11	1¼	670,128	16	0½	1730—1740
1740—1750	812,647	13	0¼	708,943	9	6¼	1740—1750
1750—1760	1,577,419	16	2½	802,691	6	10	1750—1760
1760—1770	1,763,409	10	3	1,044,591	17	0	1760—1770
1770—1780	1,331,206	1	5	743,560	10	10	1770—1780

STORES AND RESIDENCES

OF

THE MEMBERS OF THE CHAMBER OF COMMERCE.

1768.

Holt's N. Y. Journal.—Gaine's N. Y. Mercury.

ALEXANDER ROBERT. See Thompson & Alexander.

ALLICOCKE JOSEPH. Wines, Spirits, Groceries. "*Corner House fronting Wall and Queen Streets*, where Mr. Peter Remsen formerly lived," removed May, 1769, to "*the House in Wall Street* wherein Thomas William Moore lately lived."

ALSOP JOHN. General Importing Business. *Store in Hanover Square.*

AMIEL JOHN. General Groceries. *Store in South Street* nearly opposite Mr. Augustus Van Horne.

BAYARD SAMUEL, JR. Importer of European and India Goods. Store in *Queen Street.*

BACHE THEOPHYLACT. Importer of European and India Goods. Owner of ship Grace, William Chambers, Master—Bristol Trader. *Hanover Square, south side.*

BEEKMAN GERARD WILLIAM. Importer of Dry Goods. House in *Dock Street.*

BEEKMAN JAMES. Importer of European and India Goods. *Store in Queen Street.*

BOGART HENRY C. West India Goods. *Smith Street*, next door to Mr. Robert Ray's, near the Old Dutch Church.

BOOTH BENJAMIN. Importer of European Goods. "*Store near the Fly Market and the Ferry Stairs in the Street leading from thence to the Coffee House*—removed Feb. 1769 to the *large new Store of Mr. Peter Clopper, near the corner of Maiden Lane at the upper end of the Fly Market.*"

BREVOORT HENRY. Iron Mongery, at the "Sign of the Frying Pan." *Queen Street between the Fly Market and Burling's Slip.*

BUCHANAN THOMAS. See Walter & Thomas Buchanan.

BUCHANAN WALTER & THOMAS. Importers from England and Scotland, Dry Goods, &c. *Queen Street near the Fly Market.*

BULL JOSEPH. See Corsa & Bull.

CORSA & BULL. (Colonel Isaac Corsa & Joseph Bull.) Importers. Shop near *Peck's Slip.*

CRUGER HENRY & JOHN. Shipping Business. Owners of Bristol Traders. *Cruger's Dock.*

CRUGER JOHN (late Mayor), of Henry & John Cruger. House opposite to Mr. Lott's in *Smith Street.*

CRUGER JOHN HARRIS. Importer and Shipping Merchant, English and West India Trade. *Near the Exchange.*

DESBROSSES ELIAS. Importer of European Goods. Corner House, late Major Van Horne's—two doors from Abraham DePeyster's, *between the Fly Market & Merchants' Coffee House.*

DUYCKINCK GERARDUS. Drugs, Medicines, Stationery, "The Universal Store"—at the "Sign of the Looking Glass and Druggist Pot." *Dock Street*, corner of the *Old Slip Market.*

FOLLIOTT GEORGE & Co. Importers of European Goods, *Dock Street.*

FRANKLIN WALTER & Co. General Shipping and Importing Business. *Store in Wall Street.*

HOFFMAN & LUDLOW. (Nicholas Hoffman & Gabriel H. Ludlow.) Vendue Masters. *Dock Street.*

HOFFMAN NICHOLAS. See Hoffman & Ludlow.

KETELTAS & SHARPE. Peter Keteltas and Richard Sharpe, Clerks of the Old Insurance Office at the *Coffee House.*

KEMBLE SAMUEL, Captain. Commander of snow General Gage. London Trader.

LAIGHT EDWARD. Iron Mongery & Cutlery. *St. George's Square*, opposite the Hon. William Walton's.

LISPENARD LEONARD, JR. At the "Brewerie" on the *North River.*

LIVINGSTON PHILIP. General Importing Business. "Store on the *new Dock* (*Burnet's* Quay) *near the Ferry Stairs.*"

LOW ISAAC. General and Importing Business, Beaver Skins, &c. Store between the *Coenties Market and the Exchange.*

LUDLOW GABRIEL H. See Hoffman & Ludlow.

LYNSEN ABRAHAM. See Moore & Lynsen.

MCADAM WILLIAM. General Importer. *Smith Street*, near the New Dutch Church.

MCCORMICK DANIEL. See Moore, Lynsen & Co.

MCDAVITT PATRICK. Vendue Master, *corner of King Street*, opposite Alderman Desbrosses.

MCDONALD ALEXANDER, Captain. Importer of Dry Goods, Madeira Wine, &c.—"*near the Merchants' Coffee House.*"

MCEVERS CHARLES. Importer of European and India Goods. Successor to James McEvers, *Hanover Square.*

MCEVERS JAMES. Importer of European and India Goods. *Hanover Square.*

MARSTON THOMAS & JOHN. General Merchandise.

MILLER THOMAS, Captain. Commander of Ship Edward,—London Trader, at *Murray's Wharf.*

MOORE THOMAS WILLIAM. Importer and Vendue Master. See Moore & Lynsen. *Store in Wall Street, near the Coffee House.*

MOORE & LYNSEN. Vendue Masters. Thomas William Moore, Abraham Lynsen. Dissolved May, 1769. *Wall Street.*

MOORE, LYNSEN & Co. Vendue Masters. Thomas William Moore, Abraham Lynsen, Daniel McCormick. *Wall Street.*

MURRAY JOHN. See Watson & Murray.

MURRAY ROBERT. Shipping Merchant. *Store on Murray's Wharf.*

NEILSON WILLIAM. Importer of English Dry Goods. *Store in Great Dock Street.*

NICOLL CHARLES. Wine Importer *at the White-Hall.*

PHENIX DANIEL. House fronting on *Burnet's Street*, adjoining house where Mr. James De Peyster lives.

RAMADGE SMITH. Dry Goods Importer. *Queen Street.*

RAMSAY JOHN. Dry Goods Importer. *Near the Fly Market.*

RANDALL THOMAS, Captain. *Pearl Street.*

RAPALJE GARRETT. Dry Goods Importer. *Opposite the Fly Market.* Brew House (William Faulkner, Rem. & Garret Rapalje), *Brookland Ferry.*

READE JOHN. Importer of European and India Goods. Shipping. *Store corner of Wall Street*, fronting *Queen Street.*

READE & YATES. Lawrence Reade & Richard Yates. Importers of European and East India Goods. *Store Wall Street.*

REMSEN HENRY JR. & COMPANY. Importers of Dry Goods, Prints, &c. *Store in Hanover Square.*

REMSEN PETER. General Importer of Dry Goods. At the *corner of King Street.*

ROOSEVELT ISAAC. Sugar Refiner. *Wall Street.*

SEARS ISAAC. European and India Goods, Anchors, &c. *Queen Street.*

SETON WILLIAM. Importer of Dry Goods, European and India Goods. *Store on Cruger's Dock.*

SHARPE RICHARD. New York Air Furnace Company. Gilbert Forbes, Peter T. Curtemus, Richard Sharpe, &c. See Keteltas & Sharp.

SHERBROOKE MILES. (Perry, Hayes & Sherbrooke.) General Importers. *Bayard Street.*

SIMSON SAMPSON. (Sampson & Solomon Simson.) Shipping, Groceries, &c. *Store in Stone Street.*

TAYLOR JOHN. European and India Goods. *Hanover Square.*

TEMPLETON OLIVER. (Templeton & Stewart.) Vendue Masters. Opposite the *Coffee-House Bridge.*

THOMPSON & ALEXANDER. (Acheson Thompson & Robert Alexander.) Importers of Bottled Beer, Irish Beef, and Wines. *Great Dock Street, near Coenties Market.*

THOMPSON ACHESON. See Thompson & Alexander.

THURMAN JOHN, JR. General Importer. Dry Goods, West India Produce. *Wall Street, the corner of Smith Street.*

USTICK WILLIAM. Hardware Merchant. Nail Factory (William Ustick, Hubert van Waganen, Henry Ustick). Sign of "the Lock and Key," *between Burling's and Beekman's Slip.*

VAN DAM ANTHONY. Importer of Wines, and Shipping Agent. *Store in Dock Street.* Secretary of the New York Insurance Company. *Merchants' Coffee House.*

VAN HORNE AUGUSTUS. European and India Goods. *Smith Street.*

VAN ZANDT JACOBUS. General Importing Business. Dry Goods, Groceries. *Rotten Row, near the Coffee House.*

VERPLANCK SAMUEL. General Importer. European Goods. *House in Wall Street.*

WADDELL ROBERT ROSS. (Greg Cunningham & Co.) Shipping Merchants and Importers. *Hunter's Quay.*

WALLACE HUGH & ALEXANDER. Importers from Ireland. Linens, &c. "*Counting House in Burnet's Street.*"

WALTON JACOB & WILLIAM. Ship Yards on the *East River.*

WALTON WILLIAM. See Jacob & William Walton. Residence *St. George's Square.*

WATSON & MURRAY. (Jacob Watson & John Murray.) General Importers of European and India Goods, West India Produce, near *Burling's Slip.*

WETHERHEAD JOHN. Importer. Store near the *Bowling Green, in the Broadway.*

WHITE HENRY. General Importer. *Cruger's Dock*, fronting the *East River.* Removed May, 1769, to the late Treasurer's (Abraham de Peyster), between the *Fly Market and Coffee House.*

YATES RICHARD. See Reade & Yates.

DESCRIPTION

OF THE

CITY OF NEW YORK.

From Campbell's Political Survey of Great Britain.

"*THE City of New York is seated in* 41 *d.* 42 *m. north lat. The road before it, though inconvenienced with ice in very hard winters, is notwithstanding always open. This, with other circumstances, renders it a place of great resort and very extensive Commerce. They export to the West Indies, bread, peas, rye, meal, Indian Corn, horses, sheep, beef, pork, and at least eighty thousand barrels of flour; their returns are rum, sugar, and molasses. They send provisions to the Spanish Main. They have a considerable share in the logwood trade; wheat, flour, Indian corn, and timber, they send to Lisbon and Madeira. They have also a correspondence with Hamburg and Holland which, A. D.* 1769, *amounted to* 246,522*l. In the succeeding year the ships entered inwards were* 196, *sloops* 431; *cleared outwards, ships* 188, *sloops* 424."

Population of New York, in 1768, 20,000 Inhabitants.

The Worshipful WHITEHEAD HICKS, *Mayor.*

Lady Warren
The Monument
Thiebout
Sand Hill
A Elliot Esq.
Bestavers Rivulet
Abrm Mortier Esq
G. Stuyvesant
N. Stuyvesant
Herring
Lane
Road to Greenwich
Dyckman
The Bowry
James Delancy Esq.
Foundery
G. Harison Esq.
Ranelagh Garden
Fresh Water
Out Ward
Grand
Delaneys Square
The Jones Esq.
Division Street
Common
King George Street
Prince
Cherry Street
Ship Yards
Corlaers
Peck's Slip
Long I. Ferry
Murray's Wharf
Little Division Street
Southward Boundaries
Brookland Ferry
J. Rapalie
Mill Dam
E
4
5
6
3

INDEX.

Addresses of Chamber, 87, 116, 134, 182, 192.

Admissions to Chamber. See Elections.

Advertisements, 17, 28, 106, 114, 146, 148, 153, 177, 178, 196, 311, 315, 317, 330, 335, 337, 353.

Alsop, John, Founder, 3; Treas. 179; Vice-Pres. 191, 202; on Committee, 21, 42, 73, 189; absent, 217, 347. See page 306.

Almshouses, 209, 344.

Amiel, John, resigns, 171.

Anderson, John, Capt. vs. Knote, Potters, Flemings Arbitration, 47.

Arbitration Committee, 8, 29, 40, 74; Special do. 238; Cases of Schuyler vs. Kennedy, 36; Franks vs. Duyckinck, 47; Knotes, Potter, Fleming vs. Anderson, 47; Barnes vs. Garrison, 47; Rhodes vs. LaPiere, 53; Warnock vs. Franklin, 54; Watson & Murray vs. Sears, 65; Conyngham & Nesbitt vs. Capt. Warden, 108; John Dunlap vs. Lewis Pintard, 114; Peter Townsend vs. Thomas Budd, 119; Dennis McReady vs. Patrick Loughan, 119; Walter & Thomas Buchanan & Co. vs. Robert Munro, 119; William Castel vs. Capt. Joseph Smith, 122; Grant & Fine vs. Henry Law and Totten & Crosfield, 122; Lewis Johnston vs. William Bayard, 144; Ward & Selkrig vs. David Black, 215; Henry White vs. Donaldson & White, 219; Shedden & Goodrich vs. Capt. McDonald, 220; Issachar Polock vs. Barrack Hays, 220; William Pagan vs. Robert Dale, 223; Capt. Rogers vs. Privateer Auctioneer, 238; Abraham Cuyler vs. Sheffield Howard, 240; Winthrop & Kemble vs. Augustus Van Horne, 263; Banan & Burke vs. Captain Stone, 264; Thomas C. Williams vs. Thomas Roy, 267; James Douglas vs. Lowther and Hodgzard, 273; Lyon vs. McCole, 79; Wilkins vs. Porteus and Reed, 287; Strachan vs. Hoakesley, 291.

Arbuthnot, Marriott, Admiral, 237, 255, 257, 260, 360; Sketch, 380.

Articles of Chamber, 20, 25, 29.

Assembly, General, 311, 327; Thanks to Merchants, 41, 313.

Attendance, Tabular View of, 305.

Auctioneers. See Vendue Masters.

Bache, Theophylact, Founder, 3; Treas. 100; Vice-Pres. 128, 158; Pres. 179; on Committee, 21, 43, 53, 59, 64, 73, 75, 133, 177, 181. See page 306.

Backhouse, William, on Committee, 252. See page 306.

Banan & Burke vs. Capt. Stone, Arbitration, 264.

Banan, Owen, Letter, 267, 268, 270.

Banyar, Goldsbrow, Dep. Sec. 82; Sketch, 374.

Barnes, John vs. Lambert Garrison, 47.

Bayard, William vs. Lewis Johnston, Arbitration, 144; Sketch, 377.

Beef and Pork, 63, 70, 227, 323, 325.

Beekman, Gerard W., resigns, 168; James, resigns, 168. See page 306.

Biographical Sketches, Arbuthnot, Marriott, 380; Banyar, Goldsbrow, 374. Bayard, William, 377; Blake, Jonathan, 378; Bowne, Robert, 383; Bradley, James, 373; Clinton, Sir Henry, 381; Colden, Cadwallader, 374; Cuyler, Abraham, 380; Digby, Robert, 382; Dunmore, Earl of, 375; Elliot, Andrew, 379; Elphinstone, George Keith, 382; Foxcroft, William, 376; Gage, Thomas, 378; Gaine, Hugh, 375; George III., 375; Graves, Thomas, 381; Harris, Richard, 379; Hicks, Whitehead, 373; Holt, John, 372; Howard, Sheffield, 380; Johnston, Lewis, 376; Jones, Daniel, 378; Kempe, John Tabor, 374; Kennedy, Archibald, 372; McClean, Archibald, 374; Mathews, David, 382; Maerschalk, Francis, 375; Mersillis, Peter, 377; Montresor, John, 373; Morris, Robert Hunter, 377; Newman, Charles, 380; Norris, John, 379; Patterson, James, 379; Pettitt, Thomas, 375; Pratt, Matthew, 377; Ray, Cornelius, 383; Rittenhouse, David, 373; Robertson, James, 379; Romans, Bernard, 378;

Biographical Sketches—
Sands, Comfort, 383, Joshua, 383; Schuyler, John, 372; St. Clair, John, 382; Smyth, Frederick, 376; Tongue, William, 380; Tryon, William, 376; Walter, Lieut. 379; Warden, Capt. 375; Winn, Isaac L., 377; Winthrop, Francis Bayard, 381.
Black, David vs. Ward & Selkrig, Arbitration, 215.
Blake, Jonathan, 169, 171; Sketch, 378.
Block Island, 359.
Bloomandale, 314.
Bogart, Henry C., on Committee, 75.
Bolton & Sigel's Tavern, 9, 307.
Boundary Line N. Y. and N. J., 63, 319.
Bounties, Fish, 176, 190, 194, 195, 336; to Seamen, 272, 365.
Booth, Benjamin, on Committee, 207; Proposal, 211, 216.
Bowne, Robert, Sketch, 383.
Bradley, James, Dr., Sketch, 373.
Bread, Price of, 223, 225, 349, 367; Inspector, 226, 350.
Broad Street, 96, 327.
Buchanan, Thomas, Vice-President, 217, 228, 254, 284; Pres., 295; declines, 296; on Committee, 64, 73, 229, 247, 252; Walter, see page 306; Walter and Thomas & Co. vs. Robert Munro, arbitration, 119.
Budd, Thomas vs. Peter Townsend, arbitration, 119.
Bull, Joseph, Proposal, 161.
Buoys in Harbor, 74, 323.
Burr-Stones, 110, 330.
By-Laws. See Regulations.
Captains of King's Ships, 328.
Carteret Packet, 232, 352.
Cartmen, 210, 214, 344, 345.
Casks, Flour and Bread, 12, 14, 15, 17, 21, 23, 46, 49.
Castel, William vs. Capt. Joseph Smith, Arbitration, 122.
Chancellor and Vice-Admiral, 192, 338.
Chaleur Bay, 120, 331.
Charter of Chamber, 67, 70, 76, 82, 88, 89, 326, 371; for New York City, 249, 358.
Clinton, Sir Henry, 247, 250, 354, 356; Sketch, 381.
Coffee House, Merchants', 203, 212, 251; Account of, 340.
Coin, 52, 66, 69, 102, 104, 105, 316; Clipping of, 322; Table of, 386; Value of, 387.
Colden, Cadwallader, 76, 79, 88, 97, 339; Sketch, 374; Portrait of, 126, 127, 332.
Colony and Territories N. Y., 87, 326.
Commandant of N. Y., 204, 205, 209, 342.
Commerce, 203, 339.
Commissioners' Proclamation, 203, 204, 248, 340, 356.
Commissions, Mercantile, 43.
Committees to be raised, 6; on Arbitration, 8, 29; By-Laws, 20; Exchange, 17; Trade of Col. 21, 31; Flour purchase, 35; Meeting-room, 36, 251; Repairs, 38; Address to Gen. Assembly, 42; Commissions, 43; Tonnage, 44, 46, 130; Coin, 52; Lumber, 53, 57, 59; Public Packers, 64, 73; Rules, 69; Charter, 73; Whaling, 75; Gold-scales, 124; English Mail, 133; Address to Gov. Tryon, 133, 189; Cupola, 159; Portrait, 169; Fish Bounties, 177, 190, 202; Address to Gen. Gage, 181, 182; Street-cleaning, 207; Cartmen, 210; Price of Labor, 214; Powder-ship, 218, 224; Letter to Gen. Robertson, 229; Plate to Capt. Newman, 233; Letter to Gen. Clinton, 247; Charter for N. Y. City, 252; Vendue Masters, 262; of Arbitration, see Arbitration Committee.
Conyngham & Nesbitt vs. Capt. Warden. Arbitration, 108.
Convoy to Halifax, 270, 364.
Corbet's House, 63, 319.
Cornel, Inspection of, 83, 99, 326.
Corsa, Isaac, on Committee, 207.
Council of Province, 66, 324.
Cruger, John, Founder, 3; Pres. 4, 42; Thanks of Assembly, 41; Proposal, 102, 104, 118; Dissents recorded 106, 143.
John Harris, on Committee, 52, 73, 133, 181, 182, 370.
Cupola, 156, 159, 164, 335.
Currency, Penn. 10, 11, 15, 18, 308; Table of, 388; New Jersey, 10, 11, 13, 15, 104, 107, 143, 146, 151, 153, 160, 163, 168, 170, 171, 185, 296, 308, 329, 334, 370; Table of, 384, 385; New York, 12, 15, 309, 345; Table of, 388.
Customs, 246, 357; Officers of, 99, 329, 356.
Cuyler, Abraham vs. Sheffield Howard, Arbitration, 240; Sketch, 380.
Dale, Robert vs. William Pagan, Arbitration, 223.
Desbrosses, Elias, Founder, 3; Treas. 4, 42; Vice-Pres. 100; Pres. 128; Member of Committee, 21, 42, 181, 189.
Digby, Robert, 280; Sketch, 382.
Donaldson and White vs. Henry White, Arbitration, 219; Samuel, on Committee, 224, 229; Proposal, 247, 252.
Doorkeeper, 7, 212, 229, 249.

Dinner, Annual, 44, 83, 99, 126, 155, 333, 336.
Douglass, James vs. Lowther and Hodgzard, Arbitration, 273.
Dunlap, John vs. Lewis Pintard, Arbitration, 114.
Dunmore, Earl of, 116, 117, 128, 333; Sketch, 375.
Duties, Customs', 246, 356, 357.
Duyckinck, Gerardus vs. Moses Franks, Arbitration, 47; resigns, 168. See page 306.
Elections, Annual, 4; Rules for, 5, 14, 15, 67, 75, 79; Tabular View of, 304.
Elliott, Andrew, 206, 210, 247, 248, 269, 276, 355, 356, 358; Sketch, 379.
Elphinstone, George K., Capt., 270, 271; Sketch, 382.
Embargo on Shipping, 236, 354.
Exchange, Col., Table of, 388; European, 20; Inland, 15, 17, 19, 20; West India, 15, 17, 19, 20, 310.
Exchange, Room over, 36, 156, 159, 162, 311, 335, 336.
Exports of Flour, Table of Imports and, 329.
Fairholme, Johnston, on Committee, 182, 189.
Fare, 337.
Fees of Admission, 4, 74, 157, 297, 370.
Fines, 7, 10, 50, 211, 244, 245, 284.
Fire Insurance. See Insurance against Fire.
Fish Bounties, 175, 190, 194, 195, 336.
Fisheries, 285, 360.
Flatbush, 314.
Fleet, British, 236, 360, 365; Provision, 275, 366.
Fleming, Joseph and Stephen and others vs. Capt. John Anderson, 47.
Florida, Maps of, 191, 198, 202, 338, 339.
Flour, Branding, 330; Combination of Bakers, 23; Inspection of, 15, 17, 21, 29, 46, 113, 314; Prices of, 223; Weighing of, 148.
Folliot, George, Founder, 3.
Fort George, Latitude of, 61, 317, 319.
Founders of Chamber, 3, 7.
Foxcroft, William, Dep. Postmaster, 132; Sketch of, 376.
Fraunces' Tavern. See Bolton & Sigell, 307.
Franklin, John vs. Capt. William Warnock, Arbitration, 54; Walter, 3; on Committee, 42, 75.
Franks, Moses vs. Gerardus Duyckinck, Arbitration, 47.
Freight on Casks, 332, 362.
Friendship, Snow, 247, 355.
Gage, Thomas, General, 182, 183; and his Suite, 328; Departure for England, 337; Sketch, 378.
Gaine, Hugh, Printer, 108, 110; Sketch, 375.
Gardner's Bay, 360.
Garland, King's Ship, 271, 365.
Garrison, Lambert vs. John Barnes, Arbitration, 47.
Garrison, New York, 357; Gibraltar, 359.
George the Third, Sketch, 375.
Georgetown, 370.
Georgia restored to Trade, 357.
Glover, John T. See page 306.
Gold Scales, 121, 331.
Goldsmith to be appointed, 124.
Goold, Edward. See page 306.
Gouverneur Harman, resigns, 168.
Governor of New York, 249, 333, 358.
Grant and Fine vs. Law, Totten & Crosfield, Arbitration, 122.
Graves, Thomas, Admiral, Sketch, 381.
Gunpowder, 211, 216, 218, 347.
Hackensack, 331.
Halifax, Trade with, 361.
Harbor of New York, 361.
Harris, Richard, 229, 379.
Hays, Barrack vs. Issachar Polock, Arbitration, 220.
Hicks, Whitehead, Sketch, 373.
Hoakesley, Robert vs. John Strachan, Arbitration, 291.
Hodgzard, William, Arbitration, 273.
Hoffman, Nicholas, resigns, 168; on Committee, 207.
Holt, John, Printer, 37; Sketch, 372.
Howard, Sheffield vs. Abraham Cuyler, Arbitration, 240, 380.
Historical Sketches, Bolton & Sigell, Fraunces' Tavern, 307; Paper Currency of N. Y. 309; of Penn. 308; of N. J. 308; the Assembly, 311, 327; Merchants' Exchange, 311, 335; Non-Importation Agreement, 313; Fort George, 317; Latitude of New York, 319; Boundary between N. Y. and N. J. 319; Light-house on Sandy Hook, 320; Buoys in the Harbor, 323; Whale Fishery of N. Y. 323; Seal of the Province, 325; Fire Insurance, 325; Charter of the Chamber, 326; Sterling Iron Works, 331; Picture of Gov. Colden, 332; Proprietors of New Jersey, 334; Newspapers of New York, 335; Seal of the Chamber, 335; Victories in the French War, 337; Merchants' Coffee House, 340; New York Hospital, 343; Alms Houses, 344; In-

surance Offices, 346; Powder-ship, 348; Privateers, 351, 352, 359, 360, 368, 369; Cartaret Packet, 352, 353; Post Office, 353; Affairs in New York, 339, 357, 363; British Ships, 360, 361, 364, 365; New York Harbor, 361; Wharves, 367.
Hospitals, 343.
Imlaytown, 120, 331.
Imlay, William, resigns, 168.
Imports, Tables of Exports and, Duties on, 357.
Incorporators, List of, 90.
Inspection of Beef and Pork, 70, 323; of Cornel, etc. 83, 99, 326; of Flour, 15, 17, 21, 29, 46, 113, 314; of Lumber, 317; of Potashes, 21, 29, 330.
Inspector of Bread, 360.
Insurance against Fire, 82, 99, 101, 325.
Insurance, Marine, Tables of, 359, 365.
Insurance Offices, 210; Case of, 287; "Old" Account of, 346.
Jauncey, James, Founder, 3; on Committee, 133, 177; William, on Committee, 190.
Johannes, Half, 102, 104, 105, 227, 329.
Johnston, Lewis vs. William Bayard, Arbitration, 144; Sketch of, 376.
Jones, Daniel, Commandant, 204, 205, 342; Sketch, 378.
Kempe, John Tabor, Atty. Gen. 374.
Kennedy, Archibald, Capt. vs. Col. John Schuyler, Arbitration, 36; Sketch, 372.
Keteltas, Peter, on Committee, 133. See page 306.
Knote, Daniel and others vs. Capt. John Anderson, Arbitration, 47.
Kortright, Lawrence, Founder, 3; on Committee, 36, 42, 43, 207, 252.
Laight, Edward, Proposal, 39; resigns, 170, 211; William, on Committee, 207, 218, 247, 252. See page 306.
La Piere vs. Rhodes, Arbitration, 53.
Latitude of New York ascertained, 61.
Law of Colony as to Fare, 310.
Law, Henry, Arbitration, 122.
Lee & Strachan, 291.
Letters of Chamber, 204, 225, 230, 250, 252, 255, 258, 265, 269, 271, 276, 279, 281; to Chamber, 205, 210, 231, 233, 257, 260, 266, 267, 269, 270, 271, 276, 294.
Lewis, Francis, on Committee, 190. See page 306.
Lightning Conductor, 224, 348.
Lispenard, Leonard, resigns, 168.
Livingston, Robert C., on Committee, 133, 140, 159, 162, 185; Philip, Founder, 7.
Local Sketches. See Historical Sketches.
Loughan vs. Dennis McCready, Arbitration, 119.
Low, Isaac, Founder, 3; on Committee, 17, 21, 36, 38, 42, 133, 189, 207, 247; President, 203, 227, 254, 284; Proposal, 31, 46, 67, 73, 74, 75, 104, 110; Treasurer, 158; Vice-Pres. 179, 191.
Lowther, William and William Hodgzard vs. Douglas, Arbitration, 273. See page 306; William, on Committee, 247, 252.
Ludlow, Daniel, see page 306; George W., see page 306.
Lumber, Regulations of, 53, 66; Inspection of, 317.
Lyon, William vs. John McCole, Arbitration, 79.
Mahacomac, 319.
Mail for England, 132, 133.
Markets, 339.
Marschalk, Francis, Inspector of Flour, 113, 114; Sketch, 375.
Mathews, David, Mayor, 266, 276; Sketch, 382.
Mayor, 266, and Corporation, 317.
McAdam, William, Founder, 3; Proposal, 43, 74, 143; Committee, 42, 73, 133, 190, 211; Treas. 191; Vice Pres. 202; Death, 217.
McClean, Archibald, a Commissioner to ascertain the Boundary Line, 63; Sketch, 374.
McCready, Dennis vs. Patrick Loughan, Arbitration, 119.
McCole, John vs. William Lyon, Arbitration, 279.
McCormick, Daniel. See page 306.
McDavitt, Patrick. See page 306.
McDonald, Capt. vs. Shedden & Goodrich, Arbitration, 220.
McEvers, Charles, on Committee, 64, 69, 73, 182; Treasurer, 202; Letter to, 252; Letter from, 294; James, Founder, 3.
Measure, Winchester, 333.
Meetings of Chamber, Day of, 4; Special, 31; Quarterly, 4; Place of, 5, 6, 9, 36, 96, 203, 251.
Members, 6; List of, 300; Stores and Residences of, 393.
Merchants of N. Y., Thanks to, by General Assembly, 41.
Mersellis, Peter, 162, 377.
Miller, John, on Committee, 207, 211, 218, 224, 247. See Page 306. Thomas, Capt., on Committee, 177.
Montauk Point, 361.
Montresor, John, Capt., takes Latitude of Flag Bastion, 61; Sketch, 373.

Moore, John, Member of Committee, 17, 53, 59, 69, 73, 102, 133, 169, 189, 212, 224, 247, 252; Proposal, 109, 110; Thomas William, Member of Committee, 35.
Morris, Robert Hunter; Sketch, 377.
Munro, Robert vs. Walter and Thomas Buchanan & Co., Arbitration, 119.
Murray, John, on Committee, 261. See page 306. Robert, Founder, 3; on Committee, 44, 52, 252.
Neilson, William, to visit Philadelphia and Purchase Flour, 21, 22; Resigns, 168. See page 306.
New Jersey, Currency. See Currency. Proprietors of New Jersey, 334, 335.
Newman, Charles, Capt., 232, 233, 234, 352, 353, 380.
Newspapers of N. Y., 335.
New York, description of. See Biographical and Historical Sketches.
New York, Sketches of. See Biographical and Historical Sketches.
Norris, John, 212, 214, 229; Sketch, 379.
Non-Importation Agreement, 41, 313.
North Castle, 315.
Nutten Island, 65, 322.
Officers of Chamber, 3; How Chosen, 4; List of, 299; Field —— on Duty in N. Y., 333.
Oothout, John, Proposal, 219; Member of Committee, 217, 261. See page 306.
Ordinances, City, 208, 342, 345, 347.
Packers, Public, 63, 322.
Packet to England, 132, 333.
Pagan, William vs. Robert Dale, Arbitration, 223; on Committee, 251.
Pallade, Peter, Procurator for La Piere, 53.
Paper Currency. See Currency.
Parliament, Act of, 247, 355.
Pattison, James, Maj. Gen., 206; Sketch, 379.
Peltry, 333.
Pennsylvania Currency. See Currency.
Petition for Charter, 77.
Pettitt, Thomas, Doorkeeper, 101, 104, 130, 154, 155, 156, 170, 171, 179, 212; Sketch, 375.
Phenix, Daniel, resigns, 168. See page 306.
Pintard, Lewis, to Purchase Flour in Philadelphia, 22; Thanks to, 33; Hands in Accounts, 35; on Committee, 43, 64, 73, 179; —— vs. John Dunlap, Arbitration, 114.
Platt, Jeremiah. See page 306.
Police of the City, 208, 343, 355; Magistrates of, 227, 238, 261, 263, 265, 343.
Polock, Issachar vs. Barrack Hays, Arbitration, 220.
Porteous, John and Read vs. Wilkins, Arbitration, 287; Notice of, 369.
Portrait of Lieut. Gen. Colden, 126, 127, 167, 169, 332, 336.
Post-Office, 233, 353.
Potashes, Inspection of, 21, 114, 330.
Potter, Thomas and Isaac and others vs. Capt. John Anderson, Arbitration, 47.
Pratt, Matthew, Limner, 167, 169; Sketch, 377.
President, Duties of, 6, 7; Vice-Pres., Duties of, 6, 7.
Prices Current, Table of, 1765 to 1775, 389. See Rates.
Primage on Goods, 222.
Privateer Auctioneer, 238, 354.
Privateers, 204, 233, 281, 342, 351, 352, 357, 359, 360, 366, 368, 369.
Prizes. See Privateers.
Proclamations, 203, 248, 263, 340, 343, 348, 355, 367.
Proprietors of New Jersey, 334.
Proposals, to be in writing, 10; Price of Casks, 12; as to Currency, 10, 12, 15; Admission of Members, 14; Bills of Exchange, 15; Inspection of Flour, 15, 113; Printing the Articles, 21; Regulation of Trade, 21; Inspection of Potashes, 21; Special Meeting, 31; Tare on Butter and Lard, 39; Arbitrations, 39; Tonnage of Goods, 40; Rates of Commissions, 43; Fine for leaving Meetings, 43; Flour Casks, 46; to address the Chair standing, 46; Rates of Coin, 52; Regulations as to Lumber, 53; Only Merchants to be Admitted, 59; Regulations to be Printed, 64; Value of Guineas, 66; Clipping of Coin, 66; to Revise Rules for Printing, 67; Charter Proposed, 67, 70; to Alter Rules of Admission, 67; to Submit all Disputes to Arbitration Committee, 74; Limit of Number of Members, 74; Buoys in Harbor, 74; Whale Fishery, 74; Mode of Election, 75; Salary to Sec'y, 83; as to Value of Johannes, 102; Half Joes, 104; Jersey Money, 104; to read Charter every Quarterly Meeting, 110; Flour, 110; Adjournment, 118; Gold Scales, 122; Seamen's Wages, 122; to address Gov. Tryon, 133; to Publish Report of Committee on Tonnage, 146; as to Weighing of Flour, 148; as to Money of Chamber, 157; as to Jer-

sey Money, 160, 161; to offer Fish Bounties, 176; as to Resignations on account of Jersey Money, 185; as to Records of Arbitration Committee, 219; Thanks of Chamber to Capt. Newman, 232; as to Fine on Arbitration Committee, 244, 245; to address Commander on Duties, 247.
Provision Fleets, 275, 366.
Queens' Head Tavern. See Bolton & Sigell's.
Quorum, 6.
Ramadge, Smith, on Committee, 211, 224.
Ramsay John. See page 306.
Randall, Thomas, Founder, 3; on Committee, 36, 38, 159. See page 306.
Rates, 210, 211, 214, 216, 223, 342, 344, 349, 367.
Ray, Cornelius; Sketch, 383.
Rebellion, this unnatural, 271, 365.
Records, where to be kept, 5, 6.
Reed, Patrick & Porteous vs. Wilkins, Arbitration, 287.
Regulations and By-Laws, 4, 10, 20, 25, 59, 69, 83, 121.
Remsen, Henry, Proposal, 59, 74; on Committee, 73, 75; Resigns, 168. See page 306.
Peter, on Committee, 44.
Reports: Bills of Exchange, 19, 24; Revision of By-Laws, 25; Inspection of Flour, 29; Trade of Colony, 29; Room over Exchange, 38; Draught of Thanks to Assembly, 42; Value of Coin, 56; Regulation of Lumber, 57, 63, 66; Inspection of Beef and Pork, 70; of President as to Charter, 78; Visit to Mayor, as to Curing of Beef and Pork, 79; Regulations, By-Laws, 83; Address to Gov. Tryon, 134; on Tonnage, 141; on Repairs, 162; Address to Gen. Gage, 181; on Street Cleaning, 208; Letter to Gen. Robertson, 230; Address to Sir Henry Clinton, 247; on Meeting Rooms, 254; on Letter to Admiral, 255; Licensed Auctioneers, 262.
Resignation of Members, 164, 166, 168, 170.
Resolutions as to By-Laws, 4; Notice to New Members, 8; Arbitration Committee, 8, 40; to Price of Casks, 14; Admission of Members, 15; Bills of Exchange, 17, 20; tare of Casks, 17; Inspection of Flour, 17; Pennsylvania Currency, 18; Revision of By-Laws, 20; to Purchase Flour in Philadelphia, 21, 23; to Advertise Articles, 29; Special Meetings, 33; Thanks to Mr. Pintard, 33; Commission to Sec'y, 34; to Audit accounts of Flour purchase, 35; to wait on the Mayor, 36; to Repair Room over Exchange, 38; Reply to General Assembly, 42; to enter Arbitrations on the Minutes, 43; Flour Casks, 49; Fine for Addressing Chair from seat, 50; on Coin, 57; to admit none but Merchants, 64; to Print the Rules, 64; as to Value of Guineas and Half Joes, 69; to apply for Charter, 77; as to Admission of Members, 80; as to Coin, 106; as to Adjournment, 121; as to English Mail, 132; Tonnage of Goods, 143; Weighing of Flour, 151; as to Jersey Money, 152, 187; on Fish Bounties, 177; as to Maps of Florida, 191; Thanks to Gen. Clinton, 250; Address to Admiral on Distress of Commerce, 254; Thanks to Capt. Elphinstone, 270; as to Wharfage, 279; as to Letter on Privateering, 285.
Rhinelander, Frederick, on Committee, 207, 211.
Rhodes vs. La Piere, Arbitration, 53.
Rittenhouse, David, takes Latitude of Flag Bastion, 61; ascertains Boundary Line, 63; Sketch, 373.
Robertson, James, Gen., 229, 230, 231, 272, 277, 280, 285, 350, 358; Sketch, 379.
Rogers, Sam'l, Capt., 238.
Roosevelt, Isaac, Member of Committee, 36; Resigns, 168. See page 306.
Romans, Bernard, 191, 198, 201, 338; Sketch, 378.
Ross, Capt., 281, 368.
Roy, Thomas vs. T. C. Williams, Arbitration, 267.
Royal Oak Ship, 257, 360.
Rules and Regulations. See Regulations.
Sandy Hook Light, 63, 320.
Sands, Comfort; Sketch, 383.
Sands, Joshua; Sketch, 383.
Schuyler, John, Col. vs. Capt. Archibald Kennedy, Arbitration, 36; Sketch, 372. Resigns, 168.
John, Jr., 159.
Seal of Chamber, 156, 158, 159, 160, 335; of Province, George III., 325.
Seamen, advance pay of, 122, 331; Bounties to, 365; Discharge of, 361, 368, 369; Wanted, 272.
Setauket, 215.
Sears, Isaac vs. Watson & Murray, Arbitration, 65; Resigns his Seat, 164. See page 306.
Secretary, duties of, 6, 13; Salary to, 83.

Secretaries of the Council, 328.
Seton, William, 229, 252.
Sharpe, Richard, on Committee, 73, 169.
Sheddon & Goodrich vs. Capt. McDonald, Arbitration, 220.
Sherbrooke, Miles, Founder, 3 ; on Committee, 44.
Ships of War, 254.
Shrewsbury Banks, 360.
Simson, Sampson, on Committee, 38, 43, 73, 75 ; Proposal, 43, 66.
Sketches. See Historical and Biographical.
Skreens, German Mill, 113, 330.
Smith, Mrs. 212, 213, 347 ; Joseph, Capt. vs. William Cartel, Arbitration, 122.
Smyth, Frederick, Chief Justice, Sketch, 376.
St. Clair, John, Sec'y, 279, 368, 382.
Stepple, William, on Committee, 190, 207.
Sterling, 226.
Stone, Capt. vs. Banan & Burke, Arbitration, 264.
Stores and Residences, 393.
Stove for Chamber, 110, 329.
Strachan, James, 254, 358 ; ——, John vs. Robert Hoakesley, Arbitration, 291.
Street Cleaning, 208.
Sugar, 357.
Superintendent, Gen., 206, 268, 350.
Tables of attendance, 303 ; of Coins, 386 ; of Currency, 384, 385, 388 ; of Imports and Exports, 392 ; of Insurance, 390, 391 ; Prices Current, 1765–1775, 389.
Tare of Casks, 15, 17, 310 ; Butter and Lard, 39.
Taylor & Rogers, 246.
Templeton, Oliver, on Committee, 261. See page 306.
Tench, John, on Committee, 270.
Territories depending on N. Y., 326.
Thompson, Acheson, Founder, 3.
Thurman, John, on Committee, 64, 73, 75, 207 ; Proposal, 82, 160 ; Resigns, 168. See page 306.
Tongue, William, 223, 240, 380.
Tonnage of Goods, 44, 138, 141, 143, 148, 314, 333.
Totten & Crosfield vs. Grant & Fine, Arbitration, 122.
Townsend, Peter vs. Thomas Budd, Arbitration, 119.
Trade, Regulations, 21, 29 ; Georgia restored to, 248, 357 ; with Halifax, 361.
Treasurer of Chamber, 6.
Tyron, William, Gov. 133, 135, 157, 189, 192, 193 ; Departure for England, 338 ; Sketch, 376.
Ustick, William, on Committee, 218.
Van Dam, Anthony, Founder, 3 ; elected Secretary, 4, 42, 100, 128, 158, 179, 191, 202, 228, 254, 284, 295 ; hands in accounts, 35 ; on Committee, 251, 252 ; Proposal, 38, 67, 146.
Van Horne, Augustus, on Committee, 207 ; vs. Winthrop & Kemble, Arbitration, 263.
Van Zandt, Jacobus, on Committee, 69, 102. See page 306.
Vendue Masters, 261, 263, 347, 362.
Verplanck, Samuel, Founder, 3 ; on Committee, 17, 21, 52, 75, 133 ; Proposal, 59.
Victories, English, 182, 337.
Volunteers for Fleet, 272.
Waddell, Robert Ross, Founder, 3 ; on Committee, 228 ; Treas. 254, 284, 295. See page 306.
Wallace, Alexander, on Committee, 53, 124, 211 ; Hugh, Founder, 3 ; Member of Committee, 19, 36, 133, 229 ; Pres. 100, 127 ; Vice-Pres. 4, 42, 218, 228.
Walloon Bay, 224, 241, 349.
Walter, Lieut. 224, 379.
Walton, Abraham, Proposal, 244, 245 ; Gerard, on Committee, 162, 169, 182, 224, 229, 246, 252 ; Vice-Pres. 295. See page 306.
Jacob, Founder, 3 ; on Committee, 17, 124, 177 ; Vice-Pres. 254, 284.
William, Founder, 3 ; on Committee, 36, 52, 73, 133, 189, 207, 252 ; Proposal, 52, 125 ; Magistrate of Police, 266, 362 ; Treas. 128 ; President, 191 ; Vice-Pres. 158, 179, 295. See page 306.
Ward & Selkrig vs. David Black, Arbitration, 215.
Wardens of the Port, 263, 323, 362.
Warden, Capt. vs. Conyngham & Nesbitt, Arbitration, 108 ; Sketch, 375.
Warnock, William, Capt. vs. John Franklin, Arbitration, 54.
Warwick, King's Ship, 270, 364.
Watson Jacob, on Committee, 53, 207, 252 ; Proposal, 122 ; Resigns, 166.
Joshua, on Committee, 261.
—— and Murray vs. Isaac Sears, Arbitration, 65.
Watts, Robert, on Committee, 35, 190.
Whale Boats, 285, 360 ; at the Narrows, 369 ; Fishery, 74, 323.
Wharves, 277, 367.

White, Henry, Founder, 7; on Committee, 64, 229; Vice-Pres. 100, 128; Pres. 158; —— vs. Donaldson and White, Arbitration, 219.
Thomas, Founder, 3.
Wilkins, Robert vs. Porteous and Reed, Arbitration, 287.
Williams, Thomas Charles vs. Thomas Roy, Arbitration, 267.
Winchester Measure, 142, 333.
Winn, Isaac L., Capt. 156, 159; Sketch, 377.
Winthrop, Francis Bayard; Sketch, 381; —— and Kemble vs. Augustus Van Horne, Arbitration, 263; Firm of, 362.
Yates, Richard, on Committee, 44, 53, 59, 73, 75; Proposal, 83.
Young, Hamilton, on Committee, 44, 52, 124, 170.

THE END.

COLONIAL NEW YORK.

SKETCHES

BIOGRAPHICAL AND HISTORICAL

1768—1784.

BY

JOHN AUSTIN STEVENS JR.

NEW YORK:
JOHN F. TROW & CO., 50 GREENE STREET.
1867.

JOHN F. TROW & CO.,
PRINTERS, STEREOTYPERS, AND ELECTROTYPERS.
50 Greene Street, New York.

PREFACE.

THE editor tenders his grateful thanks to the Merchants of New York for the kind and generous interest they have shown in this effort to preserve the record of the Colonial Commerce of the City, and his warm acknowledgments to the many descendants of the founders and early members of the Chamber of Commerce who have aided him in his biographical researches.

He also records his obligations to those who have favored him with their counsel and personal labors in the toilsome and difficult research into the newspaper and documentary history of the last century. To Mr. George H. Moore, the judicious historian and devoted custodian of the treasures of the New York Historical Society, he is indebted for timely and valuable suggestions. To the pains-taking and courteous assistant in the care of this honored institution, Mr. William Kelby, who may be justly called a "living concordance" to the old newspapers of the city, he cheerfully owns his daily varied obligation.

Among those who have shown a practical interest in the work, the editor names with pleasure the Hon. Gulian C. Verplanck, from whose store of reminiscence he has drawn many interesting facts; Mr. S. Alofsen, of Jersey City, who kindly furnished biographical information of value; Dr. E. B. O'Callaghan, of Albany, to whose labors the State is indebted for the admirable arrangement of its valuable manuscript documents, and whose ripe judgment is ever at the service of the historical student.

John Cruger

Engd by G.R. Hall from a Picture in possession of the Chamber of Commerce

JOHN CRUGER.

FIRST PRESIDENT OF THE NEW YORK CHAMBER OF COMMERCE.

1768–1770.

THE family of CRUGER is variously stated to be of Danish and of German origin; the latter supposition being the more probable. The first of the family in England are reputed to have emigrated from the Continent in the reign of Henry VIII., and to have settled at Bristol, where numerous ancient monuments to persons of this name still exist in the church-yard attached to the cathedral. The fact that one of the American family sent to Bristol for a commercial education there received the highest political honors, at one time representing this ancient city in the British Parliament and at another its Mayor, seems to imply some previous connection with its interests and families. Yet this unusual honor to the stranger may be sufficiently accounted for, perhaps, in the extent of the trade of this thriving city with the city of New York, and the desire of its people to show their sympathy with the Colonies at a period when all American eyes were carefully scrutinizing the conduct of their English cousins in the struggle waging for civil liberty on both sides of the Atlantic.

The name of CRUGER, now rarely heard in the halls of commerce or on the marts of trade, was from the beginning to the close of the eighteenth century beloved and honored in the colonial city of New York, and the history of the family is almost that of English rule in this provincial capital.

The first emigrant of the name to America, or at least the first of whom any mention is to be found in any of the old documents of record, whether of baptisms, marriages, or wills, was John Cruger, who married Maria Cuyler, in the year 1702. He first appears as supercargo of the trading ship "The Prophet Daniel," Captain Appel, which weighed anchor at New York, Friday, 15th July, 1698, bound to the coast of Africa, where she fell into the hands of pirates—a misfortune of which he published a curious account on his return.

Entering into active business, he soon became a prosperous merchant, and was also, during the early part of the last century, a prominent public man. He was successively chosen Alderman of the Dock Ward (now the First Ward) for twenty-two years—from 1712 to 1733. In 1739 he was appointed Mayor of the city, and remained in office until his death, in 1744.

By his wife, Maria Cuyler, he left two sons, Henry and John. His son Tieliman, (or Telemon,) of whose baptism, 1705, Nov. 11, the record remains, does not seem to have survived him. He probably died at an early age.

John Cruger, the third son of John Cruger and Maria his wife, was born in the city of New York, on the 18th day of July, 1710: the record of his baptism on the following day may be found on the minutes of the Dutch Church.

He followed closely in the footsteps of his father. He also was a successful and eminent merchant. He also was the favored choice of his fellow-citizens for one after another of the highest positions of trust in their gift. In reviewing his career as a public man, it will be observed with interest that he was alike the trusted officer of the Crown, and the chosen representative of the people.

His first connection with the history of the period appears in the record of his name, JOHN CRUGER, JUNIOR, as one of the Grand Jury empannelled by the Supreme Court, 21st of April, 1741, (Robert Watts merchant, foreman,) for examination into the supposed Negro Plot of that year, which so alarmed the Colony. All of his fellows on the panel were merchants.

He was elected Alderman of the Dock Ward in 1754 and 1755, and in 1756 raised to the dignity of Mayor, which office he held for ten successive years, until 1765.

While yet in his first year of office he was called upon to check the growing insolence of the British officers, and under his lead the city authorities protested against the orders of Lord Loudon, Commander-in-Chief of the King's forces in America, quartering a large body of troops upon the inhabitants of New York. The protest was unavailing, but the magistrates promoted a subscription to defray the expenses of the officers' quarters.

In 1759 he was elected member of the General Assembly of the Colony; again re-elected in February, 1761, he became one of that famous body, the Long Assembly, as it was called, of 1761 to 1768, to whose patriotism and courage the union of the Colonies and the successful vindication of American liberties was, in a great measure, indeed, it may be properly said, chiefly due.

This Assembly was earnest in protest against the growing ursurpation of the Home Government; and as early as the 18th of October, 1764, addressed memorials to the King, the Lords, and the Commons, which for fervent appeal and bold assertion of rights are not surpassed by any of the documents of that age of manly eloquence. So decided was the tone of these papers, that it is recorded that no one of Parliament was to be found bold enough to present them. The Assembly did not stop here, but, as though instinctively aware of the probable futility of their protest, on the same day, and in the same resolutions by which they ordered the transmission of the memorials, they further raised a committee "to write to and correspond with the several Assemblies, or committees of Assemblies," of the sister Colonies on the several objectionable acts of Parliament "lately passed with relation to the trade of the Northern Colonies; and also on the subject of the impending dangers which threaten the Colonies of being taxed by laws to be passed in Great Britain." This may justly be considered the first step towards American Union. Of this Committee of Correspondence JOHN CRUGER was a leading member.

The petitions of the Colonies were of no avail, and the Stamp Act passed Parliament on the 22d March, 1765. This news reached New York in April, and was received with intense indignation. The people resolved to resist the Act, and their leaders were active to obtain harmonious and common action from all the Colonies. To this work the Committee of Correspondence assiduously devoted themselves; and from their suggestions sprung the Stamp Act Congress, held in New York City in October, 1765. In this Congress New York was represented by the persons who composed the Committee of Correspondence of the Assembly—Robert R. Livingston, JOHN CRUGER, Philip Livingston, Leonard Lispenard, and William Bayard. JOHN CRUGER was again earnest in his defence of popular rights, and the clear, concise, and able "Declaration of Rights and Grievances of the Colonists in America," issued by that Congress, was from his pen.

But the spirit of the people was not content with protests alone, and on the 31st October, 1765, the merchants assembled in mass meeting, at Burns' Coffee House, and resolved to decline importation from Great Britain until the Act should be repealed.

Meanwhile the stamps had arrived, and the Governor had announced his intention to enforce the Act. The Sons of Liberty, supported by the merchants and the people, resolved not to permit their delivery from the Fort.

The 1st of November was the day appointed for the enforcement of the Act. In the evening the people gathered on the Commons, and marching to the Fort, burned the effigy of Colden on the Bowling Green, under the muzzles of the guns. Only the moderation of General Gage, the British Commander, in his peremptory orders to the troops not to fire on the citizens, averted a rupture otherwise inevitable. The next morning Colden declared his intention "to do nothing in relation to the Stamps, but leave it to Sir Henry Moore (the newly appointed Governor) to do as he pleased on his Arrival," then daily looked for. Still the people were not satisfied, and, on the 5th of November, rallied in large numbers on the Commons, and resolved to storm the fort and seize the odious papers—the symbols of oppression.

Again the manly presence of JOHN CRUGER, then Mayor of the City, is found in the front rank of the defenders of the rights of the People—while not unmindful of his official duty to preserve the order of the city. Attended by the Aldermen of the Wards he visited the Lieut.-Governor, and warning him of the imminent danger, received from him the promise that the Stamps should be delivered into the custody of the city authorities. "They accordingly soon after, accompanied with a Prodigious Concourse of People of all

Ranks, (so runs the newspaper account of the day,) attended at the Gate of the Fort, when the Governor ordered the Paper to be given up to them; and upon the Reception of it gave three Cheers, carried it to the City Hall and dispersed. After which Tranquility was restored to the City." Thus the world saw the novel spectacle of the majesty of the King compelled to bow to the majesty of the People.

The moderation of General Gage on these occasions greatly endeared him to the people, and won from the city authorities a marked testimony of their gratitude.

The original draft of their address of thanks, in the handwriting of Mr. Cruger, still exists. In it, as in all his writings, just sentiments appear clothed in graceful and becoming language. His style was of rare beauty. To limpid clearness and great power of logical statement he united a chastened fervor which marked the even mind where warm feeling was ever subject to the cool, calm will.

To his Excellency the Honorable Thomas Gage, Major-General and Commander-in-Chief of all his Majesty's forces in North America.

The Humble Address of the Mayor, Aldermen, and Commonalty of the City of New York in Common Council convened:

It is with the greatest joy we beg leave to congratulate your Excellency upon the Restoration of the Tranquility of this City: and as its Preservation (under God) was eminently owing to your Prudence, we think ourselves bound to render your Excellency our most grateful acknowledgements.

As the Destruction of the City and the Effusion of Blood

might at this unhappy conjuncture have fed the Spirit of Discontent so prevalent in all the Colonies, and involved the whole Continent in Confusion and Distress, that Wisdom which prevented consequences not to be thought of without Horror, deserves our applause and will never be forgotten by his Majesty's faithful and loyal Subjects in this City. We are with the greatest Esteem and Regard,

May it please Your Excellency,

Your Excellency's

Most obedient and humble servants,

JOHN CRUGER, MAYOR.

Signed by order of the Common Council.

NEW YORK, 11th November, 1765.

The British ministry was not prepared for such stern action, and early in the following year the Stamp Act was repealed. The gladsome news reached the city on the 20th day of May, and was received with great demonstrations of joy. A large meeting of citizens was held on the 23d June, when the Assembly was petitioned to erect a statue to William Pitt, to whose eloquent appeals in defence of American rights the repeal was chiefly attributed. It was JOHN CRUGER, who, as the head of the New York City delegation, made this motion in the Assembly.

Thwarted in their first attempt to reduce the Colonies to submission, the ministry endeavored to enforce the provisions of the Mutiny Act, which required the citizens to supply quarters to the King's troops. The Assembly replied with a limited Supply Bill, which the King refused to receive. On the 15th December, 1766, the Assembly answered the King's refusal with a bold message refusing supplies, and was at once prorogued by the Governor. Still the ministry continued their exactions, and Townshend introduced a bill in Parliament imposing duties on tea and other articles. The merchants again renewed their non-importation agreement.

On the 11th of February, 1768, the Assembly was formally dissolved by Governor Moore, and writs were issued for a new election. To this body Philip Livingston was chosen in the place of MR. CRUGER, who does not appear to have been a candidate, but on its dissolution, in January, 1769, he was again put in nomination and elected by a large majority. On the organization of this, the last Colonial Assembly, in April, 1769, JOHN CRUGER was unanimously chosen Speaker, and retained this position until 1775, in April of which year it adjourned never to meet again, and the direction of the affairs of the Colony passed into the hands of a Council of Safety, and subsequently into the control of a Provincial Congress. MR. CRUGER, therefore, represented the city of New York in the Assembly for sixteen years.

It was during this exciting period on the 5th day of April, 1768, that JOHN CRUGER met with a few of the leading merchants of this then unconscious metropolis, and laid the foundations of the first Mercantile Society in America. The tendency of the time was towards union; a common danger drew close the bonds of friendship, sympathy, and union. To this characteristic of the day many of the most deserving societies of New York, now existing, owe their origin.

On the first organization of the Chamber of Commerce, 1768, Mr. JOHN CRUGER, the first-named of its founders, was chosen President. On the 2d May, 1769, he was unanimously re-elected, and it is recorded on the still fair minutes of the day's proceedings, "that Mr. President reported that he had it in charge from the General Assembly to give the Merchants of this city and colony the thanks of the House for their repeated disinterested, public spirited, and patriotic conduct in declining the importation of goods from Great Britain until such acts of Parliament as the General Assembly had declared unconstitutional and subversive of the rights and liberties of the people of this Colony should be repealed."

The transmission of this resolution to the Merchants came naturally by MR. CRUGER, who was at once the Speaker of the Assembly and the President of the Chamber; it owed its origin in the House to that distinguished patriot and merchant Philip Livingston, who, for a long period of years, shared with MR. CRUGER the honors and the confidence of the Colony.

Thus in the infancy of New York the patriotic devotion of its merchants to the cause of popular rights was clearly recognized: and it is a source of just pride to-day that the Chamber has lost nothing of its ancient spirit, as is abundantly shown by the records of the meeting held in its hall Tuesday the 19th day of April, 1861, when, the news of the rebellious attack upon a national fortress having reached the city, the members rallied in numbers to "pledge their hearty and cordial support to such measures as the Government of the United States should in its wisdom inaugurate," and to directly urge a blockade of the Southern ports, from whose commerce the merchants of New York derived large profits,—again, after the lapse of a century, nobly sacrificing their private interests to the public good.

At the middle of the last century the commerce of New York was yet in its infancy. It was in May, 1763, that the Sandy Hook light-house was lighted for the first time. It was in November, 1769, that the latitude of Fort George was cast for the Chamber.

Mr. Cruger retained the office of President of the Chamber until it had received its charter from the Crown and its permanent existence was secured. In the following May, 1770, he retired. As an instance of the faithfulness with which he performed the trusts reposed in him, it may be noticed that during the two years of his presidency he was absent from his seat on two occasions only, on one of which he is excused upon the minutes as "not well;" and during all the period of his connection with the institution he was one of the most punctual and regular of all the members in his attendance.

In all the early difficulties of the Chamber which sprung from differences of opinion with regard to the taking of "Jersey currency," he clung steadily to the Chamber, and manfully contended for its true interests; but a sea of trouble was soon to sweep over the commerce of the Colony, compared with which all minor differences were but as ripples on the wave.

John Cruger appears to have exercised his great influence to moderate the passions of his fellow-men and to harmonize the widely differing opinions of the opposing parties. His course during the stormy spring of 1775, when patriotic blood was boiling at fever-heat upon the news of the Lexington outrage, was marked by calm and dignified self-reliance and courage. His opinions remain on record in two able letters, the one addressed to the Committee of Safety on the 3d, and the other to General Gage on the 5th May of that year.

In the first, signed jointly with Jacob Walton, one of his colleagues in the Assembly, he declines to subscribe to the Articles of Association entered into by the citizens of New York 29th April, 1775, "to adopt and carry into execution whatever measures may be recommended by the Continental Congress or by the Provincial Convention for the purpose of preserving our constitution, and opposing the execution of several arbitrary and oppressive acts of the British Parliament," presented to him for signature, in these forcible words: "Because, as we were elected Representatives in General Assembly for the City and County of New York, we conceive that the faithful performance of that important trust requires of us a free, unbiased exercise of our judgment. To submit this to the control of any power on earth would, in our opinion, be deserting that trust; but to engage implicitly to approve and carry into execution the regulations of any other body, would justly expose us to the reproach of our own consciences, the censure not only of our constituents, but of the whole world. In our legislative capacity (he continues) we have already transmitted to the King and both Houses of Parliament representations of our grievances. Upon mature reflection, and after revolving our conduct with the most impartial deliberation, we cannot but approve what we have done, and will, therefore, patiently wait for the event, which will, we hope, be productive of much benefit, not only to this Colony, but to the cause of AMERICAN liberty in general. As the signing of this Association, therefore, would, in effect, be to deprive ourselves of our legislative powers, we cannot but suppose, from the tenor of it, an exemption of us is implied in it." And he concludes with an expression "of the most anxious concern for the distresses of the inhabitants of the Massachusetts Bay, and the most sincere wishes for the relief, and the liberty and prosperity of all the colonies."

Yet that he was not personally indifferent to the wishes of the General Committee is evident from the fact of his liberal contributions to its funds.

In a letter to General Gage, headed and doubtless

drawn by himself, and signed by fourteen members of the Assembly, on the 5th May of the same year, just two days subsequent to that last quoted, he urges that officer, then commanding the British forces in America, "that, as far as consistent with his duty, he would immediately order a cessation of public hostilities until his Majesty can be apprised of the situation of the American colonies," and expresses the wish "that no military force might land or be stationed in this province."

But in that day, as in our own, the logic of events brought more rapid conclusions than "the resources of statesmanship," and in a few months the Revolution had swept away the old landmarks. A little later the British army took possession of the city, and Washington fell back with the American troops upon White Plains.

Mr. Cruger retired, before the occupation, to Kinderhook, on the Hudson. In a letter to the Council of Safety, dated at Kinderhook, Nov. 2, 1777, he states, "it is over nineteen months since I left New York with my sister and family; since which both she and myself have suffered many inconveniences by reason of our age and bodily infirmities and the want of necessities to which they have exposed us," and asks for a pass to return to the City "for himself and family and what little furniture he has at Kinderhook." It seems that this pass was not granted, for he continued to reside at Kinderhook until the close of the war.

Through his long public career Mr. Cruger ever upheld a manly independence of character. His life presents a rare combination of moderation and firmness. Twice his judgment saved the city from violent outbreak and bloodshed. Fearless of kingly power, he resisted with a like courage the pressure of angry popular opinion. Once, when in 1747 he counselled the people against useless resistance to military exaction; again, when in 1765 he persuaded the Government to yield to the imperative popular demand.

MR. CRUGER appears the central figure of the later Colonial period, and around him are grouped the principal personages of this historic canvas. What more dramatic scenes than those which opened and closed his career as Mayor of the City. What finer instance of 'time's revenges' than that of the Magistrate, who had endured in silence the insolence of Loudon, receiving in his person a vindication of the outraged dignity of his station on the surrender to him of the stamps, by the courteous but not less arbitrary Colden.

Had fortune cast his lot a few years later in time, this early, constant choice of the people, and able advocate of American liberties, had, perchance, left a revolutionary history as brilliant as any of those eventful days; but at sixty-six years of age JOHN CRUGER had no longer the youthful vigor to plunge into the thick of the terrible struggle, and he appears to have taken no further part in public affairs.

Returning to the city, after the peace of 1783, he lived with his nephew, Nicholas Cruger, who continued in the third generation this eminent race of merchants; and here, on Tuesday, the 27th day of December, 1791, at the ripe age of eighty-two years, he died.

A notice of his death in the "New York Journal and Patriotic Register" has the touching phrase:

> "It may be truly said of him, that he was
> The upright man,
> Beloved of all his friends,
> And of whom an enemy
> (If he had one)
> Could speak no evil."

The CRUGERS were large ship-owners and engaged in

general trade, chiefly with Bristol and the West Indies. Their place of business was on Cruger's Wharf, which lay on the east side of White-Hall Slip, on the East River. The great fire of 1776, so fatal to the interests of the city for many years, broke out here. Six buildings belonging to JOHN and HENRY CRUGER were destroyed.

JOHN CRUGER never married. The name is now sustained by the descendants of his brother Henry, also a distinguished man in his day, an eminent merchant, a representative of New York for many years in the Assembly, and a member of the King's Council for this Province. He died at Bristol, February 8th, 1780, and was buried within the precincts of the cathedral in that city. Of the nephews of JOHN CRUGER, sons of this brother, John Harris Cruger was one of the earliest members of the Chamber; before the Revolution he was Chamberlain of the city. In the struggle he clung to the side of the Crown, and became a distinguished officer in Delancey's brigade. Henry Cruger was the colleague of Edmund Burke for Bristol in the British Parliament, and a staunch defender of American rights. He was afterwards Mayor of Bristol. He died in New York, in 1827, and is still remembered by many of the older citizens. Nicholas Cruger was a successful merchant in the West India trade. It was under his patronage that the illustrious Hamilton, then an adventurous boy, came to this country. Nicholas Cruger was a strong patriot and an intimate personal friend of Washington.

The engraving which prefaces this sketch is from a portrait in the possession of the Chamber of Commerce, admirably enlarged by Mr. Thomas Hicks, of New York, from a small but exquisitely painted miniature owned by Miss Eliza Cruger, daughter of the distinguished Member of Parliament above named.

HUGH WALLACE.

SECOND PRESIDENT OF THE NEW YORK CHAMBER OF COMMERCE.

1770–1771.

IN the early part of the last century New York was a favorite resort of the adventurous from all parts of the British Dominions. Many of its most distinguished Merchants were born without the Colony. Among those whom its growing trade drew to this then far-off shore were two brothers of the name of WALLACE, the elder of whom soon became a leading man in the Province, and rose to high places of honor and trust. They were of Irish origin, but from what part of the island is not now known. HUGH WALLACE, the elder brother, was probably originally the agent of some of the great linen factories which had already gained celebrity by the fineness of their textures. His name first appears in an advertisement of goods of this character in the "New York Mercury," of Monday, October 23d, 1753: "Just Imported a large Assortment of *Irish Linnens*, and to be sold cheap by HUGH WALLACE, at his Store in New-Dutch-Church Street." He did not, however, confine himself to any one branch of business, as his occasional notices show; on the 31st July, 1758, he informs the public that there was "To be sold at Private Sale, by HUGH WALLACE, *The Snow La Faveur*, lately a French Privateer, with or without her Guns and Warlike Stores as the Purchaser pleases. If said Vessel is not sold before she will be sold at Publick Vendue at the Merchants' Coffee House on Tuesday, the 8th of August next. Said WALLACE has a large Parcel of *Fyall Wines* to dispose of which he will sell reasonably." In the same year he applies for commissions for Captains of the Ship Terrible, 10 guns, and the Snow Montresor, also of 10 guns. In January, 1762, (Gaines' "New York Mercury," 18th inst.,) he advertises a cargo of *Coals* for sale, and again, on the 29th March, of the same year, he announces a curious variety of articles, common enough at that period, but now never found on the shelves of any one merchant: "HUGH WALLACE sells on very reasonable Terms Madeira, Mountain, Sherry, and benecarlo Wines; Rum, Molasses, White and Muscovado Sugar, *Oranges* and Lemmons, Sallad Oil, Olives, Capers and Anchovies, Gold and Silver Lace, Men's Shoes and Pumps, Boots and Spatterdashes, Silk Handkerchiefs, Scots Carpets, Men's and Women's Gloves, Irish Linnens and sundry European Goods."

Thriving in business, he seems to have resolved to make the new country his permanent residence. The "New York Mercury," of May 12th, 1760, notices, as an item of interesting news, that "Last week MR. HUGH WALLACE, of this City, Merchant, was married to Miss Sally Low, daughter of Cornelius Low, of Rariton, in New Jersey, an agreeable Young Lady endow'd with every Qualification requisite to render the Marriage State happy." In those days the family incidents of the high in station were presumed as of right to interest the general public. By this marriage MR. WALLACE connected himself with some of the most distinguished families of the Colony. The Lows were among the earlier English settlers, and had intermarried with the Gouverneurs, and the Cuylers, who were second to none in the aristocracy of the New York Province.

Strengthened by these alliances and his growing wealth and influence, Mr. Wallace now seems to have looked to political preferment. In 1760 he was evidently an agent of the Government, and in October of that year was authorized to impress Vessels to carry troops to Halifax. He does not appear to have filled any minor stations, but to have reached at once the higher honors. On the retirement of Mr. Walton he was called to the King's Council, a body of twelve, which acted as the advisers of the Governor, and held powers somewhat analogous to those of the modern Senate. On the 21st January, 1769, as Gov. Moore informs the Earl of Hillsborough, "Mr. Wallace took the oaths and his seat at the Board." This position he continued to hold until the downfall of the King's power in the Colony. His name last appears upon the minutes of a meeting of the Council held 11 March, 1776, on board the Ship Dutchess of Gordon in the Harbour, in which Governor Tryon had taken refuge.

But while thus occupied with the grave affairs of State, Mr. Wallace was not indifferent to his business or his calling. He was one of the founders of the Chamber of Commerce in 1768, and its first Vice-President. On the retirement of Mr. Cruger, in 1770, he was chosen President of the Institution.

Near this period Alexander Wallace first appears in this country. He had no doubt been led hither by the success of the elder brother, and a business house was formed between them. A notice of this connection appears in Gaines' "New York Gazette & Weekly Mercury," July 24th, 1769: "To be sold a handsome *Chariot*, the Box made to take off occasionally, with Harness for four Horses. Enquire of Messieurs Hugh & Alexander Wallace." This is curious as showing the state which the grandees of the Colonial days maintained.

This partnership of the two brothers, whose interests were still more closely allied by the marriage of Alexander with a sister of the wife of HUGH, continued until the close of the revolutionary war. Their advertisements, as general importers, always include a notice of "large assortments of low priced yard-wide Irish Linen by the Box."

MR. WALLACE upheld the dignity of his station, and his mansion was the resort of the great dignitaries of the Province. It is recorded in Rivington's "Gazette," of June 29th, 1775, that Governor Tryon, who came passenger by the Ship Juliana, Capt. Montgomery, landed that evening at New York, "and was conducted to the house of the HON. HUGH WALLACE by an immense number of the principal people of that city."

In the struggle between the Colonies and the Crown HUGH WALLACE stood steadfast to his allegiance, and controlled the great influence of his connections in the interest of the Mother Country. Born in Great Britain and a Councillor of the King in the Colony, no other course could be expected of him. And he maintained his loyalty as firmly in the dark as in the bright hours—nor did he desert his post. On the 4th February, 1776, he was invited to appear before the Committee of Safety and inform them what he knew of the intentions of the British fleet. It had been announced that the Mercury Frigate and two other transports were below. MR. WALLACE replied that he intended to go on board of the Governor's Ship that afternoon, and would give information of "anything of importance to the City."

Early in August, 1776, on the 17th, so runs the account given in the Upcott Coll.: iv. 383, of the conversation of a gentleman who had made his escape from the City to the British forces on Staten Island, the two brothers, HUGH and ALEXANDER WALLACE, with other persons of mark, "were committed to gaol for having refused to take the oath of allegiance to the Congress." MR. HUGH WALLACE was ordered to Connecticut by the military authorities, but the confinement of Alexander was of short duration.

The fact of his imprisonment is confirmed in a letter of Governor Tryon to Lord George Germaine, dated New York, 24th September, 1776, which gives a melancholy account of the state of the King's Government in the Colony, and reports "MR. HUGH WALLACE and Mr. James Jauncey prisoners with the Rebels."

MR. WALLACE was now to undergo something of the hardships of war. His wife remained in New York under the care of Alexander. A letter written by Mr. Alexander Wallace to a friend and influential patriot, Gouverneur Morris, 28th December, 1776, gives an account of the losses to which he was at this time subjected: "Mrs. Hugh Wallace is pretty well in health, but very unhappy about her husband being kept so long from her, and what adds to her distress is the very heavy loss she has met with about ten days ago in losing all her plate. She sent it to Mr. Richard Yates last summer at Aquacknock, to be kept there as a place of safety; but upon his leaving that place he had the box which contained the plate put on board a brig, commanded by Capt. Roche, bound to this place. About five miles below Hackinsack the brig was seized by a party of your army, and all the goods taken out. The plate cost upwards of £1500, this currency. She thinks the gentlemen belonging to the Convention, when they know it belongs to her, will order it to be sent to her immediately, as it would be very hard indeed to send her husband away to Connecticut and allow her property to be plundered. I must request the favour of you to get this affair settled as soon as possible. Enclosed is an inventory of the plate; it was all in one box. My papers are in much better order than I expected; but my brother and I shall suffer greatly by being sent away from our property. I have sent your letter to your mother, who is very well, as is all your friends. I shall go and see your mother in a few days. General Robinson assured me all the women and children who have a mind to go to their husbands or friends have liberty to go by this flag, or any other way they think proper."

He adds in a postscript: "Please deliver the enclosed letters; give the one for Hugh Wallace to Mr. Samuel Loudon, to be sent by post. My brother has lost all his clothes in the Jerseys. Mrs. Wallace sent them there."

The inventory alluded to gives the contents of the box of plate: 1 tea urn, 1 epergne, 1 very large bowl, 4 candlesticks, 1 large pudding dish, 2 large salvers, 3 small salvers, 1 large tankard, 1 coffee pot, 1 pitcher, 1 cruet stand, 4 long handled spoons, 4 scalloped spoons, 6 dozen table spoons, 1 dozen desert spoons, 1 sugar dish, 1 funnel, 1 fish trowel, 6 salts, 2 mustard pots with spoons, 6 skewers, 2 milk pots, 1 tea chest with cannisters, 1 sugar tongs, 4 labels for bottles, 4 tumblers, 4 rummers, 2 black jacks, 1 large soup ladle, 1 marrow spoon.—(*Correspondence of Prov. Cong., Vol.* 2, *p.* 237.)

With the family of Gouverneur Morris there was also a connection through the Gouverneurs: the second wife of Colonel Lewis Morris and mother of Gouverneur Morris was Sarah Gouverneur.

Meanwhile Mr. Wallace was not long detained in durance. He and his fellow captives were released upon the following written obligation:

WHEREAS, we, HUGH WALLACE, Fred Philipse, James Jauncey, and James Jauncey, Jun'r, Esqr., and Gerard Walton, William Jauncey and John Miller, all of the City and Province of New York, have for some time past resided at Middletown, in the State of Connecticut, being apprehended and sent thither by His Excellency General Washington as suspected of disaffection to the United States of America; and whereas, upon our application, His Honour Jona Trumbull, Esq., Governor of the said State of Connecticut, hath permitted us to return to our families in New York and reside there till otherwise ordered, we do hereby pledge our faith and words of honour to the said Governor Trumbull, that we will neither bear arms, nor excite or encourage others to bear arms, against this or any other of the United States of America; and that we will not do anything in prejudice of the interest or measures of this or any of the said United States; and that we will give no intelligence to the enemies of the United States of any of the councils of war or other the Transactions of this or any of the said States; and that we will return to any place in this State when required by His Honour Governor Trumbull, the General Assembly of Connecticut, or His Excellency the General of the armies of the said United States for the time being.

In witness whereto we have hereunto set our hands, this 23d day of December, A.D. 1776.

HUGH WALLACE,
FRED PHILIPS,
JAS. JAUNCEY,
JAS. JAUNCEY, JUN'R,
GERARD WALTON,
WILLIAM JAUNCEY,
JOHN MILLER.

Governor Tryon, in a letter to Lord George Germaine, of date New York, 31 Dec., 1776, alludes to the return of the prisoners. "Last Sunday evening MR. WALLACE and Mr. Jauncey, two of his Majesty's Council of this Province, with several other Inhabitants thereof, came to town from Connecticut, having been discharged by Gov. Trumbull from their confinement upon the express obligation of not taking up arms against America, and to return to captivity if required."

The brothers Wallace remained in New York during the war. The newspapers of 1782 and 1783 contain a standing advertisement that "HUGH and ALEXANDER WALLACE have for sale, on reasonable terms, a Quantity of good sweet Flour, old Lisbon Wine, a large quantity of Queens-ware in Crates, Glass and China in Boxes, Cannon, 4, 6 and 9 pounders, Shot, Swivel guns of newest construction." They were also constantly favored by the military authorities, and were agents of the Government for the payment of prize-money to the British men of war. On May 5, 1783, they give notice in Gaine's N. Y. Gazette and Mercury that they will pay the prize-money for the captures of His Majesty's Ship *Cyclops*.

The property of HUGH WALLACE was confiscated by the Provincial Legislature on the 22d October, 1779. The confiscated Estates were sold under a further act of the State Legislature of 12 May, 1784.

HUGH WALLACE did not remain to witness the new order of things, but left with the army in 1783. He returned to Great Britain, and died at Waterford in Ireland in the year 1788. No portrait of Mr. WALLACE is known to exist in this country.

ELIAS DESBROSSES.

THIRD PRESIDENT OF THE NEW YORK CHAMBER OF COMMERCE.

1771–1772.

T what period the family of Desbrosses came to the New York Colony is now unknown. They have been called of Huguenot extraction—a view to which their warm attachment to the Protestant faith gives color; but this name is not found in the Colonial records at the time when the chief part of this emigration reached the New World. The town of New Rochelle, in Westchester County, was settled as early as 1681 by French refugees, who had fled to England to avoid the persecutions which preceded the revocation of the Edict of Nantes in 1685. The name of Desbrosses does not appear on the lists of freeholders of the new settlement of 1708 or 1724.

The name is first met with in an advertisement in William Bradford's "New York Gazette," September 12th to 19th, 1737, giving notice of "Choice Good Canary Wine to be sold at Three Shillings and six pence per Gallon by the five Gallons at the Widow Desbrosses, in Hanover Square."

Elias Desbrosses was born (probably in this city) in the year 1718. The family appears, in 1737, to have consisted of the widow, her sons Elias and James (and perhaps Stephen, whose name appears later), and her daughters Magdalen and Elizabeth.

He first comes into notice in the famous report, by Horsmanden, of the Negro Plot of 1741. It was the belief of the time that the negroes were set on by Catholic priests. The shade of Guy Fawkes yet lurked near every burning house. His testimony before the Court on the 24th July, 1741, is thus given: "ELIAS DESBROSSES, of New York, Confectioner; John Ury, the popish priest, now in jail, came with one Webb, a carpenter, to him, and asked if he (deponent) had any sugar bits or wafers, &c., (the bits are usually made as the deponent apprehends in imitation of Spanish silver coin.) This deponent showed the said Ury some confectionary in imitation of dogs, hawks, owls, lambs, and swans, supposing that he wished them to give away to please children, but told him he had no bits or wafers." At this time Catholic worship was punished as a crime, and all magistrates were sworn to maintain the Protestant religion. This Ury was convicted, and executed on the 29th of the same month.

About this time James Desbrosses, a brother of ELIAS, first appears. One of his negroes, Primus, made confession concerning the Plot. He was to have stolen his master's gun and helped kill the white people. He resided at the "last house on the East River to Kip's Bay," described by David Grim as the house at which the line of Palisades of Cedar logs commenced, which was stretched across the island to the North River, in 1745, "for the security and protection of the inhabitants of the city, who were at that time much alarmed and afraid that the French and Indians were coming to invade the City." This house was near the shipyards at the foot of Catharine Street. An advertisement in the "New York Journal," April 2, 1767, shows that he was still residing there.

A part of the family, however, still occupied the house

in Hanover Square in 1755. An advertisement in Gaine's "New York Mercury," of June 16th of that year, gives an approximation to its situation. It alludes to a house on Hanover Square wherein "Mr. Lewis Morris lived, next door to Mr. Walton's, and directly opposite to Mr. Grant's and DESBROSSES." Here ELIAS DESBROSSES carried on a general business, trading with Madeira and the West India Islands. He was also part owner of the sloop Success, as his applications to Gov. Hardy for permits show.

His name now begins to appear quite often in advertisements of real estate. In Gaine's "Mercury," of February 7th, 1757, he calls attention to a tract of land in New Jersey which he has for sale. He here signs himself Merchant.

James Desbrosses appears also to have been somewhat engaged in commerce. An advertisement of "A variety of Paper Hangings, imported from London," to be sold by him, appeared in 1761. The name of still another of the family is recorded in an order issued by Governor Monckton, March 5th, 1763, to Capt. Lawrence, of Kings County, to deliver a certain negro boy, named *Touissant*, to Stephen Desbrosses, to be sent by him to Mr. Veyer, his former master at Martinico.

With these various enterprises MR. ELIAS DESBROSSES continued to increase his property and influence, and to win the esteem of his neighbors. In 1767 he was chosen Alderman of the East Ward, which he continued to represent in the City Councils until 1770.

In 1768 he was one of the founders of the Chamber of Commerce, and its first Treasurer—an office which he held until 1770, when he was chosen Vice-President, and the next year President, of this Corporation.

MR. DESBROSSES does not seem to have had any desire

for public life. He was one of the Committee of Correspondence of fifty-one, chosen by the citizens in May, 1774, but the minutes only show him in his seat at the first meeting. He took no part in the stirring and angry scenes which followed. He was too little of a partisan to meet any annoyance from either side, and passed untroubled through the occupation of both armies. He showed his strong sympathy with the English side by signing the very loyal address of Lord Howe, in October, 1776, and though not claimed by Sabine as a loyalist in his comprehensive collection of sketches, he must be classed in this body.

In May of the following year, when the British authorities undertook to raise troops for the King's service in New York, Mr. Desbrosses, whose residence is given as in Queen Street, was one of a Committee, together with Henry White, Nathaniel Marston, and Thomas White, "appointed to receive donations which will be applied for the Comfort and Encouragement of such of his Majesty's faithful Subjects as already have or hereafter shall enter into the Provincial Regiments raising in this Province."

In December, 1777, he was named first on the Vestry appointed by General Robertson for the Relief of the Poor of the City. With him were many of his old commercial associates—Miles Sherbrooke, Isaac Low, Charles Nicoll, Gabriel H. Ludlow, and others.

He seems to have taken no further active part in business, and when the meetings of the Chamber were renewed by such of the members as adhered to the Crown, he did not resume his connection with it.

Mr. Desbrosses was a very religious man, and forward in every charitable enterprise. The family were among the early and liberal contributors to the Huguenot church, L'Eglise du St. Esprit, erected in Pine Street, and James was one of the elders while the church was under the ministry of Jean Carle. ELIAS DESBROSSES early connected himself with the Established Church. He was a Vestryman of Trinity from 1759 to 1770 and Warden from 1770 to 1778, and he was a liberal contributor to the support of the Charity School of that Corporation. His name appears first signed to the report of the great loss the Corporation sustained in the fire of 1776, amounting to £22,000,—the Church, Charity Schools, Library, and Rectory being all destroyed,—and it was he who, as Churchwarden, inducted Mr. Inglis as Rector, the following year, the ceremony being completed by "placing his hand (Mr. Inglis') on the wall of the said church, the same being then a ruin."

He was one of the early patrons of the New York Hospital, and a Governor from 1775 to 1778.

The time was now rapidly approaching when the career of MR. DESBROSSES, the latter days of which appear to have been devoted to good works, was to close. He died in New York on the 26th March, 1778. An elaborate obituary notice appeared in Rivington's "Royal Gazette," for Saturday, April 4th, 1778, which gives a careful analysis of his character.

"On Thursday, the 26th of last month, departed this life, in the 60th year of his age, ELIAS DESBROSSES, ESQ., for many years an eminent Merchant in this City. By the death of this worthy man, who was much loved and respected, this Community hath lost a most useful member.

"His conduct through life was regulated by the strictest probity; and he ever supported a fine, unspotted character. He was active, sober, and just; mild, easy, and humane; devout, benevolent, and sincere. No man had a more feeling heart for the distresses, or more interested in the welfare of others. In him the poor and needy always found a generous benefactor; every scheme that could be subservient to the comforts of Society, a zealous patron—all who required his services (and their number was great), a faithful, steady Friend.

"An invariable adherence to this line of conduct evinced that it was the result of fixed principles—that it flowed from a deep and awful sense of the Supreme Being, from a conscientious regard to the dictates of his revealed will and from an habitual piety which without any ostentation always influenced his proceedings in every station.

"An ornament to the Religious Society of which he was a member, he was assiduous in promoting its interest, and indefatigable in his endeavours to extricate it from those embarassments in which the present wanton and unnatural Rebellion had involved it. Nor were his views for this purpose and the general good of his fellow creatures confined to the term of his own existence here. By his last will he bequeathed considerable sums for the education and support of orphans in the Charity School of Trinity Church, and for promoting religion. In short, few persons have deserved better of society—few have been more justly and sincerely lamented than MR. DESBROSSES. His remains were interred in the family vault in Trinity Church Yard, attended by a large number of respectable citizens, on the Saturday after his decease."

The will of MR. ELIAS DESBROSSES, on file in the Surrogate's office for New York County, dated — June, 1773, and finally proved in 1784, recounts the names of his family and recites his bequests. By it he bequeathes to his brother, James, all the town-land in Hardenbergh Patent; to his loving sisters, Magdalen and Elizabeth Desbrosses, his lot, dwelling, and store fronting King, Queen, and Dock Streets, bought of the heirs of Cornelius Van Horne; to his niece,

Mary Ann Desbrosses, the lot and dwelling-house fronting Queen Street, bought of the heirs of Piere G. Depeyster; "One thousand Pounds, lawful money of New York, unto the Rector and inhabitants of the City of New York in communion of the Church of England as by Law established, in trust, to be placed at interest by the Vestry of that Corporation for the maintenance of a French Clergyman, who shall perform Divine Service in the French language in this City according to the liturgie of the Church of England as by law established, and should it be any considerable time before such establishment is effected, then the interest arising from the said thousand pounds shall become a principal for the same use—and the sum of five hundred pounds, lawful money of New York, ... for the clothing and educating the poor children of Trinity Church School in this City."

The Mary Ann Desbrosses here named was married to Joseph Waddington, Feb. 6th, 1781. The two sisters of Mr. Desbrosses died single at a great age. On the 12th July, 1781, they made their wills, in which each styled herself a "single woman," in each other's favor. "The Daily Advertiser," for Friday, December 26th, 1794, has a notice of the death of the survivor: "Died, on Monday last, Mrs. Magdalen Desbrosses, aged 87 years."

The two wills were proved on the 9th January, 1795. That of Magdalen names as her residuary legatees her nephew James Desbrosses, (Jr.,) of New York, Merchant, and his wife Elizabeth, (he had married Elizabeth Butler, in 1762,) and two other sons of James, by name Elias and William, of whom no other mention appears.

Between this period and the 5th May, 1809, there was great mortality in the family. On this day Letters of Administration were granted to John Hunter and Elizabeth his wife, and to Henry Overing and Charlotte Magdalene his wife, "cousins of Elias Desbrosses, late of this City, Merchant, deceased." All of the legatees and executors are said to have died, and these, his grand-nieces, were next of kin. The whole property of the family, the accumulations of nearly a century, thus passed into the hands of these two ladies. The one had married John Hunter, of Hunter's Island, Westchester County, the other Captain Overing, of the British army.

The name of Desbrosses thus became extinct in the American line, and is only kept in memory by the Street on the West side of the City which was called in his honor about the beginning of this century.

The life of Mr. Desbrosses presents many pleasing traits, which, derived from his French origin, are recognized as characteristic of the Huguenot families of America. Wherever the old French blood has allied itself to the English or Dutch, a fine variety of the human race has been the product; while the traits of the Huguenot are alike marked in the new strain as it appears in Charleston and New York, the chosen resorts of the early Huguenot emigration. Integrity of character, cheerfulness and amiability of temperament, and a religious sentiment showing itself in practical charity, are the well-known marks of this noble stock; and withal a desire for the quiet social walks rather than the busy and crowded scenes of public life.

A diligent search has not discovered any portrait or sketch of Elias Desbrosses from which a picture could be made to fill his place upon the walls of the Chamber of Commerce, or to keep in memory the features of one whose character and life offer so much to imitate and revere.

Henry White

[illegible] by F. Halpin from the picture in possession of the Chamber of Commerce.

HENRY WHITE.

FOURTH PRESIDENT OF THE NEW YORK CHAMBER OF COMMERCE.

1772-1773.

BUT little is known of HENRY WHITE before his arrival in the New York Province, beyond the fact that he was of Welsh birth and origin. He first appears upon the busy scene of Colonial trade in a Petition, dated May 8, 1756, for leave to ship bread to South Carolina for the use of the Navy, and is called their agent by Samuel Bowman, Jr., and Jo. Yates, of Charleston, in their request to Governor Hardy, the same summer, for a similar authority.

His first mercantile advertisement may be seen in the New York Mercury of December 12, 1757, which sets forth that "HENRY WHITE has just imported from London and Bristol a neat assortment of goods fit for the season, which he will sell for ready money or short credit, at his store in King Street."

On the 13th May, 1761, according to the Record of New York Marriages, MR. WHITE formed an alliance with Eva Van Cortland, daughter of Frederick, and grand-daughter of Jacobus Van Cortland. In her veins ran also the blood of the Philipse, another of the wealthiest and most important families of the Colony. This connection secured the fortune of MR. WHITE.

In 1762 he appears as the owner of the sloop Moro, 10 guns. All the vessels sent out from New York at this time were armed. The war with France, ended on land, still raged on the seas.

The following year, as appears from a notice in Weyman's Gazette of March 21, 1763, he made a voyage to England. A trip across the Atlantic was at this period an important matter. He announces himself as "intending for England about the end of April next," and invites those to whom he is indebted to call for their money.

While regularly pursuing his business with Great Britain, and at times making ventures to the neighboring colonies, he seems to have looked to political preferment.

In 1769, on the refusal of Mr. Delancey to take a seat at the Council Board, MR. WHITE made urgent application to the Governor for the vacant place. Governor Moore so informs the Earl of Hillsborough in his letter of 21 January, and seems to have supported the request, for on the 8th March following MR. WHITE received the Commission, and was sworn of the Council—a post which he retained during the remaining period of English rule in America.

Hitherto he had carried on his trade at his store on Cruger's Wharf, but now, his rising fortunes and new honors requiring more state, he changes his residence. Hugh Gaine's New York Gazette and Weekly Mercury of May 1, 1769, contains the advertisement that "HENRY WHITE has removed to the house of the late Treasurer, between the Fly market and the Coffee-House, where he has to sell the following articles, viz.: Nails of all sizes, Bohea and Congo Teas, 6 by 8, 7 by 9, and 8 by 10 Window Glass, English Sail Cloth, from No. 1 to 7, Russia do., writing paper, English cordage, Bristol Beer, blue duffils, spotted rugs, Newkirk and Dutch Ozenbrigs, Madeira Wine." The late Treasurer here alluded to was Abraham De Peyster, one of the wealthiest of the City magnates, who died in 1767.

Henry White was one of the consignees of the tea the shipment of which caused great excitement on the American seaboard in the winter of 1773 to 1774. The East India Company, yielding to the urgent demands of Lord North, who had promised the King "to try the question with America," in the fall of 1773 despatched their consignments of the forbidden merchandise to all the chief coast cities from the Massachusetts Bay to the Carolinas. The ship for South Carolina had arrived at Charleston on the 2d December, 1773, and the consignees declining to receive the cargo, the duties were not paid, and the tea was left to rot in the cellar where it was stored. The three ships for Boston were boarded in the night of the 26th December, and their cargoes were emptied into the sea; the ship for Pennsylvania arrived at Chester on the 27th December, when the Philadelphians gathered in town meeting, and the captain was made to promise to return to London with ship and cargo the very next day.

Early advised by the Company of the shipment to New York, Henry White, with two of the other consignees, Abraham Lott and Benjamin Booth, addressed a memorial, Dec. 1st, 1773, to Governor Tryon for the protection of the tea.

It was not until the 18th of April, 1774, that the Nancy reached the offing. Contrary winds had blown her off the coast, and she had put into Antigua. She was boarded by a Committee of Vigilance at Sandy Hook. Captain Lockyer, her master, was permitted to bring the ship to the city, but his men were not allowed to land.

According to the account given in Hugh Gaine's New

York Gazette of April 25th, 1774, "The Committee, early next morning, conducted Captain Lockyer to the house of the HON. HENRY WHITE, ESQ., one of the Consignees, and there informed Captain Lockyer that it was the sense of the Citizens that he should not presume to go near the Custom House, &c.". . . To this he answered, "That as the Consignees would not receive his cargo, he would not go to the Custom House, and would make all the dispatch he could to leave the city."

MR. WHITE was unyielding in his opinions, and at no period showed any sympathy with those who resisted the King's authority. In the summer of 1775, he was in correspondence with Governor Martin, of North Carolina. A letter from the Governor to his address, asking for the shipment of a marquee "with the royal standard," previously asked for, was intercepted and laid before the Committee of Safety. MR. WHITE does not appear to have fallen into the hands of the revolutionists. He probably left the city before stringent measures were adopted. In the summer of 1776, he is spoken of by Governor Tryon, in his account of the breaking up of the Council, as in England. He returned to his post when the British resumed control in the fall of the same year, probably with the army, as he was one of the signers of the loyal address to Lord Howe in October following. In 1777 he was appointed first of the committee of four to receive donations for equipment of provincial regiments for the King's service, and resided here during the war, acting as the agent of the Home Government in various ways—chiefly in the sale of captured vessels and cargoes, and the distribution of prize-money among the British vessels of war. One of many of his advertisements of this kind may be seen in Rivington's Royal Gazette of the 23d April, 1783, in which he gives notice of a division of the "nett proceeds of the ship Tyger and cargo, condemned at Bermuda, and of the schooner Neptune and ship Vestal."

On the 9th October, 1780, he is said by Sabine to have appeared before the surrogate to prove the will of the unfortunate André, when he declared that he was "well acquainted with the testator's handwriting, and believed the instrument to be genuine."

He left the city and returned to England with the British on the evacuation in the fall of 1783.

His estates were among the earliest confiscated in 1779. An advertisement of sale by the Commissioners of Forfeitures, in Kollock's New York Gazette of May 23d, 1786, is curious as descriptive of a mansion of those days. This house was then in the occupation of George Clinton, the first Governor of the State of New York. "On Monday the 19th June, at the Merchants' Coffee House—That large and commodious House and Lot of Ground situated on the South Easterly side of Queen Street, in the East ward of the said City, now occupied by his Excellency the Governor; the house is three large stories high, and contains four large rooms with fire places on each floor, besides a convenient kitchen in the rear of and adjoining thereto: in the Yard is a large brick building calculated for a storehouse and coach-house with stables, also a well and cistern; the lot extends nearly through to Water Street, and has a spacious gangway for a carriage in the said street; its situation and conveniences are as well calculated for a merchant in extensive business as any in this city. The above premises were forfeited and vested in the People of this State by the attainder of HENRY WHITE, ESQ., late one of the Members of the Council of the late Colony of New York."

Mr. White did not long survive the war. He died in Golden Square, London, on the 23d day of December, 1786. His wife, Eva Van Cortland, the daughter of Frederick Van Cortland, survived him nearly half a century. She died at her residence, No. 11 Broadway, on the 19th August, 1836, in the ninety-ninth year of her age. By her Mr. White had thirteen children, seven of whom reached years of maturity. Of these, 1. Henry White married Ann Van Cortland, and lived and died in the United States. 2. John Chambers White entered the British navy, rose to the rank of Vice Admiral of the White, and was knighted. He married, first, Cordelia Fanshawe; second, Miss Dalrymple. 3. Frederick Van Cortland White entered the British army in 1781, as an Ensign, and became General. He married, first, Sophia Coore; second, Miss Davidson. 4. William Tryon White lived and died, unmarried, in the United States. Of the daughters, 1. Ann married Dr. (afterwards Sir) John McNamara Hayes, of Golden Square, London, in 1787, and lived and died in England. 2. Margaret married Peter Jay Munro, and lived and died in the United States. 3. Frances married Dr. Archibald Bruce, and also lived and died in the United States.

There is a fine portrait of Henry White, senior, by John Singleton Copley, in the possession of a great-grandson, Augustus Van Cortland, who occupies the Cortlandt House, erected at Yonkers by Frederick Van Cortlandt in 1748. A picture, also by Copley, belongs to his descendants in the line of Munro. The portrait which hangs in the hall of the Chamber of Commerce was painted from the Van Cortland picture. The engraving which prefaces this sketch is after the same picture.

Theophylact Bache

Eng[d] by G. F. Hall, from the Picture in Possession of the Chamber of Commerce, N.Y.

THEOPHYLACT BACHE.

FIFTH PRESIDENT OF THE NEW YORK CHAMBER OF COMMERCE.

1773–1774.

F the family of BACHE, in England, but little is known in America. The name is, without doubt, Norman. In English records it is printed De la Bèche and De la Bache. William Bache, the father of THEOPHYLACT and RICHARD BACHE, from whom all of the name in this country are descended, was a Collector of Excise at the town of Settle, in the West Riding of Yorkshire, England. His wife was Mary Blyckenden. They were the parents of a large family, Richard Bache being the eighteenth child.

THEOPHYLACT BACHE was born at Settle on the 17th January, 1734–5, old style; and, as appears in a memorandum in his own hand-writing, he "arrived at New York September 17th, 1751." He came out at this early age to the care of Paul Richard, whose wife, Elizabeth Garland, of London, was a relation. Paul Richard was a man of distinction in the Colony. He was a successful merchant, and had at one period held the office of Mayor of the City.

Young BACHE was no doubt the assistant of Mr. Richard in his business. He was certainly regarded by him with attachment. A codicil to his will, dated 19 Sept., 1756, shortly before his death, leaves to MR. BACHE £300 currency, and names him an Executor of his Estate.

The first mercantile notice of MR. BACHE appears in the "New York Mercury," of April 11th, 1757: "To be Sold, by THEOPHYLACT BACHE, at the house of the late Paul Richard, Esq., a choice parcel of Madeira Wine, Cheshire Cheese, Sperma-ceti Candles, with sundry sorts of European Goods, and will be disposed of reasonably to close the accounts."

In August, 1757, his name is recorded with that of Leonard Lispenard as a merchant and owner of the Ship Grace—eight guns. MR. BACHE now steadily increased his business, and his advertisements appear at intervals in the journals—sometimes of cargoes received by him, at others, of goods on hand. It is worthy of notice that many of the goods were of a kind extremely costly at that period. The "New York Mercury," for Monday, March 6th, 1758, announces that there had been "Imported on the last vessels from London, and to be sold by THEOPHYLACT BACHE, at his store in *Hanover Square*, a great variety of Velvets, Thicksets, Fustians, Jeans, Pillows, and printed Cottons suitable for the approaching season; with a fresh assortment of European Goods."

The next year he seems to have changed his location. In Gaine's "New York Mercury," for January 15th, 1759, he announces as "Just imported from Liverpool, by the snow Betsey, Nathaniel Remmer, Master, a large Assortment of European Goods proper for the present and approaching season, to be sold on reasonable Terms by THEOPHYLACT BACHE, at his Store on *Hunter's Quay*, next door to Mr. Walters. N. B.—He has also fine Blown Salt to dispose of by the 100 Baskets."

Again, in the same year, July 9th, 1759, in Weyman's "New York Gazette," appears the announcement that

"THEOPHYLACT BACHE has imported in the last vessels from Europe a general Assortment of Goods proper for the season, and has also to dispose of a Parcel of Choice Madeira Wine, Flour, Salt, and Cordage." This from his store on the Quay; meanwhile he had been making arrangements for increased accommodations for his growing business.

In the "New York Mercury," of August 15th, 1760, he announces that he "has removed from his store on Hunter's Quay to his new store in the Square, adjoining Mrs. Farmer's, where he has to dispose of a choice assortment of European and India Goods; also Madeira Wine, Sugar and Molasses; and a few boxes of excellent green Tea." The exactions of the British ministry had not yet made tea-drinking unfashionable and unpatriotic.

He now enters upon a more important charge than any which had preceded it. On the 16th of October, 1760, he married Ann Dorothy, daughter of Andrew Barclay, a wealthy gentleman who had come to New York from Curaçoa, and established himself as a merchant. This connection united him to some of the wealthiest and most distinguished families in the Province. Of his wife's sisters, Catharine married Augustus Van Cortlandt; Sarah, Anthony Lispenard; Ann Margaret, Frederick Jay; Helena, Major Moncrieff, a British officer of distinction; and Charlotte Amelia became the second wife of Dr. Richard Bailey.

This Anthony Lispenard was the brother of Leonard, who was joint owner with MR. BACHE in the ship Grace. This vessel he ran in the English trade, and on the 27th February, 1765, he advertises her in the "New York Gazette and Weekly Post Boy" as shortly to sail for Bristol, under the command of William Chambers, Master.

Meanwhile the younger brother Richard had arrived in America, and as early as 1760 established himself in business in Philadelphia. He seems to have acted for the elder brother also. A part of this agency was the underwriting of vessels and cargoes. There still remains a curious policy, issued in the name of the two brothers, at Philadelphia, 31st May, 1764, on a shipment from that port to Havana by the brig Success, Marshall, Master, for a consideration of three and a-half per cent. "Touching the Adventures and Perils which the Assurers are contented to bear—they are of *Seas, Men-of-War*, Fire, Enemies, Pirates, Rovers, Thieves, Jetisons, Letters of Mart and *Counter-Mart*, Surprisals, *Taking at Sea, Arrests, Restraints and Detainments, of all Kings, Princes, or People of what Nation, Condition, or Quality soever*, &c., &c., to be of as much force and effect as the Surest Writing or Policy of Assurance heretofore made in *Lombard Street*, or elsewhere in LONDON." In Philadelphia Richard Bache connected himself in marriage with one of those names which rescue from oblivion even its most distant alliances, and give them place on the page of history. On the 29th October, 1767, Richard Bache married Sarah, sole daughter of the illustrious Benjamin Franklin.

THEOPHYLACT BACHE stood high in the confidence of his fellow merchants, and was one of the select few who organized the Chamber of Commerce on the 5th April, 1768. In 1770 he was chosen Treasurer, in 1771 Vice-President, and in 1773 President, of this flourishing Corporation.

He was one of the first petitioners for the Marine Society, which was incorporated in April, 1770. He was one of the incorporators also of the Society of the New York Hospital in 1771.

How far MR. BACHE identified himself with the great public movements in opposition to the Stamp Act in 1765, is not known. In 1770 he united heartily with his fellow merchants in their non-importation agreements, and was one of the committee to see to their execution. He does not appear to have sought political distinction. With an important business, and with the constant demands of a large family circle, he had little inclination to mix in the turbulent scenes of this stormy period. His disposition was genial, his qualities domestic: to an open-handed hospitality he added a great love of field-sports, and his dog and gun were the constant companions of his hours of leisure. His favorite sporting-ground was at Islip, Long Island, then abounding in game. There he passed weeks in the spring and fall at the house of his friend, Judge Thompson.

That his public course had been satisfactory to all sides is evident from the fact that his name was on both the tickets for the Committee of Correspondence of fifty-one, and stands third upon this list of the magnates of the city. This Committee was organized in May, 1774, on the news reaching the city of the passage of the Boston Port Bill. Mr. Bache was a regular attendant at its meetings, and seems to have been a willing promoter of the first Continental Congress, which sprung from the suggestions of this much abused but really wise and patriotic body. With Charles McEvers, he was appointed by it to oversee the election of the Deputies to this first Congress. This Congress, it will be remembered, went no further than to adopt a "Declaration of Rights," and to recommend to the Colonies a non-exportation and a non-importation Act. To these orders Mr. Bache faithfully adhered.

In the early spring of 1775 the aspect of affairs was more alarming, and in April the news of the Lexington fight threw all into confusion. The summer of 1775 was one of great excitement and distress throughout the continent. In New York, more than in the older English

Colonies, a large proportion of the merchants were English born: many had married here. The blood about to flow in the contest was on either side the blood of friends. To all such the prospect was gloomy and forbidding.

Meanwhile the leaders of the patriot party saw and felt the danger of delay. For them the die was cast, and they were content to abide the issue; but every consideration of personal safety and public duty urged them to use all means to add to their ranks, and take from the power of the royal party. To do this they took instant steps to break down the middle party, and to draw a narrow line between the friends of King and Country. To men like MR. BACHE, whose nature was of the tender kind, such a choice was unusually painful. Besides the ties of kindred and the early recollections of his English home, his family in America were divided in opinion. His only brother in the Colonies, swayed by the logic of the master-mind of Franklin, and nerved, perhaps, by the warm, patriotic heart of his wife, one of the noblest of American women, was strong in his sympathy with the Revolutionists. On the other hand, his wife's sister had married an officer in the King's service. Still halting between two opinions, MR. BACHE remained in New York and hoped to weather the storm. A simple incident turned the scale. In the month of September (7th, 1775), one Isaac L. Winn, a Captain of a trading vessel, was brought up for examination by the Committee of Safety; and although he gave to Messrs. Livingston and Scott, who were deputed to examine him, "such sufficient satisfaction of his friendly dispositions to the liberties of America as induced them to believe the suspicions against him to be entirely groundless," and received a certificate to that effect from the Committee, his papers were taken from him. Among them was an unsigned letter directed to Major Moncrieff, at Boston, which from the hand-writing and other circumstances was believed to be by MR. THEOPHYLACT BACHE. It ran as follows:

NEW YORK, Sept. 3, 1775.

DEAR MAJOR:—I wrote to you a few days ago by the transport which sailed from hence. I hope you have received it. It is now decreed by the Congress criminal to speak, and as it would be equally so to write not knowing into whose hands this may fall before this reaches you, I am determined not to transgress. I wish to remain in this country as long as I can, and not to do anything that may cause a banishment, or the punishment of being sent to the mines of Symsbury, which are punishments daily inflicted on those poor culprits who are found or even supposed *inimical.*

Don't think of returning here while the unhappy contest continues. You will be ferreted and exposed to insults I would wish you to avoid. I will take care of your wife as much as a brother or friend can do. She is as well and as happy as can be expected. I expect that she will lay in at Flatbush, as I think it would be dangerous to bring her to town. The late firing of the Asia has been fatal to many women in her situation. The family join me in love to you, and believe me to be, dear Moncrief,

Yours,

——— ———

To Major Moncrief, Boston.

Thomas Moncrieff was a Major of Brigade in the American Establishment, and had married Helena Barclay, the sister of Mrs. Bache, in the summer of 1774.

In consequence of this letter MR. BACHE was ordered to

attend the Committee for examination—Mr. Isaac Roosevelt, to his honor be it said, dissenting; but the messenger on his return reported that MR. BACHE had gone out of town. He had probably received some friendly warning.

In the summer of 1775 he was again cited to appear before the Provincial Congress, and replied in the following letter. Throughout, the tone is that of one whose dearest wish is to preserve a strict neutrality.

FLATBUSH, Monday, 7th July, 1776.

GENTLEMEN:—I would have waited upon you this day pursuant to your Citation received on Friday last, but the distressed state of Mrs. Bache and my numerous family since the arrival of the fleet at Sandy Hook, will, I hope, be a sufficient apology for my remaining with them as they will require all my attention to save them from the horrible calamities of the approaching conflict.

My being represented to the Congress as one of the persons inimical to the cause of America, fills me with the deepest concern; be assured, Gentlemen, that the accusation is unmerited and must have proceeded from those unacquainted with my sentiments. I have not since the unhappy dispute began, contravened any order of the Congress, Continental or Provincial, nor is it my intention. I sincerely hope for a reconciliation—that this once happy country may enjoy the blessings of peace; and am, Gentlemen,

Your most obt. humble Svt.,

THEOPHYLACT BACHE.

To Philip Livingston, Esq., and the Gentlemen of Congress.

About this time he left New York and retreated to the British lines. A letter in the Upcott Collection, written on the 12th August, 1776, alludes to his arrival on Staten

Island with Mr. Augustus Van Cortlandt and others, "having narrowly escaped from their pursuers." He returned to New York with the troops a little later, and during the war divided his time between the City and his residence at Flatbush.

Some account of his residence and life at Flatbush, which was a favorite country-seat with New Yorkers, is furnished by Capt. Alexander Graydon in his memoirs of his own time. He was one of the thirty-two Captains commissioned by Congress in January, 1776, and had been taken prisoner at the battle of Harlem Heights in the following September. He relates "that he was taken to Flatbush, and billeted upon a Mr. Jacob Suydam. His house was pretty large, consisting of buildings which appeared to have been erected at different times, the front and best of which was in the occupation of MR. THEOPHYLACT BACHE and his family from New York. The morning after our arrival at this place we encountered MR. BACHE in the piazza, which extended the whole length of the building on the south side. His being an Englishman and determined royalist did not prevent him from accosting us very civilly, and manifesting a disposition to maintain a friendly intercourse with us, notwithstanding the difference in our political sentiments. . . . . Whatever was the motive, the behaviour of MR. BACHE was altogether free from intolerance and party rancour; it was more, it was hospitable and kind. In addition to frequent invitations to tea and to partake of his Madeira, to help us along a little, as he expressed, in allusion to the mean fare at Jacob's table, I was indebted to him for the offer of his purse, although he neither knew me or my connexions. As I stood in no need of it, I declined it with a due sense of the obligation the mere offer imposed. I availed myself, however, of the tender of his services in executing small commissions for me when he went to New York, which was almost every day." As a further instance of the good feeling of MR. BACHE, Captain Graydon says that he afterwards learned from MR. BACHE that he had seen him while a prisoner passing the Coffee-house in New York, and that he and some other gentlemen had been obliged to exert themselves to prevent some blackguards insulting him.

A change was soon to take place in the fortunes of the companions. In the night of the 15th June, 1778, William Mariner, one of the daring spirits of the day, made a dash into the town of Flatbush, and carried off MR. BACHE and Major Moncrieff, and freed Capt. Graydon from his captivity. Mariner left Middleton, New Jersey, in the evening with 11 men, and returned by six the next morning, having travelled by land and water above 50 miles. The attack was made in the dead of night, and MR. BACHE was hurried from the house without time being given him to put on his clothes. MR. BACHE was greatly distressed at his forcible separation from his wife and family. The prisoners were taken to Morristown, N. J., where they underwent a nominal confinement for a short time. MR. BACHE was soon sent home, a general exchange of prisoners taking place shortly after.

MR. BACHE exerted himself during the war to alleviate the distresses it occasioned. He was one of the Vestry appointed by Gen'l Robertson in 1772 to care for the Poor of the City. His kindly feeling never failed him, and he let no opportunity for its display pass. It was he who moved, in 1784, for the readmission to the Chamber of those who had been absent during the war.

In 1770 MR. BACHE appears to have been the joint owner, with Charles McEvers and Hamilton Young, of a certificate of location for a tract of 37,000 acres of land, near the tracts known by the name of Socialborough; and the next year he petitions that it may be erected into a township by the name of Newry. Newry is a port on the Irish coast, with which New York had some trade at this time. At a later period, in 1785, he was again interested, with James Barclay, in a claim to a tract of 18,000 acres, on the west side of the waters which flow into Lake Champlain. With the peace, he resumed his business at his old house in Hanover Square, No. 38, and his name appears in the first New York Directory, 1787 to 1793, at this place. From 1794 to 1801 the location is described as No. 122 Pearl Street. This house is remembered as an old-fashion brick building, on the lower side of the street, with a front of between forty and fifty feet, and an entrance nearly on the ground-level. As the land was extended into the East River, Mr. Bache, as the riparian owner, became possessed of lots on Water Street, on which he built three brick houses, which were known as 85, 86, and 87 Water Street. In 1802, Mr. Bache occupied No. 87. On the further filling in of the river-front, four houses were added on Front Street; and on its final extension to South Street, Mr. Bache put up two fine warehouses on an improved plan, which for a long time served as models for structures of this kind. These buildings were known as 44 and 45 South Street. They were later sold to Mr. John G. Coster, and were destroyed in the great fire of 1835. This locality is famous in the history of New York merchants. Here, on the ground-floor, Mr. Jonathan Goodhue, the founder of the well-known house of Goodhue & Co., at one time had an office, his firm being at that time Goodhue & Swett. No. 45 is now the counting house of one of the most distinguished merchants of this century, Mr. Moses Taylor.

Mr. Bache passed the greater part of his time at a country seat a short distance from the city, on what was then known as Turtle Bay. This is the first indentation above Kipp's Bay, and opposite the Western end of Blackwell's Island. In the later Colonial period the King's Stores were near this point. The house belonged to Mr. Francis Winthrop, a large owner of land in that neighborhood, and was on the eastern end of his property.

This place MR. BACHE called Camperdown, in honor of the great victory won by Lord Duncan, in the fall of 1797, over the Dutch fleet in the Texel under Admiral De Winton. This complete defeat of the sea-forces of the Batavian Republic was hailed throughout Great Britain with great joy, as the downfall of the naval power of Holland, long the only rival of England on the seas. With the true pride of a Briton MR. BACHE rejoiced in the triumph of his countrymen. This estate was afterwards purchased by Mr. Isaac Lawrence.

In 1803 MR. BACHE took his son Andrew into his commercial house, and carried on his business under the style of THEOPHYLACT & ANDREW BACHE. Their trade was with Bristol, Poole and the ports of the west of England, and with Newfoundland, the fisheries of which they supplied on the orders of their English friends. They were also the agents of the Phœnix Fire Insurance Office of London. Although the favored correspondent of English houses, and himself experienced in the trade of the period, MR. BACHE'S business was not prosperous towards the close of his career. In this he but shared the common fate.

The period was one of commercial disaster. All Europe was shaken by the tread of vast armies, and the arts of peace were rudely set aside in the sharp struggle which followed the French Revolution. It is not easy to measure the commercial distress of the earlier days of this century.

He died on Friday, the 30th October, 1807, in the 73d year of his age, at his old residence, and was buried from the house of his friend and kinsman, Mr. Charles McEvers, in Wall Street, on the Sunday following.

His life presents a fine example of a large manly nature. His stature was Norman in its great size, and all his instincts were noble and generous. His heart was large as the frame that contained it, and his attachments were strong and lasting. Nor were his interests bound by the circle of his family and friends. Wherever there was a good work to do, he was among the foremost.

He was one of the early projectors of the New York Hospital, of which he was Governor from 1785 to 1797, and President from 1794 to 1797.

One of the originators of the St. George Society, in 1786 he was its second President, being chosen to succeed Goldsborow Banyar in that office.

As an instance of the respect which his old companions entertained for him, notwithstanding his adherence to the British side, it may be mentioned that he was made Vice-President of the Chamber in 1788, and re-elected every year until 1792.

In religion, Mr. Bache was a warm supporter of the Church of England. He was a Vestryman of Trinity Church from 1760 to 1784, in 1788, and from 1792 to 1800.

By his wife, Ann Dorothy Barclay, whose death preceded his own some years (she died 7th November, 1795), he had a numerous issue. Of those who lived to maturity, 1. Paul Richard, his eldest son, so called after his patron and benefactor, married his cousin Helena, the eldest daughter of Anthony Lispenard; their only daughter, Sarah, was married to Robert Montgomery Livingston. 2. Andrew, married in England: of his children two sons, George Perry and William Satterthwaite, are now living; Eliza Barclay was married to G. H. Duckwith, and Sarah Bleecker to Jacob R. Nevius. 3. William, who was brought up as a lawyer, and practised his profession in New York, married Christina Cooper, daughter of Dr. Ananias Cooper of Rhinebeck: of this marriage also the only surviving issue was in the female line; one of the daughters was married to the late Mr. J. W. Schmidt, the Consul of Prussia at New York, and the other to Mr. Samuel Patterson, of Charleston, South Carolina.

Of the daughters of THEOPHYLACT BACHE, the eldest, 1. Elizabeth Garland, and some years after her death, 2. Sarah, were married to James, son of Anthony Bleecker; 3. Catharine, to an English gentleman, Thomas Wilkinson Satterthwaite; 4. Ann Dorothy, to her cousin Leonard, eldest son of Anthony Lispenard; 5. Mary, to Charles McEvers.

The Baches of Philadelphia, whose name the late Alexander Dallas Bache has so greatly distinguished by his contributions to science, are the descendants of Richard, the brother of THEOPHYLACT BACHE, and Sarah, the daughter of Dr. Franklin.

The portrait which prefaces this sketch is a copy from a crayon head drawn by the French emigré St. Memin, when in New York in 1797, now owned by Mr. Thomas Wilkinson Satterthwaite of this city, a grandson of MR. BACHE. A fine copy of this picture hangs on the walls of the Chamber of Commerce. It was taken in the winter of 1866-7, by Mr. Vincent Colyer, for its Gallery of Presidents.

There is also in the possession of a grand-daughter of MR. BACHE, wife of Judge Thomas W. Clerke of this city, a fine portrait of Mayor Richard, the early friend of the family in this country.

Wm Walton

Engd by G. R. Hall, from a picture in p[illegible] of the Chamber of Commerce.

WILLIAM WALTON.

SIXTH PRESIDENT OF THE NEW YORK CHAMBER OF COMMERCE.

1774-1775.

NO name calls up more pleasant memories of old New York than that of WALTON. For more than a hundred years this family of merchants held the first place among their fellows, and were the true princes of their time. Their descendants have left the walks of trade in which their race found wealth and honor, and the name is no more seen upon the roll of New York merchants, but the mansion in which their colonial ancestors held baronial state is still standing, a mute reminder of the splendors of a by-gone age.

The WALTONS were of English origin, and probably came from the county of Norfolk. Two families of the name appear at about the same period, the one in New York, the other in Richmond County, Staten Island. On the 12th December, 1689, an order was issued to the Justice of Richmond County to assist in taking an inventory of the estate of Thomas Walton, deceased. There is little doubt, from the sameness of the Christian names used in the two branches, that they were very nearly allied. In the New York family the name William was carried through a full century. The first William Walton of whom mention is made, was born sometime in the latter part of the seventeenth century. In 1698 he was admitted a Freeman of the City, and in the same year he is said to have married Mary Santford. In the Census of 1703 he is recorded as the head of a Family, composed of 1 Male, 1 Female, 2 Children, 1 Negro. His name appears upon the list of subscriptions towards the finishing the steeple of Trinity Church in 1711. On the 13th October, 1712, Andrew Faneuil, Charles Crommelin, Abraham Van Hoorn, and William Walton, of New York, merchants and owners of the sloop Swallow, Réné Het, Master, petition Governor Hunter for leave to convoy French prisoners to the French West Indies, under a flag of truce. In 1727 he is cited to appear at the office of the Secretary of the Colony, with an inventory of the estate of his son Thomas, deceased. About this period he purchased several lots on Water Street, and established a shipyard. But he was not alone a builder of vessels or a shipper of goods; he appears to have sailed his own vessels on his trading voyages to the West India Islands and the Spanish Main. In April, 1734, an advertisement of the removal of the printer of the New York Gazette shows "Captain Walton" to have resided at that period in Hanover Square. In 1736 he subscribed to the enlargement of Trinity Church.

All authorities concur in stating that the origin of the fortunes of this enterprising family was the preference of trade given, early in the eighteenth century, to Captain Walton by the Spaniards of St. Augustine and the West India Islands. Pintard so related it as of tradition, and Watson tells the same story. The printing of the Colonial Manuscripts of New York cleared the subject of every vestige of doubt. In a letter of Lieut.-Governor Clarke to the Duke of Newcastle, dated New York, June 2d, 1738, in which he announces the receipt of news that a land and naval force was arrived at St. Augustine from Cuba in order to make a descent in Georgia, occurs this passage:—" The Council were of opinion that there was sufficient cause to embargo Kip and Griffith sloops—both owned by one William Walton, of this town, who, as I am informed, has supplied that place for many years by contract. He protested against the Custom House officers for refusing to clear ships. Captain Walton thought it hard that his vessels entering and clearing for Carolina (as they always do for some English port) should be embargoed, while other vessells that enter for the same place should be suffered to depart; but I can not think it either hard or unjust, Walton being the only person in this place whom the Spaniards permit to trade at Augustine, where he has a Factor who has resided there many years."

In 1741 his slave Jupiter was indicted for his participation in the Negro Plot.

On Monday, the 25th May, 1747, " The New York Gazette, revived in The Weekly Post Boy," contained a notice of his death. " Saturday last, departed this life, Capt. William Walton, a very eminent merchant in this city." His wife survived him many years. Hugh Gaine's New York Mercury for Monday, 12th September, 1768, among the deaths, announces, " The 3d instant, Madam Walton, of this city in the 90th year of her age."

William Walton, by his wife Mary Santford, left two sons, Jacob and William, the latter of whom rose quickly to posts of great distinction in the colony, and added largely to the family wealth.

William Walton, the younger of the sons, appears also as sailing his father's vessels. He thus acquired the title of captain, by which he is sometimes called.

In the New York Weekly Post Boy of June 11th,

1744, among the Inward Entries is the report of the ship Mermaid, William Walton (master), from North Carolina, and among the Clearances on the 6th February, 1745-6, that of the ship William and Mary, William Walton (master), for Curaçoa. Whether this was the father or the son is not certain; but it is hardly probable that the father, whose affairs were entirely easy, would have exposed himself in sea-voyages at his advanced age.

After the father's death, the two brothers formed a partnership: on the 26th May, 1747, Jacob and William Walton appear as merchants and owners of the ship Mary Magdalen. They continued the profitable business established by their enterprising father, and enjoyed the "preferences" which had been granted to him, by the Spaniards of South America and Cuba. The brothers still further united their interests by matrimonial alliances with the same family. As appears by the records of the Dutch Church, Jacob Walton married May 14th, 1726, Maria, daughter of Gerard Beekman and Magdalen Abeel, and William Walton, January 27th, 1731, Cornelia, daughter of Dr. William Beekman and Catharine Peters de la Noy. Cornelia was the niece of the lady who had married the elder brother.

The partnership of the two brothers was soon ended by the death of Jacob, the elder, on the 17th October, 1749. He was then in his 47th year, and left behind him, to the care of William, a large family. Happily for them, their uncle had no children of his own.

The surviving brother continued to carry on the business of the family, uniting some of his nephews with him, under the firm of William Walton & Company. On the 24th December, 1753, under this name they joined the leading merchants of the city in an agreement not to receive, after that day, "copper Half-pence otherwise than fourteen for a shilling;" their declared object being to check the growing debasement of this coin. This curious document may be seen in Hugh Gaine's New York Mercury of that date.

On the 17th December, 1757, Mr. Walton applies for a commission for the Captain of the ship William and Mary, 10 guns; and on the 24th March, 1762, the firm make the same request for Capt. Jonathan Lawrence, of the sloop Live Oak, 10 guns. While thus adding to their fleet of vessels, they kept up the old and lucrative trade with the southern ports of the Continent, the Spanish West India Islands, and the Spanish Main. Their old friends in Florida still gave them the sole preference of their trade. On the 3d June, 1757, Lt. Governor De Lancey informed the Lords of Trade that Sir Charles Hardy (the Governor) had desired him to transmit to their Lordships "copies of the Memorial of Mr. Walton to him, of the 29th of January, praying leave to continue supplies to the Spanish Garrison at St. Augustine, according to his Contract with the Government and Royal Officers."

Growing in wealth and power, Mr. Walton was now looked upon as fitted for political honors. On the election in June, 1751, "for a member to serve in the General Assembly, for the City and County of New York, in the room of David Clarkson, Esq., deceased, Captain William Walton was unanimously chosen." A new summons being issued, the next season, he was again re-elected, February 24th, 1752, together with Captain Paul Richard, Henry Cruger, and Major Cornelius Von Hoorn, and continued to serve until 1759.

In the Assembly he attached himself to the party of the Lieut. Governor, James Delancey, then the ruling spirit in the province, and Mr. Smith relates that he also secured for the Delancey interest the support of "his cousin," also a William Walton, who sat for Richmond County. This connection with the Lieut. Governor led to promotion. On 3d December, 1756, Governor Hardy recommended to the Board of Trade, "John Watts, William Walton, and Robert R. Livingston, to supply vacancies which may happen in the Council; these gentlemen are possessed of considerable estate in the Province and . . . fully qualified for the trust." In the summer of 1757, the favorite nephew, namesake, and heir of Mr. Walton, married the daughter of Lieut. Governor Delancey. The next year Mr. Walton received his appointment. He first took his seat at the Council Board on the 14th November, 1758, and was a constant attendant at its sessions until the 22d March, 1768, a few months before his death. The benefit of his political position to his business has been illustrated in the interference of Delancey with the Home Government. Another instance is recorded. On the 20th April, 1765, William Walton & Co. applied to Lieut. Governor Colden "for a letter to the Governor of Havana, desiring his countenance and aid in collecting divers sums of money due them from officers, soldiers, and inhabitants of St. Augustine." From this it seems that they supplied the whole settlement. Two days later they receive a passport for their sloop Live Oak to proceed to Pensacola, touching at Havana.

About the time of his first entrance into political life Mr. William Walton, who had been living in the heart of the city, resolved to change his residence. In the year 1752 he erected the mansion-house which now bears his name, on one of the lots which he had inherited from his father near the shipyards. The first notice of this house appears in the New York Gazette or the Weekly Post Boy for May 14th, 1753, in an advertisement of a house for sale "in the upper end of Queen Street, next door but one to Captain Walton's new House, near Peck's Slip." This house is still standing, although in a dilapidated state, in Franklin Square, and is known as No. 326 Pearl Street. In 1752, Pearl was called Queen Street. An inscription (*The Old Walton House*), coarsely painted in dingy white on its muddy red walls, arrests the eye of the passing stranger.

The WALTON HOUSE is indeed a most interesting relic of "the good old colony time." Now that the Hancock House, once the abode of the great New England merchant and patriot, has been destroyed by the march of improvement, the New York building remains sole witness to the power and state of the merchant of the last century. An account of the Walton House, written by John Pintard, to whose antiquarian taste and graphic pen New York is indebted for many of its most pleasing reminiscences, was published in the New York Mirror of Saturday, March 17th, 1832, with a picture of the building as it then appeared. "This family dwelling-house was in its day—indeed, still is—a noble specimen of English architecture a century ago. It is a brick edifice, fifty feet in front, and three stories high, built with Holland bricks relieved by brown stone water-tables, lentils and jams, with walls as substantial as many modern churches, standing along the south side of Pearl-street, formerly called Queen Street. The superb staircase in its ample hall, with mahogany handrails and bannisters, by age as dark as ebony, would not disgrace a nobleman's palace. It is the only relic of the kind, that probably at this period remains in the city, the appearance of which affords an air of grandeur not to be seen in the lighter staircases of modern buildings.

"This venerable mansion is one of the very few remaining in uninterrupted succession in the family of the original proprietor. It was erected in 1754(2) by William Walton, Esq., and bequeathed by him to his nephew, the late (*honorable*) WILLIAM WALTON, whose son, advanced in years, now occupies the premises . . . Mr. Walton was a merchant, and resided in Hanover Square. He acquired an ample fortune by an advantageous contract with some Spaniards at St. Augustine, which enabled him to build by far the most expensive, capacious, elegant house at that period in New York.

"Mr. Walton was very hospitable, and gave, as he could well afford, the most sumptuous entertainments of any person in those plain but bountiful days. At the termination of the old and last French War with this country in 1759 (which was crowned by the conquest of Canada, whereby the British Colonies in America, and especially the Province of New York, were relieved from the incursions and aggression of the French, and the dreadful terrors and sufferings by the tomahawk and scalping-knife of their savage allies, the Indians), every demonstration of joy was evinced by the good citizens of Albany and New York. The British army, on its return from Canada, was hailed and treated with the most profuse prodigality. Among others, Mr. Walton entertained the chief officers in a magnificent manner. His table was spread with the choicest viands, and a forest of decanters, sparkling with the most delicious wines. The sideboard groaned with the weight of brilliant massive silver. . . .

"After the peace of 1763, the English Parliament manifested its intention of taxing the Colonies for the purpose of refunding the debt incurred by the recent war." The Colonists objected their poverty and exhaustion consequent on the struggle. "The plea was rebutted in Parliament by an appeal to the elegant entertainments given by the citizens of

New York to the officers of the British army, and the dazzling display of silver plate at their dinners, equal if not superior to any nobleman's, which hospitality and exhibitions were adduced as proofs of the wealth and prosperity of the Colonies."

When this sketch was written the memory of the scene was still green. The father of John Pintard was a contemporary of the old merchant, and had often sat at his hospitable board, and tasted of his choice wines.

Another antiquarian has left the report of an eye-witness to the splendor of its festivities. Watson, in his Annals of old New York, written in 1830, says, "it was deemed the nonpareil of the city in 1766, when seen by my mother greatly illuminated in celebration of the Stamp Act repealed. It has even now an air of ancient stately grandeur. It has five windows in front, constructed of yellow Holland brick; has a double-pitched roof, covered with tiles, and a double course of balustrades thereon. Formerly its garden extended down to the river."

When these notices were written the mansion was still "a noble wreck in ruinous perfection," and its approaches suited to its dignity and grandeur. Fluted columns, surmounted with armorial bearings, richly carved and ornamented, upheld its broad portico; and the heads of lions, cut from the freestone, looked down from between the windows upon the passers. To-day the house is but a ruin. Its pitched tilings have given place to a flat roof; its balustrades are seen no more; its portico and columns, its carvings and hatchments, even its doorways, are gone. The broad halls and spacious chambers where the courtly aristocracy of the Province was wont to meet in gay and joyous throng, have been broken into small rooms which now serve as petty shops for tailors and cobblers, or the humble abode of seamen. The fluted pillars in the hall are fast rotting away, yet in their decay convey, to an eye not unused to massive structures, a sense of stately grandeur; while without, only the dull and stony stare of the dilapidated old lion, who still wearily looks down as he did a hundred years ago upon the everlasting movements of the seething life below, serves to mark this once princely mansion from its vulgar and upstart neighbors.

Here, in the full enjoyment of wealth and honor, the first merchant of his time, the honored councillor of his Sovereign, beloved of his friends, and his life only clouded by the thought that he was childless and his estates must descend to another, no son of his succeeding, passed from the structure of his raising to a " mansion not made with hands."

Gaine's New York Gazette and Weekly Mercury for Monday, 18th July, 1768, announces that there "Died on Monday last (July 11th), at his house in this city the Honorable William Walton, Esquire, in the 63d Year of his age. He was one of his Majesty's Council for this Province, and for many Years an Eminent Merchant of this City. His remains were interred in the Family Vault of this City on the Wednesday following."

His wife survived him many years. When the British took possession of the city, this scion of a patriotic stock abandoned her honors and station, and took refuge in a neighboring colony. An obituary notice in the New York Packet of Monday, May 15th, 1786, alludes to this fact. " On Monday evening last, the 10th instant, departed this life, in the 78th year of her age, Mrs. Cornelia Walton, relict of the late Hon. William Walton, Esq., and eldest daughter of Dr. William Beekman, deceased. Though childless herself, many there are who will in her death experience the loss of a *mother*, and during her residence in the Jersies through the late contest, her benevolence and acts of charity will endear her memory to all those who have tasted of her liberality. . . . Thus, as she lived beloved, she died justly lamented; and, on the Friday evening following, her remains, attended by a Concourse of the most respectable inhabitants, were interred in Trinity Church Yard, in the family vault where her husband lay, agreeable to her own request, where she now rests from all her labors, and her works will follow her."

The will of Hon. William Walton, dated 8th June, 1768, and proved on the 14th July, 1768, is still on file in the Surrogate's Office (liber 26, folio 318). After leaving to his wife Cornelia, during her life, the house in which they lived (the Walton House) and £800, the amount received "with her on our marriage as a marriage portion;" to his nephew Jacob Walton, Lot on Water Street, No. 3, and Lot No. 4, bounded by or belonging to estate of "my brother Jacob Walton, deceased, which were of the estate of my (his) late father William Walton, deceased," and to the other children of his brother Jacob handsome legacies; he devises to his nephew William Walton, son of his brother Jacob Walton, the rest of his large property, with remainder to his grand-nephew William, son of his nephew William Walton, and William, son of his nephew Jacob Walton. He thus took every means possible to keep his name in memory.

William Walton, son of Jacob Walton and Maria Beekman, was born in the city of New York in the year 1731. Connected, at an early age, in business with his uncle and patron, the name of the young merchant is rarely found alone. An instance appears, however, in the deposition of William Walton, Junior, of New York, merchant, as to a declaration of one Christopher, Lieut. of the ship Peggy, dated November 3d, 1758. It is not probable that he ever sailed the vessels of the house in person, like the elder Walton. The Captain William Walton who appears in command of the ship Prince of Wales, July 23d, 1753, was probably some other person, perhaps of the Richmond County family.

William Walton, with his great advantages, fine person, and prospective wealth, was one of the most distinguished young men of his day, and it is natural to find him forming an alliance with one of the highest and proudest of the landed aristocracy of the New York Colony. On the 3d October, 1757, the Record of New York Marriages gives the date of the Bond. William Walton, Junr., married Mary, daughter of Lieut. Governor James Delancey. The Delanceys were of French Huguenot descent, had early intermarried with the Van Cortlandts, and were at this period, under the lead of their great chief, the Lieut. Governor, the most powerful family in the province. The estates of the Delanceys were at Mamaroneck, Westchester County.

Upon the death of the uncle, in 1768, William Walton associated himself with his brother, and carried on the business of the family under the style of "William and Jacob Walton & Co." Jacob was also a man of mark. He had married a daughter of Henry Cruger, a wealthy and distinguished merchant, and was a representative of New York in General Assembly. About this period, (April 8, 1772,) they are found among the owners of large tracts of land granted at Socialborough, in the northern part of the State. They appear too to have been engaged in manufacturing of some kind, as on the 3d June, 1773, they advertise in the N. Y. Mercury, for sale "the well-known and convenient mills of William & Jacob Walton & Co. at Pembroke, thirty miles from New York." These were probably flour mills.

MR. WILLIAM WALTON took the part which became his wealth and station in the public affairs of the time. He was one of the founders of the Chamber of Commerce in 1768, was its Treasurer in 1771, Vice-President in 1772, and President from 1774 to 1775.

He was one of the first petitioners for the Marine Society, incorporated in 1770, "for the purpose of improving Maritime Knowledge, and for relieving indigent and distressed (and the Wives and Children of deceased) Masters of Vessels."

He was warm in support of the measures adopted by the merchants to resist the Stamp Act, and the subsequent attempts of the British ministry to restrict the liberties of the Colonies. He was one of the Committee of Correspondence of Fifty-One, chosen in May, 1774, when the citizens learned of the closing of the Port of Boston. The minutes of the Committee show him to have been one of its most regular attendants. From the recommendations of this Committee sprung the First Continental Congress of 1774, whose only act of resistance to the Home Government was the adoption of a non-importation and non-exportation ordinance. MR. WILLIAM WALTON was one of the Committee of Sixty chosen to carry out this order in New York. He was also one of the Committee of Safety of One Hundred, chosen in May, 1775

So far MR. WALTON appears to have been willing to go with the more patriotic party. His sympathies appear to have been on the side of the popular cause, but his family connections were divided. The Delanceys had nearly all taken the side of the Crown, while the WALTONS were inclined to be neutral in the contest. When the hour finally came for a decision, MR. WALTON withdrew from the city to his country residence in New Jersey. But he was too marked a man to be left in peace, and he was finally forced to return to the city when the British authority was restored. His Jersey estates were in consequence confiscated. He remained in New York during the war, and devoted his time and large means to relieve the distress the war brought upon so many. He was one of the Vestry named by Governor Robertson, December 29, 1779, to look to the poor and suffering of the city. It is gratefully remembered of him that he was unceasing in his efforts to soften the terrors of the confinement to which the American prisoners were subjected.

He was one of those merchants who resumed the meetings of the Chamber of Commerce 21st June, 1779, and he appears quite regularly in his seat until the close of the war. In fact, he was again chosen Vice-President in 1783.

During this period MR. WALTON did not engage in active business, though he continued to reside in the city. His death is recorded in "Greenleaf's New York Journal and Patriotic Register," under date of Tuesday, 23d Aug., 1796: "Died, on the 18th instant, sixty-fifth year of his age, MR. WILLIAM WALTON, a native and respectable inhabitant of this city." He had been long a widower. Holt's "New York Journal," of Thursday, 21st May, 1767, contains the notice of his wife's death: "DIED, Saturday last (16th) departed this Life in the 31st Year of her Age Mrs. Mary Walton of this Place (and Daughter of the late Hon. James De Lancey, Esqr.) a Lady whose Death is much regretted." By his wife Mary De Lancey, Mr. William Walton left three sons, who in turn inherited his estates: William; James De Lancey; Jacob, who entered the British Navy, and rose to the rank of Rear Admiral. Ann, a daughter, was the wife of Daniel Crommelin Verplanck.

The old name is now continued by the Rev. William Walton, a son of the Admiral.

ISAAC LOW.

SEVENTH PRESIDENT OF THE NEW YORK CHAMBER OF COMMERCE.

1775-1783.

FROM the earliest period of English settlement in the New York Colony, the name of Low appears upon its annals. The first of the family native to this country was Cornelius, whose birth is recorded as having taken place at Kingston, in the year 1670. His son Cornelius was born in the City of New York, on the 31st day of March, 1700. Cornelius Low married, in 1729, Johanna, daughter of Isaac Gouverneur (a gentleman of Huguenot extraction), and Mary, daughter of Jacob Leisler, and widow of Jacob Milbourne—names which recall one of the darkest pages in the history of New York. They were tried, convicted, and executed in 1691 for political offences, and have been aptly termed "the first victims to arbitrary power in the Colony."

Of the fruits of this marriage two sons, ISAAC and Nicholas, became leading men in the province. Nicholas, the younger, was a warm and active patriot during the War of the Revolution, and an honored and trusted Whig. He was one of the New York Convention for deliberating on the adoption of the Constitution of the United States, assembled at Poughkeepsie, June 17, 1788. Two daughters were married to the brothers Hugh and Alexander Wallace, gentlemen of Irish birth, both of whom were merchants in New York, and strong loyalists.

Isaac Low, son of Cornelius Low and Johanna Gouverneur, was born in April, 1731, at Raritan landing, near New Brunswick, in New Jersey.

He married a younger daughter of Cornelius Cuyler, for many years Mayor of Albany. The Cuylers were a family of distinction, and were connected in marriage with the Schuylers, the Van Cortlandts, and other notables of the Colony.

Soon after his majority Mr. Low appears as a merchant. He had formed a partnership with Mr. Abraham Lott, one of a family long and well known in the City. Precisely at what date the partnership of Lott & Low was formed is uncertain. The Lott of this firm was Abraham Lott, afterwards Treasurer of the Province. The name of the subsequent partner of Mr. Low, then Abraham Lott, Jr., appears as that of one of "a number of the principal merchants" who signed an Agreement on the 24th December, 1753 (N. Y. Mercury, No. 72), not to receive coppers "otherwise than fourteen for a shilling," in order to check the growing debasement of this coin. Had the connection with Mr. Low existed at this time, the joint name of the house would have been signed, as in other cases. Abraham Lott, Senior, then member of the Assembly, died July 29, 1754.

The first notice of the young firm (Mr. Low was then in his 24th year) appeared in the New York Mercury, May 13, 1754. "Lott and Low have just imported in the Brig Maria, Capt. Thomas Miller, from London, a neat assortment of European and India Goods proper for the Season, and are to be disposed of on the cheapest terms, at their Store, in the house wherein Mr. Henry Clopper, Sadler, lately lived, opposite to Mr. Joseph

Reade's, and facing the Meal Market." The "*Meal Market*," stood, as Mr. Devoe states in his admirable History of the Markets of New York, at "the South end of Clark's Slip, at the East end of Wall Street." It was sometimes called the "Wall Street Market." It was erected in 1709, but became such a nuisance that, on the petition of the neighbors, the Common Council, in 1762, ordered it to be removed.

In the New York Mercury for Monday, June 17, 1755, it is announced that "LOTT AND LOW have removed to the house in Hanover Square, wherein Mr. Lewis Morris lately lived, next door to Mrs. Walton's, where they offer for sale their late importations from Bristol and London, chiefly of European and India goods." Their business must have been large to have warranted this step. Mr. Morris, whose house they entered, was one of the wealthiest men of the day; he was one of the proprietors of New Jersey, as well as heir to the Morrisania Estates. Hanover Square was the centre of trade. Here were the counting-houses of Walton, Desbrosses, Bache, and other great Merchants of the City. MR. LOW was then in his twenty-fifth year. They remained here in active trade, as their repeated advertisements show, until the fall of 1765. Among the many changes which were made in the circle of trade at this time, was the breaking up of their house. On the 26th December, 1765, LOTT & LOW gave notice in Holt's New York Gazette or Weekly Post Boy that their partnership, which was probably to end on the 1st of the new year, was "renewed until the first of May next" (1766), to allow of the gathering in of the debts due to them. A closing notice followed in the same journal, April 10, 1766: "The Co-Partnership of LOTT AND LOW expiring on the First Day of May next: They beg leave to introduce themselves to their Friends under the separate stiles of

Abraham Lott and Isaac Low; the former living at the old store of Lott & Low, and the latter nearly opposite to the Queen's Head Tavern, between Coenties Market and the New Exchange; where they each continue to keep an Assortment of dry Goods, which they will sell on the most reasonable terms: And as our principal Motive of dissolving this Partnership is to collect the debts due to it. . . . . Those persons who are in Arrear upwards of twelve months must not take amiss (after the repeated and earnest Requests made them to discharge the same) to be now informed that this is the last Time of asking, and that if it should not have the desired Effect, Process will certainly commence against them. Debts will be received by either of the Parties, at their respective places of Abode above-mentioned."

Mr. Abraham Lott does not appear to have long remained in active business. On the death of Abraham De Peyster, Treasurer of the Colony, he was, on the 12th December, 1767, appointed to that office. Mr. Isaac Low appears at this time to have carried on an extensive business in the importation of dry goods. His first notice, issued in Holt's New York Journal and General Advertiser for Thursday, Nov. 6, 1766, announces that he "Has just imported an assortment of goods suitable to the season, consisting of friezes, coatings, broad cloths, flannels, embossed serges; Penistons and half-thicks, spotted ermine, shalloons, rattinets, callimancoes, Oznabrigs, sheeting; Russia drilling, dowlass, garlix, Callicoes, cottons, cambricks, lawns; both muslen, taffaties, Persians, cotton, lungee and new silk romalls, bandannos and women's gloves; worsted and cotton hose, &c., &c., which he will sell on the most reasonable terms at his store, between the Exchange and Coenties market.——Imported since the above: A fresh assortment of beautiful checks and callicoes from the fountain head;

Scots handkerchiefs, bed bunts, bed ticks, gartering, binding, &c."

To this curious assortment he adds the next year, as appears in Gaine's N. Y. Mercury (Oct. 12, 1767), "red and beaver coatings, blue and red ratteen, best London strouds and Auroras, Shrewsbury cottons, felt hats, men's 4 thread worsted breeches patterns, women's worsted mitts, Marseilles quilting; cloves, cinnamon, meal, and nutmegs; best Scot's snuff, by the hogshead, tierce, or less quantity; best Pistol Powder; a few Pipes of Madeira Wine, &c., &c., for which he will take in barter most kinds of country produce, such as flour, pork, flax seed, bar iron, potash, beaver.—Has also to sell a few packs of best Michillimachinac beaver." A further notice in Holt's N. Y. Journal and General Advertiser (May 12, 1768) gives the further quaint names of flowered petticoating, silk Sooses, and Damascus silk Lorettos, silk burdels, and dressed deer skins.

The Beaver and Deer Skins which Mr. Isaac Low here and often offers for sale, probably came to him from the northern border of the Colony, where his wife's connections (the Schuylers) had their great estates, and constant dealings with the Indians, whose chief staple of trade was the skins of the Beaver. He seems to have had almost a monopoly of the Fur trade at this time.

The great rivals of Mr. Low at this time in the Dry Goods trade were the houses of Remsen and Beekman. Others, with foreign agencies, soon made their appearance.

At an early age Mr. Low came into notice for his attention to political questions. In December, 1764, he was one of the "Committee on Agriculture and Oeconomy of the Society of the Promotion of Arts," the chief association of that period.

The year 1765 was marked by a serious attempt on

the part of the Home Government to abridge the liberties of the Colonies, and to bring them to a state of vassalage to their mother Country. The French war had greatly added to the debt of England. Undertaken to check the power of France in the New World, it was really but an incident in the old rivalry of the neighbor kingdoms, and the British ministry were well content to try the wager of battle in a far-off land. The issue of such a struggle could not be doubtful. England, with her naval power and able seamen, aided by a hardy people with the better part of the American continent at their back, entered into the war with every advantage. The struggle closed with the surrender of Canada. The fruits of victory had hardly been secured when the ministry brought into Parliament a bill to tax the Colonies to pay their cost. The Colonies, well versed in the principles of liberty, objected to pay a tax voted by a Parliament in which they were not represented. They claimed equality; they spurned inferiority or servitude.

All America united in resistance; all classes joined together with a singleness of purpose to which the after-history of the long contest presents no parallel. The merchants of New York led the van, and the great popular triumph gained in the repeal of the Stamp Act may be fairly claimed as the result of their action. Not less than two hundred merchants signed their names to the solemn agreement of the 31st October, 1765, to trade no more with Britain till the Act was repealed. It is a never-ending source of regret to the inquirer into the early history of New York that the details of this struggle are nowhere preserved. The credit due to individuals has all been merged, in the lapse of time, into the honor of a class.

The part taken by Mr. Low in these interesting movements has shared the common fate. Enough remains to show that there was no holding back by the young and high-spirited merchant.

His name appears with those of James De Lancey, William Walton, Jun., John Thurman, Jun., Henry White and John Harris Cruger, all leading men, "signed by order of and at the request of a considerable number of the respectable inhabitants of the City of New York," June 26th, 1766, to a petition to the City Members to ask the General Assembly to erect "an elegant statue of brass to William Pitt in honor of his manly stand in behalf of Colonial rights." The history of this statue has been too often written to need more than passing mention.

A few years later Mr. Low again changes his place of business. In Holt's N. Y. Journal and General Advertiser of May 4th, 1769, he announces his removal "into the House of Mrs. Lawrence next door to Theodorus Van Wyck." The streets do not seem to have been numbered as early as this.

In the year 1770 he again appears in public positions of a nature which show that he was the trusted leader of his merchant associates. A record of his name as one of the "Committee of Merchants appointed to inspect the importation of goods" is given in Holt's New York Journal of May 31st of that year.

The continued encroachments of the ministry had led to a second renewal of the old agreements as to non-importation and exportation, into which all the Colonies had heartily entered. Yet the sequel showed that they were only faithfully kept by New York.

The merchants of New York becoming aware of the continued importations of their neighbors, grew restive, and in the summer the Committee of Inspection directed Mr. Isaac Low, their chairman, to inform the Boston Committee, composed of Thomas Cushing, John Hancock, and others, of their discontent. On the 24th July they reply, and express a doubt of the New York letter, because only signed by four of its numbers. To this the New York Committee, 18th Aug., 1770, returned an indignant rejoinder, rejecting the idea that Mr. Low could be unknown to them as the "chairman of the New York Committee and a gentleman of character," and renewing the charge of a breach of the agreements on the part of Boston merchants.

The letter is worthy of careful study as a proof of the early leaning of New York towards a Congress of the Colonies, and its resolve to enter into no new agreements except in that form. It explains the settled purpose which was evident in the course of its merchants at a later period. A few extracts will give a clear idea of the tenor of the New York letter. It may be seen in Holt's New York Journal of 30th August, 1770.

"This Committee used every endeavour in their power to harmonize and act in concert with their neighbours, not only by the proposal of a Congress, in consequence of instructions from our inhabitants at a general and very full meeting, but by faithfully communicating their *real* sentiments on every occasion afterwards. Your concurrence in so salutary a measure as that of a Congress would undoubtedly have satisfied the minds of our inhabitants, and in all probability might have had a happy tendency to unite them in one system for the whole Continent. This was rejected, and gave much discontent—in so much that numbers said it was only a scheme in you to continue importing under pompous ostentatious resolves against it.

"The Bills of Entry made at the Custom House in London contain the Entries of all kinds of goods, as usually shipped for your Port, as if no Agreement existed, and at the same time the Pamphlet appearing of Imports and Exports confirming those Entries at your Town, together with your former neglect (which some construed wilful) to give orders, to the masters of your vessels, not to take in any Goods contrary to Agreement.

"Your merchants coming into Connecticut, particularly Middletown, soliciting the custom of people there, alledging that as NEW YORK WAS OUT OF GOODS, and they having GENERAL Assortment, it must be of great advantage to them to come to Boston and trade; and the Goods run into this City from your Province and Rhode Island, were all very aggravating circumstances, which conspired to raise such murmurings and clamours in our Inhabitants as no arguments could appease, unless at the proposed general Congress sufficient evidence had appeared to their Deputies to have assured their constituents at their Return that the different Reports which had been current were void of all JUST foundation, and the Pamphlet SPURIOUS.

"We would long since have inclosed you one of the Pamphlets you mention, if we could have possibly supposed you ignorant of its true contents, especially as it was originally sent us from Boston, and not New-Port as is suggested.

"That you may not, however, any longer plead ignorance of matters it so highly Concerns you to know and clear up, too, if possible, we now inclose you the Pamphlet for those Purposes.

"The Conduct of the Merchants of this City has always been agreeable to their public declarations and agreements; they have never DECEIVED their Neighbours, but have most religiously maintained their engagements."

This letter was addressed to Messrs. Cushing, Hancock, and others, the Committee at Boston. There could not have been any ignorance of the facts charged or the pamphlet concerning them. The Boston Chronicle of Thursday, Feb. 8, 1770, both makes the charges and provides the proof in the publication of the manifests. It even accuses the Committee of a neglect to expose those "who are deceiving the Public by false accounts."

The plan of a Congress was generally entertained in New York. An anonymous suggestion of the kind so much in fashion, published in Holt's N. Y. Journal and General Advertiser, June 20, 1770, says: "a suitable place *for a Congress*, provided a convenient time be given for a meeting from Boston, New York, and Philadelphia, is an open and eligible mode of proceeding."

The New York Committee went so far as to address their correspondents, desiring a Congress of Merchants to meet at Norwalk. But nothing seems to have come of this plan. The neighboring Colonies found their advantage in what New York felt to be a great burden. Failing in their efforts, there was a general resumption of trade by New York, except as to Tea.

Whether a strict adherence to these agreements, and an entire stoppage of British trade, would have caused such suffering in Great Britain as to force the withdrawal of the obnoxious Acts of Parliament, is mere matter of conjecture. Many of the wisest observers of that day differed in idea. From their failure the Colonies, at least New York, which was the greatest sufferer, learned one great lesson, that agreements were useless, unless there were some power to enforce their observance.

This was the germ of the idea of American Union. The Committees of Inspection were the forerunners of the Delegations to Congress. Indeed, the only *act* of the first Continental Congress was to recommend the Colonies to give legal powers to new Committees regularly chosen to enforce the observance of the agreements. So at a later period when the old Colonies, then new States, had won their freedom, they turned from the weak Confederacy they had formed to "a more perfect union." It is an error to suppose that the great Republic which to-day stands first in power among the nations of the earth, self-sustained and self-sustaining, was the result of the deliberations of any body of men. It was the growth of years of experience, and the wisest of its statesmen were little in advance of the spirit of the age.

In the first days of May, 1774, the agitation in America was at fever-heat. The Colonies waited in anxiety for news from the mother country. Each in turn had added action to protest. Boston had boarded the tea-ships and thrown their cargoes into the sea; New York and Philadelphia had forced the vessels to return; Charleston had permitted a landing, but refused to drink the offered cup. A nameless Nation had with one accord defied a Power beneath whose heavy hand kingdoms had crumbled to decay. The letters of their agents had given word to the Colonies of the King's purpose to force them to submission. Every eye was turned seaward in eager watching for the coming messenger; every ear was strained to catch the first note of England's answer to the Colonial defiance.

On the 12th of May, the Packet-Ship Samson, Coupar master, sailed into the offing. In the letters to merchants came copies of a Bill which had passed the Commons and the Lords without a dissenting voice, and received the King's sanction on the 31st March. This Bill closed the Port of Boston, removed the Board of Customs to Marblehead, and its seat of government to Salem. News came too that General Gage had been named civil Governor of the Massachusetts Colony, and was about to sail in the Lively Frigate for his new government. The news spread rapidly through the city. To indignation at the arbitrary measures of the Ministry, was added consternation and surprise that all Parliament had joined in the cruel measure. Even the great Whig leader Fox had been content to suggest that the powers of relief should be lodged with Parliament and not in the Crown, and when the final vote was taken his voice was still. The excitement in the city was heightened by the report of a captain of a schooner that "as they came past Boston, Tuesday, the 10th, they heard great firing, by which there was reason to suppose General Gage had arrived there." This was an error. The firing was from the Castle in honor of the appointment, the news of which reached Boston that day by a merchant-vessel. The Lively Frigate did not arrive till the 13th.

If Parliament was of one mind, there were those in England who held other views, and looked upon the issue to be tried in the Colonies as a common cause. Letters from some of these friends of America were received by the Samson, three by private hand. Those dated 5th, 7th, and 8th of April, were of an important nature. One was "from a military officer of eminence, both on account of his rank and literary abilities." Who this officer was is uncertain. It was probably Colonel Barre, a leading Whig, and an officer of high merit, well known in America; he had been the bosom friend of Wolfe; was with him at Quebec; and, badly wounded himself, had seen his friend and commander fall in the moment of victory. Colonel Barre had greatly endeared himself to the Colonies by his manly and eloquent appeals in their defence in Parliament in opposition to the Stamp Act of 1765. To him was by many ascribed the authorship of the Letters of Junius (1769-1772). He had held the post of Adjutant-General of the British army, and his military talents were of a high order. He fully answers the description given of the author of one of these Letters.

The letter of the 7th pointed out the encroachments of the Ministry on Constitutional rights, the weakness of the minority to "stem the torrent of corruption," and urged that nothing stood in the way of an assumption of arbitrary power but the struggles of the Americans to preserve their liberties. It warned the Americans to firmness and vigilance. "It behooves the Colonies to be united in their intelligence, council, and measures; it is a matter of the last importance to them to stand by and support one another: the most favoured can only expect to be the last devoured. The Ministry are determined to try your metal to the utmost. Depend upon it, every Colony is to be subdued into a slavish obedience to the tyrannical imposition of Great Britain: nothing less will suffice; nothing less is intended."

The letter of the 8th urged instant reprisals, and added: "the preservation of England itself and her excellent Constitution require it of you."

These vigorous letters, printed on the back of the Boston Port Bill, and spread over the city in handbills, aroused the city to a high pitch of excitement.

At this period the political state of New York was peculiar. The harmony which marked the movement of 1765, in resistance to the Stamp Act, had been broken. Party feeling was warm on more than one ground of difference. The old struggle between the Episcopalians and the Presbyterians had been carried to the polls. The Church-party and the landed aristocracy held the Government House and its patronage. The Dissenters had their voice in the Assembly, and the ear of the tradesman and the mechanic. More than all, the people were restless; the spirit of liberty was abroad, and would not be restrained. And it is as true that license is often the first assertion of liberty as that oppression is the last stage of arbitrary power. The nightly processions and effigy-burnings alarmed the men of property. The merchants saw with uneasiness that their interests were jeopardized by men whom they could not influence or control.

They now resolved to guide the movement. On Saturday, the 14th, while handbills were freely passing through the city, a notice was posted in the Coffee-house, calling a meeting of merchants and others at the house of Samuel Fraunces, then known as "The Queen's Head Tavern." The same day the Vigilance Committee of the Sons of Liberty, an order kept alive by the radical leaders of the old organization so famous in 1765, addressed a letter to the Committee at Boston, announcing the intended meeting, and pledging the merchants to a line of conduct not yet adopted by them. "*The merchants are to have a meeting tomorrow evening to agree upon a non-Importation and non-Exportation of Goods to and from Great Britain.*" This step was not known until a later day, when a curious mistake gave rise to much ill feeling and caused a serious division in the city.

The assemblage, proving too large for the rooms of Mr. Francis, adjourned to the Exchange, a few paces distant. Two parties appeared at this meeting, with printed lists of candidates. The one, a list of twenty-five members, was offered by the Sons of Liberty—the mechanics and traders; the other, of fifty members, had been arranged by the merchants. One of these tickets was the base of both; there are but two names upon the smaller not found in the same order on the larger ticket. Both, in their original form, may be seen in the admirable collection of the New York Historical Society: as neither is dated, it is at this day impossible to say whether that of fifty had been enlarged from the one of twenty-five, or that of twenty-five reduced from that of fifty. Both were headed with the name of John Alsop, and both were chiefly made up of merchants.

The merchants' party was headed by Mr. Isaac Low. On him all eyes were turned at this crisis. The vigor of his intellect, the independence of his character, and his manly self-reliance, marked him as a leader of men; he had long since proved his abilities in the political discussions which were the fashion of the day, and had for many years been the favorite chairman of public meetings. A handbill, preserved in the New York Historical Society Collection of Broadsides, gives a clear account of the proceedings at the meeting.

"At a Meeting at the Exchange, 16th May, 1774,

Isaac Low chosen Chairman,

1st. Question put,—Whether it is necessary for the present to appoint a Committee to correspond with the neighboring colonies on the present important crisis? Carried in the affirmative by a great Majority."

2d. Whether a Committee be nominated this evening for the Approbation of the Public? Carried in the affirmative by a great Majority.

3d. Whether the Committee of 50 be appointed, or 25? Carried for 50 by a great Majority."

The handbill then names the Committee.

From a subsequent notice it appears that a quorum was fixed at 15 members. This was a bitter disappointment to the more radical, who hoped to retain the direction of affairs. But the wisdom of the merchants, the wider range of interest represented on their ticket, the high character of the persons named and their great stake in the community, and, above all, the demand for union and harmony, happily met by them in the appointment of some of the more respected of their opponents, carried the day.

On the 17th, another public notice summoned a meeting of the inhabitants of all ranks at the Merchants' Coffee-house to confirm the choice. Previous to the vote being taken, as is related in the journals of the day—

"Mr. Low addressed his fellow citizens in the following words, viz.:

"Gentlemen,—You have been duly apprised, both by Hand Bills and Advertisements in this Day's Papers of the intention of your present meeting. I hope, gentlemen, you will manifest by your conduct that you are actuated by the Dictates of calm reason *only* in the choice of the Committee I am to propose for your approbation.

"It is but charitable to suppose we all mean the same thing, and that the only Difference amongst us is, or at least ought to be, the mode of affecting it,—I mean the Preservation of our just Rights and Liberties. Let us then call down Wisdom to our aid, and endeavor to walk in her hallowed paths. Zeal in a good cause is most laudable; but when it transports beyond the Bounds of Reason, it often leaves Room for bitter Reflection. We ought therefore, Gentlemen, to banish from our Hearts all little Party Distinctions, Feuds, and Animosities—for to our Unanimity and Virtue we must at last recur for Safety, and that Man will approve himself the best Friend to his Country whose highest Emulation is to inculcate these Principles both by Precept and Example."

The Committee, of fifty nominated at the meeting of the 16th, was then carried, and the honored name of Francis

Lewis was added to the list, thus raising the number to Fifty-one.

The manuscript minutes of the Committee hint at no difference of sentiment on this occasion, and the journals are discreetly silent; but a letter of Mr. Gouverneur Morris, who was present, addressed to Mr. Penn the next day, the 20th May, shows that there was a warm contest.

The Committee organized on the 23d, with the appointment of MR. ISAAC LOW Chairman, and Mr. John Alsop Deputy-Chairman. At this meeting a letter was read from the Body of Mechanics, signed by Jonathan Blake, Chairman, concurring in the nomination. At this first meeting Paul Revere, the active and patriotic Liberty Boy, and Express from Boston to Philadelphia, delivered in the official Report of the town meeting held at Boston on the 13th May, which had adopted strong importation resolutions, and recommended a similar course to the other Colonies. McDougall, an active and radical son of Liberty, ISAAC LOW, James Duane, and John Jay, were appointed to prepare a reply, and the same evening the general committee met and ordered the signing of the following letter.

This letter, as an early announcement of the settled purpose and views of the majority of the Committee, is of great value, and is in itself a sufficient defence against all the attacks made upon its course in that day or this.

NEW YORK, May 23, 1774.

GENTLEMEN:

The alarming measures of the British Parliament relative to your ancient and respectable town, which has so long been the Seat of Freedom, fills the inhabitants of this city with inexpressible concern. As a sister Colony, suffering in defence of the rights of America, *We consider your injuries as a common cause*, to the redress of which it is equally our duty and our interest to contribute. But what ought to be done in a situation so truly critical, while it employs the anxious thoughts of every generous mind, is very hard to be determined. Our citizens have thought it necessary to appoint a large committee of fifty-one persons to correspond with our sister Colonies in this and every other matter of public moment; and at ten o'clock this forenoon we were first assembled. Your letter, enclosing the vote of the Town of Boston and the letter of your Committee of Correspondence were immediately taken into consideration.

While we think you justly entitled to the thanks of your sister Colonies for asking their advice in a case of such extensive consequences, we lament our inability to relieve your anxiety by a decisive opinion. *The cause is general and concerns a whole Continent* who are equally interested with you and us, and we foresee no remedy can be of any avail unless it proceeds from the *joint act and approbation of all.* From a virtuous and spirited union much may be expected, while the feeble efforts of a few will only be attended with mischief and disappointment to themselves, and triumph to the adversaries of our liberty. Upon these reasons we conclude that a Congress of deputies from the Colonies in general is of the utmost moment; that it ought to be assembled without delay, and some unanimous resolutions formed in this fatal emergency, not only respecting *your* deplorable circumstances, but for the security of our common *right.* Such being our sentiments it must be premature to pronounce any judgement on the expedient which you have suggested. We beg, however, that you will do us the justice to believe that we shall continue to act with a firm and becoming regard to *American Freedom*, and to co-operate with our sister colonies in every measure which shall be thought salutary and conducive to the public good.

We have nothing to add but that we sincerely condole with you in your unexampled distresses, and to request your speedy opinion of the proposed Congress, that if it should meet with your approbation we may exert our utmost endeavours to carry it into execution.

By order of the Committee of Correspondence,

Isaac Low, Chairman.

This letter is ascribed by Sparks to John Jay, but no authority is given. There is little doubt but that it was written by Mr. Low. The style is that of Mr. Low in the many communications, which appeared in the journals of the period, known to be from his pen, and is in thorough accord with that of the subsequent letter to Boston, by a committee of which Mr. Jay did not make part. Nor is it probable that one of the first merchants of the time, who had presided over their earlier committees, and whose habit was that of the pen, would have given way to any person at this important crisis.

The merchants of New York had not yet forgotten the result of the old non-importation agreements, which, dating from the original resolve in 1765, had been often renewed, nor the bitter correspondence between the New York Committee of Inspection, of which Mr. Isaac Low was Chairman, and the Boston Committee. This agreement, rigidly adhered to by New York Merchants to their great detriment, had been broken by all the other Colonies. As the New England historian of the United States, Mr. George Bancroft, strikingly states it: "Canada, Carolina and Georgia, and even Maryland and Virginia, had increased their importations, and New England and Pennsylvania had imported nearly one half as much as usual; New York alone had been perfectly true to its agreements, and its imports had fallen off nearly five parts in six. It was impatient of a system of voluntary renunciation which was so unequally kept, and the belief was common that if the others had adhered to it as strictly, all the grievances would have been shortly redressed."

The Merchants of New York had set their faces as flint against any plan but that of a General Congress of the Colonies, similar to the famous Stamp Act Congress, in which most of the Colonies took part, in 1765, and the results of which were so happy.

A strange mistake occurred at this time which, for some time unexplained, gave rise to doubts in the minds of many of the Committee, and has surely been the cause of grave errors since by all historians who have written of the action of New York in the spring of 1774. This error has left a shadow on the fame of the Committee of Fifty-one.

While the Merchants of New York were weighing their course, the letter of the Vigilance Committee of the 14th, pledging them in advance to non-importation agreements, had reached the Boston Committee of Correspondence, whose reply came to the hands of the Committee of Fifty-one. The Committee met on the 6th June, and ordered an answer signifying their adherence to the measures of a Congress at any time or place, requesting the names of the Boston Committee, and informing them of their mistake in answering the letter which mentioned not a word of the "suspension of trade," a measure they leave entirely to the Congress. It appears from this and abundant other proofs, that the mind of New York was set on a Congress. The Boston Letter called forth a second statement of their fixed views. From it as from the first it is clear that New York was resolved on a Congress, and nothing but a Congress, of the Colonies:

"NEW YORK, June 7, 1774.

"GENTLEMEN:

"We have received your favor of the 30th May, and you may rest assured we shall eagerly embrace all proper opportunities of contributing our mite towards bringing to a favorable issue the unhappy disputes which at present exist between the Parent State and her Colonies.

"You say that 'a speedy and united and vigorous effort is certainly all that can be depended upon to yield us any effectual relief, and that this effort is on all hands acknowledged to be the suspension of trade so wisely defined by you.' To the first we entirely concur; but in the last we apprehend you have made a mistake, for on revising our letter to you, far from finding a word mentioned of a 'suspension of trade,' the idea is not even conceived. That and every other resolution we have thought most prudent to leave for the discussion of the proposed General Congress.

"*Adhering, therefore, to that* measure, as most conducive to promote the grand system of politics we all have in view, we have the pleasure to acquaint you that we shall be ready on our part to meet at any time and place that you shall think fit to appoint; either of Deputies from the General Assemblies, or such other Deputies as shall be chosen, not only to speak the sentiments, but also to pledge themselves for the conduct of the people of the respective Colonies they represent.

"We can undertake to assure you in behalf of the people in this Colony that they will readily agree to any measure that shall be adopted by the General Congress. It will be necessary that you give a sufficient time for the Deputies of the Colonies as far southward as the Carolinas to assemble and acquaint them as soon as possible with the proposed measure of a Congress. These letters to the southward we will forward with great pleasure.

"You may have seen all the names of our Committee in the public prints, and as we have never heard the names of those which constitute your Committee, we request the favor of you to give us that satisfaction in your next.

"We beg that your letters for the future may be sealed and directed to our Chairman.

"We are, Gentlemen, your friends and most humble servants. By order of the Committee,

"I. Low, Chairman."

In July the concurrence of other Colonies being obtained, and the Boston Committee, acting upon the suggestion of New York, having named Philadelphia as the place and September as the time for the meeting of the Congress, the Committee of Correspondence, on the 4th (July, 1774), nominated Philip Livingston, James Duane, John Alsop, Isaac Low, and John Jay, as delegates for the City and County of New York, and called a public meeting to ratify their choice.

The "Body of Mechanics," whose leaders, John Morin Scott and Alexander McDougall, had been refused by the Committee of Fifty-one as Delegates, presented a new ticket, upon which Alexander McDougall and Leonard Lispenard were named in the place of James Duane and John Alsop. Some difference of opinion arose as to the true mode of choosing the delegates, but the Committee holding firmly to their purpose the rival candidates withdrew their names. All differences were finally healed by an appeal to the people at the polls, and at an election held in the seven wards of the City on the 28th July, the candidates of the Committee were chosen. Three of these delegates were merchants and members of the Chamber of Commerce.

Meanwhile the radical leaders, discontented with their loss

of control, and without doubt urged by the Boston Committee with whom they were leagued in close and friendly ties, called a public meeting in the Fields, on the 6th July, over which Mr. McDougall (a member of the New York Committee of Fifty-one) presided. This meeting, among other expressions of opinion, resolved "*That a non-importation agreement would prove the salvation of North America;*" instructed the deputies to Congress to establish a non-importation act; and ordered that the Committee of Correspondence be instructed to carry their resolutions into effect.

The next day the call for the "Meeting in the Fields" and the course of Mr. McDougall in acting as its Chairman were discussed in the Committee-room. It was justly claimed that it was unfair to the Committee for a member of it to submit "resolves calculated for partial purposes, no motion having been made for such resolves in the Committee." Warm feeling was shown on both sides, and on the passage by a vote of 21 to 9 censuring such proceedings as calculated to throw an odium upon the Committee, as well as create disunion in the city, the minority withdrew from the room and proclaimed that the Committee was dissolved.

The Committee then proceeded to express their views of the Boston Port Bill, and of the measures proposed for the relief of the sister colony.

In a report, made on the 13th July, they urged that "the proposed Congress of Delegates is the most prudent measure that could be devised;" that the whole subject should be left in the hands of Congress; . . . that no measures calculated to "injure our brethren the manufacturers, traders, and merchants in England" should be adopted, except in case of dire necessity (and expressed reliance on the co-operation of friends in England); . . . "*that if a non-importation agreement be adopted by Congress, it ought to be very general and faithfully adhered to, and that a non-importation, partially observed like the last, would answer no good purpose, but, on the contrary, serve to expose all the Colonies to further injuries;* . . . . finally, that the Delegates should be so instructed that they may be able to pledge themselves for the good conduct of the people of the Colonies they represent."

With the election of the delegates to Congress, the object for which the Committee was raised was attained. Although occasional meetings were held afterwards, no other action was ever taken by it, and on the 15th November it was finally ordered, that after a Committee to enforce the association of the Congress should be elected, they should consider themselves dissolved. There was no later meeting.

From first to last this Committee never lost sight of the object which it set forth in its first letter. Every effort was made at the time to force it to adopt again the old and weak measure of a breaking up of commercial intercourse with Great Britain, and both in that day and in this their refusal has been harshly judged and misrepresented. Had they yielded, the scheme of a Congress would, for the time at least, have fallen to the ground. It was only when Massachusetts found that New York would be satisfied with nothing else than a Congress, that she came into the often proposed but always rejected scheme.

Towards the end of August the Eastern delegates arrived in the city on their way to Philadelphia, to the first Continental Congress, and were entertained with great hospitality. John Adams' account alludes to the courtesy with which they were received. "We dined in the Exchange Chambers at the invitation of the Committee of Correspondence, with more than fifty gentlemen, at the most splendid dinner I ever saw; a profusion of rich dishes, &c., &c."

He has left a record, too, of the style in which Mr. Low then lived, and of the charms of his family. His house was at this time in Little Dock Street. "We breakfasted with Mr. Low, a gentleman of fortune and in trade. His lady is a beauty. Rich furniture, again, on the tea-table."

Abundant concurrent testimony bears witness to the fascination of the wife of Mr. Low.

Mrs. Grant, in her "Memoirs of an American lady" (Madame Schuyler), pays a beautiful tribute to the merits and graces of the two unmarried daughters of Mr. Cuyler, nieces and constant companions of Mrs. Schuyler. "They were, from their beauty and their manners, the ornaments of her society, while their good sense, ripened by being called early into action, made these amiable and elegant young women more a comfort and assistance than a care or charge. . . . . The eldest niece, a remarkably fine young woman, was married to Mr. C. (Cortland) of C. (Cortland) manor, which was accounted one of the best matches, or rather the very best, in the province. She was distinguished by a figure of uncommon grace and dignity, a noble and expressive countenance, and a mind such as her appearance led one to expect. . . . . Her younger sister, equally admired, though possessing a different style of beauty, more soft and debonair, with the fairest complexion, and a most cheerful simplicity of aspect, was the peculiar favorite of her aunt above all that she ever had charge of. She, too, was soon after married to that highly esteemed patriot, the late Isaac L(ow), revered, through the whole continent, for his sound good sense and genuine public spirit. He was indeed happily tempered, mild, and firm."

The departure of the city delegates for this the first Continental Congress on the 1st September, was the occasion of a popular demonstration, of which Mr. Low received a marked share. "Gaines's New York Gazette" of September 5th thus describes it: "Mr. Low being under the Necessity of going by Way of Powles Hook, he was escorted to the Ferry Stairs by a considerable number of respectable persons, with Colours flying, Music playing, and loud Huzzas at the End of each Street. When they got down to the River, he in a very polite Manner took Leave of the Inhabitants, six of whom accompanied him and his Lady over, with Music playing God save the King. The Inhabitants then returned to the Coffee House to testify the like Respect to the other delegates."

On the 5th September, 1774, the Congress assembled at the Carpenter's Hall, Philadelphia. All the New York members were present.

The next day two Committees were appointed, one upon the Rights of the Colonies; the other "to examine and report the several statutes which affect the trade and manufactures of the Colonies." Upon this latter, composed of eleven delegates, one from each Colony represented in the Congress, Mr. Isaac Low sat for New York.

The opinions of Mr. Low are given in John Adams' sketches of the debate. On the 6th of October Mr. Low said,

"Gentlemen have been transported by their zeal into reflections upon an order of men who deserve it the least of any men in the community. (It is clear that he was defending the merchants from some unjust attack.)

"We ought not to deny the just rights of our mother country. We have too much reason in this Congress to suspect that independency is aimed at.

"I am for a resolution against any tea, Dutch as well as English.

"We ought to consider the consequences, possible as

well as probable, of every resolution we take, and provide ourselves with a retreat or a resource.

"What would be the consequence of an adjournment of the Congress for six months? or a recommendation of a new election of another to meet at the end of six months? Is not it possible they may make it criminal, as treason, misprision of treason, or felony, or a *præmunire*, both in the Assemblies who choose and in the members who shall accept the trust? Would the assemblies or members be intimidated? Would they regard such an act?

"Will, can the people bear a total interruption of the West India trade? Can they live without rum, sugar, and molasses? Will not this impatience and vexation defeat the measure? This would cut up the revenue by the roots, if wine, fruit, molasses, and sugar were discarded as well as tea.

"But a prohibition of all exports to the West Indies will annihilate the fishery, because they cannot afford to lose the West India market, and thus would throw a multitude of families in our fishing towns into the arms of famine."

On the 20th October the Congress formed itself into an ASSOCIATION of Non-Importation and Non-Exportation, and to this agreement Mr. Low subscribed his name.

The first Continental Congress, although but ill fitted, from the want of uniformity in the representation of the different Colonies to assume the functions of government, was a great step towards union. They styled themselves "the guardians of the rights and liberties of the Colonies." They walked in the old beaten track trodden in 1765. They put forth a "Declaration of Rights," but their sole measure of redress was the Non-Exportation Act, to take effect after the 10th of September, 1774, and the Non-Importation Act, to date from the 1st of December of the same year. It finally dissolved itself on the 26th October, 1774.

Agreeably to the resolution of Congress, the Committee of Correspondence appointed a day for an election of sixty Persons, who were styled "The Committee for carrying into execution the Association entered into by the Continental Congress." Of this Committee of Sixty, or Observation, as it is generally called, elected by the freeholders at large of the city, Mr. Low was also the Chairman.

In March, 1775, the New York Assembly, having refused to appoint delegates to the second continental Congress, the Committee of Observation (*of Sixty*) recommended the voters of the city to elect deputies to a Provincial Convention, "for the *sole* purpose of appointing out of their own Body delegates for the next Congress." This election was the occasion of a fresh dispute in the city. Mr. Low, and the more moderate men of the old Committee of Correspondence, were desirous of confining the number of the New York Delegates to Five, well satisfied that the delegates to the First Congress would be renominated, while the friends of McDougall, determined to put him upon the Convention, proposed to raise the number to eleven, and carried this point in the Committee Chamber.

An election was held in the city the 15th March, 1775, and Philip Livingston, John Jay, James Duane, John Alsop, Isaac Low, Francis Lewis, Abraham Walton, Abraham Brasher, Alexander McDougall, Leonard Lispenard and Isaac Roosevelt were returned by a great majority of the Delegates for New York.

The next day the counties were asked to join in the Convention.

A Letter addressed to them by Mr. Low, on this occasion, urged "that the Honour, as well as the Interest of the Provinces, requires that New York also should be fully and properly represented in the next Congress," and expressed the belief that they are "fully sensible that the Happiness of this Colony, and the Preservation of our Rights and Liberties, depend on their acceding to the General Union, and observing such a Line of conduct as may be *firm* as well as *Temperate*."

Upon the organization of the Convention, which met at the Exchange in New York, 20th April, 1775, Mr. Low did not appear with his colleagues, and, on being called upon by the Secretary, to inform the Convention whether it was to consider him as a member, (as by the terms of their appointment delegates could only be selected out of their own body,) he replied, that as he had given notice to the Committee that, if the number of Delegates for New York was raised to eleven, he should decline to serve and had afterwards published a declaration to the same effect, that the city might fill the vacancy, he should not serve in the Convention. The old wound given by McDougall the year before was not yet healed, and with his usual independence and tenacity, Mr. Low refused to recede from the position he had taken. The respect in which he was held is seen in the mode in which the Convention excuse themselves from not renominating him to the Congress. They Resolved unanimously "that this Convention, sensible of the services of the Delegates from this Colony, who attended the Continental Congress, in order to express their approbation of their conduct, and as a mark of the confidence reposed in them, have unanimously re-elected all of their Delegates to attend the next Continental Congress at Philadelphia, except Mr. Isaac Low, who had previously declared that the Convention was not to consider him as a member of this Convention, and is therefore ineligible."

The Convention adjourned on Saturday the 22d.

The next day, Sunday, 23d April, "reports were received from Rhode Island and New London, that an Action had happened between the King's Troops and the Inhabitants of Boston which were not credited;" but about 12 o'clock an express arrived from Watertown with the details of the fight at Lexington, and later a second Express from Fairfield, with an account of the affair, attested to (as a "true copy, as received by Express from New Haven") by *Jonathan Sturges* and others of the Fairfield Committee of Correspondence.

"The news,"—says Colonel Willet, an eye-witness and actor in the scenes he narrates,—"produced a general insurrection of the Populace, who assemblyed and not being able to procure the key of an arsnell where a number of arms belonging to the Colonial Government were deposited, forced open the door and took possession of those arms, consisting of about 600 muskets, with Bayonets and Cartridge boxes to each, filled with ball cartridges. These arms were distributed among the most active of the citizens who formed themselves into a Voluntary Corps, and assumed the Government of the City. They possessed themselves of the keys of the Custom House, and took possession of all the public stores. There was a general stagnation of business. The armed citizens were constantly parading about the city without any Definite object."

The letter to the Counties, dated 28th April, alluded to "the distressed and alarming situation of our country, occasioned by the sanguinary measures adopted by the British ministry (to enforce which the sword has actually been drawn against our brethren in the Massachusetts), threatening to involve this Continent in all the horrors of a civil war," as obliging the Committee to "call for the united aid and council of the Colony at this dangerous crisis;" and urged that no arguments could be wanting to evince the "necessity of a perfect union;" and that there was no method in which the united sense of the people of the Province could be collected but the one proposed.

This state of affairs called for new powers, and the Committee of Observation resolved to propose to the people the choosing of a new Committee, and the calling of a Provincial Congress.

NEW YORK COMMITTEE CHAMBER,
26th April, 1775.

The Committee, having taken into consideration the commotions occasioned by the sanguinary measures pursued by the British Ministry, and that the Powers with which this Committee is invested respect only the Association, are unanimously of opinion that a new Committee be elected by the Freeholders and Freemen of this City and County for the present unhappy exigency of Affairs, as well as to observe the Conduct of all Persons touching the Association; That the said Committee consist of 100 Persons; that 33 be a Quorum, and that they dissolve within a Fortnight next after the end of the next Session of the Continental Congress . . . And this Committee is further unanimously of Opinion, That, at the present alarming Juncture, it is highly advisable that a Provincial Congress be immediately summoned, &c. &c. ISAAC LOW, Chairman.

The Committee appointed the Friday succeeding for the election. But it appears that another division occurred, as on Friday an appeal was addressed to the citizens by the Chairman.

"To the Freeholders and Freemen of the City and County of New York:

"We regret, Gentlemen, the necessity we are under of

addressing you upon this occasion; and perceive, with anxiety, the disorder and confusion into which this city has been unfortunately involved.

"From cool and temperate counsels only, good consequences may be expected; nor can union (so essential to the success of our cause) be preserved unless every member of society will consent to be governed by the sense of the majority, and join in having that sense fairly and candidly ascertained.

"Conscious that the powers you conferred upon us were not adequate to the present exigency of affairs, we were unanimously of opinion that another Committee should be appointed; and well knowing that questions of the highest moment and last importance would come under their consideration, and call for their determination, we thought it most advisable that it should consist of a large number in order that by interesting many of weight and consequence in all public measures, they might meet with the more advocates, receive less opposition, and be attended with more certain success.

"The names of 100 persons were mentioned by this Committee,—you were at liberty to approve or reject them and appoint others in their room; and that your sense might be the better taken, polls in each ward were directed to be opened: What could be more fair?

"By all means, Gentlemen, let us avoid divisions; and instead of cherishing a spirit of animosity against one another, let us join in forwarding a reconciliation of all parties, and thereby strengthen the general cause.

"Many, no doubt, have become objects of distrust and suspicion; and perhaps not without reason. You have now an opportunity of trying them. It surely never can be good policy to put it out of their power to join us heartily.

It is time enough to reject them when they refuse us their aid. In short, Gentlemen, consider that our contest is for *Liberty*, and therefore we should be extremely cautious how we permit our struggles to hurry us into acts of violence and extravagance inconsistent with freedom.

"Permit us to entreat you to consider these matters seriously, and act with temper as well as firmness; and by all means join in the appointment of some Committee to whom you may resort for counsel, and who may rescue you from tumult, anarchy, and confusion.

"We take the liberty therefore of recommending it to you to go to the usual places of election in each of your wards on Monday next at 9 o'clock in the morning, and then and there give your voices for a committee of 100; to consist of such persons as you may think most worthy of confidence, and most capable of the arduous task.

"Being also fully persuaded of the necessity of a Provincial Convention being summoned with all possible expedition, we recommend it to you, at the same time, to choose 21 deputies to represent this city and county, in such Convention; to meet here on the 22d day of May next.

"By Order of the Committee,

"Isaac Low, Chairman.

"New York, April 28th, 1775."

This Address seems to have had the desired effect, and on Monday the 1st May the General Committee of 100 and the twenty-one deputies to the Provincial Congress were elected.

Of this Committee, known by the name of the Committee of One Hundred, Mr. Isaac Low was also chosen chairman.

The Provincial Congress met in this city at the Exchange on the 22d May, and assumed the direction of affairs. Mr. Low was a constant attendant at its meetings, and was appointed to its most important duties. He was made one of the Committee selected to consider the expediency of emitting a Continental paper currency, and reported in favor of the plan early in June. He was also upon the Committee to prepare a plan for an accommodation between Great Britain and the Colonies, and to advise Congress of the same. As yet only the most radical of the New York members entertained the idea of a formal and permanent separation from the mother-country.

This Provincial Congress finally adjourned on the 30th June, 1776. A new Provincial Congress met at White Plains on the 9th July of the same year, which on the 15th changed its title to "the Convention of the Representatives of the State of New York."

In the intervals between the sessions of these bodies, New York was governed by a Committee of Safety raised by them.

Mr. Low's opinions, like those of many of the time, were all against a separation from the mother-country. A redress of the wrongs of the Colonies, within the British Empire, was the object of his hopes. There were many who felt that it was a desertion of the men who had fought their battles in the British Parliament to break away from them forever. New York was closely connected with Great Britain. Letters passed freely between her merchants and the leaders of the great Whig party. Many in England looked upon the struggle as a common cause. Indeed, the sword was drawn in America in the King's name, and the early commissions granted, ordered their holders to act in his interest.

In the Congress of '74, Mr. Low had strongly expressed himself against Independence; and when the Congress of '76 broke the last tie which bound the Colonies to the mother-country, and ushered into the world a new nation, his sympathies were all against the movement.

He retired from the city to the Raritan. Here it seems that he was at one time arrested and confined by the New Jersey Convention, in consequence of a letter of General Washington "advising that body that a number of persons deemed unfriendly to the interests of America were suspected of holding a correspondence with the enemy from Shrewsbury;" but upon the General's statement that he had received satisfaction with respect to Mr. Low, he was released. On the occupation of New York by the British he returned to the city, and in 1777 was named one of the Vestry for the relief of the poor.

At a later period Mr. Low seems to have entered heart and soul into the British cause, while his brother, Nicholas Low, rendered valuable services to the American cause, and was one of the tried and trusty counsellors of the Patriot party.

The family connections of Mr. Low mostly shared his opinions. The brothers Hugh and Alexander Wallace—the former of whom was a member of the King's Council—had married sisters of Mr. Low, and were strong loyalists; and the family of his wife (the Cuylers) were equally devoted to the Royal cause. One of her brothers, Cornelius Cuyler, was in the British service, and rose to high rank and honors: he became a Major General, and was knighted.

To Mr. Low may probably be attributed the revival of the Chamber of Commerce and the exercise of its functions and influence in aid of the military authorities.

Mr. Low had been elected President of this mercantile body in May, 1775; but the state of public affairs was such that no meetings had been held from that day until June, 1779, when, the business of the city having somewhat revived under the authority granted by the King's Commissioners (the Earl of Carlisle, Sir Henry Clinton, and Mr. William Eden), in the preceding fall, a Chamber was convened. There was, however, little or no healthy commerce in the city. The packet had given way to the privateer; the white-winged messenger of Peace and Civilization was turned into the instrument of death and destruction; the creature of commerce, its powers were used against the author of its being. The extent to which privateering was carried is quite surprising. The columns of the newspapers teem with lists of captured vessels and notices of public vendues of their cargoes. Between the eighteenth of September, 1778, and the eighth of March, 1779, one hundred and twenty-one Letters of Marque were issued by Governor Tryon, and their holders brought in one hundred and sixty-five vessels which, with their cargoes, were valued at six hundred thousand pounds. On the other hand the patriots were not idle, and the hardy seamen of the coast pursued and captured the British traders on every sea, and at times cut out whole fleets of merchantmen from under the guns of their convoys. Until the close of the war the Chamber continued to render most efficient service to the authorities; in fact, the city was governed by its advice. The records contain but little else than debates on regulations asked of the Chamber by the Commandant and his subordinates.

In 1779 the property of Mr. Low was confiscated. At the close of the war he withdrew from the city and made his residence in England. He died at Cowes, in the Isle of Wight, 25th July, 1791. His only son, Isaac, was, in 1815, a Commissary General in the British Army, and living near Lyndhurst, in the New Forest, Hants.

ANTHONY VAN DAM.

FIRST SECRETARY OF THE NEW YORK CHAMBER OF COMMERCE.

1768-1783.

ONG after the downfall of the power of Holland in the New Netherlands, a scion of the sturdy old Dutch stock rose, in spite of the prejudice of race with which the early settlers were looked upon by the English Colonists, to the chief post of honor in the State, and revived the memory of the Great Republic.

The early history of Albany preserves the name of Claes Ripse Van Dam, a leading trader in the little settlement which had clustered about Fort Orange before its surrender to the English in 1664. He was an Alderman, Commissioner to the Indians, and held other places of trust in the infant village.

Rip Van Dam, whose short rule of the New York Colony fills a bright page in its annals, is thought to have been a son of the old Dutch trader. He was born at Albany about the middle of the seventeenth century, though at what date is now unknown. Members of his family resided and traded there many years after his removal to New York.

From trading as a captain in one of his own vessels, the Sloop Catharine, with the West Indies, he rose as early as the beginning of the eighteenth century to the first rank among the merchants of the city; his name appears even before this period (in 1690), together with those of De Lancey, Van Cortlandt, De Peyster, Stuyvesant, Bayard, and De Forest, the principal inhabitants of the Province, in a petition to William and Mary for relief against the measures of Leisler. From this time forward he took open and manly stand against all abuses, and watched eagerly over all that affected the Trade of the young Colony. Indeed, his first entrance into the exciting scenes of politics seems to have been on occasion of the seizure of his vessels for alleged infringements of the Customs Laws during Bellomont's administration. Mr. Van Dam eagerly threw himself into the opposition which shortly secured the upper hand in the Government. On the arrival of Lord Cornbury he was, in June, 1702, appointed one of the Council. The Republican party, of which Mr. Van Dam was an active leader, had gained great power. William Nicoll and Lewis Morris, in the Assembly, had taken advantage of the needs of the Government, at the time of the expedition to Canada, to wring from it certain concessions. They had refused all supplies until they were granted the power to issue bills of credit for the Colony, and until their chief, Morris, was made Chief Justice of the Province—the first native of America who held that office.

Mr. Van Dam held his seat in the Council for a long period. On the 1st July, 1731, on the death of Governor Montgomerie, he became, as senior councillor, President of the Council and acting Governor of the Province. This position he held until the arrival of Governor Crosby, Aug. 1, 1732.

Smith, the great authority upon the history of this period, speaks in terms of slight of the administrative abilities of President Van Dam. On the death of Governor Montgomerie, July 1, 1731, "the chief command then devolved upon Rip Van Dam, Esquire, he being the oldest councillor and an eminent merchant of a fair estate, though distinguished more for the integrity of his heart than his capacity to hold the reins of government. This administration is unfortunately signalised by the memorable encroachments at Crown Point;"—the reason for his poor opinion of Mr. Van Dam's powers being what he terms his tardy notice of the danger which would result to the English Colonies from the French fort at Crown Point. Smith charges that the first news of this danger came from Governor Belcher of Massachusetts. A reference to the New York Council Minutes disproves the correctness of this statement. It there appears (vol. xvi. 174) that the letter of Belcher was in answer to one written by Van Dam. The Government of New York had notice of the design of the French as early as Dec. 3, 1730 (ibid. 73), and two months after the Executive power fell into his hands, the subject was laid before the New York General Assembly by President Van Dam.

On the 2d November, 1731, Van Dam wrote to the Board of Trade, London, on the subject. (Col. Doc. v. 925.) The letter of Governor Belcher was not received until some months later, and was communicated by Van Dam 4th February, 1732. (Smith, 220.)

"Die Jovis, 9 ho. A. M., Sept. 30, 1731. *Col. Myndert Schuyler* brought from the President a Letter from the Commissioners of *Indian* affairs at *Albany;* as also a minute of their meeting dated the 25th inst., importing, that the *French*, with about eighty men, had built a Fort and inclosed it with Stockadoes, at the *Crown Point* on the south end of *Corlar's* Lake, near the CARRYING PLACE above *Saratoga;* that they had also built a House of forty feet, and were busy to erect two more there; and that the Persons who brought this account did add, that they were credibly informed in *Canada*, that the *French* designed to inclose the said Fort and Buildings with a Stone Wall, next spring; and they positively designed to go up at the same time with 200 men to *Fiederodequat*, lying on the south side of *Cadaragua* Lake, above *Oswego*, near the *Seneka's* Country, in order to stop the *English* trade in *Oswego*.

"The House, taking the same into consideration, are justly apprehensive that if these attempts and encroachments are not prevented, they may prove of the last consequence not only to this Colony, but also to several others of his Majesty's Colonies on this continent. Inasmuch as the *French* can march from *Crown Point* in three Days to *Albany* itself (whereby the frontiers would be extreamely exposed), in case a Rupture should happen between that crown and *Great Britain*, and in the meanwhile they may at *Fiederodequat* obstruct the Beaver and Fur Trade at *Oswego*, which has been acquired there at a vast expence;" and therefore came to sundry Resolutions: '1. That the President represent the case to the King. 2. That the Commissioners of Indian affairs at Albany dispose the Six Nations, particularly the Senekas, to prevent the French from obstructing the trade; and finally, that his Honor be further addressed that he will be pleased to send Copies of the above-mentioned Letter and Minute to the Governor of *Connecticut*, of the *Massachusetts*, and *Pennsylvania*, in as much as the said attempts may affect them likewise.'

So far as the judgment of the historian depended on his incorrect information on this important matter, it is clear that it was erroneous. The error of Smith, in his statement, was first pointed out by Dr. O'Callaghan, in a MS. note, communicated to the New York Historical Society.

The pride of power worked no change in the heart or conduct of Mr. Van Dam. As chief of the State he was always faithful to his views of right and duty, without a thought of self. His course offers one of those rare instances of a use of office to secure the rights of the governed rather than to add to the power of the governors. There is no axiom of government more true, than that authority seeks to increase rather than abate the extent of its power. Perhaps he had drawn his lesson from the then late example of the self-denying character of the great Stadtholder. Tenacity has always been a leading trait in the Dutch character.

Rip Van Dam married Sarah Vanderspiegle in the city of New York on the 14th day of September, 1684. By her he had many children. The baptisms of fifteen are given in the records of the Dutch church, between the years 1685 and 1707. The tenth and eleventh of these children were twins.

Many of this large family lived to years of maturity, and allied themselves with some of the most powerful families of New York. Rip, Richard, and Isaac, continued the name in the male line. Rip married Judith Bayard; Richard, Cornelia Beekman; Isaac, Isabella ——. Of the daughters, Maria was married to Nicholas Parcel; Catalyntie to Walter Thong, whose daughter Mary was the wife of Robert, third proprietor of the manor of Livingston. Elizabeth married, 1st, John Sybrandt; 2d, Jacobus Kiersted.

Isaac Van Dam, son of Rip Van Dam and Sarah Vanderspiegle, was born in New York, and baptized in the Dutch Church on the 9th January, 1704. Of his life little is known now; his marriage does not appear upon the Book of New York marriages. He was named one of the executors of the will of his father, whom he outlived but a few months.

He died on the 10th December, 1749, the last surviving son of Rip Van Dam. His will, proved 7th May, 1750, is recorded in the Surrogate's office of New York. In it he names six children—four sons, ANTHONY, Rip, Isaac, John; and two daughters, Sarah and Catharine Mary.

ANTHONY VAN DAM, the eldest son of Isaac Van Dam and Isabella his wife, was born (doubtless in the City of New York) in 1731, the year of his grandfather's administration of the government of New York Colony. Of his early life nothing is known. The first notice of him as a merchant, to be met with, appeared in the *New York Mercury* for November 12, 1753.

"CORNE & VAN DAM, at their store in King Street, next to Captain Waddell's, Have Imported Yard-wide venetians, and cross-barred hungarians, watered chines, callimancoes, blue, red and green worsted plush, tammies, garlix, bed-ticks, china blue calicoe cambricks, common and white chapel needles, pins in packs and pounds, best London pewter, pint and quart mugs, tea and milk pots, porringers, a large assortment of tin ware, nales, sod irons, corks of all kinds, shovels, tongs, brass cocks, jew's-harps, iron coffee-mills, mouse traps, gimlets, knitting-needles, frying-pans, candlesticks, spades, compasses, saws, bellowses, hob-nails, with sundry other goods too tedious to mention." The CORNE of this firm was Peter Corne, one of the most noted captains of the Port of New York. On the 24th December of the same year the name of the firm was signed to the agreement entered into, by the principal merchants, no longer "to receive Copper halfpence otherwise than fourteen for a shilling." On the first of May, 1754, they removed to the house of the Widow Henderson in Queen Street, between the Fly and Meal Markets, where they again advertise "a choice assortment of hosiery and all sorts of iron-mongery for ready money or short credit." Notices of importation, from London, of European and India goods by the Packets occasionally appear. Their business does not seem to have been prosperous, and the firm was shortly broken up. They announce in the *New York Mercury* of Oct. 10, 1757, that, their partnership having been some time dissolved, their debtors must pay before 20th November, "as they intend for England this winter;" and on the 12th December following they inform their delinquent debtors that they are indulged till 24th December, after which they will have their accounts to settle with an attorney, the firm being "determined to have their business settled by the 1st January."

Though their mercantile house was dissolved, the partners had many subsequent joint transactions. On the 28th October, 1757, Peter Corne and ANTHONY VAN DAM, merchants and owners of the Brigantine "Betsey" (6 guns), applied for a Commission for the captain of this vessel. She was evidently about to start on a privateering expedition against the French, the war between England and France then being at its height. On the 24th October of the next year ANTHONY VAN DAM and Company again apply for a captain's commission, this time for Peter Corne himself, who resumed his old profession and took command of the Brigantine "Nebuchadnezzar," of 8 guns. Captain Corne was used to this adventurous life, and had long experience in trading on the coast of Africa, and in the private cruises which were the fashion of the day. The records of the Colonies in the last century are full of accounts of these ventures, and it may be truly said that the whole American coast from Maine to Georgia swarmed with bold, adventurous, and too often unscrupulous privateers, who preyed upon the commerce of each of the great European nations in turn. Large fortunes were rapidly made in this manner. Rich Spanish Galleons, laden with the wealth of Mexico and

Peru; French ships, filled with the spices and coffee of their Indian provinces, and cargoes of West India Sugars and Rum, were constantly being brought into port to the joy of the inhabitants, who followed the career of their townsmen with interest, and to their own great benefit. By sea, as well as by land, the Colonies were gaining an experience and self-reliance, which was soon to be used in a mode then little dreamed of by British statesmen.

The next year MR. VAN DAM made some other business connection. He had probably been to England during the summer, and selected his goods for the coming season. On the 18th December, 1758, ANTHONY VAN DAM & Co. announce, in the "New York Mercury," that "they have just opened the store next door to Mr. Stuyvesant's, in King Street, and have to sell, for ready money only, a variety of India and European Goods at the Lowest Prices." This rather unusual demand warrants the inference that the young merchant had but little money in his business.

In 1759 he appears to have given up the idea of supporting himself by trade only, and accepted the post of Clerk of the New York Insurance Office. Their first notice appeared in the "New York Mercury," on the 29th October, 1759. The office was opened at the House of the Widow Smith, adjoining the *Merchants' Coffee House*, which stood on the site recently occupied by the Journal of Commerce. Here MR. VAN DAM, "Clerk of the Office," promised constant attendance from the Hours of Eleven to One, and from Six to Eight in the Evening. He was connected with this office for many years. He signed, for the office, the subscription list for the publication of Bernard Roman's Maps of Florida in 1775.

The quiet, simple old Dutch habits were fast changing. The "Englishmen from Britain" brought in new fashions and customs with their new tongue. The shops which in the good old days of the Stuyvesants and Van Dams were plain and substantial, now shone "with painted glare and display." The English shopkeepers brought over the last London styles. The Hollanders, who loved long and easy lives, always closed their stores early enough for an afternoon ride or drive in the Bowerie or Bloomendale roads in the spring and fall, a walk on the river-banks in the summer evenings, or a sleighing in the winter, and all classes of the people joined in the amusements. The English opened their stores at night as well as by day, and pursued the dollar as ardently in the last century as the most eager in this. The old language too was almost forgotten, and schoolmasters announced instruction in the Dutch and Latin, as though both tongues were alike strange.

With new habits and hours of business they also introduced a new beverage, which was destined to become one of the civilizers of the world, and to do more to refine society than any invention of science or act of legislation. Ale-drinking had given way to tea-drinking. The fair hands of lovely dames no longer swung the heavy tankard, and the foam of beer marred no more the beauty of their rosy lips. Men left their deep potations to watch the graceful play of taper fingers dallying with delicate cups of porcelain and light spoons of precious metal. At the tea-table woman reigned supreme. That soft influence which could humanize a Johnson, soon modified the relations of the sexes and added to social life a charm before unknown: yet not without a murmur here and there from some conservative Englishman, who would fain cling to the old customs. In 1754 the muse herself was invoked in their support. A poem which appeared in the *New York Mercury* has these lines:

"'Twas better for each British Virgin,
When on roast Beef, strong Beer, and Sturgeon,
Joyous to Breakfast they sat round,
Nor was ashamed to eat a Pound.
These were the Manners, these the Ways,
In good Queen *Bess's* golden Days."

The tea-table is now a recognized institution the world over, and that region is indeed benighted which has not been visited by some John Bull with his national tea-pot and felt the influence of the fragrant plant.

The business of Insurance which MR. VAN DAM undertook was quite different from what it is at the present day. The mutual and the company systems are the product of a later age. The "Office" was the rendezvous of the rich and adventurous, who would underwrite risks in full or in part at rates agreed upon with the shippers or owners of vessels.

There is still in existence, in the Walton family, a Book of Insurance kept by William Walton from 1773 to 1776, and by Jacob Walton from 1777 to 1781. Some of the entries in the first part are in the writing of MR. VAN DAM, clerk of the office.

The care and precision of MR. VAN DAM rendered him a most suitable person for certain kinds of business, and his well-known probity ensured him employments of public trust. On the 20th January, 1763, he was commissioned, by Lieutenant Governor Colden, Master and Warden of the Port, and held the office for seven years, until 1770. There were seven Wardens in the City at this time.

The store of MR. VAN DAM was on the water, and near the Ferry Stairs.

On the organization of the Chamber of Commerce, in the spring of 1768, MR. VAN DAM was one of the founders, and was chosen its Secretary. The fair and exact minutes still remain to testify to the faithfulness and care which he brought to the execution of his duties.

The meetings of the Chamber in the last century were of a different fashion from that of the present day. Pleasure and business were joined together in these gatherings of the solid men of old New York. The hour of meeting was at six o'clock, and the debates were held over long tables, where "Bread and Cheese, Beer, Punch, Pipes and Tobacco," were regularly provided by the Treasurer, as ordered in the By-laws. The pipe was still in fashion among the old Knickerbockers; not the modern meerschaum, but the good old Dutch clay of Holland, hogsheads of which appear in the lists of importations. Cigars were then uncommon, if at all known, to New Yorkers. How the practice of smoking, in New York, appeared to strangers, is amusingly shown in the narration of Brissot (Warville), of his voyage in the United States in 1788. "The habit of smoking has not disappeared from the town with other customs brought in by its first Dutch founders. They chiefly smoke *cigars* from the Spanish islands: These are leaves of a fragrant tobacco six inches in length which are smoked without the aid of any instrument. This habit shocks the French. It must be distasteful to women, as it destroys the sweetness of the breath. It will be condemned by the Philosopher as a superfluous want. But it has one merit. It tends to meditation; it checks loquacity; the smoker asks a question; the reply does not come for two minutes after, and is a sound one. The cigar performs the part which the Philosopher drew from the glass of water which he drank when angry."

At a much later time the cigar was little known. It has no mention in the gastronomical works which appeared from 1800 to 1815. Even *Brillat Savarin*, the famous author of the *Phisiologie du Goût*, passes by in silence this now common part of a well-ordered feast.

Who will say in this latter day that the inevitable cigar of the great soldier of the Republic had not a share in his victories!

The business of MR. VAN DAM, from this period, appears to have been chiefly confined to the products of the West India and Cape de Verde Islands. An advertisement in "Holt's New York Journal" of April 5th, 1770, is a fair example of this. In it he offers "Madeira wine of the vintage of 1765, 1767, and 1768, West India Rum, Muscovado Sugars, Mollasses, Cotton, Cocoa, and Deer Skins in the hair."

There was a great intimacy, perhaps some nearer tie, between MR. VAN DAM and the Walton family. On the 15th March, 1770, the Land Papers show that Letters Patent were granted to William Walton, Gerard Walton, and ANTHONY VAN DAM for a tract of land on the south side of the Mohawk River, in what is now known as Delaware County.

MR. VAN DAM took no active part in the politics of the time. When the citizens seized the City, he was elected one of the Committee of One Hundred who took charge of the Government until a Provincial Congress was assembled; but this appears to be the only instance in his career. An unflinching loyalist, he remained in the City during the British occupation. On the 1st September, 1779, he was again appointed one of the Wardens of the Port by General Pattison, and had charge of the military patrol for the safety of vessels at the wharves, from the Fly Market to the Old Slip. The Fly Market was at the foot of Maiden Lane.

When the Chamber resumed its meetings, in 1779, he

returned to his old post, and faithfully attended to its duties. He was last present on the 6th May, 1783. Mr. John Pintard, who knew him well, bore testimony to his precise and methodical habits. As an instance of his economy and carefulness, he related of him, that for his engrossing he used but one pen a year. His long service, covering the whole Colonial period of the Chamber, is evidence of the esteem in which his fellow merchants held him.

Towards the close of the war, he is noticed in *Gaine's New York Gazette*, April 8th, 1782, as having removed to 13, corner of Nassau and Crown Streets, near the new Dutch Church. On the evacuation of New York by the British, MR. ANTHONY VAN DAM retired to England, where he is said by *Sabine* to have been an agent of the Underwriters at Lloyd's.

He never married. The *London Annual Register* for 1808 announced his death, in Guilford Street, at the age of seventy-seven. Some years later, a tablet was erected to his memory on the south side wall of the chancel of St. Paul's Church in New York. It is said to have been put up under the direction of Mr. John Pintard. It bears this inscription:

"Sacred to the Memory of ANTHONY VAN DAM, Esq., Grandson of the Honourable Rip Van Dam, President of the Council of the Province of New York, 1731. He was for many years a Vestryman of Trinity Church. Distinguished for his attachment and services. The earliest part of his life he passed in his native city. From the year 1788 he resided in London, where he died on the 25th September, 1808, in the 77th year of his age. Highly esteemed by a large circle of friends. His remains were interred in the Chapel of the Foundling Hospital in that city. This Monument was erected by his affectionate surviving sister Catharine Van Dam of London, A. D. 1824."

BIOGRAPHICAL SKETCHES

OF THE

MEMBERS OF THE NEW YORK CHAMBER OF COMMERCE.

1768–1784.

ALEXANDER ROBERT.—Of the firm of Thompson & Alexander, merchants. He married Jane Willett on the 5th March, 1772; and on the 22d April of the same year sailed in the Ship Britannia, Captain Thomas Miller, for London. He visited England again in 1774, taking passage for Bristol on the 16th June, "with his lady," in the Ship Grace, Capt. William Chambers. His house, during the War, was styled Robert Alexander & Co., their office at 917 Water Street. Their business was in provisions, chiefly Irish beef, wines, and bottled beer. On the 16th April, 1783, he was appointed by General Carleton one of five commissioners to act as a Board for the settling and adjusting all matters of debt, case, or accounts, of the value of *Ten Pounds* or upwards, contracted by any of the inhabitants at New York since the first day of November, 1776. He was in business in Augusta, Georgia, in 1800, and lost his wife there in that year.

ALLICOCKE JOSEPH.—A dealer in Wines, Spirits, Teas, &c. He was one of the Sons of Liberty and a member of its chief Committee in 1766. On the organization of the Committee of Correspondence, 30th May, 1776, it was resolved to appoint a Secretary not of the Board, and MR. ALLICOCKE was chosen; but on the 20th June he "requested, for particular reasons, to resign." He was at this period Inspector of Pot and Pearl Ashes. He was also Secretary of the United Whaling Company. He remained in the City during the War. A letter to Lieut. Butricke, of the Royal Irish Fusileers, August 23, 1775, published in the Correspondence of the Provincial Congress, alludes to his "expensive family." A daughter, Sarah, was married to James Bouchier, Commander of the Raynham Hall Indiaman, at New York, July, 1781.

ALSOP JOHN.—The family of Alsop in America is descended from Richard Alsop, who emigrated from England towards the close of the seventeenth century, and under the patronage of Thomas Wandell, a brother of his mother, settled at Mespat Kills, since called Maspeth, and now known as Newtown, Long Island. Mr. Wandell, dying without issue, left his estate in Newtown to his nephew, who continued to reside upon it until his death. By his wife, Hannah, who is said to have been a Dutch lady, he left a numerous issue. His third son, John Alsop, was bred to the legal profession, and early located himself at New Windsor, in Orange County, New York; but soon removed to the City of New York, where he was admitted a freeman, in 1749. He continued in the practice of his profession until his death, in 1761. He married Abigail, daughter of Joseph Sackett, of Newtown, by whom he had two sons, John and Richard, both of whom survived him.

JOHN ALSOP was the eldest son of John Alsop and Abigail Sackett.

The precise date of his birth is not known. He was brought up as a merchant, as was also his brother Richard; the latter in the counting-house of Philip Livingston. For a time young ALSOP seems to have transacted business alone, as his name appears signed JOHN ALSOP, JUNIOR, to the agreement entered into by the principal merchants of the city in December, 1753, "not to receive Copper Halfpence otherwise than fourteen for a shilling." About this time the two brothers engaged in business together under the firm of John & Richard Alsop, and were for some time engaged in the importation of dry goods. Their partnership was dissolved on the 30th September, 1757—Richard removing to Middletown, Conn., and JOHN continuing the business in New York in his own name. He soon reached the first rank among the merchants of the City. During the period which preceded and followed the passage and repeal of the Stamp Act in 1765 and 1766, he was active with his fellow merchants in measures of resistance to the oppressive laws of the British Parliament, and in May, 1769, was chosen to read the acknowledgment of the merchants of the resolution adopted by the Assembly, thanking them for their faithful observance of the Non-Importation agreements. He was then a member of the Chamber of Commerce, which he had aided in founding the year before. In 1770 he was one of the Committee of Inspection to enforce the agreements which were still continued. When the news of the passage of the Boston Port Bill reached New York, in May, 1774, and a committee of correspondence was raised to concert measures of resistance, JOHN ALSOP was the first named of the fifty-one members; and on the organization of the committee was chosen deputy chairman. In the summer of the same year he was elected one of the New York Delegates to the First Continental Congress. In May, 1775, he was one of the committee of One Hundred chosen by the citizens to take charge of the Government till a convention could be assembled: the following year he was re-elected to Congress. On the adoption of the Declaration of Independence, and its immediate ratification by the Provincial Convention of New York, MR. ALSOP resigned his seat. In a letter to the Convention he expressed surprise and indignation at the slight put upon the New York Delegation in leaving it without instructions on this point, although such instructions had been repeatedly sought for, and disapprobation as to the course of Congress in closing the door against reconciliation with Great Britain. Withdrawing to Middletown, where his brother's family was settled, he resided there until the close of the War. On his return to the City in 1784, he renewed his connection with the Chamber of Commerce, and was one of the petitioners for a confirmation of the Charter from the State in April of that year. On the reorganization of the Chamber he was the unanimous choice of his fellow merchants for the Presidency of the Chamber—a high tribute, from men who had not always agreed with him in opinion, to the integrity of his character and the fidelity of his attachment to his native land. In 1785 he declined a re-election, owing to his failing health and advanced years, and he gradually withdrew from business, in which he had been largely engaged, as well as in underwriting, from which he reaped large profits.

MR. ALSOP was, for many years, a Vestryman of Trinity Church; President of the Society of the New York Hospital from 1770 to 1784; and also served as Governor from 1784 to 1788. He was one of the incorporators of the Hospital.

MR. ALSOP married on the 8th June, 1766, Mary Frogat, who died on the 14th April, 1772, at the early age of 28 years, leaving to his care an only child, Mary, who was married 30th March, 1786, to Hon. Rufus King, then a Delegate from Massachusetts to the Congress sitting in New York. MR. ALSOP died on the 22d November, 1794, "at an advanced age."

The descendants of JOHN ALSOP are well known in New York. Hon. John Alsop King, formerly Governor of the State of New York; Hon. Charles King, LL.D., late President of Columbia College; Hon. James Gore King, of the great banking house of Prime, Ward & King, and Representative for New Jersey in the 31st Congress; he was also President of the Chamber of Commerce in 1845 and 1848.

The name of ALSOP, extinct in the line of John, is sustained by the descendants of his brother Richard. His son, Richard, was distinguished for his literary culture and poetical productions; and his grandson, Richard, was a distinguished merchant of Philadelphia, and the founder of the great house of Alsop & Chauncey, which, with its connections on the west coast of America, has carried the name of Alsop to the four corners of the earth, and made it a familiar sound on the commercial marts of the eastern and western worlds.

AMIEL JOHN.—Was engaged chiefly in the grocery trade. His store was in Smith Street in 1768. In May, 1770, he married Elizabeth Farquhar, and in 1774 was still importing and selling groceries at his old stand. He remained in the city during the British occupation, and was one of the loyal addressers of Lord and General Howe in 1776. He was Major of the City Volunteer Corps raised by General Robertson in 1780.

ASHFIELD VINCENT PEARCE.—Was descended from the Right Hon. Richard Ashfield, a member of Cromwell's Parliament and colonel in the army of the Commonwealth, and Patience Hart, of Enfield, England, sister of Thomas Hart, a merchant of the same place, and one of the twelve original proprietors of East Jersey. Upon his death, Richard Ashfield, a merchant of New York, inherited the proprietary right from his mother. He married Isabella Morris, daughter of Lewis Morris, first Governor of New Jersey. Their issue were Lewis Morris Ashfield, Richard, who died young, and Vincent Pearce Ashfield. The last named was the first President of the Marine Society, which was incorporated in 1770. He was lost at sea on a visit to England, the vessel on which he sailed being never heard from. His wife survived him but a short time, and died in 1779.

VINCENT PEARCE ASHFIELD, the member of the Chamber of Commerce, was son of Lewis Morris Ashfield. He is styled Captain in the list of officers of the Marine Society given by Gaine in 1778, where he appears as Vice-President.

The name of Ashfield is now extinct, the only descendants being in the female line.—*Communicated by Dr. Samuel Corp Ellis.*

BACHE THEOPHYLACT.—Fifth President of the Chamber of Commerce. (See Sketch of Life, page 41, *ante.*)

BACKHOUSE WILLIAM.—He was one of the addressers of Lord Howe in October, 1776. In 1778 he was engaged in trade, chiefly domestic, under the firm-name of William Backhouse & Co. The first New York Directory, published in 1786 by David Franks, gives his place of business as 163 Water Street. The next year he appears at 14 Duke Street. In 1790 he made a partnership with William Laight, under the firm of BACKHOUSE & LAIGHT. The business was carried on at the old store of Mr. Laight, No. 200 Queen Street.

WILLIAM BACKHOUSE died suddenly Saturday morning, 25th August, 1792. An obituary notice in the N. Y. Journal styles him "one of the oldest and most respectable merchants in the City."

BAYARD SAMUEL, Jr.—He appears as a merchant 24th July, 1769. In 1774 he was appointed Deputy Secretary of the Province—an office which he held till the close of the War. On the 9th December, 1775, he deposited the Records of Patents and commissions and the minutes of the council with Governor Tryon on board the Duchess of Gordon, then lying in the bay under the guns of the Asia. In 1776 he appears again in charge of a portion of the Records under guard at the house of his kinsman, Nicholas Bayard. He entered the British Army, and was commissioned Major of the King's Orange Rangers, February 9, 1781. On Sunday, the 26th April, 1778, he married Catharine Van Horne.

BEEKMAN GERARD WILLIAM.—Was the second son of Dr. William Beekman and Catharine Peters de la Noy. He was born at Jamaica, Long Island, December 13, 1718, and married Mary Duyckinck in 1751. Of his ten children, only five survived their infancy. During the War his family resided in Philadelphia. He had been engaged in an importing and commission business until the breaking out of hostilities. His abandoned residence on the corner of Sloat Lane and Hanover Square became the abode of many of the British naval officers. Here Admiral Digby entertained as a ward or pupil Prince William Henry, afterwards King of England. The young Prince was a frequent skater on the Kolch Pond, surrounded by a crowd of curious city boys and better skaters.

Cornelia, the sister of Gerard W. and William Beekman, was the wife of William Walton, who built the Walton House, still standing in Franklin Square.—*Communicated by Hon. James W. Beekman, of New York City.*

BEEKMAN JAMES.—Was born in New York, March 5th, 1732. He was the fifth son of Dr. William Beekman and Catharine Peters de la Noy. Before he was twenty-one years old he married, in October, 1752, Jane Keteltas, who was also a native of New York. James Beekman was the great-grandson of William Beekman, the first of the name, who emigrated from Holland, and arrived in New Netherlands, in the year 1647, with Petrus Stuyvesant.

At the breaking out of the War of the Revolution, James Beekman took open part with the Whigs. He was one of the General Committee of One Hundred chosen, May 1st, 1775, to take control of the City until a Provincial Congress should be assembled. He served as 2d Lieutenant in Captain Lott's Company (called the Sportsman's Company), in a Battalion of Independent Foot raised in New York.

When the British took possession of the city, he gathered the remains of his fortune, and, hiring a farm at Esopus, devoted his entire estate to the education of his children. Seven years afterwards, when the family returned to the city, both girls and boys were ready to enter college. His wife, a very clever and accomplished woman, superintended the instruction of her children.

The author of "An Excursion to the United States," published in 1794, mentions a dinner-party at the country house of Mr. Bridgens, three miles out of New York, on the East River (Rose Hill). He says, "there was an addition to our party at tea—a Mrs. Beekman, the mother of twelve sons and daughters. Three of the Miss Beekman's accompanied their mother, one of whom, it was said, was well skilled in Greek and Latin."

During the War, James Beekman's country house was the quarters of several British officers. By a record of the successive tenants, kept by the Gardener, it appears that General Howe occupied the place seven months; General Clinton more than three years and six months; General Robertson until May 1st, 1782; General Carleton five months, to the evacuation of the city by the English troops. The Baroness Reidesel resided here during the summer of 1780. She speaks of the visit paid her while there by General Clinton, "accompanied by the ill-fated Major André, who on the succeeding day set out upon the fatal expedition." Family traditions point out the room in which Major André passed the night before he went forward into Westchester. During September, 1776, in the greenhouse, which at that season was emptied of plants, sat the Court Martial which tried and condemned to death Nathan Hale the patriot, who afterwards suffered such cruelties at the hands of Provost Cunningham, and who died "regretting that he had but one life to give for his country." On "Evacuation Day," November 25th, 1783, punch was made from the lemons that grew in this greenhouse, and General Washington and his staff were entertained at the house while the American army marched by on their progress to the city. While residing at Esopus he was again called upon to serve his country, and sat as a member for the City and County of New York in the Convention which assembled at Kingston, Ulster County, on the 20th April, 1777, to frame a constitution for the "State of New York."

With the return of peace JAMES BEEKMAN again engaged in commerce. His wife took upon herself the duties of bookkeeper, for no salaries could be afforded; and so well qualified was she for the office, that on one occasion, when a ship arrived in her husband's absence at Philadelphia, she had transacted all the customs' business perfectly before his return.

His place of business was in Hanover Square; the family lived in the same building. By diligent industry he retrieved his fortunes. It is said of him, that having remitted over sixty thousand dollars to London at the breaking out of the War, he found at its close that the money had not been received. He paid the debt again, but not without very severe exertion and economy. After a time, his family resided through the year at his country seat, called "Mount Pleasant," and his habit was, when business had detained him late, to pass the night at his compting house in Hanover Square. Next morning, by dawn of day, he walked four miles to surprise his wife and children before they had risen, and after breakfasting with the family, he would walk back in good season for business. In 1784 he formed a partnership with his sons, and, under the name of JAMES BEEKMAN & SONS, carried on a dry-goods importing business at 241 Queen Street.

He died in New York, April 6th, 1817, at the age of eighty-two.—*Communicated by Hon. James W. Beekman of New York City.*

BOGART HENRY C.—The son of Cornelius Bogart, of New York. He was descended from one of the French Huguenot refugees, who abandoned his native land for conscience sake, and came to this country on the revocation of the Edict of Nantes. Cornelius Bogart, the father of HENRY C. BOGART, was born in 1699, and became during the first half of the succeeding century a large land-holder in the City of New York, and carried on an extensive mercantile business. At a later period he withdrew from active connection with commercial affairs, and left his large trade to his sons—HENRY C. and Nicholas. Cornelius died on the 19th April, 1793, at the great age of ninety-four years.

HENRY C. BOGART, the elder son of Cornelius, was born in 1733. He is said to have been "a man greatly admired for the elegance of his person, his accomplished manners, and the sterling integrity of his private and public character." He seems to have confined his business chiefly to trade with the West Indies, the English Colonies of which he is known to have visited. His place of business was in Smith Street.

In 1771 he married Helena Van Wyck, of Bergen, New Jersey—the record of New York marriages giving the date of license March 4th, 1791. His marriage was of short duration. He died on the 30th May, 1774, at the age of 41, and was buried in the family vault in the New Dutch Church. An obituary notice said of him: "It may with the greatest propriety be said that he was an affectionate husband, a dutiful and obedient child, and indulgent master; a very useful member of the community by his extensive connection in trade, and a friend to all who stood in need of his assistance; benevolence and charity sat perching on his right hand; the fatherless and widow have tasted of his unceasing bounty. He bore his long illness with the patience of a Christian and the fortitude of a good man.

> "*Mature for Heaven, the fatal mandate came,*
> *With it a chariot of ethereal flame,*
> *In which, Elijah like,* he *past the spheres,*
> *Brought joy to Heaven, but left his friends in tears.*"

The young widow soon abandoned her establishment, for she had borne her husband no children, and on the 8th August, 1774, the executors advertised for sale "the House and Lot of Ground of the late HENRY C. BOGART, deceased, situate in Smith Street, and facing the Street leading to the Old Dutch Church—being an easy and convenient dwelling with two good kitchens and dry cellars under the whole, with a large storehouse and stable on the rear of said lot; a good pump cistern and grass plot in the yard."

The family name in this branch was continued by his brother, Nicholas C. Bogart, who married Ann, daughter of Myndert Schuyler, merchant, of New York, and Elizabeth Wessels. The family were strong Whigs. Mr. Nicholas C. Bogart removed from the city on the British occupation to Tappan, Rockland County, where he was taken prisoner by the British, and only released through the interposition of General Washington. During the American occupation the headquarters of the Commander-in-Chief of the patriots were in the immediate neighborhood of Mr. Bogart's residence, and he was at times the guest as well as the host of the General and his Staff. "It was at the house of Mr. Bogart that the unfortunate Major André was confined after his arrest, and from it, October 2d, 1780, he was led forth to execution."—*Communicated by Miss Eliza Bogart, of N. Y. City.*

BOOTH BENJAMIN.—In a letter to Mr. Charles Thompson, of Philadelphia, dated 17th June, 1774 (which made part of an angry correspondence concerning the observance of a Fast in Philadelphia on the 1st June), Mr. Booth says that "he had fixed his residence in America out of Choice, and in preference to his native country, and that he bids fair to leave behind him a numerous offspring *all* Americans." He married Elizabeth Willet on the 26th June, 1766. The next year he revisited England. On the 29th October, 1767, he announced his return from London with a stock of goods, which he offered for sale "exceeding cheap for cash."

He was one of the consignees of the East India Company, and on the 1st December, 1773, addressed a memorial to Governor Tryon for the protection of the expected tea. Although one of the Committee of Correspondence of Fifty-one, and inclined to active measures of resistance within the limits of loyalty, he does not appear to have ever wavered in his allegiance. On the 23d September, 1778, as secretary of the Royal Refugees, he called a meeting of deputies from the several provinces at the house of Mrs. de la Montanye, in the Fields—now the City Park. His property was confiscated. In 1771 the house of Pigou & Booth advertised for sale a variety of Wares, Writing-paper, Kidderminster Carpeting, Bottled Porter, &c.

BREVOORT HENRY.—He was Assistant Alderman of the East Ward from 1771 to 1773. His name appears signed to the loyal address to Lord and General Howe, in October, 1776, and he was one of the Vestry who on the 20th July, 1778, petitioned Sir Henry Clinton to permit them to rent for the use of the poor the "houses belonging to persons not under protection of government," or to give some directions so that "they may be relieved and kept from perishing by some other means."

In the *New York Gazette* of June 6, 1774, there may be found the advertisement of a most elaborate assortment of ironmongery, cutlery, hosiery, &c., imported from Bristol and London, for sale either wholesale or retail by MR. BREVOORT at the sign of the Golden Frying Pan, in Queen Street, between the Fly Market and Burling's Slip. He is presumed to have been the son of Henry and brother of Elias Brevoort, who lived about the middle of the last century in the "Bowerie Lane." The late Henry Brevoort, who so distinguished the name by his varied attainments and elegant culture, was distantly if at all related to this colonial merchant.

BUCHANAN THOMAS.—The eldest son of George Buchanan and Jean Lowden, his wife, was born at Glasgow, in Scotland, on the 24th day of December, 1744. His father was a gentleman of fortune and liberal education, and a leading merchant in Glasgow during the early part of the last century. He was descended from a branch of the ancient and distinguished family of Buchanan of Buchanan, a clan which always held a prominent position in the annals of Scotland. In the Buchanan history honorable mention is made of Sir Alexander Buchanan, grandson and heir-apparent of Sir Walter Buchanan, the eleventh Laird of Buchanan, and of his heroic achievements in the wars in France, especially at the battle of Beaujé, March 22d, 1421.

The mother of MR. THOMAS BUCHANAN, Jean Lowden, was a Scottish lady of birth, refinement, and education, and was connected with many of the leading families of Scotland.

THOMAS BUCHANAN, as the eldest son, was educated with great care by his parents. After finishing his studies at the University of Glasgow, he determined to visit America, and arrived in New York soon after he had completed his eighteenth year.

Mr. Walter Buchanan, a cousin of the father of THOMAS, was at that time engaged in business in New York. THOMAS in a short time entered into partnership with this relative, and together they transacted business under the firm of "Walter & Thomas Buchanan." The first advertisement of this firm appears in the "Post Boy," November 17th, 1763. The store of the Buchanans was for many years in Queen Street, opposite the upper end of the Fly Market; their business was principally confined to importing and selling goods from Glasgow. It appears, however, from their numerous advertisements in the papers of the day, that they were constantly receiving consignments from London, Liverpool, and Bristol, as well as from Scotland.

THOMAS BUCHANAN was thus a partner in a prominent mercantile house engaged in a large foreign and domestic trade before he was nineteen years of age. The business of the house of Walter and Thomas Buchanan, even at this early period, was varied and extensive, and THOMAS BUCHANAN soon acquired, and retained until his death, the standing of one of the leading foreign merchants in New York.

It does not appear that MR. BUCHANAN had originally intended to become a permanent resident in New York, but a youthful attachment was soon to change all his plans of life. As soon as he was of age, about the close of the year 1765, he was married to Almy Townsend, daughter of

Jacob and Mary Townsend, of Oyster Bay, Long Island. This lady was possessed of great personal attractions, and always exercised a strong influence over her husband. The difficulties between the Colonies and the mother country were then impending, and his wife's family had taken a deep interest in the struggle. They were all zealous republicans. These new ties were probably the reason why MR. BUCHANAN never returned to Scotland. His business relations in this country were also steadily increasing. About a year after his marriage the name of the firm was changed to "Walter and Thomas Buchanan & Co.," his younger brother being admitted as a partner. The character of their business was also altered and its extent enlarged. The firm became at this time one of the largest ship-owners in New York.

Mr. Walter Buchanan afterwards withdrew from the firm, and the business was conducted for several years by the two brothers, under the name of "Thomas Buchanan & Co." This continued from 1785 until the 1st of May, 1794, when this partnership was dissolved, and the business was then carried on by THOMAS BUCHANAN alone, at No. 41 Wall Street. In the early part of 1807 his son, George Buchanan, became a partner, and the name of the firm was then changed to "Thomas Buchanan & Son," and so remained until its dissolution by MR. BUCHANAN'S death, in 1815.

MR. BUCHANAN has been spoken of as a large ship-owner. In addition to his importations from England and Scotland, he was constantly receiving cargoes from the West Indies and Madeira, and the wines of his house were well known and highly appreciated.

MR. BUCHANAN was never in public life. As he was by birth a British subject, and arrived in this country at a time when men were already beginning to take sides in the struggle soon to break out in active hostilities, his feelings and prejudices were naturally in favor of his native land. His wife's family, however, were closely identified with the cause of the Colonies, and his sentiments were very much influenced by these strong republican connections. During the British occupation of the city, he resided partly at New York and partly at Oyster Bay. He endeavored to remain neutral during the contest, continuing his business as far as was possible in the disturbed state of the country. As his motives in refraining from taking an active part in the struggle were well understood, he retained the esteem of both the Americans and the British, and he seems to have been enabled to pursue an independent course, which would have been difficult except to one in his situation—impossible to an American born, but which his birth abroad and his marriage into a strong republican family justified him in taking.

His house was rendered unusually conspicuous in the history of the time from the fact that to it was consigned the tea-ship Nancy, Captain Lockyer, which was returned to London with its cargo by the indignant citizens of New York, in April, 1774. He was one of the General Committee of One Hundred chosen from all parties to take control of the city when the people seized the Government and public buildings, in May, 1775.

His name is found with that of many other leading merchants, who remained in the city after the entry of the British troops, in September, 1776, as one of the signers of the loyal address to Lord and General Howe on the 24th October of that year. Sabine, in his "Sketches of the Loyalists," justly claims him as an adherent to the royal cause.

On the other hand, his influence with the royalists was often exerted in behalf of his friends. Thompson, in his "History of Long Island," relates an instance in which his personal exertions and interference preserved from plunder and destruction the property of his wife's family, attacked by a marauding party of Delancey's corps. The officers of this battalion were quartered in the house of Mr. Samuel Townsend, at Oyster Bay. This gentleman was the brother of Mrs. Buchanan's father, and as a delegate to the Provincial Congress of 1776, and a zealous patriot, was subjected to constant annoyance by the British, who were in full possession of Long Island. It is of interest to relate that Solomon Townsend, the son of this gentleman, and the cousin of MR. BUCHANAN'S wife, was master of the ship Glasgow, which belonged to the Buchanans. Mr. Samuel Townsend was afterwards a Senator of the State of New York.

MR. BUCHANAN was always deeply interested in the prosperity of his adopted city. He was a constant friend and promoter of its public institutions and charities. Although not one of the founders of the Chamber of Commerce, he was among those elected at its second meeting, May 3d, 1768. At this time he was only in his twenty-fourth year. He was Vice-President of the Institution from 1780 to 1783; in May of which year he was elected to the Presidency, but declined to serve. He was one of the original promoters of that noble charity, the New York Hospital, his name being recorded upon the charter granted to it by George III., on the 13th June, 1771, and he served it faithfully as one of its Governors from 1785 to 1800—a period of fifteen years. He was active and zealous in various offices of commercial trust.

After his marriage MR. BUCHANAN built a house in Wall Street, on the site of the Merchants' Exchange, now used as the Custom House. This dwelling-house was a large double building, spacious and convenient, the grounds extending back to Sloat Lane, where his warehouse stood. In the latter part of his life he had his private office at his residence in Wall Street, in which he transacted the business of the firm. Here he continued to reside until his death.

There is no portrait of MR. BUCHANAN in this country. Soon after his marriage his miniature was sent to his parents in Glasgow, and since that time has passed into the hands of some distant members of the family. His personal appearance, however, is still fresh in the memory of his descendants. In his early years he is described as displaying in his figure all the marks of his Scottish origin. His hair was sandy; his eyes light blue; his complexion florid. He was of middle height, and not very stout in his youth, but grew larger as he advanced in years. He then wore his hair powdered and tied in a cue, which was daily arranged with much particularity. His usual dress was a blue coat with bright buttons, light waistcoat, small-clothes, and silk stockings. He always wore a white stock and gold buckles. The style of his dress was that generally adopted by gentlemen of the Old School of his age and position.

During his latter years MR. BUCHANAN passed much of his time at his country seat, on the East River, near Hurl-Gate. He was always domestic in his habits and pleasures, and was never more happy than when he gathered around him the large circle of his children and grandchildren. Here, in the bosom of his family, and surrounded by his friends, he enjoyed the leisure and comforts resulting from a well-spent life of activity and usefulness.

He died at his residence in Wall Street, on the 10th September, 1815, after an illness which had partly withdrawn him from his business for several years, and left behind him, as a precious legacy to his descendants, an unstained reputation and the example of an honorable and highly successful merchant and honest man. He was buried in his family-vault in the First Presbyterian Church in Wall Street, where he had always attended public worship. After the sale of that property, his remains were removed to a vault in the yard of the same church, in the Fifth Avenue.

Mr. Buchanan left eight children, none of whom are now living. Of these, Jean, his eldest daughter, died unmarried; Almy married Peter P. Goelet; Margaret married Robert R. Goelet; Martha married Thomas Hicks, son of Whitehead Hicks, Mayor of New York; Elizabeth married Samuel Gilford; George Buchanan, his only son, died unmarried; Hannah died unmarried; Frances, the youngest child, married Thomas C. Pearsall. Mr. Buchanan thus left no descendants of his own name, but many of his grandchildren and great-grandchildren are now residents of New York.—*Communicated by Henry R. Winthrop, Esq., of New York.*

BUCHANAN WALTER.—Of Glasgow, Scotland. He was the first of the family afterwards distinguished in the annals of American commerce. In 1762 he advertised in *Gaine's New York Mercury*, March 15, a variety of dry goods, Sagothees, duroys, Plyden leather breeches, &c., at his Store on "Peck's Slip, next Door to the Sign of the Half Moon," as imported in the last vessels from London, Liverpool, and Glasgow. He afterwards took Thomas Buchanan into partnership. He remained in New York during the War, but does not appear to have taken any part in the politics of the time. It is to be mentioned to the honor of the Buchanans, that they nowhere appear as engaged in privateering—an exception to the almost universal practice of the day.

BULL JOSEPH.—Of the house of "Corsa & Bull." On the 2d June, 1766, they advertised for sale, "Salt Petre, made in this Province by Doctor Robert Graham," and describe it to be an expensive undertaking. In 1770 they sold tea at their store between Beekman's and Peck's Slip. Joseph Bull was chosen one of the Committee of One Hundred, May 1, 1775, and appears to have acted with the patriots; but his views gradually changed. On the 1st June, 1776, he wrote to Colonel Henry Remsen that some other person should be appointed in the place in the regiment to which he had been elected, and added that he was "by no means a friend to independency, and would not, in any capacity, arm in defence of it." He was later taken prisoner at New Rochelle, and pleaded his early services to General Scott to avoid being sent to Norwich. He then said that all his friends were, "if the country is conquered, ruined; ties, if nothing else, which would induce him to be friendly to the American cause." His old partner, Col. Corsa, was prisoner at the same time. He alludes to his wife in the same letter. The New York marriages give a record of a marriage-bond of Joseph Bull and Esther Gedney, Nov. 16, 1761.

BURNLEY HARDING.—Of this person no mention has been discovered either in the journals or local histories.

CLARKSON LEVINUS.—He was a strong Whig. During the early part of the War he resided at Flatbush. On the approach of the British he left his house, which was badly used by the Hessians. He was permitted to return to it shortly after. He had married, in 1763, Mary Van Horne; the date of the bond is given in the Book of New York marriages, Feb. 19, 1763. Captain Graydon, in his memoir, says there were "five Misses Van Hornes (avowed Whigs), all handsome and well bred, who returned to Flatbush with Mr. Clarkson." The Levinus Clarkson of Stratfield and Levinus Clarkson who was in business in New York City at 37 Water Street from 1787, for many years, was probably the son of this old merchant. He died at Jamaica, May 24, 1798, aged fifty-eight.

CORSA ISAAC.—Of the firm of "Corsa & Bull." He was a distinguished officer in the old French War. He received his commission as Captain on the 25th September, 1755. He led a detachment of Queens County men as Colonel at the capture of Fort Frontenac (Kingston), August, 1758; and on the night of the 25th August, volunteered to erect a battery under the enemy's fire. He was here slightly wounded. The next day the fort surrendered under the fire. On the breaking out of the Revolution he clung to the Crown; and on the 12th August, 1776, was arrested by order of General Washington, and sent prisoner to Norwich and Middletown. He was released, on his parole and promise to return when sent for, the following December. He married Sarah Franklin in April, 1758. She was the sister of Walter Franklin, a wealthy New York merchant who resided at Maspeth. After his death, in 1780, COLONEL CORSA occupied his mansion. COLONEL CORSA died at Flushing 3d May, 1807, in the eightieth year of his age, respected and beloved. He is said to have been "small in stature and juvenile in appearance, though an intrepid officer." His only child, Maria Franklin, was married to John I. Staples.

CRUGER JOHN.—First President of the New York Chamber of Commerce. (See page 5, *ante.*)

CRUGER JOHN HARRIS.—The son of Henry Cruger and Elizabeth Harris, was born at Jamaica, West India Islands, on the 25th December, 1737. He appears to have transacted a considerable business under his own name (near the Exchange), chiefly in the despatch of vessels and the importation of goods from Bristol, England, with the interests of which city his family were closely connected.

In 1762 he married Anne DeLancy, daughter of Oliver DeLancy, afterwards General in the British service. The record of New York marriages gives the date of the bond as November 25, 1762.

On the 26th August, 1773, his father having resigned his seat at the King's Council Board, an advisory body of twelve, whose functions were those of the modern Senate, JOHN HARRIS CRUGER was sworn in his place, and continued to hold the position till the Revolution swept the Board away with the rest of the authority of the King.

In 1772 he was appointed the Treasurer of the Corporation, and held this office until the breaking out of the War. In 1777 he entered the British service, and, raising a battalion of men, was commissioned Lieut. Colonel in the Brigade of which his father-in-law, Oliver DeLancy, was commander. His was the 1st Battalion. He was in constant and difficult service, and caused great annoyance to the patriots about New York, his knowledge of the country and habits of the population giving him peculiar advantages in this way. He was taken prisoner on the King's birth-day while at dinner in Georgia, but soon exchanged. In 1780 he was at Ninety-six. In 1781 he maintained his post against a siege and assault by the American army under General Greene with a steady gallantry against great odds which has rarely been equalled, and he held on until relieved by Rawdon. His wife was with him at this time. At the battle of Eutaw Springs he held the centre, and again won distinction by his conduct and courage. On leaving Charleston, in July, 1782, he was warmly addressed by the citizens. His furniture was sold on the 5th June, 1783, from his quarters, No. 8 Hanover Square, and he shortly retired to England. His estate was confiscated. He died in London on the 3d June, 1807, at the age of sixty-nine. His wife died at Chelsea, England, in 1822, aged seventy-eight.

DESBROSSES ELIAS.—Third President of the New York Chamber of Commerce. (See page 27, *ante.*)

DONALDSON SAMUEL.—An Importer of Wines. In 1783 his place of business was at No. 20 Smith (now William Street), next door to the corner of Wall Street, where he advertised Port and Benecarlo Wines for sale, together with Tea and Dry Goods. He was one of the fifty-five loyalists who, in July, 1783, petitioned Sir Guy Carleton in New York for large grants of land in Nova Scotia, to which they declared it to be their desire to remove. In this petition they say that previous to the Revolution they were men of influence and property. Sabine says he was of Virginia. He does not appear in New York before the War.

DOUGLASS JAMES.—Of the house of "William & James Douglass." They did a general business. They advertise the sale of Loaf Sugar from Cuyler's Sugar House Company on the 30th April, 1781. At the peace William Douglass, with his family, went from New York to Nova Scotia. JAMES DOUGLASS last took his seat in the Chamber of Commerce in April, 1782.

DUYCKINCK GERARDUS.—He was the son of Gerardus Duyckinck and Anna Rapalje. The proprietor of the "Universal Store." His advertisements are among the most curious of the period, and are unique in their fashion of display. He was one of the Committee of Correspondence of Fifty-one chosen, in May, 1774, to concert with the other Colonies some plan of resistance to the oppressive measures of Parliament. He was also one of the Committee of One Hundred selected to take charge of the city, May 1, 1775, on the announcement of blood being shed at Lexington.

In 1775 he married Susannah, daughter of Dr. Henry Livingston, of Poughkeepsie, a strong and influential Whig. The date of the bond is given as the 16th November of that year. He suffered greatly by the fire of 1778, losing seven houses. It appears that he had accumulated a large property.

ELAM SAMUEL.—Was born at Leeds, in the County of Yorkshire, England, in the year 1750.

His uncle, Emanuel Elam, was largely interested in the exportation of woollen goods to the American Colonies, and had, as early as 1768, sent out Mr. John J. Glover to take charge of his business in this country. SAMUEL ELAM was a favored nephew of this rich merchant, and under his auspices came out to America at an early age. There is no record of any mercantile career under his own name; but from the fact that he was elected member of the Chamber of Commerce on the 4th March, 1783, it is probable that he was in some form identified with the business of his uncle, probably connected with the agency of Mr. Glover, his friend and townsman and companion in youth, who was chosen to the Chamber on the same day. His connection with the Chamber was of short duration, for in the succeeding year, 1784, his name disappears from the record, and he became a citizen of the State of Rhode Island, where he continued to reside. Emanuel Elam left him a large fortune, and he is not known to have engaged afterwards in any active mercantile business.

Of great public spirit and philanthropy, he devoted the remainder of his life to public duties, at one time representing the town of Portsmouth in the General Assembly, at another Senator of the State. He early purchased an estate at Portsmouth, which he named "Vaucluse," after the celebrated retreat of the lover of Laura, the "divine Petrarch." It lies upon the eastern side of the island, upon the water, nearly five miles from the gay town of Newport, which was then, as now, the scene of perennial fashion, gayety, and luxury,—a residence which the happy accident of tempered climate, the lavish gifts of nature, and a generous expenditure of taste and labor, have contributed to render one of the most attractive in the world. To the adornment of Vaucluse MR. ELAM gave of his time and fortune without stint. This charming seat still retains the mark of his cultivated taste in its open groves, its wooded walks, shaded with the rarest and finest foliage; its easy slopes, and spreading lawns, and gently undulating fields; while through its openings the distant sea may be discovered and the low murmur of its swelling tides is borne to the attentive ear.

This alone of the old Newport residences (the homes of the Malbones, the Overings, and the Bannisters, the gentry of the time, whose walls echoed by turns the loud laughter of English officers, the fervent enthusiasm of Colonial patriots, and the sprightly merriment of the gay companions of DeGrasse and Rochambeau, and down whose long halls, high dignitaries, victorious generals, and courtly parlor knights led graceful dames in stately minuet or gayer dance), still bears some traces of its ancient grandeur.

Here MR. ELAM maintained a noble hospitality, of which the fame spread far and wide. One day of each week, throughout the season when Newport was most frequented, Vaucluse was thrown open for the entertainment of strangers: every luxury in food which taste could command, or unbounded means supply, was spread upon his board, and the choicest wines flowed fast and free. An amusing incident is related of him which well accords with his general disposition and hospitality. A member of the Society of Friends of the Orthodox School, and subject to the discipline of the church, the gayety of his mansion, which was doubtless, after the manner of the day, not always subdued, was at times a subject of remark among his religious peers. Hearing, on one occasion, that it had been resolved upon to discipline him at an early day, he invited the scandalized companion and the threatened judges to a dinner at Vaucluse, where, under the mixed influences of kindness and good cheer, it is said that they were compelled to confess, before they bade him adieu, that they were but fellow sinners, and none cared to throw the first stone.

But it must not be inferred that conviviality was the measure of the heart or habit of MR. ELAM. In his elegant leisure he drew about him many of the most celebrated of the literary men and artists of the time, and many a work of charity was planned within his walls. Even in the cultivation of his lands he sought rather the public benefit by the example he set at his own cost than any profit to himself. He was constantly importing the newest varieties in seeds and roots, and distributing them broadcast over the whole country with a bounteous hand.

Here, in the loveliest season of the year, when the October sun had warned the fogs to sea and was touching with magic pencil the foliage of each shrub and tree,—far from his native home, but amid troops of friends, full of years and at peace with God and man,—this lovely, generous nature passed to his rest, and was laid beneath the broad branches of the tall elms his own hands had planted and his own watchful care had nursed. MR. ELAM having never married, "Vaucluse" soon felt the loss of its master's tender care.

"But O, the heavy change, now thou art gone!
Now thou art gone and never must return!
Thee shepherd, thee the woods and desert caves
With wilde Thyme and the gadding Vine o'ergrown,
And all their echoes mourn."—

Vaucluse has long since passed into the hands of the stranger, but something of the old spirit yet haunts its pictured grounds. The gate stands ever open and the latch hangs outside the door to any that would evoke the shade of its whilom master, and but the shade. A small, unpretending tombstone, about one foot square, stands in the south-west corner of the Friends' Burying Ground, in the town of Newport (on either side the stones of John Slocum and Benjamin Haven), and tells the visitor that there now lies—

SAMUEL ELAM, DIED 1813, AGED 63 YEARS.

But the name and the fame of Vaucluse will be a household story when this too shall have passed away, and even its own glories be but a tradition of the past.

An obituary notice of MR. ELAM, in the Newport Mercury of October 30, 1813, gives the date of his death as the 25th October, 1813.

FAIRHOLME JOHNSTON.—At the breaking out of the War he withdrew to Perth Amboy, New Jersey. In July, 1776, he was arrested by Major Duyckinck, and sent to General Livingston at Elizabethtown. He was subsequently sent to the Provincial Congress, which directed him to remain on parole at Trenton. He was later allowed to live at Bordentown.

FOLLIOT GEORGE.—An extensive importer. In 1775 he was elected to the Committee of One Hundred, but refused to serve. He was also chosen member of the Provincial Congress for the City and County of New York in 1775, but declined to act. His estate of twenty-one acres was confiscated and sold in 1784. A record of his marriage to Jane Harison appears in the Book of New York marriages November 16, 1758. He announced his intention to go to Europe by the first conveyance, and called in his outstanding accounts Nov. 5, 1781, by an advertisement in the New York Gazette.

FORTEATH ALEXANDER.—The house of ALEXANDER FORTEATH was at 52 Burling Slip in 1781, in the West India trade. Nothing more is known of MR. FORTEATH.

FRANKLIN WALTER.—Born in England of a highly respectable Quaker family. Of his early life little is known until, with his brother, he emigrated to America and fixed his home in the City of New York. The name "Walter & Samuel Franklin" was for a long period well and honorably known among New York merchants. In 1761 they were actively engaged in the importation of dry goods from Liverpool and other English ports. In 1768 MR. WALTER FRANKLIN appears to have been alone. At this time he joined with a few of the leading merchants of the day in the organization of the Chamber of Commerce. On the 12th May, 1774, he married Mary, daughter of Daniel Bowne, of Flushing, a lady of great beauty and many estimable qualities. He was one of the Committee of One Hundred chosen to look to the safety of the city in May, 1775. Both he and his brother Samuel remained in the city during the War, and were signers of the loyal address to Lord and General Howe in October of 1776.

The city residence of WALTER FRANKLIN was in Pearl Street, near Cherry, in the building later known as the Franklin Bank. He had besides a country place at Maspeth, which was for a long time a Quaker community. This beautiful seat was afterwards the residence of Hon. De Witt Clinton.

MR. FRANKLIN did not survive the War. His death is recorded in Rivington's Royal Gazette, Wednesday, Aug. 9, 1780. "Last Sunday (6th) died of an apoplexy, MR. WALTER FRANKLIN, an old inhabitant and formerly an eminent merchant and underwriter of this City."

By his wife, Mary Bowne, he had three children, all daughters—Sarah, who married John Norton, a gentleman of wealth from Georgia; Mary, the wife of De Witt Clinton; and Hannah, of George Clinton, brother of the last named.

MR. FRANKLIN acquired a large fortune in trade and was much loved and respected, as the tender affection in which his memory is still cherished, particularly among Quakers of all sects, abundantly shows.—*Communicated by Walter Franklin Jones, Esq.*

GLOVER JOHN I.—The son of John and Alice Glover, of Leeds, Yorkshire, England, was born in that town in the year 1749. He came to America in the year 1768 in charge of the business of Emanuel Elam, of Leeds, who was at that period and for many years after extensively engaged in the woollen trade with this country. MR. GLOVER, although but nineteen years of age when he established himself in New York, managed his agency with such a happy mixture of caution and enterprise, that in the course of six years he doubled the amount of his principal's business with the Colonies, without incurring a single bad debt.

His chief characteristics as a merchant were industry, punctuality, directness, and good faith. It is related of him that he won the entire confidence of those to whom he was introduced by strict silence with regard to such information as was entrusted to him, and that the mutual confidence thus engendered invariably grew into strong and lasting friendships.

So young and so lately from the old country, with which his relations were yet warm, and bound to great caution by consideration for the interests of his patron, he could not be expected to take part in the discussion of the great political questions which were agitating men's minds and deranging the regular course of trade.

MR. GLOVER was in the city during the British occupation; at least he was elected to the Chamber of Commerce on the 4th March, 1783, and must have been then engaged in business here: it was not until the following December that the British withdrew from the city. His friend and companion, Samuel Elam, his junior by a year only and the nephew of his principal, was chosen member of the Chamber the same day. The reorganization of the Chamber under a Charter from the State the next year involved the necessity of a re-election, and he was again chosen, June, 1784.

After closing his agency for Emanuel Elam, MR. GLOVER entered into copartnership with Thomas Pearsall, under the style of PEARSALL & GLOVER, in the dry goods business, in the course of which he removed to New Haven, Connecticut, and opened a dry goods house in that town. Many of the customers of this as well as of other New York importing houses were in the New England States.

This movement of an important business house,—doubtless one of many similarly situated,—presents a striking instance of the difficulties under which commerce labored at the period which immediately followed the Revolution, and which were a natural continuance of those which had caused so much bitterness and bad feeling between the different Colonies during the voluntary "non-importation agreements" which immediately preceded the appeal to arms. Each State, claiming to be sovereign, had such navigation and revenue laws as it thought best suited to foster its own trade and attract that of its neighbors, in total disregard of the general interest,—a state of things which, if it had lasted, would have required the establishment of internal custom houses and revenue guards on the frontier lines of each State—have led to a general system of smuggling from State to State, and in the end to civil war; for it is not to be supposed that the larger States, whose taxes were in proportion to their population and heavier expenditure, would have consented quietly to the flooding of their markets with goods brought in from other States at a lower rate of duty than they exacted from their own citizens. Thus in Connecticut the duties on foreign goods were five per cent. less than those levied by the State of New York.

A brief review of the subject will not be without interest. The articles of "Confederation and Perpetual Union" submitted by the Congress sitting at Yorktown, in a Circular Letter to the several States on the 17th November, 1777, were after long struggle and many delays finally adopted by all the States in March, 1781, and the confederacy styled THE UNITED STATES OF AMERICA was formally established. The State of New Jersey, in an able memorial of its Legislature laid before Congress in reply to the Circular Letter of that body on the 25th June, 1781, called attention to the insufficient nature of the powers vested in Congress over the foreign trade of the country. "By the sixth and ninth articles the regulation of trade seems to be committed to the several States within their separate jurisdictions in such a degree as may involve many difficulties and embarrassments, and be attended with injustice to some States in the Union. We are of opinion that the sole and exclusive power of regulating the trade of the United States with foreign nations ought to be clearly vested in the Congress; and that the revenue arising from all duties and customs imposed thereon ought to be appropriated to the building, equipping and manning a navy for the protection and defence of the coasts, and to such other public and general purposes as to the Congress shall seem proper and for the common benefit of the States. This principle appears to us to be just, and it may be added, that a great security will by this means be derived to the Union from the establishment of a common and mutual interest."

This wise suggestion was unheeded by the Congress, the great subject of difference between the States as to the proposed confederation being the claims of the larger States to the vast vacant territory comprised within the boundaries fixed by their Colonial Charters from the Crown. It is worthy of notice that each of the thirteen original Colonies, now States, had a seaport of its own—a fact which partially accounts for their indifference on the subject of a general revenue system. Had there been a single State without such facility, as a majority of all are to-day, there can be no doubt that the disadvantage under which it would labor would have been at once seen. Such State could never have voluntarily made part of a Union which placed it at the mercy of its neighbors. The State of New York closed the great dispute and removed the last bar to the confederation by the noble example of a voluntary surrender of her vast territorial claims. But of what real avail were the waste lands to those States which did not lie contiguous to them, if the States which had this advantage could impose on the population, soon to enter upon them, a revenue tax on all the foreign articles it should consume?

The working of the new government soon developed its weakness and brought home to the minds of men the stern fact that a confederation of sovereignties, without more central power, especially that of regulating intercourse with foreign nations, was not a proper system for this country. With this strong conviction, and under the lead and direction of men of unequalled wisdom, foresight, statesmanship and patriotism, the American people resolved to re-form their Government and "establish a more perfect Union." The Constitution of the United States (an instrument in which the words "Sovereign States" and "Federal Government" are nowhere to be found), was finally adopted, and Congress held its first session under it in New York, April 1, 1789.

It is a curious fact, and one to which Mr. Webster called attention, that the first petition to this Congress was from "certain tradesmen, manufacturers and others of Maryland, praying an imposition of such duties on all foreign articles which can be made in America, as will give a just and decided preference to the labors of the petitioners;" and the second "a petition of the shipwrights of the city of Charlestown, in the State of South Carolina, praying that the wisdom and policy of the national legislature may be directed to such measures, in a general regulation of trade and the establishment of a proper navigation act, as will tend to relieve the particular distresses of the petitioners, and in common with them that of their fellow-shipwrights throughout the United States."

It is difficult, at this distance of time, to estimate the extent of suffering caused by the depression of commerce during the interval from the ratification of peace in 1783 to the adoption of the Constitution in 1789. The memory of them fortunately remained, and in no small degree served to strengthen the solemn resolve of the American people, in its late great struggle, to preserve a government obtained through such trials and at such cost.

To return from this digression, the adoption of the Constitution was the signal for the breaking up of the New Haven establishment, and the return of MR. GLOVER to New York. He had been married in 1786 to Miss Sarah Cornell, of Success, Long Island.

Besides the dry goods establishment which he continued to direct at 222 Pearl Street, his enterprising spirit and great industry led him into other transactions and occupations. He was interested for many years in equal shares with Peter Schermerhorn, John Titus, and Thomas C. Pearsall, in ships and cargoes. He was partially engaged in the trade with Calcutta, and constantly took ventures in other enterprises as favorable opportunities offered.

He was a director in the First United States Bank, in the United Marine Insurance Company, and the Globe Fire Insurance Company. He was also a Governor of that ancient charity, the New York Hospital, from 1796 to 1802.

By his wife, Sarah Cornell, MR. GLOVER had a large family of children, twelve of whom survived him. His death occurred at his house on the corner of Broadway and Leonard Street, in September, 1824, at the age of 75 years.

One who knew him well says of him, "He was lovely at his death as in his life; to the Rev. the late Dr. Milnor, of St. George's Church, he declared his entire belief of the atonement of his Saviour, expressed himself as ready and willing to die, adding, that had he his life to live over again he did not know one thing he should wish to alter."—*The biographical details communicated by John Glover, Esq., of Fairfield, Conn.*

GOODWIN THOMAS.—Nothing appears of this person. He seems to have remained in the city till the close of the War.

GOOLD EDWARD.—A large general importer in Hanover Square. He remained in the city during and after the War. In 1774 he married Sarah Child Huggins, who is said to have been a West Indian lady of some fortune (the date of the bond is given as March 2, 1774). After the peace he formed a connection with one of the Ludlows, and they carried on an importing business at 49 Wall Street, under the firm of LUDLOW & GOOLD.

GOUVERNEUR HERMAN.—The family of Gouverneur in America is descended from Nicholas Gouverneur, a French Huguenot who established himself as a merchant in Amsterdam, and had early connection with the trade of the New Netherlands. His son Abraham, having received an extended education, which included the speaking and writing of three languages, English, French, and Dutch, emigrated to this country. He is distinguished in the history of the time as the Secretary to Leisler during his administration of the government of the province. As such he attested his public acts, and was included in the indictment and conviction under which Leisler and Milbourne suffered on the 19th March, 1691. The Secretary was reprieved by Governor Slaughter, and the sentence being reversed by Act of Parliament, his property was partially restored, and £1000 was paid to him by a vote of the Colonial Legislative Assembly in further compensation. After this restoration he became a leader of the Dutch party and was elected Speaker of the Assembly and Recorder of the City. After the execution of Milbourne, Abraham Gouverneur married his widow, who was the daughter of Leisler.

From him HERMAN GOUVERNEUR was descended. He was a merchant in general business, chiefly with the West Indies and Curacoa, on Hunter's Quay, near the Coffee House. He was also the owner of "large commodious Store Houses" on Gouverneur's Wharf, which stood on the corner of Front Street and Gouverneur's Alley. He was lost at sea in returning from Curacoa, where Isaac Gouverneur, his uncle, possessed a large estate. The vessel on which he embarked was never after heard from, and is supposed to have foundered. This occurred about the year 1773. In June of the next year, 1774, Mary Gouverneur, Hugh Wallace, and Nicholas Gouverneur, his executors, advertised for sale six thousand and eighty-six acres of land in the patent of Kayaderosses, in the County of Albany. These valuable lands were near to the City, and formed part of his large estate.—*Chiefly contributed by Gouverneur Kemble, Esq., of Cold Spring.*

GOUVERNEUR NICHOLAS.—This gentleman, who was one of the earliest members of the Chamber of Commerce in 1768, was the brother-in-law of its first President, John Cruger, whose sister Sarah he married in 1755, the date of the bond being recorded as of the 15th August of that year. She was the daughter of John Cruger, the first mayor of the name, and Maria Cuyler. In 1764 he advertised for sale iron mines, with furnaces and forges, dwellings and coal-houses, on a good stream, 28 miles from Acquackanung landing, and 30 miles from New York; application to be made to himself at New York, or to David Ogden, or Samuel Gouverneur. NICHOLAS GOUVERNEUR appears in 1774 as one of the executors of Herman Gouverneur, then recently deceased. He was then residing at Mount Pleasant, near Newark, New Jersey.

All the Gouverneurs were strong Whigs during the war of the Revolution. Isaac Gouverneur, who had been established in business by his uncle of the same name at Curacoa, St. Eustatia, and who was afterwards of New York, presented the Provincial Congress of New York with "one pair of nine pound cannon" in October, 1775, and received a vote of thanks for the timely and patriotic gift. The house of Curson & Gouverneur, of which he was a member, supplied the American army with arms and ammunition. On the capture of St. Eustatia by Admiral Rodney, in the summer of 1781, the partners were made prisoners and taken to England, and "Mr. Gouverneur was committed to New Prison charged with High Treason in carrying on a correspondence with the American agent, Adams, at Amsterdam, and with furnishing the colonists with ammunition and every other species of military stores for the support of the war." They are naively stated in the account published in the Political Magazine, 1781, to have been "plainly dressed, but had the entire appearance of gentlemen, in light brown clothes and white hats. The house of which they were the heads was deemed the first in St. Eustatia, and the firm of the partnership was estimated at no less a sum than three hundred thousand pounds." He was released at the peace.—*Chiefly contributed by Gouverneur Kemble, Esq., of Cold Spring.*

HAKE SAMUEL.—A general importer of European and India goods, doing business in 1771 at the lower end of Wall Street, and in 1772 in Queen Street. He married Helen, daughter of Robert Gilbert Livingston, who was a distinguished merchant of New York. The date of the bond is recorded as of 4th January, 1769. He remained in New York during the War.

HASENCLIVER PETER.—He was a merchant of great consideration. On the 12th January, 1767, Governor Moore wrote to the Board of Trade, advising them that he had given "MR. PETER HASENCLIVER a Letter of Introduction, as he was then ready to sail for England, imagining that from his character and knowledge of the Country a more perfect Account might be obtained from him of what was required in the before mentioned Letter than I could possibly give by that opportunity. . . . . As to the Foundaries which MR. HASENCLIVER has set up in the different parts of this country, I do not mention them, as he will be able to give your Lordships a full account of them and of the progress he has already made; can only say that I think this Province is under very great obligations to him for the large sums of money he has laid out here in promoting the cultivation of Hemp and introducing the valuable manufacture of Iron and Pot Ash."—*London Doc., XL.* These were the Ringwood Iron Works in East Jersey. On the 26th June, 1766, he advertised the runaway of a number of miners who were "still engaged by contract for 3 years and 4 months, who have been brought into this country from Europe at a very great expense." They were arrested shortly after. He here signs himself PETER HASENECLEVER, but the name is differently spelled on the minutes of the Chamber.

HODGZARD WILLIAM.—Of the house of "Hodgzard & Graham," whose business was chiefly the sale of provisions from Cork; Irish Beef, Pork, and Rose butter—the latter a famous commodity in that day. To these they added a stock of "Piece Goods," consisting of colored broadcloths, ribbons, &c. Their store was in 1780 at 853 Hanover Square. In 1781 it is described as No. 38 Hanover Square.

HOFFMAN NICHOLAS.—Of the house of "Hoffman & Ludlow," auctioneers. He was the son of Colonel Martinus Hoffman and Wyntie Benson, and was born in Dutchess County in the year 1736. In 1768 the firm were in business in Dock Street. At a later period the connection with Mr. Ludlow appears to have been broken off, for in 1780 MR. HOFFMAN advertises teas for sale "purchased out of the India prize ship," from his store No. 907 Water Street. He married Sarah Ogden, of Newark, New Jersey, by whom he had children, Martin Hoffman, Josiah Ogden Hoffman, and Mary, wife of James Seton. He was one of the General

Committee of One Hundred chosen in May, 1775, when the citizens seized the Government, but he does not appear to have taken a prominent part in public affairs. He clung to the faith of his ancestors, and was a Deacon of the Dutch Reformed Church in 1773. He is described as "a Dutchman, slow, inflexible in honesty and pure in character." He died at Redhook in 1800. His descendants are the families of the late Ogden Hoffman, Judge Murray Hoffman, and the late Lindley Murray Hoffman, the latter of whom honorably sustained the mercantile reputation of his ancestor.

IMLAY WILLIAM.—Of "John & William Imlay," importers of European and India Goods (1771). He was a member of the Social Club, which met at Sam. Fraunces' tavern, and included in its number many of the most distinguished men of the day. In a note upon the political views of the members, made by John Moore, a fellow member, and preserved in MSS. in the Historical Society, he is described as having been "loyal at first to the Crown but doubtful after 1777." Sabine says of him that he was in Pennsylvania in 1777, and was sent prisoner to Virginia by the Whig authorities.

JAMESON NIEL.—The head of the dry goods house of "Niel Jameson & Co.," whose place of business was at No. 933 Water Street. After the fashion of the day they added to their stock of broadcloths and serges an assortment of cutlery, window glass, and other incongruous articles.

JAUNCEY JAMES.—He was one of the foremost figures of the time. During the French war he was largely interested in privateering ventures. In 1758 he was appointed one of the Wardens of the Port, and held the post until 1775. In 1765 he was one of the twelve who addressed the General Assembly on the state of the country in behalf of the meeting of twelve hundred freemen and freeholders held on the 26th November. In 1768 he was elected to the Assembly after a sharp struggle, and in 1769 re-elected. During the latter canvass there appeared a song in the Poet's Corner of the New York Journal, to the tune of Hearts of Oak, in which occurs this verse :

> " To JAUNCEY my Souls ! let your Praises resound ;
> With Health and Success may his Goodness be crowned !
> May the Cup of his Joy never cease to run o'er,
> For he gave to us *all* when he gave to the *Poor*."

He sat in this Assembly until the breaking out of the War. He was one of the Committee of Correspondence of Fifty-one, raised in May, 1774, to concert measures of resistance to the arbitrary measures of Parliament. It does not appear that he ever had much sympathy with the revolutionary movement. His son, James, was a member of the King's Council. Both were made prisoners in 1776, and sent to Middletown, Conn., but were released shortly after and returned to the city. The son, who married Eleanor Elliot in 1773, died in New York in 1777. The father was one of the Vestry appointed by General Robertson for the relief of the Poor the same year. For his course during the War his property was confiscated, and he removed to England and resided in Charlotte Street, Rathbone Place, London. He died in London on the 6th February, 1790. "As he was entering the door of Providence Chapel, he dropped down and expired immediately." He seems to have retained his reputation for great benevolence, and it is recorded that he "was well known for his constant practice of relieving the poor at chapel-doors and in the street." Notwithstanding the loss of his large landed estate in New York, he is said to have died worth £100,000.

JAUNCEY WILLIAM.—A brother of James. His name rarely appears. He was prisoner with James at Middletown in 1776. He was a Governor of the New York Hospital from 1797 to 1802. His residence was at No. 20 Wall Street.

KEMBLE SAMUEL.—He was the eldest son of Peter Kemble and Gertrude, daughter of Samuel Bayard of New York. He was born at New Brunswick, in the Colony of New Jersey, about the year 1732. Although at one time engaged in commercial business as an auctioneer with Walter Spens, under the firm of Kemble & Spens, his profession was that of a sailor. He commanded in turn the General Gage and the Lady Gage, London traders. A portrait of him in the uniform of a Lieutenant is in the possession of his nephew, Mr. Gouverneur Kemble, of Cold Spring.

In October, 1773, he was appointed Naval Officer of New York in the place of Charles Williams. This post he retained until the close of the War, when he retired to England. He never afterwards returned to this country. He established a mercantile house in London, but not succeeding in his new commercial venture, he removed to the East Indies. There he married a Miss French, by whom he had three children. He died in the island of Sumatra about the year 1796.

His loyalty to the Crown, during the American struggle, was not forgotten, and his family continued to receive the protection of the British Government. Of his three sons, Peter, George, and Gideon, Peter, the eldest, held rank in the navy. He died in England. Gideon, the youngest, died Collector of the Port of Kingston in Jamaica, where he had married. Gideon, in turn, left four sons: Frederick, a Captain in the British navy; Edward and Henry, lawyers in Jamaica; and William, Secretary of the Colonial Parliament.—*From memoranda contributed by Gouverneur Kemble, Esq., of Cold Spring.*

KENYON WILLIAM.—An importing merchant, chiefly of provisions. From 1779 to 1783 his store was at 190 Queen Street, opposite to Beekman's Slip. He remained in the city after the War, and carried on his business from the same place for many years. In 1792 he was at 39 Beekman Street. He was a Governor of the New York Hospital from 1795 to 1797.

KERR ANDREW.—Of the house of "Moore & Kerr," dealers in groceries in Wall Street. ANDREW KERR was one of the signers of the loyal address to Lord Howe in October, 1776. In June, 1783, he was residing at No. 16 Wall Street. He does not appear to have remained in the city after the War.

KETELTAS PETER.—As early as 1756 MR. PETER KETELTAS appears as occupying a house, and storehouse adjoining, fronting on Queen Street. In 1757 he was a part owner and agent of the privateer Snow Royal Ester, which brought in the French ships Le Leger and Le Debonier. In 1754 he is again found as a petitioner for a commission for the Captain of the Sloop Anne, of 6 guns. When the War broke out with the mother country he sided with the patriots. At its close he returned to the city and carried on his business from No. 10 Princess Street. He died in the city on Monday the 22d August, 1792. An obituary notice of him in the New York Journal says, "that he had been for many years a respectable merchant, and was not only esteemed, as he truly was, an upright and honest man, but enjoyed the singular faculty of passing through life unsuspected of an unworthy action. In his loss, although at an advanced period, his family laments a tender husband, a fond parent, and a most indulgent master."

KORTRIGHT LAWRENCE.—He was extensively engaged in privateering in the old French war. He was part owner of the Harlequin, of 8 guns, in 1756; of the brigantine DeLancey, of 14 guns, commanded by the noted Captain Thomas Randall; of the Prince Edward, of 8 guns; owner of the Snow Royal Hester, of 16 guns; Prince Ferdinand, 14 guns, and Ship Hunter, 18 guns; in 1758 of the brigantine John, 14 guns. He was largely interested in land in Tryon County, and the township of Kortright was settled on his patent. The War having broken up the settlement, in 1783, in order to encourage the return of the families, he offered to waive any rent until May, 1788.

In 1790 he was in business as a merchant at No. 90 Broadway.

LAIGHT EDWARD.—He was the son of Edward Laight, the first of the name who emigrated to this country from England in the year 1692, and settled in New York Colony. His son EDWARD was born in the City of New York on the 24th August, 1721. He was in partnership with Charles Nicoll, under the firm-name of Edward Laight & Charles Nicoll, in 1764; on the 19th of March of which year they advertise for sale from their store in Burling's Slip a variety of West India Goods, Sugars, Molasses, Rum, &c.

These two partners were strong friends, both of them belonging to the organization of the Sons of Liberty, revived in 1765 to resist the operation of the Stamp Act. EDWARD LAIGHT was one of the nine Corresponding Members or Committee of this Association. On the repeal of the Act, in March, 1776, the Society was dissolved, but the interest of MR. LAIGHT in the cause of freedom does not appear to have diminished, for on the 10th of October of the same year his name appears second of the Committee which addressed a letter to Nicholas Ray, the Agent in London, in which, while announcing the dissolution of the organization and the inexpediency of forming a Club as suggested by Mr. Ray in his letter of 28th July, 1766, they pledge themselves to use their "utmost endeavours to keep up that glorious spirit of liberty which was rapidly and so generally kindled throughout this extensive continent."

The partnership with Mr. Nicoll was soon dissolved, for on the 26th February, 1767, MR. EDWARD LAIGHT alone advertised a general assortment of "Ironmongery," as hardware was then styled, to be sold by him from the house to which he had removed, opposite the Hon. William Walton's, Esquire. This was in St. George's, now Franklin Square. To hardware he added the articles used in the tanning trade.

In 1770 he was associated with Gabriel, Lewis, and Moses Ogden, of Newark, East New Jersey, in the "Vesuvius Air-Furnace" Company, under the name of Ogdens, Laight & Co.

MR. EDWARD LAIGHT had married a Miss Luther, by whom he had a son, William, born in 1749, who also became a merchant in the city.

EDWARD LAIGHT was one of the Committee of Fifty-one appointed at the Exchange in May, 1774, and served with great regularity, being absent only from the last three meetings. He was one of the nine delegates chosen in July of the same year to confer with the Committee of Mechanics for the selection of delegates to represent the City in the first Continental Congress, and was also one of the Committee of Inspection (of Sixty) elected in November of the same year, to carry out the non-importation and non-exportation agreements recommended by the first Continental Congress.

When the final appeal to arms came, MR. LAIGHT appears to have withdrawn from public affairs. It seems that he was one of those who were unwilling to support the revolutionary movement. There were many who were willing to make every effort "consistent with loyalty" to obtain their liberties, but who would not draw the sword against the mother country.

MR. LAIGHT remained in New York during the British occupation. In April, 1778, he took his son into partnership with him. They carried on the hardware trade until the close of the War. He was one of the Overseers of the Poor appointed by General Robertson in 1778. Gaine's New York Gazette of June 7, 1783, contains a notice of the death of his youngest son, Benjamin, at the age of nineteen, who is described as "a youth of most amiable manners and promising genius, beloved by his friends and esteemed by the whole circle of his acquaintance." His remains were interred in the yard of Trinity Church, of which his father was a vestryman from 1762 to 1784.

MR. EDWARD LAIGHT was the owner of a country residence near Corlear's Hook. He died on the 18th December, 1794, and was buried in Trinity Church yard. A likeness of him remains in the possession of his descendants. His family and the name of Laight were continued in the line of his son William, who has been named as a merchant of New York.—*Partly from memoranda contributed by Edward Laight, Esq., of New York.*

LAIGHT WILLIAM.—The son of Edward Laight and —— Luther. He was born in New York, 19th February, 1749. He was graduated from King's (now Columbia) College, on Tuesday, 19th May, 1767. The Commencement was held at St. Paul's Church, and "His Excellency the Governor, the members of his Majesty's Council, the Clergy of the City and neighbouring Governments, and a very numerous and splendid Audience, honoured the Day with their presence. The salutatory oration was delivered by MR. LAIGHT, whose graceful action and correct manner of expression were justly admired by every Gentleman of Learning present." After some other performances by Messrs. Jay and Harrison, "MR. LAIGHT favored the assembly with a discourse in *Praise of a City Life*, which, for genteel delivery, argument and Propriety of Language, gave much Satisfaction to the polite audience."

In November, 1772, he married Frances Sackett. On the breaking out of War he was chosen one of the General Committee of One Hundred which assumed the charge of the City. His sympathies were with the royal party, and in May, 1777, he carried despatches from Governor Tryon to Lord George Germaine, certifying him to be "a good and faithful subject, which testimony he desired."

The next year he was engaged in the hardware business with his father, at 190 Queen Street, and this connection continued throughout the War. After the peace he formed a partnership with William Backhouse, and carried on a trade with China. This connection was dissolved in 1792 by the death of Mr. Backhouse. In 1787 MR. LAIGHT was elected Secretary of the Chamber of Commerce, and as such took part in the grand Federal procession in July, 1788. John Broome, President of the Chamber, and William Maxwell, headed the Merchants and Traders in a chariot. WILLIAM LAIGHT followed "on horseback, having a standard representing, in an oval field, surrounded by thirteen stars, Mercury, supporting the arms of the

City, surrounded by emblems of Commerce, and the motto, 'non nobis nati solum.'" This was the device of the Chamber.

MR. LAIGHT died in New York on the 2d April, 1802, at the age of 54 years, and was buried in Trinity Church yard.

MR. LAIGHT was called to many important offices of trust. He was Director in the United Insurance Company, the Mutual Assurance Company, the United States Branch Bank, a Trustee of the Society Library, and a Governor of the New York Hospital from 1787 till his death—a period of sixteen years. His residence was at 112 Greenwich Street. By his wife, Frances Sackett, he had ten children, and numerous of his descendants are now living. A miniature portrait of him remains in the possession of the family.—*Partly communicated by Edward Laight, Esq.*

LECKIE ALEXANDER.—A large dry goods importer, chiefly of English and Scotch goods. His store was at No. 22 Hanover Square. As his name disappears after the War, it is probable that he retired with the British troops on the evacuation of the City.

LEWIS FRANCIS.—He was the son of the Rev. William Lewis, a clergyman of the Church of England, and his wife, the daughter of Rev. Dr. Pettingall, residing in South Wales, and was born at Landaff, South Wales, in 1713. He received his education at Westminster. Having turned his patrimony into merchandise, he sailed in 1735 for New York, where he formed a connection with Mr. Richard Annely, which continued until the death of the latter in 1743, when he appears to have continued the importation of dry goods for his own account. MR. LEWIS married Miss Annely, a sister of his partner. On the 18th May, 1747, he advertises a choice assortment, after the manner of the time, in Parker's Post Boy. He was established near the "Fly Market." During his mercantile career MR. LEWIS visited the different countries of Europe, and even Russia. He was twice shipwrecked on the coast of Ireland. In the French war he was much in Government employ. An agent for the supply of the British troops at Fort Oswego, he was taken prisoner when it surrendered to Montcalm, after Colonel Mercer had been killed at his side. He was taken to Montreal, and afterwards to France. During the Stamp Act period he was one of the most active of the Sons of Liberty. In 1774 he was unanimously added to the Committee of Fifty. He was one of the representatives of New York in the First Continental Congress which sat in Philadelphia the same year. In 1775 he was chosen on the Committee of One Hundred, and again re-elected to the Second Continental Congress. He signed the Declaration of Independence in 1776. He was employed by Congress in the importation of stores and on secret service. In the summer of 1776 he took his family to Flushing, where his house and library were destroyed in the fall by British troops. His wife was taken prisoner and cruelly treated. MR. LEWIS received a vote of thanks from the Colony for his services. The last 20 years of his life he spent at Flushing in retirement and comparative poverty. He died December 30, 1803, in his 90th year. The Hon. Morgan Lewis, Governor of the State of New York, was his son.

LISPENARD LEONARD, JR.—The family of Lispenard, now extinct in the male line in this country, was descended from Anthony Lispenard, a Huguenot refugee from La Rochelle, by the way of Holland, who arrived in New Amsterdam about the middle of the seventeenth century. His will, on record in the registry office, under date of 1696, shows the name of his only son to have been Anthony.

Anthony Lispenard 2d married Elizabeth Huygens de Kleyn, daughter of Barent de Kleyn and grand-daughter of Barentsen Huygens. Leonard Lispenard, Senior, was a child of this marriage.

Leonard Lispenard, Senior, whose parentage is thus mentioned, was born in the City of New York, in the year 1716. In 1741 he was married to Alice, daughter of Anthony Rutgers. Mr. Rutgers was the owner of land-grants from the Crown by two patents to him from King George the Second, the first dated September 28, 1732, the second December 31, 1733—embracing with other ground that known in the early part of this century as "Lispenard Hill" and "Lispenard Meadows." On the death of Anthony Rutgers in 1746, Leonard Lispenard, Senior, inherited through his wife one third of these grants, and purchased, September 24, 1748, from the co-heiresses, Mary, wife of Reverend Dr. Barclay, Rector of Trinity Church, and Aletta, wife of Dirk Lefferts, the other two thirds; thus becoming proprietor of the whole. This was the origin of what is since known as the Lispenard Estate. Leonard Lispenard, Senior, besides his large property, was a prominent citizen in many ways. He was admitted a freeman of the city, under the appellation of Merchant, in 1750. He was the Assistant Alderman of the North Ward from 1750 to 1755, and Alderman from 1756 to 1762. He was also a delegate from New York to the First Colonial Congress, familiarly known as the Stamp Act Congress, which met at New York in October, 1765, and opened the scenes, which closed with American Independence, by a Declaration of Rights and Grievances. He was one of the Committee of Fifty-one chosen by the citizens on the 16th May, 1774, "to correspond with the neighboring colonies" on the impending crisis. He was early identified with the Sons of Liberty, and was no doubt a member of that organization. He was one of the nine members who withdrew from the Committee of Fifty-one on the 7th July, 1774, because of its disavowal of the action of McDougall—a member also—in calling a public meeting in the Fields and presiding over it. The more radical members were dissatisfied with the course pursued by the majority, and, after leaving the rooms of the Committee, published an address to the public in justification of their conduct, to which Mr. Lispenard also signed his name. Unlike the majority of the discontents, Mr. Lispenard returned to the Committee in November, and took part in the final resolves which redeemed it from the reproaches of the time and concluded its patriotic effort to unite the Colonies in a general Congress. He was delegate to the General Assembly of the Province from 1765 to 1767. He was also one of the Committee of One Hundred chosen by the citizens to take control of public affairs on the 5th May, 1775. A month later, on the 25th June, 1775 (as the incident is recorded in Rivington's Gazette of the 29th), "General Washington, attended by Generals Lee and Schuyler and the light horse of Philadelphia, on the way for the American camp at Cambridge, landed at COLONEL LISPENARD'S seat, about a mile above New York, from whence they were conducted to the City by nine companies of foot, in their uniforms, and a greater number of the principal inhabitants of the City than ever appeared on any occasion before." After the breaking out of hostilities he seems to have remained in the city, his age (he was then sixty years), no doubt protecting him from personal interference. Mr. Lispenard was a generous patron of the infant public institutions of New York City. He was one of the original members of the Society of the New York Hospital and one of its first Governors from 1770 to 1777. He was also Treasurer of King's College as early as 1772, and for a long period of years subsequently. He died February 20th, 1790, at his residence on Lispenard Hill, a mansion which was situated at its highest elevation, and overlooked what is now known as St.

John's Square. The centre of this hill was the junction of Hudson and Desbrosses Streets in the present maps of the city. He was buried in the family vault in the rear of Trinity Church.

By his wife, Alice Rutgers, he had three children, LEONARD LISPENARD, JUNIOR, Anthony Lispenard, and Cornelia, who married Thomas Marston, of New York.

LEONARD LISPENARD, JUNIOR, the son of Leonard Lispenard and Alice Rutgers, was born in the City of New York in the year 1743. His name is mentioned in the New York Mercury of June 14, 1762, as one of nine young gentlemen who received from the President of King's College, at St. George's Chapel, the degree of Bachelor of Arts. In 1768 he was admitted freeman of the city under the title of Gentleman, but as early as 1769 he seems to have engaged in some commercial business to have qualified him to receive an election to the Chamber of Commerce on the 4th July, 1769.

He was an active member of this body and a constant attendant at its meetings until the divisions which occurred among the members, owing to their different political views, in 1774. He is last recorded as in his seat on the 4th October of that year, but he had not dissolved his connection with it on the 3d May, 1775, on which day he was named as one of the monthly Committee to "hear and determine disputes" left to the Chamber. This was the last Committee appointed until the month of June, 1779, when a few of the members who remained in the city during the British occupation met together for the first time in four years.

In the MSS. notes of Mr. John Moore as to the political sentiments of the different members of the Social Club, which after many joyous gatherings finally dispersed in December, 1775, mention is made of LEONARD LISPENARD and his brother Anthony, as of "doubtful loyalty to the crown, but as remaining quiet at New York" during the British occupation. There can be little doubt that he partook of his father's sentiments, but family considerations may have governed his actions during those troublous times.

He was one of the founders of the Masonic Society of New York, and appears first on the list of its members January 8, 1770. He is here styled "Captain." It is of well-known family tradition that he travelled extensively in Europe and acquired wealth independent of his father. He was a man of fine education, and of marked intelligence and energy of character. He was the proprietor of the property known as "Davenport's Neck," near New Rochelle, Westchester County, where he had a summer residence. He was never married, and died comparatively young. He was buried in the family vault in Trinity Church yard.

Anthony Lispenard, the second son of Leonard Lispenard, Senior, and only brother of LEONARD LISPENARD, JUNIOR, married Sarah Barclay, daughter of Andrew Barclay, merchant, and niece of the Reverend Dr. Barclay, of Trinity Church. The record of the license of this marriage is of the 10th December, 1764. They were cousins. He was the proprietor of the extensive breweries on the Greenwich road, near the foot of Canal Street. His attention to this business no doubt sprung from the large interest of his maternal grandfather with this profitable manufacture. Anthony Rutgers had been the owner of large breweries and mills located on the North River not far from the foot of the present Cortlandt Street. These with his dwelling-house, "on the Broadway, opposite Maiden Lane," passed on his death in 1746 by will to his grandson, Anthony A. Rutgers, only son of his only son Anthony, then deceased. Anthony Lispenard, by his wife, Sarah Barclay, had three sons and three daughters: Leonard Lispenard, 3d, who continued the name in the next generation, Anthony, and Thomas, who died unmarried. Leonard, Anthony (now Worth), and Thomas Streets were respectively named by the father after the three brothers, and Lispenard Street was so named by the Corporation of the City in honor of the family. Of the three daughters, Helena Roosevelt Lispenard married Paul Bache, son of Theophylact Bache and brother of the wife of Leonard Lispenard, 3d; Sarah married Alexander Stewart, father of Lispenard Stewart, of this City; Alice Lispenard died unmarried. Bache Street, now incorrectly spelled Beach, which was opened through the Lispenard farm, was so called after Paul Bache.

Leonard Lispenard, 3d, was also engaged in one of the breweries on the Greenwich road, perhaps in partnership with his father. He went to England shortly after the peace in 1783, and remained some years in London with the Barclays, relatives of his mother, the founders of the famous breweries of that city bearing their name. One purpose of this visit may have been the better to fit himself for the management of a business of this kind on his return. In 1802 Leonard Lispenard, 3d, formed a partnership with Bernard Hart, under the firm of "Lispenard & Hart." Mr. Hart was one of the leading Jewish merchants at the close of the last century. The business of the house was partly as auctioneers, added to which was a large commission business. They were originally located at 89 Water Street, but in 1806 moved to 141 Pearl Street, where they remained until the dissolution of the partnership in 1813. Mr. Lispenard died in 1816.

Leonard Lispenard, 3d, married Anna Dorothea, daughter of Mr. Theophylact Bache, a distinguished merchant and Fifth President of the Chamber of Commerce. They were cousins also, their mothers being both daughters of Andrew Barclay. Their issue were, 1st, Theophylact Bache Lispenard, who settled in Montreal, married a Canadian lady, and died in 1832, leaving three daughters; 2d, Sarah, still living and unmarried; 3d, Anthony, died unmarried; 4th, Helen, married to Major Nicholson, Paymaster in the United States Marine Corps, and the mother of the present Captain Somerville Nicholson, of the United States Navy, and Captain Augustus Nicholson, of the United States Marine Corps, as also of other children, daughters.

Thus to-day, while the honored name of Lispenard is no longer borne by any male descendant of this once powerful family, there are many representatives by the female line, in the fifth and sixth generations from the old Huguenot refugee, in the families of Stewart, Webb, Nicholson, Livingston, LeRoy, and Winthrop.—*Communicated by Lispenard Stewart, Esq., of New York.*

LIVINGSTON PHILIP.—The family of Livingston in America is descended from John Livingston, a Scotch clergyman of the parish of Ancram, Roxburghshire, Scotland. His son, Robert, emigrated to America about the year 1676, and shortly after married Alida, daughter of Philip Pieterse Schuyler, and widow of the Patron Nicholas Van Renselaer. He soon acquired a large landed estate by purchase from the Indians, which was incorporated into the manor of Livingston by patent dated 22d July, 1686. This grant was confirmed in 1715, and to it was added the privilege of a "close-borough;" that is, of a right to the tenants of electing a representative to the General Assembly. Philip, the second son, succeeded to the estate on the death of the eldest brother, and is known as the second proprietor of the manor. He married Catharine, daughter of Captain Peter Van Brugh, of Albany.

PHILIP LIVINGSTON, grandson of Robert 1st, and son of Philip Livingston 2d (proprietor), and Catharine Van Brugh, was born at Albany on the

10

15th January, 1716. He graduated from Yale College in the year 1737, and soon after, settling in New York, established himself in business and rapidly acquired a large fortune. His place of business was on Burnet's Key. An advertisement of the "Brigantine Nebuchadnezar, Captain Peter Corne, for London, (for freight or passage, agree with Philip Livingston, Junior,)" appears in "Bradford's New York Gazette, revived in the New York Post Boy," 2d January, 1748. During the French war he was extensively engaged in privateering. He appears as an applicant for commissions for captain of the Schooner Albany, of 8 guns, in 1757; of the Ship Tartar, 16 guns, and Amherst, 12 guns, in 1758. He seems early to have turned his attention to public affairs, in which the family of Livingston was deeply interested.

In 1754 he was elected Alderman for the East Ward, and held this office until 1762. He was a member of the Assembly from 1759 to 1769, and during his last term of office was Speaker of the House. He was a member of the First and Second Continental Congress, elected in 1774 and 1775, and was one of the signers of the Declaration of Independence. He was also a member of the Convention which met at Kingston to form a Constitution for the State of New York in 1777. He was a Representative in Congress at the time of his death, which occurred at York, Pennsylvania, on the 12th June, 1771. His great patriotism was shown by the sale of part of his private property to support the public credit.

LIVINGSTON ROBERT CAMBRIDGE.—The son of Robert, third proprietor of the manor of Livingston, and Mrs. Gertrude Schuyler, his second wife. He took his middle name as a distinction, from his having graduated from Cambridge University, England, where he was a fellow-student with Bishop Prevoost, afterwards Chaplain to the Senate of the United States.

In September, 1775, having informed the Committee of Safety of "his intention to go to Britain for the recovery of his health, at present very much impaired," he received a permission attested by the officers of the committee: "The Committee, firmly persuaded of his attachment to the liberties of this country, approve of his intended voyage, wish him the restoration of his health and a happy return to his native country." He married Alice, daughter of John Swift, Esq., of Pennsylvania. He died at Hudson, in September, 1794, at the age of fifty-three years. His descendants are in the families of Robert Swift, John S. and James Duane Livingston. His New York residence was at 13 Dock Street.

LIVINGSTON ROBERT GILBERT, Jr.—The son of Robert Gilbert Livingston and Catharine McPheadres. His sisters, Helen and Catharine, were married to Samuel Hake and John Reade; both of whom were merchants of New York. In 1771 he was engaged in the dry goods trade in Dock Street, "next door to Messrs. Hugh & Alexander Wallace, near the Coffee House." In July, 1773, he announced that he had "declined trade and intended leaving the city." On the 2d August, 1776, he addressed to the Provincial Congress a complaint that Mr. Rutgers had refused to receive payment for principal and interest due upon a bond in Continental currency, and stated that he "had received lately very large sums in that way with as great readiness as he would gold and silver." He resided subsequently at Redhook, on the Hudson. After the War his New York residence was in the "Bowerie Lane."

LOW ISAAC.—He was seventh President of the Chamber of Commerce. For sketch of his life see page 69, *ante*.

LOWTHER WILLIAM.—In 1775 he was owner of the sloop Francis, which was permitted to sail with her cargo for the Carolinas by the Committee of Safety. He remained in New York. After the War he was in business at 78 Cherry Street.

LUDLOW DANIEL.—The Ludlows of New York are all descended from Gabriel Ludlow, who emigrated to this country from England towards the close of the seventeenth century, and married Sarah Hanmer, daughter of the Rev. Mr. Hanmer. His son Gabriel married, first, Frances Duncan, and afterwards his cousin, Elizabeth Crommelin.

DANIEL LUDLOW was the third son of Gabriel Ludlow and Elizabeth Crommelin, and was born about the year 1750. He followed in the footsteps of his father and grandfather, and early devoted himself to commerce. A part of his mercantile training he received at Amsterdam, in the counting-house of the great bankers, his relatives, Daniel Crommelin & Son.

In 1773 (the date of the bond is given as of September 13th, 1773), he married Arabella Duncan, daughter of Mr. Thomas Duncan. A few years later MR. LUDLOW entered into partnership with Mr. Edward Goold, and transacted a general importing business at No. 47 Wall Street. This connection was terminated about 1790, and MR. LUDLOW continued business under his own name at 38 Dock Street, his residence being at No. 48 Wall. In 1793 his counting-house was at 42 Wall Street, and in 1795 at 51 Wall, and the title of his firm, Daniel Ludlow & Co.

MR. LUDLOW visited Europe to extend the business of his house, and it is related of him that he was present in Paris at the execution of Lewis XVI. and Marie Antoinette. On his return to this country he took his son Daniel Ludlow, Jr., into partnership. The house was engaged in general trade. They did an extensive business with the East Indies, and were heavy underwriters.

The country-seat of MR. LUDLOW was at Baretto's Point, on the East River, from which it was his habit to drive into town four-in-hand in the summer season. He died in New York about 1813. The name of Ludlow, in his branch, is continued by the children of his son, Dr. Edward G. Ludlow, of New York.

LUDLOW GABRIEL H.—Of the firm of "Ludlow & Hoffman," auctioneers. He was one of the Committee of Correspondence of Fifty-one in 1774, and also a member of the Committee of One Hundred which assumed charge of the city in May, 1775. His sympathies were with the Royal cause, however, and he remained in the city during the War. He was one of the Vestry appointed by General Robertson, in 1778, to look to the poor. He married Ann Williams in March, 1771. His residence in 1780 was at No. 11 Wall Street. In 1783 he was in partnership with Mr. Shaw in the importation of wines — the style of the house being Ludlow & Shaw. In 1787 his place of business was at 50 Smith Street. In 1789 his widow resided at 16 Little Queen Street.

LUDLOW GEORGE W.—He is mentioned by John Moore as a member of the Social Club which met in New York during the War. He says of him that he was loyal to the Crown, but remained on Long Island in quiet.

LYNSEN ABRAHAM.—The son of Abraham Lynsen, of New York. In 1757 he married Magdalen Beekman, and soon after appears to have made a partnership with some one of his wife's family under the name of

Beekman & Lynsen. This connection was dissolved in 1763, and for a time MR. LYNSEN carried on his business, which was chiefly with the West Indies, under his own name. Later he formed a partnership with Thomas William Moore in the Vendue business, as auctioneering was called in that day. He died before 1783. The death of his widow is thus recorded in Gaine's New York Gazette of 29th September, 1783: "the 2d instant died at Verplanck's Point, in the County of Westchester, in this Province, Mrs. Magdalen Lynsen, Relict of MR. ABRAHAM LYNSEN, formerly of this place, Merchant."

McADAM JOHN LOUDON.—He was distinguished as the inventor of the MacAdamised stone-road. He was born in Scotland in 1756, and emigrated to America shortly before the Revolution, his uncle being established in business in New York. In 1778 he married Gloriana Margaretta, daughter of William Nicoll, by whom he had several children. After her death he married Anne Charlotte, daughter of John Peter Delancy, of Marmaroneck, and great niece of Judge Thomas Jones, who had adopted her as his daughter. MR. McADAM was engaged as agent for the sale of British prizes, and accumulated some property, but returned to England at the close of the War with but little of his fortune. The name of his house was McAdam, Watson & Co. For his discovery in road-making the British Government gave him £10,000, and offered him Knighthood, which he declined. The honor was then conferred on his son, James Nicoll McAdam. MR. McADAM died at Moffat, County of Dumfries, in 1836, aged eighty. His widow, Anne Charlotte, died at Hoddeson, Hertfordshire, England, May, 1852.

McADAM WILLIAM.—He was in business near the New Dutch Church in 1766, where he advertised for sale "Iron-bound Butts and Puncheons, genuine Batavia Arrack in Bottles, Frontiniack, Priniack and Madeira," etc. He was one of the Committee of Correspondence of Fifty-one, but later took part with the Crown. His estate was confiscated. He died in New York on the 1st day of October, 1779.

McCORMICK DANIEL.—He was of the house of Moore, Lynsen & Co., auctioneers. At a later period he carried on the same business alone. He made a large fortune in the sale of prizes during the War. His vendue store was in Wall Street. He was a bachelor, noted for his hospitality. Of a fine afternoon he would sit with his friends upon the stoop of his house, 39 Wall Street, for hours. Notwithstanding his conviviality, he is described as a man of strict religious principles, and was a member of the First Presbyterian Church in Wall Street.

McDAVITT PATRICK.—He was of the firm of Fargie & McDavitt, vendue masters, which dissolved on 6th November, 1766. In 1771 he was importing English and India goods at his store near the Fly Market. He remained in the city during the War, and carried on an extensive auction business under his own name in Queen Street.

McDONALD ALEXANDER.—He was a sea-captain. On the 1st October, 1764, he married Susannah Myers. In 1771 his store was in King Street, where he bartered Madeira wine for country produce, and gave notice that "the one article is to be received when the other is delivered."

He was charged, 14th June, 1775, in Provincial Congress, "with concerting measures and employing agents to enlist men, to be employed against the liberties of America." A committee was sent to Staten Island to arrest him and search his house, but they reported that he had gone to Boston, and that they found "no papers relating to the raising of troops."

McEVERS CHARLES.—The brother of James McEvers, who declined to distribute the Stamps as Stamp Officer, in 1765. Upon his brother's death, in 1768, he succeeded to his business. He had previously been established, first near the Meal Market, where he sold dry goods, teas, and Irish goods as early as 1759, and later in Dock Street. One of the Committee of Correspondence in 1774, his statement that he wished the disavowal of the Meeting in the Fields printed, that it might go to England in the Packet, was the cause of a serious division among its members. One of the Committee, in a handbill in his defence, calls him "one of the most amiable characters among us." He remained in the city during the War, and was one of the addressers of Lord and General Howe in the fall of 1776, when the British troops entered the city. His wife, Mary, died at Jamaica, Long Island, 23d December, 1778. He died in New York, Sunday, September 4, 1808, aged sixty-nine years, and was buried from No. 34 Wall Street, the house of his son, Charles McEvers, Jr. Charles McEvers, Jr., married Mary, daughter of Theophylact Bache, in 1787, and after her death, Margaret Cooper. He was of the famous house of LeRoy Bayard and McEvers.

McEVERS JAMES.—He was largely engaged in the importation of European and India goods at Hanover Square about the middle of the last century. The family were well established in New York at that period. Besides his brother Charles, mention is made, in Parker's Post Boy of July 22, 1752, of John and William McEvers.

On the passage of the Stamp Act, JAMES McEVERS was appointed Stamp Distributor for New York and accredited by Act of Parliament. In August, 1765, he found that the sentiment of the people was so strongly opposed to the Act that he resigned his office. On the 26th August he wrote to Jared Ingersoll, who had been appointed "Stamp Master" for Connecticut, asking what course he intended to pursue. It appears from the correspondence that neither of them were in favor of the Act. Ingersoll replied, "the truth is that I love the Stamp Act about as little as you do." The people, however, were not satisfied, and the Stamps having arrived, and it being understood that a commission had been received by McEVERS, he was waited on by Isaac Sears and Joseph Allicocke in behalf of the Sons of Liberty, and signed a public renunciation of the office on the 2d December, 1765, which was published in the newspapers of the day.

One of the earliest members of the Chamber, illness prevented his taking his seat. He died in New York City, 8th September, 1768. His executors were Elizabeth McEvers, Charles McEvers his brother, and Charles William Apthorpe.

McKENZIE JOHN.—He is said by Sabine to have been a Captain, and to have commanded a vessel engaged under the royal flag in the transportation of supplies for the British troops. "He removed to Shelburne, Nova Scotia, at the peace, and died at Liverpool, in that Province, in 1825." He left several children.

MARSTON THOMAS.—This family, now extinct in the male line in this city, was among the most distinguished of the colonial period. He was one of the earliest members of the Chamber. In 1759 (the date of the bond is given as February 7th), he married Cornelia, daughter of Leonard Lispenard. She died on the 18th November, 1775. His eldest daughter married Francis Bayard Winthrop, in April, 1779. He was one of the Committee of One Hundred raised in 1775, but his name does not again appear in the history of the time. His portrait, taken in 1798, is No. 74 of the St. Memin collection. He died in New York on the 11th January, 1814, in the 75th year of his age.

MILLER JOHN.—He was one of the addressers of Lord and General Howe in October, 1776, and remained in the city during the War. His place of business was in 1782 at No. 14 Water Street, where he sold a variety of goods, chiefly provisions.

MILLER THOMAS, CAPTAIN.—One of the most noted Captains in the London trade. He commanded the ship Britannia, which "arrived on Monday evening (28th May, 1770), in 6 weeks from the Downs." She "brought over the Statues of His Majesty and Mr. Pitt," which had been ordered by the Assembly of the Colony in gratitude for the repeal of the Stamp Act. He remained loyal to the Crown. He was an addresser of Lord Howe in 1776, and sailed for England with his family in the fleet which took over Governor Tryon, in September, 1780. He married Martha Willett, in October, 1756.

MOORE JOHN.—In 1762 he kept the "compleat Soap and Candle Store and sold coffee and tobacco in the house where the late David Fleming lived, between the Market and Burling Slip." He is presumed to be the JOHN MOORE who married Elizabeth Taylor, in 1759. He formed a partnership later with Andrew Kerr, and carried on the ship chandlery business from their store in Wall Street. A notice of his death appears in Gaine's New York Gazette: "Last Monday night, December 31, 1781, died MR. JOHN MOORE, merchant of this city in partnership with Mr. Kerr; as he possessed the general esteem of mankind, from the excellent qualities of his heart and the urbanity of his manners, his death is most sincerely regretted by an extensive and a very genteel acquaintance."

MOORE THOMAS WILLIAM.—He was the seventh child of Judge William Moore, of Moore Hall, Pennsylvania, and was born the 17th June, 1735.

Judge William Moore was a son of John Moore, who died Collector of the Port of Philadelphia in 1732, and who was the first of this branch of the family who emigrated to this country from England. He first established himself at Charleston, South Carolina, then an important commercial city, and his son, John Moore, was there born as early as 1686.

The first record of the presence of THOMAS W. MOORE in New York is to be found in the recorded publishment of his marriage with Anne Ascough, 6th July, 1761, at which period he had just entered on his 27th year. This lady was the widow of Dr. Richard Ascough, a surgeon in the British army resident in New York in the middle of the last century. In 1762 MR. MOORE appears to have been engaged in mercantile business for his own account. In Gaine's Mercury of 23d August of that year he advertises "Sugar by THOMAS WILLIAM MOORE at his store in King's Street, next door to James Duane, Esq."

In 1768, on the 4th October, he was admitted to membership in the Chamber of Commerce, and in the course of the next year, 1769, he was made a freeman of the city under the appellation of Gentleman.

He was of the firm of Moore & Lynsen, afterwards Moore, Lynsen & Co., auctioneers, Daniel McCormick having been admitted to the firm.

MR. MOORE seems never to have hesitated in his allegiance to the Crown. When the British army arrived from Halifax, in 1776, he immediately entered the service. When General Oliver DeLancey raised his Loyal Brigade, he offered Captains' and subordinate commissions to all well recommended characters who should engage a company of seventy men. In the 2d Battalion of this Brigade, commanded by Colonel George Brewerton, MR. MOORE enlisted as Captain. Notwithstanding the inducements held out by General DeLancey, his Brigade filled up but slowly, and the three Battalions did not number over seven hundred men in 1778 instead of the fifteen hundred required to fill his ranks. Towards the close of the year 1778 the large force which had been gathering in New York, to the great solicitude of Washington and the colonists, was sent out on various expeditions. About the end of November a body of troops under Lieutenant-Colonel Campbell sailed for Georgia in the squadron of Commodore Hyde Parker. The object of this expedition was to attack Georgia from the seaboard, while General Prevost should make a flank attack on the banks of the Savannah River.

CAPTAIN MOORE sailed with his command in this expedition, and was present at the taking of Savannah at the end of December of that year. After the capture of the town Colonel Campbell appointed MOORE Barrack Master to the Garrison.

General Prevost, arriving shortly after, assumed the general command, and detached Colonel Campbell against Augusta. CAPTAIN MOORE remained in Savannah as Provincial Aid-de-Camp to General Prevost, and took part in the defence of the city in October of the succeeding year, 1779, during the memorable siege by the Americans under Major-General Lincoln and the French under Admiral D'Estaing, one of the most hotly contested actions of the War, from which, after a spirited assault led in person by their commanders, the allies were forced to retreat, with a large loss of officers and men, including the gallant Count Pulaski.

On the evacuation of Savannah by the British troops, CAPTAIN MOORE returned to New York. Whether he continued in the corps of loyalists commanded by DeLancey, which gave so much annoyance to the American forces and scourged the counties of Westchester, New York, and Long Island, in 1781, does not appear.

Upon the entry of the troops under Washington, in 1783, CAPTAIN MOORE withdrew to Nova Scotia; thence he crossed the Atlantic to England, and was rewarded by the Government for his services with the appointment of Consul to Rhode Island and Connecticut. A disagreement taking place between the Governor of Rhode Island and MR. MOORE, his exequatur was withdrawn by President Washington. After again twice crossing the Atlantic, he died in England.

By his wife, the widow of Dr. Ascough, MR. MOORE had several children. Thomas William Moore, his son, was well known and greatly esteemed in this city, and was for many years the Agent of the British Packets at New York. He was celebrated for his genial and generous hospitality. He was twice married, first to Mary, daughter of George Gibbs, Esq., of Newport, Rhode Island, who died in 1813, secondly to Miss Bibby, of New York, who still survives him. Their son, Thomas Bibby Moore, served gallantly in the U. S. Cavalry during the recent War. The other children of CAPTAIN MOORE were William Moore, and a daughter who married first Mr. Campbell, and later became the wife of Lieutenant, afterwards Captain, Jones, of the British Navy, a distinguished officer.

The widow of CAPTAIN MOORE, after the death of her husband in England, resided and died in Brooklyn, Long Island.—*Chiefly contributed by T. W. C. Moore, Esq., of New York.*

MURRAY JOHN.—The son of John Murray. He was of Scotch parentage, born in the town of Swataca, Pennsylvania, in 1737. Early in life he came to New York City and entered the counting-house or store of an older brother, Robert, with whom he was at a later period associated in partnership under the name of ROBERT & JOHN MURRAY. The name was later continued under the styles of JOHN MURRAY, JOHN MURRAY & SON, and JOHN MURRAY & SONS. He was a man of quiet and unobtrusive manners, and plain, simple habits, particularly averse to display of any kind; as a citizen, among the foremost in the support of all the religious and philanthropic institutions of the day; in his religious belief a Presbyterian, and for many years an elder in Dr. Rodgers' Church. As a business man he was comprehensive in his views, of strict integrity, and successful. He took no prominent part in public affairs, and is not known ever to have held any office. In his political opinions he was a Federalist, and among his intimate friends were Rufus King and Alexander Hamilton. During the later years of his life MR. MURRAY was much engaged in acting as a referee and arbitrator in cases of mercantile differences, and an appeal was rarely taken from his decision. He was President of the Chamber of Commerce from 1798 to 1806.

MR. MURRAY died at his country seat on New York Island, then three miles from the City, now that part of it known as "Murray Hill," on the 17th October, 1808, aged 71. There is a fine portrait of him by Trumbull, from which the painting in the Hall of the Chamber of Commerce is a copy. —*Communicated by John R. Murray, Esq., of Cazenovia.*

MURRAY ROBERT.—The son of John Murray. He was born at Swataca, Pennsylvania, about the year 1714. He was one of the most important merchants of the last century. It is said of him, that his firm owned more tons of shipping than any other house in America. Together with the Franklins, who were of the same religious belief, both being Quaker families, he despatched, April 21st, 1768, the first whaling sloop which had left the city on a cruise for many years. His place of business was on Murray's Wharf, where he had two stores. In 1771 his younger brother, John, was in business with him; the house was then styled ROBERT & JOHN MURRAY. At a later period the firm-name was MURRAY, SANSOM & CO. He accumulated a large property. He married Mary Lindley in 1744. His farm-house at Incleberg, now Murray Hill, became historical as the spot where Mrs. Murray entertained Lord Howe and his officers, and by her good cheer and pleasant conversation detained the march long enough to allow of the escape of the division of the American troops under Putnam, which had otherwise been cut off. He was one of the addressers of Lord Howe shortly after this occurrence. Of course, with his Quaker opinions, he was not expected to take an active part with either side. He resided in the city during the War, in Chapel Street. He died in New York on the 22d of July, 1786, at No. 188 Queen Street. His children were John Murray, jr., Lindley Murray the Grammarian, Mrs. Martin Hoffman, and Mrs. Gilbert Willett; his later descendants, David Colden Murray, Lindley Murray, Robert Lindley Murray, and John Murray, jr.—*Chiefly communicated by David Colden Murray, Esq., of New York City.*

NEILSON WILLIAM.—One of the largest dry goods importers of the last century. His place of business was in Dock Street. He does not appear to have taken any part in public affairs. He died in New York on the 26th of November, 1820, at the age of 83; "the last survivor of the original members of the New York Chamber of Commerce."

NICOLL CHARLES.—He was the posthumous son of William Nicoll, of Islip, Long Island, by his second wife, Ruth Northen, and born 3d January, 1724. He was one of the earliest of the Sons of Liberty, and a member of its most important Committee in 1766. For some time a partner of Edward Laight in the importing of European and India goods, he appears alone in the wine business at a later period. He remained in New York during the War, and was one of the Vestry to take charge of the poor in 1778. He died Tuesday, 12th December, 1780, in the City of New York, "in the 59th year of his age." An obituary by the hand of a friend said of him, "that his loyalty endeared him to his country; his good nature and sincerity to his friends; his humanity to the indigent; his benevolent and social spirit to his companions, and his candor and integrity to all men."

OOTHOUT JOHN.—He was admitted freeman of the city in 1765. In 1771 he was a candidate for the office of Church Warden. He does not appear to have taken a prominent part in public affairs. He remained in the city during the War. Of the house of OOTHOUT & DUMONT, 13 Smith Street, after the War.

PAGAN WILLIAM.—He was admitted freeman of the city in 1769. He was one of the addressers of Lord Howe in 1776. His name does not appear after the Peace.

PHŒNIX DANIEL.—He was the son of Alexander Phœnix and Elizabeth Bockee his wife, and was born in the City of New York in 1742. He died at his residence in this city, 138 Water Street, on the 17th of May, 1812, and was buried in a vault beneath the Wall Street Presbyterian Church. He was the great-grandson of Alexander Phœnix, who is traditionally reported to have been a younger son of Sir John Fenwick, Bart., a representative of the great Northumbrian family of Fenwicks. It is well known to those who have studied the history of surnames, that Phœnix is simply a corrupt form of Fenwick (which is pronounced as if written Fennick); but whether the tradition referred to rests on any further basis of truth than this, it is now impossible to say. Little is known of Alexander Phœnix (or Fennick, as he wrote it), than that he was born in England about 1620—that he embraced non-conformist principles in religion—and that the persecution to which he was subjected in consequence drove him to the New World. He removed to New York, then New Amsterdam, in 1640. His descendants have remained here from that day to this, and during a period of *two hundred and twenty years* have lived in what is now the first ward of the city.

DANIEL PHŒNIX, having received a liberal education, entered at an early age into the business of importing goods from Great Britain, and by his intelligence and uprightness soon acquired the confidence of the community. Beginning with a moderate capital which he had inherited from his father, he soon amassed what was in those days a large fortune, and was considered throughout his long life one of our wealthiest and most influential citizens.

His interest in religious affairs was manifested at an early age and continued unabated to the day of his death. His name is identified with the history of the Presbyterian Church in this city. He was chosen a trustee of the Wall Street (now Dr. Phillips') Church in 1772, and served faithfully and zealously in that capacity until the city fell into the hands of the British troops. On the evacuation of New York and the consequent re-opening of the Church, he was called upon to resume his old seat in the board of trustees—a position which he continued to occupy, with hardly an interval, till his death, in 1812. Such was the confidence of his associates in his integrity, and such their estimate of his ability, that the financial matters of the Church were entrusted almost entirely to him.

In politics he was an uncompromising Whig, and took an active part in all measures calculated to resist the tyranny of the mother country. News of the passage of the Stamp Act having reached New York in April, 1765, he at once joined the association known as the "Sons of Liberty," which had been formed at the stormy time of Zenger's trial, to protect the liberties of the people and resist the aggressions of the Crown. To the patriotic measures of that organization—its Non-Importation Act; its persistent resistance to Governor Colden in his attempts to enforce the Stamp Act; its rejoicings over the repeal of that odious measure; its almost daily conflicts with the British soldiery quartered here under the command of General Gage; its loud protests against the disfranchisement of the Provincial Assembly; its rigorous opposition to the Tea Bill—he lent his active co-operation. It deserves to be remembered that he was one of the last who adhered to the non-importation measures adopted by the colonists in opposition to the Stamp Act, though they fell with particular severity upon himself, and indeed entirely suspended his business for several years.

On the reception of the news of the battle of Lexington, 24th April, 1775, the Arsenal, Custom House, and other public buildings in New York were seized by the people, and at a meeting on the 5th May, a "General Committee of One Hundred" influential citizens was appointed to carry on the government of the city till further action on the part of the Provincial Congress. Of this Committee DANIEL PHŒNIX was a prominent member. It continued in power until the capture of the city by the British army under General Howe, on the 15th of September, 1776, when MR. PHŒNIX retired with his family to Morristown, New Jersey. Here he resided during the War. On the evacuation of New York, November 25, 1783, he returned to the city, to find his house burned, his business ruined, and much of his property irretrievably lost. His sacrifices in the cause of liberty were not, however, unappreciated by his fellow citizens. He was at once chosen one of a Committee of thirteen (representing the original States), to receive General Washington on his triumphal entry into the city, and at the first municipal election he was elected Alderman of the East Ward—an honor then highly esteemed and eagerly courted by our best citizens. In 1790 he was again returned to the Board of Aldermen, then seven in number, from the Out Ward. Such was the general confidence in his integrity and financial ability, that in 1789 he was appointed by the Mayor and Aldermen to the honorable and responsible office of City Treasurer, or Chamberlain—a position which he continued to hold till the year 1809, when declining health compelled him to resign it. During this long period of twenty-one years there was but one opinion of his eminent fitness for the position and of the uprightness with which the affairs of his department were administered.

DANIEL PHŒNIX took an active part in the inception of the many noble charitable and literary institutions which adorn this city, and contributed liberally to their support. He was Governor of the New York Hospital from

1784 to 1787, and by his untiring efforts aided largely in placing that memorable institution in a position to fulfill in 1791 the intentions of its founders. He was elected a Trustee of the Society Library in 1775, and continued to occupy that position till the year 1810, when his feeble health forced him to resign. During most of this time he acted as the Treasurer of the Society. He aided materially in erecting the first Free School ever built in this city. This was a small building, founded and maintained at the expense of a few public-spirited citizens, in Madison near Pearl Street, and was opened on the 7th of May, 1806, with accommodation for only forty scholars; but as the germ of our present Common School System, its founders deserve an honorable place in the history of the city.

In the commercial world, MR. PHŒNIX's wealth and integrity gave him a high position. He was connected with almost all the mercantile institutions of his day. Two years after its formation in 1768, (on the 4th day of December, 1770,) he was elected a member of the Chamber of Commerce (being then only twenty-eight years of age), and he continued an active member of that institution to the day of his death. On the 20th of April, 1784, he was among the petitioners to the Legislature for a confirmation of the Chamber's Charter, which he believed had been forfeited by the disloyal action of some of the members during the British occupation.

He was Secretary of the New York Insurance Company from 1795 to 1799 (being succeeded in that position by his son Sidney), and Director of the Manhattan Company (chartered in 1799 with a capital of two millions and a half to supply the city with water, but afterwards merged into a banking company) from 1803 to 1810. He was one of the original subscribers to the celebrated Tontine Association, which was composed of the most eminent merchants of the day, taking his share in the name of his daughter Rebecca, who was born on the 17th of January, 1781, and died on the 3d of February, 1818.

He died, as has been said, on the 17th day of May, 1812, leaving behind him an enviable reputation as an honorable and successful merchant, a public-spirited and patriotic citizen, a courteous, urbane gentleman, and an earnest Christian.

DANIEL PHŒNIX was twice married; to Hannah Tredwell, on the 8th of February, 1770, and to Elizabeth Platt, on the 3d of November, 1772. It is mentioned as a curious fact by our city chroniclers, that at the funeral of the latter, in 1784, "the pall-bearers were ladies."

His children were: 1. Gerard, born 10th of July, 1774; died in infancy. 2. Alexander, born 28th of February, 1777; graduated at Columbia College, 1794; admitted to the bar in 1798, but afterwards studied for the ministry; pastor of the Congregational Church at Chicopee, Mass., 1824-35; died at Harlem, New York, 31st of August, 1863; (an appreciative memoir of this excellent man was recently published by the Pastor of the Congregational Church at Harlem.) 3. Elizabeth, born 23d of April, 1776; died 1st of October, 1844; married Nathaniel Gibbs Ingraham, by whom he had three children, one of whom, Daniel P. Ingraham, is a Judge of the Supreme Court of New York. 4. Rebecca, born 17th of January, 1781 (Tontine Life); died 3d of February, 1818; married Eliphalet Williams, of Northampton, Mass. 5. Amelia, born 30th of March, 1784; died in infancy. 6. Jennet, married Richard Riker, the well-known District Attorney and Recorder of the city. 7. Sidney, born in 1779; died in 1800, unmarried.

The male line of the descendants of DANIEL PHŒNIX was continued only in the children of his second son, Alexander.—*Contributed by S. Whitney Phœnix, Esq., of New York.*

PINTARD LEWIS.—In 1762 he appears as the owner of the schooner Catherine, of 6 guns. A prominent merchant in the time of the Stamp Act, he was called upon by the Sons of Liberty in reference to a bond and Mediterranean pass, which the Committee at Philadelphia informed the New York Committee he had sent on stamped paper. He disavowed any intention of using the stamp. He was one of the Committee of Correspondence of Fifty-one of 1774, and of the Committee of One Hundred of 1775. He was connected with the Commission for the relief of American prisoners in this city during the War. His wife Susannah died March 11th, 1772. He died March 16th, 1818, at the age of 86, "one of the three last survivors of the original members of the Chamber of Commerce."

PLATT JEREMIAH.—There was a firm of WATSON & PLATT in 1762, who were engaged in the domestic trade, selling "Long Island Pork and Gammons, and Connecticut Cheese, at Burling's Slip." In August, 1769, he married Mary Ann Vanderspiegle. It is presumed he was of the Fairfield County (Conn.) family. He was on the Committee of One Hundred in 1775.

PONSONBY JOHN.—Nothing occurs concerning this person. He no doubt went out with the British troops.

RAMADGE SMITH.—A dry goods importer, at No. 10 Water Street. He married Mary Jones on New Year's Day, 1777. He was arrested in 1776 and committed to gaol for refusing to take the oath to the Continental Congress. On the 9th of April, 1781, he announced that he "intends embarking for Europe with the first convoy, and calls in his outstanding debts." He also offered for sale his store in Water Street, and his dwelling-house, No. 35 Hanover Square.

RAMSAY JOHN.—The son of James Ramsay, of Perthshire, Scotland, was born in Perthshire, in the year 1731.

The family of Ramsay has been established in the old County of Perth for many generations, and claims descent from Adam de Ramsay, of Banff, one of the Scottish barons who is recorded as having submitted to Edward I. of England.

JOHN RAMSAY, after receiving a liberal education in the professions of law and physic, left his home in Scotland, and, in companionship with his young friend, Mercer, went up to London, where they entered a counting-house together. There was probably some family tie between these two young men; in fact, Burke, in an account of the family in the landed gentry, states that George Ramsay, of Banff, Perthshire, married Elizabeth, daughter of Mercer, of Aldie. When MR. RAMSAY reached twenty-one years of age the two friends emigrated to New York, and, forming a partnership, entered into the business of importing.

In 1763 MR. RAMSAY was married to Mrs. Elizabeth Marshall, of Charleston, South Carolina. He is said to have continued in partnership with his friend until the breaking out of the Revolutionary War; perhaps such was the case, and the business was at first carried on under the sole name of one partner, who advertises in Hugh Gaine's Mercury of January 21, 1768, "MR. JOHN RAMSAY, merchant in New York, near the Fly Market." At a later period the name of the house was MERCER & RAMSAY. He seems to have been in high consideration among his countrymen, for on February 13th, 1769, he summoned together the Sons of St. Andrew, as the Secretary of the Society.

On the 5th March, 1771, he was elected a member of the Chamber of Commerce.

The course of MR. RAMSAY on the approach of the struggle was a firm and consistent one. A member of the Dutch Reformed Church, it was natural that he should ally himself with the party which favored a larger liberty than the views of either Church or King promised in that day. On these questions it was to be expected that every Scotchman would have clearly defined opinions. Differing in views from his partner, their connection was now dissolved, and Mr. Mercer, whose sentiments were strongly with the Crown, returned to Great Britain, where soon after, on the death of an elder brother, he became Lord Keith.

After the retirement of Mr. Mercer, MR. RAMSAY continued the business alone. Through his many influential connections abroad, he received many brilliant offers from the British Government, but he always refused to take part against the land of his adoption or the cause of human rights. Although he does not seem to have taken an active part in the contest, and his name does not appear in any of the numerous committees of the period, yet when the British army took possession of the city, he removed to New Jersey, where he remained until the close of the War.

He returned to New York for a short period, and while here was, on the 1st June, 1784, re-elected to the Chamber of Commerce. He does not seem to have been contented with the position of affairs in New York, and removing to Philadelphia, he established himself there, but in a few years, in consequence of the failing state of his wife's health, he returned to New York and renewed his old business at his store in Pearl Street—his residence being in Greenwich Street. A few years later he withdrew from active life, and retired to his farm in Westchester County, where he died on the 1st day of December, 1816, at the full age of 85. There remains, unfortunately, no likeness of this worthy man, except a small silhouette.

MR. RAMSAY, by his marriage mentioned, had six children, of whom one was a son, Charles; of the daughters, Martha married Mr. John Cruger, of Belmont, Hudson River, a seat between Sing Sing and Fishkill. It is this Mr. Cruger whose portrait is No. 43 of the St. Memin series. Another, and the only surviving child, is Mrs. Isabella Bloomfield, of Philadelphia.—*From MSS. memoranda contributed by Mrs. Isabella Bloomfield, of Philadelphia.*

RANDALL THOMAS, CAPTAIN.—He was one of the noted Captains of the day, and took a prominent part in public affairs. In 1748 he commanded the privateer brigantine The Fox, which brought in the French ship L'Amazone. In 1757 he took out the brigantine DeLancey, of 14 guns. The next year he seems to have withdrawn from active service, and to have sent out privateers under the command of others. In 1758 he was joint owner of the snow General Abercrombie, 16 guns, and the ship Mary, 10 guns. In 1760 the DeLancey in her turn was captured by the Dutch off Curacoa, and her commander and crew imprisoned. In 1762 he appears as the owner of the Charming Sally, of 6 guns. On the breaking out of the War of the Revolution he took active part with the patriots. He was a member of the Committee of Fifty-one, and took part with the radical members on the division caused by the meeting called in the Fields by McDougall. He was also on the Committee of One Hundred. When the British entered the city he withdrew to Elizabethtown, and appears to have aided the Provincial Congress in the care of the Privateers commissioned by it. His house in New York, on the west side of Broadway, was one of those spared by the destructive fire of 1776. On the return of the exiles to New York, a meeting was held at Cape's tavern, 18th November, 1783, which appointed a Committee to prepare an address to General Washington. The name of CAPTAIN RANDALL leads the signatures to this paper. He was also one of the Committee of thirteen to conduct the procession to meet Governor Clinton on his entrance into the city, 26th November. He was one of the gentlemen who presented Washington with the "President's Barge," used by him during his stay in New York. On the President's return to Virginia, in 1789, he returned the barge to the donors, with a warm letter to CAPTAIN RANDALL.

The residence of CAPTAIN RANDALL was at No. 8 Whitehall. He died Friday, October 27, 1797, aged 74 years. His remains were interred in the family vault in Trinity Church Yard.

RAPALJE GARRET.—The son of John Rapalje and Diana, daughter of Garret Middah, was born in Brooklyn, May 31, 1730. In 1768, together with William Faulkner and Rem Rapalje, he opened a Brew-House at the Brookland Ferry. He had been for some time engaged in the importation of ironmongery and dry goods at his store opposite the Fly Market. He was the owner of the Wallabout. He married Helen Denys, of New Utrecht, and moved to New Orleans.

READE JOHN.—He was a general importer. He was in business under his own name, first in Wall Street and later in King Street. He married Catharine, daughter of Robert Gilbert Livingston.

REMSEN HENRY, JUNIOR.—He was the son of Henry Remsen and Catalina, daughter of Joris Remsen, and was born 5th April, 1736. On the 28th December, 1761, he married Cornelia Dickenson. He entered into the dry goods business, and soon became one of the largest importers of the day. The style of the firm was HENRY REMSEN & COMPANY, and their store was in Hanover Square, the centre of business. Some years later, MR. REMSEN united with him David Seabury, and they continued the same business until the first of April, 1774, when the firm was dissolved, MR. REMSEN retiring.

In politics MR. REMSEN was a strong Whig. He was one of the Committee of Correspondence of Fifty-one, and also of the Committee of Association of One Hundred, of which he was Deputy Chairman. As such he signed the address of the General Committee to Lieut. Governor Colden, on the 18th May, 1775. In 1776 he was active in aid of the Provincial Congress, importing stores and supplies for the troops. He had then retired to Morristown, New Jersey, with his wife and family. He returned to the city after the Peace, and resumed his business at No. 8 Hanover Square. He died 13th March, 1792. Of nine of his children, Henry was the only one who married; his wife was Catharine, daughter of Captain DePeyster.

REMSEN PETER.—The son of Rem Remsen and Dorothy his wife, was born in 1722. He was in partnership in New York with his brother Henry, in the dry goods business. The firm was PETER & HENRY REMSEN. They dissolved in May, 1762, and PETER REMSEN continued the business in his own name, at his store on the corner of King Street, until his death, in 1771.

RHINELANDER FREDERICK.—A large importer of china, glass, and earthen ware. His store was at the corner of Burling's Slip. He remained in the city during the War, and was, with his brother Philip, an addresser of Lord and General Howe, in October, 1776. He appears, in July, 1778, as one of the Vestry of the city, charged with the care of the poor. On the 28th July, 1783, he was summoned by Lewis Duboys, Sheriff of Dutchess County, to show cause why his estates should not be forfeited for "adhering to the enemies of the people of the State of New York."

On the 10th December, 1783, FREDERICK & PHILIP RHINELANDER announced their intention to "dissolve business." Their advertisement was dated from Rhinelander's store, "168 Water Street, corner of Burling's Slip."

After the War they continued their business from the corner of Barclay and Greenwich Streets, North River.

ROOSEVELT ISAAC.—His business was that of sugar-refining, his store originally in Wall Street. He afterwards removed to St. George's Square. On the 25th April, 1772, he issued the following advertisement: "ISAAC ROOSEVELT is removed from his House in Wall Street to the House of his late Brother, Jacobus Roosevelt, Jun'r, deceased, near the Sugar House, and opposite to Mr. William Walton's, being on the North West side of Queen Street, where his customers may be supplied as usual, with double, middling, and single refined loaf sugars, clarified, muscovado, and other molasses, &c." He was one of the most noted Whigs of the time. He was one of the General Committee of Association of One Hundred, chosen in May, 1775, to take control of the Government. On the entry of the British he withdrew from the city. His sacrifices were rewarded by the confidence of his countrymen. He represented the City of New York in the Convention which met at Kingston, Ulster County, April 20, 1777, to form a Constitution for this State, and of the New York Convention which assembled at Poughkeepsie, June 17, 1788, to deliberate on the adoption of the Constitution of the United States. After the Peace he was Senator of the State. On the death of General McDougall, in 1786, MR. ROOSEVELT succeeded him in the Presidency of the Bank of New York, which had been organized two years before in the Walton House, opposite to the residence of MR. ROOSEVELT, which was then known as 159 Queen Street. He had resumed his business of sugar-refining, in partnership with his son, under the firm of ISAAC ROOSEVELT & SON. MR. ROOSEVELT continued in the Presidency of the Bank until May, 1791, when he retired, and was succeeded by Mr. Gulian Verplanck. He was the Fourth President of the Society of the New York Hospital, from 1790 to 1794. He died in October, 1794, at the age of sixty-eight years, beloved and honored as a tried, true, and consistent patriot.

SCHUYLER JOHN, JUNIOR.—The son of Col. John Schuyler, the wealthy proprietor of the Belleville Copper Mines in New Jersey. He was engaged in the importation of European and India Goods, at his store in Dock Street, between the Coenties' and Slip Market in 1771. In 1774 he dropped the Junior. His store was still in Great Dock Street. He then advertised domestic produce chiefly. He married Mary Hunter, on the 16th February, 1769. His wife died on the 23d March, 1806, in the 56th year of her age.

SEABURY DAVID.—Of the house of "Remsen & Seabury." This was a large dry goods importing house. Their place of business was on Hanover Square. This partnership was dissolved in April, 1774. MR. SEABURY remained in the city during the British occupation, and carried on his business at No. 353 Smith Street. In June, 1783, he charitably aided the loyal refugees, who were about embarking for Nova Scotia. The 9th August following, all the household furniture of Mrs. Anne Lyne was sold at auction, at the "house formerly occupied by MR. DAVID SEABURY, No. 17 Smith Street." MR. SEABURY had married Anne Lyne, probably a daughter of this lady, on the 5th September, 1770. It seems from this notice that he had withdrawn from the city.

SEAGROVE JAMES.—In 1775 his name appears as Captain Lieutenant, in an Independent Company of Foot, called the Royal Artillery. He was one of the addressers of Lord and General Howe, in October, 1776. He is mentioned by Mr. John Moore, in his account of the Social Club, as one of its members. He describes him as "disaffected" to the Crown, and as having gone to the southward as a merchant.

SEARS ISAAC.—He was one of the foremost figures in the stirring scenes enacted in America during the latter half of the last century. His profession as the Captain of a peaceful trader being broken up by the French war, he entered at once into privateering. In 1757 he took out the Dogger Decoy of 6 guns, and later the sloop-of-war Catharine; but his most daring exploits were while in charge of the sloop Belle Isle, of 14 guns, owned by John Schermerhorn & Co., merchants, which put to sea in 1759. In September he fell in with a large French ship of 24 guns and eighty men, and attacked her without hesitation. He was twice disabled and forced to withdraw to refit. The third time he grappled the Frenchman and a long contest took place, but the grappling giving way, the sloop sheered off with nine men killed and twenty wounded. A gale springing up separated the vessels. In 1761 he was shipwrecked on the Isle of Sables, and with difficulty saved his own and the lives of his crew. The prestige of these exploits gave him a strong moral ascendancy over his fellow-citizens, and he seems to have fairly won the title of *King* which was given to him. In the resistance to the Stamp Act, and the daily struggles which took place with the soldiery about the Liberty Pole, SEARS was always in the front rank and exposed himself without hesitation. A complete sketch of his life would make a history of this stormy period, for there is hardly an event connected with it in which he does not appear. Fresnau, in his poetical squib upon Gaine, the trimming editor of the New York Mercury, gives an amusing account of him:

"At this time arose a certain King SEARS,
Who made it his study to banish our fears.
He was without doubt a person of merit,
Great knowledge, some wit, and abundance of spirit;
Could talk like a lawyer, and that without fee,
And threatened perdition to all that drank TEA."

He was one of the Committee of Correspondence of Fifty-one, in 1774, and clung steadfastly to his old friend McDougall in the divisions in that body. He was also one of the General Committee of One Hundred chosen by the citizens in 1775. He was known from one end of America to the other as a daring Son of Liberty. When John Hancock passed through New York in May, 1775, he lodged with MR. SEARS. In the autumn of that year SEARS entered the city at noonday with a Company of Connecticut Light Horse, and destroyed the Tory press of Rivington, which had made itself obnoxious to the Whigs. Before the War he was engaged in a small importing business, which does not appear to have been very satisfactory, as he accepted the post of Inspector of Pot and Pearl

Ashes, which he held till 1772. During the War he was engaged in some business in Boston, but returned to New York at the peace, and made a partnership with his son-in-law, Paschal N. Smith, who appears at an earlier period as a Captain of an eastern trader. Their business was not successful, and MR. SEARS again resumed his voyages. He died in China, on the 28th October, 1786. His son Isaac died at Martinique, in February, 1795.

SETON WILLIAM.—The family of Seton is one of the oldest and most renowned of Scotland, and the name is familiar alike to the lover of history, ballad, and romance. From a remote period in history it has been settled in the County of Fife.

WILLIAM SETON, the son of John Seton, Gentleman of Parfroth, Fifeshire, Scotland, and Elizabeth Seton, of the House of Carriston (also Seton), was born in the year 1746. He came to America at an early age. What motive induced his emigration is not known. His family were then, or soon after, well established at home. His brother James was a banker at Edinburgh. Three of his sisters were married—Lady Sinott, Lady Cayley, Mrs. Berry, mother of the Misses Berry, the faithful friends and favorites of Sir Horace Walpole in his latter days. A fourth, Margaret, came later to this country and married a cousin of the same name.

WILLIAM married, soon after his arrival, Rebecca Curson, as appears by the record, in the Book of New York Marriages, of the license granted under date March 2, 1767, being then not over twenty-one years of age. This lady was a daughter of Mr. Richard Curson, of Maryland, a gentleman of English family, whose descendants are now well-known residents of Baltimore. After her death he was again married to a second sister, Anna Maria Curson, whom he also survived some years. This order of marriage was a vexed ecclesiastical question at this period, especially in the Episcopal Church, in which faith MR. SETON had been reared.

In the year 1768 the young merchant must have already enjoyed the respect and confidence of his seniors, for on the 2d August he was admitted to membership in the Chamber of Commerce. He seems at this period to have determined on a permanent residence in New York. In 1770 his name appears, WILLIAM SETON, GENTLEMAN, admitted freeman of the city. He was engaged in the shipping and importing business, at first in partnership with his brother-in-law, Richard Curson, under the name of CURSON & SETON. In the New York Gazette, April 15, 1771, is published a notice: "CURSON & SETON, removed from Dock Street to Hunter's Quay (alias Rotten Row), opposite Mr. Gouverneur's." At a later period he was the head of the house of SETON, MAITLAND & CO.

MR. SETON does not appear to have taken part in the events which immediately preceded the Revolution. His youth and the influence of his friends; his comparative isolation and slender ties in this country; his family at home, to whom he was devotedly attached, and their large and influential connections, would naturally lead him to great caution in his conduct. But it is probable that he needed none of these to hold him steadfast in his allegiance. His sympathy with the Episcopalian Church, and the antagonism to the Presbyterian element natural to the descendant of an old Scotch Catholic family, doubtless attached him to the Episcopalian party, when Church and King were alike the objects of attack by the bold dissenting element then struggling for mastery. Perhaps, too, a natural pride in that brave loyalty which was the distinguishing characteristic and honor of the race, had no small part in the decision of the question in his mind.

On the 5th May, 1775, when the excited people, aroused by the news of the Lexington fight, took possession of the public buildings, and elected a

Committee of One Hundred to control the city, WILLIAM SETON was named eighth on the list; but it will be remembered that all shades of opinion were included in this Committee, whose duty was not so much to promote the objects of revolution as to secure the peace and order of the city.

Though moderate in his opinions, his leanings were to the royal side, and he of course remained in the city when the British troops took possession, in the fall of 1776, and every sincere Whig retired with the retreating American army under the personal command of Washington.

His business was probably not prosperous at this period of general derangement, for on the establishment, by General Howe, of a Superintendent's Department, 27th July, 1777, MR. SETON was appointed Assistant Ware House Keeper—an office which he retained for several years, certainly until 1780, and probably to the close of the War.

In 1779 he was appointed Notary Public under the British Government. This Notarial seal, in the name of King George the Third, is still in the possession of his namesake and grandson, Mr. William Seton, of Cragdon, Westchester County.

In 1782 he was named Secretary to the Superintendent of Police of the city.

In 1783, on the 10th December, he advertised himself in the Royal Gazette as Deputy Agent of the French Packets, office at 215 Water Street.

During this period MR. SETON retained his connection with the Chamber of Commerce, and when, after a lapse of four years, the resident members, on the 21st June, 1779, petitioned General Daniel Jones, the commandant of the city, for permission to resume their meetings, he appears to have been in his seat.

The moderation of MR. SETON, and the kindness which marked his whole life, as well during this troubled period as in the more peaceful years which immediately succeeded the British evacuation in 1783, was soon to meet its reward. On the organization, in 1784, of the Bank of New York, the first fiscal institution in the country, preceding by seven years the Bank of the United States, established in 1791, Mr. Alexander McDougall was appointed President, and MR. WILLIAM SETON Cashier—a position for which the known uprightness of his character, the sterling nature of his integrity, so honorably shown in his mercantile career, eminently qualified him, and in which he found a broad field for the exercise of his rare diligence, precision, and methodical habits. His appointment in connection with Mr. McDougall, the early, constant Son of Liberty and a distinguished officer of the Revolutionary forces, is an evidence of the esteem in which he was held, even by the most determined of the liberal party. He continued in this important position, commending himself to the affection of his fellow citizens by his amiable and courteous manner, until the 10th June, 1794, when he retired, and was succeeded by Mr. Charles Wilkes. His death occurred in the month of June, 1798, in the 52d year of his age—a want of timely attention to a fall he had met with on his own doorstep the preceding winter, while escorting a friend in freezing rain to a carriage with his wonted politeness. The loss of such a man, before his allotted years were ripe, was a public calamity, and was so felt by the community, large numbers of whom followed his remains to their last resting-place. He was buried in the vault of John Fell, on the south side of Trinity Church yard.

MR. SETON resided at one period at the Banking House, in Hanover Square, afterwards at the corner of Stone and Mill Streets—the store and office being in the rear, in Mill Street. It was the usage of the times for merchants to occupy the lower story of their dwelling-houses for business purposes. The year of the first yellow fever, the family remained in town, in the vicinity of Old Slip, all in health, but the following summer MR. SETON purchased a country residence, which he named CRAG-DON, probably in memory of scenes of his youth among the "rocks and brooks" of Scotland. Its locality was in Bloomingdale, nearly opposite the present site of the New York Orphan Asylum. At the time of his death he was engaged in building a mansion-house not far from what is called Carmansville.

The features of this worthy gentleman are preserved in a fine and faithful portrait, painted in 1795 by the celebrated Stuart, in the possession of the family.

MR. SETON had a family of fourteen children, ten of whom married. They intermarried with the families of Hoffman and Ogden of this city. The last survivor of this large family is Samuel W. Seton, now 78 years of age, well known from his connection of more than a half-century with the cause of public education in New York City. In the third and later generations there are 87 surviving descendants, the name being continued in the families of Mr. William Seton, of Crag-don, Westchester County, of Messrs. Alfred and E. A. Seton, of Opelousas, Louisiana; while in the female line the old blood runs in the veins of the Lyles of Virginia; Maitlands of Baltimore; Beans of Massachusetts; McCallisters of Pennsylvania; Roberts, Gilmans of New York; Ogdens of New York and Oregon; in England, in the children of Dr. Paterson, of London; in Africa, in the family of Rev. C. C. Hoffman, of the Episcopal mission at Cape Palmas; and Miss Catharine Seton has consecrated her life to charitable deeds as a Sister of Mercy in this city.—*From memoranda furnished by Samuel W. Seton, Esq.*

SHARPE RICHARD.—He appears in 1756 with the McEvers, Alsops, Rutgers, and others, as an owner of the patents of Minisink and Wayawanda, then encroached upon by the people of New Jersey. During the French war he was joint owner, with Lawrence Kortright and Jacobus Van Zandt, in several privateers. He was a partner in the Iron Furnace of Peter T. Curtenius, and also one of the Clerks of the Old Insurance office, which was opened at the Merchants' Coffee House for the convenience of the Underwriters. He remained in New York during the War, and was one of the Vestry named by Governor Robertson to oversee the poor of the city. His store was opposite the Mayor's, in 1778, and his business the sale of wines.

SHERBROOKE MILES.—He was one of the auction-house of "Perry, Hays & Sherbrooke." In 1774 he was one of the Committee of Correspondence of Fifty-one. He remained in the city during the War, and carried on his business from his store in Mill Street. Part of the time he resided at Flatbush, L. I., where he was captured in June, 1778, by Captain Mariner, who owed him a personal grudge. This was the expedition upon which Mr. Bache and Major Moncrieffe were taken prisoners. He was one of the Vestry appointed by General Robertson to relieve the poor. In 1779 his property was confiscated and he was banished. In 1784 he petitioned the Legislature for a reversal of the attainder. He was living at No. 9 Whitehall Street in 1790.

SIMSON SAMPSON.—The son of Joseph Simson and Rebekah Simson, was born in the City of New York. He was in partnership with his brother Solomon, the style of their advertisements of Beaver Coating and numerous other articles of their importation being "at Simson's in Stone Street." He was greatly respected, and one of the prominent men of his time. "It is said of him that he was a remarkably pious and conscientious Jew, celebrated for punctuality and strict honesty." He died of a consumption on Sunday night, the 28th August, 1773, and was buried in the grounds of the Congregation "Shearith Israel." In June of the next year, Solomon, as Executor, called in all the outstanding claims of the partnership of Sampson & Solomon Simson.—*Partly communicated by Rev. Ansel Leo, of New York.*

SMITH RICHARD.—He was an addresser of Lord and General Howe in October, 1776. He was an importer from England, chiefly of flour and provisions. His store was at No. 11 Queen Street.

SPENS WALTER.—A merchant in the English and Scotch trade. He came passenger from Greenock in the snow Georgia, which was ordered by the Provincial Congress "to return with her cargo from whence she came," in October, 1775. MR. SPENS had an invoice of goods on board, and there were also consignments to the Buchanans, but they were not permitted to be landed. MR. SPENS adhered to the Crown. In 1778 he was engaged in business at 1091 Water Street, receiving and clearing packets for London and selling European goods. In 1780 he was at 45 Maiden Lane. In September of that year he sailed in the fleet which took off Governor Tryon. In his absence his business, then chiefly in Port and Lisbon Wines, was transacted by Hugh Smith, at No. 21 Little Dock Street, as appears by advertisement of the latter in the *N. Y. Gazette*, Feb. 26, 1781. He was in partnership at one time with Mr. Samuel Kemble, under the firm of "Kemble & Spens."

STEPPLE WILLIAM.—His name was signed to the loyal address to Lord and General Howe, in October, 1776, and it is known that he remained in New York during the War; but what was the nature of his business does not appear.

STRACHAN JOHN.—Nothing appears of this person. He was probably of the firm of "Lee & Strachan."

TAYLOR JOHN.—He was born at Fintry, Scotland, in the year 1752, and emigrating to America, soon after reaching his majority, settled in the City of New York. In 1778 he was engaged in the auction business, his Vendue Store being near the Fly Market. He returned home before the close of the War, and was married to Margaret Scott at Glasgow, October 27, 1783. He returned to New York and engaged in the importation of dry goods shortly after, from 225 Queen Street. At a later period he united with him his two sons, James and Andrew, and continued the business chiefly on Commission, under the style of JOHN TAYLOR & SONS, at 185 Pearl Street. He died in New York City, June 30, 1833, and was buried in the Murray Street Church. His remains have been since removed to Greenwood Cemetery. He is said to have been a "man of strong, vigorous, and discriminating mind, of the strictest integrity, perfectly reliable, and most punctual in meeting his engagements." He was a man of earnest religious convictions, and "the influence of his faith was visible in all the relations and doings of life—in the family, the counting-house, and in his general intercourse with society." He had seven children. 1. Margaret, widow of John Johnston, of "Boorman, Johnston & Co."

2. Elizabeth, who died at New Haven. 3. John R., deceased. 4. Andrew, residing in England. 5. Jennet, who died at Duffield, Conn. 6. Robert L., shipping merchant of New York. 7. Scott, who died in Brooklyn.—*Communicated by John Taylor Johnston, Esq., of New York.*

TEMPLETON OLIVER.—Of the house of "Templeton & Stewart," Vendue Markers, one of the most prominent auction houses of the time. The partnership was dissolved by mutual consent, by public advertisement, September 1, 1783. OLIVER TEMPLETON was an old merchant of New York. His advertisements of English goods are to be found in 1764. On the 13th June, 1774, it was announced in the New York Gazette that "last week Mr. OLIVER TEMPLETON was married by the Rev. Dr. Cooper, President of King's College, to Miss Betty Brownjohn, daughter of Mr. William Brownjohn, an eminent druggist in this city." MR. TEMPLETON died in New York, in November, 1792.

TENCH JOHN.—Of the house of "John Tench & Co." auctioneers, in the city during the British occupation. He joined the Loyalist Association, organized in New York in 1782, to settle at Shelbourne, Nova Scotia, the following year with his family. He married Rachel Evans on the 12th September, 1778.

THOMPSON ACHESON.—He was in 1764 engaged in the despatch of vessels and cargoes to Ireland, and an importer in return of Irish Beef, Linens, &c. His store was opposite that of John Alexander & Co., near Burling Slip. He afterwards was in partnership with Robert Alexander, but his name disappears from the records of commerce soon after his election to the Chamber in 1768.

THOMPSON HENRY.—In 1780 he was at 954 Water Street, in the dry goods trade. He was engaged in 1781 in the ship-chandlery business at No. 51 Water Street, between Burling Slip and the Fly Market. His name is not found after the peace.

THURMAN JOHN, JUNIOR.—In a deposition made by John Thurman, Sr., on the 19th March, 1742, with regard to the famous Negro Plot of that year, he appears as a baker. He had married Nealta Quick in 1737. The son was a dry goods importer in Wall Street, on the corner of South Street, in 1765. He seems to have risen early to a position of honor among the merchants of the city. He took an active part with the Sons of Liberty in 1765. He was one of the Committee who, in the name of the Freemen and Freeholders of the City of New York, requested the Representatives to move for a brass statue of William Pitt, in gratitude for his exertions in the repeal of the Stamp Act. He was also one of the Committee of Inspectors to enforce the observance of the non-importation agreement, which was again resolved on in the renewal of the aggressions of Parliament. His sympathies were not with the radical leaders of the organization, and he was as determined in his resistance to the later movements as he had been earnest in the support of the earlier efforts of the Sons of Liberty. He was one of the Committee of Correspondence of Fifty-one, chosen in May, 1775, and made the motion to disavow the meeting in the Fields, called and presided over by McDougall. From this time he appears to have acted against McDougall and his friends. He presided over the meeting held at the house of De LaMontagnie, in March, 1775, to thwart the purposes of the Committee who had recommended a general meeting to elect delegates to the Second Congress. He remained in the city during the War, but he does not appear to have taken an active part with the royal party. In 1784, at the petition of the Whigs, his old friends, he was permitted to return to the State.

TRENHOLM WILLIAM.—Nothing appears of this person in the records of the period.

USTICK WILLIAM.—Of the firm of WILLIAM & HENRY USTICK. These brothers were heavily engaged in the hardware business. In 1774 Henry Ustick had a nailery on Pot Bakers Hill, in Smith Street, and at the same period WILLIAM was an importer of ironmongery of all kinds, at the sign of the Lock and Key, between Burling's Slip and Beekman's Slip. They were both strong loyalists, and signers of the address to Lord and General Howe, in 1776. In fact, in April of that year they had made themselves unusually obnoxious to the Sons of Liberty by their breach of the non-importation agreement and the supply of the royal troops at Boston with pickaxes.

WILLIAM USTICK was in the iron business as early as 1763. In 1757 he married Susannah Pelletrau. She died on Sunday, the 14th day of September, 1783, and was buried in Trinity Church yard. His daughter Betsey was married to Lawrence Hartshorne, of Monmouth County, New Jersey, January 20, 1780. She died at Halifax in 1793. The firm of Hartshorne & Ustick sprung from this connection. After the peace MR. USTICK resided in Flushing. His son, William Ustick, Jr., was in the nail business, at 33 Queen Street, during the War, and continued in the same business after the peace. The latter died Jan 31st, 1836, aged 72 years.

VAN DAM ANTHONY.—First Secretary of the Chamber of Commerce. For a sketch of his life see page 105, *ante*.

VAN HORNE AUGUSTUS.—The son of Cornelius Garret Van Horne. One of the most respected of the merchants of the last century, and of a family which from the earliest period held a leading position in the Colony, alike under the Dutch and English rule. On the 21st May, 1764, he advertises a cargo of Jamaica rum by the puncheon. In 1765 (the date of the bond was February 13), he married Anne Marston. He does not appear to have taken any decided stand in the politics of the time, and although arrested in August, 1776, by General Washington, in Queens County, and sent to Norwich, with a number of other persons, he was shortly after released on parole and permitted to return to his home. Part of the Van Horne family were ardent Whigs. Captain Graydon, in his memoirs, describes young ladies of this name as at Flatbush during his confinement, as "handsome and well bred," and "avowed Whigs." MR. VAN HORNE appears to have remained quiet in the city. He was one of the Vestry for the relief of the poor in 1777. In 1781 he resided at No. 7 Little Dock Street, fronting Princess Street. After the War he resided No. 58 Smith Street.

VAN ZANDT JACOBUS.—Of the dry goods house of JACOBUS VAN ZANDT & SON. One of the active Sons of Liberty of 1768. In 1769 he signed, with Lamb, Sears, McDougall, and others, the address to the Representatives of New York in the Assembly, in favor of a secret ballot, as a protection to the popular liberties. He was a member of the Committee of

Correspondence chosen in May, 1774, to concert measures of union with the other Colonies, but was not present during the struggles which ensued between the two wings of the body. He had already discontinued attendance on the meetings of the Committee, but as his name does not appear among those who withdrew, it seems probable that he was absent from the city. He was a member of the General Committee of One Hundred chosen in May, 1775, to take control of the city. He withdrew from the city on the British occupation, but returned after the War. He died before 1788.

VERPLANCK SAMUEL.—The eldest of this name was the eldest son of Gulian Verplanck, merchant, of the City of New York, and his wife Mary, a daughter of Charles Crommelin, also of New York. By the father's side he was descended from an old Dutch race, the ancestors of which came from Holland to this country in the time of Governor Stuyvesant; by his mother he was of French Huguenot extraction, her father having been born in France. Their eldest son inherited many characteristics of both races.

He was born in the City of New York, 13th of September, 1739—was educated there, and was among the earliest students and graduates of King's (now Columbia) College. Hugh Gaine's Universal Register for 1779 calls this institution "The New York College," and among its Governors records the name of SAMUEL VERPLANCK. It had been founded under royal charter in the year 1754. Among the fellow students of SAMUEL VERPLANCK were John Jay, Peter Van Schaick, and Egbert Benson. With the two last especially he kept up an unbroken intimacy, and they were accustomed to pay him frequent visits to the last years of his long life.

His father died before he arrived at years of manhood. After his college course he went to Holland, and was for some years in the counting-house of his maternal uncle, Daniel Crommelin, of Amsterdam, who was then at the head of one of the great banking and commercial houses of Holland. At Amsterdam, in 1761, he married his cousin Judith Crommelin, a daughter of Daniel Crommelin. Gulian Verplanck, who was also a distinguished merchant in New York, was his younger brother, to whom he was most tenderly attached. He carefully superintended his education, and after a collegiate course at King's College sent him to Europe to be trained commercially in the counting-house of David Crommelin.

The only child of SAMUEL VERPLANCK who reached maturity was Daniel Crommelin Verplanck, of Fishkill, Dutchess County, who was a Representative in Congress from this State from 1803 to 1809, and who filled other honorable public stations. His only living descendants are Gulian C. Verplanck, William Walton Verplanck, M. D., James DeLancey Verplanck, Mrs. Elizabeth V. Knevels, and their children and grandchildren. His other descendants died without issue.

SAMUEL VERPLANCK, after extensive travel in Europe, returned in 1763 and established himself in business in the City of New York, as an importing wholesale merchant, and, so far as the limited business of the city allowed, as a banker. The style of the house was SAMUEL VERPLANCK. Under this name he advertised to be sold "the new Brigantine Three Sisters," in Holt's N. Y. Journal, on the 23d of December, 1767. His residence was in Wall Street, on the site of the building formerly owned by the Bank of Commerce, and since sold to the United States. His counting-room was adjoining. In 1768 he was one of the twenty-four founders of the Chamber of Commerce, although then but a young man. He was successful in business, and at the beginning of the troubles in 1774 was a marked man. His name is to be found among those of the Committee of One

Hundred who were chosen to take charge of the City Government upon the seizure of the public buildings in May, 1775. His impaired health and the disturbed state of the country induced his withdrawal from business, and about this period he removed to Fishkill, Dutchess county, where he was a large landholder, being one of the three original patentees of the Rumbout patent, which included the tract between the Matteawan and Wappingin Creek and some lands north and south of each. He resided first at Fishkill Plains, in what is now the township of East Fishkill, and afterwards, until his death, at Mount Gulian, on the banks of the Hudson, which had been a country residence of his father. He recovered his health with his change of life. Though never leaving his immediate neighborhood, except on indispensable business, he had much regular exercise in walking, and enjoyed good health to old age.

He died 27th of January, 1820, and is buried in the burying-ground of the Episcopal Church in the village of Fishkill.

There is an excellent half-length portrait of him by Copley, taken shortly before that eminent artist removed to England, where he soon became celebrated. He was intimate with Copley, who also painted for him a full-length portrait, size of life, of his son, still a boy, playing with a squirrel. This is probably a variation of the portrait of "a boy and a squirrel," which was exhibited about that time in London, and led to Copley's celebrity and fortune.

Both of these fine portraits are now at Mount Gulian on the Hudson, in the possession of Dr. W. W. Verplanck.

With many characteristics of his Dutch ancestry and of Holland, to whose institutions, habits, and principles he cherished a warm attachment, he yet manifested clearly his French descent by his excitability, his gesticulation, and his general manners, which were those of the old-fashioned French gentleman.

He was a good Latin scholar, and kept up his familiarity with the best Latin Classics. He spoke Dutch and French with fluency. His English had nothing, either in pronunciation or idiom, of the peculiarities which designate foreign origin.

From the ease and fluency with which he spoke French, and his living hospitably, he became acquainted with many Frenchmen of note who visited this country, some before and during the War, and others as emigrants during the revolution which succeeded it. He is mentioned by more than one of them in the published accounts of their travels.

St. Jean de Crèvecoeur was often his guest. St. Jean's letters from America were first published in English, and long a popular book upon this country. In the large edition in French, Paris, 1801, he gives in a couple of pages a story of *M. S. Verplanck de Fishkill*, who used the Bald Eagle and the Fish-Hawk to catch large fish for his table. The story is a whimsically exaggerated version of an accidental fact. A copy of the book is to be found in the Astor Library.—*Contributed by Hon. Gulian C. Verplanck.*

[*The following is the story above alluded to.*]

Note.—"I was visiting MR. S. VERPLANCK, whose mansion was but a short distance from Fishkill, when he said to me, 'Come with me; I wish to show you with what skill my purveyors will take the fish we shall have for dinner to-day.' Walking in profound silence to the east bank of the shore, and hidden under thick bushes, we watched with attention the river in sight, until, at a short distance astern of a vessel which was coming up the stream in full sail, I saw a considerable undulation in the middle of the channel, as though a large stone had been thrown into it; out from which soon after a fish-hawk rose with difficulty from the midst of the water, holding in its claws a large fish, whose length and tortuous motions seemed to impede its flight. By turns he rose into the air, seemed as though about to fail in the effort, rose again; at last after many efforts, taking advantage of a puff of favorable wind, he was flying towards his eyrie, not far from where we were hidden, when MR. VERPLANCK called my attention to a bald-headed eagle, his fierce antagonist, right above our heads, who, to judge from the flapping of his wings, and his fierce look, was preparing for a combat, or rather to claim the right of the strongest.

"The fish-hawk, too heavy laden to make any resistance, dropped his prey, which was about to escape the eagerness of its enemy, when the bald eagle, with a skillful turn and an incredible increase of velocity, seized it at the very moment it was about to fall into the river. He in turn was approaching his nest when, surprised and frightened by the cries of MR. VERPLANCK, he dropped the fish. It was a *sea-bass* weighing 21 pounds. 'It is thus,' said my friend, 'that the prey of the weak often become that of the strong. However (he continued), I rarely disturb these birds, whose flights, skill and combats, are so interesting, for fear of driving them from the neighborhood. I have been indiscreet to-day in order to show you one of the most curious spectacles of natural history which this fine stream affords.

"'Just as the corsair (he continued), whose prey an enemy carries off from his clutches in sight of port, cruises anew in the hope of better fortune, so the fish-hawk soars anew high up in air, and darting again with the speed of lightning beneath the waves, reappears holding in his claws a new prey, which he succeeds in saving from his fierce rival more easily if it be lighter than to-day. These birds remain here until the *bass* returns to the sea. Then the bald-headed eagle wings his way to the mountains and the fish-hawk flies to the sea-shore, where he pays tribute no more.'"

This scene, which, if the weight of the fish be taken with allowance, is not an uncommon one in northern streams, is illustrated by a curious plate, in which the sloops, the village of Fishkill, the contending birds, and the luckless fish, are all represented.—*Editor.*

WADDELL ROBERT ROSS.—He was connected for many years with the great shipping house of Greg, Cunningham & Co., and, together with Hamilton Young, advertised the closing of their business in August, 1775. He was one of the addressers of Lord Howe in 1776. In 1778 his store was in King Street, and he was engaged in the sale of groceries, chiefly teas, sugar, and claret. He remained in the city after the War. His store was in 1790 at 61 King Street.

WALLACE ALEXANDER.—Of the house of HUGH & ALEXANDER WALLACE, merchants, extensively engaged in the Irish trade. The two brothers married sisters, the daughters of Cornelius Low, of Raritan, New Jersey. Born in Ireland, he was a thorough loyalist. He was one of the Committee of Correspondence of Fifty-one. He lived at Jamaica during the War. Captain Graydon dined with him during his captivity, and testifies to his good cheer and hospitality. His property was confiscated. A letter written by him to Governor Morris, in 1776, preserved in the correspondence of the Provincial Congress, speaks of a son Hugh.

WALLACE HUGH.—Second President of the Chamber of Commerce. For a sketch of his life see page 19, *ante*.

WALTON ABRAHAM.—He was a son of Jacob Walton and Maria Beekman. He married Grace Williams, in 1766 (the date of the bond is given as of August 6th). In May, 1772, he was engaged in brewing, carrying on the brewery of Mrs. Elizabeth Rutgers. In the beginning of the Revolution his sympathies were with the patriots; he was one of the Committee of One Hundred who were chosen to take charge of the city government in 1775, and one of the delegates to the Provincial Congress the same year. His residence was at Pembroke, Musquito Cove, Long Island. As the struggle progressed he withdrew from the position he had taken. His house was sacked in 1779, by the Whigs, and he lost largely in plate and money. He was taken out of his bed and carried into Connecticut. After the War he resided in New York, at 137 Water Street. He died in 1796.

WALTON GERARD.—A son of Jacob Walton and Maria Beekman. He was sent prisoner to Middletown, Connecticut, by the patriots, in 1776. He remained in the city during the War. In 1790 he resided at 68 Queen Street. He died at 328 Pearl Street, in the year 1821, in the eightieth year of his age. His will, proved May 21 of this year, names his brothers and sisters (Mary, the wife of General Lewis Morris, is spoken of as deceased), and, after sundry bequests, makes particular disposition of his guns, swords, fishing tackle, &c. He was a sportsman as well as a distinguished merchant. He never married.

WALTON JACOB.—One of the firm of WILLIAM AND JACOB WALTON & Co. He was a son of Jacob Walton and Maria Beekman. On the death of his uncle, William Walton, he received a share of his landed estate. On the 17th March, 1760, he married Miss Polly Cruger, the daughter of Henry Cruger, Esq., afterwards member of the King's Council. In 1769 he was elected to the General Assembly. A piece of verse in the Poet's Corner of Holt's New York Journal of January 26, 1769, says of him:

> "For worth and for truth and good nature renowned,
> Let the name and applauses of WALTON go round.
> His Prudence attracts—but his free honest Soul
> Gives a Grace to the Rest and enlivens the whole."

He signed the address to General Gage, issued by some of the members of the Assembly, entreating him to send no troops into this Province. In 1776 he was residing at Horne's Hook, when General Lee ordered him to leave the house for the accommodation of the Whig troops. He was loyal to the crown, and one of the addressers of Lord and General Howe in 1776. His wife died at Flatbush, August 1, 1782, in the 38th year of her age, and MR. WALTON followed her in eight days. His death occurred also at Flatbush, on the 9th August, 1782.

WALTON THOMAS.—The son of Jacob Walton and Maria Beekman. He does not appear to have married. His will, proved on the 14th June, 1773, names his brothers William, Jacob, Abraham, Gerard (all of whom were members of the Chamber of Commerce); his sisters, Mrs. Mary, wife of Lewis Morris, Magdalene, wife of David Johnston, and Catharine, wife of James Thompson. He was a leading member of the Non-importation Association from 1765 to 1770.

WALTON WILLIAM.—Sixth President of the New York Chamber of Commerce. For a sketch of his life see page 55, *ante*.

WATSON JACOB.—A general importer, chiefly of dry goods. In 1776 he carried on a trade in barter with the river counties. His letters, preserved in the correspondence of the Provincial Congress, show him to have been a Quaker. He remained in New York during the War, and was one of the loyal addressers of Lord Howe. When in 1777 the Quakers of New York set on foot a subscription for the relief of their distressed fellow subjects, he and William Backhouse were appointed a committee to receive the funds. In 1781 he was an agent for the sale of the sugar of Cuyler's Sugar House. In 1790 he was in business at 72 Cherry Street.

WATSON JOSHUA.—What was his business does not appear. A Joshua Watson married Sarah Pell in 1780: the Book of New York marriages gives the date of the bond as 28th September.

WATTS ROBERT.—He is presumed to have been the oldest son of John Watts and Anne De Lancey. He was born August 23, 1743, in the City of New York, and graduated at King's College in May, 1760. He married Lady Mary, daughter of Lord Stirling, the Revolutionary General. MR. WATTS remained loyal to the crown. "His residence was at Rose Hill, near Fordham, Westchester County, now the grounds of the Roman Catholic Seminary of St. Johns." He appears in the Directory of 1790 as living in Great Dock Street. He died in Philadelphia.

WETHERHEAD JOHN.—He was a merchant in large general business in King Street. He was one of the addressers of Lord Howe in 1776. His property was confiscated. His name does not appear after the peace.

WHITE HENRY.—Fourth President of the Chamber of Commerce. For a sketch of his life see page 35, *ante.*

WHITE THOMAS.—What was the business of THOMAS WHITE at the period of his connection with the Chamber does not appear. In 1750 he was a large importer of European and East India goods, and his place of business was "at the Dwelling House of Mr. Daniel Shatford, in Smith's Street near Hanover Square." He was one of the loyal addressers of Lord Howe in 1776, and in 1777 was appointed one of the committee to receive subscriptions for the raising of loyal Provincial Regiments. His residence was then in Wall Street. In 1760 (the date of the bond was May 7), he married Anne Hinson. He died in New York on the 6th August, 1781, in the 57th year of his age. An obituary in Gaine's New York Gazette of the 20th says of him, that he was "a gentleman of great respectability, benevolence and humanity; he was a tender husband, an indulgent parent, a good master and a most steady and uniform friend; in short, he possessed those sympathetic feelings in an eminent degree which characterize good men." On the 12th November of the same year, Ann, his widow and executrix, advertised her desire to close up his estate. His property was confiscated in 1779.

WILLIAMS THOMAS CHARLES.—He was a large importer of Linens and East India goods. In 1774 he had a house under the name of THOMAS CHARLES WILLIAMS & Co., of Annapolis, Maryland. Some tea being consigned to this house, it was destroyed by the people, and information was sent to New York on the 20th October, and MR. WILLIAMS, who arrived on the 26th in the ship Samson from London, found himself compelled to issue a card, assuring the citizens that the report that "he had shipped the tea was groundless."

He returned to the city during the British occupation, and continued his business from his store in Great Dock Street. He died on board a flag of truce from the Chesapeake in June, 1782. "He had been to settle accounts of a very considerable amount in Virginia, and on his return was seized with a bilious disorder, which in a very short time carried him off, to the extreme regret of a most valuable wife and a numerous circle of sympathizing friends." He is described as a "respectable and universally beloved merchant of this city."

YATES RICHARD.—Of the firm of READE & YATES. On the death of his partner, Laurence Reade, in 1774, he continued the business, which was chiefly carried on between St. Kitts and the Windward Islands, in his own name. He was one of the Committee of One Hundred chosen to take control of the city in 1775. Taking sides with the British in 1776, he went into New Jersey, but returned when Lord Howe took possession in the fall. He was one of the vestry to oversee the poor in 1778. After the War he remained in the city and carried on his business in 1786 from No. 28 Maiden Lane, and in 1787 and afterwards from No. 9 Princess Street.

YOUNG HAMILTON.—In 1768 he was engaged in a small general business in Little Dock Street, between the Coffee House and Old Slip. He was connected at a later period with the great shipping house of Greg, Cunningham & Co., and, with Robert Ross Waddell, wound up their business from "the house of MR. YOUNG, late Herman Gouverneur's," on Hunter's Quay, in August, 1775. He was one of the Committee of Correspondence of 1774, and of the General Committee of One Hundred in 1775. He remained in the city during the War, and was one of the loyal addressers of Gen. Howe in 1776. In 1778 he was one of the vestry appointed by Gen. Robertson to oversee the poor. He does not appear in New York after the War.

THE END.

Correction of Page 341.

NOTE 121. The presumption that the Chamber of Commerce continued to hold its meetings at the *Merchants' Coffee House* until 1804, is an error as may be seen by reference to Note 80, Page 332. The correction was inadvertently omitted. Mitchell's Picture of New York, printed in 1807, states that the Chamber had its rooms in the *Tontine Coffee House.* Its sessions were then discontinued.

www.ingramcontent.com/pod-product-compliance
Lightning Source LLC
LaVergne TN
LVHW021223110826
845150LV00002B/231

* 9 7 8 1 4 2 5 5 6 4 2 9 2 *